BY THE EDITORS OF
CONSUMER GUIDE®

PRESCRIPTION DRUGS

Cheryl Nunn-Thompson, Pharm.D., BCPS
Joan Stachnik, Pharm.D., BCPS

pil
Publications
International, Ltd.

This book is for information purposes and is not intended to provide medical advice. Neither the Editors of Consumer Guide® and Publications International, Ltd., nor the authors or publisher take responsibility for any possible consequences from any treatment, procedure, exercise, dietary modification, action, or application of medication or preparation by any person reading or following the information in this book. The publication of this book does not constitute the practice of medicine, and this book does not attempt to replace your physician or other health care provider. Before undertaking any course of treatment, the authors, editors, and publisher advise the reader to check with a physician or other health care provider.

Cheryl Nunn-Thompson, Pharm.D., BCPS, is a doctor of pharmacy and is on faculty at the University of Illinois College of Pharmacy. She is a member of the American College of Clinical Pharmacy (ACCP) and the American Pharmaceutical Association (APhA). In addition, she has written extensively for consumers.

Joan Stachnik, Pharm.D., BCPS, is a doctor of pharmacy and a clinical assistant professor at the University of Illinois College of Pharmacy. She has practiced in various health care settings and has published and lectured on drug information and pharmacotherapy topics.

Louis Weber, CEO
Publications International, Ltd.
7373 North Cicero Avenue
Lincolnwood, Illinois 60712

Manufactured in U.S.A.

8 7 6 5 4 3 2 1

ISBN: 1-4127-1117-7

Contents

Introduction

The right drug for the right patient in the right dose by the right path at the right time: This rule sums up the decisions made when your doctor gives you a prescription. You've helped to make these decisions by giving your doctor a complete medical history, which should include any previous allergic reactions you've suffered, any other drugs or supplements you may be taking, any chronic health problems you may have, and whether you are pregnant or breast-feeding an infant. Once you leave your doctor's office with your prescription in hand, however, you have still more to do as a responsible patient and informed consumer.

Drug therapy is an important component of health care. When you receive a prescription, you must know how and when to properly administer your medication. You must understand and comply with your dosage schedule. You must know what to do to prevent certain side effects and how to handle any side effects that might occur. You must recognize the signals that indicate the need to call your doctor.

Yet all too often, patients leave their doctors' offices without a full understanding of the drug therapy they're about to start. This may result in a failure to fully comply with their doctors' instructions. For example, patients may stop taking the medication too soon because it doesn't seem to work or because they feel better or because it causes bothersome side effects. They may take the drug improperly, at the wrong time, too often, or not often enough. They may continue drinking alcohol or taking other drugs when they shouldn't be. Perhaps they don't even realize that taking cold pills, oral contraceptives, aspirin, or vitamins could affect the action of the prescribed drug. The end result may be that they do not get better; they may get worse and may even suffer a dangerous reaction.

Few of us would buy a car without shopping around, a house or condominium without an appraisal, or an appliance without knowing how to work it. Prescription medications should be approached like these other purchases—with understanding. You will be the end user. As an informed consumer you should know what you are buying and how to get the most out of your purchase.

Prescription medications are dispensed on the basis of two assumptions: 1) instructions for proper use are provided to the patient, and 2) those instructions will be followed. In many states, pharmacists are required to provide drug information for each prescription medication by means of written information, verbal counseling, or both. Nevertheless, as a consumer, you have the responsibility to understand your own drug therapy. The National Council on Patient Information and Education (NCPIE) is made up of health care professionals, lay people, and consumer advocates. It has published guidelines that are designed to provide consumers with the information they need regarding proper drug therapy. This is important since the Council estimates that half of all prescription drugs dispensed in any one year are taken incorrectly. Moreover, almost 40 million prescriptions go unclaimed every year (11 percent of women and 7 percent of men don't fill or don't pick up their prescription medication). This leads to unnecessary side effects, worsening of illnesses, and, in rare cases, even death. The economic losses from taking medicine incorrectly and not filling prescriptions have been estimated at more than $1.5 billion annually for lost workdays due to preventable illness. NCPIE recommends that you ask your health care professional the following six questions about each prescription medication you receive:

1. What is the name of the medicine, and what is it supposed to do? Is this the brand or generic name? (Is a generic version available?)

2. How and when do I take it and for how long?

3. What foods, drinks, other medicines, dietary supplements, or activities should I avoid while taking this drug?

4. What are the possible side effects, and what do I do if they occur?

5. When should I expect the medication to begin working, and how will I be able to tell if the medication is working?

6. Will this new prescription work safely with the other prescription and nonprescription medicines I am taking?

Prescription Drugs provides the information you need to take prescription medications safely and effectively. Along with general information on how to read a prescription and how to buy, store, and administer drugs, this publication provides an introduction to the action of drugs—how they work to stop infection, to lower blood pressure, or to relieve pain. It then provides detailed information on hundreds of the most commonly prescribed drugs. Included in the drug profiles is information on how to alleviate certain side effects, whether the drug should be taken on an empty stomach or with meals, whether it is likely to affect your ability to drive, and whether generic equivalents are available for a prescribed trade-name medication. You will discover which side effects are common to some medications and which side effects signal the need for immediate attention from your physician.

Of course, *Prescription Drugs* is not a substitute for consulting your doctor, your pharmacist, and other health care professionals directly involved in your care. They are your primary reference sources on the use of prescription drugs. To assure that you receive the best health care possible, however, you, too, must be informed and knowledgeable about the prescription drugs you use.

Filling Your Prescription

While you're having your prescription filled, you should make sure you understand what the drug is used for, your dosage schedule, and how to store the medication properly. You should be clear about what kinds of precautions to take to prevent or reduce side effects, whether you should restrict your diet or drinking habits while taking the drug, which side effects are expected or unavoidable, and which side effects signal a need for a doctor's attention. Your first step in having your prescription filled is reading and understanding what your doctor has written.

READING YOUR PRESCRIPTION

Prescriptions may appear mysterious, but they contain no secret messages. Many of the symbols and phrases doctors use on prescriptions are abbreviated Latin or Greek words; they are holdovers from the days when doctors actually wrote in Latin. For example, *gtt* comes from the Latin word *guttae,* which means *drops,* and *bid* is a shortened version of *bis in die,* which is Latin for *twice a day.*

You do not have to be a doctor, nurse, or pharmacist to read a prescription. You can (and should) learn how to read one yourself—after all, the prescription describes the drug you will be taking. You should understand what your doctor has written on the prescription form to be sure that the label on the container you receive from your pharmacist coincides with the prescription form your doctor gave you.

The table below and on the facing page lists the most common prescription symbols and abbreviations. Use it as a guide as you practice deciphering the sample prescriptions that appear on page 8.

Common Abbreviations and Symbols Used in Writing Prescriptions

Abbreviation	Meaning	Derivation and Notes
aa	of each	*ana* (Greek)
ac	before meals	*ante cibum* (Latin)
AD	right ear	*auris dextra* (Latin)
AL	left ear	*auris laeva* (Latin)
AM	morning	*ante meridiem* (Latin)
AS	left ear	*auris sinistra* (Latin)
au	both ears	*auris* (Latin)
bid	twice a day	*bis in die* (Latin)
C	100	—
c̄	with	*cum* (Latin)
cap	capsule	—

Abbreviation	Meaning	Derivation and Notes
cc *or* cm^3	cubic centimeter	30 cc equals one ounce
disp	dispense	—
dtd#	give this number	*dentur tales doses* (Latin)
ea	each	—
ext	for external use	—
gtt	drops	*guttae* (Latin)
gt	drop	*gutta* (Latin)
h	hour	*hora* (Latin)
hs	at bedtime	*hora somni* (Latin)
M ft	make	*misce fiat* (Latin)
mL	milliliter	30 mL equals one ounce (1 mL=1 cc)
O	pint	*octarius* (Latin)
OD	right eye	*oculus dexter* (Latin)
OL	left eye	*oculus laevus* (Latin)
OS	left eye	*oculus sinister* (Latin)
OU	each eye	*oculus uterque* (Latin)
pc	after meals	*post cibum* (Latin)
PM	evening	*post meridiem* (Latin)
po	by mouth	*per os* (Latin)
prn	as needed	*pro re nata* (Latin)
$\bar{q}$	every	*quaqua* (Latin)
qd	once a day; every day	*quaqua die* (Latin)
qid	four times a day	*quater in die* (Latin)
qod	every other day	—
$\bar{s}$	without	*sine* (Latin)
sig	label as follows	*signa* (Latin)
sl	under the tongue	*sub lingua* (Latin)
SOB	shortness of breath	—
sol	solution	—
ss	half unit	*semis* (Latin)
stat	at once; first dose	*statim* (Latin)
susp	suspension	—
tab	tablet	—
tid	three times a day	*ter in die* (Latin)
top	apply topically	—
ung *or* ungt	ointment	*unguentum* (Latin)
UT	under the tongue	—
ut dict *or* UD	as directed	ut dictum (Latin)
x	times	—

John D. Jones MD
Anytown, U.S.A.

DEA# 123456789 PHONE# 123-4567

NAME *Your Name* AGE *47*
ADDRESS *Anytown, U.S.A.* DATE *5/10/04*

Rx *Fiorinal*
#24
Sig: caps i q̄ 4h prn pain

REFILLS *5x*
LABEL *yes*

DISPENSE AS WRITTEN
John D. Jones M.D.
SUBSTITUTION

The first sample prescription is for a medication called Fiorinal. The prescription tells the pharmacist to give you 24 (#24) capsules (caps), and it tells you to take one (i) of those capsules every four hours (q̄ 4h) as needed (prn) for pain. The prescription indicates that you may receive five refills (5x), that the label on the drug container should state the name of the drug (yes), and that the pharmacist may substitute (substitution) a less expensive equivalent generic product.

Look at the second prescription. It shows that you will receive 100 (dtd C) tablets of Lanoxin, 0.125 mg. You will take three tablets at once (iii stat), then two (ii) tomorrow morning (AM), and one (i) every (q̄) morning (AM) thereafter with (c̄) orange juice (OJ). You will receive the specific brand noted (dispense as written), you may receive refills as needed (prn), and the name of the drug will be on the package (✔).

John D. Jones MD
Anytown, U.S.A.

DEA# 123456789 PHONE# 123-4567

NAME *Your Name* AGE *55*
ADDRESS *Anytown, U.S.A.* DATE *5/23/04*

Rx *Lanoxin 0.125*
dtd C
Sig: iii stat, ii tomorrow AM,
then i q̄ AM c̄ OJ

John D. Jones, M.D.
DISPENSE AS WRITTEN

REFILLS *prn*
LABEL *✔*

SUBSTITUTION

Remember to check the label on the drug container when you receive your medicine. If the label information differs from what is written on the prescription, ask your pharmacist for an explanation. Be certain that you are receiving the right medication and the correct instructions for taking it.

TALKING TO YOUR PHARMACIST

Once you have read the prescription, its directions may seem clear enough, but will they seem clear when you get home? For example, the prescription for the Fiorinal states that you should take one capsule every four hours as needed. How many capsules can you take each day—four, six, . . . more? The phrase "as needed" is not clear, and unless you understand what it means, you don't know how much medication you can take per day. What if your prescription instructs you to take "one tablet four times a day?" What does "four times a day" mean? For some antibiotics, it may mean one tablet every six hours around the clock. For other medications, it may mean one tablet in the morning, one at noon, one in the early evening, and one at bedtime. For still others, it may mean one tablet every hour for the first four hours after you get up in the morning. Don't leave the pharmacy with unanswered questions; ask your pharmacist for an explanation of any confusing terms on your prescription.

Your pharmacist is a valuable resource in your health care. He or she should have a record of ALL the prescription and over-the-counter drugs you take in order to detect any possible life-threatening drug interactions. It is therefore a good idea to choose a pharmacy that maintains careful records and then to stick with that pharmacy.

The pharmacist will be able to tell you if your medication is likely to cause drowsiness or nausea and if your therapy may be affected by smoking, eating certain foods, or drinking alcohol. He or she can tell you what to expect from the medication and about how long you will have to take it. Of course, treatments vary tremendously, but you should ask whether you will likely have to take medication for a few days, a few months, or even longer.

You should discuss with your pharmacist the possible side effects of your medication and ask for a description of symptoms. The pharmacist can tell you which side effects require prompt attention from your physician. For example, one of the major side effects of the drug carbamazepine is a blood disorder. Since a sore throat can be one of the early symptoms of a blood disorder, your pharmacist may instruct you to consult your physician if this symptom occurs.

Your pharmacist can also explain how to take your medicine. You need to know whether to take the medication with meals or between meals. The timing of the doses of a drug can make a big difference, and the effectiveness of each drug depends on following the directions for its use. Your pharmacist can tell you what is meant by such phrases as "as needed," "as directed," and "take with fluid." For example, you may take water, but not milk, with some drugs. With other medications, you should drink milk. Your pharmacist can also tell you how many refills you are allowed and whether you are likely to need them.

OVER-THE-COUNTER DRUGS

Drugs that can be purchased without a prescription are referred to as over-the-counter (OTC) drugs. The largest selection is found in drugstores, of course, but they are also sold in grocery and convenience stores, airports, and even hotel lobbies. There are no legal requirements or limitations as to who may buy or sell them.

Products sold OTC contain amounts of active ingredients considered safe for self-treatment by consumers when instructions on the label are followed. Many people visit a doctor for ailments that can be treated effectively by taking nonprescription drugs. Actually, prescriptions are sometimes written for such drugs. Your pharmacist will be able to recommend appropriate OTC medications and how to use them.

On the other hand, if your pharmacist urges you to avoid certain OTC drugs, follow the advice. For one thing, OTC drugs could affect the way your body reacts to prescription drugs you may be taking. For instance, people taking tetracycline should avoid taking antacids or iron-containing products at the same time; their use should be separated by an interval of at least two hours. Antacids and iron interfere with the body's absorption of tetracycline, thereby decreasing its effectiveness. So be sure you know what you are taking. If you are unsure of the type or contents of your medications, ask your doctor or pharmacist.

In the last several years, many medicines that formerly could be obtained only through a doctor's prescription have become available over the counter. These medicines can now be purchased OTC because of their established history of safety and efficacy. The Food and Drug Administration (FDA) understands that certain medications, if available OTC, allow consumers to self-treat minor health problems. Accordingly, important medicines such as clotrimazole (a medicine to treat fungal infections), ibuprofen and naproxen (pain relievers), and nicotine gum (to help patients stop smoking) have been "switched" from prescription to OTC availability. Some medicines now available OTC are not identical to the prescription form, however. For example, cimetidine, famotidine, and ranitidine have been available for several years only by prescription to treat stomach ulcers. These medicines are now also available OTC, but the OTC forms are indicated for use on different health problems (preventing and treating heartburn) than those treated with the prescription versions, and the OTC forms are offered at a reduced dosage. Therefore, if you need medication for stomach ulcer disease, a prescription is still required in order to provide the correct dosage. Note also that OTC availability of a medicine you've been taking by prescription does not mean you should automatically stop the prescription form and change to the OTC form. If this situation arises, discuss it with your doctor or pharmacist first.

GENERIC DRUGS

One way your pharmacist can help you save money is by dispensing generic medications. The term generic has two slightly different meanings in terms of medicines. When applied to the name of a medication, *generic* means "not protected by trademark registration." The generic *name* of a drug is usually a shortened form of its chemical name. Every medication has a generic name. However, not every drug is available for purchase in its generic *form*.

Generally, the manufacturer that researches and develops a new drug will hold a patent on that drug for a specified period of time, keeping other companies from producing and/or marketing the drug and allowing the original manufacturer to recoup the costs of the research and development. The original manufacturer generally gives the drug a trademarked, or brand, name in addition to its generic name. The brand name is registered, and only the manufacturer who holds the trademark can use the brand name when marketing a drug, even after the patent on the drug has expired. So, for example, only GlaxoSmithKline can call their amoxicillin product Amoxil, and only Bristol-Myers Squibb can use the brand name Capoten for captopril. (Brand names are capitalized in this publication.)

Once the patent on the drug expires, other companies may begin to manufacture or sell the drug, but they cannot use the original brand name. They can sell it under their own brand name or as a generic drug, using its generic name.

Many people think that drugs with brand names are made by large manufacturers while generic drugs are made by smaller companies. In fact, a manufacturer may market large quantities of a drug under a brand name and also sell the base chemical to several other companies, some of which then sell the drug under its generic name and some under their own brand names. For example, the antibiotic ampicillin is the base for over 200 different products, yet all ampicillin is produced by only a few dozen drug companies.

Generic drugs are generally priced lower than their trademarked equivalents, largely because they are not as widely advertised and because the companies that sell them did not pay for the original research and development costs. Not every drug is available generically, however, and not every generic is significantly less expensive than its trademarked equivalent. Nevertheless, consumers may be able to save money by purchasing a generic product. To cite one example, 30 capsules of Prozac (20 mg) cost about $105, while the same quantity of the generic equivalent costs about $42—a savings of $63 or an impressive 60 percent.

For some drugs, it's inadvisable to shop around for a generic equivalent. Although the FDA has stated that no evidence exists to suspect serious differences between brand-name drugs and generic drugs, some differences are seen when the two types of drugs are compared. For example, because of variations in the way they are made or the fillers (nonactive ingredients) used, capsules from different manufacturers may not dissolve in the stomach at the same rate or to the same extent. This is especially true for the various generic carbamazepine, digoxin, phenytoin, and warfarin products. It is therefore important to discuss the advantages or disadvantages of any particular generic product with your doctor and pharmacist.

All states have some form of substitution law that allows pharmacists to fill prescriptions with the least expensive equivalent product. However, your doctor can authorize the use of a specific brand of medication on the prescription form (see the sample prescriptions on page 8). You should be aware that certain patients can sometimes respond in different ways to various equivalent products, and your doctor may have good reasons for being specific. Again, discuss this with your doctor, and be sure you know both the brand and generic names of all the medicines you take.

MAIL-ORDER PRESCRIPTION DRUGS

Traditionally, Americans have purchased prescription medication at their neighborhood drugstore. Today this is no longer always the case. Some patients—especially those who may be very ill or unable to get around easily—simply find it more convenient to have their medications mailed directly to their homes. There are also many people who take medication on a regular basis for a chronic disease, such as high blood pressure or heart disease, who prefer home delivery. Actually, mail-order pharmacies are not all that new. The Veteran's Administration (VA) started a mail-order operation in the late 1940s. And the AARP (formerly the American Association of Retired Persons) Pharmacy Service, which provides both OTC and prescription medication by mail, has been supplying medication to its members for more than 35 years. Still, the majority of people who get their medication by mail have been encouraged to do so because of group contracts with employers and insurers.

Most mail-order pharmacies maintain toll-free telephone lines to respond to questions from patients and physicians. And they may provide printed information about your prescription, just as many local pharmacies do. But when you do business by mail, there is an unavoidable loss of face-to-face interaction with your pharmacist, which is important to many people. Thus, before deciding whether buying prescription medications by mail is best for you and your family, carefully consider the various advantages and drawbacks.

BUYING PRESCRIPTION DRUGS ONLINE

Buying medicines *online,* or over the Internet, has become a more widely used method of obtaining prescribed medications. Many Internet pharmacies exist to provide consumers with a safe, high-quality, private, and convenient source of prescription medications. In addition, online pharmacies offer an easy way to comparison shop to find the best prices on the medications you take.

Unfortunately, Web sites that engage in illegal, unsafe pharmacy practices do exist. These rogue Web sites may violate the law and put unwitting consumers at risk by selling medications not approved by the FDA (many foreign sites offer unapproved drugs); selling medications without requiring that a doctor's prescription be submitted to the pharmacy; prescribing medication based solely on a questionnaire, without medical evaluation; selling expired or tainted medications; filling orders with the incorrect drug or dosage strength; and/or sharing the consumer's private health information or not offering secure transactions.

As part of its mission to ensure that only safe and useful medications are available for use in the United States, the FDA oversees the manufacturing of medications as well as the prescribing process. With the growth of the Internet, the FDA and other regulatory agencies are very concerned that consumers be able to identify and use only reputable pharmacy Web sites and avoid those engaging in unlawful selling. So beginning in 1999, the FDA and the National Association of Boards of Pharmacy (NABP) created a voluntary certification program, which companies can apply for, that assures quality Internet pharmacy services. Pharmacies that are certified in this way are allowed to display the Verified Internet Pharmacy Practice Site (VIPPS) seal, and it is important to look for this seal when you are shopping for an Internet pharmacy site. Clicking on the VIPPS seal links you to the VIPPS Web site, which verifies that the seal is indeed posted on a VIPPS-certified site. By visiting the NABP Web site (www.nabp.net/vipps/intro.asp) or calling the NABP (847-698-6227), you can obtain additional information about a specific VIPPS-certified pharmacy site. You can also find further information at the FDA Web site (www.fda.org).

HOW MUCH TO BUY

On a prescription, your doctor specifies exactly how many tablets or capsules or how much liquid medication you will receive. But if you must take a drug for a long period of time or if you are very sensitive to drugs, you may want to consider purchasing more or less than the amount specified.

The amount of medication to buy depends on several factors. One is the condition being treated. For example, drugs to treat high blood pressure or diabetes may be purchased in large quantities because patients with such chronic conditions take medication for long periods. In most cases the price per dose decreases with the amount purchased. In other words, a drug that usually costs six cents per tablet may cost four or five cents per tablet if you buy 100 at a time. Another factor is how much you can afford or—for those whose prescriptions are covered by insurance—how much your insurance company will pay. A third factor is the length of time your medication can be stored. Nitroglycerin tablets, for example, lose their effectiveness after about six months and should be replaced with a fresh supply. There is no reason to ask for more nitroglycerin in tablet form than will be needed during that period of time.

Many doctors prescribe only a single month's supply of a drug, even if it will be taken for a long time. If you wish to buy more, check with your pharmacist. It is also important to have enough medication on hand so you'll be covered—if you're away from your pharmacy while traveling, for example. Serious side effects could occur if you miss even a few doses of drugs such as propranolol or prednisone.

If you have been plagued by annoying side effects or have had allergic reactions to some drugs in the past, you may want to ask your pharmacist to dispense only enough medication on an initial prescription for a few days or a week. That way you can determine how your body reacts to the drug. Pharmacists cannot allow the return of a prescription medication once it has left the pharmacy. You may have to pay more per dose if the pharmacist dispenses a small quantity, but at least you will not be paying for a supply of medication your body can't tolerate. Be sure you can get the remainder of the prescribed amount of the drug if no serious or intolerable side effects occur. With some drugs, after you have received part of the intended amount, you cannot receive the remainder without another prescription.

STORING YOUR DRUGS

Before you leave the pharmacy, find out how you should store your medication. Drugs that are not protected from heat and moisture may lose potency.

All medications should be kept in their original containers. One reason for this is that some drugs may lose potency when stored with other medications. A more important reason is to prevent confusion about which drug is being taken. And never remove the label from a prescription vial. It contains the name of the medication, directions for proper use, and the prescription number (helpful at refill time).

You can safely store most prescription drugs at room temperature and out of direct sunlight. But even drugs dispensed in colored bottles or in containers that reflect light should be kept out of direct sunlight.

Some drugs require storage in the refrigerator; others should not be refrigerated. For example, some liquid cough suppressants thicken as they become cold and will not pour from the bottle. Some people keep nitroglycerin tablets in the refrigerator in the mistaken belief that the drug will be more stable when kept cold. This is not the case, however: Nitroglycerin should not be stored in the refrigerator.

Even if the label on your drug states "keep refrigerated," you should not keep the drug in the freezer compartment. If a drug is frozen and then thawed, coated tablets may crack and some liquids may separate into layers that can't be remixed.

Many people keep prescription drugs and other medications in the bathroom medicine cabinet, but this is one of the worst places to keep drugs. Small children can easily climb onto the sink and reach drugs stored above it. Meanwhile, the temperature and humidity changes in the bathroom may adversely affect the stability of both prescription and OTC medications.

Definitions of Terms Used for Storage Temperatures

Excessive cold	Less than 36°F (2°C)
Refrigerated	Between 36°F and 46°F (2° and 8°C)
Cool	Between 46°F and 59°F (8° and 15°C)
Room temperature	Between 59°F and 86°F (15° and 30°C)
Excessive heat	More than 104° F (40° C)

The law requires all prescription drugs for oral use be dispensed in childproof containers unless the prescribing doctor or patient requests otherwise. If you find the container difficult to open AND if there are no small children in your home, ask your pharmacist to dispense your medication in a container that is not childproof.

Do not keep unused prescription drugs. Flush leftover medication down the toilet or pour it down the sink, then wash and discard the empty container. Clean out your medicine cabinet yearly, and remove any drugs that are not being used or that have expired (the expiration date is sometimes shown on the container label). Such drugs can be dangerous to your children and guests, and you might be tempted to take them yourself if you develop similar symptoms in the future. Similar symptoms may not be due to the same disease, however, and you may be denied proper medication or even make your condition worse by taking the wrong medication.

It cannot be repeated too often: KEEP ALL MEDICATIONS AWAY FROM CHILDREN. If a child accidentally swallows medication or receives too much of a prescribed medication, IMMEDIATELY CALL YOUR LOCAL POISON CONTROL CENTER, A NEARBY EMERGENCY ROOM, OR YOUR DOCTOR for instructions and recommendations. These phone numbers should be written down in a readily accessible place. (To be safe, it is wise to keep a list of these and other important telephone numbers—such as those for the police and fire departments—near every telephone in your home.) You should also have an over-the-counter emetic (a vomit-inducing agent) such as syrup of ipecac on hand in case you are directed to empty a child's stomach. But do not administer an emetic unless specifically instructed to do so by a medical professional.

Administering Medication Correctly

To derive the maximum benefit from your drug therapy, you must use your medicine correctly. If you use drugs improperly, you may not receive their full therapeutic effects. Indeed, improper administration can be dangerous, since some medications may become toxic if used incorrectly.

Before administering medications to older adults (that is, people who are 65 years of age or older) or children, ask your doctor for specific instructions. These groups of patients can be more sensitive to dosage amounts and side effects of medications than young and middle-aged adults.

As a person ages, the function of the kidneys, liver, and other organ systems in the body slows down. Compared with younger adults, people over 65 may have a reduced capacity to break down and remove medicines from their bodies. Therefore, it is sometimes recommended that older people receive lower initial doses of drugs and that drug dosages be increased more slowly. In other cases, a different drug within the same class of medication may be administered because the side effects from the alternative drug may be less bothersome. For example, in the elderly population with diabetes, the oral antidiabetic agent glyburide may be more appropriate than chlorpropamide (another oral antidiabetic agent), which is associated with an increased chance of dangerously low blood sugar in the elderly. In general, physicians "start low and go slow" when prescribing medications and adjusting dosages for older patients. The drug profiles in this publication will indicate in the WARNINGS section when caution is warranted for drugs given to older adults.

Infants and children also differ from adults in how their bodies respond to medication. Depending on age and weight, the best dose of a medicine for a younger patient may be different than an adult dose. Accordingly, children may be given lower dosages of some medications (including antibiotics) and higher dosages of others (including phenytoin, carbamazepine, and phenobarbital).

AEROSOL SPRAYS

Many topical (applied to the skin) medications are packaged as pressurized aerosol sprays. These sprays usually cost more than the cream or ointment form of the same product. They are especially useful on very tender or hairy areas of the body where it is difficult to apply a cream or ointment. Aerosols can have a cooling effect on burns, rashes, and other skin inflammations.

Before using an aerosol spray, shake the container to evenly disperse the particles of medication. Hold the container upright four to six inches from the skin. Press the nozzle for a few seconds, then release.

Never use an aerosol around the face or eyes. If your doctor tells you to treat part of your face, simply spray the solution onto your hand, then rub it in. Getting the solution in your eyes, nose, or mouth may cause pain and may even damage your eyes.

Aerosol sprays may feel cold when they are first applied. If this sensation bothers you, ask your pharmacist or doctor whether another form of the same product is available and appropriate for your needs.

BUCCAL TABLETS

A few drugs, including some forms of nitroglycerin, are prepared as tablets that must be placed between the lip and gum or in the cheek. These products are designed to release a dose of the drug over a period of time. To take a buccal tablet properly, place it between the upper lip and gum (above the front teeth) or between the cheek and gum. If you eat or drink during the three to five hours it takes for the tablet to dissolve, place the tablet between the upper lip and gum. Do not go to sleep with a tablet in your mouth because it could slip down your throat and cause choking.

CAPSULES, TABLETS, AND ORAL POWDERS

Many people find it hard to swallow a tablet or capsule. If tablets or capsules tend to catch in your throat, rinse your mouth with water, or at least wet your mouth, before attempting to swallow them. Then place the tablet or capsule on the back of your tongue, take a drink, and gulp it down. If it seems too large to swallow or tends to stick in your throat, there is another possible option: Empty the capsule or crush the tablet in a spoon and mix it with applesauce, soup, or even chocolate syrup. But BE SURE TO CHECK WITH YOUR PHARMACIST BEFOREHAND, since some tablets and capsules must be swallowed whole and should not be crushed or opened. Your pharmacist can tell you which ones can and cannot be taken this way. If it cannot be crushed or chewed and you prefer to not mix it with food, ask your doctor if the drug can be prescribed in a liquid or chewable tablet form instead.

Occasionally medications come in oral powder form (for example, cholestyramine and colestipol). Such preparations should be carefully mixed with liquids, then swallowed; they are not meant to be swallowed dry.

EARDROPS

Eardrops must be administered so they fill the ear canal. To use eardrops properly, tilt your head to one side, turning the affected ear upward. Grasp the earlobe and gently pull it upward (toward the top of the head) and back to straighten the ear canal. When administering eardrops to a child younger than three years old, gently pull the child's earlobe downward (toward the shoulder) and back. Fill the dropper and place the prescribed number of drops (usually a dropperful) into the ear. Be careful to avoid touching the sides or edge of the ear canal, because the dropper can easily become contaminated by such contact.

Keep the ear tilted upward for five to ten seconds while continuing to hold the earlobe. Your doctor may want you to gently insert a small wad of clean cotton into the ear to prevent the medication from seeping out. Do not wash or wipe the dropper after use; replace it in the bottle and tightly close the bottle to keep out moisture.

Before administering eardrops, you may warm the drops to body temperature simply by rolling the container back and forth between your hands. Do not place the bottle in boiling water, however: The eardrops may become so hot that they cause pain or damage when placed in the ear. Boiling water can also cause the container's label to loosen or peel off and might even ruin the medication.

EYEDROPS AND EYE OINTMENTS

Before administering eyedrops or ointments, wash your hands. Then sit or lie down and tilt your head back. Using your thumb and forefinger, gently and carefully pull your lower eyelid down to form a pouch. Hold the dropper close to your eyelid without touching it. Squeeze the prescribed amount of medicine into this pouch and slowly close your eye. Try not to blink. Keep your eye closed, and use your finger to apply slight pressure at the inner corner of the eye for a minute or two to prevent loss of medication through the duct that drains fluid from the surface of the eye. If more than one drop per eye is prescribed, wait at least five minutes before administering the next drop. This pause helps ensure that the first drop is not flushed away by the second or that the second is not diluted by tears from the first. When finished, wipe away any tears or excess solution from the eye area with a clean tissue. Do not wash or wipe the dropper before replacing it in the bottle—this may contaminate the remaining medication. Close the bottle tightly.

To administer an eye ointment, squeeze a line of ointment in the prescribed amount into the pouch formed as just described for eyedrops (avoid touching the tube to your eyelid), and close your eye. Roll your eye a few times to spread the ointment.

Be sure the drops or ointments are intended for use in the eye (all products made for use in the eye must be sterilized to prevent eye infections). And check the expiration date on the label or container. Don't use a drug product after the specified date, and never use any eye product that has changed color. If it appears that your medication contains particles that weren't visible at the time of purchase, discard it.

LIQUIDS

Liquid medications are used in several different ways. Some are intended to be used externally on the skin; some are placed in the eye, ear, nose, or throat; still others are taken internally. Before taking or using any liquid medication, carefully read the label for specific directions.

A suspension is a liquid product containing particles that settle to the bottom of the container. It must be shaken before use so each application contains the right proportion of ingredients. If you don't shake it well each time, you may not get the correct amount of the active ingredient, and as the amount of liquid remaining in the bottle becomes smaller, the drug could become more concentrated. Thus, you may be getting more of the active ingredient than you need. A dose could even reach toxic levels.

If a liquid medication is for application to the skin, pour a small quantity onto a cotton pad, a piece of gauze, or a cotton-tipped applicator. (Don't use a large piece of cotton or gauze, since it will absorb more medication than is needed, resulting in waste.) Don't pour the medication into your cupped hand; you may spill some of it. Never dip cotton-tipped applicators, pieces of cotton or gauze, or your fingers directly into the bottle itself, however.

Liquid medications that are to be swallowed must be measured accurately. When your doctor prescribes one teaspoonful of medication, he or she is thinking of a 5-milliliter (mL) medical spoon. The ordinary teaspoons you have at home can hold anywhere from 2 to 10 mL of liquid. If you use one of these to measure your medication, you may get too little or too much drug with each dose. Ask your pharmacist for a medical teaspoon or one of the other plastic devices for accurately measuring liquid medications. Most of these cost only a few cents; they are well worth their cost in ensuring accurate dosage. Incidentally, while it's true that many children balk at medication taken from a teaspoon, they often enjoy taking it from a "special" spoon.

NOSE DROPS AND SPRAYS

Before using nose drops or sprays, gently blow your nose if you can. To administer nose drops, fill the dropper, tilt your head back, and place the prescribed number of drops into your nose. To prevent contamination of the rest of the medicine, do not touch the dropper to the nasal membranes. Keep your head tilted for five to ten seconds, and sniff gently two or three times.

When using a nasal spray, do not tilt your head back. Insert the sprayer into the nose, but try to avoid touching the inner nasal membranes. Sniff and squeeze the sprayer at the same time, according to the product directions. Do not release your grip on the sprayer until you have withdrawn it from your nose (to prevent nasal mucus and bacteria from entering the plastic bottle and contaminating its contents). After you have sprayed the prescribed number of times in one or both of your nostrils, gently sniff two or three times.

Unless your doctor has told you otherwise, you should not use nose drops or sprays for more than two or three days at a time. If they have been prescribed for a longer period, do not administer nose drops or sprays from the same container for more than one week. Bacteria from your nose can easily enter the container and contaminate the solution. If you must take drops or spray for more than a week, purchase a new container. Never allow anyone else to use your nose drops or spray.

RECTAL SUPPOSITORIES

Rectal suppositories are used to deliver various types of medication, including laxatives, sleep aids, tranquilizers, and even medications to relieve nausea and vomiting. Regardless of the type of medicine that they are delivering into the body, all rectal suppositories are inserted in the same way.

In extremely hot weather, a suppository may become too soft to handle properly. If this happens, place it in the refrigerator, in a glass of cool water, or under cold running water until it becomes firm. (A few minutes is usually sufficient.) Before inserting a suppository, remove any aluminum wrappings. Rubber finger coverings or disposable rubber gloves may be worn when inserting a suppository, but they are not necessary unless your fingernails are unusually long or sharp.

To insert a suppository, lie on your left side with your right knee bent. Push the suppository, pointed end first, into the rectum as far as is comfortable. You may quickly feel as if you want to have a bowel movement, but ignore that feeling and lie still for a few minutes. Delay trying to have a bowel movement for at least an hour. If you have trouble inserting a suppository or if the process is painful, coat the suppository with a thin layer of petroleum jelly or mineral oil.

Some manufacturers of suppositories used for hemorrhoids suggest that their product should be stored in the refrigerator. But don't assume that this is always the case. Ask your pharmacist for advice about proper storage.

SUBLINGUAL TABLETS

Some drugs, such as nitroglycerin, are prepared as tablets that must be placed under the tongue. Such drugs are more rapidly or completely absorbed into the bloodstream from the lining of the mouth than they are from the stomach and intestinal tract.

To take a sublingual tablet properly, place it under your tongue, close your mouth, and hold the saliva under your tongue for as long as you can before swallowing to allow the tablet to dissolve. A bitter taste in your mouth five minutes after taking a nitroglycerin tablet indicates that the drug has not yet been completely absorbed. Wait at least five minutes longer before drinking liquids. Drinking too soon may wash the medication into the stomach before it has been completely absorbed. Do not smoke, eat, or chew gum while the medication is dissolving.

THROAT LOZENGES AND DISCS

Both lozenges and discs contain medication that is released in the mouth to soothe a sore throat, to reduce coughing, or to treat laryngitis. Neither should be chewed; they should be allowed to dissolve in the mouth. After the lozenge or disc has dissolved, try not to swallow or drink any fluids for a while.

THROAT SPRAYS

To administer a throat spray, open your mouth fully and spray the medication as far back as possible. Hold the liquid in your mouth for as long as you can, trying not to swallow, and do not drink any fluids for several minutes. Swallowing a throat spray is not harmful, but if you find that your throat spray upsets your stomach, don't swallow it; simply spit it out.

TOPICAL OINTMENTS AND CREAMS

Most topical (applied to the skin) ointments and creams exert only local effects—that is, they affect only the area to which they are directly applied. Most creams and ointments are expensive (especially steroid products) and should be applied to the skin in as thin a layer as possible. A thin layer is just as effective as a thick layer but less expensive. Moreover, some steroid-containing creams and ointments can cause toxic side effects if applied too heavily.

Before applying the medication, moisten the skin by immersing it in water or dabbing the area with a clean, wet cloth. Blot the skin almost dry and apply the medication as directed. Gently massage it into the skin until the medication disappears.

If your doctor has not indicated whether you should receive a cream or an ointment, ask your pharmacist for the one you prefer. Creams are greaseless and do not stain your clothing; they are best to use on the scalp or other hairy areas of the body. However, if your skin is dry, ask for an ointment. Ointments help keep skin soft.

If your doctor tells you to place a wrap on the skin after the cream or ointment has been applied, you may use transparent plastic film like that used for wrapping food. A wrap holds the medication close to the skin and helps to keep the skin moist so the drug can be absorbed. To use a wrap correctly, apply the cream or ointment as directed, then wrap the area with a layer of transparent plastic film. Follow your doctor's directions EXACTLY, and keep the wrap in place only as long as you are told to do so. If you keep a wrap on the skin too long, too much of the drug may be absorbed, which may lead to increased side effects. Do not use a wrap without your doctor's approval, and never use one for an oozing lesion.

TRANSDERMAL PATCHES

Transdermal patches allow controlled, continuous release of medication. They are convenient and easy to use. Apply the patch to a hairless or clean-shaven area of skin, avoiding scars and wounds. Choose an area of skin, such as the chest or upper arm, that is not subject to excessive movement. For best results and to minimize skin irritation, each time you replace a patch, apply the new patch to a different area of the body. In the event that a patch falls off, ask your pharmacist or doctor for advice on whether to re-apply the same patch or replace it with a new patch. It is alright to bathe, shower, or swim with a patch in place.

If redness or irritation develops at the application site, consult your physician. Some people are sensitive to the materials used to make patches.

VAGINAL OINTMENTS AND CREAMS

Most vaginal products are packaged with complete instructions for use. If a woman is not sure how to administer vaginal medication, she should ask her pharmacist.

Before using any vaginal ointment or cream, read the directions. They will probably tell you to attach the applicator to the top of the tube and to squeeze the tube from the bottom until the applicator is completely filled. Then lie on your back with your knees drawn up. Hold the applicator horizontally or pointed slightly downward, and insert it into the vagina as far as it will go comfortably. Press the plunger down to empty the cream or ointment into the vagina. Withdraw the plunger and wash it in warm, soapy water. Rinse it thoroughly and allow it to dry completely before storing.

VAGINAL TABLETS AND SUPPOSITORIES

Most packages of vaginal tablets or suppositories include complete directions for use, but you may wish to review these general instructions.

Remove any foil wrapping. Place the tablet or suppository in the applicator that is provided. Lie on your back with your knees drawn up. Hold the applicator horizontally or tilted slightly downward, and insert it into the vagina as far as it will comfortably go. Depress the plunger slowly to release the tablet or suppository into the vagina. Withdraw the applicator and wash it in warm, soapy water. Rinse it thoroughly and then let it dry completely before storing.

Unless your doctor has told you otherwise, do not douche for two to three weeks after you use vaginal tablets or suppositories. Be sure to ask your doctor for specific recommendations on douching.

Coping with Side Effects

Medications are prescribed and taken precisely because they have certain desirable effects on the human body. The desirable reaction caused by a medication is known as the drug's activity, or therapeutic effect. But medications sometimes have undesirable effects as well. These unwanted effects are referred to as side effects, adverse reactions, or, in some rare cases, lethal effects.

Even if you experience minor side effects, it is very important that you continue to take your medication exactly as it was prescribed. You should take the full dose at the appropriate times throughout the day for the length of time prescribed by your doctor. It is simply not appropriate to take a lesser amount of medication to avoid side effects or because your condition appears to be improving. It is not valid to assume that taking half of the regular dose will provide half of the therapeutic effects. Indeed, a smaller dose may not provide any benefit whatsoever.

Some side effects are expected and unavoidable, but others may surprise the doctor as well as the patient. Such unexpected reactions may be due to an individual's particular response to the drug.

Side effects generally fall into one of two major categories—those that are obvious and those that can be detected only through laboratory testing. Discussion between you and your doctor about your medication should not be limited to the most easily recognized side effects. Other, less obvious, side effects may also be harmful, and you should be sure you understand what they are.

If you know a particular side effect is expected from a specific drug, you can relax a little. Most expected side effects are temporary and need not cause alarm. You'll merely experience discomfort or inconvenience for a short time. For example, you may become drowsy after taking an antihistamine or develop an upset stomach after taking the antibiotic erythromycin. Of course, if you find minor side effects especially bothersome, you should discuss them with your doctor, who may be able to prescribe another drug or at least assure you that the benefits of the drug you are taking far outweigh its side effects. Sometimes side effects can be minimized or eliminated by changing your dosage schedule or taking the drug with meals. Be sure to consult your doctor or pharmacist if you have questions.

Some side effects signal a serious, perhaps even dangerous, problem. When a new medication is prescribed for you, you should ask your doctor what side effects might occur that would signal the need for immediate attention. The discussion that follows should also help you determine whether any side effects you experience require attention. The side effects have been divided into two main categories, those that are obvious and those that are more subtle or discernable only through laboratory testing. With subtle side effects, you may not be aware of any symptoms at all, or you may notice only slight ones. Therefore, your doctor may want you to have periodic laboratory tests or examinations to ensure that no subtle damage is occurring while you are on certain medications. Within the main discussions of obvious and subtle side effects, the discussions have been further broken down into an alphabetical listing of the body parts or systems affected.

OBVIOUS SIDE EFFECTS

Circulatory System

Drugs may slow down or speed up the heartbeat. If a drug slows the heartbeat, you may feel drowsy and tired or even dizzy. If a drug accelerates the heartbeat, you probably will experience palpitations (thumping in the chest). You may feel as though your heart is skipping a beat occasionally. For most people, these symptoms do not indicate a serious problem. If they occur frequently, however, consult your doctor, who may prescribe other medication or adjust your dosage.

Some drugs can cause edema (fluid retention), in which fluid from the blood collects outside the blood vessels. Ordinarily, edema is not a serious condition. But if you are steadily gaining weight or have gained more than three pounds within a week, be sure to consult your doctor.

Drugs may decrease or increase blood pressure. When blood pressure decreases, you may feel drowsy or tired; you may become dizzy, or may even faint, especially when you rise suddenly from a sitting or reclining position. If a drug makes you dizzy or light-headed, sit or lie down for a while. To avoid light-headedness when you stand, contract and relax the muscles of your legs for a few moments before rising. Do this by pushing one foot against the floor while raising the other foot slightly, alternating feet so you are "pumping" your legs in a pedaling motion. Get up slowly, and be careful on stairs. When blood pressure increases, you may feel dizzy, have a headache or blurred vision, hear a ringing or buzzing in your ears, or experience frequent nosebleeds. If these symptoms occur, contact your doctor.

Ears and Hearing

Although a few medications may cause loss of hearing if they are taken in large quantities, hearing loss is an uncommon drug side effect. Drugs that are used to treat problems of the ear may cause dizziness, and many medications produce tinnitus (a sensation of ringing, buzzing, thumping, or hollowness in the ears). Discuss any persistent hearing or ear problem with your doctor.

Eyes and Vision

Blurred vision is a common side effect of many drugs. Medications such as digoxin may cause you to see a halo around a lighted object, such as a television screen or a traffic light, and other drugs may cause night blindness. Chlordiazepoxide and clidinium combination makes it difficult to judge distance accurately while driving and also makes the eyes sensitive to sunlight. While the effects caused by chlordiazepoxide and clidinium combination are to be expected, the effects on the eyes caused by digoxin are danger signs of toxicity. In any case, if an eye-related problem occurs while you are taking medication, contact your physician.

Gastrointestinal System

The gastrointestinal system includes the mouth, esophagus, stomach, small intestine, large intestine, and rectum. Almost any medication has the potential to cause a side effect involving some part of the gastrointestinal system. Many medications produce diarrhea, constipation, dry mouth, mouth sores, difficulty swallowing, heartburn, nausea, vomiting, loss of appetite, or abnormal cramping. Other drugs cause bloating and gas, and some cause rectal itching.

Diarrhea can be expected after taking many medications, but in most cases it is temporary and self-limiting; that is, the diarrhea should stop within three days. During this time, do not take any diarrhea remedy (even over-the-counter or herbal ones), and drink plenty of liquids to replace the fluid you are losing. If the diarrhea lasts more than three days or is accompanied by fever, call your doctor.

In some cases, diarrhea signals a problem. For example, some antibiotics can cause severe diarrhea. When diarrhea is severe—it lasts more than three days or the stools contain blood, pus, or mucus—the intestine may become ulcerated and begin to bleed. If severe diarrhea develops while you are taking an antibiotic or shortly after you complete a course of antibiotic therapy, contact your doctor.

As a side effect of drug use, constipation is more common but less serious than diarrhea. It occurs when a drug slows down the activity of the bowel. Medications such as amitriptyline and chlorpromazine have this effect. Constipation also develops when drugs cause moisture to be absorbed from the bowel, resulting in a more solid stool. Finally, constipation may arise if a drug acts on the nervous system to decrease nerve impulses to the intestine—an effect produced, for example, by methyldopa. Constipation caused by a drug can last for several days.

You may help relieve constipation by drinking eight to ten glasses of water a day, including more fiber in your diet, and getting plenty of exercise (unless your doctor directs you to do otherwise). Do not take laxatives unless your doctor directs you to do so. If constipation continues for more than three days, call your doctor.

Nervous System

Medications that act on the nervous system may cause drowsiness or stimulation (excitation). If a medication causes drowsiness, you may become dizzy or your coordination may become impaired. If a drug causes stimulation, you may become nervous or have insomnia or tremors. Neither drowsiness nor stimulation is cause for concern for most people. When you are drowsy, however, you should be careful around machinery and should avoid driving.

Some medications cause throbbing headaches, and others produce a tingling sensation in the fingers or toes. If these symptoms don't disappear within a few days to a week, be sure to notify your doctor.

Respiratory System

Side effects common to the respiratory system include stuffy nose, dry throat, shortness of breath, and slowed breathing. A stuffy nose and dry throat usually disappear several days after starting a medication. If these side effects are bothersome, you may use nose drops (consult your doctor first) or throat lozenges, or you may gargle with warm salt water to relieve them. Shortness of breath is a characteristic side effect of some drugs (for example, propranolol). If you experience shortness of breath, check with your doctor. It may be a sign of a serious side effect.

Skin

Skin reactions include itching, swelling, redness, rash, and sweating. Itching, swelling, redness, and rash frequently indicate a drug allergy. You should not continue to take a medication if you develop an allergy to it, but you need to contact your doctor before stopping the drug.

Some drugs increase sweating; others decrease it. Drugs that decrease sweating may cause problems during exercise or hot weather when your body needs to sweat to reduce body temperature.

If you have a minor skin reaction not diagnosed as an allergy, ask your pharmacist for advice on how best to manage the problem.

Another type of skin reaction is photosensitivity (also called phototoxicity or sun toxicity)—that is, unusual sensitivity to sunlight. Tetracycline antibiotics can cause photosensitivity. If, while taking such a medication, you are exposed to the sun for even a brief period (10 or 15 minutes), you may get a severe sunburn. This doesn't mean you have to stay indoors while taking these drugs, but you should be fully clothed while outside and not remain in the sun too long. You should also use sunscreen on all exposed skin while in the sun—ask your pharmacist to help you choose one—and wear some type of head covering. Since medications may remain in your bloodstream after you stop taking them, you should continue to follow these precautions for several days after ending treatment with drugs that lead to photosensitivity.

SUBTLE SIDE EFFECTS

Blood

Many drugs affect the blood and circulatory system but do not produce noticeable symptoms for some time. Some drugs decrease the number of red blood cells, the cells responsible for carrying oxygen and nutrients throughout the body. If you have too few red blood cells, you become anemic; you appear pale and feel tired, weak, dizzy, and perhaps hungry. Other drugs may decrease the number of white blood cells, the cells responsible for combating infection. Having too few white blood cells increases susceptibility to infection and may prolong illness. If a sore throat or a fever begins after you start taking a drug and continues for a few days, you may have an infection and too few white blood cells to fight it. Call your doctor.

Common Minor Side Effects

Side Effect	Management
Constipation	Increase amount of fiber in diet*; drink plenty of fluids*; exercise*
Decreased sweating	Avoid working or exercising in the sun or under warm conditions
Diarrhea	Drink lots of water to replace lost fluids; if diarrhea lasts more than three days, call doctor
Dizziness	Avoid operating machinery or driving a car
Drowsiness	Avoid operating machinery or driving a car
Dry mouth	Suck on candy or ice chips, or chew sugarless gum
Dry nose/throat	Use a humidifier or vaporizer
Fluid retention (mild)	Avoid adding salt to foods; keep legs elevated when seated
Headache	Remain quiet; take aspirin* or acetaminophen*
Insomnia	Take dose of drug earlier in the day*; avoid caffeine after noon; ask doctor about exercise program
Itching	Take frequent baths or showers, or use wet soaks
Nasal congestion	If necessary, use nose drops*
Palpitations (mild)	Rest often; avoid tension; do not drink coffee, tea, or cola; stop smoking
Upset stomach	Take drug with milk or food*

*Consult your doctor first

Kidneys

If one of the side effects of a specific medication is to reduce the kidneys' ability to remove chemicals and other substances from the blood, then these substances begin to accumulate in body tissues. Over time, this accumulation may cause vague symptoms, such as swelling, fluid retention, nausea, headache, or weakness. Obvious symptoms, especially pain, are rare.

Liver

Since the liver is responsible for converting many medications and body chemicals into compounds that can be eliminated by other body organs (such as the kidneys, lungs, and gastrointestinal tract), drug-induced liver damage can result in a buildup of these substances. Because liver damage may be quite advanced before it produces any symptoms, periodic blood tests of liver function are recommended during therapy with certain medications.

DRUG USE DURING PREGNANCY AND BREAST-FEEDING

Before taking any medication, it is very important that you tell your doctor if you are pregnant, if you are planning to become pregnant, or if you are breast-feeding an infant. For most medications, complete information on safety during pregnancy and while breast-feeding an infant is not available. This is not due to negligence or lack of concern on the part of regulatory agencies but to the fact that it would be unethical to conduct drug experiments on pregnant and nursing women. With this in mind, you and your doctor should discuss the risks versus benefits of taking any medication in pregnancy or while nursing an infant.

MANAGEMENT OF SIDE EFFECTS

Consult the individual drug profiles to determine whether any side effects that you are experiencing are minor (relatively common and usually not serious) or major (symptoms that indicate the need to consult your doctor). If your side effects are minor, you may be able to compensate for them (see the table on the previous page for suggestions). However, notify your doctor if you consider minor side effects to be persistent or particularly bothersome.

If you experience any major side effects, contact your doctor immediately. Your dosage of the medication may need adjustment, you may have developed an allergy or sensitivity to the drug, or you simply may not be able to tolerate the particular medication well. Your doctor may therefore decide to discontinue the drug and possibly switch you to an alternative medication. However, never stop taking a prescribed medication unless you discuss it with your doctor first.

How Drugs Work

Prescription medications can be placed into several broad categories based on the body systems that they are designed to affect. The drugs in these major categories can be further separated into groupings based on the disease or symptom they are used for, the specific effect they have on an organ or body system, or the particular body function they act upon. The following pages discuss several of the common, broad categories of prescription medications, as well as the subgroupings within them, to give you a better understanding of the types of drugs prescribed for different body systems and different medical conditions.

CARDIOVASCULAR DRUGS

Antianginals

Since the heart is a muscle that must work continuously, it requires a constant supply of nutrients and oxygen. Those nutrients and oxygen are carried to the heart muscle in the blood. The chest pain known as angina can occur when there is an insufficient supply of blood, and consequently of oxygen, to the heart muscle. There are several types of antianginal medications. These include beta blockers (acebutolol, atenolol, betaxolol, bisoprolol, labetalol, metoprolol, nadolol, pindolol, propranolol, timolol), calcium channel blockers (diltiazem, nifedipine, verapamil), and vasodilators (nitroglycerin, isosorbide dinitrate). These drugs act by increasing the amount of oxygen that reaches the heart muscle.

Antiarrhythmics

If the heart does not beat rhythmically or smoothly (a condition called arrhythmia), its rate of contraction must be regulated. Antiarrhythmic drugs (disopyramide, mexiletine, procainamide, propranolol, amiodarone, tocainide) prevent or alleviate arrhythmias by altering nerve impulses in the heart.

Anticoagulants

The blood has a natural ability to clot; otherwise, we would bleed to death from the slightest wound. Sometimes, however, this natural clotting mechanism can be problematic; for instance, blood clots that develop on the interior wall of an artery can end up completely blocking blood flow. Drugs that prevent blood clotting are called anticoagulants (blood thinners). Anticoagulants fall into two categories.

The first category contains medications that must be given by injection. These medications are used in both the hospital and home-care settings. They work by preventing or treating blood clots that could interfere with circulation. Examples of such drugs are dalteparin, enoxaparin, and heparin.

The second category includes oral anticoagulants (those taken by mouth), principally derivatives of the drug warfarin. Warfarin may be used in the treatment of conditions such as stroke, heart disease, and abnormal blood clotting. Warfarin is also used to prevent the movement of a clot, a development that could cause serious problems. It acts by preventing the liver from manufacturing the proteins that are responsible for blood clot formation.

People who are taking warfarin must be careful to avoid using many other medications (including certain doses of aspirin, which itself can have a blood thinning effect), because the interaction of the other medications with the anticoagulant medication could cause internal bleeding. Indeed, patients who are taking warfarin should check with their pharmacist or physician before using any other medications, including any herbal products; natural or homeopathic remedies; vitamins, minerals, or other supplements; and any over-the-counter medications. People taking warfarin should also have their blood checked frequently by their physician to ensure that the correct degree of blood thinning is maintained.

Antihyperlipidemics

Medications for treating atherosclerosis, or hardening of the arteries, act to reduce the serum (the liquified portion of blood) levels of cholesterol and triglycerides (fats), which form plaques (deposits) on the walls of arteries. Some antihyperlipidemics, such as cholestyramine, colestipol, and colesevelam, bind to bile acids in the gastrointestinal tract, thereby decreasing the body's production of cholesterol. Atorvastatin, simvastatin, lovastatin, and pravastatin also decrease the body's production of cholesterol. Use of such drugs is generally recommended only after diet and lifestyle changes have failed to lower blood lipids to desirable levels. Even then, however, diet therapy should be continued.

Antihypertensives

Basically, high blood pressure is a condition in which the pressure of the blood against the walls of the blood vessels is higher than what is considered normal. High blood pressure, or hypertension, which can eventually cause damage to the brain, eyes, heart, or kidneys, is controllable. If medication for high blood pressure has been prescribed, it is very important that you continue to take it regularly, even if you don't notice any symptoms of hypertension. If hypertension is controlled, other damage can be prevented. Medications that counteract or reduce high blood pressure can prolong the life of people with hypertension.

Several different drug actions produce an antihypertensive effect. Some drugs block nerve impulses that cause arteries to constrict; others slow the heart rate and decrease its force of contraction; still others reduce the amount of a certain hormone in the blood that causes blood pressure to rise. The effect of any of these medications is to reduce blood pressure. The mainstay of antihypertensive therapy is often a diuretic, a drug that reduces body fluids. Examples of antihypertensive drugs include beta blockers, calcium channel blockers, ACE (angiotensin-converting enzyme) inhibitors (including benazepril, captopril, enalapril, lisinopril, and quinapril), and the agents valsartan, losartan, prazosin, and terazosin.

Beta Blockers

Beta-blocking medications block the response of the heart and blood vessels to nerve stimulation, thereby slowing the heart rate and lowering blood pressure. They are used in the treatment of a wide range of diseases, including angina, high blood pressure, migraine headaches, arrhythmias, and glaucoma. Metoprolol and propranolol are examples of beta blockers.

Calcium Channel Blockers

Calcium channel blockers (diltiazem, nifedipine, verapamil) are used for the prevention of angina (chest pain). Verapamil is also useful in correcting certain arrhythmias (heartbeat irregularities) and lowering blood pressure. This group of drugs is thought to prevent angina and arrhythmias and lower blood pressure by blocking or slowing calcium flow into muscle cells, which results in vasodilation (widening of the blood vessels) and greater oxygen delivery to the heart muscle.

Cardiac Glycosides

Cardiac glycosides include drugs that are derived from digitalis (digoxin is an example). This type of drug slows the rate of the heart but increases its force of contraction. Cardiac glycosides act as both heart depressants and stimulants: They may be used to regulate irregular heart rhythm or to increase the volume of blood pumped by the heart in heart failure.

Diuretics

Diuretic drugs, such as chlorothiazide, chlorthalidone, furosemide, hydrochlorothiazide, and spironolactone, promote the loss of water and salt from the body (which is why they are sometimes called water pills). This loss of water and salt results in lower blood pressure. They also lower blood pressure by increasing the diameter of blood vessels. Because some antihypertensive medications cause the body to retain salt and water, they are often used concurrently with diuretics. Most diuretics act directly on the kidneys, but there are different types of diuretics, each with different actions. This allows therapy for high blood pressure to be adjusted to meet the needs of individual patients.

Thiazide diuretics, such as chlorothiazide, chlorthalidone, and hydrochlorothiazide, are the most commonly prescribed water pills available today. They are generally well tolerated and can be taken either once or twice per day. Since patients do not develop a tolerance to their antihypertensive effect, these diuretics can be taken for prolonged periods. However, a major drawback of thiazide diuretics is that they often deplete the body of potassium. This can be compensated for with a potassium supplement. Potassium-rich foods and liquids, such as apricots, bananas, and orange juice, can also be used to help correct a potassium deficiency. Salt substitutes are another source of potassium. If necessary, your doctor will direct you to a source of potassium appropriate for you.

Loop diuretics, such as furosemide, act more vigorously than thiazide diuretics. (Loop refers to the structures in the kidneys on which these specific diuretic medications act.) Loop diuretics promote more water loss than thiazide diuretics but they also deplete more potassium from the body.

To remove excess water from the body while retaining its store of potassium, manufacturers developed potassium-sparing diuretics. Medications such as amiloride, spironolactone, and triamterene are effective in treating potassium loss, heart failure, and high blood pressure. Potassium-sparing diuretics are combined with thiazide diuretics in combination medications such as amiloride and hydrochlorothiazide combination, spironolactone and hydrochlorothiazide combination, and triamterene and hydrochlorothiazide combination. Such blends of drugs enhance the antihypertensive effect and reduce potassium loss.

Vasodilators

Vasodilating medications cause the blood vessels to dilate, or widen. Some of the antihypertensive medications, such as hydralazine and prazosin, lower blood pressure by dilating the arteries or veins. Other vasodilating medicines are used in the treatment of stroke and diseases that are characterized by poor blood circulation. Ergoloid mesylates, for example, are used to reduce the symptoms of senility by increasing the flow of oxygen-rich blood to the brain.

DRUGS FOR THE EARS

For an ear infection, a physician usually prescribes an antibiotic drug and a steroid drug or a single medication that contains a combination of the two. The antibiotic attacks the infecting bacteria, and the steroid reduces the inflammation and pain from the infection. Often, a local anesthetic, such as benzocaine or lidocaine, may also be administered or prescribed to relieve pain.

DRUGS FOR THE EYES

Almost all drugs that are used to treat eye problems can be used to treat disorders of other parts of the body as well.

Glaucoma is one of the major disorders of the eye, causing increased pressure within the eyeball. It is of special concern to people over 40 years of age. Although glaucoma is sometimes treated surgically, pressure in the eye can usually be reduced, and blindness prevented, through use of eyedrops. Frequently prescribed drugs for this purpose are timolol, betaxolol, dorzolamide, and latanoprost.

Timolol and betaxolol are beta-blocking drugs that work against glaucoma by decreasing the production of aqueous humor (fluid) in the eye. Unless they have a history of heart failure or asthma, most patients with glaucoma can use a beta blocker. Beta-blocking drugs account for most of the glaucoma medications sold. Dorzolamide is known as a carbonic anhydrate inhibitor, which works differently than the beta blockers to decrease the amount of fluid the eye produces. Sometimes, a beta blocker and a carbonic anhydrate inhibitor will be combined in a single drug product. Latanoprost is a prostaglandin analogue that works to treat glaucoma by increasing the outflow of fluid from the eye.

Eyedrops containing steroids or nonsteroidal anti-inflammatory drugs (NSAIDs) can be used to treat noninfectious eye inflammations as long as they are not used for an extended period of time. Pharmacists carefully monitor refill requests for eyedrops, particularly if the drops contain steroids. They may refuse to refill such prescriptions until you have revisited your doctor. Such caution is necessary because with long-term use, these products can cause additional eye problems. Topical antibiotic medications are also used to treat bacterial eye infections. Other types of eyedrops are sometimes prescribed for the treatment of eye infections, itchy eyes associated with allergies, or redness due to minor eye irritation.

GASTROINTESTINAL DRUGS

Anticholinergics

Anticholinergic medications—for example, dicyclomine—slow the action of the bowel and reduce the amount of stomach acid. Because these medications slow the action of the bowel by relaxing the muscles and relieving spasms, they are said to have an antispasmodic action.

Antidiarrheals

Diarrhea may be caused by many conditions, including influenza (the flu) and ulcerative colitis, and it can sometimes occur as a side effect of a medication. Narcotic drugs and anticholinergic medications slow the action of the bowel and can thereby help alleviate diarrhea. An antidiarrheal medication such as diphenoxylate and atropine combination contains both a narcotic and an anticholinergic.

Antiemetics

Antiemetic medications reduce the urge to vomit. One of the most effective of these medications is the phenothiazine derivative prochlorperazine. This medication acts on the vomiting center in the brain. It is often administered rectally and usually alleviates nausea and vomiting within a few minutes to an hour. Other drugs that are used to combat nausea and vomiting include dolasetron, granisetron, and ondansetron. Antihistamines are also often used to prevent nausea and vomiting, especially when these problems are caused by motion sickness. This type of medication may also work on the vomiting center in the brain.

Antiulcer Medications

Antiulcer medications are prescribed to relieve the symptoms and promote the healing of peptic ulcers as well as to treat acid-reflux disease, which can cause severe heartburn pain in some people. Histamine (H-2) blockers, including cimetidine, famotidine, nizatidine, and ranitidine, work by preventing histamine from attaching to receptors on acid-secreting cells, thus keeping the histamine from triggering the secretion of stomach acid. Another group of antiulcer drugs are the proton pump inhibitors (PPIs); they limit stomach-acid secretion by shutting down the "acid pumps" in the acid-secreting cells themselves. PPIs, which include omeprazole, pantoprazole, and lansoprazole, are commonly prescribed to treat and prevent many stomach problems. Another antiulcer drug, sucralfate, works by forming a chemical barrier over an exposed ulcer that protects the ulcer from stomach acid, much as a bandage protects a wound from debris. These medications provide sustained relief from ulcer and heartburn pain and promote healing.

HORMONES

Hormones are substances that are normally produced and secreted by various glands in the body; they act to stimulate and regulate body functions. Hormone medications mimic the effects of naturally produced hormones and are commonly given when naturally occurring hormones are not being produced in sufficient amounts to regulate specific body functions. This category of medication also includes oral contraceptives (birth control pills) as well as certain types of medications that are used to combat inflammatory reactions.

Antidiabetic Drugs

Insulin, a hormone that is secreted by the pancreas, regulates the level of glucose (a form of sugar) in the blood, as well as the metabolism of carbohydrates and fats. Insulin's counterpart, glucagon, stimulates the liver to release stored glucose. Both insulin and glucagon must be present in the right amounts to maintain the proper blood sugar levels in the body.

Treatment of diabetes mellitus (inability of the body to produce and/or utilize insulin) may involve an adjustment of diet and/or the administration of insulin or oral antidiabetic drugs. Glucagon is given only in emergencies, such as insulin shock, when blood sugar levels must be raised quickly.

People with type 1, or insulin-dependent, diabetes must use insulin to control their blood sugar levels. People who have type 2, or non-insulin-dependent, diabetes may be able to regulate their blood sugar levels through diet modification alone. If not, they may be prescribed oral antidiabetic medications, such as glimepiride, metformin, acarbose, or rosiglitazone. Oral antidiabetics induce the pancreas to secrete more insulin by acting on small groups of pancreatic cells that make and store insulin. Some people with type 2 diabetes may need both insulin and oral antidiabetic drugs.

Sex Hormones

Although small amounts of sex hormones are secreted by the adrenal glands in both males and females, for the most part these hormones are produced by the sex glands. Estrogens and progesterone are the female hormones responsible for secondary sex characteristics such as development of the breasts and maintenance of the lining of the uterus. Testosterone (androgen) is the corresponding male hormone. It is responsible for secondary sex characteristics such as facial hair, a deepened voice, and the maturation of external genitalia.

Testosterone reduces elimination of protein from the body, thereby producing an increase in muscle size. Athletes sometimes take drugs called anabolic steroids (which are chemicals similar to testosterone) for this effect, but using medication for this purpose is dangerous, since anabolic steroids can adversely affect the heart, the nervous system, and the kidneys and cause long-term damage.

Most oral contraceptives (birth control pills) combine estrogen and progestin (natural or synthetic progesterone), but some contain only progestin. Examples of progestin-only contraceptives include the Norplant implant and the Depo-Provera contraceptive device. Progestin aids in preventing ovulation, alters the lining of the uterus, and thickens cervical mucus—processes that help to prevent conception and implantation. The estrogen in birth control pills prevents egg production. Oral contraceptives have many side effects, so their use should be discussed with a physician.

Conjugated estrogens are occasionally used in hormone replacement therapy to treat more severe symptoms of menopause in women whose bodies are no longer able to produce estrogen in sufficient quantities. However, they are no longer recommended for long-term treatment or replacement therapy in most patients. Medroxyprogesterone is used to treat uterine bleeding because of its ability to induce and maintain a lining in the uterus that resembles the lining produced during pregnancy. It also suppresses the release of the pituitary hormone that initiates ovulation, and it is used for menstrual problems.

Steroids

The pituitary gland secretes adrenocorticotropic hormone (ACTH), which directs the adrenal glands to produce adrenocorticosteroids, such as cortisone. Oral steroid preparations (prednisone, for example) may be used to treat poison ivy, hay fever, or insect bites as well as inflammatory diseases such as arthritis, allergies, and asthma. How these drugs relieve inflammation is currently unknown.

Thyroid Drugs

In the past, thyroid preparations were made by drying and pulverizing the thyroid glands of animals and then forming them into tablets. That medication is in minimal use today because people who are unable to produce a sufficient amount of thyroid hormone are usually prescribed a synthetic form, such as levothyroxine.

ANTI-INFECTIVES

Antibiotics

Antibiotics are used to treat a wide variety of bacterial infections. They inhibit the growth of bacteria by interfering with the production of certain biochemicals necessary to sustain the bacteria's life or by interfering with the bacteria's ability to use nutrients. The body's defenses then have a much easier time eliminating the infection.

When used properly, antibiotics are usually effective. To treat an infection adequately, however, antibiotics must be taken regularly for a specified time. If they are not taken for the prescribed period, microorganisms resistant to the antibiotic may continue growing, and the infection could recur. Aminoglycosides, cephalosporins, erythromycins, penicillins (including ampicillin and amoxicillin), quinolones, and tetracyclines are some examples of antibiotics.

Antibiotics do not counteract viruses, including those that cause the common cold, so their use in cold therapy is inappropriate.

Antivirals

Antiviral medications are used to combat viral infections. An antiviral drug called acyclovir is being used in the management of herpes infection. This medication reduces the reproduction of the herpes virus in initial outbreaks, lessens the number of outbreaks of recurrent infection, and speeds the healing of herpes blisters. Acyclovir does not cure the disease, however.

Vaccines

Vaccines were used long before antibiotics became available. A vaccine contains weakened or dead disease-causing microorganisms or parts of such organisms, which activate the body's immune system to produce a natural defense against a particular disease (such as polio or measles). A vaccine is usually given to prevent a specific disease, but it may also be used in certain circumstances to alleviate or treat an infectious disease that has already taken hold.

Other Anti-infectives

Drugs called anthelmintics are used to treat worm infestations. Fungal infections are treated with antifungals, such as nystatin, that destroy and prevent the growth of fungi. A pediculicide is a drug used to treat a person infested with lice. And a scabicide is prescribed to deal with scabies.

ANTINEOPLASTICS

Antineoplastic medications are used in the treatment of cancer. Most of these drugs prevent the growth of body cells that divide rapidly, which include cancer cells (unfortunately, there are also normal, healthy cells that naturally grow rapidly, and these can be damaged or destroyed by antineoplastic drugs as well). Antineoplastic medications are, without exception, extremely toxic substances and can cause serious side effects. But for many cancer victims, the benefits derived from chemotherapy with antineoplastic drugs far outweigh the risks.

TOPICAL DRUGS

Medications are often applied topically (locally to the skin) to treat skin disorders so that there are minimal systemic (throughout the body) side effects from their use. For example, antibiotic and antifungal creams or ointments are prescribed for skin infections. And steroids may be applied to deal with certain inflammatory skin conditions. Many different topical steroid medicines, of varying potency, are available. Examples include hydrocortisone (considered low-potency) and triamcinolone (considered to be a higher-potency product).

Some medications that are applied to the skin have more far-reaching effects in the body, however. For example, nitroglycerin can be placed on the skin in the form of an ointment or patch and then absorbed into the bloodstream. The absorbed nitroglycerin dilates blood vessels and alleviates the chest pain known as angina. Clonidine, estrogen, scopolamine, nicotine, and a birth-control-hormone combination are also available in the form of transdermal patches.

CENTRAL NERVOUS SYSTEM DRUGS

Alzheimer's Disease Drugs

Several medications are available to help slow the decline in mental abilities in people who suffer from Alzheimer's disease, an incurable disease that causes gradual deterioration in brain function. These medications work by increasing the amount of a substance called acetylcholine in the brain. Commonly used medicines are donepezil, rivastigmine, and galantamine.

Amphetamines

Amphetamines, or adrenergic drugs, are sometimes prescribed as anorectics (drugs that are used to reduce the appetite). These drugs temporarily quiet the part of the brain that causes hunger, but they also keep a person awake, speed up the heart, and raise blood pressure. After two to three weeks, these medications begin to lose their effectiveness as appetite suppressants.

Amphetamines stimulate most people, but they have the opposite effect on children who have attention deficit hyperactivity disorder (ADHD), which is marked by inattention, impulsiveness, and an abnormal degree of overactivity. ADHD is difficult to diagnose properly and requires a specialist to treat. But when children with ADHD take an amphetamine such as methylphenidate, their level of activity diminishes. Most likely, amphetamines quiet these youngsters by selectively stimulating parts of the brain that ordinarily control activity.

Analgesics

Pain is not a disease but a symptom of some other problem. Drugs used to relieve pain are called analgesics, which form a rather diverse group. We do not fully understand how most analgesics work. Analgesics fall into two categories: They may be either narcotic or nonnarcotic.

Narcotics are derived from the opium poppy. They act on the brain to relieve pain, often bringing on drowsiness and a feeling of well-being. Some narcotics relieve coughing spasms and are used in prescription cough syrups. Unfortunately, narcotics can be addictive. To date, attempts by manufacturers to produce nonaddictive synthetic narcotic derivatives have not succeeded.

Nonnarcotic pain relievers are also used. Aspirin and related medications, called nonsteroidal anti-inflammatory drugs (NSAIDs), are the most frequently used pain relievers in the United States today. Aspirin does not require a prescription, but doctors often write prescriptions for it to treat diseases such as arthritis.

Acetaminophen, which is not an NSAID, may be used in place of aspirin to relieve pain, but it does not reduce inflammation.

A number of analgesic medications contain codeine or other narcotics in combination with nonnarcotic analgesics (such as aspirin, ibuprofen, or acetaminophen). These combination analgesics are not as potent as pure narcotics but are frequently as effective. Because these medications contain narcotics, however, they have the potential for abuse and must be used with caution.

Antianxiety/Sedative Drugs

Medications used in the treatment of anxiety, panic disorder, and insomnia selectively reduce the activity of certain chemicals in the brain. Drugs formulated to relieve anxiety include benzodiazepines (such as lorazepam, alprazolam, clorazepate, and diazepam) and buspirone. These medications are not offered to relieve the stresses of everyday life; they are used only when indicated by your doctor. Drugs used to induce sleep in insomniacs may include benzodiazepines, antihistamines (such as diphenhydramine), and zaleplon.

Anticonvulsants

Drugs such as carbamazepine, phenytoin, and gabapentin are used to control seizures and other symptoms of epilepsy. They selectively reduce excessive stimulation in the brain. In addition, these medications may be used to prevent and treat certain types of pain. The manner in which they work is not clearly understood.

Antidepressants

Tricyclic antidepressants (such as amitriptyline), selective serotonin reuptake inhibitors (such as fluoxetine, paroxetine, and sertraline), tetracyclic antidepressants (such as maprotiline), and monoamine oxidase (MAO) inhibitors (such as phenelzine) are types of medication used to treat depression. Antidepressant medications are also used for panic attacks and obsessive-compulsive disorder (OCD) and in the prevention of migraine headaches and other types of pain, although the manner in which they help to provide relief is not clearly understood.

Antidepressants may produce serious side effects, and they can interact with other drugs. MAO inhibitors can also mix with certain foods, resulting in dangerous increases in blood pressure. Therefore, they should be used very carefully.

Anti-inflammatory Drugs

Inflammation is the body's natural response to injury. An inflammatory response is generally marked by swelling, pain, fever, redness, and itching. Aspirin is one of the most effective anti-inflammatory drugs. Other drugs, called nonsteroidal anti-inflammatory drugs (NSAIDs)—for example, fenoprofen, ibuprofen, indomethacin, naproxen, and tolmetin—relieve inflammation and may be more effective than aspirin in certain individuals. Steroids are also used to treat inflammatory diseases.

When sore muscles tense up or tighten, they can cause pain, inflammation, and spasm. Skeletal muscle relaxants (such as orphenadrine and meprobamate) may help to relieve these symptoms. Skeletal muscle relaxants are often given in combination with an anti-inflammatory pain-relieving medication such as aspirin or ibuprofen. Some doctors, however, believe that aspirin or another NSAID and rest are better than skeletal muscle relaxants for alleviating the symptoms of muscle strain.

Antipsychotics

Major tranquilizers or antipsychotic medications are usually prescribed for patients who are suffering from psychoses (certain types of mental disorders). These medications calm certain areas of the brain but permit the rest of the brain to function normally. They act as a screen that allows the transmission of some nerve impulses but restricts the passage of others. The drugs most frequently used include haloperidol, lithium, chlorpromazine, and thioridazine. Other newer agents that may be used include clozapine, olanzapine, and quetiapine.

Parkinson's Disease Drugs

Parkinson's disease is a progressive neurological disorder caused by a chemical imbalance in the brain. People who have Parkinson's disease experience uncontrollable tremors, develop a characteristic stoop, and eventually become unable to walk. Medications such as benztropine, bromocriptine, levodopa, selegiline, and trihexyphenidyl are used to correct the chemical imbalance in the brain, thus helping to relieve the symptoms of the disease (although these medications can have unwanted side effects of their own). Benztropine and trihexyphenidyl are used to relieve tremors that are caused by other medications as well.

RESPIRATORY DRUGS

Antihistamines

Histamine is a body chemical that, when released in the body, typically causes swelling and itching. Antihistamines counteract these allergy symptoms by blocking the effects of histamine and are used for mild respiratory allergies, such as hay fever. Diphenhydramine and other antihistamines are relatively slow-acting. Severe allergic reactions sometimes require the use of epinephrine (which is not an antihistamine). In its injectable form, epinephrine acts very quickly.

Some types of antihistamines are also used to prevent or treat motion sickness. The antihistamines diphenhydramine, meclizine, and scopolamine, for example, are often used specifically for this purpose.

Antitussives

Antitussive medications control coughs. There are many nonprescription antitussives available; most contain dextromethorphan. Codeine is a narcotic antitussive that is an ingredient in many prescription cough medications. Before they can relieve a cough, these preparations must be absorbed into the blood, circulate through the system, and then act on the brain.

Bronchodilators

Bronchodilators (agents that open airways in the lungs) and medications that relax smooth-muscle tissue (such as that found in the lungs) are used to improve breathing. Aminophylline and theophylline are oral bronchodilators commonly used to relieve the symptoms of asthma and pulmonary emphysema. Albuterol and metaproterenol are bronchodilators available orally or as inhalants and act directly on the muscles of the bronchi (breathing tubes).

Decongestants

Decongestants constrict blood vessels in the nose and sinuses to open air passages. They are available in different forms: as oral preparations, nose drops, and nose sprays. Oral decongestants are slow-acting but do not interfere with the production of mucus or movement of the cilia, hairlike structures in the respiratory tract that help sweep mucus and debris out of the air passages. They can increase blood pressure, however, so they should be used cautiously by patients who have high blood pressure. Topical decongestants (nose drops or spray) provide almost immediate relief. They do not increase blood pressure as much as oral decongestants, but they do slow the movement of the cilia. People who use these products may develop a tolerance for them. (Tolerance can be described as a need for ever-increasing dosages to achieve a beneficial effect.) One disadvantage of developing a tolerance is that as the dosage increases, the risk of side effects also increases. Topical decongestants should not be used for more than a few days at a time.

Expectorants

Expectorants are used to change a dry, nonproductive cough into a productive one (that is, one that brings up phlegm). Expectorants are supposed to increase the amount of mucus that is produced, but drinking extra water or using a vaporizer or humidifier is probably more effective at increasing mucus production.

VITAMINS AND MINERALS

Vitamins and minerals are chemical substances that are vital to the maintenance of normal body function. Most of us can obtain enough vitamins and minerals from our regular diet, but some people develop vitamin deficiencies. Serious nutritional deficiencies lead to diseases such as pellagra and beriberi, which must be treated by a physician. People who have an inadequate or restricted diet, people who have certain disorders or debilitating illnesses, and women who are pregnant or breast-feeding are among those who may benefit from taking supplemental vitamins and minerals. Even these people should consult a doctor to verify the need for supplements.

Drug Profiles

Immediately following this chapter are profiles of the most commonly prescribed drugs and selected over-the-counter medications. The drug profiles are arranged alphabetically by the generic name of each drug. To look up a drug by its brand name, use the Index, at the back of the publication, which will tell you the drug's generic name. Then see the generic name in the Index for the page number of the profile.

A drug profile summarizes the most important information about a particular drug. By studying a profile, you will learn what to expect from the drug, when to be concerned about side effects, which other drugs may interact with it, and how to take the drug to get the most benefit. Each profile includes the following information:

generic name

The drugs profiled in this publication are listed by generic names. You should know both the generic and the trade names of all of the medications you are taking. If you are unsure of the generic name of one of your drugs after checking the Index at the back of this publication, consult your pharmacist.

BRAND NAMES (Manufacturers)
The most common trade names of each generic product are listed, along with the manufacturers' names. Not every available trade name is included, but as many as possible have been listed. "Various manufacturers" is listed for some of the generic names—this indicates that there are generic products available.
TYPE OF DRUG
The chemical or pharmacologic class or effect is listed for each generic drug.
INGREDIENTS
The pharmaceutically active components (the ingredients in the drug that are supposed to achieve the desired medicinal effect) of each drug product are itemized. Many drugs contain more than one active chemical component; all of these components are included under this category.
DOSAGE FORMS
The most common forms (for example, tablets, capsules, liquid, suppositories) of each profiled drug are listed, as well as the drug's alcohol content, if any. Strengths or concentrations are also provided.
STORAGE
Storage requirements for each of the dosage forms listed are discussed. These directions should be followed carefully in order to ensure the potency of your medications.

USES

It is important that you understand why you are taking each of your medications. This section includes the most important and most common clinical uses for each profiled drug. Your doctor may prescribe a drug for a reason that does not appear on this list. The exclusion does not mean that your doctor has made an error. However, if the use for which you are taking a drug does not appear in this category and if you have any questions about why the drug was prescribed, consult your doctor. A description of how the drug is thought to work is also given in this section.

TREATMENT

Instructions are provided on how to take each profiled medication in order to obtain its maximum benefit. Information can be found on whether the drug can be taken with food. Advice is given on how to use the various forms that the drug might be available in, such as ointments, creams, aerosol sprays, eardrops, eyedrops, or suppositories. This is also where you will find information on what to do if you miss a scheduled dose of your medication.

SIDE EFFECTS

Minor. The most common and least serious reactions to a drug are listed in this section. Most of these side effects, if they occur, disappear in a day or two. Do not expect to experience these side effects; but if they occur and are particularly annoying, do not hesitate to seek medical advice.

Suggestions for preventing or relieving some of these side effects are also provided in this section of the profile.

Major. Major side effects are less common than minor side effects, and you will probably never experience them. However, should any of the reactions listed in this section occur, you should call your doctor. These reactions indicate that something may be going wrong with your drug therapy. You may have an allergy to the drug, or some other problem could have developed. If you experience a major side effect, it may be necessary to adjust your dosage or to substitute a different medication in your treatment. It is important to discuss this with your doctor.

New side effects are being reported daily. If you experience a reaction that is bothersome or severe, consult your doctor immediately, even if that particular side effect is not mentioned in this publication.

INTERACTIONS

This section lists the medications (both prescription and over-the-counter drugs) and foods that can interact with the profiled drug. Certain drugs are safe when used alone but may cause serious reactions or lose potency when taken in combination with other drugs or chemicals or certain foods. A description of how the profiled medication interacts with other drugs or foods, and what to expect if the two are taken together, is also provided. Not all possible drug combinations have been tested. So it is important that your pharmacist and health care providers be aware of all the drugs you are taking (including prescription, over-the-counter, homeopathic, and natural products as well as any vitamin and/or mineral supplements).

WARNINGS

This section lists the precautions necessary for safe use of the profiled drug. It provides information on drugs that should be avoided if you have had a previous allergic reaction or severe drug reaction, as well as information on the conditions or disease states that require close monitoring while this drug is being taken. In this section you will also find out whether the profiled drug is likely to affect your driving ability, whether you are likely to become tolerant to its effects over time, if it is dangerous to stop taking the medication abruptly, and if you should discuss with your doctor temporarily stopping therapy with the medication before having surgery or any other medical or dental procedure.

Certain individuals are allergic to the color additive FD&C Yellow No. 5 (tartrazine). This section provides information on the tartrazine content of the various dosage forms. Other information included in this category might concern supplemental therapy—for example, drinking extra fluids while treating a urinary tract infection or wearing cotton underpants while treating a vaginal infection.

A discussion of the known risks of treatment with this medication during pregnancy or while breast-feeding an infant is provided. It should be kept in mind that for the majority of medications on the market, the risks to a fetus or nursing infant are simply not known. Experiments are not usually conducted on pregnant women and infants (for ethical reasons). You should therefore discuss the risks and benefits of any particular drug therapy with your doctor if you are pregnant, are planning to become pregnant, or are breast-feeding an infant.

abacavir

BRAND NAME (Manufacturer)
Ziagen (GlaxoSmithKline)
TYPE OF DRUG
Antiviral
INGREDIENT
abacavir
DOSAGE FORMS
Tablets (300 mg)
Oral solution (20 mg per mL)
STORAGE
Store tablets and oral solution at room temperature in a tightly closed container. Do not expose to excess heat. The oral solution may be refrigerated but should not be frozen.

USES

Abacavir is used in the treatment of human immunodeficiency virus (HIV) infection. HIV is the virus that causes AIDS. Abacavir works by inhibiting the reproduction, or growth, of the virus, which slows down the progression of AIDS. Abacavir does not cure HIV infection or AIDS, but it may delay the onset of other infections and diseases caused by AIDS.

TREATMENT

This medication works best when the level of medicine in your bloodstream is kept constant. It is best to take the drug at evenly spaced intervals throughout the day.

If you miss a dose of this medication, take it as soon as possible. However, if it is almost time for your next dose, skip the missed dose and go back to your regular dosing schedule. Do not double the doses.

SIDE EFFECTS

Minor. Diarrhea, difficulty sleeping, insomnia, loss of appetite, nausea, or vomiting. These side effects should decrease or disappear as your body adjusts to the medication.
Major. Tell your doctor about any side effects that are persistent or particularly bothersome. IT IS ESPECIALLY IMPORTANT TO TELL YOUR DOCTOR about abdominal pain, achiness or a general feeling of being unwell, diarrhea, fever, muscle pain or cramping, nausea, severe tiredness or exhaustion, skin rash, vomiting, or yellowing of the skin or the whites of the eyes.

INTERACTIONS

Abacavir may interact with a number of other medications; be sure to contact your doctor or pharmacist about possible interactions with any other medications that you are currently taking.

Use of alcohol during treatment with abacavir may increase the amount of abacavir in the body by preventing its breakdown.

WARNINGS

• A small percentage of patients have experienced a severe and potentially fatal allergic (hypersensitivity) reaction while taking this medication. IF YOU DEVELOP A SKIN RASH WHILE TAKING ABACAVIR, YOU SHOULD DISCONTINUE USE OF THE MEDICATION AND CONTACT YOUR DOCTOR IMMEDIATELY. OTHER SIGNS OF AN ALLERGIC REACTION INCLUDE DIARRHEA, VOMITING, MOUTH SORES, DIFFICULTY BREATHING, ABDOMINAL PAIN, SEVERE TIREDNESS, ACHES, OR A GENERAL FEELING OF BEING UNWELL. IF YOU DEVELOP ANY OF THESE SIDE EFFECTS, YOU SHOULD CONTACT YOUR DOCTOR IMMEDIATELY. A medication guide and warning card explaining the signs and symptoms of an allergic reaction to abacavir should be given to you with your prescription; ask your pharmacist for these materials if they are not included with your prescription.

• Tell your doctor if you have ever had an allergic reaction to abacavir or to any other medication. If you develop an allergic reaction to abacavir, it is important to know that you cannot take this medication again.

• Although it is not common, abacavir may cause a condition known as lactic acidosis. IT IS IMPORTANT TO TELL YOUR DOCTOR IMMEDIATELY if you experience severe muscle pain or cramping, diarrhea, shallow or fast breathing, and unusual tiredness or weakness.

• Before taking this medication, be sure to tell your doctor about any medical problems you may have, especially liver problems.

• Be sure to tell your doctor if you are pregnant. Although birth defects have not been documented in humans, abacavir has been shown to cause birth defects in animals. It is unknown if abacavir is safe to use during human pregnancy. It is also not known if abacavir passes into human breast milk. However, because of the risk of passing the HIV virus to infants, it is recommended that mothers who are infected with the HIV virus NOT breast-feed their infants.

---

acarbose

BRAND NAME (Manufacturer)
Precose (Bayer)
TYPE OF DRUG
Oral antidiabetic
INGREDIENT
acarbose
DOSAGE FORM
Tablets (50 mg and 100 mg)
STORAGE
Store at room temperature in a tightly closed container. Do not refrigerate or freeze this medication. Discard any outdated medication.

USES

Acarbose is used for the treatment of the form of diabetes that appears most frequently in adulthood—known as type 2 or non–insulin-dependent diabetes—when it cannot be managed by exercise and control of diet alone. Acarbose works differently from other antidiabetic medications: It does not act to lower your blood sugar. Instead, it works to reduce the amount of sugar that your body can absorb from food. Acarbose can be used alone or with other oral antidiabetic agents (such as sulfonylureas).

TREATMENT

For this medication to work correctly, it must be taken at the beginning of each main meal, as directed by your doctor. It is important to avoid missing any doses of acarbose. However, if you have already finished a meal and forgot to take your dose of the medication, do not take the missed dose at all. Just return to your regular dosing schedule, taking the next dose at the beginning of your next main meal. Do not double the dose of this medication.

SIDE EFFECTS

Minor. Abdominal pain, diarrhea, and stomach gas. These side effects should decrease or disappear as your body adjusts to the medication.

Major. Tell your doctor about any side effects from this medication that are persistent or particularly bothersome. IT IS ESPECIALLY IMPORTANT TO TELL YOUR DOCTOR if you experience severe abdominal pain or discomfort as well as any persistent diarrhea or stomach gas.

INTERACTIONS

Acarbose interacts with several types of medications:
1. This medication may reduce the effectiveness of digestive enzymes.
2. Medications such as activated charcoal or other absorbents may interfere with the action of acarbose.

WARNINGS

• Tell your doctor if you have ever had an unusual or allergic reaction to any medication, especially to acarbose.
• Tell your doctor if you now have or if you have ever had anemia or liver disease, any type of stomach or intestinal disorders, kidney disease, or any complications from diabetes.
• Before having surgery or any other medical or dental treatment, be sure to tell your doctor or dentist that you are taking acarbose.
• Follow the special dietary guidelines provided by your doctor. This is an important part of controlling your blood sugar levels and is necessary in order for this medication to work properly.
• Test for sugar in your blood or urine as directed by your doctor. It is a convenient way to determine whether your diabetes is being controlled by this medication.
• Acarbose does not cause hypoglycemia (low blood sugar), even if it is taken without food. However, acarbose is sometimes used with other antidiabetic agents that may cause hypoglycemia. IT IS IMPORTANT TO REMEMBER THAT acarbose will interfere with your body's ability to absorb table sugar. If you experience symptoms of hypoglycemia (such as anxiety, chills, cold sweats, cool or pale skin, drowsiness, excessive hunger, headache, nausea, nervousness, rapid heartbeat, shakiness, or unusual tiredness or weakness), you need to eat or drink something containing GLUCOSE OR DEXTROSE right away. Table sugar will not be absorbed by your body if you are taking acarbose. It is important for your family and friends to know the symptoms of low blood sugar. They should understand what to do if they observe any of these symptoms in you.
• Tell your doctor if you are pregnant or plan to become pregnant. This drug has not been studied for use in pregnancy. Your doctor may switch you to insulin while you are pregnant. Also tell your doctor if you are breast-feeding an infant. Small amounts of acarbose may pass into breast milk.

---

acetaminophen and codeine combination

BRAND NAMES (Manufacturers)
acetaminophen with codeine (various manufacturers)
Capital with Codeine (Carnrick)
Phenaphen-650 with Codeine (Robins)
Phenaphen with Codeine (Robins)
Tylenol with Codeine (McNeil)
TYPE OF DRUG
Analgesic combination
INGREDIENTS
acetaminophen and codeine

DOSAGE FORMS

Tablets (300 mg acetaminophen with 15 mg, 30 mg, or 60 mg codeine; 325 mg acetaminophen with 30 mg or 60 mg codeine; 650 mg acetaminophen with 30 mg codeine)

Capsules (325 mg acetaminophen with 15 mg, 30 mg, or 60 mg codeine)

Oral elixir (120 mg acetaminophen and 12 mg codeine per 5-mL spoonful, with 7% alcohol)

Oral suspension (120 mg acetaminophen and 12 mg codeine per 5-mL spoonful, alcohol-free)

On the label of the vial of tablets or capsules, the name of this drug may be followed by a number that refers to the amount of codeine present (#2 has 15 mg codeine, #3 has 30 mg codeine, and #4 has 60 mg codeine).

STORAGE

Store all forms of this medication at room temperature. Do not store this medication in the freezer.

USES

Acetaminophen and codeine combination is used to relieve mild to severe pain (the formulations of this medication that have the higher codeine contents are used to relieve more severe pain). Codeine is a narcotic analgesic that acts on the central nervous system (brain and spinal cord) in order to relieve pain.

TREATMENT

To avoid stomach upset, take this medication with food or with milk.

This medication works most effectively if you take it at the onset of pain, rather than waiting until the pain becomes more intense.

Measure the dose of the liquid form of this medication carefully with a specially designed 5-mL measuring spoon. An ordinary kitchen teaspoon is not accurate enough for measuring the dosage.

If you are taking this medication on a regular schedule and you miss a dose, take the missed dose as soon as possible. However, if it is almost time for the next dose, don't take the missed dose at all; just return to your regular dosing schedule. Do not double the next dose.

SIDE EFFECTS

Minor. Constipation, dizziness, drowsiness, dry mouth, false sense of well-being, flushing, light-headedness, loss of appetite, nausea, painful or difficult urination, or sweating. These side effects should disappear as your body adjusts to the medication.

If you are constipated, increase the amount of fiber in your diet (fresh fruits and vegetables, salads, bran, and whole-grain breads), exercise, and drink more water (unless your doctor directs you to do otherwise).

To reduce mouth dryness, chew sugarless gum or suck on ice chips or hard candy.

If you feel dizzy or light-headed, sit or lie down for a while; get up slowly from a sitting or reclining position; and be careful on stairs.

Major. Tell your doctor about any side effects that are persistent or particularly bothersome. IT IS ESPECIALLY IMPORTANT TO TELL YOUR DOCTOR about anxiety, difficulty in breathing, excitation, fatigue, heart palpitations, rash, restlessness, sore throat and fever, tremors, unusual bleeding or bruising of the skin, weakness, or yellowing of the skin or the whites of the eyes.

INTERACTIONS

This medication interacts with several other types of drugs:

1. Concurrent use with other central nervous system depressants (such as alcohol, antihistamines, barbiturates, benzodiazepine tranquilizers, muscle relaxants, and phenothiazine tranquilizers) or with tricyclic antidepressant medications can cause extreme drowsiness.
2. A monoamine oxidase (MAO) inhibitor taken within 14 days of this medication can lead to unpredictable and severe side effects.
3. Long-term use and high doses of the acetaminophen portion of this medication can increase the effects of oral anticoagulants (blood-thinning medications, such as warfarin and heparin); combining these medications in this manner, therefore, may lead to bleeding complications.
4. Anticonvulsants (antiseizure medications), barbiturates, and alcohol can increase the toxic effects on the liver that are caused by large doses of the acetaminophen portion of this medication.

BE SURE TO TELL YOUR DOCTOR about any medications you are currently taking, especially any of the medications listed above.

WARNINGS

• Tell your doctor about unusual or allergic reactions you have had to any medications, especially to acetaminophen or to codeine or other narcotic analgesics (such as hydrocodone, hydromorphone, meperidine, methadone, morphine, oxycodone, and propoxyphene).

• Tell your doctor if you now have or if you have ever had an acute abdominal condition, asthma, a blood disorder, brain disease, colitis, epilepsy, gallstones or gallbladder disease, a head injury, heart disease, kidney disease, liver disease, lung disease, mental illness, prostate disease, thyroid disease, or urethral strictures.

• If you experience dizziness or drowsiness from use of this medication, do not take part in any activity that requires alertness, such as driving a car or operating potentially dangerous equipment.

• Before having surgery or any other medical or dental treatment, be sure to tell your doctor or dentist that you are taking this medication.

• Because this product contains codeine, it has the potential for abuse and must be used with caution. Usually, it should not be taken on a regular schedule for longer than ten days at a time. Tolerance develops quickly; do not increase the dosage or stop taking the drug abruptly unless you first consult your doctor. If you have been taking large amounts of this medication for long periods, you may experience a withdrawal reaction (diarrhea, excessive yawning, gooseflesh, irritability, muscle aches, nausea, runny nose, shivering, sleep disorders, stomach cramps, sweating, trembling, vomiting, or weakness). Your doctor may, therefore, want to reduce your dosage of the medication gradually to avoid this reaction.

• Because this product contains acetaminophen, additional prescription or over-the-counter medications that contain acetaminophen should not be taken without first getting your doctor's approval. Be sure to check the labels on over-the-counter pain, sinus, allergy, asthma, diet, cough, and cold products before you use them in order to see if they also contain acetaminophen.

• Be sure to tell your doctor if you are pregnant. The effects of this medication during pregnancy have not been thoroughly studied in humans. Codeine used regularly in large doses during pregnancy can result in addiction of the fetus, leading to withdrawal symptoms (such as diarrhea, excessive crying, excessive yawning, irritability, fever, sneezing, tremors, or vomiting) in the infant at birth. Also be sure to tell your doctor if you are breast-feeding an infant. Small amounts of this medication may pass into the breast milk and cause drowsiness in the nursing infant.

acetaminophen and hydrocodone combination

BRAND NAMES (Manufacturers)
acetaminophen with hydrocodone (various manufacturers)
Anexsia (Mallinckrodt)
Lorcet (Forest)
Lortab (UCB)*
Vicodin (Abbott)
Vicodin ES (Abbott)
Vicodin HP (Abbott)
Zydone (DuPont)
*Available in different strengths

TYPE OF DRUG
Analgesic combination

INGREDIENTS
acetaminophen and hydrocodone

DOSAGE FORMS
Tablets (500 mg acetaminophen with 2.5 mg, 5 mg, 7.5 mg, or 10 mg hydrocodone; 650 mg acetaminophen with 7.5 mg or 10 mg hydrocodone; 660 mg acetaminophen with 10 mg hydrocodone; 750 mg acetaminophen with 7.5 mg hydrocodone)
Capsules (500 mg acetaminophen with 5 mg hydrocodone)
Liquid (167 mg acetaminophen with 2.5 mg hydrocodone per 5-mL spoonful, with 7% alcohol)

STORAGE
Store all forms at room temperature in tightly closed, light-resistant containers.

USES

This medication is used to relieve moderate to severe pain. Hydrocodone is a narcotic analgesic that acts on the central nervous system (the brain and spinal cord) to relieve pain.

TREATMENT

To avoid stomach upset, take this medication with food or with milk.

Measure each dose of the oral liquid form of this medication carefully with a specially designed 5-mL measuring spoon. An ordinary kitchen teaspoon is not accurate enough for this purpose.

This medication works most effectively if you take it at the onset of pain rather than waiting until the pain becomes intense.

If you are taking this medication on a regular schedule and you miss a dose, take the missed dose as soon as possible. However, if it is almost time for your next dose, don't take the missed dose at all; just return to your regular dosing schedule. Do not double the next dose.

SIDE EFFECTS

Minor. Constipation, dizziness, dry mouth, false sense of well-being, flushing, lightheadedness, loss of appetite, nausea, painful or difficult urination, or sweating. These side effects should disappear as your body adjusts to the medication.

If you are constipated, increase the amount of fiber in your diet (fresh fruits and vegetables, salads, bran, and whole-grain breads), exercise, and drink more water (unless your doctor directs you to do otherwise).

To reduce mouth dryness, chew sugarless gum or suck on ice chips or hard candy.

If you feel dizzy, sit or lie down for a while; get up from a sitting or reclining position slowly; and be careful on stairs.

Major. Tell your doctor about any side effects that are persistent or particularly bothersome. IT IS ESPECIALLY IMPORTANT TO TELL YOUR DOCTOR about anxiety, difficulty in breathing, excitation, fatigue, palpitations, rash, restlessness, sore throat and fever, tremors, unusual bleeding or bruising, weakness, or yellowing of the eyes or the skin.

INTERACTIONS

This medication interacts with several other types of drugs:

1. Concurrent use of this medication with other central nervous system depressants (such as alcohol, antihistamines, barbiturates, benzodiazepine tranquilizers, muscle relaxants, and phenothiazine tranquilizers) or with tricyclic antidepressants can cause extreme drowsiness.

2. A monoamine oxidase (MAO) inhibitor taken within 14 days of this drug can lead to severe side effects.

3. Long-term use and high doses of the acetaminophen portion of this medication can increase the effects of oral anticoagulants (blood thinners, such as warfarin); this combination may lead to bleeding complications.

4. Anticonvulsants (antiseizure medications), barbiturates, and alcohol can increase the liver toxicity caused by large doses of the acetaminophen portion of this medication.

TELL YOUR DOCTOR about any medications you are currently taking, especially any of those listed above.

WARNINGS

• Tell your doctor about unusual or allergic reactions you have had to any medications, especially to acetaminophen, hydrocodone, or other narcotic analgesics (such as codeine, hydromorphone, meperidine, methadone, morphine, oxycodone, and propoxyphene).

• Tell your doctor if you now have or if you have ever had acute abdominal conditions, asthma, blood disorders, brain disease, colitis, epilepsy, gallstones or gallbladder disease, a head injury, heart disease, kidney disease, liver disease, lung disease, mental illness, prostate disease, thyroid disease, or urethral strictures.

• If this medication makes you dizzy or drowsy, do not take part in any activity that requires you to remain alert, such as driving an automobile or operating potentially dangerous equipment.

• Before having surgery or any other medical or dental treatment, be sure to tell your doctor or dentist that you are taking this medication.

• Because this product contains hydrocodone, it has the potential for abuse and must be used with caution. Usually, it should not be taken on a regular schedule for longer than ten days at a time. Tolerance develops quickly; do not increase the dosage or stop taking the drug abruptly unless you first consult your doctor. If you have been taking large amounts of this medication for long periods, you may experience a withdrawal reaction (with symptoms including diarrhea, excessive yawning, gooseflesh, irritability, muscle aches, nausea, runny nose, shivering, sleep disorders, stomach cramps, sweating, trembling, vomiting, or weakness). Your doctor may, therefore, want to reduce the dosage of this medication gradually.

• Because this product contains acetaminophen, additional medications that contain acetaminophen should not be taken without your doctor's approval. Check the labels on over-the-counter (nonprescription) pain, sinus, allergy, asthma, diet, cough, and cold products to see if they contain acetaminophen.

• Be sure to tell your doctor if you are pregnant. The effects of this medication during pregnancy have not been thoroughly studied in humans. Regular use of hydrocodone in large doses during pregnancy can result in addiction of the fetus, leading to withdrawal symptoms (diarrhea, excessive crying, excessive yawning, fever, irritability, sneezing, tremors, or vomiting) at birth. Also be sure that you tell your doctor if you are breast-feeding an infant. Small amounts of this medication may pass into breast milk and cause excessive drowsiness in the nursing infant.

---

acetaminophen and oxycodone combination

BRAND NAMES (Manufacturers)
oxycodone hydrochloride with acetaminophen (various manufacturers)
Percocet (DuPont)
Roxicet (Roxane)
TYPE OF DRUG
Analgesic combination
INGREDIENTS
acetaminophen and oxycodone
DOSAGE FORMS
Tablets (325 mg acetaminophen with 2.5 mg oxycodone; 325 mg acetaminophen with 5 mg oxycodone; 500 mg acetaminophen with 5 mg oxycodone; 500 mg acetaminophen with 7.5 mg oxycodone; 650 mg acetaminophen with 10 mg oxycodone)
Caplets (500 mg acetaminophen with 5 mg oxycodone)
Capsules (500 mg acetaminophen with 5 mg oxycodone)
Oral liquid (325 mg acetaminophen with 5 mg oxycodone per 5-mL spoonful, with 0.4% alcohol)
STORAGE
Store all forms of this medication at room temperature in a tightly closed container.

USES

Acetaminophen and oxycodone combination is used to relieve moderate to severe pain. Oxycodone is a narcotic analgesic that acts on the central nervous system (brain and spinal cord) to relieve pain.

TREATMENT

To avoid stomach upset, you can take this medication with food or with milk.

This medication works most effectively if you take it at the onset of pain rather than waiting until the pain becomes intense.

If you are taking this medication on a regular schedule and you miss a dose, take the missed dose as soon as possible. However, if it is almost time for your next dose, don't take the missed dose at all; just return to your regular dosing schedule. Do not double the next dose.

SIDE EFFECTS

Minor. Constipation, dizziness, drowsiness, dry mouth, false sense of well-being, flushing, light-headedness, loss of appetite, nausea, painful or difficult urination, or sweating. These side effects should disappear as your body adjusts to the medication.

If you are constipated, increase the amount of fiber in your diet (fresh fruits and vegetables, salads, bran, and whole-grain breads), exercise, and drink more water (unless your doctor directs you to do otherwise).

To reduce mouth dryness, chew sugarless gum or suck on ice chips or hard candy.

If you feel dizzy or light-headed, sit or lie down for a while; get up from a sitting or reclining position slowly; and be careful on stairs.

Major. Tell your doctor about any side effects that you find persistent or particularly bothersome. IT IS ESPECIALLY IMPORTANT THAT YOU TELL YOUR DOCTOR about anxiety, difficulty in breathing, excitation, fatigue, heart palpitations, rash, restlessness, sore throat and fever, tremors, unusual bleeding or bruising, weakness, or yellowing of the eyes or skin.

INTERACTIONS

This medication interacts with several other types of drugs:

1. Concurrent use of this medication with other central nervous system depressants (such as alcohol, antihistamines, barbiturates, benzodiazepine tranquilizers, muscle relaxants, and phenothiazine tranquilizers) or with tricyclic antidepressants can cause extreme drowsiness.

2. A monoamine oxidase (MAO) inhibitor taken within 14 days of this medication can cause severe side effects.

3. Long-term use and high doses of the acetaminophen portion of this medication can increase the effects of oral anticoagulants (blood thinners, such as warfarin); combining these drugs in this way may lead to bleeding complications.

4. Anticonvulsants (antiseizure medications), barbiturates, and alcohol can increase the liver toxicity caused by large doses of the acetaminophen portion of this medication.

BE SURE TO TELL YOUR DOCTOR about any medications you are currently taking, especially any listed above.

WARNINGS

• Tell your doctor about unusual or allergic reactions you have had to any medications, especially to acetaminophen, oxycodone, or other narcotic analgesics (such as codeine, hydrocodone, hydromorphone, meperidine, methadone, morphine, and propoxyphene).

• Tell your doctor if you now have or if you have ever had an acute abdominal condition, asthma, blood disorders, brain disease, colitis, epilepsy, gallstones or gallbladder disease, a head injury, heart disease, kidney disease, liver disease, lung disease, mental illness, prostate disease, thyroid disease, or urethral strictures.

• If this drug makes you dizzy or drowsy, do not take part in any activity that requires alertness, such as driving a car or operating potentially dangerous equipment.

• Before having surgery or any other medical or dental treatment, be sure to tell your doctor or dentist that you are taking this medication.

• Because this product contains oxycodone, it has the potential for abuse and must be used with caution. Usually, it should not be taken on a regular schedule for longer than ten days at a time. Tolerance develops quickly; do not increase the dosage or stop taking the drug abruptly unless you first consult your doctor. If you have been taking large amounts of this medication for long periods, you may experience a withdrawal reaction (muscle aches, diarrhea, gooseflesh, runny nose, nausea, vomiting, shivering, trembling, stomach cramps, sleep disorders, irritability, weakness, excessive yawning, or sweating). Your doctor may, therefore, want to reduce the dosage gradually.

• Because this product contains acetaminophen, additional drugs containing acetaminophen should not be taken without your doctor's approval. Check the labels on nonprescription pain, sinus, allergy, asthma, diet, cough, and cold products to see if they contain acetaminophen.

• Be sure to tell your doctor if you are pregnant. The effects of this medication during pregnancy have not been thoroughly studied in humans. Oxycodone, used regularly in large doses during pregnancy, can result in addiction of the fetus, leading to the appearance of withdrawal symptoms (such as irritability, excessive crying, tremors, fever, vomiting, diarrhea, sneezing, or excessive yawning) at birth. Also tell your doctor if you are breast-feeding an infant. Small amounts of this medication may pass into breast milk and cause excessive drowsiness in the nursing infant.

acyclovir

BRAND NAME (Manufacturer)
Zovirax (GlaxoSmithKline)
TYPE OF DRUG
Antiviral
INGREDIENT
acyclovir
DOSAGE FORMS
Capsules (200 mg)
Ointment (5%)
Oral suspension (200 mg per 5-mL spoonful)
Tablets (400 mg and 800 mg)
STORAGE
Store the ointment, capsule, and tablet forms of the drug in a cool, dry place. Keep the suspension form of this medication at room temperature.

USES

Acyclovir is used to treat genital herpes and herpes infections of the skin including chicken pox and zoster (shingles). Acyclovir prevents the growth and multiplication of the herpes virus. This drug does not cure a herpes infection but may relieve the pain associated with the viral infection and may shorten the duration of an outbreak.

TREATMENT

Take oral acyclovir or apply topical acyclovir as soon as possible after the symptoms of a herpes infection appear. Wash the infected area with soap and water, and allow it to dry. To avoid spreading the infection, use a rubber glove or a finger cot to apply the ointment to the affected area. Apply enough acyclovir so that you completely cover the area of the infection.

Complete the full course of therapy with acyclovir as prescribed by your doctor, even if your symptoms disappear before you have finished the prescribed amount. The full course usually lasts about ten days.

If you miss a dose of this medication, take or apply the missed dose as soon as possible. However, if you do not remember until it is almost time for the next dose, do not take or apply the missed dose of medication at all; just return to your regular dosing schedule. Do not double the next dose of the medication.

SIDE EFFECTS

Minor. You may experience temporary pain, burning, stinging, itching, or rash when this medication is applied topically. These side effects should disappear as your body adjusts to the medication.

After oral therapy, you may experience diarrhea, difficulty sleeping, dizziness, fatigue, headache, rash, upset stomach, or vomiting. These side effects should disappear as your body adjusts to the medication.

Major. Tell your doctor about any side effects that are persistent or particularly bothersome. IT IS ESPECIALLY IMPORTANT TO TELL YOUR DOCTOR if you experience fever or muscle pain.

INTERACTIONS

Acyclovir should not interact with other medications if it is used according to directions.

WARNINGS

- Be sure to tell your doctor about unusual or allergic reactions you have had to any medications.

• Acyclovir ointment is intended for use on the skin only; it should not be used in or around the eyes.
• Try to avoid sexual activity while you have signs or symptoms of genital herpes; this medication does not prevent the transmission of herpes to other individuals, nor does it prevent recurrences.
• This medication has been prescribed for your current infection only. A subsequent infection, or one that someone else has, may require a different medication. Do not use your medication to treat other infections, unless your doctor directs you to do so.
• Be sure to tell your doctor if you are pregnant. Although this drug appears safe in animal pregnancy, studies in humans during pregnancy have not been conducted. Also be sure to tell your doctor if you are breast-feeding an infant. Although acyclovir passes into breast milk, no toxicity has been observed in any infants.

---

adalimumab

BRAND NAME (Manufacturer)
Humira (Abbott Labs)
TYPE OF DRUG
Antiarthritic
INGREDIENT
adalimumab
DOSAGE FORM
Injection (40 mg per 0.8 mL prefilled syringe)
STORAGE
Store in the refrigerator and protect from light. Do not freeze this medication.

USES

Adalimumab is used to treat the symptoms of rheumatoid arthritis, such as pain and swelling of the joints. This medication may also help prevent further damage to the bones and joints. Adalimumab is in a new class of medication for arthritis called TNF blockers. It works by blocking the effects of a chemical called TNF-alpha, which is part of your body's immune system. People who have rheumatoid arthritis have too much TNF-alpha. Although TNF-alpha is an important defense mechanism that the body uses to help fight off infections, too much TNF-alpha can cause healthy tissues (especially tissues in the bones and joints) to become inflamed and painful. However, blocking TNF-alpha may make you more susceptible to infections.

TREATMENT

Take this medication exactly as prescribed by your doctor. Adalimumab is given by injection under the skin (subcutaneously), every other week. Complete instructions on proper use of adalimumab are included with the medication. Be sure to review these instructions before using adalimumab. If you have any questions about the medication or its administration, be sure to contact your doctor or pharmacist. In many cases, a nurse or other health care specialist will train you on how to inject this medication and how to monitor for side effects.

Since adalimumab is given by injection, you will need a special container to dispose of used needles and syringes. Also, check the vial before using adalimumab; the solution should be clear. Do not use the medication if there are particles floating in the liquid or if the solution has become colored or cloudy. Do not mix adalimumab with any other medications or dilute the solution before injecting it. Adalimumab contains no preservatives; therefore, any portion of the medication that remains after injection of the proper dose should be discarded. The contents of a used syringe should not be saved for later use.

If you miss a dose of this medication, take the missed dose as soon as possible. However, if it is almost time for your next dose of the medication, do not take the missed dose at all; just return to your regular dosing schedule. Do not double the next dose.

SIDE EFFECTS

Minor. Headache; nausea; redness, rash, swelling, itching, or bruising at the site of the injection; or sinus infections.

The swelling, rash, and redness at the injection site should go away in a few days. Applying a cold towel may help relieve some of the discomfort. If the swelling, redness, and rash persist for more than a few days, or if the other side effects persist, contact your doctor.

Major. Tell your doctor about any side effects you experience that are persistent or particularly bothersome. IT IS ESPECIALLY IMPORTANT TO TELL YOUR DOCTOR about any type of infection, chest pains, dizziness, joint pain, numbness or tingling, a rash on your chest or face, shortness of breath, vision problems, or any weakness in your legs.

INTERACTIONS

If it is taken exactly as directed, adalimumab is unlikely to interact with any other medications.

However, before you start taking this medication, BE SURE TO TELL YOUR DOCTOR about any medications you are currently taking, including natural or herbal products or over-the-counter medications.

WARNINGS

• Tell your doctor if you currently have or have ever had infections that keep returning, any conditions that may increase your risk of getting an infection, tuberculosis, any type of disorder or disease of the nervous system, or lupus or lupuslike symptoms. Also be sure to tell your doctor if you are scheduled to have any type of surgery or receive any type of vaccination.

• Tell your doctor about unusual or allergic reactions you have ever had to any medications, especially to adalimumab or to any other medications that are used in the treatment of arthritis.

• Adalimumab may increase your risk of getting a serious infection, including tuberculosis and life-threatening fungal or bacterial infections. Your doctor may want to test you for tuberculosis before beginning adalimumab.

• Some patients who have rheumatoid arthritis have an increased risk of getting certain types of cancers, including lymphoma, a cancer that can affect the lymph system. Discuss your risk of cancer with your doctor before beginning treatment with adalimumab.

• The risk of a condition known as lupus may be increased with adalimumab. Symptoms include joint pain, a rash across the cheeks of the face or arms that is sensitive to sunlight, and shortness of breath. If you experience these symptoms, call your doctor. It may be necessary to stop treatment with adalimumab.

• If you develop a severe rash, swelling of the face, or difficulty breathing after taking adalimumab, call your doctor immediately.

• Before having surgery or any other medical or dental treatment, be sure to tell your doctor that you are taking this medication.

• Be sure to tell your doctor if you are pregnant. Effects of this drug during pregnancy have not been thoroughly studied in either humans or animals. Also tell your doctor if you are breast-feeding an infant. It is unknown whether adalimumab passes into breast milk or what the effects of adalimumab would be on a nursing infant whose mother is being treated with adalimumab.

adefovir

BRAND NAME (Manufacturer)
Hepsera (Gilead)
TYPE OF DRUG
Antiviral
INGREDIENT
adefovir dipivoxil
DOSAGE FORM
Tablets (10 mg)
STORAGE
Store this medication at room temperature in a tightly closed container. Do not expose to excess heat.

USES

Adefovir is used in the treatment of hepatitis that is caused by the hepatitis B virus. Adefovir works by inhibiting the reproduction or growth of the virus, which slows down the infection in the liver. Adefovir may not completely eliminate the virus from the liver, but it does keep levels of the virus low enough to prevent liver damage.

TREATMENT

This medication works best when the level of medicine in your bloodstream is kept constant. It is best to take the drug at the same time every day. If you miss a dose of this medication, take it as soon as possible. However, if it is almost time for your next dose, skip the missed dose and go back to your regular dosing schedule. Do not double the next dose of this medication.

SIDE EFFECTS

Minor. Diarrhea, flatulence (gas), headache, heartburn, indigestion, nausea, skin rash, or vomiting. These side effects should diminish or disappear as your body adjusts to the medication.

Major. Tell your doctor about any side effects that are persistent or particularly bothersome. IT IS ESPECIALLY IMPORTANT TO TELL YOUR DOCTOR about a cold feeling in your arms or legs, dizziness or light-headedness, fast heartbeat, feelings of weakness or tiredness, stomach pain with nausea and vomiting, trouble breathing, unusual muscle aches, or yellowing of the skin or eyes.

INTERACTIONS

Adefovir may interact with a number of other drugs:

1. Certain nonsteroidal anti-inflammatory drugs, such as ibuprofen, may increase the side effects of adefovir.

2. The side effects—especially as they relate to the kidneys—of furosemide, bumetanide, ethacrynic acid, colistin, vancomycin, polymyxin B, and aminoglycoside antibiotics can be increased by adefovir.

WARNINGS

- About 25% of patients who stop taking adefovir have a worsening or return of symptoms of hepatitis. This is usually seen within 12 weeks of stopping adefovir. Therefore, you should not stop taking adefovir unless directed by your doctor. Your doctor may order certain blood tests to monitor your liver function after stopping adefovir.
- Adefovir may worsen kidney function, especially in patients who had kidney problems before starting adefovir. Your doctor may order regular blood tests to monitor how your kidneys are working while on adefovir.

• Adefovir may cause a condition called lactic acidosis, which is a buildup of acid in the blood. IF YOU DEVELOP ANY SIGNS OF LACTIC ACIDOSIS, INCLUDING FEELINGS OF WEAKNESS OR TIREDNESS, UNUSUAL MUSCLE ACHES, TROUBLE BREATHING, STOMACH PAIN WITH NAUSEA AND VOMITING, COLD FEELING IN YOUR ARMS OR LEGS, DIZZINESS OR LIGHT-HEADEDNESS, OR FAST HEARTBEAT WHILE TAKING ADEFOVIR, YOU SHOULD CONTACT YOUR DOCTOR IMMEDIATELY.
• Tell your doctor if you have ever had an allergic reaction to adefovir or to any other medication (especially to medications that are used in the treatment of viral infections, including HIV infection).
• If you are at risk for infection with HIV (the virus that causes AIDS) or if you may have been exposed to HIV, it is important that you discuss with your doctor being tested for HIV before beginning adefovir. If you are infected with HIV and are not being treated for that infection, adefovir may allow the virus to become resistant to some medications used to treat HIV infection.
• Before taking this medication, be sure to tell your doctor about any medical problems you may have, especially any liver or kidney problems. The dose of adefovir prescribed may need to be lower than usual if you have kidney or liver problems.
• Be sure to tell your doctor if you are pregnant or if you are nursing an infant. Although birth defects have not been documented in humans, adefovir has been shown to cause birth defects in animals when given at very high doses. It is unknown if adefovir is safe during human pregnancy. It is not known if adefovir passes into human breast milk, and its safety in breast-feeding is unknown.

---

albuterol

BRAND NAMES (Manufacturers)
albuterol (various manufacturers)
Proventil (Schering)
Proventil HFA (Schering)
Ventolin (GlaxoSmithKline)
Volmax (Muro)
TYPE OF DRUG
Bronchodilator
INGREDIENT
albuterol
DOSAGE FORMS
Tablets and extended-release tablets (2 mg, 4 mg, and 8 mg)
Inhalation aerosol (each spray delivers 90 mcg)
Inhalation solution (0.5% and 0.083%)
Oral syrup (2 mg per 5-mL spoonful)
Rotocaps for inhalation (200 mcg)
STORAGE
Store at room temperature in a tightly closed, light-resistant container. Store the inhalation aerosol away from excessive heat. The contents are pressurized and can explode if heated.

USES

Albuterol is used to relieve wheezing and shortness of breath caused by lung diseases such as asthma, bronchitis, and emphysema. This drug acts directly on the muscles of the bronchi (breathing tubes) to relieve bronchospasms (muscle contractions of the bronchi), which allows air to move more freely to and from the lungs.

TREATMENT

To lessen stomach upset, take the tablets and syrup with food (unless your doctor directs you to do otherwise).

Measure each dose of syrup carefully with a specially designed 5-mL measuring spoon. Ordinary kitchen teaspoons are not accurate enough.

The inhalation aerosol form of this medication is usually packaged with an instruction sheet. Read the directions carefully before using this medication. You may wish to consult your doctor or pharmacist about the proper administration of this drug. Shake the container well just before each use in order to distribute the ingredients evenly and equalize the doses. The contents tend to settle on the bottom of the bottle. If more than one inhalation is necessary, wait at least one full minute between doses to receive the full benefit of the first dose.

If you miss a dose of this medication and remember within an hour, take the missed dose immediately; then follow your regular dosing schedule for the next dose. If you miss the dose by more than an hour, just wait until the next scheduled dose. Do not double the dose.

SIDE EFFECTS

Minor. Anxiety, dizziness, dryness or irritation of the mouth or throat (from the inhalation aerosol), flushing, headache, insomnia, irritability, loss of appetite, muscle cramps, nausea, nervousness, restlessness, sweating, tremors, vomiting, or weakness. These side effects should disappear as your body adjusts to the medication.

To help prevent dryness or irritation of the mouth or throat from the inhalation aerosol, rinse your mouth with water after each dose.

To avoid difficulty in falling asleep, check with your doctor to see if you can take the last dose of this medication several hours before bedtime each day.

If you feel dizzy, sit or lie down for a while; get up from a sitting or reclining position slowly; and be careful on stairs.

Major. Tell your doctor about any side effects that are persistent or particularly bothersome. IT IS ESPECIALLY IMPORTANT TO TELL YOUR DOCTOR about chest pain, difficult or painful urination, itching, palpitations, or rash.

INTERACTIONS

Albuterol interacts with several other types of drugs:

1. The beta blockers (acebutolol, atenolol, labetalol, metoprolol, nadolol, pindolol, propranolol, timolol) antagonize (act against) this medication, decreasing its effectiveness.

2. Monoamine oxidase (MAO) inhibitors, tricyclic antidepressants, antihistamines, levothyroxine, digoxin, quinidine, and over-the-counter (nonprescription) cough, cold, asthma, allergy, diet, and sinus medications may increase the side effects of this medication.

3. There may be a change in the dosage requirements of insulin or oral antidiabetic medications when albuterol is started.

4. The use of albuterol with other bronchodilator drugs (either oral or inhalant drugs) can have additive side effects. Discuss this with your doctor.

BE SURE TO TELL YOUR DOCTOR about any medications you are taking, especially any listed above.

WARNINGS

- Tell your doctor about unusual or allergic reactions you have had to medications, especially to albuterol or any related drug (amphetamines, ephedrine, epinephrine, isoproterenol, metaproterenol, norepinephrine, phenylephrine, phenylpropanolamine, pseudoephedrine, or terbutaline).

• Tell your doctor if you now have or if you have ever had diabetes mellitus, an enlarged prostate gland, epilepsy, glaucoma, heart disease, high blood pressure, or thyroid disease.
• This medication can cause dizziness. Your ability to perform tasks that require alertness, such as driving a car or operating potentially dangerous equipment, may be decreased. Take appropriate caution.
• Before having surgery or any other medical or dental treatment, be sure to tell the doctor or dentist that you are taking this medication.
• Do not exceed the recommended dosage of this medication; excessive use may lead to an increase in side effects or a loss of effectiveness.
• Avoid contact of the aerosol inhalation with your eyes.
• Do not puncture, break, or burn the aerosol container. The contents are under pressure and may explode.
• Contact your doctor if you do not respond to the usual dose of this medication. It may be an indication that your asthma is getting worse, which may mean that you require additional therapy.
• Be sure to tell your doctor if you are pregnant. The effects of this medication during pregnancy have not been thoroughly studied in humans, but it has caused side effects in the offspring of animals that received large doses of this medication during pregnancy. Also tell your doctor if you are breast-feeding an infant. It is not known if albuterol passes into breast milk.

alendronate

BRAND NAME (Manufacturer)
Fosamax (Merck)
TYPE OF DRUG
Bone resorption inhibitor
INGREDIENT
alendronate
DOSAGE FORM
Tablets (5 mg, 10 mg, 35 mg, 40 mg, and 70 mg)
STORAGE
Store at room temperature in a tightly closed container.

USES

Alendronate represents a new class of medication that works by increasing the development of new bone in the body and by preventing the weakening and breakdown of the bones themselves. This medication is used in the treatment of postmenopausal osteoporosis and in the treatment of patients who have Paget's disease.

TREATMENT

Alendronate must be taken with a full glass (six to eight ounces) of plain water only (not coffee, mineral water, tea, or juice) on an empty stomach. Because food, certain beverages, and other medications will decrease the amount of alendronate absorbed by the body, you should take this medication at least 30 minutes before the first food, beverage, or other medication of the day. Your doctor will advise you on the use of supplemental calcium while taking alendronate. In addition, to avoid irritation or pain in your esophagus, it is very important that you not lie down for at least 30 minutes after taking alendronate.

If you miss a dose of alendronate, take the missed dose as soon as possible unless it is later in the day. In that case, do not take the missed dose at all; just wait until the next scheduled dose. Do not double the next dose. If the dose you missed was a once-weekly dose, continue the usual schedule beginning the next morning.

SIDE EFFECTS

Minor. Abdominal pain, muscle pain, nausea, or skin rash. These side effects should diminish or disappear as your body adjusts to the medication.
Major. Tell your doctor about any side effects that are persistent or particularly bothersome to you. IT IS ESPECIALLY IMPORTANT THAT YOU TELL YOUR DOCTOR about constipation, diarrhea, difficulty swallowing, gas, headache, heartburn or a sense of irritation or pain in your esophagus, or unusually full or bloated feelings in your stomach.

INTERACTIONS

Alendronate can only be absorbed by your body when your stomach is empty. Therefore it is very important you do not take any other medications (including antacids) or foods for at least 30 minutes after your morning dose of alendronate.

This drug can interact with aspirin and aspirin-containing medications, increasing the frequency of problems with stomach upset or heartburn.

WARNINGS

• Tell your doctor about any unusual or allergic reactions you have had to any medications, especially to alendronate. Also be sure to tell your doctor if you have ever had kidney disease, peptic ulcer disease, esophageal reflux disease, low blood calcium, or a deficiency of vitamin D.
• Be sure to tell your doctor if you are pregnant. The effects of this medication have not been thoroughly studied in humans. Also be sure to notify your doctor if you are breast-feeding an infant. It is not known if alendronate passes into breast milk.

---

allopurinol

BRAND NAMES (Manufacturers)
allopurinol (various manufacturers)
Zyloprim (Faro)
TYPE OF DRUG
Antigout
INGREDIENT
allopurinol
DOSAGE FORM
Tablets (100 mg and 300 mg)
STORAGE
Store this medication at room temperature in a tightly closed container.

USES

This medication is used to treat chronic gout and to lower blood uric acid levels. Allopurinol blocks the body's production of uric acid. Allopurinol should not be used to treat acute gout attacks.

TREATMENT

To avoid stomach irritation, take allopurinol with food or with a full glass of water or milk. It may take one to three weeks before the full effects of this medication are observed.

Drink at least 10 to 12 glasses (eight ounces each) of fluids per day while taking this medication to prevent the formation of kidney stones.

If you miss a dose of this medication, take the missed dose as soon as possible. However, if it is almost time for the next dose, do not take the missed dose at all; just return to your regular dosing schedule. Do not double the next dose.

Take this medication for the full duration of prescribed therapy, as the full benefit of allopurinol may not be achieved for several weeks.

SIDE EFFECTS

Minor. Diarrhea, drowsiness, nausea, stomach upset, or vomiting. These side effects should disappear as your body adjusts to the medication.

Major. Tell your doctor about any side effects that are persistent or particularly bothersome that may be the result of this medication. IT IS ESPECIALLY IMPORTANT TO TELL YOUR DOCTOR about blurred vision, chills, difficult or painful urination, fatigue, fever, loss of hair, muscle aches, numbness or tingling sensations, paleness, rash, sore throat, unusual bleeding or bruising, or yellowing of the skin or the whites of the eyes.

INTERACTIONS

Allopurinol interacts with several other types of drugs:

1. Alcohol, diuretics (water pills), and pyrazinamide can increase blood uric acid levels, thus decreasing the effectiveness of allopurinol.

2. Allopurinol can increase the body's store of iron salts, which can lead to iron toxicity.

3. When combined with allopurinol, ampicillin can increase the chance of skin rash; thiazide diuretics and captopril can increase the chance of allergic reactions; and cyclophosphamide can increase the chance of blood disorders. Allopurinol can also increase the blood levels, therapeutic effects, and toxicity of mercaptopurine, azathioprine, oral anticoagulants (blood thinners), and theophylline.

4. Vitamin C can make the urine acidic, which can increase the risk of kidney stone formation in people who are taking this medication.

Before starting to take allopurinol, BE SURE TO TELL YOUR DOCTOR about any medications you are currently taking, especially any of those listed above.

WARNINGS

• Tell your doctor about unusual or allergic reactions you have had to any medications, especially to allopurinol.

• Tell your doctor if you now have or ever had blood disorders, kidney disease, or liver disease. Also tell your doctor if you have a relative with idiopathic hemochromatosis (a disorder of iron metabolism).

• This drug may cause dizziness or drowsiness. Do not take part in any activity that requires alertness, such as driving a car or operating potentially dangerous equipment.

• Be sure to tell your doctor if you are pregnant. Although this drug appears to be safe in animals, studies in pregnant women have not been conducted. Also be sure to tell your doctor if you are breast-feeding an infant. Although the medication passes into breast milk, no problems have been observed in nursing infants. Still, if this drug has been prescribed for you, it is best to inform your physician that you are nursing an infant.

---

alprazolam

BRAND NAMES (Manufacturers)

alprazolam (various manufacturers)
Xanax (Pharmacia)

TYPE OF DRUG
Benzodiazepine sedative/hypnotic
INGREDIENT
alprazolam
DOSAGE FORM
Tablets (0.25 mg, 0.5 mg, 1 mg, and 2 mg)
STORAGE
Store at room temperature in a tightly closed, light-resistant container. If not protected from heat and moisture, the medication's potency could be impaired.

USES

Alprazolam is prescribed to treat symptoms of anxiety and anxiety associated with depression. It may work by acting as a depressant of the central nervous system. This drug is currently used to relieve nervousness and panic disorder. Alprazolam is effective for this purpose for short periods, but it is important to try to identify and remove the cause of the anxiety as well.

TREATMENT

Take exactly as directed by your doctor. This medication can be taken with food or with a full glass of water if stomach upset occurs.

If you are taking this medication regularly and you miss a dose, take the missed dose immediately if you remember within an hour of the scheduled dose. If more than an hour has passed, skip the dose you missed and wait for the next scheduled dose. Do not double the dose.

SIDE EFFECTS

Minor. Bitter taste in mouth, constipation, diarrhea, dizziness, drowsiness (after a night's sleep), dry mouth, excessive salivation, fatigue, flushing, headache, heartburn, loss of appetite, nausea, nervousness, sweating, or vomiting. These side effects should disappear as your body adjusts to the medication.

To relieve constipation, increase the amount of fiber in your diet (fresh fruits and vegetables, salads, bran, and whole-grain breads), exercise, and drink more water (unless your doctor directs you to do otherwise).

Dry mouth can be relieved by chewing sugarless gum or by sucking on ice chips.

If you feel dizzy, sit or lie down for a while; get up slowly from a sitting or reclining position; and be careful on stairs.

Major. Tell your doctor about any side effects that are persistent or particularly bothersome. IT IS ESPECIALLY IMPORTANT TO TELL YOUR DOCTOR about blurred or double vision, chest pain, severe depression, difficulty in urinating, fainting, falling, fever, hallucinations, joint pain, mouth sores, nightmares, palpitations, rash, shortness of breath, slurred speech, sore throat, uncoordinated movements, unusual excitement, unusual tiredness, or yellowing of the eyes or skin.

INTERACTIONS

Alprazolam interacts with several other types of drugs:

1. To prevent oversedation, this drug should not be taken with alcohol, other sedative drugs, central nervous system depressants (such as antihistamines, barbiturates, muscle relaxants, pain medications, narcotics, medications for seizures, and phenothiazine tranquilizers), or antidepressants.

2. This medication may decrease the effectiveness of carbamazepine, levodopa, and oral anticoagulants (blood thinners such as warfarin).

3. Disulfiram, oral contraceptives (birth control pills), isoniazid, fluvoxamine, nefazodone, fluoxetine, propoxyphene, and cimetidine can increase the blood levels of alprazolam, which can lead to toxic effects.

4. Concurrent use of rifampin may decrease the effectiveness of alprazolam.

Before starting to take alprazolam, BE SURE TO TELL YOUR DOCTOR about any medications you are currently taking, especially any of those listed above.

WARNINGS

- Tell your doctor about any unusual or allergic reactions you have had to any medications, especially to alprazolam or other benzodiazepine tranquilizers (such as chlordiazepoxide, clorazepate, diazepam, flurazepam, halazepam, lorazepam, oxazepam, prazepam, temazepam, or triazolam).
- Tell your doctor if you now have or have ever had liver disease, kidney disease, epilepsy, lung disease, myasthenia gravis, narrow-angle glaucoma, porphyria, mental depression, mental illness, or sleep apnea.
- This medicine can cause drowsiness. Avoid tasks that require mental alertness, such as driving a car or using potentially dangerous equipment.
- This medication has the potential for abuse and must be used with caution. Tolerance may develop quickly; do not increase the dosage of the drug without first consulting your doctor. It is also important not to stop this drug suddenly if you have been taking it in large amounts or if you have used it for several months. Your doctor will want to reduce the dosage gradually.
- This is a safe drug when used properly. When it is combined with other sedative drugs or alcohol, however, serious side effects can develop.
- Be sure to tell your doctor if you are pregnant. This medicine may increase the chance of birth defects in the infant if it is taken during the first three months of pregnancy. In addition, too much use of this medication during the final six months of pregnancy may result in the fetus becoming addicted to the medication—leading to withdrawal side effects in the newborn. Use of this medication during the last weeks of pregnancy may cause drowsiness, slowed heartbeat, and breathing difficulties in the infant. In addition, be sure to tell your doctor if you are breast-feeding an infant. This medication can pass into breast milk and cause excessive drowsiness, slowed heartbeat, and breathing difficulties in the nursing infant.

---

amitriptyline

BRAND NAMES (Manufacturers)
amitriptyline hydrochloride (various manufacturers)
Elavil (AstraZeneca)
TYPE OF DRUG
Tricyclic antidepressant
INGREDIENT
amitriptyline
DOSAGE FORM
Tablets (10 mg, 25 mg, 50 mg, 75 mg, 100 mg, and 150 mg)
STORAGE
Store at room temperature in a tightly closed container.

USES

Amitriptyline is used to relieve the symptoms of mental depression. This medication belongs to a group of drugs referred to as the tricyclic antidepressants. These medicines are thought to relieve depression by increasing the concentration of certain chemicals necessary for nerve transmission in the brain.

TREATMENT

Take this medication exactly as your doctor prescribes. This medication can be taken with water or with food to lessen the chance of stomach irritation, unless your doctor directs otherwise.

The effects of therapy with this medication may not become apparent for two or three weeks.

If you miss a dose of this medication, take the missed dose as soon as possible, and then return to your regular dosing schedule. However, if the dose you missed was a once-a-day bedtime dose, do not take that dose in the morning; check with your doctor instead. If the dose is taken in the morning, it may cause some unwanted side effects. Never double the dose.

SIDE EFFECTS

Minor. Constipation, cramps, diarrhea, dizziness, drowsiness, dry mouth, fatigue, heartburn, loss of appetite, nausea, peculiar tastes in the mouth, restlessness, sweating, vomiting, weakness, or weight gain or loss. As your body adjusts to the medication, these side effects should disappear.

This medication may cause increased sensitivity to sunlight. Avoid prolonged exposure to sunlight and sunlamps, wear protective clothing, and use an effective sunscreen.

Amitriptyline may cause your urine to turn blue-green; this effect is harmless.

Dry mouth can be relieved by chewing sugarless gum or by sucking on ice chips or hard candy.

To relieve constipation, increase the amount of fiber in your diet (fresh fruits and vegetables, salads, bran, and whole-grain breads), exercise, and drink more water (unless your doctor directs you to do otherwise).

To avoid dizziness when you stand, contract and relax the muscles of your legs for a few moments before rising. Do this by alternately pushing one foot against the floor while raising the other foot slightly, so that you are "pumping" your legs in a pedaling motion.

Major. Tell your doctor about any side effects that are persistent or particularly bothersome. IT IS ESPECIALLY IMPORTANT TO TELL YOUR DOCTOR about agitation, anxiety, blurred vision, chest pain, confusion, convulsions, difficulty in urinating, enlarged or painful breasts (in both sexes), fainting, fever, fluid retention, hair loss, hallucinations, headaches, impotence, mood changes, mouth sores, nervousness, nightmares, numbness in the fingers or toes, palpitations, ringing in the ears, seizures, skin rash, sleep disorders, sore throat, tremors, uncoordinated movements or balance problems, unusual bleeding or bruising, or yellowing of the skin or the whites of the eyes.

INTERACTIONS

Amitriptyline interacts with a number of other types of medications:

1. Extreme drowsiness can occur when this medicine is taken with central nervous system depressants (such as alcohol, antihistamines, barbiturates, benzodiazepine tranquilizers, muscle relaxants, narcotics, pain medications, phenothiazine tranquilizers, and sleeping medications) or with other antidepressants.

2. Amitriptyline may decrease the effectiveness of antiseizure medications and may block the blood-pressure-lowering effects of clonidine and guanethidine.

3. Oral contraceptives (birth control pills) or drugs containing estrogen can increase the side effects and reduce the effectiveness of the tricyclic antidepressants (a drug type that includes amitriptyline).

4. Cimetidine can decrease the elimination of amitriptyline from the body, thus increasing the risk of side effects.

5. Tricyclic antidepressants may increase the side effects of thyroid medication and of nonprescription cough, cold, allergy, asthma, sinus, and weight-control medications.

6. The concurrent use of tricyclic antidepressants and monoamine oxidase (MAO) inhibitors should be avoided because the combination may result in fever, convulsions, or high blood pressure. At least 14 days should separate the use of amitriptyline and the use of an MAO inhibitor.

Before starting to take amitriptyline, BE SURE TO TELL YOUR DOCTOR about any medications you are currently taking, especially any of those listed above.

WARNINGS

- Tell your doctor if you have had unusual or allergic reactions to medications, especially to amitriptyline or any of the other tricyclic antidepressants (imipramine, doxepin, trimipramine, amoxapine, protriptyline, desipramine, maprotiline, and nortriptyline).
- Tell your doctor if you have a history of alcoholism or if you have ever had asthma, diabetes, high blood pressure, liver or kidney disease, heart disease, a heart attack, circulatory disease, stomach problems, intestinal problems, difficulty in urinating, enlarged prostate gland, epilepsy, glaucoma, thyroid disease, mental illness, or electroshock therapy.
- If this drug makes you dizzy or drowsy, do not take part in any activity that requires alertness, such as driving a car or operating potentially dangerous equipment.
- Before having surgery or other medical or dental treatment, tell your doctor or dentist you are taking this drug.
- Do not stop taking this drug suddenly. Abruptly stopping it can cause nausea, headache, stomach upset, fatigue, or a worsening of your condition. Your doctor may want to reduce the dosage gradually.
- The effects of this medication may last as long as seven days after you have stopped taking it, so continue to observe all precautions during that period.
- Be sure to tell your doctor if you are pregnant. Studies have not been done in humans; however, studies in animals have shown that this type of medication can cause side effects to the fetus when given to the mother in large doses during pregnancy. Also tell your doctor if you are breast-feeding an infant. Small amounts of this drug can pass into breast milk and may cause unwanted side effects, such as irritability or sleeping problems, in nursing infants.

---

amlodipine

BRAND NAME (Manufacturer)
Norvasc (Pfizer)
TYPE OF DRUG
Antianginal and antihypertensive
INGREDIENT
amlodipine
DOSAGE FORM
Tablets (2.5 mg, 5 mg, and 10 mg)
STORAGE
Store at room temperature in a tightly closed container away from heat and direct sunlight.

USES

Amlodipine belongs to a group of drugs known as calcium channel blockers and is used to prevent the symptoms of angina (chest pain). It can also be used to treat high blood pressure. Amlodipine dilates the blood vessels of the heart and increases the amount of oxygen that reaches the heart muscle, though it is unclear exactly how it operates.

TREATMENT

Take exactly as prescribed by your doctor. Amlodipine can be taken with meals or with a full glass of water if stomach upset occurs. Try to develop a set schedule for taking it.

Amlodipine does not relieve chest pain once it has begun; it is only used to prevent angina attacks.

If you miss a dose and remember within 12 hours, take the missed dose and resume your regular schedule. If more than 12 hours have passed, skip the dose you missed and then take your next dose as scheduled. Do not double the next dose.

This medication does not cure angina or high blood pressure, but it can help to control the condition as long as you continue to take it.

SIDE EFFECTS

Minor. Constipation, diarrhea, dizziness, drowsiness, headache, insomnia, light-headedness, nausea, nervousness, stomach pain, or vomiting. These side effects should disappear as your body adjusts to the medication.

To relieve constipation, increase the amount of fiber in your diet (fresh fruits and vegetables, salads, bran, and whole-grain breads), exercise, and drink more water (unless your doctor directs you to do otherwise).

Major. Tell your doctor about any side effects that are persistent or particularly bothersome. IT IS ESPECIALLY IMPORTANT TO TELL YOUR DOCTOR about confusion, depression, eye pain, fatigue, flushing, palpitations, skin rash, swelling of the ankles or feet, or vision changes.

INTERACTIONS

Amlodipine interacts with several other types of medications:

1. Concurrent use of this drug with beta blockers (including acebutolol, atenolol, labetolol, metoprolol, nadolol, pindolol, propranolol, and timolol) may cause your heart to beat slower and may cause your blood pressure to be too low.

2. Cyclosporine levels may be increased during therapy with this medication.

3. Concurrent use of this medication and other medications for high blood pressure may cause your blood pressure to be too low.

Before starting to take amlodipine, BE SURE TO TELL YOUR DOCTOR about any medications you are currently taking, especially any of those listed above.

WARNINGS

• Tell your doctor about unusual or allergic reactions you have had to any medications, especially amlodipine.

• Tell your doctor if you have ever had liver disease, obstructive coronary artery disease, or heart failure.

• If this drug makes you drowsy or dizzy, avoid taking part in any activity that requires alertness, such as driving a car or operating potentially dangerous equipment.

• Be sure to tell your doctor if you are pregnant. Extensive studies in pregnant women have not been conducted, but side effects have been reported in the offspring of animals that received large doses of amlodipine during pregnancy. Also be sure to tell your doctor if you are breast-feeding an infant. It is not known if amlodipine passes into breast milk.

---

amoxicillin

BRAND NAMES (Manufacturers)

amoxicillin (various manufacturers)
Amoxil (GlaxoSmithKline)
Trimox (Apothecon)
Wymox (Wyeth-Ayerst)

TYPE OF DRUG

Antibiotic

INGREDIENT
amoxicillin
DOSAGE FORMS
Capsules (250 mg and 500 mg)
Chewable tablets (125 mg and 250 mg)
Oral suspension (125 mg and 250 mg per 5-mL spoonful)
Oral suspension drops (50 mg per mL)
STORAGE
Store tablets and capsules at room temperature in tightly closed containers. Store the suspension form of this medication at room temperature or in the refrigerator in a tightly closed container: Follow manufacturer's directions. Any unused portion of the suspension should be discarded after 14 days because the drug loses its potency after that time. Do not freeze.

USES

Amoxicillin antibiotic is used to treat a wide variety of bacterial infections, including infections in the middle ear, skin, upper and lower respiratory tracts, and urinary tract. Amoxicillin acts by severely injuring the cell walls of the infecting bacteria, thereby preventing them from growing and multiplying.

Amoxicillin kills susceptible bacteria but is not effective against viruses, parasites, or fungi.

TREATMENT

Amoxicillin can be taken either on an empty stomach or with food or milk (in order to prevent stomach upset).

Shake the suspension well just before measuring each dose to distribute the ingredients evenly and equalize the doses. The contents tend to settle on the bottom of the bottle. Measure each dose carefully with a specially designed 5-mL measuring spoon or the 1-mL dropper provided, as directed by your doctor or pharmacist. An ordinary kitchen teaspoon is not accurate enough.

It is important to continue to take this medication for the entire time prescribed by your doctor (usually 7 to 14 days), even if the symptoms of infection disappear before the end of that period. If you stop taking the drug too soon, resistant bacteria are given the chance to continue growing, and the infection could recur.

Amoxicillin works best when the level of medicine in your bloodstream is kept constant. It is best, therefore, to take the doses at evenly spaced intervals throughout the day and night. For example, if you are supposed to take three doses of the medication each day, the doses should be spaced eight hours apart.

If you miss a dose of this medication, take the missed dose immediately. However, if it is almost time for your next dose, take the missed dose at once; space the following dose about halfway through the regular interval between doses; then return to your regular schedule. Do not skip any doses of this medication.

SIDE EFFECTS

Minor. Diarrhea, heartburn, nausea, or vomiting. These side effects should disappear as your body adjusts to the drug.

Major. Tell your doctor about any side effects that are persistent or particularly bothersome. IT IS ESPECIALLY IMPORTANT TO TELL YOUR DOCTOR about bloating, chills, cough, darkened tongue, difficulty in breathing, fever, irritation of the mouth, muscle aches, rash, rectal or vaginal itching, severe or bloody diarrhea, or sore throat. If your symptoms of infection seem to be getting worse rather than improving, you should contact your doctor.

INTERACTIONS

Amoxicillin interacts with other types of medications:

1. Probenecid can increase the blood concentration of this medication.
2. Amoxicillin may decrease the effectiveness of oral contraceptives (birth control pills), and pregnancy could result. You should, therefore, use a different or additional (barrier) form of birth control while taking this medication. Discuss this with your doctor.
3. The concurrent use of amoxicillin and allopurinol can increase the risk of developing a rash.

BE SURE TO TELL YOUR DOCTOR about any medications you are currently taking, especially those listed above.

WARNINGS

- Tell your doctor about unusual or allergic reactions you have had to any medications, especially to amoxicillin, ampicillin, or penicillin or to cephalosporin antibiotics, penicillamine, or griseofulvin.
- Tell your doctor if you now have or ever had kidney disease, asthma, or allergies.
- This medication has been prescribed for your current infection only. Another infection later on, or one that someone else has, may require a different medicine. You should not give your medicine to other people or use it for other infections, unless your doctor specifically directs you to do so.
- People with diabetes taking amoxicillin should know that this drug may cause a false-positive sugar reaction with a Clinitest urine glucose test. To avoid this problem while taking amoxicillin, you should switch to Clinistix or Tes-Tape to test your urine for sugar.
- Be sure to tell your doctor if you are pregnant. Although amoxicillin appears to be safe during pregnancy, extensive studies in humans have not been conducted. Also tell your doctor if you are breast-feeding an infant. Small amounts of this medication pass into breast milk and may temporarily alter the bacterial balance in the intestinal tract of the nursing infant, resulting in diarrhea.

---

amoxicillin and clavulanic acid combination

BRAND NAME (Manufacturer)
Augmentin (GlaxoSmithKline)
TYPE OF DRUG
Antibiotic
INGREDIENTS
amoxicillin and clavulanic acid
DOSAGE FORMS
Tablets (250 mg amoxicillin and 125 mg clavulanic acid; 500 mg amoxicillin and 125 mg clavulanic acid; 875 mg amoxicillin and 125 mg clavulanic acid)
Tablets, chewable (125 mg amoxicillin and 31.25 mg clavulanic acid; 200 mg amoxicillin and 28.5 mg clavulanic acid; 250 mg amoxicillin and 62.5 mg clavulanic acid; 400 mg amoxicillin and 57 mg clavulanic acid)
Oral suspension (125 mg amoxicillin and 31.25 mg clavulanic acid per 5-mL spoonful; 200 mg amoxicillin and 28.5 clavulanic acid per 5-mL spoonful; 250 mg amoxicillin and 62.5 mg clavulanic acid per 5-mL spoonful; 400 mg amoxicillin and 57 mg clavulanic acid per 5-mL spoonful)
STORAGE
Store the tablet form of this medication at room temperature in a tightly closed container. Store the suspension in the refrigerator in a tightly closed container. Discard any unused portion of the suspension after ten days because the drug loses its potency after that time. Do not freeze.

USES

Amoxicillin and clavulanic acid combination is used to treat a wide variety of bacterial infections, including infections of the middle ear, skin, sinuses, lower respiratory tract, and urinary tract. Amoxicillin is an antibiotic that acts by severely injuring the cell membranes of infecting bacteria, thereby preventing them from growing and multiplying. Clavulanic acid has no antibacterial activity. It acts to prevent the breakdown of amoxicillin in the body.

Amoxicillin and clavulanic acid combination kills susceptible bacteria, but it is not effective against viruses, parasites, or fungi.

TREATMENT

Amoxicillin and clavulanic acid combination can be taken either on an empty stomach or with food or milk in order to prevent stomach upset.

Shake the suspension well just before measuring each dose to distribute the ingredients evenly and to equalize the doses. The contents tend to settle on the bottom of the bottle. Measure each dose carefully with a specially designed 5-mL measuring spoon. An ordinary kitchen teaspoon is not accurate enough.

It is important to continue to take this medication for the entire time prescribed by your doctor (usually seven to ten days), even if the symptoms of infection disappear before the end of that period. If you stop taking the drug too soon, resistant bacteria are given the chance to continue growing, and the infection could recur.

Amoxicillin and clavulanic acid combination works best when the level of medicine in your bloodstream is kept constant. It is best, therefore, to take the doses of this medication at evenly spaced intervals throughout the day and night. For example, if you are to take three doses a day, the doses should be spaced eight hours apart.

If you miss a dose, take the missed dose of this medication immediately. However, if it is almost time for your next dose, take the missed dose and space the next dose about halfway through the regular interval between doses; then return to your regular schedule. Try not to skip any doses.

SIDE EFFECTS

Minor. Abdominal discomfort, bloating, diarrhea, gas, headache, heartburn, nausea, or vomiting. These side effects should disappear as your body adjusts to this medication.

Major. Tell your doctor about any side effects that are persistent or particularly bothersome. IT IS ESPECIALLY IMPORTANT TO TELL YOUR DOCTOR about bloody or prolonged diarrhea, chills, cough, darkened tongue, difficulty in breathing, fever, irritation of the mouth, itching, muscle aches, rash, rectal or vaginal itching, sore throat, or unusual bleeding or bruising. If your symptoms of infection seem to be getting worse rather than improving, contact your doctor.

INTERACTIONS

Amoxicillin and clavulanic acid can interact with several other types of medications:

1. Probenecid can increase the blood concentration of amoxicillin.

2. Amoxicillin may decrease the effectiveness of oral contraceptives (birth control pills), and pregnancy could result. You should, therefore, use a different or additional (barrier) form of birth control while taking this medication. Discuss this with your doctor.

3. Amoxicillin and clavulanic acid combination can increase the risk of side effects from the medication disulfiram (Antabuse).

4. The risk of skin rash is increased when amoxicillin and allopurinol are taken concurrently.

Before starting this medication, BE SURE TO TELL YOUR DOCTOR about any medications you are currently taking, especially any of the medications listed above.

WARNINGS

• Tell your doctor about unusual or allergic reactions you have had to any medications, especially to penicillin, amoxicillin, ampicillin, cephalosporin antibiotics, penicillamine, griseofulvin, or clavulanic acid.
• Tell your doctor if you now have or ever had allergies, asthma, kidney disease, or mononucleosis.
• This medication has been prescribed for your current infection only. A subsequent infection, or one that someone else has, may require an entirely different medication. You should not give your medicine to other people for their use, nor should you use it to treat other infections, unless your doctor specifically indicates that you do so.
• People with diabetes who are taking amoxicillin and clavulanic acid combination should know that this medication may cause a false-positive sugar reaction with a Clinitest urine glucose test. To avoid this problem while taking this drug, you should switch to Clinistix or Tes-Tape to test your urine for sugar.
• Be sure to tell your doctor if you are pregnant. Although amoxicillin and clavulanic acid combination appears to be safe during pregnancy, studies in humans have not been conducted. Also tell your doctor if you are breast-feeding an infant. Small amounts of this medication pass into breast milk and may cause diarrhea in the nursing infant

---

ampicillin

BRAND NAMES (Manufacturers)
ampicillin (various manufacturers)
Omnipen (Wyeth-Ayerst)
Principen (Apothecon)
Totacillin (GlaxoSmithKline)
TYPE OF DRUG
Antibiotic
INGREDIENT
ampicillin
DOSAGE FORMS
Capsules (250 mg and 500 mg)
Oral suspension (125 mg and 250 mg per 5-mL spoonful)
STORAGE
Store capsules at room temperature. The suspension is stable for 7 days at room temperature or 14 days when refrigerated; it should never be frozen. Do not keep any of these medications beyond the expiration date written on the container. All containers should be closed tightly to keep out moisture.

USES

Ampicillin is an antibiotic used to treat a wide variety of bacterial infections, including middle ear infections in children and infections of the respiratory, urinary, and gastrointestinal tracts. This type of antibiotic acts by severely injuring the cell walls of the infecting bacteria, thereby preventing the bacteria from growing and multiplying. Ampicillin kills susceptible bacteria, but it is not effective against viruses, parasites, or fungi.

TREATMENT

It is best to take ampicillin on an empty stomach (one hour before or two hours after a meal) with a full glass of water (not juice or soda pop). Always follow your doctor's directions for use.

Shake the suspension well just before measuring each dose to distribute the ingredients evenly and equalize the doses. The active ingredients tend to settle on the bottom of the bottle. Measure each dose carefully with a specially designed 5-mL measuring spoon. An ordinary kitchen teaspoon is not accurate enough.

This medication works best when the level of medicine in your bloodstream is kept constant. It is best to take the doses at evenly spaced intervals day and night. For example, if you are to take four doses a day, the doses should be spaced six hours apart.

If you miss a dose, take it as soon as possible. If it is already time for the next dose, take it, then space the next two doses at half the normal time interval. (For example, if you were supposed to take one capsule every six hours, take your next two doses every three hours.) Then resume your normal dosing schedule.

It is very important that you continue to take this medication for the entire time prescribed by your doctor (usually 7 to 14 days), even if the symptoms disappear before the end of that period. If you stop taking this medication too soon, resistant bacteria are given the chance to continue growing, and the infection could recur.

SIDE EFFECTS

Minor. Diarrhea, nausea, or vomiting. These side effects should disappear as your body adjusts to the medication.

Major. Tell your doctor about any side effects that are persistent or particularly bothersome. IT IS ESPECIALLY IMPORTANT TO TELL YOUR DOCTOR about darkened tongue, difficulty in breathing, fever, joint pain, mouth sores, rash, rectal or vaginal itching, severe or bloody diarrhea, or sore throat. If your symptoms of infection seem to be getting worse rather than improving, you should contact your doctor.

INTERACTIONS

This drug interacts with other types of medications:

1. Probenecid may increase the blood concentration of ampicillin.

2. Concurrent use of allopurinol and ampicillin increases the risk of skin rash.

3. Ampicillin may decrease the effectiveness of oral contraceptives (birth control pills), and pregnancy could result. You should, therefore, use a different or additional (barrier) form of birth control while taking ampicillin.

BE SURE TO TELL YOUR DOCTOR about any medications you are currently taking, especially any of the medications listed above.

WARNINGS

• Tell your doctor about unusual or allergic reactions you have had to any medications, especially to penicillin, ampicillin, amoxicillin, cephalosporin antibiotics, penicillamine, or griseofulvin.

• Tell your doctor if you have or ever had liver or kidney disease, asthma, hay fever, or other allergies.

• This medication has been prescribed for your current infection only. Another infection that you experience at a later time, or an infection that someone else has, may require a different medication. Do not give your medication to other people or use it for other infections unless your doctor directs you to do so.

• People who have diabetes who have been prescribed ampicillin should be aware that this medication may cause a false-positive sugar reading with a Clinitest urine glucose test. To avoid such false-positive readings during treatment with ampicillin, you should switch to Clinistix or Tes-Tape to test your urine for sugar.

• Be sure to tell your doctor if you are pregnant. Although ampicillin appears to be safe when used during pregnancy, extensive scientific studies in humans have not been conducted. Also be sure to tell your doctor if you are breast-feeding an infant. Small amounts of this medication pass into the breast milk and may temporarily alter the natural bacterial balance in the intestinal tract of the nursing infant, resulting in diarrhea.

aripiprazole

BRAND NAME (Manufacturer)
Abilify (Bristol-Myers Squibb)
TYPE OF DRUG
Antipsychotic
INGREDIENT
aripiprazole
DOSAGE FORM
Tablets (10 mg, 15 mg, 20 mg, and 30 mg)
STORAGE
Store in a tightly closed container at room temperature, away from heat and direct sunlight.

USES

Aripiprazole is prescribed to treat symptoms of mental illness, such as the emotional symptoms of psychosis and schizophrenia. This medication is thought to relieve the symptoms of mental illness by blocking certain chemicals involved with nerve transmission in the brain.

TREATMENT

This medication should be taken exactly as prescribed by your doctor. It may be taken with or without food. To avoid stomach irritation, take aripiprazole with food or a full glass of water (unless your doctor directs you to do otherwise).

The full effects of this medication for the control of emotional or mental symptoms may not become apparent for two weeks after you begin treatment.

If you miss a dose of this medicine, take the missed dose as soon as possible and return to your regular dosing schedule. However, if it is almost time for your next dose of the medication, skip the missed dose and then return to your regular dosing schedule. Never take a double dose to make up for the dose that you missed unless directed to do so by your doctor.

SIDE EFFECTS

Minor. Anxiety, blurred vision, constipation, dizziness or light-headedness, drowsiness, dry mouth, headache, nausea, rash, restlessness, trouble sleeping, vomiting, or weakness. These side effects should diminish or disappear as your body adjusts to the medication.

Dry mouth can be relieved by chewing sugarless gum or sucking on hard candy.

To relieve constipation, increase the amount of fiber in your diet (fresh fruits and vegetables, salads, bran, and whole-grain breads), exercise, and drink more water (unless your doctor directs you to do otherwise).

If you feel dizzy or light-headed, sit or lie down for a while, get up slowly from a sitting or lying position, and be careful on stairs.

To avoid dizziness or light-headedness when you stand, contract and relax the muscles in your legs for a few moments before rising. You can do this by pushing one foot against the floor while raising the other foot slightly, alternating feet so that you are "pumping" your legs in a pedaling motion.

Major. Tell your doctor about any side effects that are persistent or particularly bothersome. IT IS ESPECIALLY IMPORTANT TO TELL YOUR DOCTOR about chest pain; difficulty in breathing or swallowing; fainting; fever; heart palpitations; impotence; involuntary movements of the face, mouth, tongue, or jaw; seizures; skin rash or hives; sleep disorders; sore throat; tremors; uncoordinated movements; unusual bleeding or bruising; or yellowing of the skin or the whites of the eyes.

INTERACTIONS

Aripiprazole interacts with several other types of drugs:

1. Extreme drowsiness can occur when this medication is taken with other central nervous system depressants such as alcohol, antihistamines, antidepressants, barbiturates, benzodiazepine tranquilizers, muscle relaxants, narcotics, pain medications, and sleeping medications.

2. The drugs carbamazepine, valproate, and famotidine may decrease the effects of aripiprazole.

3. Quinidine, fluoxetine, paroxetine, fluvoxamine, ketoconazole, and itraconazole may increase the amount of aripiprazole in the blood and, as a result, increase the side effects from this medication.

Before taking aripiprazole, BE SURE TO TELL YOUR DOCTOR about any medication you are taking, especially any of those listed above.

WARNINGS

• Tell your doctor about any unusual or allergic reactions you have had to any medications, especially to aripiprazole or other antipsychotics.

• Tell your doctor if you have a history of alcoholism or if you now have or ever had heart or circulatory disease, kidney disease, liver disease, irregular or fast heartbeats, or epilepsy.

• To prevent oversedation, avoid drinking alcoholic beverages while taking this medication.

• If this medication makes you drowsy or dizzy, do not take part in any activity that requires alertness, such as driving a car or operating dangerous equipment.

• This medication may decrease sweating and heat release from the body. Therefore avoid getting overheated by strenuous exercise in hot weather, and avoid taking hot baths, showers, or saunas.

• While taking this medication, do not take any over-the-counter (nonprescription) medication for weight control or for cough, cold, asthma, allergy, or sinus problems unless you first check with your doctor.

• Before having surgery or any other medical or dental treatment, be sure to tell your doctor or dentist that you are taking aripiprazole.

• Be sure to tell your doctor if you are pregnant. The effects of this medication during pregnancy have not been thoroughly studied in humans. It is also not known if aripiprazole passes into breast milk in humans, so be sure to tell your doctor if you are breast-feeding an infant.

---

aspirin

BRAND NAMES (Manufacturers)

aspirin* (various manufacturers)
Bayer* (Glenbrook)
Bayer Children's* (Glenbrook)
Ecotrin* (GlaxoSmithKline)
ZORprin (Abbott)
*Available over the counter (without a prescription)

TYPE OF DRUG

Analgesic and anti-inflammatory

INGREDIENT

aspirin

DOSAGE FORMS

Tablets (81 mg, 162.5 mg, 325 mg, 500 mg, and 650 mg)
Chewable tablets (81 mg)

Chewing gum (227 mg)
Enteric-coated tablets (81 mg, 325 mg, 500 mg, 650 mg, and 975 mg)
Sustained-release tablets (650 mg, 800 mg, and 950 mg)
Suppositories (60 mg, 120 mg, 125 mg, 130 mg, 195 mg, 200 mg, 300 mg, 325 mg, 600 mg, 650 mg, and 1.2 g)

STORAGE

Store at room temperature in a tightly closed container. Moisture causes aspirin to decompose. Discard the medicine if it has a vinegary odor.

USES

Aspirin is used to treat mild to moderate pain, fever, and inflammatory conditions, such as rheumatic fever, rheumatoid arthritis, and osteoarthritis. Because it prevents the formation of blood clots, aspirin has also been shown to be effective in reducing the risk of transient ischemic attacks (small strokes) and to have a protective effect against heart attacks in patients with angina (chest pain).

Aspirin is a useful medication that is utilized in the treatment of a wide variety of diseases. Because it is so common and so readily available, you may not think of it as "real medicine." This is a common misconception; aspirin certainly is "real medicine." If your doctor prescribes or recommends aspirin for your condition, it is for a good reason. FOLLOW YOUR DOCTOR'S DIRECTIONS CAREFULLY!

TREATMENT

To avoid stomach irritation, take aspirin with food or with a full glass of water or milk.

Chewable aspirin tablets may be chewed, dissolved in fluid, or swallowed whole.

Be sure to swallow the sustained-release or enteric-coated tablets whole. Crushing, chewing, or breaking these tablets destroys their sustained-release activity and increases their side effects.

To use the suppository, remove the foil wrapper and moisten the suppository with water (if it is too soft to insert, refrigerate the suppository for half an hour or run cold water over it before you remove the wrapper). Lie on your left side with your right knee bent. Push the suppository into the rectum, pointed end first. Lie still for a few minutes. Avoid having a bowel movement for at least an hour in order to give the drug time to be absorbed into your system.

If you are using aspirin to treat an inflammatory condition, it may take two or three weeks for the full benefits of the medication to be observed.

If you are taking aspirin on a regular schedule and you miss a dose, take the missed dose as soon as possible. However, if it is almost time for the next dose, do not take the missed dose at all; just return to your regular dosing schedule. Do not double the next dose.

SIDE EFFECTS

Minor. Heartburn, nausea, or vomiting. These side effects should disappear as your body adjusts to the medication.

Major. Tell your doctor about any side effects that are persistent or particularly bothersome. IT IS ESPECIALLY IMPORTANT TO TELL YOUR DOCTOR about bloody or black, tarry stools; confusion; difficult or painful urination; difficulty in breathing; dizziness; hearing loss or ringing in the ears; severe stomach pain; skin rash; or unusual weakness.

INTERACTIONS

Aspirin interacts with a number of other medications:

1. Aspirin can increase the effects of anticoagulant medications (blood thinners), such as warfarin, leading to bleeding complications.

2. The antigout effects of probenecid and sulfinpyrazone may be blocked by aspirin.

3. Aspirin can increase the gastrointestinal side effects of nonsteroidal anti-inflammatory drugs, alcohol, phenylbutazone, and adrenocorticosteroids (cortisonelike medications).
4. Ammonium chloride, methionine, and furosemide can increase the side effects of aspirin.
5. Acetazolamide, methazolamide, antacids, and phenobarbital can decrease the effectiveness of aspirin.
6. Aspirin can increase the side effects of methotrexate, penicillin, thyroid hormone, phenytoin, sulfinpyrazone, naproxen, valproic acid, insulin, and oral antidiabetic medications.
7. Aspirin can decrease the effects of spironolactone.

Before starting to take aspirin, BE SURE TO TELL YOUR DOCTOR about any medications you are currently taking, especially any of those listed above.

WARNINGS

• Tell your doctor about unusual or allergic reactions you have had to any medications, especially to aspirin, methyl salicylate (oil of wintergreen), tartrazine, diclofenac, diflunisal, flurbiprofen, fenoprofen, ibuprofen, indomethacin, ketoprofen, meclofenamate, mefenamic acid, naproxen, piroxicam, sulindac, tolmetin, or etodolac.
• Before starting to take aspirin, be sure to tell your doctor if you now have or ever had asthma, bleeding disorders, congestive heart failure, diabetes, glucose-6-phosphate dehydrogenase (G6PD) deficiency, gout, hemophilia, high blood pressure, kidney disease, liver disease, nasal polyps, peptic ulcers, or thyroid disease.
• Before having surgery or any other medical or dental treatment, be sure to tell your doctor or dentist that you are taking aspirin. Aspirin is usually discontinued five to seven days before surgery, in order to prevent bleeding complications.
• The use of aspirin in children (about 16 years of age or less) with the flu or chicken pox has been associated with a rare, life-threatening condition called Reye's syndrome. Aspirin should, therefore, not be given to children with signs of an infection.
• Large doses of aspirin (greater than eight 325 mg tablets per day) can cause erroneous urine glucose test results. People with diabetes should, therefore, check with their doctor before changing insulin doses while taking this medication.
• Additional medications that contain aspirin should not be taken without your doctor's approval. Be sure to check the labels on over-the-counter (nonprescription) pain, sinus, allergy, asthma, cough, and cold preparations to see if they contain aspirin.
• Be sure to tell your doctor if you are pregnant. Aspirin has been shown to cause birth defects in the offspring of animals that received large doses during pregnancy. Large doses of aspirin given to a pregnant woman close to term can prolong labor and cause bleeding complications in the mother and heart problems in the infant. Also tell your doctor if you are breast-feeding an infant. Small amounts of aspirin pass into breast milk.

---

aspirin and oxycodone combination

BRAND NAMES (Manufacturers)
oxycodone hydrochloride, oxycodone terephthalate, and aspirin (various manufacturers)
Percodan (DuPont)
Percodan-Demi (DuPont)
TYPE OF DRUG
Analgesic combination
INGREDIENTS
aspirin and oxycodone

DOSAGE FORM

Tablets (325 mg aspirin with 2.25 mg oxycodone hydrochloride and 0.19 mg oxycodone terephthalate; 325 mg aspirin with 4.5 mg oxycodone hydrochloride and 0.38 mg oxycodone terephthalate)

STORAGE

Store at room temperature in a tightly closed container. Moisture causes the aspirin in this product to decompose. Discard the medicine if it has a vinegary odor.

USES

This combination medication is used to relieve moderate to severe pain. Oxycodone is a narcotic analgesic that acts upon the central nervous system (brain and spinal cord) to alleviate pain.

TREATMENT

To avoid stomach upset, take this medication with food or with milk.

This medication works most effectively if you take it at the onset of pain, rather than waiting until the pain becomes more intense.

If you are taking this medication on a regular schedule and you miss a dose, take the missed dose as soon as possible. However, if it is almost time for your next dose of the medication, don't take the missed dose at all; just return to your regular dosing schedule. Do not double the next dose of the medication.

SIDE EFFECTS

Minor. Constipation, dizziness, drowsiness, dry mouth, false sense of well-being, flushing, indigestion, light-headedness, loss of appetite, nausea, sweating, or vomiting. These side effects should disappear over time as your body adjusts to the medication.

If you are constipated, increase the amount of fiber in your diet (fresh fruits and vegetables, salads, bran, and whole-grain breads), drink more water, and exercise (unless your doctor directs you to do otherwise).

Chew sugarless gum or suck on ice chips or a piece of hard candy to reduce mouth dryness.

If you feel dizzy, light-headed, or nauseated, sit or lie down for a while; get up from a sitting or lying position slowly; and be careful on stairs.

Major. Tell your doctor about any side effects that are persistent or particularly bothersome. IT IS ESPECIALLY IMPORTANT TO TELL YOUR DOCTOR about bloody or black, tarry stools; chest tightness; difficult or painful urination; difficulty in breathing; fatigue; itching; palpitations; rash; ringing in the ears; severe abdominal pain; tremors; or yellowing of the eyes or skin.

INTERACTIONS

This medication interacts with several other types of medications:

1. Concurrent use of this medication with other central nervous system depressants (such as alcohol, antihistamines, barbiturates, benzodiazepine tranquilizers, muscle relaxants, and phenothiazine tranquilizers) or with tricyclic antidepressants can cause extreme drowsiness.

2. The concurrent use of aspirin and oxycodone combination and monoamine oxidase (MAO) inhibitors should be avoided. At least 14 days should separate the use of this drug and the use of an MAO inhibitor.

3. Alcohol and anti-inflammatory medications can increase the gastrointestinal side effects of this medication.

4. The side effects caused by anticoagulants (blood thinners, such as warfarin), oral antidiabetic agents, phenytoin, and methotrexate may be increased by the aspirin contained in this product.

5. Large doses of antacids increase the elimination of the aspirin portion of this medication from the body and decrease its effectiveness.

6. The aspirin portion of this medication may decrease the antigout effects of probenecid and sulfinpyrazone.

BE SURE TO TELL YOUR DOCTOR about any medications that you are currently taking.

WARNINGS

• Tell your doctor about unusual or allergic reactions you have had to medications, especially to aspirin, methyl salicylate (oil of wintergreen), diclofenac, diflunisal, flurbiprofen, fenoprofen, ibuprofen, indomethacin, ketoprofen, meclofenamate, mefenamic acid, naproxen, piroxicam, sulindac, or tolmetin or to oxycodone or other narcotic analgesics (such as codeine, hydrocodone, hydromorphone, meperidine, methadone, morphine, or propoxyphene).

• Tell your doctor if you now have or ever had abdominal disease, Addison's disease, bleeding or blood disorders, brain disease, colitis, epilepsy, gallstones or gallbladder disease, head injuries, heart disease, hemophilia, kidney disease, liver disease, lung disease, peptic ulcers, porphyria, enlarged prostate gland, or thyroid disease.

• If this medication makes you dizzy or drowsy, do not participate in any activity that requires alertness, such as driving an automobile or operating any potentially dangerous equipment.

• Before having surgery or any other medical or dental treatment, be sure to tell your doctor or dentist that you are taking this medication. Aspirin-containing medications are usually stopped five to seven days before surgery in order to prevent bleeding complications.

• The use of aspirin in children (about 16 years of age or younger) who have the flu or chicken pox has been associated with a rare, life-threatening condition called Reye's syndrome. Aspirin-containing products should, therefore, not be given to children who show any signs of having an infection. Check the labels on all nonprescription products.

• Because this drug contains oxycodone, it has the potential for abuse and must be used with caution. Usually, it should not be taken on a regular schedule for longer than ten days at a time. Tolerance develops quickly; do not increase the dosage or stop taking the drug abruptly unless you first consult your doctor.

• If you have been taking large amounts of this medication for long periods, you may experience a withdrawal reaction (muscle aches, diarrhea, gooseflesh, runny nose, nausea, vomiting, shivering, trembling, stomach cramps, sleep disorders, irritability, weakness, excessive yawning, or sweating). Your doctor may, therefore, want to reduce the dosage gradually to prevent or minimize this response.

• Because this product contains aspirin, additional medications that contain aspirin should not be taken without your doctor's approval. Check the labels on over-the-counter (nonprescription) pain, sinus, allergy, asthma, cough, and cold products to see if they contain aspirin.

• People who have diabetes should be aware that large doses of aspirin (more than eight 325 mg tablets per day) may interfere with urine sugar testing. Such individuals should check with their doctor before making any adjustments to their dosage of insulin based on results from this testing.

• Be sure to tell your doctor if you are pregnant. The effects of this drug during pregnancy have not been thoroughly studied in humans. Oxycodone used regularly in large doses during pregnancy may result in addiction of the fetus, leading to withdrawal symptoms (irritability, excessive crying, tremors, fever, vomiting, diarrhea, sneezing, or excessive yawning) at birth. Large amounts of aspirin taken close to the end of pregnancy may prolong labor and cause bleeding problems in the mother and heart problems in the newborn infant. Also tell your doctor if you are breast-feeding an infant. Small amounts of this drug may pass into breast milk and cause excessive drowsiness in the nursing infant.

atenolol

BRAND NAMES (Manufacturers)
atenolol (various manufacturers)
Tenormin (Astra Zeneca)
TYPE OF DRUG
Beta-adrenergic blocking agent
INGREDIENT
atenolol
DOSAGE FORM
Tablets (25 mg, 50 mg, and 100 mg)
STORAGE
Store this medication at room temperature in a tightly closed, light-resistant container; do not freeze.

USES

Atenolol is most commonly used to treat high blood pressure and angina (chest pain) and to help regulate heart rate after a heart attack. It belongs to a group of medicines known as beta-adrenergic blocking agents or, more commonly, beta blockers. These drugs work by controlling impulses along certain nerve pathways. The result is a decreased workload for the heart.

TREATMENT

Atenolol can be taken with a glass of water, with meals, immediately following meals, or on an empty stomach, depending on your doctor's instructions. Try to take the medication at the same time(s) each day.

Try not to miss any doses of this medication. If you do miss a dose, take the missed dose as soon as possible. However, if your next scheduled dose of the medication is within eight hours (if you are taking this medicine only once a day) or within four hours (if you are taking this medicine more than once a day), do not take the missed dose of medication at all; just return to your regular dosing schedule. Do not double the next dose.

It is important to remember that atenolol does not cure high blood pressure, but it will help to control the condition as long as you continue to take it.

SIDE EFFECTS

Minor. Anxiety; constipation; decreased sexual ability; diarrhea; difficulty in sleeping; drowsiness; dryness of the eyes, mouth, and skin; headache; nausea; nervousness; stomach discomfort; tiredness; or weakness. These side effects should disappear as your body adjusts to the medicine.

If you are extra-sensitive to the cold, be sure to dress warmly during cold weather.

To relieve constipation, increase the amount of fiber in your diet (fresh fruits and vegetables, salads, bran, and whole-grain breads), and drink more water (unless your doctor directs you to do otherwise).

Plain, nonmedicated eyedrops (often called artificial tears) may help to relieve eye dryness.

Sucking on ice chips or chewing sugarless gum can help to relieve mouth or throat dryness.

Major. Tell your doctor about any side effects that are persistent or particularly bothersome. IT IS ESPECIALLY IMPORTANT TO TELL YOUR DOCTOR about breathing difficulty or wheezing; cold hands or feet (due to decreased blood flow to skin, fingers, and toes); confusion; dizziness; fever and sore throat; hair loss; hallucinations; light-headedness; mental depression; nightmares; reduced alertness; skin rash; swelling of the ankles, feet, or lower legs; or unusual or unexplained bleeding or bruising.

INTERACTIONS

This medication interacts with a variety of other types of medications:

1. Indomethacin and other nonsteroidal anti-inflammatory drugs (including diclofenac, etodolac, ibuprofen, ketoprofen, naproxen, and piroxicam) have been shown to decrease the blood-pressure-lowering effects of the beta blockers. This may also happen with aspirin or other salicylates.

2. Concurrent use of beta blockers and calcium channel blockers (diltiazem, nifedipine, and verapamil) or disopyramide can lead to heart failure or to very low blood pressure.

3. Cimetidine and oral contraceptives (birth control pills) can often increase the side effects caused by beta blockers.

4. Side effects may be increased when beta blockers are taken with clonidine, digoxin, epinephrine, phenylephrine, phenylpropanolamine, phenothiazine tranquilizers, prazosin, or monoamine oxidase (MAO) inhibitors. At least 14 days should separate the use of a beta blocker and the use of an MAO inhibitor.

5. Alcohol, barbiturates, and rifampin can decrease the effectiveness of atenolol.

6. Beta blockers may antagonize (work against) the effects of theophylline, aminophylline, albuterol, isoproterenol, metaproterenol, and terbutaline.

7. Beta blockers can also interact with insulin or oral antidiabetic agents—raising or lowering blood sugar levels or masking the symptoms of low blood sugar.

8. The action of beta blockers may be increased if they are used with chlorpromazine, furosemide, or hydralazine, which may have a negative effect.

9. In patients who have congestive heart failure treated with digitalis glycosides (for example, digoxin or digitoxin), caution should be used as both atenolol and digitalis products may slow heart conduction.

BE SURE TO TELL YOUR DOCTOR about any medications you are currently taking, especially any of those listed above.

WARNINGS

• Before starting to take this medication, it is important to tell your doctor if you have ever had unusual or allergic reactions to any beta blocker (acebutolol, atenolol, betaxolol, bisoprolol, carteolol, esmolol, labetalol, metoprolol, nadolol, penbutolol, pindolol, propranolol, and timolol).

• Tell your doctor if you now have or if you have ever had allergies, asthma, hay fever, eczema, slow heartbeat, bronchitis, diabetes mellitus, emphysema, heart or blood vessel disease, kidney disease, liver disease, thyroid disease, or poor circulation in the fingers or toes.

• In people who have diabetes, this medication may block some of the warning signs of low blood sugar, such as rapid pulse rate, but not others, such as dizziness or sweating.

• You may want to check your pulse regularly while you are being treated with this medication. If your pulse is much slower than your usual rate (or if it is less than 50 beats per minute), check with your doctor. A pulse rate that is too slow may cause circulation problems.

• Atenolol may affect your body's response to exercise. Make sure you discuss with your doctor a safe amount of exercise for your medical condition.

• It is important that you do not stop taking this medicine without first checking with your doctor. Some conditions may become worse when the medicine is stopped suddenly, and the danger of a heart attack is increased in some patients. Your doctor may want you to gradually reduce the amount of medicine you take before stopping completely. Make sure that you have enough medicine on hand to last through vacations and holidays.

• Before having surgery or any other medical or dental treatment, tell the physician or dentist that you are taking this medicine. Often, this medication will be discontinued 48 hours prior to any major surgery.

• This medicine can cause decreased alertness, dizziness, light-headedness, or drowsiness. Therefore, exercise caution while driving a car or operating any potentially dangerous equipment.

• While taking this medicine, do not use any over-the-counter (nonprescription) asthma, allergy, cough, cold, sinus, or diet preparations unless you first check with your pharmacist or doctor. Some of these medicines can cause high blood pressure when taken at the same time as a beta blocker.

• Be sure to tell your doctor if you are pregnant. Animal studies have shown that some beta blockers can cause problems in pregnancy when used at very high doses. Adequate studies have not been done in humans, but there has been some association between beta blockers used during pregnancy and low birth weight, as well as breathing problems and slow heart rate in the newborn infants. However, other reports have shown no effects on newborn infants. Also tell your doctor if you are breast-feeding an infant. Small amounts of atenolol may pass into breast milk.

---

atomoxetine

BRAND NAME (Manufacturer)
Strattera (Eli Lilly)
TYPE OF DRUG
Adrenergic
INGREDIENT
atomoxetine
DOSAGE FORM
Capsules (5 mg, 10 mg, 18 mg, 25 mg, 40 mg, and 60 mg)
STORAGE
Store at room temperature in a tightly closed, light-resistant container.

USES

Atomoxetine is a nonstimulant agent that increases mental alertness and decreases fatigue. The medication does this by increasing a certain chemical in the brain (called norepinephrine). It is used in the treatment of children and adolescents who suffer from attention-deficit/hyperactivity disorder. The way this medication works in this behavioral syndrome is not clearly understood.

TREATMENT

Atomoxetine can be taken on an empty stomach or with food. It can be taken once daily (usually in the morning) or as evenly divided doses in the morning and late afternoon or early evening. It is best not to take this medication too late in the evening since it may cause difficulty sleeping. Discuss with your doctor the best time to take this medication.

If you miss a dose, take the missed dose as soon as possible. However, if it is almost time for your next dose, do not take the missed dose; just return to your regular dosing schedule. Do not double the next dose.

SIDE EFFECTS

Minor. Abdominal pain, constipation, dizziness, drowsiness, dry mouth, headache, insomnia, irritability, mood swings, weakness, or weight loss. These side effects should disappear as your body adjusts to the medication.

Dry mouth can be relieved by sucking on ice chips or a piece of hard candy or by chewing sugarless gum.

To relieve constipation, increase the amount of fiber in your diet (fresh fruits and vegetables, salads, bran, and whole-grain breads), exercise, and drink more water (unless your doctor directs you to do otherwise).

To avoid dizziness or light-headedness when you stand, contract and relax the muscles of your legs for a few moments before rising.

If you feel dizzy, sit or lie down for a while, get up from a sitting or lying position slowly, and be careful on stairs.

Major: Tell your doctor about any side effects that are persistent or particularly bothersome. IT IS ESPECIALLY IMPORTANT TO TELL YOUR DOCTOR about chest pain, difficulty in urinating, hallucinations, hives, mood changes, palpitations, seizures, or uncoordinated movements.

The effects of atomoxetine on the growth (height and weight) of children are unknown. If this medication is to be used for a long period of time, discuss with your doctor whether a drug-free period is needed to allow for normal height and weight gain in children.

INTERACTIONS

Atomoxetine interacts with several other medications:

1. Use of atomoxetine within 14 days of using a monoamine oxidase (MAO) inhibitor, such as isocarboxazid, pargyline, phenelzine, or tranylcypromine, can result in severe high blood pressure.

2. Atomoxetine should be used carefully with certain asthma medications such as albuterol. The effects on the heart may be increased with this combination.

3. Do not take medications that may increase blood pressure, such as diet pills, caffeine, or stimulants, while taking atomoxetine.

4. Paroxetine, fluoxetine, quinidine, and sertraline increase the side effects of atomoxetine. Avoid taking any of these medications while taking atomoxetine.

Before starting this medication, BE SURE TO TELL YOUR DOCTOR about any medications you are currently taking, especially any of those listed above.

Tell your doctor about unusual or allergic reactions you have had to any medications, especially to atomoxetine or antidepressants.

WARNINGS

- Tell your doctor if you have ever had epilepsy, glaucoma, high blood pressure, motor tics, Tourette's syndrome, anxiety, agitation, heart problems, fast or irregular heartbeats, kidney or urinary tract problems, depression, or tension.
- Atomoxetine may mask the symptoms of extreme fatigue and can cause dizziness. Your ability to perform tasks that require alertness, such as driving a car or operating potentially dangerous machinery, may be decreased. Appropriate caution should be taken. A child taking atomoxetine should be careful while engaging in physical activity.
- Call your doctor immediately if you experience difficulty breathing, have facial swelling, or develop a rash after taking atomoxetine.
- Before having surgery or any other medical or dental treatment, be sure to tell your doctor that you are taking this medication.
- Children may be more sensitive to certain side effects from this drug, such as loss of appetite, stomach pain, trouble sleeping, and weight loss.
- Be sure to tell your doctor if you are pregnant. Effects of this medication during pregnancy have not been thoroughly studied in either humans or animals. Also tell your doctor if you are breast-feeding an infant. Small amounts of atomoxetine may pass into breast milk.

atorvastatin

BRAND NAME (Manufacturer)
Lipitor (Pfizer)
TYPE OF DRUG
Antihyperlipidemic (lipid-lowering drug)
INGREDIENT
atorvastatin
DOSAGE FORM
Tablets (10 mg, 20 mg, and 40 mg)
STORAGE
Store in a tightly closed container at room temperature, away from heat and direct sunlight. Do not refrigerate or freeze.

USES

Atorvastatin is used to treat hyperlipidemia (high blood fat levels). It may be prescribed with nondrug therapies such as diet control and exercise to regulate lipid and cholesterol levels. Atorvastatin chemically interferes with an enzyme in the body that is responsible for synthesizing cholesterol. This enzyme blockade decreases the LDL (low-density lipoprotein) type of cholesterol, which has been associated with coronary artery disease and atherosclerosis. In addition, this drug significantly decreases triglyceride levels.

TREATMENT

Take this medication exactly as prescribed by your doctor. If you are supposed to take the medication once a day, it is best to take it at the same time every day. Atorvastatin can be taken with meals or with a large glass of water if you experience stomach upset.

While using this medication, try to develop a set schedule for taking it. If you miss a dose and remember within a few hours, take the missed dose and resume your regular schedule. If many hours have passed, skip the dose you missed and take your next dose as scheduled. Do not double the next dose.

SIDE EFFECTS

Minor. Abdominal pain or cramps, constipation, diarrhea, gas, nausea, or stomach pain. These effects may be relieved by taking atorvastatin with a meal, adding fiber to your diet, or using mild stool softeners.
Major. Tell your doctor about any side effects that are persistent or particularly bothersome, including giddiness, headache, impaired short-term memory (forgetfulness). or mild confusion. IT IS ESPECIALLY IMPORTANT TO TELL YOUR DOCTOR about blurred vision (or any other visual changes or difficulties) or muscle pain or tenderness, especially accompanied by extreme tiredness or fever.

INTERACTIONS

Atorvastatin may increase the effectiveness of oral anticoagulants (blood thinners, such as warfarin) and digoxin.
1. Because of the risk of severe myopathy (muscle weakness), the combined use of atorvastatin with gemfibrozil or clofibrate should generally be avoided.
2. Cyclosporine, erythromycin, nicotinic acid, niacin, itraconazole, and ketoconazole may increase the side effects of atorvastatin and should be used with extreme caution.
3. Cholestyramine, colestipol, or aluminum- or magnesium-containing antacids may decrease the effectiveness of this medication by decreasing its absorption. It is best

to take these medications either one hour before or several hours after your dose of atorvastatin to avoid this drug interaction.

4. Do not eat grapefruit or drink grapefruit juice during treatment with atorvastatin, as these products may interfere with your body's ability to excrete this drug.

BE SURE TO TELL YOUR DOCTOR about any medications you are taking, especially any of the medications that are listed above.

WARNINGS

- Tell your doctor about unusual or allergic reactions you have had to any medications.
- Be sure to tell your doctor if you have ever had liver disease, heart disease, stroke, or digestive-tract disorders.
- Patients taking another drug in the same class as atorvastatin developed eye-related problems during treatment. It is advisable to have regular checkups with your ophthalmologist, who should be informed of your use of this drug.
- It is very important to limit your intake of alcoholic beverages while taking this medication to avoid increased side effects from it.
- This medication can cause increased sensitivity to sunlight. Therefore, you should avoid prolonged exposure to sunlight and sunlamps, wear protective clothing and sunglasses, and use an effective sunscreen.
- This drug should not be taken if you are pregnant. Serious side effects have been reported in the offspring of animals given this drug during pregnancy. Also, be sure to tell your doctor if you are breast-feeding an infant. This drug should not be used while breast-feeding.

---

azithromycin

BRAND NAME (Manufacturer)
Zithromax (Pfizer)
TYPE OF DRUG
Antibiotic
INGREDIENT
azithromycin
DOSAGE FORMS
Tablets (250 mg and 600 mg)
Oral suspension (100 mg per 5-mL spoonful; 200 mg per 5-mL spoonful; 1 g single-dose packet)
STORAGE
Store tablets at room temperature in a tightly closed, light-resistant container. Store the suspension at room temperature; do not refrigerate. Discard any unused portion of the suspension after ten days.

USES

Azithromycin is used to treat a wide variety of bacterial infections, including those of the upper and lower respiratory tracts and skin and certain sexually transmitted diseases. This medicine acts by preventing bacteria from manufacturing protein and thereby preventing their growth. Azithromycin kills certain bacteria but is not effective against viruses, parasites, or fungi.

TREATMENT

Shake the suspension well before each use. To prepare solution from the packet, mix the contents from the one-gram packet in a glass with two ounces of water and drink it immediately. Then add two more ounces of water to the glass, and drink it to make sure all of medication has been taken.

It is best to take the suspension on an empty stomach (one hour before or two hours after a meal). The tablets may be taken with or without food, as directed by your doctor. Azithromycin works best when the level of medicine in your bloodstream is kept constant. Therefore, it is best to take the doses at the same time every day.

If you miss a dose, take it immediately. However, if you don't remember to take your scheduled dose until the next day, skip the missed dose and go back to your regular dosing schedule. Do not double the next dose.

It is important to continue to take this medicine for the entire time period prescribed by the doctor (usually five days), even if the symptoms disappear before the end of that period. If you stop taking this drug too soon, resistant bacteria (bacteria that will not be killed by the antibiotic) are given a chance to continue to grow, and the infection could recur.

SIDE EFFECTS

Minor. Abdominal pain, diarrhea, dizziness, headache, nausea, or vomiting. These effects should disappear as your body adjusts to the medication.

This medication can cause increased sensitivity to sunlight. It is important to avoid prolonged exposure to sunlight and sunlamps. Wear protective clothing, and use an effective sunscreen.

If you feel dizzy or light-headed, sit or lie down for a while; get up slowly from a sitting or reclining position; and be careful on stairs.

Major. Tell your doctor about any side effects that are persistent or particularly bothersome. IT IS ESPECIALLY IMPORTANT TO TELL YOUR DOCTOR about fever, palpitations, rash, rectal or vaginal itching, shortness of breath, swelling of the face or neck, sore throat, unusual bruising or bleeding, or yellowing of the eyes or skin. If your symptoms of infection seem to be getting worse rather than improving, you should contact your doctor.

INTERACTIONS

Azithromycin interacts with several medications:

1. Azithromycin may increase blood levels of aminophylline, theophylline, carbamazepine, cyclosporine, tacrolimus, disopyramide, phenytoin, digoxin, triazolam, phenobarbital, ergotamine, dihydroergotamine, or oral anticoagulants (blood thinners, such as warfarin) when they are used concurrently; this may lead to serious side effects.

2. Antacids containing aluminum or magnesium will decrease the efficacy of azithromycin. Take antacids one hour before or two hours after your dose of azithromycin.

3. Do not take this medication if you are taking pimozide; increased adverse effects on the heart may result.

BE SURE TO TELL YOUR DOCTOR about any medications you are currently taking, especially any listed above.

WARNINGS

• Tell your doctor about any unusual reactions you have had to any medications, especially to azithromycin, clarithromycin, dirithromycin, or erythromycin.

• Tell your doctor if you have or if you have ever had kidney disease, liver disease, or heart disease.

• This medication has been prescribed for your current infection only. Another infection later on, or one that someone else has, may require a different medicine. You should not give your medication to other people or use it for other infections, unless your doctor specifically directs you to do so.

• Before having surgery or any other medical or dental treatment, be sure to tell your doctor or dentist you are taking azithromycin.

• Be sure to tell your doctor if you are pregnant. The effects of this medicine during pregnancy have not been thoroughly studied in humans. Also tell your doctor if you are breast-feeding an infant. It is not known if azithromycin passes into breast milk.

beclomethasone

BRAND NAMES (Manufacturers)
Beclovent (GlaxoSmithKline)
Vanceril (Schering-Plough)
Vanceril Double Strength (Schering-Plough)
TYPE OF DRUG
Corticosteroid inhalant (antiasthmatic)
INGREDIENT
beclomethasone
DOSAGE FORM
Inhalation aerosol (each actuation delivers approximately 42 mcg or 84 mcg)
STORAGE
Store at room temperature and away from excessive heat, as the contents are pressurized and can explode if heated. Do not puncture the container. Do not refrigerate or freeze this medication.

USES

Inhalation corticosteroids are cortisonelike medicines. They are used to help prevent the symptoms of asthma. When used regularly every day, inhalation corticosteroids decrease the number and severity of asthma attacks. However, they will not relieve an asthma attack that has already started. This medicine works by preventing certain cells in the lungs and breathing passages from releasing substances that cause asthma symptoms.

TREATMENT

This medication should be packaged with an instruction sheet. Read the directions carefully before using this medication. You may wish to consult your doctor or pharmacist about the proper administration of this drug. Shake the container well just before each use to distribute the ingredients evenly and equalize the doses, as the medication tends to settle on the bottom. If more than one inhalation is necessary, wait at least one full minute between doses of the medication, in order to receive the full benefit of the first dose.

This medication should be taken exactly as prescribed by your doctor. Do not use more of it and do not use it more often than recommended by your doctor. To do so may increase the chance that you will experience side effects. While using this medication, try to develop a set schedule for taking it. If you miss a dose of the medication and remember within a few hours, take the missed dose and use any remaining doses for that day at regularly spaced intervals. Do not double the dose. This medication does not cure asthma, but it will help to control the condition as long as you continue to take it. It may be several weeks before you notice the full effects of this medication.

SIDE EFFECTS

Minor. Cough, dry mouth, hoarseness or other voice changes, sore throat, or unpleasant taste. These side effects should disappear as your body adjusts to the medication.

Chew sugarless gum or suck on ice chips or a piece of hard candy to relieve mouth or throat dryness.

In order to prevent dryness or irritation of the mouth and throat and infection of the mouth, rinse your mouth or gargle with water after each dose. DO NOT SWALLOW the water after rinsing.

Major. Tell your doctor about any side effects that are persistent or particularly bothersome. IT IS ESPECIALLY IMPORTANT TO TELL YOUR DOCTOR about behavior changes; creamy white, curdlike patches in the mouth or throat and/or pain when eating or swallowing; difficulty breathing; mental depression; nervousness; pain or burning in the chest; restlessness; tightness in the chest; or wheezing.

INTERACTIONS

This medication should not interact with other medications when used according to directions.

Before starting to take this medication, BE SURE TO TELL YOUR DOCTOR about any medications you are taking.

WARNINGS

- Tell your doctor about unusual or allergic reactions you have had to any cortisone-like medications, especially to this medication.
- Be sure to tell your doctor if you have ever had bone disease of any sort (including osteoporosis), diabetes mellitus, emotional instability, glaucoma, fungal infections, heart disease, high blood pressure, high cholesterol levels, myasthenia gravis, ulcerative colitis, peptic ulcers, kidney disease, liver disease, or tuberculosis.
- Before having surgery or other medical or dental treatment, tell your doctor or dentist you are taking this medication. Depending on how long you have been taking this medication, you may need to receive higher doses if you are exposed to stress, such as serious infection, injury, or surgery. Discuss this with your doctor or dentist.
- Avoid contact of the aerosol inhalation with your eyes.
- Do not puncture, break, or burn the aerosol container. The contents are under pressure and may explode. In addition, avoid exposure of this medication to cold or freezing temperatures; this medication may be less effective if it is cold when you use it.
- Do not stop taking this medication without first checking with your doctor. Your doctor may want to gradually reduce the amount of medicine you are taking before completely stopping the treatment. Make sure that you have enough medicine on hand to last through vacations, holidays, and weekends.
- Do not take any over-the-counter (nonprescription) medications for weight control or for asthma, sinus, cough, cold, or allergy problems unless you first check with your pharmacist or doctor.
- Your doctor may want you to carry a medical identification card stating that you are using this medicine and that you may need additional medicine during times of emergency, stress, severe asthma attack, or other illness.
- If you are using a bronchodilator (albuterol, metaproterenol, etc.) by inhalation, you must use the bronchodilator several minutes BEFORE you take beclomethasone. Discuss this with your doctor or pharmacist.
- Notify your doctor immediately if you are exposed to any person with chicken pox or the measles.
- This medication is for preventative therapy only. DO NOT use it to treat an acute asthmatic attack. This medication should be used at regularly scheduled intervals throughout the day as prescribed by your doctor, even if you are not having any symptoms of asthma.
- Be sure to tell your doctor if you are pregnant. This medication has been shown to cause birth defects in the offspring of animals that received large doses of it during pregnancy. Adequate studies have not been done in humans. Also tell your doctor if you are breast-feeding an infant. Small amounts of this medication pass into breast milk and may cause growth suppression or a decrease in natural corticosteroid production in the nursing infant.

benazepril

BRAND NAME (Manufacturer)
Lotensin (Novartis)
TYPE OF DRUG
Antihypertensive
INGREDIENT
benazepril
DOSAGE FORM
Tablets (5 mg, 10 mg, 20 mg, and 40 mg)
STORAGE
Store benazepril at room temperature in a tightly closed container.

USES

Benazepril is used to treat high blood pressure and congestive heart failure. It is a vasodilator (it widens the blood vessels) that acts by blocking the production of chemicals that may be responsible for constricting, or narrowing, the blood vessels. This medication is in a class of medications called angiotensin-converting enzyme (ACE) inhibitors.

TREATMENT

Benazepril can be taken with food if it causes irritation or stomach upset when taken on an empty stomach. To become accustomed to taking this medication, try to take it at the same time(s) every day.

It may be several weeks before you notice the full effects of this medication.

If you miss a dose of benazepril, take the missed dose as soon as possible. However, if it is almost time for the next dose of medication, do not take the missed dose at all; just wait until it's time for your next scheduled dose. Do not double the dose.

This drug does not cure high blood pressure, but it will help to control the condition as long as you continue to take the medication.

SIDE EFFECTS

Minor. Abdominal pain, cough, diarrhea, dizziness, drowsiness, fatigue, headache, insomnia, nausea, nervousness, sweating, or vomiting. These side effects should disappear as your body adjusts to the medication.

To avoid dizziness when you stand, contract and relax the muscles of your legs for a few moments before rising. Do this by alternately pushing one foot against the floor while lifting the other foot slightly.

Major. Tell your doctor about any side effects that are persistent or particularly bothersome. IT IS ESPECIALLY IMPORTANT TO TELL YOUR DOCTOR about chest pain; difficulty breathing; fainting; fever; itching; light-headedness (especially during the first few days); muscle cramps; palpitations; rash; sore throat; swelling of the face, eyes, lips, or tongue; tingling in the fingers and toes; or yellowing of the eyes or skin.

INTERACTIONS

Benazepril interacts with several other types of medications:

1. Diuretics and other antihypertensive medications can cause an excessive drop in blood pressure when they are combined with benazepril (especially with the first dose).

2. The combination of benazepril with amiloride, potassium supplements, salt substitutes, spironolactone, or triamterene can lead to hyperkalemia (dangerously high levels of potassium in the bloodstream).

3. Nonsteroidal anti-inflammatory agents (including ibuprofen, indomethacin, and naproxen) may reduce the effectiveness of this medication.

4. Antacids containing aluminum or magnesium may decrease the efficacy of benazepril. Therefore, take antacids one hour before or two hours after taking your prescribed dose of benazepril.
5. The concurrent use of this medication with probenecid, rifampin, lithium, or allopurinol may result in an unwanted drug interaction.

Before starting to take benazepril, BE SURE TO TELL YOUR DOCTOR about any medications you are currently taking, especially any of those listed above.

WARNINGS

• Tell your doctor about any unusual or allergic reactions you have had to any medications, especially to benazepril or other ACE inhibitor drugs.
• Tell your doctor if you now have or if you have ever had blood disorders, heart failure, renal disease, or systemic lupus erythematosus.
• Excessive perspiration, dehydration, or prolonged vomiting or diarrhea can lead to an excessive drop in blood pressure while you are taking this medication. Contact your doctor if you have any of these symptoms.
• Before having surgery or other medical or dental treatment, tell your doctor or dentist you are taking this drug.
• If this drug makes you dizzy or drowsy, do not take part in any activity that requires alertness, such as driving a car or operating potentially dangerous equipment.
• If you have high blood pressure, do not take any over-the-counter (nonprescription) medications for weight control or for asthma, sinus, cough, cold, or allergy problems unless you first check with your doctor.
• Be sure to tell your doctor if you are pregnant. Drugs in the same class as benazepril have been shown to cause birth defects, including kidney damage, low blood pressure, and improper skull development, and may even cause death when taken in the second and third trimesters. Also tell your doctor if you are breast-feeding an infant. Small amounts of benazepril may pass into breast milk.

---

benztropine

BRAND NAMES (Manufacturers)
benztropine (various manufacturers)
Cogentin (Merck)
TYPE OF DRUG
Anticholinergic and antiparkinsonism agent
INGREDIENT
benztropine
DOSAGE FORM
Tablets (0.5 mg, 1 mg, and 2 mg)
STORAGE
Store at room temperature in a tightly closed container. Do not refrigerate.

USES

Benztropine is used to treat the symptoms of Parkinson's disease or to control the side effects of phenothiazine tranquilizers. It is not understood how this medication works, but benztropine may act by helping to balance certain chemicals in the brain.

TREATMENT

To reduce the possibility of stomach irritation, you can take this medication with food or just after a meal.

If you miss a dose of this medication, take the missed dose as soon as possible. However, if it is within two hours of your next dose, don't take the missed dose at all; just return to your regular dosing schedule. Do not double the next dose of the medication.

SIDE EFFECTS

Minor. Bloating; blurred vision; constipation; dizziness; drowsiness; dry mouth, throat, and nose; false sense of well-being; headache; increased sensitivity of the eyes to light; muscle cramps; nausea; nervousness; reduced sweating; or weakness. These side effects should disappear as your body adjusts to the medication.

If you are constipated, increase the amount of fiber in your diet (fresh fruits and vegetables, salads, bran, and whole-grain breads), exercise, and drink more water (unless your doctor directs you to do otherwise).

Chew sugarless gum or suck on ice chips or a piece of hard candy to reduce mouth dryness.

If your eyes become sensitive to light, avoid exposure to the sun or wear sunglasses.

To avoid dizziness and light-headedness when you stand, contract and relax the muscles of your legs for a few moments before rising. Do this by pushing one foot against the floor while raising the other foot slightly, alternating feet so that you are "pumping" your legs in a pedaling motion.

Major. Tell your doctor about any side effects that are persistent or particularly bothersome. IT IS ESPECIALLY IMPORTANT TO TELL YOUR DOCTOR about depression, difficulty in urinating, difficulty sleeping, hallucinations, involuntary muscle movements, loss of balance, memory loss, mood changes, numbness of the fingers, palpitations, or unusual excitement.

Some side effects may occur for a short time after discontinuing this drug. Consult your doctor if they become bothersome.

INTERACTIONS

Benztropine can interact with several other types of medications:

1. It can cause extreme drowsiness when combined with alcohol or other central nervous system depressants (such as antihistamines, barbiturates, benzodiazepine tranquilizers, muscle relaxants, narcotics, and pain medications) or with tricyclic antidepressants.

2. Amantadine, antihistamines, haloperidol, monoamine oxidase (MAO) inhibitors, phenothiazine tranquilizers, procainamide, quinidine, and tricyclic antidepressants can increase the side effects from benztropine. At least 14 days should separate the use of this medication and the use of an MAO inhibitor.

3. Antacids and antidiarrheal medicines prevent absorption of this medication, so at least one hour should separate doses of benztropine and one of these medicines.

Before starting to take this medication, BE SURE TO TELL YOUR DOCTOR about any medications that you are currently taking, especially any of the medications that are discussed above.

WARNINGS

- Be sure to tell your doctor about unusual or allergic reactions you have had to any medications, especially any reactions to benztropine.
- Tell your doctor if you now have or if you have ever had achalasia (difficulty in relaxing certain muscles), glaucoma, heart disease, high blood pressure, kidney disease, liver disease, myasthenia gravis, blockage of the intestinal tract or urinary tract, enlarged prostate gland, stomach ulcers, or thyroid disease.
- If this drug makes you dizzy or drowsy, be sure to avoid any activity that requires alertness, such as driving a car or operating potentially dangerous equipment. Be careful when using stairs, and avoid getting up suddenly from a lying or sitting position.
- This medication can decrease sweating and heat release from the body. You should, therefore, avoid getting overheated by strenuous exercise in hot weather and should avoid taking hot baths, showers, and saunas.

• Elderly patients are more sensitive to the effects of this medication. Contact your doctor if you experience confusion, disorientation, agitation, or hallucinations.
• Be sure to tell your doctor if you are pregnant. Extensive studies of benztropine use during pregnancy have not been conducted. Also tell your doctor if you are breast-feeding an infant. Small amounts of this medication may pass into breast milk. In addition, benztropine can reduce milk formation in lactating women.

---

betamethasone dipropionate (topical)

BRAND NAMES (Manufacturers)
Alphatrex (Savage)
betamethasone dipropionate (various manufacturers)
Diprolene (Schering-Plough)
Diprosone (Schering-Plough)
Maxivate (Bristol-Myers Squibb)
TYPE OF DRUG
Adrenocorticosteroid hormone
INGREDIENT
betamethasone
DOSAGE FORMS
Ointment (0.05%)
Cream (0.05%)
Lotion (0.05%)
Aerosol (0.1%)
Gel (0.05%)
STORAGE
Store all forms at room temperature in tightly closed containers. Do not freeze.

The aerosol form of this medication is packaged under pressure. It should not be stored near heat or an open flame or in direct sunlight. Do not puncture the container.

USES

Your adrenal glands naturally produce certain cortisonelike chemicals. These chemicals are involved in various regulatory processes in the body (such as those involving fluid balance, temperature, and reaction to inflammation). Betamethasone dipropionate belongs to a group of drugs known as adrenocorticosteroids (or cortisonelike medications). It is used to relieve the skin inflammation (redness, swelling, itching, and discomfort) associated with conditions such as dermatitis, eczema, and poison ivy. How betamethasone dipropionate acts to relieve these dermatological conditions is not completely understood.

TREATMENT

Before applying this medication, wash your hands. Then, unless your doctor gives you different instructions, gently wash the area of the skin where the medication is to be applied. With a clean towel, pat the area until it is almost dry; it should be slightly damp when you put the medicine on it.

Shake the lotion well to distribute the ingredients evenly and equalize the doses before pouring it out. The contents tend to settle on the bottom of the bottle.

Apply a small amount of the medication to the affected area in a thin layer. Do not bandage the area unless your doctor tells you to do so. If you are to apply an occlusive dressing (like kitchen plastic wrap), be sure you understand the instructions for proper use. Wash your hands again after application.

Shake the aerosol spray form of this medication in order to disperse the medication evenly. Hold the can upright, six to eight inches from the area to be sprayed, and spray the area for one to three seconds. DO NOT SMOKE while you are using the aerosol spray; the contents are under pressure and may explode when exposed to heat or flames.

Avoid applying this medication to areas with cuts or open wounds.

If you miss a dose, apply it as soon as possible. However, if it is almost time for the next application, do not apply the missed dose; just return to your regular schedule. Do not put twice as much of the medication on your skin at the next application.

SIDE EFFECTS

Minor. Acne, burning sensation, itching, skin dryness, or rash. These side effects should diminish or disappear as your body adjusts to the medication.

If the affected area is extremely dry or scaling, the skin may be moistened before the medication is applied by soaking the area in water or by applying water to the area with a clean cloth. The ointment form of this medication is probably the most appropriate for dry skin.

A mild, temporary stinging sensation may occur after this medication is applied. If this persists, contact your doctor.

Major. Tell your doctor about any side effects that are persistent or particularly bothersome. IT IS ESPECIALLY IMPORTANT TO TELL YOUR DOCTOR about blistering, increased hair growth, irritation of the affected area, loss of skin color, secondary infection in the area being treated, or thinning of the skin with easy bruising.

INTERACTIONS

This medication should not interact with any other medications as long as it is used according to directions.

WARNINGS

• Tell your doctor about unusual or allergic reactions you have had to any medications, especially to betamethasone dipropionate or any other adrenocorticosteroid (such as amcinonide, clocortolone, cortisone, desonide, desoximetasone, dexamethasone, diflorasone, flumethasone, fluocinolone, fluocinonide, fluorometholone, flurandrenolide, halcinonide, hydrocortisone, methylprednisolone, prednisolone, prednisone, and triamcinolone).

• Tell your doctor if you now have or ever had blood vessel disease, chicken pox, diabetes mellitus, fungal infection, peptic ulcer, shingles, tuberculosis, tuberculosis of the skin, or any other type of infection, especially at the site currently being treated.

• If irritation develops while using this drug, immediately discontinue its use and notify your doctor.

• This product is not for use in the eyes, on mucous membranes, or on broken skin; contact may result in side effects.

• Do not use this product with an occlusive wrap unless your doctor directs you to do so. Systemic absorption of this drug is increased if extensive areas of the body are treated, particularly if occlusive bandages are used. If it is necessary for you to use this drug under a wrap, follow your doctor's instructions exactly; do not leave the wrap in place longer than specified.

• If you are using this medication on a child's diaper area, do not put tight-fitting diapers or plastic pants on the child. This may lead to increased systemic absorption of the drug and a possible increase in side effects.

• Elderly patients and younger children have thinner skin, and, therefore, betamethasone dipropionate is more likely to be absorbed into the system. Watch for and report any adverse effects to your doctor.

• To avoid freezing skin tissue when using the aerosol form of this medication, make sure that you do not spray continuously for more than three seconds, and hold the container at least six inches from the skin.

• When using the aerosol form of this medication near the face, cover your eyes and do not inhale the spray.
• Use this medication only for your current condition. Do not use it for another problem later or give it to other people to use.
• Tell your doctor if you are pregnant. If large amounts of this drug are applied for prolonged periods, some of it may cross the placenta. Although studies in humans have not been conducted, birth defects have been observed in the offspring of animals that were given large oral doses of this type of drug during pregnancy. Also tell your doctor if you are breast-feeding an infant. If absorbed through the skin, small amounts of the drug may pass into breast milk and may cause growth suppression or a decrease in natural adrenocorticosteroid production in the nursing infant.

---

betamethasone valerate (topical)

BRAND NAMES (Manufacturers)
betamethasone valerate (various manufacturers)
Betatrex (Savage)
Beta-Val (Lemmon)
Valisone (Schering-Plough)
Valisone Reduced Strength (Schering-Plough)
TYPE OF DRUG
Adrenocorticosteroid hormone
INGREDIENT
betamethasone
DOSAGE FORMS
Cream (0.01% and 0.1%)
Lotion (0.1%)
Ointment (0.1%)
STORAGE
Store at room temperature in a tightly closed container. Do not freeze.

USES

Your adrenal glands naturally produce certain cortisonelike chemicals. These chemicals are involved in various regulatory processes in the body (such as those involving fluid balance, temperature, and reaction to inflammation). Betamethasone valerate belongs to a group of drugs known as adrenocorticosteroids (or cortisonelike medications). It is used to relieve the skin inflammation (redness, swelling, itching, and discomfort) associated with conditions such as dermatitis, eczema, and poison ivy. How this drug acts to relieve these disorders is not completely understood.

TREATMENT

Wash your hands before applying this medication. Then, unless your doctor gives you different instructions, gently wash the area of the skin where the medication is to be applied. With a clean towel, pat the area almost dry; it should be slightly damp when you put the medicine on.

Shake the lotion well to distribute the ingredients evenly and equalize the doses before pouring out the medicine and applying it.

Apply a small amount of the medication to the affected area in a thin layer. Avoid applying medication to cuts or open wounds. Do not bandage the area unless your doctor specifically tells you to do so. If you are to apply an occlusive dressing (like kitchen plastic wrap), be sure that you understand the instructions. Wash your hands again after applying the medication.

If you miss a dose, apply it as soon as possible. However, if it is almost time for the next application, do not apply the missed dose; just return to your regular dosing schedule. Do not put twice as much on your skin at the next application.

SIDE EFFECTS

Minor. Acne, burning sensation, itching, rash, or skin dryness. These side effects should diminish as your body adjusts to the medication.

If the affected area is extremely dry or scaling, the skin may be moistened before applying the medication by soaking the area in water or by applying water to the area with a clean cloth. The ointment form is probably better for dry skin than other forms.

A mild, temporary stinging sensation may occur after this medication is applied. If this persists, contact your doctor.

Major. Tell your doctor about any side effects that are persistent or particularly bothersome. IT IS ESPECIALLY IMPORTANT TO TELL YOUR DOCTOR about blistering, increased hair growth, irritation of the affected area, loss of skin color, secondary infection of the area being treated, or thinning of the skin with easy bruising.

INTERACTIONS

This medication should not interact with any other medications as long as it is used according to directions.

WARNINGS

• Tell your doctor about unusual or allergic reactions you have had to any medications, especially to betamethasone valerate or other adrenocorticosteroids (such as amcinonide, clocortolone, cortisone, desonide, desoximetasone, dexamethasone, diflorasone, flumethasone, fluocinolone, fluocinonide, fluorometholone, flurandrenolide, halcinonide, hydrocortisone, methylprednisolone, prednisolone, prednisone, and triamcinolone).

• Tell your doctor if you now have or ever had blood vessel disease, chicken pox, diabetes mellitus, fungal infection, peptic ulcers, shingles, tuberculosis, tuberculosis of the skin, or any other type of infection, especially at the site currently being treated.

• If irritation develops while using this drug, immediately discontinue its use and notify your doctor.

• This product is not for use in the eyes, on mucous membranes, or on broken skin; contact may result in side effects.

• Use this drug only for your current condition. Do not use it for another problem or give it to others to use.

• Do not use this product with an occlusive wrap unless your doctor directs you to do so. Systemic absorption of this drug is increased if extensive areas of the body are treated, particularly if occlusive bandages are used. If it is necessary for you to use this drug under a wrap, follow your doctor's instructions exactly.

• If you are using this medication on a child's diaper area, do not put tight-fitting diapers or plastic pants on the child. This may lead to increased systemic absorption of the drug and a possible increase in side effects.

• Elderly patients and younger children have naturally thinner skin, and, therefore, the drug is more likely to be absorbed. Report any adverse effects.

• Be sure to tell your doctor if you are pregnant. If large amounts of this drug are applied for prolonged periods, some of it will be absorbed and may cross the placenta. Although studies in humans have not been conducted, birth defects have been observed in the offspring of animals that were given large oral doses of this type of drug during pregnancy. Also tell your doctor if you are breast-feeding an infant. If absorbed through the skin, small amounts of this type of drug pass into breast milk and may cause growth suppression or a decrease in natural adrenocorticosteroid production in the nursing infant.

betaxolol (systemic)

BRAND NAME (Manufacturer)
Kerlone (Pharmacia)
TYPE OF DRUG
Beta-adrenergic blocking agent
INGREDIENT
betaxolol
DOSAGE FORM
Tablets (10 mg and 20 mg)
STORAGE
Store at room temperature in a tightly closed container.

USES

Betaxolol is prescribed for the treatment of high blood pressure. It belongs to a group of medicines known as beta-adrenergic blocking agents or, more commonly, beta blockers. These drugs work by controlling impulses along certain nerve pathways. This results in a decreased workload for the heart.

TREATMENT

Betaxolol can be taken with a glass of water, with meals, immediately following meals, or on an empty stomach, depending on your doctor's instructions. It is important that you try to take the medication at the same time(s) each day.

Try not to miss any doses of this medication. If you do miss a dose, take it as soon as possible. However, if the next scheduled dose is within eight hours (if you are taking this medication only once a day) or within four hours (if you are taking this medication more than once a day), do not take the missed dose at all; just return to your regular dosing schedule. Do not double the next dose of the medication.

It is important to remember that betaxolol does not cure high blood pressure.

SIDE EFFECTS

Minor. Decreased sexual ability, diarrhea, fatigue, headache, indigestion, or nausea. These side effects should diminish as your body becomes accustomed to the medication.

Major. Tell your doctor about any side effects that are persistent or particularly bothersome. IT IS ESPECIALLY IMPORTANT TO TELL YOUR DOCTOR about breathing difficulty or wheezing; cold hands or feet due to decreased blood circulation to the skin, fingers, and toes; confusion; dizziness; fever and sore throat; hair loss; hallucinations; light-headedness; mental depression; nightmares; reduced alertness; skin rash; swelling of the ankles, feet, or lower legs; or unusual bleeding or bruising.

INTERACTIONS

Betaxolol interacts with a number of other medications:

1. Indomethacin, other nonsteroidal anti-inflammatory agents (including diclofenac, etodolac, ibuprofen, ketoprofen, naproxen, and piroxicam), aspirin, and other salicylates may decrease the blood-pressure-lowering effects of beta blockers.

2. Calcium channel blockers (nifedipine, verapamil, and diltiazem) may be used with beta blockers such as betaxolol unless the patient has heart trouble. Very low blood pressure and heart failure have been observed in patients with impaired heart function who take beta blockers.

3. Side effects may also be increased if beta blockers are taken along with epinephrine, phenylephrine, phenylpropanolamine, phenothiazine tranquilizers, reserpine, clonidine, prazosin, or monoamine oxidase (MAO) inhibitors. At least 14 days should separate the use of a beta blocker and the use of an MAO inhibitor.

4. Beta blockers may antagonize (work against) the effects of theophylline, aminophylline, albuterol, isoproterenol, metaproterenol, and terbutaline.
5. Beta blockers can also interact with insulin or oral antidiabetic agents—raising or lowering blood sugar levels or masking symptoms of low blood sugar.
6. Furosemide, hydrochlorothiazide, or hydralazine may increase the blood-pressure-lowering effects of beta blockers.
7. Alcohol, barbiturates, and rifampin can decrease blood concentrations of this drug, which can result in a decrease in effectiveness.
8. If you are on both betaxolol and clonidine, and both of these medications are to be discontinued, it is recommended that the betaxolol be tapered off over several days before the gradual reduction of clonidine.

Before starting to take betaxolol, BE SURE TO TELL YOUR DOCTOR about any medications you are already taking—including over-the-counter products—especially any of the medications listed above.

WARNINGS

• Tell your doctor about any unusual or allergic reactions you have had to any medications, especially to betaxolol or any other beta blocker (acebutolol, atenolol, bisoprolol, carteolol, esmolol, labetolol, metoprolol, nadolol, penbutalol, pindolol, propranolol, and timolol).
• Be sure to tell your doctor if you now have or ever had asthma, bronchitis, diabetes mellitus, heart block, heart failure, kidney disease, liver disease, peripheral vascular disease (poor circulation in the fingers or toes), severe bradycardia (slowed heart rate), or thyroid disease.
• Betaxolol therapy may increase the risk of cardiac failure in some patients. Be sure to report any abnormal heart function to your doctor.
• Patients with severe bronchospastic disease (such as asthma) should, in general, not receive beta blockers. Inform your physician if breathing is difficult.
• In people with diabetes, betaxolol may block some of the warning signs of low blood sugar (hypoglycemia), such as a rapid pulse rate, but not others, such as sweating or feelings of dizziness.
• You may want to check your pulse while taking this drug. If your pulse is much slower than usual or less than 50 beats per minute, check with your doctor. A pulse that is too slow may cause circulation problems.
• This medication may affect your body's response to exercise. Ask your doctor what an appropriate amount of exercise would be for you.
• It is important that you do not stop taking this medication without first checking with your doctor. Some conditions, such as angina pectoris (chest pain), may become worse when the medication is stopped suddenly, and the danger of a heart attack is increased in some patients. Your doctor may want you to gradually reduce the amount of the drug you take before stopping completely. Make sure you have enough medication to last through vacations and holidays.
• Tell your doctor or dentist that you are taking this drug before having surgery or any other medical or dental treatment. Often, this medication will be discontinued 48 hours prior to any major surgery.
• While taking this drug, do not use any over-the-counter (nonprescription) allergy, asthma, cough, cold, sinus, or diet preparations without first checking with your doctor or pharmacist. The combination of these medications with a beta blocker can result in high blood pressure.
• Betaxolol may reduce intraocular pressure and give a misleading negative glaucoma test.
• Be sure to tell your doctor if you are pregnant. Animal studies have shown that some beta blockers can cause problems in pregnancy when used at very high doses. Adequate studies have not been conducted in humans, but there has been some association between beta blockers used during pregnancy and low birth weight, breath-

ing problems, and slow heart rate in the newborn. Also tell your doctor if you are breast-feeding an infant. Although this medication has not been shown to cause problems in breast-fed infants, it may pass into breast milk, so caution is warranted.
• The safety of this medication for use in children has not been established.

bupropion

BRAND NAMES (Manufacturers)
Wellbutrin (GlaxoSmithKline)
Wellbutrin SR (GlaxoSmithKline)
Zyban (GlaxoSmithKline)
TYPE OF DRUG
Antidepressant
INGREDIENT
bupropion hydrochloride
DOSAGE FORMS
Tablets (75 mg and 100 mg)
Sustained-release tablets (150 mg)
STORAGE
Store this medication at room temperature in a tightly closed container.

USES

Bupropion is used to relieve the symptoms of mental depression in patients who cannot take other medications. In addition, this medication has been used as a non-nicotine aid to assist in the treatment of nicotine addiction and help individuals stop smoking. The exact mechanism of action of bupropion is unknown, but it is thought to relieve depression by altering the concentration of certain chemicals that are necessary for nerve transmission in the brain.

TREATMENT

It is important to take your medication on a regular schedule as recommended by your physician. If you miss a dose, take it, unless the next regular dose should be taken in less than six hours; in that case, simply skip the missed dose, and take the next dose at the scheduled time. Never double the dose.

The effects of this medication may not become apparent for several weeks.

If you are taking this medication to help you stop smoking, it is very important that you and your doctor set a target "quit date" after which you will attempt to stop smoking cigarettes. This "quit date" will usually be scheduled after you have been taking bupropion for a few weeks.

SIDE EFFECTS

Minor. Constipation, decreased appetite, decreased sexual ability, diarrhea, dizziness, dry mouth, excessive sweating, fatigue, headache, insomnia, irregular heartbeat, sedation, or vomiting. These side effects should decrease or disappear as your body adjusts to the medication.

To help relieve constipation, increase the amount of fiber in your diet (eat more fresh fruits and vegetables, salads, bran, and whole-grain breads and cereals). You can also increase your exercise level and drink more water (unless your doctor directs you to do otherwise).

To decrease dry mouth, chew sugarless gum or suck on ice chips or hard candy.

To avoid dizziness or light-headedness when you stand, contract and relax the muscles in your legs for a few moments before rising from a sitting or reclining position. Do this by pushing one foot against the floor while raising the other foot slightly, alternating feet so that you are "pumping" your legs in a pedaling motion.

Major. Tell your doctor about any side effects that are persistent or particularly bothersome. IT IS ESPECIALLY IMPORTANT TO TELL YOUR DOCTOR about agitation, blurred vision, movement disorders, rash, seizures, or tremors.

INTERACTIONS

Bupropion hydrochloride interacts with other types of medications:

1. The drugs carbamazepine, phenobarbital, and phenytoin may decrease the efficacy of bupropion.
2. Bupropion can interact with monoamine oxidase (MAO) inhibitors. At least 14 days should separate the use of this drug and the use of an MAO inhibitor.
3. Cimetidine may increase the blood level and adverse effects of bupropion.
4. Alcohol may increase the side effects of bupropion.

Be sure to tell your doctor about any medications you are currently taking, especially any of the medications that are listed above.

WARNINGS

• Tell your doctor about unusual or allergic reactions you have had to any medications, especially any reactions to bupropion.
• Tell your doctor if you now have or have ever had cataracts or other vision problems, seizures or epilepsy, bulimia, anorexia nervosa, mania, liver or kidney disease, or respiratory disorders.
• This medication may make you tired or drowsy or affect your thinking ability. You should not operate potentially dangerous equipment or drive an automobile until you know how this drug affects you.
• Do not stop taking this medication abruptly or increase the dose unless so directed by your physician. Stopping abruptly or increasing your dose in large amounts can lead to reduced effectiveness or increased side effects.
• Do not take any over-the-counter (nonprescription) medication or new prescription drug without discussing it with your doctor or pharmacist. Many over-the-counter preparations and some prescription medications may interact with bupropion.
• Medications that may increase the risk of seizures, such as antidepressants and antipsychotics, should be avoided when taking bupropion.
• Tell your doctor if you are pregnant. In high doses, bupropion has caused chromosomal changes in animals, but the effects in humans are unknown. In addition, be sure to tell your doctor if you are breast-feeding an infant. This medication can pass into the breast milk and lead to adverse effects in the infant.

---

buspirone

BRAND NAME (Manufacturer)
BuSpar (Bristol-Myers Squibb)
TYPE OF DRUG
Antianxiety agent
INGREDIENT
buspirone hydrochloride
DOSAGE FORM
Tablets (5 mg,10 mg, and 15 mg)
STORAGE
Store this medication at room temperature in a tightly closed container. Avoid exposing the medication to high temperatures (greater than 86°F).

USES

This medication is prescribed as a treatment for the symptoms of anxiety or panic attacks. It is not yet understood exactly how this medication works. Buspirone has been shown to be effective in relieving symptoms of anxiety, but it is important that you try to identify and remove the cause of the anxiety as well.

TREATMENT

Buspirone should be taken exactly as directed by your doctor. It can be taken with food or a full glass of water if stomach upset occurs.

If you are taking this drug regularly and miss a dose, take the missed dose immediately if you remember within an hour. If more time has passed, however, skip the dose you missed and wait for the next scheduled dose. Do not double the dose.

SIDE EFFECTS

Minor. Diarrhea, dizziness, excitement, fatigue, headache, light-headedness, nasal congestion, nausea, nervousness, sleeping problems, sweating, or weakness. These side effects should disappear as your body adjusts to this medication.

If you feel dizzy or light-headed, sit or lie down for a while; get up slowly from a sitting or reclining position; and be careful on stairs.

Major. Tell your doctor about any side effects that are persistent or particularly bothersome. IT IS ESPECIALLY IMPORTANT TO TELL YOUR DOCTOR about chest pain, confusion, feelings of anger, lack of coordination, muscle pain, numbness, rash, ringing in the ears, sore throat, tingling in your fingers or toes, tremors, or other changes in your senses (smell, hearing, vision).

INTERACTIONS

Although extensive studies on buspirone have not yet been completed, this drug may interact with several other medications.

1. Concurrent use of this medication with other central nervous system depressants (such as alcohol, antihistamines, pain medicines, barbiturates, benzodiazepine tranquilizers, muscle relaxants, and phenothiazine tranquilizers) or with tricyclic antidepressants can cause extreme drowsiness.

2. This medication may increase the adverse effects of digoxin and haloperidol.

3. This medication should not be taken with a monoamine oxidase (MAO) inhibitor. At least 14 days should separate the use of this drug and the use of an MAO inhibitor.

Before starting buspirone, BE SURE TO TELL YOUR DOCTOR about any medications you are currently taking, especially any of those listed above.

WARNINGS

- Before starting buspirone, be sure to tell your doctor about any unusual or allergic reactions you have had to any medications, especially to buspirone.
- Be sure to tell your doctor if you now have or if you have ever had kidney disease, liver disease, or any type of psychiatric disorder.
- Until you experience how this medication affects you, do not drive a car or operate potentially dangerous machinery.
- Erythromycin and itraconazole may increase the side effects of buspirone.
- Be sure to tell your doctor if you are pregnant. Although buspirone does appear to be safe in animals, complete studies in pregnant women have not been conducted. Also be sure to tell your doctor if you are breast-feeding an infant. Small amounts of buspirone have been shown to pass into the milk of animals, and its use in nursing women is not recommended.

---

calcifediol

BRAND NAME (Manufacturer)

Calderol (Organon)

TYPE OF DRUG
Vitamin D analog
INGREDIENT
calcifediol (25-hydroxycholecalciferol)
DOSAGE FORM
Capsules (20 mcg and 50 mcg)
STORAGE
Store at room temperature in a tightly closed, light-resistant container. Do not refrigerate this medication.

USES

Vitamin D is essential to many body systems, including building and maintenance of bone structure, regulation of blood calcium levels, and heart and muscle contraction. Since vitamin D is activated in the kidneys, patients with chronic (long-term) kidney failure are unable to produce enough active vitamin D on their own. Calcifediol is one of the active forms of vitamin D. This medication is used to treat bone disease and hypocalcemia (low blood calcium levels) in patients on dialysis.

TREATMENT

Calcifediol can be taken either on an empty stomach or with food or milk (as directed by your doctor). Swallow the capsules whole; do not crush or chew them.

If you miss a dose, take the missed dose as soon as possible. However, if it is almost time for the next dose of the medication, do not take the missed dose at all; return to your regular dosing schedule. Do not double the next dose.

SIDE EFFECTS

Minor. None, at the dosages normally prescribed.
Major. The side effects associated with calcifediol therapy are usually the result of too much medication (vitamin D toxicity). Tell your doctor about any side effects that are persistent or particularly bothersome. IT IS ESPECIALLY IMPORTANT TO TELL YOUR DOCTOR about blurred vision, bone pain, constipation, dry mouth, headache, heart palpitations, increased thirst, increased urination, irritability, loss of appetite, mental disorders, metallic taste in the mouth, muscle pain, nausea, runny nose, vomiting, weakness, or weight loss.

INTERACTIONS

Calcifediol interacts with several types of medications:
1. The dosage of calcifediol may need to be altered if anticonvulsant medication (such as phenytoin, phenobarbital, and primidone) is started.
2. Cholestyramine, colestipol, and mineral oil (taken internally) can decrease the absorption of calcifediol from the gastrointestinal tract.
3. Use of magnesium-containing antacids along with calcifediol may cause high blood levels of magnesium.
4. Calcifediol may lower the effectiveness of verapamil and other calcium channel blockers.
5. Corticosteroid drugs may counteract the effects of Vitamin D analogs such as calcifediol.
6. Digoxin and digitoxin can cause irregular heart rate when taken with calcifediol.
7. Be sure to tell your doctor if you are taking a thiazide diuretic (water pill); some patients may experience elevated calcium levels when thiazide diuretics are combined with calcifediol.

BE SURE TO TELL YOUR DOCTOR about any medications that you are currently taking, especially any of the medications listed above.

WARNINGS

- Be sure to tell your doctor about unusual or allergic reactions you have had to any medications, especially to calcifediol, calcitriol, dihydrotachysterol, ergocalciferol, or vitamin D.
- Before starting to take this medication, be sure to tell your doctor if you now have or ever had heart or blood-vessel disease, hypercalcemia (high levels of calcium in the bloodstream), hyperphosphatemia (high levels of phosphate in the bloodstream), kidney disease, vitamin D intoxication, or sarcoidosis.
- Before taking any over-the-counter (nonprescription) products that contain vitamin D, calcium, phosphates, or magnesium, consult your doctor. These ingredients can increase the side effects of calcifediol.
- Be sure to tell your doctor if you are pregnant. Although calcifediol (in normal doses) appears to be safe when used during pregnancy, extensive scientific studies in humans have not been conducted. Birth defects have been reported in the offspring of animals that received large doses of this medication during pregnancy. Also tell your doctor if you are breast-feeding an infant. Small amounts of calcifediol pass into breast milk.

---

calcitriol

BRAND NAME (Manufacturer)
Rocaltrol (Roche)
TYPE OF DRUG
Vitamin D analog
INGREDIENT
calcitriol (1.25-dihydroxycholecalciferol)
DOSAGE FORM
Capsules (0.25 mcg and 0.5 mcg)
STORAGE
Store at room temperature in a tightly closed, light-resistant container.

USES

Vitamin D is essential to bone structure, regulation of blood calcium levels, and heart and muscle contraction. Since vitamin D is activated in the kidneys, patients with chronic kidney failure are unable to produce enough active vitamin D on their own. Calcitriol is one of the active forms of vitamin D. This drug is used to treat bone disease and hypocalcemia (low blood calcium levels) in dialysis patients. It has also been used in the treatment of psoriasis and rickets.

TREATMENT

Calcitriol can be taken either on an empty stomach or with food or milk (as directed by your doctor). Swallow the capsules whole.

If you miss a dose of this drug, take the missed dose as soon as possible. However, if it is almost time for the next dose, do not take the missed dose at all; return to your regular dosing schedule. Do not double the next dose.

SIDE EFFECTS

Minor. None, at the dosages normally prescribed.
Major. Side effects result from too much medication (vitamin D toxicity). Tell your doctor about any side effects that are persistent or particularly bothersome. IT IS ESPECIALLY IMPORTANT TO TELL YOUR DOCTOR about appetite loss, blurred vision, bone pain, constipation, dry mouth, headache, increased thirst, increased urination, irritability, mental disorders, metallic taste in mouth, muscle pain, nausea, palpitations, runny nose, vomiting, weakness, or weight loss.

INTERACTIONS

Calcitriol interacts with several types of medications:

1. The dosage of calcitriol may need to be adjusted if anticonvulsant medication (phenytoin, phenobarbital, or primidone) is started.

2. Cholestyramine, colestipol, and mineral oil can decrease the absorption of calcitriol from the gastrointestinal tract.

3. Use of magnesium-containing antacids along with calcitriol may cause high blood levels of magnesium.

4. Calcitriol may lower the effectiveness of verapamil and other calcium channel blockers.

5. Corticosteroids may counteract the effects of Vitamin D analogs such as calcitriol.

6. Digoxin and digitoxin can cause irregular heart rate when taken with calcitriol.

7. Be sure to tell your doctor if you are taking a thiazide diuretic (water pill); some patients may experience elevated calcium levels when thiazide diuretics are combined with calcitriol.

BE SURE TO TELL YOUR DOCTOR about any medications you are currently taking, especially any of the medications listed above.

WARNINGS

• Be sure to tell your doctor about unusual or allergic reactions you have had to any medications, especially reactions to calcitriol, calcifediol, dihydrotachysterol, ergocalciferol, or vitamin D.

• Before starting to take this drug, tell your doctor if you have ever had heart or blood vessel disease, hypercalcemia (high blood levels of calcium), hyperphosphatemia (high levels of blood phosphate), kidney disease, vitamin D intoxication, or sarcoidosis.

• Check with your doctor before taking any over-the-counter (nonprescription) products that contain calcium, phosphates, magnesium, or vitamin D. These ingredients can increase the side effects of calcitriol.

• Be sure to tell your doctor if you are pregnant. Although calcitriol appears to be safe during pregnancy in humans, birth defects have been reported in the offspring of animals that received large doses of the medication during pregnancy. Also be sure to tell your doctor if you are breast-feeding an infant. Studies have shown that small amounts of calcitriol may pass into breast milk.

---

captopril

BRAND NAMES (Manufacturers)

Capoten (Bristol-Myers Squibb)

captopril (various manufacturers)

TYPE OF DRUG

Antihypertensive

INGREDIENT

captopril

DOSAGE FORM

Tablets (12.5 mg, 25 mg, 50 mg, and 100 mg)

STORAGE

Store this medication at room temperature in a tightly closed container.

USES

Captopril is used to treat high blood pressure, heart damage after a heart attack, and congestive heart failure. Captopril is also used to slow the development of kidney disease in patients with diabetes. Captopril is a vasodilator (it expands the blood vessels) that acts by blocking the production of chemicals that may be responsible for constricting, or narrowing, blood vessels.

TREATMENT

To obtain maximum benefit from captopril, you should take it on an empty stomach one hour before meals. In order to become accustomed to taking this medication, try to take it at the same time(s) every day.

It may be several weeks before you notice the full effects of this medication.

If you miss a dose of captopril, take the missed dose as soon as possible. However, if it is almost time for the next dose, do not take the missed dose at all; just wait until the next scheduled dose. Do not double the dose.

Captopril does not cure high blood pressure, but it will help you to control this condition as long as you continue to take the medication.

SIDE EFFECTS

Minor. Abdominal pain, constipation, cough, diarrhea, dizziness, dry mouth, fatigue, flushing, headache, insomnia, loss of appetite, loss of taste, nausea, or vomiting. These side effects should disappear over time as your body adjusts to the medication.

This medication can increase your sensitivity to sunlight. It is important to avoid prolonged exposure to sunlight and sunlamps. Always wear protective clothing and sunglasses when outdoors, and use an effective sunscreen.

To relieve constipation, increase the amount of fiber in your diet (fresh fruits and vegetables, salads, bran, and whole-grain breads). You can also increase your level of exercise and drink more water (unless your doctor directs you to do otherwise).

To relieve mouth dryness, suck on ice chips or a piece of hard candy or chew sugarless gum.

To avoid dizziness or light-headedness when you stand, contract and relax the muscles of your legs for a few moments before rising. Do this by pushing one foot against the floor while raising the other foot slightly, alternating feet so that you are "pumping" your legs.

Major. Tell your doctor about any side effects that are persistent or particularly bothersome. IT IS ESPECIALLY IMPORTANT TO TELL YOUR DOCTOR about chest pain; chills; coughing; difficult or painful urination; fever; itching; mouth sores; palpitations; prolonged vomiting or diarrhea; rash; sore throat; swelling of the face, hands, or feet; tingling in the fingers or toes; unusual bleeding or bruising; or yellowing of the eyes or skin.

INTERACTIONS

Captopril interacts with several other types of medications:

1. Diuretics (water pills) and other antihypertensive medications can cause an excessive drop in blood pressure when combined with captopril (especially with the first dose).

2. The combination of captopril with spironolactone, triamterene, amiloride, potassium supplements, or salt substitutes can lead to hyperkalemia (dangerously high levels of potassium in the bloodstream).

3. Antineoplastic agents (anticancer drugs) or chloramphenicol can increase the bone marrow side effects caused by captopril.

4. Concurrent use of captopril and allopurinol can increase the risk of developing an allergic reaction to the medication.

5. Indomethacin and other nonsteroidal anti-inflammatory drugs can decrease the blood-pressure-lowering effects of captopril.

6. Captopril can delay the body's elimination of lithium. Concurrent use of captopril and lithium may cause lithium toxicity.

7. Antacids containing aluminum or magnesium may decrease the efficacy of captopril. Take antacids one hour before or two hours after your dose of captopril.

Before starting captopril, BE SURE TO TELL YOUR DOCTOR about any drugs you are taking, especially any of those listed above.

WARNINGS

• Tell your doctor about any reactions you have had to medications, especially to benazepril, captopril, enalapril, lisinopril, quinapril, or ramipril.
• Tell your doctor if you now have or ever had aortic stenosis, a blood disorder, kidney or liver disease, a kidney transplant, lupus, a heart attack, or a stroke.
• Be sure to drink plenty of liquids (unless your doctor advises otherwise)—excessive perspiration, dehydration, or prolonged vomiting or diarrhea can lead to an excessive drop in blood pressure while you are taking this medication. Contact your doctor if you experience any of these symptoms.
• Before having surgery or any other medical or dental treatment, be sure that you tell your doctor that you are taking this medication.
• The first few doses of this medication may cause dizziness. Try to avoid any sudden changes in posture.
• If you have high blood pressure, do not take any over-the-counter (nonprescription) medications for weight control or for allergy, asthma, a sinus condition, cough, or cold unless you first check with your doctor.
• Do not stop taking this medication unless you first consult your doctor. Stopping this drug abruptly may lead to a rise in blood pressure.
• Be sure to tell your doctor if you are pregnant. Captopril has been found to cause birth defects in the fetus if taken during the second or third trimester of pregnancy. Also tell your doctor if you are breast-feeding an infant. Captopril passes into breast milk. The potential effects of this drug on the infant have not been determined.

---

carbamazepine

BRAND NAMES (Manufacturers)
carbamazepine (various manufacturers)
Carbatrol (Athena Neurosciences)
Epitol (Teva)
Tegretol (Novartis)
Tegretol-XR (Novartis)
TYPE OF DRUG
Anticonvulsant
INGREDIENT
carbamazepine
DOSAGE FORMS
Tablets (200 mg)
Chewable tablets (100 mg)
Extended-release tablets (100 mg, 200 mg, and 300 mg)
Extended-release capsules (200 mg and 300 mg)
Oral suspension (100 mg per 5-mL spoonful)
STORAGE
Store all forms at room temperature in tightly closed containers.

USES

This medication is used for the treatment of seizure disorders, for relief of neuralgia (nerve pain), for alcohol withdrawal, and for a wide variety of mental disorders. The mechanism of carbamazepine's antiseizure activity is unknown, but it is not related to other anticonvulsants. Carbamazepine is not an ordinary pain reliever—it should not be used for minor aches or pains.

TREATMENT

Carbamazepine should be taken with meals to avoid stomach upset, unless your doctor directs otherwise. The extended-release forms should not be crushed or chewed.

Carbamazepine works best when the level of medicine in your bloodstream is kept constant. It is best, therefore, to take it at evenly spaced intervals day and night. For example, if you are to take four doses a day, the doses should be spaced six hours apart.

Try not to miss any doses of this medication. If you do miss a dose, take the missed dose as soon as possible. However, if it is almost time for the next dose, do not take the missed dose at all; just return to your regular dosing schedule. Do not double the next dose unless your doctor directs you to do so. If you are taking carbamazepine for a seizure disorder and you miss two or more doses, be sure to contact your doctor.

SIDE EFFECTS

Minor. Agitation, blurred vision, confusion, constipation, diarrhea, dizziness, drowsiness, dry mouth, headache, loss of appetite, muscle or joint pain, nausea, restlessness, sweating, vomiting, or weakness. These side effects should disappear over time and as your body adjusts to the medication.

This medication can increase your sensitivity to sunlight. It is important, therefore, for you to avoid prolonged exposure to sunlight as well as to sunlamps. Always wear protective clothing and sunglasses when outdoors, and use an effective sunscreen.

To relieve constipation, increase the amount of fiber in your diet (fresh fruits and vegetables, salads, bran, and whole-grain breads), exercise, and drink more water (unless your doctor directs you to do otherwise).

To relieve mouth dryness, suck on ice chips or hard candy or chew sugarless gum.

If you feel dizzy or light-headed, sit or lie down for a while; get up slowly from a sitting or reclining position; and be careful on stairs.

Major. Be sure to tell your doctor about any side effects that are persistent or particularly bothersome. IT IS ESPECIALLY IMPORTANT FOR YOU TO TELL YOUR DOCTOR about abdominal pain, chills, depression, difficulty in breathing, difficulty in urinating, eye discomfort, fainting, fever, hair loss, hallucinations, impotence, loss of balance, mouth sores, nightmares, numbness or tingling sensations, palpitations, ringing in the ears, skin rash, sore throat, swelling of the hands and feet, twitching, unusual bleeding or bruising, or yellowing of the eyes or skin.

INTERACTIONS

Carbamazepine interacts with other types of medications:

1. Concurrent use of it with central nervous system depressants (such as alcohol, antihistamines, barbiturates, benzodiazepine tranquilizers, muscle relaxants, narcotics, pain medications, and phenothiazine tranquilizers) or with tricyclic antidepressants can cause extreme drowsiness.

2. Phenobarbital, phenytoin, and primidone can decrease blood levels and therefore the effectiveness of carbamazepine.

3. Concurrent use of this medication with isoniazid, propoxyphene, verapamil, cimetidine, troleandomycin, diltiazem, erythromycin, fluconazole, itraconazole, clarithromycin, tricyclic antidepressants, propoxyphene, fluoxetine, fluvoxamine, or verapamil may result in increased blood levels of and adverse effects from carbamazepine.

4. The combination of lithium and carbamazepine can lead to central nervous system side effects.

5. Carbamazepine can decrease the effectiveness of phenytoin, oral anticoagulants (blood thinners, such as warfarin and heparin), doxycycline, oral contraceptives (birth control pills), ethosuximide, aminophylline, theophylline, valproic acid, lamotrigine, risperidone, cyclosporine, bupropion, and haloperidol.

6. The use of carbamazepine within 14 days of the use of a monoamine oxidase (MAO) inhibitor can lead to serious side effects.

Before you start to take carbamazepine, BE SURE TO TELL YOUR DOCTOR about any medications you are currently taking, especially any of those listed above.

WARNINGS

• Tell your doctor about unusual or allergic reactions you have had to any medications, especially to carbamazepine or to tricyclic antidepressants (such as amitriptyline, desipramine, doxepin, imipramine, protriptyline, or nortriptyline).
• Tell your doctor if you now have or ever had bone marrow depression, blood disorders, difficulty urinating, glaucoma, heart or blood vessel disease, kidney disease, or liver disease.
• Before having surgery or any other medical or dental treatment, be sure to tell your doctor or dentist that you are taking this medication.
• If this medication makes you dizzy or drowsy, do not take part in any activity that requires alertness, such as driving a car or operating potentially dangerous equipment.
• If you are taking this medication to control a seizure disorder, do not stop taking it suddenly. If you stop taking the medication abruptly, you may experience uncontrollable seizures.
• The coating on the extended-release carbamazepine tablet is not absorbed by the body and is eliminated in the feces; these coatings may be noticed in the stools and should not cause alarm.
• Be sure to tell your doctor if you are pregnant. Birth defects have been reported more often in infants whose mothers have seizure disorders. It is unclear if the increased risk of birth defects is associated with the disorder or with the anticonvulsant medications, such as carbamazepine, that are used to treat the condition. The risks and benefits of treatment should be thoroughly discussed with your doctor. Also tell your doctor if you are breast-feeding an infant. Relatively large amounts of carbamazepine pass into breast milk. Therefore, this medication is not recommended for women who are breast-feeding.

---

cefaclor

BRAND NAMES (Manufacturers)
cefaclor (various manufacturers)
Ceclor (Lilly)
Ceclor CD (Lilly)
TYPE OF DRUG
Cephalosporin antibiotic
INGREDIENT
cefaclor
DOSAGE FORMS
Capsules (250 mg and 500 mg)
Extended-release tablets (375 mg and 500 mg)
Oral suspension (125 mg, 187 mg, 250 mg, and 375 mg per 5-mL spoonful)
STORAGE
Store the capsule and the extended-release tablet forms of this medication at room temperature in tightly closed containers. Store the suspension form in the refrigerator in a tightly closed container. Discard any unused portion of the suspension after 14 days because the suspension form loses its potency after that time. Do not freeze this medication.

USES

Cefaclor is used to treat a wide variety of bacterial infections, including those of the middle ear, skin, upper and lower respiratory tract, and urinary tract. This drug acts by severely injuring the cell walls of the infecting bacteria, thereby preventing them from growing and multiplying. Cefaclor kills susceptible bacteria, but it is not effective against viruses, parasites, or fungi.

TREATMENT

Take the capsules and tablets with food and swallow them whole; do not crush or chew them. The suspension can be taken on an empty stomach or with food, as directed by your doctor.

Shake the suspension form of this medication well to distribute the ingredients evenly and to equalize the doses just before measuring each dose. The contents tend to settle on the bottom of the bottle. Measure each dose with a specially designed 5-mL measuring spoon or with the dropper provided with the medication. An ordinary kitchen teaspoon is not accurate enough.

Cephalosporin antibiotics work best when the level of medicine in your bloodstream is kept at a constant level. It is best, therefore, to take the prescribed doses of this medication at evenly spaced intervals day and night. For example, if you are to take three doses a day, the doses should be spaced eight hours apart.

If you miss a dose of this medication, take the missed dose immediately. If you do not remember to take the missed dose until it is almost time for your next dose, take the missed dose, space the following dose halfway through the regular interval between doses, then return to your regular dosing schedule. Try not to skip any doses.

It is important to continue to take this medication for the entire time prescribed by your doctor (usually 7 to 14 days), even if the symptoms disappear before the end of that period. If you stop taking this drug too soon, resistant bacteria are given a chance to continue growing, and the infection could recur.

SIDE EFFECTS

Minor. Abdominal pain, diarrhea, dizziness, fatigue, headache, heartburn, loss of appetite, nausea, or vomiting. These minor side effects can be expected to disappear as your body becomes accustomed to the medication.

If you feel dizzy, sit or lie down for a while; get up slowly from a sitting or reclining position; and be careful on stairs.

Major. Tell your doctor about any side effects that are persistent or particularly bothersome. IT IS ESPECIALLY IMPORTANT TO TELL YOUR DOCTOR about darkened tongue, difficulty in breathing, fever, itching, joint pain, rash, rectal or vaginal itching, severe diarrhea (which can be watery or can contain pus or blood), sore mouth, stomach cramps, tingling in the hands or feet, or unusual bleeding or bruising. If symptoms of infection seem to be getting worse rather than improving, contact your doctor.

INTERACTIONS

Cefaclor interacts with several other types of medications:

1. Probenecid can increase the blood concentrations and side effects of this medication.

2. The side effects, especially effects on the kidneys, of furosemide, bumetanide, ethacrynic acid, colistin, vancomycin, polymyxin B, and aminoglycoside antibiotics can be increased by cefaclor.

3. Antacids containing aluminum or magnesium may decrease the efficacy of cefaclor extended-release tablets. Take antacids one hour before or two hours after your dose of cefaclor.

4. Concurrent use of anticoagulants (blood-thinning medications, including warfarin) and cefaclor may increase the adverse effects of the anticoagulants. IT IS VERY IMPORTANT THAT YOU ALERT YOUR DOCTOR IF YOU TAKE AN ANTICOAGULANT AND CEFACLOR HAS BEEN PRESCRIBED FOR YOU.

5. Cephalosporins may decrease the effectiveness of oral contraceptives. An additional method of contraception (such as a barrier) may be needed during treatment with this drug. Ask your doctor for more information.

BE SURE TO TELL YOUR DOCTOR about any medications you are currently taking, especially any listed above.

WARNINGS

• Be sure to tell your doctor about any unusual or allergic reactions you have had to any medications, especially to cefaclor or other cephalosporin antibiotics (such as cefamandole, cefepime, cephalexin, cephradine, cefadroxil, cefazolin, cefdinir, cefixime, cefmetazole, cefoperazone, cefotaxime, cefoxitin, cefpodoxime, cefprozil, ceftizoxime, cephalothin, cephapirin, cefuroxime, and moxalactam) or to any penicillin antibiotics.
• Tell your doctor if you now have or ever had any kidney disease.
• This medication has been prescribed for your current infection only. Another infection you experience later on, or one that someone else has, may require a different medicine. You should not give your medication to other people or use it for other infections, unless your doctor specifically directs you to do so.
• People who have diabetes should know that cefaclor can cause a false-positive sugar reaction with a Clinitest urine glucose test. To avoid this problem while taking cefaclor, they should switch to Clinistix or Tes-Tape to test their urine sugar content.
• Be sure to tell your doctor if you are pregnant. Although the cephalosporin antibiotics appear to be safe when administered during pregnancy, extensive and conclusive studies in human subjects have not been conducted. Also be sure that you tell your doctor if you are breast-feeding an infant. Small amounts of this medication can pass into breast milk and may temporarily alter the bacterial balance in the intestinal tract of the nursing infant, resulting in diarrhea or other gastrointestinal disturbance.

---

cefadroxil

BRAND NAMES (Manufacturers)
cefadroxil (various manufacturers)
Duricef (Bristol-Myers Squibb)
TYPE OF DRUG
Cephalosporin antibiotic
INGREDIENT
cefadroxil
DOSAGE FORMS
Tablets (1 g)
Capsules (500 mg)
Oral suspension (125 mg, 250 mg, and 500 mg per each 5-mL spoonful)
STORAGE
Store the tablets and capsules at room temperature in tightly closed containers. Store the suspension in the refrigerator in a tightly closed container. Discard any unused portion of the suspension after 14 days because the drug loses its potency after that time. Do not freeze this medication.

USES

Cefadroxil is used to treat a wide variety of bacterial infections, including those of the middle ear, skin, upper and lower respiratory tract, and urinary tract. This drug acts by severely injuring the cell walls of the infecting bacteria, thereby preventing them from growing and multiplying. Cefadroxil kills susceptible bacteria, but it is not effective against viruses, parasites, or fungi.

TREATMENT

You can take cefadroxil either on an empty stomach or, to avoid getting an upset stomach, with food or a glass of milk.

Shake the suspension well just before measuring each dose to distribute the ingredients evenly and equalize the doses. The contents tend to settle on the bottom of the bottle. Measure each dose of medication carefully with a specially designed 5-mL measuring spoon or with the dropper provided. An ordinary kitchen teaspoon is not accurate enough for medicinal purposes.

Cephalosporin antibiotics work best when the level of medicine in your bloodstream is kept constant. It is best to take the doses at evenly spaced intervals day and night. For example, if you are supposed to take two doses a day, the doses should be spaced 12 hours apart.

If you miss a dose of this medication, take the missed dose immediately. However, if you do not remember to take the missed dose until it is almost time for your next dose, take the missed dose, space the following dose halfway through the regular interval between doses, then return to your regular schedule. Try not to skip any doses.

It is important to continue to take this medication for the entire time prescribed by your doctor (usually 7 to 14 days), even if the symptoms disappear before the end of that period. If you stop taking this drug too soon, resistant bacteria could continue growing, and the infection could recur.

SIDE EFFECTS

Minor. Abdominal pain, diarrhea, dizziness, fatigue, headache, heartburn, loss of appetite, nausea, or vomiting. These side effects should disappear as your body adjusts to the drug.

If you feel dizzy, sit or lie down for a while; get up slowly from a sitting or reclining position; and be careful on stairs.

Major. Tell your doctor about any side effects that are persistent or particularly bothersome. IT IS ESPECIALLY IMPORTANT TO TELL YOUR DOCTOR about darkened tongue, difficulty in breathing, fever, itching, joint pain, rash, rectal or vaginal itching, severe diarrhea (which can be watery or contain pus or blood), sore mouth, stomach cramps, tingling in the hands or feet, or unusual bleeding or bruising. If your symptoms of infection seem to be getting worse rather than improving, contact your doctor.

INTERACTIONS

Cefadroxil interacts with several other types of medications:

1. Concurrent use of probenecid can increase the blood concentrations and side effects of this medication.

2. The side effects, especially effects on the kidneys, of furosemide, bumetanide, ethacrynic acid, colistin, vancomycin, polymyxin B, and aminoglycoside antibiotics can be increased by cefadroxil.

3. Cephalosporins may decrease the effectiveness of oral contraceptives. Another method of contraception, such as a barrier method, may be needed while taking this medication. Ask your doctor for more information.

Before you start to take this medication, BE SURE TO TELL YOUR DOCTOR about any other medications you are currently taking, especially any of those that are listed above.

WARNINGS

• Tell your doctor about unusual or allergic reactions you have ever had to any medication, especially to cefadroxil or other cephalosporin antibiotics (such as cefamandole, cephalexin, cefaclor, cephradine, cefazolin, cefixime, cefoperazone, cefotaxime, cefpodoxime, cefprozil, ceftizoxime, cephalothin, cephapirin, cefoxitin, cefuroxime, and moxalactam) or to penicillin antibiotics.

• Tell your doctor if you now have or if you have ever had kidney disease.

• This medication has been prescribed for your current infection only. Another infection later on, or one that someone else has, may require a different medicine. You should not give your medication to other people or use it for other infections, unless so directed by your doctor.

• People with diabetes should know that cefadroxil can cause a false-positive sugar reaction with a Clinitest urine glucose test. They should switch to Clinistix or Tes-Tape to test their urine for sugar.
• Be sure to tell your doctor if you are pregnant. Although the cephalosporin antibiotics appear to be safe during pregnancy, extensive studies in humans have not been conducted. Also inform your doctor if you are breast-feeding an infant. Small amounts of this drug pass into the breast milk and may temporarily alter the bacterial balance in the intestinal tract of the nursing infant, possibly resulting in diarrhea.

---

cefdinir

BRAND NAME (Manufacturer)
Omnicef (Parke-Davis)
TYPE OF DRUG
Cephalosporin antibiotic
INGREDIENT
cefdinir
DOSAGE FORMS
Capsules (300 mg)
Suspension (125 mg per 5-mL spoonful)
STORAGE
Store either form of this medication in a tightly closed container at room temperature, away from heat and direct sunlight. Discard any unused portion of the suspension after ten days, because this form of the medication loses its potency after that time. Do not freeze this medication.

USES

This medication is an antibiotic that is used to treat a wide variety of bacterial infections, including those of the middle ear, upper and lower respiratory tract, and skin. This medication acts by severely injuring the cell walls of the infecting bacteria, thereby preventing them from growing and multiplying. This medication kills susceptible bacteria, but it is not effective against viruses (which cause common colds), parasites, or fungi.

TREATMENT

This medication can be taken either on an empty stomach or with food or a glass of milk to avoid stomach upset. Shake the suspension well just before measuring each dose to distribute the ingredients evenly and equalize the doses, as the medication tends to settle on the bottom of the bottle. Each dose should then be measured carefully with a specially designed 5-mL measuring spoon. An ordinary kitchen teaspoon is not accurate enough.

Cephalosporin antibiotics work best when the level of medicine in your bloodstream is kept constant. It is best to take the doses at evenly spaced intervals day and night. For example, if you are to take two doses a day, the doses should be spaced twelve hours apart.

It is very important to continue this medication for the entire time prescribed by your doctor (usually 10 to 14 days), even if your symptoms improve before the end of that period. If you stop taking this medication too soon, resistant bacteria are given a chance to grow and the infection may recur.

It is very important that you do not miss any doses of this medication. While using this medication, try to develop a set schedule for taking it. If you miss a dose and remember within a few hours, take the missed dose and space the following dose halfway through the regular interval between doses, then return to your regular schedule. Try not to skip any doses.

SIDE EFFECTS

Minor. Abdominal pain, diarrhea, dizziness, fatigue, heartburn, light-headedness, loss of appetite, nausea, or vomiting. These side effects should disappear as your body adjusts to the medication.

To avoid dizziness when you stand, contract and relax the muscles of your legs for a few moments before rising. Do this by alternately pushing one foot against the floor while lifting the other foot slightly.

Major. Tell your doctor about any side effects that are persistent or particularly bothersome. IT IS ESPECIALLY IMPORTANT TO TELL YOUR DOCTOR about darkened tongue, difficulty in breathing, fever, itching, joint pain, rash, rectal or vaginal itching, severe diarrhea (which may be watery or contain blood or pus), sore mouth, stomach cramps, tingling in your hands or feet, or unusual bleeding or bruising. If your symptoms of infection seem to be getting worse rather than improving, contact your doctor.

INTERACTIONS

Cefdinir interacts with several other types of medications:

1. Concurrent use of antacids or iron (including iron-fortified foods) with this drug may decrease the effectiveness of cefdinir. To avoid this, it is recommended that you take these medications two to four hours before or after taking cefdinir.

2. The side effects, especially on the kidneys, of furosemide, bumetanide, ethacrynic acid, colistin, polymyxin B, vancomycin, and aminoglycoside antibiotics can be increased by this medication.

3. Probenecid can increase the blood levels and adverse effects of this medication.

4. The concurrent use of this medication with anticoagulants (blood-thinning medications, including warfarin) may result in an increase in the adverse effects of warfarin. It is very important to tell your doctor if you are taking this combination of medicines.

5. Cephalosporins may decrease the effectiveness of oral contraceptives. Another method of contraception, such as a barrier method, may be necessary while taking this medication. Ask your doctor for more information.

Before starting to take cefdinir, BE SURE TO TELL YOUR DOCTOR about any medications you are taking, especially those listed above.

WARNINGS

• Tell your doctor about unusual or allergic reactions you have had to any medications, especially to penicillin or to any cephalosporin antibiotics (including cefamandole, cephalexin, cefaclor, cefadroxil, cefazolin, cefoperazone, cefotaxime, ceftizoxime, cephalothin, cephradine, cefoxitin, cefmetazole, cefepime, or ceftibuten).

• Before starting to take this medication, be sure to tell your doctor if you now have or ever had kidney disease or gastrointestinal disease, particularly colitis.

• People with diabetes should know that this medication can cause a false-positive sugar reaction with a Clinitest urine glucose test. To avoid this problem while taking this medication, they should contact their doctor or pharmacist for recommendations for alternatives to monitor their urine glucose levels.

• This medication has been prescribed for your current infection only. A subsequent infection, or one that someone else has, may require a different medication. Therefore, you should not give your medication to someone else or use it for other infections unless your doctor specifically directs you to do so.

• Be sure to call your doctor immediately if you experience rash, swelling of the face, or difficulty breathing after you take this medication.

• Be sure to tell your doctor if you are pregnant. Although the cephalosporin antibiotics appear to be safe when used during pregnancy, extensive studies in humans have not been conducted. Also be sure to tell your doctor if you are breast-feeding an infant. This drug may pass into breast milk and may temporarily alter the bacterial balance in the intestinal tract of the nursing infant, which can cause the infant to have diarrhea.

cefditoren

BRAND NAME (Manufacturer)
Spectracef (TAP Pharmaceuticals)
TYPE OF DRUG
Cephalosporin antibiotic
INGREDIENT
cefditoren pivoxil
DOSAGE FORM
Tablets (200 mg)
STORAGE
Store this medication at room temperature in a tightly closed container; keep it away from moisture and out of the reach of children.

USES

This medication is used to treat a wide variety of bacterial infections, including those of the middle ear, skin, and upper and lower respiratory tract. This drug acts by severely injuring the cell walls of the infecting bacteria, thereby preventing them from growing and multiplying. Cefditoren kills susceptible bacteria, but it is not effective against viruses, parasites, or fungi.

TREATMENT

Take this medication with meals to increase the absorption of the medication.

Cephalosporin antibiotics work best when the level of medicine in your bloodstream is kept constant. It is best to take the doses at evenly spaced intervals day and night. For example, if you are to take two doses a day, the doses should be spaced 12 hours apart.

If you miss a dose of this medication, take the missed dose immediately. However, if you do not remember to take the missed dose until it is almost time for your next dose, take the missed dose, space the following dose halfway through the regular interval between doses, then return to your regular dosing schedule. It is important that you try not to skip any doses of this medication.

It is important to continue to take cefditoren for the entire time prescribed by your doctor (usually 7 to 14 days), even if the symptoms disappear before the end of that period. If you stop taking this drug too soon, resistant bacteria are given a chance to continue growing, and the infection could recur.

SIDE EFFECTS

Minor. Abdominal pain, diarrhea, dizziness, fatigue, headache, heartburn, loss of appetite, nausea, or vomiting. These side effects should disappear as your body adjusts to the medication.

If you feel dizzy or light-headed, sit or lie down for a while; get up slowly from a sitting or reclining position; and be careful on stairs.

To avoid dizziness or light-headedness when you stand, contract and relax the muscles in your legs for a few moments before rising. Do this by pushing one foot against the floor while raising the other foot slightly, alternating feet so that you are "pumping" your legs in a pedaling motion.

Tell your doctor about any side effects that are persistent or particularly bothersome. IT IS ESPECIALLY IMPORTANT TO TELL YOUR DOCTOR about darkened tongue, difficulty in breathing, fever, itching, joint pain, rash, rectal or vaginal itching, severe diarrhea (which can be watery or contain pus or blood), sore mouth, stomach cramps, tingling in the hands or feet, or unusual bleeding or bruising. If your symptoms of infection seem to be getting worse rather than improving, you should contact your doctor immediately.

INTERACTIONS

Cefditoren interacts with several other types of medications:

1. Probenecid can increase the blood concentrations and side effects of this drug.

2. The side effects—especially as they relate to the kidneys—of furosemide, bumetanide, ethacrynic acid, colistin, vancomycin, polymyxin B, and aminoglycoside antibiotics can be increased by cefditoren.

3. Some cephalosporins may decrease the effectiveness of oral contraceptives. You may need to use a different form of contraception (such as a barrier method) while taking this medication. Discuss this with your doctor.

4. Antacids, cimetidine, famotidine, ranitidine, and nizatidine may decrease the absorption of cefditoren and reduce its effectiveness.

BE SURE TO TELL YOUR DOCTOR about any medications you are currently taking, especially any of the medications that are listed above.

WARNINGS

• Tell your doctor about unusual or allergic reactions you have had to any medication, especially to cefditoren or other cephalosporin antibiotics (such as cefaclor, cefadroxil, cefamandole, cefazolin, cefepime, cefixime, cefonicid, cefoperazone, cefotaxime, cefoxitin, cefpodoxime, cefprozil, ceftibuten, ceftizoxime, cefuroxime, cephalexin, cephalothin, and cephapirin) or to penicillin antibiotics.

• Tell your doctor if you are allergic to milk or milk proteins. Cefditoren contains milk caseinate (a milk protein) and should not be used in patients with an allergy to milk proteins.

• Tell your doctor if you now have or have ever had kidney disease.

• Call your doctor immediately if you experience any difficulty in breathing or any swelling of the face after taking this medication.

• This medication has been prescribed for your current infection only. Another infection later on, or one that someone else has, may require a different medicine. You should not give your medication to other people or use it for other infections, unless your doctor specifically directs you to do so.

• People with diabetes need to know that cefditoren can cause a false-positive sugar reaction with a Clinitest urine glucose test. To avoid this problem while taking cefditoren, they should switch to Clinistix or Tes-Tape in order to test their urine sugar content accurately.

• Be sure to tell your doctor if you are pregnant. Although the cephalosporin antibiotics appear to be safe during pregnancy, extensive studies in humans have not been conducted. Also tell your doctor if you are breast-feeding. Small amounts of this medication pass into breast milk and may alter the bacterial balance in the intestinal tract of the nursing infant, resulting in diarrhea.

---

cefixime

BRAND NAME (Manufacturer)
Suprax (Lederle)

TYPE OF DRUG
Cephalosporin antibiotic

INGREDIENT
cefixime

DOSAGE FORMS
Tablets (200 mg and 400 mg)
Oral suspension (100 mg per 5-mL spoonful)

STORAGE
Store tablets at room temperature in a tightly closed container. Store the suspension in the refrigerator or at room temperature in a tightly closed container. Discard any un-

used portion of the oral suspension after 14 days because the suspension form loses its potency after that time. This medication should never be frozen.

USES

Cefixime is used to treat a wide variety of bacterial infections, including those of the middle ear, skin, upper and lower respiratory tract, and urinary tract. This medication acts by severely injuring the cell walls of the infecting bacteria, thereby preventing the bacteria from growing and multiplying. This medication is not effective against viruses, parasites, or fungi.

TREATMENT

Cefixime can be taken on an empty stomach or with food or milk (to avoid stomach upset).

Shake the suspension well just before measuring each dose to distribute the ingredients evenly and equalize the doses. The contents tend to settle on the bottom of the bottle. Measure each dose carefully with a specially designed 5-mL measuring spoon or with the dropper that is provided. An ordinary kitchen teaspoon is not accurate enough for medicinal purposes.

Cephalosporin antibiotics work best when the level of medicine in your bloodstream is kept constant. It is best to take the doses at evenly spaced intervals day and night. For example, if you are to take two doses a day, the doses should be spaced 12 hours apart.

If you miss a dose of this medication, take the missed dose immediately. If you do not remember to take the missed dose until it is almost time for your next dose, take the missed dose, space the following dose halfway through the regular interval between doses, then return to your regular dosing schedule. Try not to skip any doses of this medication.

It is important to try to take this medication for the entire time prescribed by your doctor (usually 7 to 14 days), even if the symptoms disappear before the end of that period. If you stop taking the drug too soon, resistant bacteria could continue growing, and the infection could recur.

SIDE EFFECTS

Minor. Abdominal pain, diarrhea, dizziness, fatigue, headache, heartburn, loss of appetite, nausea, or vomiting. These side effects should disappear as your body adjusts to the medication.

If you feel dizzy while you are taking this medication, sit or lie down for a while; get up slowly from a sitting or reclining position; and be careful on stairs.

Major. Tell your doctor about any side effects that are persistent or particularly bothersome. IT IS ESPECIALLY IMPORTANT TO TELL YOUR DOCTOR about darkened tongue, difficulty in breathing, fever, itching, joint pain, rash, rectal or vaginal itching, severe diarrhea (which can be watery or contain pus or blood), sore mouth, stomach cramps, tingling in the hands or feet, or unusual bleeding or bruising. If your symptoms of infection seem to be getting worse rather than improving, contact your doctor.

INTERACTIONS

Cefixime interacts with several other types of medications:

1. Probenecid can increase the blood concentrations and side effects of this drug.

2. The side effects (especially those that affect the kidneys) of furosemide, bumetanide, ethacrynic acid, colistin, vancomycin, polymyxin B, and aminoglycoside antibiotics can be increased by cefixime.

3. Cephalosporins may decrease the effectiveness of oral contraceptives. Another method of contraception, such as a barrier method, may be needed while taking this medication. Ask your doctor for more information.

BE SURE TO TELL YOUR DOCTOR about any medications you are currently taking, especially any of the medications listed above.

WARNINGS

• Tell your doctor about any unusual or allergic reactions you have had to any medication, especially to cefixime or other cephalosporin antibiotics (such as cefaclor, cefadroxil, cefamandole, cefdinir, cefditoren, cefepime, cefixime, cefonicid, cefoperazone, cefotaxime, cefotetan, cefoxitin, cefpodoxime, cefprozil, ceftazidime, ceftibuten, ceftizoxime, ceftriaxone, cefuroxime, cephalexin, cephapirin, and cephradine) or to penicillin antibiotics.
• Call your doctor immediately if you experience rash, swelling of the face, or difficulty breathing after taking this medication.
• Tell your doctor if you now have or have ever had kidney disease.
• Tell your doctor if you now have or ever had any type of gastrointestinal disease, particularly colitis.
• This medication has been prescribed for your current infection only. Another infection that you experience later on, or an infection that someone else has, may require a different medicine. You should not give your medication to other people or use it for other infections, unless your doctor specifically directs you to do so.
• People who have diabetes should know that cefixime can cause a false-positive sugar reaction with a Clinitest urine glucose test. To avoid this problem while taking cefixime, they should switch to Clinistix or Tes-Tape to test their urine sugar content.
• Cefixime may also cause a false-positive result for urinary ketones when people with diabetes use tests that involve nitroprusside.
• Be sure to tell your doctor if you are pregnant. Although the cephalosporin antibiotics, such as cefixime, appear to be safe when taken during pregnancy, extensive studies in humans have not been conducted. Also tell your doctor if you are breast-feeding an infant. Small amounts of this medication pass into breast milk and may temporarily alter the bacterial balance in the intestinal tract of the nursing infant, resulting in diarrhea.

---

cefpodoxime

BRAND NAME (Manufacturer)
Vantin (Pharmacia)
TYPE OF DRUG
Cephalosporin antibiotic
INGREDIENT
cefpodoxime proxetil
DOSAGE FORMS
Tablets (100 mg and 200 mg)
Oral suspension (50 mg and 100 mg per 5-mL spoonful)
STORAGE
Store tablets in a tightly closed container at room temperature, away from heat and direct sunlight. Store the suspension in the refrigerator in a tightly closed container. Discard any unused portion of the suspension after 14 days because the suspension loses potency after that time. This medication should never be frozen.

USES

This medication is used to treat a wide variety of bacterial infections, including those of the middle ear, upper and lower respiratory tract, and urinary tract. This drug acts by severely injuring the cell walls of the infecting bacteria, thereby preventing them from growing and multiplying. Cefpodoxime kills susceptible bacteria, but it is not effective against viruses, parasites, or fungi.

TREATMENT

Take cefpodoxime with food to improve its absorption.

Shake the suspension well just before measuring each dose to distribute the ingredients evenly and equalize the doses. The contents tend to settle on the bottom of the bottle. Measure each dose carefully with a specially designed 5-mL measuring spoon. An ordinary kitchen teaspoon is not accurate enough for this purpose.

Cephalosporin antibiotics work best when the level of medicine in your bloodstream is kept constant. It is best to take the doses at evenly spaced intervals day and night. For example, if you are to take two doses a day, the doses should be spaced twelve hours apart.

It is very important that you continue to use this medication for the entire time prescribed by your doctor (usually 7 to 14 days), even if your symptoms disappear before the end of that time period. If you stop taking this drug too soon, resistant bacteria are given the chance to grow, and the infection may recur.

If you miss a dose of this medication, take the missed dose as soon as you remember. If it is almost time for your next dose, take the missed dose and space the following dose halfway through the regular interval between doses, then return to your regular dosing schedule. Try not to skip any doses.

SIDE EFFECTS

Minor. Abdominal pain, diarrhea, dizziness, fatigue, headache, heartburn, loss of appetite, nausea, or vomiting. These side effects should disappear as your body adjusts to the medication.

If you feel dizzy or light-headed, sit or lie down for a while; get up slowly from a sitting or reclining position; and be careful on stairs.

Major. Tell your doctor about any side effects that are persistent or particularly bothersome. IT IS ESPECIALLY IMPORTANT TO TELL YOUR DOCTOR about darkened tongue, difficulty in breathing, fever, itching, joint pain, rash, rectal or vaginal itching, severe diarrhea (which may be watery or contain blood or pus), sore mouth, stomach cramps, tingling in the hands or feet, or unusual bleeding or bruising. If your symptoms of infection seem to be getting worse rather than improving, contact your doctor.

INTERACTIONS

Cefpodoxime interacts with a number of other types of medications:

1. Probenecid can increase the blood concentrations of cefpodoxime.

2. The side effects, especially effects on the kidneys, of furosemide, bumetanide, ethacrynic acid, colistin, vancomycin, polymyxin B, and aminoglycoside antibiotics can be increased by cefpodoxime.

3. High-dose antacids or H2 blockers (cimetidine, ranitidine, famotidine, and nizatidine) can decrease the effectiveness of cefpodoxime.

3. Antacids containing aluminum or magnesium may decrease the efficacy of cefpodoxime. To avoid this problem, take antacids one hour before or two hours after your dose of cefpodoxime.

4. Cephalosporins may decrease the effectiveness of oral contraceptives. Another form of contraception, such as a barrier method, may be needed while taking this medication. Ask your doctor for more information.

BE SURE TO TELL YOUR DOCTOR about any medications you are currently taking, especially any listed above.

WARNINGS

• Tell your doctor about any unusual or allergic reactions you have had to any medications, especially to cefpodoxime or other cephalosporin antibiotics (such as cefaclor, cefadroxil, cefamandole, cefdinir, cefditoren, cefepime, cefixime, cefonicid, cefoperazone, cefotaxime, cefotetan, cefoxitin, cefprozil, ceftazidime, ceftibuten, ceftizoxime, ceftriaxone, cefuroxime, cephalexin, cephapirin, and cephradine) or to penicillin antibiotics.

• Tell your doctor if you experience rash, swelling of the face, or difficulty breathing after you take this medication.

• Tell your doctor if you now have or have ever had kidney disease.

• This medication was prescribed for your current infection only. Another infection you experience later on or an infection that someone else has may require a different medication. You should not give your medicine to other people or use it for other infections unless your doctor specifically instructs you to do so.

• People with diabetes should know that cefpodoxime may cause a false-positive sugar reaction with a Clinitest urine glucose test. To avoid this problem while taking cefpodoxime, they should switch to Clinistix or Tes-Tape to test their urine for sugar.

• Be sure to tell your doctor if you are pregnant. Although the cephalosporin antibiotics appear to be safe during pregnancy, extensive studies in humans have not been conducted. Also tell your doctor if you are breast-feeding an infant. Small amounts of this medication pass into breast milk and may temporarily alter the bacterial balance of the intestinal tract of the nursing infant. This alteration could cause diarrhea in the nursing infant.

---

cefprozil

BRAND NAME (Manufacturer)
Cefzil (Bristol-Myers Squibb)
TYPE OF DRUG
Cephalosporin antibiotic
INGREDIENT
cefprozil
DOSAGE FORMS
Tablets (250 mg and 500 mg)
Oral suspension (125 mg and 250 mg per 5-mL spoonful)
STORAGE
Store tablets at room temperature in a tightly closed container. Store the suspension in the refrigerator in a tightly closed container. Discard any unused portion of the suspension after 14 days because the suspension loses potency after that time. This medication should never be frozen.

USES

This medication is used to treat a wide variety of bacterial infections, including those of the middle ear, skin, and upper and lower respiratory tract. This drug acts by severely injuring the cell walls of the infecting bacteria, thereby preventing them from growing and multiplying. This medication kills susceptible bacteria, but it is not effective against viruses, parasites, or fungi.

TREATMENT

Cefprozil can be taken either on an empty stomach or with food or milk (in order to avoid an upset stomach).

Shake the suspension well just before measuring each dose to distribute the ingredients evenly and equalize the doses. The contents tend to settle on the bottom of the bottle. Measure each dose of the medication carefully with a specially designed 5-mL measuring spoon or with the dropper provided. An ordinary kitchen teaspoon is not accurate enough for medical purposes.

Cephalosporin antibiotics work best when the level of medicine in your bloodstream is kept constant. It is best, therefore, to take the doses at evenly spaced intervals throughout the day and night. For example, if you are supposed to take two doses of the medicine each day, the doses should be spaced 12 hours apart.

If you miss a dose of this medication, take the missed dose immediately. If you do not remember to take the missed dose until it is almost time for your next dose, take the missed dose, then space the following dose halfway through the regular interval between doses; then return to your regular dosing schedule. Try not to skip any doses of this medication.

It is important to try to take this medication for the entire time prescribed by your doctor (usually 7 to 14 days), even if the symptoms disappear before the end of that period. If you stop taking the drug too soon, resistant bacteria could continue growing, and infection could recur.

SIDE EFFECTS

Minor. Abdominal pain, diarrhea, dizziness, fatigue, headache, heartburn, loss of appetite, nausea, or vomiting. These side effects should disappear as your body adjusts to the medication.

If you feel dizzy while you are taking this medication, sit or lie down for a while; get up slowly from a sitting or reclining position; and be careful when you are going up and down stairs.

Major. Tell your doctor about any side effects that are persistent or particularly bothersome. IT IS ESPECIALLY IMPORTANT TO TELL YOUR DOCTOR about darkened tongue, difficulty in breathing, fever, itching, joint pain, rash, rectal or vaginal itching, severe diarrhea (which may be watery or may contain pus or blood), sore mouth, stomach cramps, tingling in the hands or feet, or unusual bleeding or bruising of the skin. If your symptoms of infection seem to be getting worse rather than improving while you are on this medication, be sure to contact your doctor.

INTERACTIONS

Cefprozil interacts with several other types of medications:

1. Probenecid can increase the blood concentrations as well as the side effects of this medication.

2. The side effects, especially those involving the kidneys, of furosemide, bumetanide, ethacrynic acid, colistin, vancomycin, polymyxin B, and aminoglycoside antibiotics can be increased by cefprozil.

3. Cephalosporins may decrease the effectiveness of oral contraceptives. Another form of contraception, such as a barrier method, may be needed while taking this medication. Ask your doctor for more information.

BE SURE TO TELL YOUR DOCTOR about any medications you are currently taking, especially any listed above.

WARNINGS

• Tell your doctor about any unusual or allergic reactions you have had to any medication, especially to cefprozil or other cephalosporin antibiotics (such as cefaclor, cefadroxil, cefamandole, cefdinir, cefditoren, cefepime, cefixime, cefonicid, cefoperazone, cefotaxime, cefotetan, cefoxitin, cefpodoxime, ceftazidime, ceftibuten, ceftizoxime, ceftriaxone, cefuroxime, cephalexin, cephapirin, and cephradine) or to penicillin antibiotics.

• Tell your doctor if you now have or have ever had kidney disease.

• Tell your doctor if you now have or ever had any type of gastrointestinal disease, particularly colitis.

• This medication has been prescribed for your current infection only. Another infection that you experience later on or one that someone else has may require a different medicine. You should not give your medication to other people or use it for other infections unless your doctor specifically directs you to do so.

• People who have diabetes should know that cefprozil can cause a false-positive sugar reaction with a Clinitest urine glucose test. To avoid this potential problem while taking cefprozil, they should switch to Clinistix or Tes-Tape to test the sugar content of their urine.
• Cefprozil may also cause a false-positive result for urinary ketones when tests using nitroprusside are used.
• Be sure to tell your doctor if you are pregnant. Although the cephalosporin antibiotics appear to be safe during pregnancy, extensive studies in humans have not been conducted. Also tell your doctor if you are breast-feeding an infant. Small amounts of this medication pass into breast milk and may temporarily alter the bacterial balance in the intestinal tract of the nursing infant, resulting in diarrhea.

---

ceftibuten

BRAND NAME (Manufacturer)
Cedax (Schering-Plough)
TYPE OF DRUG
Cephalosporin antibiotic
INGREDIENT
ceftibuten
DOSAGE FORMS
Capsules (400 mg)
Suspension (90 mg and 180 mg per 5-mL spoonful)
STORAGE
Store capsules in a tightly closed container at room temperature, away from heat and direct sunlight. Store the suspension in the refrigerator in a tightly closed container. Discard any unused portion of the suspension after 14 days because the suspension loses potency after that time. This medication should never be frozen.

USES

This medication is an antibiotic that is used to treat a wide variety of bacterial infections, including those of the middle ear, upper and lower respiratory tract, and urinary tract. This medication acts by severely injuring the cell walls of the infecting bacteria, preventing them from growing and multiplying. This medication kills susceptible bacteria, but it is not effective against viruses, parasites, or fungi.

TREATMENT

Take the capsules either on an empty stomach or with food or a glass of milk to avoid stomach upset. However, the suspension MUST be taken at least two hours before a meal or one hour after a meal.

Shake the suspension well just before measuring each dose to distribute the ingredients evenly and equalize the doses. The contents of the suspension tend to settle on the bottom of the bottle. Measure each dose carefully with a specially designed 5-mL measuring spoon. An ordinary kitchen teaspoon is not accurate enough.

Cephalosporin antibiotics work best when the level of medicine in your bloodstream is kept constant. It is therefore desirable to take the doses at evenly spaced intervals throughout the day and night. For example, if you are supposed to take two doses a day, the doses should be spaced twelve hours apart (unless your doctor directs otherwise).

It is very important to continue this medication for the entire time prescribed by your doctor (usually ten days). This medication should be taken exactly as prescribed by your doctor, even if your symptoms improve. If you stop taking this drug too soon, resistant bacteria are given a chance to grow and the infection may recur.

If you miss a dose of this medication, take the missed dose immediately. If you do not remember to take the missed dose until it is almost time for your next dose, take the missed dose, then space the following dose halfway through the regular interval between doses; then return to your regular dosing schedule. Try not to skip any doses of this medication.

SIDE EFFECTS

Minor. Abdominal pain, diarrhea, dizziness, fatigue, heartburn, light-headedness, loss of appetite, nausea, or vomiting. These side effects should disappear as your body adjusts to the medication.

If you feel dizzy while you are taking this medication, sit or lie down for a while; get up slowly from a sitting or reclining position; and be careful when you are going up and down stairs.

Major. Tell your doctor about any side effects that are persistent or particularly bothersome. IT IS ESPECIALLY IMPORTANT TO TELL YOUR DOCTOR about darkened tongue, difficulty in breathing, fever, itching, joint pain, rash, rectal or vaginal itching, severe diarrhea (which may be watery or contain blood or pus), sore mouth, stomach cramps, tingling in your hands or feet, or unusual bleeding or bruising. If your symptoms of infection seem to be getting worse rather than improving, contact your doctor.

INTERACTIONS

Ceftibuten interacts with several other types of medications:

1. The side effects, especially those involving the kidneys, of furosemide, bumetanide, ethacrynic acid, colistin, vancomycin, polymyxin B, and aminoglycoside antibiotics can be increased by this medication.

2. Using probenecid with this medication can increase the blood levels and adverse effects of this medication.

3. Concurrent use of ranitidine can decrease the effectiveness of ceftibuten.

4. The concurrent use of this medication with anticoagulants (blood-thinning medications, including warfarin) may result in an increase in the adverse effects of the anticoagulants. It is very important to tell your doctor if you are taking this combination of medicines.

5. Cephalosporins may decrease the effectiveness of oral contraceptives. Another method of contraception, such as a barrier method, may be needed while taking this medication. Ask your doctor for more information.

Before starting to take ceftibuten, BE SURE TO TELL YOUR DOCTOR about any medications you are taking, especially those listed above.

WARNINGS

- Tell your doctor about unusual or allergic reactions you have had to any medications, especially to penicillin or to any cephalosporin antibiotics (such as cefaclor, cefadroxil, cefamandole, cefdinir, cefditoren, cefepime, cefixime, cefonicid, cefoperazone, cefotaxime, cefotetan, cefoxitin, cefpodoxime, cefprozil, ceftazidime, ceftizoxime, ceftriaxone, cefuroxime, cephalexin, cephapirin, and cephradine).
- Before starting to take this medication, be sure to tell your doctor if you now have or ever had kidney disease or gastrointestinal disease, particularly colitis.
- People who have diabetes should know that ceftibuten can cause a false-positive sugar reaction with a Clinitest urine glucose test. To avoid this problem while taking this medication, they should contact their doctor or pharmacist to get recommendations for alternative products for monitoring their urine glucose levels.
- This medication has been prescribed for your current infection only. A subsequent infection you experience, or an infection that someone else has, may require a different medicine. You should not give your medication to someone else or use it for other infections unless your doctor specifically directs you to do so.

• Be sure to call your doctor immediately if you experience rash, swelling of the face, or difficulty breathing after you take this medication.
• Be sure to tell your doctor if you are pregnant. Although the cephalosporin antibiotics appear to be safe during pregnancy, extensive studies in humans have not been conducted. Also tell your doctor if you are breast-feeding an infant. This medication may pass into breast milk and may temporarily alter the bacterial balance of the intestinal tract of the nursing infant, which could cause diarrhea.

---

cefuroxime

BRAND NAME (Manufacturer)
Ceftin (GlaxoSmithKline)
TYPE OF DRUG
Cephalosporin antibiotic
INGREDIENT
cefuroxime axetil
DOSAGE FORMS
Tablets (125 mg, 250 mg, and 500 mg)
Oral suspension (125 mg and 250 mg per 5-mL spoonful)
STORAGE
Store tablets at room temperature in a tightly closed container and protect from moisture. Store the suspension in the refrigerator or at room temperature in a tightly closed container, and discard any unused portion after 14 days because the suspension loses potency after that time. This medication should never be frozen.

USES

This medication is used to treat a wide variety of bacterial infections, including those of the middle ear, lower respiratory tract, skin, and urinary tract. It is also effective in the treatment of pharyngitis and tonsillitis. This drug acts by severely injuring the cell walls of the infecting bacteria, thereby preventing them from growing and multiplying. Cefuroxime kills susceptible bacteria, but it is not effective against viruses, parasites, or fungi.

TREATMENT

Cefuroxime tablets can be taken either on an empty stomach or with food or milk (in order to avoid an upset stomach). The tablets may be crushed and mixed with food (such as applesauce or ice cream); however, a strong, persistent, bitter taste may be noted. Cefuroxime oral suspension should always be taken with a meal.

Shake the suspension well just before measuring each dose to distribute the ingredients evenly and equalize the doses. The contents tend to settle on the bottom of the bottle. Measure each dose carefully with a specially designed 5-mL measuring spoon or with the dropper provided with the medication. An ordinary kitchen teaspoon is not accurate enough for medicinal purposes.

Cephalosporin antibiotics work best when the level of medicine in your bloodstream is kept constant. It is best, therefore, to take the doses at evenly spaced intervals throughout the day and night. For example, if you are supposed to take two doses each day, the doses should be spaced 12 hours apart.

If you miss a dose of this medication, take the missed dose immediately. However, if it is almost time for your next dose, take it and space the following dose halfway through the regular interval between doses; then return to your regular dosing schedule. Try not to skip any doses.

It is important to continue to take this medication for the entire time prescribed by your doctor (usually 7 to 14 days), even if the symptoms disappear before the end of that period. If you stop taking this drug too soon, resistant bacteria are given a chance to continue growing, and the infection could recur.

SIDE EFFECTS

Minor. Abdominal pain, diarrhea, dizziness, fatigue, headache, heartburn, loss of appetite, nausea, or vomiting. These side effects should disappear over time as your body adjusts to the medication.

If you feel dizzy, sit or lie down for a while; get up slowly from a sitting or reclining position; and be careful on stairs.

Major. Tell your doctor about any side effects that are persistent or particularly bothersome. IT IS ESPECIALLY IMPORTANT TO TELL YOUR DOCTOR about darkened tongue, difficulty in breathing, fever, itching, joint pain, rash, rectal or vaginal itching, severe diarrhea, sore mouth, stomach cramps, tingling in the hands or feet, or unusual bleeding or bruising. If your symptoms of infection seem to be getting worse rather than improving, you should contact your doctor.

INTERACTIONS

Cefuroxime interacts with several other types of medications:

1. Probenecid can increase the blood concentrations and side effects of this medication.

2. The side effects, especially effects on the kidneys, of furosemide, bumetanide, ethacrynic acid, colistin, vancomycin, polymyxin B, and aminoglycoside antibiotics can be increased by cefuroxime.

3. This medication may decrease the efficacy of certain birth control pills, and pregnancy could result. Use a different or additional (barrier) form of birth control while taking this medication. Discuss this with your doctor.

BE SURE TO TELL YOUR DOCTOR about any medications you are currently taking, especially any listed above.

WARNINGS

• Tell your doctor about any unusual or allergic reactions you have had to any medication, especially to cefuroxime or other cephalosporin antibiotics (such as cefaclor, cefadroxil, cefamandole, cefdinir, cefditoren, cefepime, cefixime, cefonicid, cefoperazone, cefotaxime, cefotetan, cefoxitin, cefpodoxime, cefprozil, ceftazidime, ceftibuten, ceftizoxime, ceftriaxone, cephalexin, cephapirin, and cephradine) or to penicillin antibiotics.

• Cefuroxime may cause a false-positive result for urinary ketones when tests using nitroprusside are used.

• Call your doctor immediately if you experience rash, swelling of the face, or difficulty breathing after you take this medication.

• Tell your doctor if you now have or if you have ever had kidney disease or gastrointestinal disease, especially colitis.

• This medication has been prescribed for your current infection only. Another infection that you experience later on, or one that someone else has, may require a different medicine. You should not give your medication to other people or use it for other infections, unless your doctor specifically directs you to do so.

• People with diabetes should know that cefuroxime can cause a false-positive sugar reaction with a Clinitest urine glucose test. To avoid this problem while taking cefuroxime, they should switch to Clinistix or Tes-Tape.

• Be sure to tell your doctor if you are pregnant. Although the cephalosporin antibiotics, such as cefuroxime, appear to be safe during pregnancy, extensive studies in humans have not been conducted. Also tell your doctor if you are breast-feeding an infant. Small amounts of this medication pass into breast milk and may temporarily alter the bacterial balance in the intestinal tract of the nursing infant, resulting in diarrhea.

celecoxib

BRAND NAME (Manufacturer)
Celebrex (Searle)
TYPE OF DRUG
Nonsteroidal anti-inflammatory drug (NSAID)
INGREDIENT
celecoxib
DOSAGE FORM
Capsule (100 mg and 200 mg)
STORAGE
Store this medication at room temperature in a tightly closed container.

USES

Celecoxib is used to treat the inflammation (pain, swelling, and stiffness) of certain types of arthritis. Celecoxib has been shown to block the production of certain body chemicals, called prostaglandins, that may trigger pain. Celecoxib works by inhibiting a specific enzyme, cyclooxygenase 2 (COX-2). Celecoxib is also used to reduce the risk of developing polyps in the colon in patients with hereditary colon disease.

TREATMENT

Celecoxib can be taken with or without food.

It is important to take celecoxib on schedule and not to miss any doses. If you miss a dose of this medication, take the missed dose as soon as possible. However, if it is almost time for the next dose, do not take the missed dose at all; just wait until the next scheduled dose. Do not double the next dose of medication.

Celecoxib does not cure arthritis, but it will help to control your symptoms as long as you continue to take it.

SIDE EFFECTS

Minor: Abdominal pain, diarrhea, dizziness, dyspepsia, flatulence, insomnia, nausea, skin rash, and sore throat. These side effects should disappear as your body adjusts to the medication.

If you become dizzy or light-headed while taking this medication, sit or lie down for a while, get up slowly from a sitting or reclining position, and be careful on stairs. Be careful when driving a car or operating potentially dangerous equipment.

Major: Tell your doctor about any side effects that are persistent or particularly bothersome. IT IS ESPECIALLY IMPORTANT TO TELL YOUR DOCTOR about bloody or black, tarry stools; skin rash, hives, or itching; swelling of the ankles; unexplained bruising or bleeding; unexplained sore throat and fever; unexplained weight gain; unusual fatigue or weakness; wheezing; or yellowing of the eyes or skin.

INTERACTIONS

Celecoxib interacts with several other types of medications:

1. The blood-pressure-lowering effects of drugs called angiotensin-converting enzyme (ACE) inhibitors may be decreased by celecoxib.

2. Blood levels of lithium may be increased by the use of celecoxib.

3. Low-dose aspirin can be used during treatment with celecoxib. However, it may increase the risk of gastrointestinal ulcers or bleeding.

4. The effects of certain diuretic medications, such as furosemide or the thiazide diuretics, may be decreased by celecoxib.

5. The medication fluconazole may increase blood levels of celecoxib.

6. Antiplatelet agents such as clopidogrel, ticlopidine, and warfarin may increase the risk of bleeding when used during treatment with celecoxib.

BE SURE TO TELL YOUR DOCTOR about any medications that you are currently taking, especially any of the medications just mentioned.

WARNINGS

• Tell your doctor about any unusual or allergic reactions you have had to medications, especially to celecoxib, other NSAIDs, or sulfonamides. Celecoxib should not be given to any patient who has experienced allergic-type reactions (asthma, itching, rash) after taking aspirin or other NSAIDs or to patients with nasal polyps who experienced aspirin-induced bronchospasms.
• Celecoxib should be used with caution in patients with a history of ulcers or who have had a gastrointestinal bleeding episode. Since gastrointestinal bleeding may be more dangerous in the elderly, celecoxib should be used cautiously in this group.
• Celecoxib should not be used in patients with severe kidney disease.
• If celecoxib tends to make you dizzy, do not take part in any activity that requires mental alertness, such as driving an automobile or operating potentially dangerous machinery or equipment.
• Stomach problems are more likely to occur if you take aspirin or other salicylates regularly or if you drink alcoholic beverages while you are being treated with this medication. This combination of medications should be avoided (unless your doctor directs you to do otherwise).
• Be sure to tell your doctor if you are pregnant or become pregnant while taking celecoxib. Celecoxib is classified in Pregnancy Category C: The effects of this medication during pregnancy have not been thoroughly studied in humans. In addition, be sure to tell your doctor if you are breast-feeding an infant. It is not known if celecoxib passes into human breast milk.

---

cephalexin

BRAND NAMES (Manufacturers)
cephalexin monohydrate (various manufacturers)
Keflex (Lilly)
Keftab (Lilly)
TYPE OF DRUG
Cephalosporin antibiotic
INGREDIENT
cephalexin
DOSAGE FORMS
Tablets (250 mg and 500 mg)
Capsules (250 mg and 500 mg)
Oral suspension (125 mg and 250 mg per 5-mL spoonful)
Pediatric oral suspension (100 mg per mL)
STORAGE
Store the tablet and capsule forms of this medication at room temperature in tightly closed containers. Keep the suspension forms of this medication in the refrigerator in tightly closed containers. Discard any unused portion of the oral suspension after 14 days because the suspension loses its potency after that time. This medication should never be frozen.

USES

This medication is used to treat a wide variety of bacterial infections, including those of the bones, middle ear, prostate, skin, upper and lower respiratory tract, and urinary tract. This drug acts by severely injuring the cell walls of the infecting bacteria, thereby preventing them from growing and multiplying. Cephalexin kills susceptible bacteria, but it is not effective against viruses, parasites, or fungi.

TREATMENT

You should take cephalexin on an empty stomach if possible. To avoid stomach upset, this medication can be taken with food or milk.

Shake the suspension form of this medication well just before measuring each dose to distribute the ingredients evenly and equalize the doses. The contents tend to settle on the bottom of the bottle. Measure each dose of medication carefully with a specially designed 5-mL measuring spoon or with the dropper provided. An ordinary kitchen teaspoon is not accurate enough.

Cephalosporin antibiotics work best when the level of medicine in your bloodstream is kept constant. It is best to take your doses of this medication at evenly spaced intervals throughout the day and night. For example, if you are to take four doses of the medication a day, the doses should be spaced six hours apart.

If you miss a dose, take the missed dose immediately. However, if you do not remember to take the missed dose until it is almost time for your next dose, take the missed dose, space the following dose halfway through the regular interval between doses, then return to your regular schedule. Do not skip any doses of this medication.

It is important to continue to take this medication for the entire time prescribed by your doctor (usually 7 to 14 days), even if the symptoms disappear before then. If you stop taking this drug too soon, resistant bacteria are given a chance to continue growing, and the infection could recur.

SIDE EFFECTS

Minor. Abdominal pain, diarrhea, dizziness, fatigue, headache, heartburn, loss of appetite, nausea, or vomiting. These side effects should disappear over time as your body adjusts to the medication.

If you feel dizzy, sit or lie down for a while; get up slowly from a sitting or reclining position; and be careful on stairs.

Major. Tell your doctor about any side effects that are persistent or particularly bothersome. IT IS ESPECIALLY IMPORTANT TO TELL YOUR DOCTOR about darkened tongue, difficulty in breathing, fever, itching, joint pain, rash, rectal or vaginal itching, severe diarrhea (which can be watery or contain pus or blood), sore mouth, stomach cramps, tingling in the hands or feet, or unusual bleeding or bruising. If your symptoms of infection seem to be getting worse rather than improving, you should contact your doctor.

INTERACTIONS

Cephalexin interacts with several other types of drugs:

1. Probenecid can increase the blood concentrations of this medication.

2. The side effects, especially effects on the kidneys, of furosemide, bumetanide, ethacrynic acid, colistin, vancomycin, polymyxin B, and aminoglycoside antibiotics can be increased by cephalexin.

3. The use of this medication may result in a decrease in the efficacy of certain birth control pills, and pregnancy could result. You should, therefore, use a different or additional (barrier) form of birth control while taking this medication. Discuss this with your doctor.

BE SURE TO TELL YOUR DOCTOR about any medications you are currently taking, especially any of those listed above.

WARNINGS

• Tell your doctor about unusual or allergic reactions you have had to any medication, especially to cephalexin or other cephalosporin antibiotics (such as cefaclor, cefadroxil, cefamandole, cefdinir, cefditoren, cefepime, cefixime, cefonicid, cefoperazone, cefotaxime, cefotetan, cefoxitin, cefpodoxime, cefprozil, ceftazidime, ceftibuten, ceftizoxime, ceftriaxone, cefuroxime, cephapirin, and cephradine) or to any penicillin antibiotics.

• Call your doctor immediately if you experience rash, swelling of the face, or difficulty breathing after you take this medication.

• Tell your doctor if you now have or if you have ever had kidney disease.

• This medication has been prescribed for your current infection only. Another infection later on, or one that someone else has, may require a different medicine. You should not give your medication to other people or use it for other infections, unless your doctor specifically directs you to do so.

• People with diabetes should know cephalexin can cause a false-positive sugar reaction with a Clinitest urine glucose test. To avoid this problem while taking cephalexin, they should switch to Clinistix or Tes-Tape.

• Be sure to tell your doctor if you are pregnant. Although the cephalosporin antibiotics appear safe during pregnancy, extensive studies in humans have not been done, and caution is warranted. Also tell your doctor if you are breast-feeding an infant. Small amounts of this drug pass into breast milk and may temporarily alter the balance of bacteria in the intestinal tract of the nursing infant, resulting in diarrhea.

---

cephradine

BRAND NAMES (Manufacturers)
cephradine (various manufacturers)
Velosef (Bristol-Myers Squibb)
TYPE OF DRUG
Cephalosporin antibiotic
INGREDIENT
cephradine
DOSAGE FORMS
Capsules (250 mg and 500 mg)
Oral suspension (125 mg and 250 mg per 5-mL spoonful)
STORAGE
Store capsules at room temperature in a tightly closed container and out of the reach of children. Keep the suspension in the refrigerator in a tightly closed container. Discard any unused portion of the suspension after 14 days because the suspension loses its potency after that time. This medication should never be frozen.

USES

This medication is used to treat a wide variety of bacterial infections, including those of the middle ear, prostate, skin, upper and lower respiratory tract, and urinary tract. This drug acts by severely injuring the cell walls of the infecting bacteria, thereby preventing them from growing and multiplying. Cephradine kills susceptible bacteria, but it is not effective against viruses, parasites, or fungi.

TREATMENT

You can take cephradine either on an empty stomach or, to avoid an upset stomach, with food or milk.

Shake the oral suspension form of this medication well just before measuring each dose to distribute the ingredients evenly and to equalize the doses. The contents tend to settle on the bottom of the bottle. Measure each dose of the medication carefully with a specially designed 5-mL measuring spoon or with the dropper provided with your prescription. An ordinary kitchen teaspoon is not accurate enough for medicinal purposes.

Cephalosporin antibiotics work best when the level of medicine in your bloodstream is kept constant. It is best, therefore, to take the doses at evenly spaced intervals day and night. For example, if you are to take four doses a day, the doses should be spaced six hours apart.

If you miss a dose of this medication, take the missed dose immediately. However, if you do not remember to take the missed dose until it is almost time for your next dose, take it and space the following dose halfway through the regular interval between doses; then return to your regular dosing schedule. It is important that you try not to skip any doses of this medication.

It is important to continue to take cephradine for the entire time prescribed by your doctor (usually 7 to 14 days), even if your symptoms of infection disappear before the end of that period. If you stop taking this drug too soon, resistant bacteria are given a chance to continue growing, and the infection could recur.

SIDE EFFECTS

Minor. Abdominal pain, diarrhea, dizziness, fatigue, headache, heartburn, loss of appetite, nausea, or vomiting. These side effects should disappear as your body adjusts to the medication.

If you feel dizzy, sit or lie down for a while; get up slowly from a sitting or reclining position; and be careful when using stairs.

To avoid dizziness when you stand, contract and relax the muscles of your legs for a few moments before rising. Do this by alternately pushing one foot against the floor while lifting the other foot slightly.

Major. Tell your doctor about any side effects that are persistent or particularly bothersome. IT IS ESPECIALLY IMPORTANT TO TELL YOUR DOCTOR about darkened tongue, difficulty in breathing, fever, itching, joint pain, rash, rectal or vaginal itching, severe diarrhea (which can be watery or contain pus or blood), sore mouth, stomach cramps, tingling in the hands or feet, or unusual bleeding or bruising. If your symptoms of infection seem to be getting worse rather than improving while you are taking this medication, you should contact your doctor immediately.

INTERACTIONS

Cephradine interacts with several other types of medications:

1. Probenecid can increase the blood concentrations as well as the side effects of this medication.

2. The side effects—especially as they relate to the kidneys—of furosemide, bumetanide, ethacrynic acid, colistin, vancomycin, polymyxin B, and aminoglycoside antibiotics can be increased by cephradine.

3. The use of this medication may result in a decrease in the efficacy of certain birth control pills, and pregnancy could result. You should, therefore, use a different or additional (barrier) form of birth control while taking this medication. Discuss this with your doctor.

BE SURE TO TELL YOUR DOCTOR about any medications you are currently taking, especially any of the medications that are listed above.

WARNINGS

• Tell your doctor about unusual or allergic reactions you have had to any medication, especially to cephradine or other cephalosporin antibiotics (such as cefaclor, cefadroxil, cefamandole, cefdinir, cefditoren, cefepime, cefixime, cefonicid, cefoperazone, cefotaxime, cefotetan, cefoxitin, cefpodoxime, cefprozil, ceftazidime, ceftibuten, ceftizoxime, ceftriaxone, cefuroxime, cephalexin, and cephapirin) or to penicillin antibiotics.

• Call your doctor immediately if you experience rash, swelling of the face, or difficulty breathing after you take this medication.

• Be sure to tell your doctor if you now have or have ever had kidney disease.

• This medication has been prescribed for your current infection only. Another infection you experience later on, or one that someone else has, may require a different medicine. You should not give your medication to other people or use it for other infections, unless your doctor specifically directs you to do so.

• People with diabetes need to know that cephradine can cause a false-positive sugar reaction with a Clinitest urine glucose test. To avoid this problem while taking cephradine, they should switch to Clinistix or Tes-Tape in order to test their urine sugar content accurately.

• Be sure to tell your doctor if you are pregnant. Although the cephalosporin antibiotics appear to be safe during pregnancy, extensive studies in humans have not been conducted. Also tell your doctor if you are breast-feeding. Small amounts of this medication pass into breast milk and may alter the bacterial balance in the intestinal tract of the nursing infant, resulting in diarrhea.

---

cetirizine

BRAND NAME (Manufacturer)
Zyrtec (Pfizer)
TYPE OF DRUG
Antihistamine
INGREDIENT
cetirizine
DOSAGE FORMS
Tablets (5 mg and 10 mg)
Syrup (5 mg per 5-mL spoonful)
STORAGE
Store at room temperature in a tightly closed container.

USES

Cetirizine belongs to a group of drugs known as antihistamines, which act by blocking the action of histamine, a chemical released by the body during an allergic reaction. This medication is used to treat or prevent symptoms of allergy. It is also used as part of the treatment of some patients with asthma.

TREATMENT

This medication can be taken with or without food. If you experience stomach upset after taking cetirizine, you may take it with food or with a full glass of milk or water (unless your doctor directs you to do otherwise).

If you miss a dose of cetirizine, take the missed dose as soon as possible. However, if it is almost time for the next dose, do not take the missed dose at all; just wait until the next scheduled dose. Do not double the dose.

SIDE EFFECTS

Minor. Dizziness, drowsiness, dry mouth, and sore throat. These side effects should disappear as your body adjusts to the medication.

Dry mouth can be relieved by chewing sugarless gum or sucking on ice chips or a piece of hard candy.

Major. Tell your doctor about any side effects that are persistent or particularly bothersome. IT IS ESPECIALLY IMPORTANT TO TELL YOUR DOCTOR about blurred vision, convulsions, feeling faint, increased sweating, irritability, mental confusion, rash, shakiness, trembling, or weight gain.

INTERACTIONS

Cetirizine can interact with other types of drugs:

1. Concurrent use of other central nervous system depressants (such as alcohol, barbiturates, benzodiazepines, muscle relaxants, narcotics, pain medications, and phenothiazine tranquilizers) or with tricyclic antidepressant medications can cause extreme drowsiness.

2. MAO inhibitors (such as phenelzine, tranylcypromine, and isocarboxazid) may increase the side effects of cetirizine. Do not take MAO inhibitors with this drug.

3. Anticholinergic agents, such as atropine, may increase the side effects of cetirizine.

Before starting to take cetirizine, BE SURE TO TELL YOUR DOCTOR about any medications you are currently taking, especially any of those listed above.

WARNINGS

- Tell your doctor about any unusual or allergic reactions you have had to any medications, especially to cetirizine or any other antihistamines.
- Cetirizine can cause drowsiness or dizziness. Your ability to perform tasks that require mental alertness, such as driving an automobile or operating potentially dangerous tools or machinery, may be decreased. Appropriate caution should therefore be taken.
- Elderly patients may be more sensitive to side effects, especially confusion, drowsiness, and irritability. Report any such effects to your doctor.
- Before having surgery or any other medical or dental treatment, be sure to tell your doctor or dentist that you are taking this medication.
- Be sure to tell your doctor if you are pregnant. The effects of this medication have not been thoroughly studied in humans. Also be sure to tell your doctor if you are breastfeeding an infant. It is not known if cetirizine is distributed into breast milk.

---

chlordiazepoxide

BRAND NAMES (Manufacturers)

chlordiazepoxide hydrochloride (various manufacturers)
Libritabs (ICN)
Librium (ICN)

TYPE OF DRUG

Benzodiazepine sedative/hypnotic

INGREDIENT

chlordiazepoxide

DOSAGE FORMS

Capsules (5 mg, 10 mg, and 25 mg)
Tablets (10 mg and 25 mg)

STORAGE

Store at room temperature in a tightly closed, light-resistant container.

USES

Chlordiazepoxide is prescribed to treat the symptoms of anxiety and alcohol withdrawal. It is not clear exactly how this medicine works, but it may relieve anxiety by acting as a depressant of the central nervous system. This drug is used to relieve nervousness. It is effective for this purpose, but it is important to remove the cause of the anxiety as well.

TREATMENT

This medication should be taken exactly as directed by your doctor. It can be taken with food or a full glass of water if stomach upset occurs. Do not take this medication with a dose of antacids, since the antacids may retard the absorption of chlordiazepoxide.

If you are taking this medication regularly and you miss a dose, take the missed dose immediately. However, if more than an hour has passed, skip the dose that you missed and simply wait for the next scheduled dose. Do not double the dose of this medication.

SIDE EFFECTS

Minor. Bitter taste in the mouth, constipation, depression, diarrhea, dizziness, drowsiness (after a night's sleep), dry mouth, excessive salivation, fatigue, flushing, headache, heartburn, loss of appetite, nausea, nervousness, sweating, or vomiting. As your body adjusts to the medicine, these side effects should disappear.

To relieve constipation, increase the fiber in your diet (fresh fruits and vegetables, salads, bran, and whole-grain breads), exercise, and drink more water (unless your doctor instructs you to do otherwise).

Dry mouth can be relieved by chewing sugarless gum or by sucking on ice chips.

If you feel dizzy, sit or lie down for a while; get up slowly from a sitting or reclining position; and be careful on stairs.

Major. Tell your doctor about any side effects that are persistent or particularly bothersome. IT IS ESPECIALLY IMPORTANT TO TELL YOUR DOCTOR about blurred or double vision, chest pain, difficulty in urinating, fainting, falling, fever, hallucinations, joint pain, mouth sores, nightmares, palpitations, rash, severe depression, shortness of breath, slurred speech, sore throat, uncoordinated movements, unusual excitement, unusual tiredness, or yellowing of the skin or the whites of the eyes.

INTERACTIONS

Chlordiazepoxide interacts with several other drugs:

1. To prevent oversedation, this drug should not be taken with alcohol, other sedative drugs, central nervous system depressants (such as antihistamines, barbiturates, muscle relaxants, pain medicines, narcotics, seizure medications, and phenothiazine tranquilizers), or antidepressants.

2. Chlordiazepoxide may decrease the effectiveness of oral anticoagulants (blood thinners) and of levodopa.

3. Chlordiazepoxide may increase the effects of phenytoin and carbamazepine.

3. Disulfiram, oral contraceptives (birth control pills), isoniazid, diltiazem, erythromycin, grapefruit juice, nefazodone, fluvoxamine, fluoxetine, itraconazole, ketoconazole, and cimetidine can increase the blood levels of chlordiazepoxide, which can lead to toxic effects.

4. Concurrent use of rifampin may decrease the effectiveness of chlordiazepoxide.

BE SURE TO TELL YOUR DOCTOR about any medications you are currently taking, especially any of the medications listed above.

WARNINGS

- Tell your doctor about unusual or allergic reactions you have had to any medications, especially to chlordiazepoxide or other benzodiazepine tranquilizers (such as alprazolam, clorazepate, diazepam, flurazepam, halazepam, lorazepam, oxazepam, prazepam, temazepam, and triazolam).
- Tell your doctor if you now have or ever had liver disease, kidney disease, epilepsy, lung disease, myasthenia gravis, porphyria, sleep apnea, mental depression, or mental illness.
- This medicine can cause drowsiness. Avoid tasks that require alertness, such as driving an automobile.
- Before having surgery or any other medical or dental treatment, tell your doctor or dentist that you are taking this drug.
- This medication has the potential for abuse and must be used with caution. Tolerance may develop quickly; do not increase the dosage of the drug without first consulting your doctor. It is also important not to stop taking this medication suddenly if you have been taking it in large amounts or if you have used it for several weeks. Your doctor may want to reduce your dosage of this medication gradually in order to avoid withdrawal symptoms.
- This is a safe drug when used properly. When it is combined with other sedative drugs or alcohol, however, serious side effects may develop.

• Be sure to tell your doctor if you are pregnant. This medicine may increase the chance of birth defects if it is taken during the first three months of pregnancy. In addition, too much use of this medicine during the last six months of pregnancy may lead to addiction of the fetus, resulting in withdrawal symptoms in the newborn. Use of this medicine during the last weeks of pregnancy may also cause excessive drowsiness, slowed heartbeat, and breathing difficulties in the infant. Tell your doctor if you are breast-feeding an infant. This medicine can pass into breast milk and cause excessive drowsiness, slowed heartbeat, and breathing difficulties in the nursing infant.

---

chlorhexidine gluconate

BRAND NAME (Manufacturer)
Peridex (Procter & Gamble)
TYPE OF DRUG
Oral rinse
INGREDIENT
chlorhexidine as the gluconate salt
DOSAGE FORM
Mouthwash (11.6% alcohol)
STORAGE
Store at room temperature in a tightly closed, light-resistant container. Do not freeze.

USES

Chlorhexidine gluconate solution is prescribed by dentists for the treatment of gingivitis and mouth infections and for the reduction of dental plaque. Gingivitis is a medical term for inflammation of the gums characterized by redness, swelling, and bleeding upon probing. Although it is unknown exactly how the product works, it is believed to eliminate bacteria, which can cause dental plaque. Dental plaque is one of several causes of gingivitis.

TREATMENT

Treatment with chlorhexidine gluconate solution should begin following a thorough cleaning of your teeth by your dental practitioner.

Measure one-half fluid ounce (as marked in the cap of the product container) of chlorhexidine gluconate solution, and swish in the mouth for at least 30 seconds twice daily. Do not dilute it in water or other liquids. It should be used full strength. Chlorhexidine gluconate solution should be used after brushing and flossing.

Do not swallow chlorhexidine gluconate solution following use. It should be expectorated (spit out) after you rinse your mouth with it.

Do not rinse your mouth with water after using this medication; doing so may increase the bad taste of this medicine. And do not eat or drink for several hours after using the medication.

SIDE EFFECTS

Minor. Irritation of the inside of the mouth can occur following use of this product In addition, some patients may experience temporary taste disturbances. However, there have been no permanent taste disturbances reported with continued use of chlorhexidine gluconate. Other adverse effects from this medication include tongue irritation and stomach upset.

Major. Be sure to tell your dentist about any side effects that are persistent or particularly bothersome. IT IS ESPECIALLY IMPORTANT TO TELL YOUR DENTIST about any inflammation and swelling of the parotid salivary gland.

Chlorhexidine may cause staining of the teeth and tongue. This staining will be more noticeable in patients who have a heavy accumulation of tartar. Usually, this staining is temporary and can be easily removed from most tooth surfaces with dental cleaning. Rarely, some persons, especially those with tartar, will have permanent stains. Use a tartar-control toothpaste and floss regularly to help reduce tartar buildup unless directed otherwise by your dentist.

INTERACTIONS

There do not appear to be any significant drug interactions with chlorhexidine gluconate. However, you should make sure that your dentist knows about all the medications you are currently taking.

WARNINGS

• Tell your doctor and dentist about any reactions you have had to any medications, especially to chlorhexidine gluconate solution.
• Chlorhexidine gluconate solution has not been fully evaluated for safety in children under the age of 18. Therefore, the medication should not be used by children who are in this age group.
• To determine the effectiveness of treatment with chlorhexidine gluconate, it is advisable to have dental checkups at least every six months.
• Be sure to tell your dentist if you are pregnant or are breast-feeding an infant. Scientific studies have not yet determined the effects of the administration of chlorhexidine gluconate to pregnant or nursing women or their babies. Therefore, use of this product during pregnancy or while breast-feeding should be carefully considered.

---

chlorpromazine

BRAND NAMES (Manufacturers)
chlorpromazine hydrochloride (GlaxoSmithKline)
Thorazine (GlaxoSmithKline)
Thorazine Spansules (GlaxoSmithKline)
TYPE OF DRUG
Phenothiazine tranquilizer
INGREDIENT
chlorpromazine hydrochloride
DOSAGE FORMS
Tablets (10 mg, 25 mg, 50 mg, 100 mg, and 200 mg)
Sustained-release capsules (30 mg, 75 mg, and 150 mg)
Oral concentrate (30 mg per mL and 100 mg per mL)
Oral syrup (10 mg per 5-mL spoonful)
Suppositories (25 mg and 100 mg)
STORAGE
Store the tablet and capsule forms of this medication at room temperature in tightly closed, light-resistant containers. Keep the syrup and suppository forms in the refrigerator in tightly closed, light-resistant containers. If the concentrate or syrup turns to a slight yellow color, the medicine is still effective and can be used. However, if the concentrate or syrup changes color markedly or has particles floating in it, it should not be used; instead, it should be discarded down the sink. Chlorpromazine should never be frozen.

USES

Chlorpromazine is prescribed for pain relief and to treat the symptoms of certain types of mental illness, such as the emotional symptoms of psychosis and the manic phase of manic-depressive illness (sometimes called bipolar disorder). This medication is thought to relieve the symptoms of mental illness by blocking certain chemicals involved with nerve transmission in the brain.

Chlorpromazine may also be used to treat tetanus, porphyria, uncontrollable hiccups, anxiety before surgery, and nausea and vomiting.

TREATMENT

To avoid stomach irritation, take the tablets or capsules with a meal or with a glass of water or milk (unless your doctor directs you to do otherwise). The sustained-release capsules should be taken whole; do not crush, break, or open them prior to swallowing. Breaking the capsule would release the medication all at once, defeating the purpose of the extended-release capsules.

Be sure to measure the syrup form of this medication carefully with a specially designed 5-mL measuring spoon. An ordinary kitchen teaspoon is not accurate enough for medicinal purposes.

Measure the concentrate carefully with the dropper provided, then add it to four ounces (one-half cup) or more of water, milk, a carbonated beverage, applesauce, or pudding just before taking it. Be careful that the serving size is not more than the patient is willing or able to drink or eat; otherwise, the full dose may not be consumed. To prevent possible loss of effectiveness, the medication should not be diluted in tea, coffee, or apple juice.

To use the suppository, remove the foil wrapper and moisten the suppository with water (if the suppository is too soft to insert, refrigerate it for half an hour or run cold water over it before removing the wrapper). Lie on your left side with your right knee bent. Push the suppository into the rectum, pointed end first. Lie still for a few minutes. Try to avoid having a bowel movement for at least an hour.

If you miss a dose of this medication, take the missed dose as soon as possible, then return to your regular schedule. However, if it is almost time for the next dose, skip the one you missed and return to your regular schedule. Do not double the dose of this medication (unless your doctor directs you to do so).

Antacids and antidiarrheal medicines may decrease the absorption of this medication from the gastrointestinal tract. Therefore, at least one hour should separate doses of any of these medicines and chlorpromazine.

The full effects of this medication for the control of emotional or mental symptoms may not become apparent for two weeks after you start to take it.

SIDE EFFECTS

Minor. Blurred vision, constipation, decreased sweating, diarrhea, dizziness, drooling, drowsiness, dry mouth, fatigue, jitteriness, menstrual irregularities, nasal congestion, restlessness, tremors, vomiting, or weight gain. As your body adjusts to the medication, these side effects should disappear.

This medication can cause increased sensitivity to sunlight. It is, therefore, important to avoid prolonged exposure to sunlight or sunlamps. Wear protective clothing and use an effective sunscreen.

Chlorpromazine can also cause discoloration of the urine to red, pink, or red-brown. This is a harmless effect.

If you experience constipation as a side effect of this medication, increase the amount of fiber in your diet (eat more fresh fruits and vegetables, salads, bran, and whole-grain breads), exercise, and drink more water (unless your doctor directs you to do otherwise).

Chew sugarless gum or suck on ice chips or a piece of hard candy to help reduce mouth dryness.

To avoid dizziness or light-headedness when you stand, contract and relax the muscles of your legs for a few moments before rising. Do this by pushing one foot against the floor while raising the other foot slightly, alternating feet so that you are "pumping" your legs in a pedaling motion.

Major. Tell your doctor about any side effects that are persistent or particularly bothersome. IT IS ESPECIALLY IMPORTANT TO TELL YOUR DOCTOR about breast enlargement (in both sexes); chest pain; convulsions; darkened skin; difficulty in swallowing or breathing; fainting; fever; impotence; involuntary movements of the face, mouth, jaw, or tongue; palpitations; rash; sleep disorders; sore throat; uncoordinated movements; unusual bleeding or bruising; visual disturbances; or yellowing of the eyes or skin.

INTERACTIONS

Chlorpromazine will interact with several other types of medications:

1. Chlorpromazine can cause extreme drowsiness when combined with alcohol or other central nervous system depressants (such as barbiturates, benzodiazepine tranquilizers, muscle relaxants, narcotics, and pain medications) or with tricyclic antidepressants, fluoxetine, fluvoxamine, paroxetine, or maprotiline.

2. Chlorpromazine can decrease the effectiveness of amphetamines, guanethidine, anticonvulsants, levodopa, and oral anticoagulants.

3. The side effects of cyclophosphamide, epinephrine, monoamine oxidase (MAO) inhibitors, phenytoin, and tricyclic antidepressant medications may be increased by concurrent use of this medication.

4. Chlorpromazine can increase the absorption of propranolol, which can increase the risk of side effects.

5. Lithium may increase the side effects and may decrease the effectiveness of this medication.

6. The side effects of disopyramide, erythromycin, pimozide, probucol, procainamide, and quinidine may be increased with this medication.

Before starting to take chlorpromazine, BE SURE TO TELL YOUR DOCTOR about any medications you are currently taking, especially any of those listed above.

WARNINGS

• Tell your doctor about unusual or allergic reactions you have had to any medications, especially to chlorpromazine or any other phenothiazine tranquilizers (such as fluphenazine, mesoridazine, perphenazine, prochlorperazine, promazine, thioridazine, and trifluoperazine) or to the drug loxapine.

• Tell your doctor if you are allergic to dyes, especially to FD&C Yellow No. 5 (tartrazine).

• Tell your doctor if you have a history of alcoholism or if you now have or ever had blood disease, bone marrow disease, brain disease, breast cancer, blockage in the urinary or digestive tract, drug-induced depression, epilepsy, high or low blood pressure, diabetes mellitus, glaucoma, heart or circulatory disease, liver disease, lung disease, Parkinson's disease, peptic ulcers, or an enlarged prostate gland.

• Tell your doctor about any recent exposure to a pesticide or an insecticide. Chlorpromazine may increase the side effects from the exposure.

• To prevent oversedation, avoid drinking alcoholic beverages while you are taking this medication.

• If this drug makes you dizzy or drowsy, avoid any activity that requires alertness, such as driving a car or operating potentially dangerous equipment.

• Before having surgery or any other medical or dental treatment, be sure to tell your doctor or dentist that you are taking this medication.

• Some of the side effects caused by this drug can be prevented by taking a drug for Parkinson's disease. Discuss this with your doctor.

• This medication can decrease sweating and heat release from the body. You should, therefore, avoid becoming overheated by strenuous exercise in hot weather and should avoid taking hot baths, showers, and saunas.

• Do not stop taking this medication suddenly. If the drug is stopped abruptly, you may experience nausea, vomiting, stomach upset, headache, increased heart rate, insomnia, tremors, or a worsening of your condition. Your doctor may want to reduce the dosage of this medication gradually before stopping it completely.

• If you are planning to have a myelogram or any other medical procedure in which dye will be injected into your spinal cord, be sure to tell the doctor that you are taking this medication.
• Avoid spilling the oral concentrate or oral syrup forms of this medication on your skin or clothing: It may cause redness and irritation of the skin.
• While you are being treated with this medication, do not take any over-the-counter (nonprescription) medications for weight control or for cough, cold, allergy, asthma, or sinus problems without first checking with your doctor. The combination of these medications with chlorpromazine may cause high blood pressure.
• Be sure to tell your doctor if you are pregnant. Small amounts of this medication cross the placenta. Although there have been reports of safe use of this drug during pregnancy, there have also been reports of liver disease and tremors in newborn infants whose mothers received this medication close to term. Also tell your doctor if you are breast-feeding an infant. Small amounts of this medication pass into breast milk and may affect the nursing infant.

cholestyramine

BRAND NAMES (Manufacturers)
cholestyramine (various manufacturers)
Questran (Bristol-Myers Squibb)
Questran Light (Bristol-Myers Squibb)
TYPE OF DRUG
Antihyperlipidemic (lipid-lowering drug)
INGREDIENT
cholestyramine
DOSAGE FORM
Oral powder (4 g of cholestyramine per 5 g, 5.5 g, or 9 g powder)
STORAGE
Store this medication at room temperature in a tightly closed container, and protect it from moisture. Do not refrigerate.

USES

This medication is used to lower levels of cholesterol in the blood and to treat the itching that is associated with liver disease. Cholestyramine chemically binds to bile salts in the gastrointestinal tract and thereby prevents the body from producing cholesterol.

TREATMENT

Cholestyramine is usually taken before meals. Measure each dose of the medication carefully and then add it to two to six ounces of water, milk, fruit juice, or another noncarbonated beverage. To avoid swallowing air while taking the medication, drink the mixture slowly. The powder can also be mixed with applesauce, cereal, crushed pineapple, or soup. You should never take cholestyramine dry because you might accidentally inhale the powder, and that could irritate your throat and lungs.

If you miss a dose of this medication, take the missed dose as soon as possible. However, if it is almost time for the next dose of medication, do not take the missed dose at all; just return to your regular dosing schedule. Do not double the next dose of this medication.

Cholestyramine does not cure hypercholesterolemia (high blood cholesterol levels), but it will help to control the condition as long as you continue to take the medication as directed.

SIDE EFFECTS

Minor. Anxiety, belching, constipation, diarrhea, dizziness, drowsiness, fatigue, gas, headache, hiccups, loss of appetite, nausea, stomach pain, vomiting, or weight loss or gain. These side effects should disappear as your body adjusts to the medication.

To relieve constipation, increase the amount of fiber in your diet (fresh fruits and vegetables, salads, bran, and whole-grain breads), exercise, and drink more water (unless your doctor directs you to do otherwise).

If this medication makes you feel dizzy, sit or lie down for a while; get up slowly from a sitting or reclining position; and be careful on stairs.

Major. Tell your doctor about any side effects you experience that are persistent or particularly bothersome. IT IS ESPECIALLY IMPORTANT TO TELL YOUR DOCTOR about backaches; bloody or black, tarry stools; difficult or painful urination; fluid retention; muscle or joint pains; rash or irritation of the skin, tongue, or rectal area; ringing in the ears; swollen glands; tingling sensations; unusual bleeding or bruising; or unusual weakness.

INTERACTIONS

Cholestyramine interacts with a number of other types of medications:

1. Cholestyramine interferes with the absorption of a number of other medications, including phenylbutazone, thiazide diuretics (water pills), digoxin, penicillins, tetracycline, oral vancomycin, phenobarbital, folic acid, iron, thyroid hormones, cephalexin, clindamycin, and trimethoprim, as well as with the fat-soluble vitamins (A, D, E, and K). The effectiveness of these medications, therefore, will be decreased by cholestyramine. To avoid this interaction, take the other medications one hour before or four to eight hours after a dose of cholestyramine.

2. Cholestyramine may prevent the absorption of warfarin, a blood thinner, reducing its effect. However, cholestyramine may also increase the effects of warfarin by depleting the body of vitamin K. Close monitoring of the effects of warfarin on the blood are needed if you take both these medications. At least six hours should separate your doses of warfarin and cholestyramine.

BE SURE TO TELL YOUR DOCTOR about any medications you are currently taking, especially those listed above.

WARNINGS

• Tell your doctor about unusual or allergic reactions you have had to any medications, especially any reactions to cholestyramine.

• Tell your doctor if you now have or if you have ever had a bleeding disorder, a biliary obstruction, heart disease, hemorrhoids, gallstones or gallbladder disease, kidney disease, any malabsorption problem, stomach ulcers, or an obstructed intestine.

• Cholestyramine should be used only in conjunction with dietary therapy, a weight-reduction plan, and/or correction of other conditions that could be causing the elevated levels of blood cholesterol.

• This product contains the color additive FD&C Yellow No. 5 (tartrazine), which can cause allergic-type reactions (including fainting, rash, shortness of breath) in certain susceptible individuals.

• The color of cholestyramine powder may vary from batch to batch. This variation in color does not alter the effectiveness of the medication.

• Be sure to tell your doctor if you are pregnant. Although cholestyramine appears to be safe (because very little is absorbed into the bloodstream), extensive studies in humans during pregnancy have not been conducted. In addition, be sure to tell your doctor if you are breast-feeding an infant. It is not known whether cholestyramine passes into breast milk. However, cholestyramine can decrease the absorption of some vitamins in the mother, which could result in decreased availability of the vitamins for the nursing infant.

cimetidine

BRAND NAMES (Manufacturers)
cimetidine (various manufacturers)
Tagamet (SmithKline Beecham)
Tagamet HB* (SmithKline Beecham)
*Available over the counter (without a prescription)
TYPE OF DRUG
Gastric-acid-secretion inhibitor (decreases stomach acid)
INGREDIENT
cimetidine
DOSAGE FORMS
Tablets (100 mg, 200 mg, 300 mg, 400 mg, and 800 mg)
Oral liquid (300 mg per 5-mL spoonful, with 2.8% alcohol)
STORAGE
Store at room temperature in a tightly closed, light-resistant container. This medication should never be frozen. If cimetidine is not properly stored (especially if it is exposed to light or heat), it may develop a strong, unpleasant odor.

USES

When obtained by prescription, cimetidine is used for the treatment of duodenal and gastric ulcers, for the long-term treatment of excessive stomach acid secretion, and for the prevention of recurrent ulcers. It is also used to treat gastroesophageal reflux (backflow of stomach contents into the esophagus), which can cause heartburn. Cimetidine works by blocking the effects of histamine in the stomach, which reduces stomach acid secretion.

A lower-strength version of cimetidine is now available over the counter for heartburn (sour stomach). When purchased without a doctor's prescription, this medication should not be used continuously for more than two weeks. If your symptoms of heartburn persist after two weeks, you should consult your doctor.

TREATMENT

Take cimetidine with, or shortly after, meals and again at bedtime, unless your doctor has provided you with other instructions for use.

Do not crush or chew the tablets because cimetidine has a bitter taste and an unpleasant odor.

Measure the liquid carefully with a specially designed 5-mL measuring spoon. An ordinary kitchen teaspoon is not accurate enough.

If you miss a dose of cimetidine, take the missed dose as soon as possible. However, if it is almost time for the next dose, do not take the missed dose at all; just return to your regular dosing schedule. Do not double the next dose of this medication.

SIDE EFFECTS

Minor. Diarrhea, dizziness, drowsiness, headache, or muscle pain. These side effects should disappear as your body adjusts to the medication.

If you feel dizzy, sit or lie down for a while; stand up slowly; and be careful on stairs.

Major. Tell your doctor about any side effects that are persistent or particularly bothersome. IT IS ESPECIALLY IMPORTANT TO TELL YOUR DOCTOR about confusion, enlarged or painful breasts (in both sexes), fever, hair loss, hallucinations, impotence, palpitations, rash, sore throat, unusual bleeding or bruising, weakness, or yellowing of the skin or the whites of the eyes.

INTERACTIONS

Cimetidine interacts with several other types of medications:

1. It can decrease the elimination, and thus increase the side effects, of theophylline, aminophylline, oxtriphylline, phenytoin, carbamazepine, beta blockers, benzodiazepine tranquilizers (such as chlordiazepoxide, diazepam, and midazolam), tricyclic antidepressants, oral anticoagulants (blood thinners, such as warfarin), lidocaine, calcium channel blockers (such as verapamil and nifedipine), quinidine, paroxetine, metronidazole, codeine, and morphine.

2. The combination of cimetidine and antineoplastic agents (medications that fight cancer) may increase the risk of blood disorders.

3. The absorption of ketoconazole and itraconazole is decreased by cimetidine. Therefore, at least two hours should separate a dose of cimetidine and a dose of either of these two medications.

4. Cimetidine may decrease the blood levels and effectiveness of digoxin.

5. Antacids can block the absorption of cimetidine. If you are taking antacids as well as cimetidine, at least one hour should separate doses of the two medications.

BE SURE TO TELL YOUR DOCTOR about any medications that you are currently taking, especially any of the medications listed above.

WARNINGS

- Cimetidine is now available in an over-the-counter (nonprescription) form. However, this does not mean that you should stop taking the prescription version of the medication and switch to the less expensive OTC version. The OTC version is only for the treatment of occasional heartburn. If you have stomach ulcer disease, your doctor will continue the prescription version. If you have any questions about which version is best for you, discuss the matter with your doctor or pharmacist.
- Tell your doctor about any unusual or allergic reactions you have had to medications, especially to cimetidine, famotidine, nizatidine, or ranitidine.
- Be sure to tell your doctor if you now have or if you have ever had arthritis, kidney disease, liver disease, or organic brain syndrome.
- Cimetidine can decrease the elimination of alcohol from the body, which can prolong its intoxicating effects.
- Cimetidine should be taken continuously for as long as your doctor prescribes. Stopping therapy early may result in ineffective treatment.
- Cigarette smoking may block the beneficial effects of therapy with cimetidine.
- If this medication makes you dizzy or drowsy, do not take part in any activity that requires alertness, such as driving an automobile or operating potentially dangerous equipment.
- Be sure to tell your doctor if you are pregnant. Cimetidine appears to be safe during pregnancy; however, extensive testing has not been conducted. Also tell your doctor if you are breast-feeding an infant. Small amounts of cimetidine pass into breast milk.

---

ciprofloxacin (systemic)

BRAND NAME (Manufacturer)
Cipro (Miles)
TYPE OF DRUG
Antibiotic
INGREDIENT
ciprofloxacin
DOSAGE FORMS
Tablets (250 mg, 500 mg, and 750 mg)
Suspension (250 mg and 500 mg per 5-mL spoonful

STORAGE

Store tablets at room temperature in a tightly closed container away from direct light. The suspension may be stored in a tightly closed container either at room temperature or in the refrigerator; do not freeze. Discard any unused portion of the suspension after 14 days because it loses potency at that point.

USES

Ciprofloxacin is an antibiotic that is used to treat a wide variety of bacterial infections. It chemically attaches to the infecting bacteria and prevents their growth and multiplication. Ciprofloxacin is not effective against viruses, parasites, or fungi.

TREATMENT

Ciprofloxacin is best taken two hours after a meal with a full glass (eight ounces) of water; however, it can be taken with or without meals. You should drink several additional glasses of water every day, unless your doctor directs you to do otherwise. Drinking extra water will help to prevent unwanted effects of ciprofloxacin.

Shake the suspension well just before measuring each dose to distribute the ingredients evenly and equalize the doses. The contents tend to settle on the bottom of the bottle. Measure each dose with a 5-mL medication spoon; an ordinary kitchen teaspoon is not accurate enough.

Ciprofloxacin works best when the level of medicine in your bloodstream is kept constant. It is best, therefore, to take the doses at evenly spaced intervals day and night. For example, if you are to take two doses a day, the doses should be spaced 12 hours apart.

It is very important that you do not miss any doses of this medication. If you do miss a dose, take it as soon as you remember. However, if you do not remember to take the missed dose until it is almost time for your next dose, skip the missed dose and go back to your regular dosing schedule. Do not double the next dose.

Ciprofloxacin therapy may be required for four to six weeks or longer, depending on the condition being treated. It is important to continue to take this drug for the entire time prescribed, even if the symptoms of infection disappear before the end of that period. If you stop taking the drug too soon, resistant bacteria are given a chance to continue growing, and your infection could recur.

SIDE EFFECTS

Minor. Diarrhea, headache, light-headedness, nausea, stomach irritation, or vomiting. These side effects should disappear as your body adjusts to the medication.

Major. Tell your doctor about any side effects that are persistent or particularly bothersome. IT IS ESPECIALLY IMPORTANT TO TELL YOUR DOCTOR about agitation, blood in your urine, change in your vision, confusion, convulsions (seizures), dizziness, hallucinations, lower back pain, muscle or joint pain, painful or difficult urination, restlessness, skin rash, tremor, unpleasant taste in the mouth, unusual bleeding or bruising, or yellowing of the eyes or skin. If the symptoms of your infection do not improve in several days, contact your doctor.

INTERACTIONS

Ciprofloxacin interacts with several other drugs:

1. Use of antacids or iron-containing vitamins with ciprofloxacin can decrease the absorption of this medicine. Do not take antacids or iron products within six hours of taking this medicine.

2. Use of sucralfate with ciprofloxacin can decrease the absorption of ciprofloxacin. Do not take a dose of sucralfate within two hours of a dose of ciprofloxacin unless directed to do so by your doctor.

3. Use of medicine containing theophylline along with ciprofloxacin can lead to increased bloodstream levels of theophylline and therefore to an increased chance of theophylline-related side effects.
4. Regular consumption of large quantities of caffeine-containing products (coffee, tea, or caffeine-containing soft drinks) with ciprofloxacin may lead to exaggerated or prolonged effects of caffeine. Your doctor may wish for you to restrict intake of caffeine during treatment.
5. Use of probenecid with ciprofloxacin can increase the bloodstream levels of ciprofloxacin and thus increase the risk of ciprofloxacin-related side effects.
6. Do not use ciprofloxacin at the same time as didanosine, digoxin, phenytoin, or warfarin. It is very important that you consult your doctor or pharmacist for advice on avoiding drug interactions if you are taking any of these medicines in addition to ciprofloxacin.
7. Calcium supplements may lead to decreased efficacy of ciprofloxacin if taken at the same time. Take ciprofloxacin two hours before or two hours after taking a calcium supplement.

Before starting to take ciprofloxacin, BE SURE TO TELL YOUR DOCTOR about any other medications that you are currently taking, especially any of the medications that are listed above.

WARNINGS

• Tell your doctor about unusual or allergic reactions you have had to any medications, especially to cinoxacin, ciprofloxacin, enoxacin, gatifloxacin, moxifloxacin, nalidixic acid, norfloxacin, ofloxacin, and sparfloxacin.
• Before starting to take this medication, be sure to tell your doctor if you now have or ever had brain or spinal cord disease, epilepsy, kidney disease, or liver disease.
• To decrease the potential for harmful effects on your kidneys, increase your intake of fluids (nonalcoholic) unless your doctor directs you to do otherwise.
• Ciprofloxacin can cause dizziness or light-headedness, so patients taking this medicine should know how they react to this medicine before they operate an automobile or machinery or engage in other activities requiring alertness or coordination.
• This medicine can make your skin more sensitive to the sun's ultraviolet rays. When you first begin taking this drug, limit sun exposure and do not use a sunlamp until you see how your skin responds to short periods of exposure to ultraviolet light. This is especially important if you tend to sunburn easily.
• Ciprofloxacin has been prescribed for your current infection only. Another infection that you experience later on, or an infection that someone else has, may require a different medicine. You should not give your medicine to other people or use it for other infections, unless your doctor specifically directs you to do so.
• Call your doctor if you experience a rash, swelling of the face, or difficulty breathing after taking ciprofloxacin.
• Be sure to tell your doctor if you are pregnant. This drug is not recommended for use in pregnant women because it can result in serious adverse effects in the developing fetus. And tell your doctor if you are breast-feeding an infant. Ciprofloxacin passes into breast milk; it is not recommended for use if you are breast-feeding.

---

citalopram

BRAND NAME
Celexa (Forest Labs/Warner Lambert)
TYPE OF DRUG
Cyclic antidepressant
INGREDIENT
citalopram

DOSAGE FORM
Tablets (10 mg, 20 mg, and 40 mg)
STORAGE
Store at room temperature in a tightly closed container. Do not store in the bathroom. Excess heat or moisture may cause this medicine to break down.

USES

Citalopram is used to treat the symptoms of mental depression. It increases the concentration of certain chemicals necessary for nerve transmission in the brain.

TREATMENT

This medication should be taken exactly as prescribed by your doctor. To avoid stomach irritation, you can take citalopram with food or with a full glass of water (unless your doctor tells you to do otherwise).

The effects of therapy with this medication may not be apparent for four weeks.

If you miss a dose, ask your doctor for instructions. However, you should not double the doses or take more than your doctor prescribes.

SIDE EFFECTS

Minor. Changes in taste, diarrhea, dizziness, drowsiness, dry mouth, increased sweating, increased yawning, insomnia, loss of appetite, muscle or joint pain, nausea, nervousness, stomach cramps, stuffy nose, vomiting, watering of the mouth, or weight gain or loss. These side effects should disappear as your body adjusts to the medication.

Dry mouth can be relieved by chewing sugarless gum or sucking on hard candy.

To avoid dizziness or light-headedness when you stand, contract and relax the muscles of your legs for a few moments before rising.

Major. Tell your doctor about any side effects that are persistent or particularly bothersome. IT IS ESPECIALLY IMPORTANT TO TELL YOUR DOCTOR about abnormal bleeding, anxiety, blurred vision, breast enlargement or tenderness (in both men and women), chills or fever, fainting, irregular heartbeat, memory loss, mood changes, painful or difficult urination, skin rash or itching, or sexual problems.

INTERACTIONS

Citalopram may interact with a number of other drugs:

1. Extreme drowsiness may occur when this medicine is taken with central nervous system depressants (alcohol, antihistamines, barbiturates, benzodiazepine tranquilizers, muscle relaxants, narcotics, pain medications, phenothiazine tranquilizers, and medications to induce sleep) or with other antidepressants.

2. Serious side effects may occur if a monoamine oxidase (MAO) inhibitor (such as furazolidone, isocarboxazid, pargyline, phenelzine, procarbazine, or tranylcypromine) is used at the same time as citalopram. Therefore, at least 14 days should separate the use of citalopram and the use of an MAO inhibitor.

3. Ketoconazole, itraconazole, fluconazole, erythromycin, cimetidine, and omeprazole may increase the amount of citalopram in the body and increase the risk of side effects.

4. Citalopram may increase the risk of side effects from other antidepressants and from some antimigraine agents, such as sumatriptan.

WARNINGS

• Tell your doctor immediately if you develop a skin rash or hives while taking this medication or if you have ever had an allergic reaction to citalopram.

• Tell your doctor if you have allergies to any substances, such as foods, sulfites, or other preservatives.

• Before starting this medication, be sure to tell your doctor if you have or ever had a heart attack, asthma, circulatory disease, difficulty in urinating, electroshock therapy, enlarged prostate gland, epilepsy, glaucoma, high blood pressure, intestinal problems, liver or kidney disease, mental illness, stomach problems, or thyroid disease.

• If this drug makes you dizzy or drowsy, do not take part in any activity that requires alertness, such as driving a car or operating potentially dangerous equipment.

• Do not stop taking this drug suddenly. Abruptly stopping it may cause nausea, headache, stomach upset, anxiety, dizziness, trembling, or worsening of your condition. Your doctor may want you to reduce the dose gradually.

• Use of alcohol while taking this medication may cause extreme drowsiness.

• The elderly may be at increased risk for side effects. Use the drug cautiously, and report any mental-status changes to your doctor immediately.

• The effects of this medication may persist for as long as seven to ten days after you stop taking it, so continue to observe all precautions during that period.

• Be sure to tell your doctor if you are pregnant. Although birth defects have not been documented in humans, in animal studies citalopram caused decreased survival rates and slowed growth in offspring. It is not known if citalopram is safe during human pregnancy. Citalopram can also pass into human breast milk, causing drowsiness, decreased feeding, and weight loss in infants. Be sure to tell your doctor if you are breast-feeding an infant, and discuss the risks and benefits of this medication.

---

clarithromycin

BRAND NAME (Manufacturer)
Biaxin (Abbott)
TYPE OF DRUG
Antibiotic
INGREDIENT
clarithromycin
DOSAGE FORMS
Tablets (250 mg and 500 mg)
Oral suspension (125 mg and 250 mg per 5-mL spoonful)
STORAGE
Store at room temperature in a tightly closed, light-resistant container. Do not refrigerate or freeze the suspension. Discard any unused suspension after 14 days because it will no longer be effective against infections.

USES

Clarithromycin is used to treat a wide variety of bacterial infections including infections of the upper and lower respiratory tracts and skin. It acts by preventing the bacteria from manufacturing protein, which prevents their growth. Clarithromycin kills susceptible bacteria, but it is not effective against viruses (such as those that cause the common cold), parasites, or fungi. This medication is also used, along with other medications, in the treatment of stomach ulcers.

TREATMENT

Clarithromycin may be taken without regard to meals. If you find that the medication upsets your stomach, it may be taken with food or milk, unless your doctor has directed you otherwise. Swallow the coated tablets whole; do not crush or chew them.

Clarithromycin works best when the level of medicine in your bloodstream is kept constant. It is best, therefore, to take the doses at evenly spaced intervals throughout the day and night. For example, if you are supposed to take two doses of the medication each day, the doses should be spaced 12 hours apart.

It is very important that you do not miss any doses of this medication. If you do miss a dose, take it as soon as you remember. However, if you do not remember to take the missed dose until it is almost time for your next dose, skip the missed dose and go back to your regular dosing schedule. Do not double the next dose.

It is important to continue to take this medication for the entire time prescribed by your doctor (usually 7 to 14 days), even if the symptoms disappear before the end of that period. If you stop taking the drug too soon, resistant bacteria are given a chance to continue growing and the infection could recur.

Shake the suspension well just before measuring each dose to distribute the ingredients evenly and equalize the doses. The contents tend to settle on the bottom of the bottle. Measure each dose carefully with a specially designed 5-mL measuring spoon or with the dropper provided with your prescription. An ordinary kitchen teaspoon is not accurate enough for therapeutic purposes.

SIDE EFFECTS

Minor. Abdominal pain/discomfort, abnormal taste, diarrhea, headache, nausea, or upset stomach. These side effects should disappear as your body adjusts to this medication.

Major. Tell your doctor about any side effects that are persistent or particularly bothersome. IT IS ESPECIALLY IMPORTANT TO TELL YOUR DOCTOR about fever, hearing loss, persistent diarrhea, rash, rectal or vaginal itching, or yellowing of the eyes or skin. If your symptoms of infection seem to be getting worse rather than improving, you should contact your doctor.

INTERACTIONS

Clarithromycin interacts with several other types of drugs:

1. Clarithromycin can decrease the elimination of the drugs carbamazepine, aminophylline, theophylline, and oxtriphylline from the body, which can lead to serious side effects. Blood levels of digoxin and of oral anticoagulants (blood thinners, such as warfarin) may also be increased by clarithromycin.

2. Clarithromycin can increase the possibility of irregular heart rate when taken with cisapride, fluconazole, or pimozide; the concurrent use of these medications should be avoided.

3. Clarithromycin can decrease the blood level and effectiveness of zidovudine. If you are taking both of these medications, you must take them at least four hours apart.

4. Clarithromycin can boost blood levels of carbamazepine (a seizure medicine) into the toxic range. Your doctor may monitor you more closely to avoid this drug interaction if you are taking both clarithromycin and carbamazepine.

5. Rifampin can decrease blood levels of clarithromycin, reducing its effectiveness.

6. While taking this medication, it is important to tell your doctor or pharmacist if you are taking bromocriptine, disopyramide, lovastatin, phenytoin, or valproate. Drug interactions may occur.

BE SURE TO TELL YOUR DOCTOR about any medications you are currently taking, especially any of those listed above.

WARNINGS

- Tell your doctor about any unusual or allergic reactions you have had to any medications, especially to clarithromycin, erythromycin, or azithromycin.
- Tell your doctor if you now have or ever had kidney disease or liver disease.
- This medication has been prescribed for your current infection only. Another infection that you experience later on, or an infection that someone else has, may require a different medication. You should not give your medicine to other people or use it for another infection, unless your doctor specifically directs you to do so.
- Before having surgery or any other medical or dental treatment, be sure to tell your doctor or dentist that you are taking clarithromycin.
- Be sure to tell your doctor if you are pregnant. The effects of using this medication during pregnancy have not been thoroughly studied in humans. Also, be sure to tell

your doctor if you are breast-feeding an infant. Clarithromycin passes into breast milk in small amounts.

• Tell your doctor about any heart problems or irregular heart rate before taking clarithromycin.

clindamycin (systemic)

BRAND NAMES (Manufacturers)
Cleocin HCl (Upjohn)
Cleocin Pediatric (Upjohn)
clindamycin (various manufacturers)
TYPE OF DRUG
Antibiotic
INGREDIENT
clindamycin palmitate hydrochloride
DOSAGE FORMS
Capsules (75 mg, 150 mg, and 300 mg)
Oral solution (75 mg per 5-mL spoonful)
STORAGE
Store the capsules and oral solution at room temperature in tightly closed containers. Do not refrigerate or freeze the solution form of this medication; when chilled, it thickens and becomes difficult to pour. Discard the solution after 14 days, because it loses potency after that time.

USES

Clindamycin is an antibiotic that is used orally to treat a wide variety of bacterial infections. It chemically attaches to the bacteria and prevents their growth and multiplication. Clindamycin kills susceptible bacteria, but it is not effective against viruses, parasites, or fungi.

TREATMENT

To prevent irritation to your esophagus (the tube connecting your mouth to your stomach) or your stomach, take clindamycin with food or with a full glass of water or milk (unless your doctor directs you to do otherwise).

Each dose of the solution form of this medication should be measured carefully with a specially designed 5-mL measuring spoon. An ordinary kitchen teaspoon is not accurate enough to ensure that the proper dose will be taken.

Clindamycin works best when the level of medicine in your bloodstream is kept constant. It is best, therefore, to take the doses at evenly spaced intervals day and night. For example, if you are to take four doses a day, the doses should be spaced six hours apart.

Try not to miss any doses of this medication. If you do miss a dose, take the missed dose as soon as you remember. However, if you do not remember to take the missed dose until it is almost time for your next dose, take the missed dose immediately; space the following dose about halfway through the regular interval between doses; then continue with your regular dosing schedule.

It is important to continue to take this medication for the entire time prescribed by your doctor (usually 7 to 14 days), even if your symptoms of infection disappear before the end of that period. If you stop taking the drug too soon, resistant bacteria are given a chance to continue growing, and your infection could recur.

SIDE EFFECTS

Minor. Diarrhea, loss of appetite, nausea, stomach or throat irritation, or vomiting. These side effects should disappear as your body adjusts to the medication. If the di-

arrhea becomes prolonged, CONTACT YOUR DOCTOR. Do not take any antidiarrheal medications.
Major. Tell your doctor about any side effects that are persistent or particularly bothersome. IT IS ESPECIALLY IMPORTANT TO TELL YOUR DOCTOR about bloody or pus-containing diarrhea, hives, itching, muscle or joint pain, skin rash, unusual bleeding or bruising, or yellowing of the eyes or skin. If the symptoms of your infection do not improve in several days, contact your doctor. This medication may not be effective for your particular infection.

INTERACTIONS

Clindamycin may interact with other medications.

Chloramphenicol and erythromycins may interfere with the actions of clindamycin.

BE SURE TO TELL YOUR DOCTOR about these or any medications you are currently taking.

WARNINGS

• Tell your doctor about any unusual or allergic reactions you have had to any medications, especially to clindamycin or lincomycin.
• Before starting this medication, tell your doctor if you now have or ever had colitis, kidney disease, or liver disease.
• Before having surgery or any other medical or dental treatment, be sure to tell your doctor or dentist you are taking clindamycin.
• The 75 mg and 150 mg capsules of this medication contain the color additive FD&C Yellow No. 5 (tartrazine), which can cause allergic-type symptoms (fainting, shortness of breath, rash) in certain susceptible individuals.
• Clindamycin has been prescribed for your current infection only. Another infection later on may require a different medicine. You should not give your medicine to other people or use it for other infections unless your doctor specifically directs you to do so
• Be sure to tell your doctor if you are pregnant. Although clindamycin appears to be safe during pregnancy, extensive studies in humans have not been conducted. Also tell your doctor if you are breast-feeding an infant. Small amounts of clindamycin pass into breast milk.

---

clindamycin (topical)

BRAND NAME (Manufacturer)
Cleocin T (Upjohn)
TYPE OF DRUG
Antibiotic
INGREDIENT
clindamycin phosphate
DOSAGE FORMS
Topical gel (1%)
Topical solution (1%)
Topical lotion (1%)
STORAGE
Store this medication at room temperature in a tightly closed container. Keep the solution and lotion forms away from flames and heat because they are flammable (they contain alcohol).

USES

Clindamycin topical solution is used to treat acne vulgaris. It is an antibiotic that is thought to act by suppressing the growth of certain bacteria that may be responsible for the formation of the acne sores.

TREATMENT

Before applying topical clindamycin, wash the affected area thoroughly with a mild soap and warm water. Then rinse well and pat dry. To avoid skin irritation from the alcohol, wait at least 30 minutes after washing or shaving before applying the solution or lotion.

The solution is packaged in a bottle with an applicator tip that can be used to apply the solution directly to the skin. Press the applicator tip firmly against your skin. The pressure applied determines the amount of medicine that will be released. Use the applicator with a dabbing motion rather than a rolling motion.

Before using the topical lotion, shake the container well.

A thin film of medication should be applied to the entire area of skin affected by acne.

Topical clindamycin does not cure acne, but it will help to control the condition as long as you continue to use the medication.

If you miss a dose of this medication, apply it as soon as possible. However, if it is almost time for the next dose, do not apply the missed dose at all; just return to your regular dosing schedule.

It is important to continue to apply this medication for the entire time prescribed by your doctor (which may be several months), even if your symptoms disappear in several days. If you stop applying the medication too soon, the bacteria are given a chance to continue growing, and your infection could recur.

If there is no improvement in your condition after six weeks of using this medication, check with your doctor. However, it may take up to 12 weeks before improvement in your acne is readily apparent.

SIDE EFFECTS

Minor. You may experience diarrhea, dry skin, fatigue, headache, nausea, oily skin, or stomach irritation. These minor side effects should disappear as your body adjusts to the medication.

If diarrhea becomes severe or prolonged, CONTACT YOUR DOCTOR. Do not take any antidiarrheal medicine.

Major. Tell your doctor about any side effects that are persistent or particularly bothersome. IT IS ESPECIALLY IMPORTANT TO TELL YOUR DOCTOR about diarrhea that is bloody or that contains pus, increased urination, itching, sore throat, or swelling of the face.

INTERACTIONS

If you are using another topical medication as well as clindamycin, apply them at different times to increase effectiveness and reduce the chance of skin irritation.

Use of abrasive or medicated cleansers, medicated cosmetics, or any topical, alcohol-containing preparations (such as aftershave lotions or perfume) in conjunction with topical clindamycin can result in excessive skin dryness and irritation.

WARNINGS

- Tell your doctor about unusual or allergic reactions you have had to any drugs, especially to clindamycin or lincomycin.
- Tell your doctor if you have ever had colitis.
- Because this medication contains alcohol, it can cause skin irritation in sensitive areas. In addition, it has an unpleasant taste if it gets on the mouth or lips. You should avoid getting this medication in your eyes, nose, or mouth or in the areas surrounding scratches or burns.
- You may continue to use cosmetics while applying this medication (unless otherwise directed by your doctor), but it is best to use only water-based cosmetics rather than ones with an oil base.

• Be sure to tell your doctor if you are pregnant. Although topical clindamycin appears safe when used during pregnancy, extensive studies in humans have not been conducted. Also tell your doctor if you are breast-feeding an infant. It is not known whether this drug passes into breast milk.

---

clomiphene

BRAND NAMES (Manufacturers)
clomiphene (various manufacturers)
Clomid (Aventis)
Serophene (Serono)
TYPE OF DRUG
Fertility drug
INGREDIENT
clomiphene
DOSAGE FORM
Tablets (50 mg)
STORAGE
Store this medication at room temperature in a tightly closed, light-resistant container and well out of the reach of children and pets.

USES

Clomiphene is used to treat infertility, primarily in women. This drug reverses some types of infertility in women by stimulating ovulation.

TREATMENT

Clomiphene can be taken either on an empty stomach or with food or milk, as directed by your doctor.

It is very important to follow your dosing schedule carefully. If you have any questions about taking this medication, BE SURE TO CHECK WITH YOUR DOCTOR.

If you miss a dose of this medication, take the missed dose as soon as possible. If you do not remember to take this medication until it is time for the next dose, it is okay to double that next dose and then return to your regular dosing schedule. If you miss more than one dose, CHECK WITH YOUR DOCTOR.

SIDE EFFECTS

Minor. Abdominal discomfort, bloating, dizziness, headache, insomnia, nausea, nervousness, or vomiting. These side effects should disappear over time as your body adjusts to the medication.

If you feel dizzy, sit or lie down for a while; get up slowly from a sitting or reclining position; and be careful on stairs.

Major. Tell your doctor about any side effects that are persistent or particularly bothersome. IT IS ESPECIALLY IMPORTANT TO TELL YOUR DOCTOR about breast tenderness, depression, fatigue, hair loss, hot flashes, pelvic pain, skin rash, or visual disturbances.

INTERACTIONS

Clomiphene should not interact with other medications if it is taken according to the directions for use.

WARNINGS

• Tell your doctor about unusual or allergic reactions you have had to any medications, especially to clomiphene.

• Before beginning treatment with clomiphene, tell your doctor if you now have or ever had any of the following symptoms: abnormal vaginal bleeding, clotting problems, tumors or cysts of the uterus or ovaries, liver disease, or mental depression.
• If clomiphene makes you dizzy, do not take part in any activity that requires alertness, such as driving a car or operating potentially dangerous equipment, and take care going up and down stairs.
• While taking this medication, it is important to carefully follow your doctor's directions for recording your body temperature and for timing sexual intercourse.
• The risk of a multiple pregnancy is increased when clomiphene is used. This medication should not be taken if you are already pregnant. If you should become pregnant during treatment with clomiphene, tell your doctor immediately and, unless directed to do otherwise, discontinue the medication at once. It has been reported to cause birth defects in the offspring of animals that received large doses of clomiphene during pregnancy. Also tell your doctor if you are breast-feeding an infant. It is not known whether clomiphene passes into breast milk.

---

clonazepam

BRAND NAME (Manufacturer)
Klonopin (Roche)
TYPE OF DRUG
Benzodiazepine anticonvulsant
INGREDIENT
clonazepam
DOSAGE FORM
Tablets (0.5 mg, 1 mg, and 2 mg)
STORAGE
Store at room temperature in a tightly closed, light-resistant container.

USES

This medication is used to treat certain seizure disorders and other mental disorders, including panic disorders, bipolar disorder (manic-depressive disorder), and schizophrenia. It has also been used to treat periodic leg movements during sleep. It is unclear exactly how clonazepam works to treat convulsions, but it appears that this drug prevents the spread of seizures to all parts of the brain.

TREATMENT

This medication can be taken either on an empty stomach or with food or milk. Follow your doctor's directions.

Clonazepam works best when the level of medicine in your bloodstream is kept constant. It is best, therefore, to take the doses at evenly spaced intervals day and night. For example, if you are to take three doses a day, the doses should be spaced eight hours apart.

Try not to miss any doses of this medication. If you do miss a dose and remember within an hour, take the missed dose immediately. If more than an hour has passed, however, do not take the missed dose at all; just return to your regular dosing schedule. Do not double the next dose. If you miss two or more doses, be sure to CONTACT YOUR DOCTOR.

SIDE EFFECTS

Minor. Constipation, diarrhea, drowsiness, dry mouth, headache, increased appetite, insomnia, loss of appetite, nausea, runny nose, or weight loss or gain. These side effects should disappear as your body adjusts to the medication.

To relieve constipation, increase the amount of fiber in your diet (fresh fruits and vegetables, salads, bran, and whole-grain breads), exercise, and drink more water (unless your doctor directs you to do otherwise).

To relieve mouth dryness, chew sugarless gum or suck on ice chips or a piece of hard candy.

Major. Tell your doctor about any side effects that are persistent or particularly bothersome. IT IS ESPECIALLY IMPORTANT TO TELL YOUR DOCTOR about behavioral problems, confusion, depression, fever, fluid retention, hair loss, hallucinations, hysteria, increased or decreased urination, muscle weakness, palpitations, skin rash, slurred speech, sore gums, tremors, unusual bleeding or bruising, unusual body movements, or yellowing of the eyes or skin.

Clonazepam can also produce an increase in salivation, so it should be used cautiously by people who have swallowing difficulties. Contact your doctor if a change in the level of salivation becomes a problem.

INTERACTIONS

Clonazepam interacts with several other types of drugs:

1. Concurrent use of it with other central nervous system depressants (such as alcohol, antihistamines, barbiturates, benzodiazepine tranquilizers, muscle relaxants, narcotics, pain medications, phenothiazine tranquilizers, and sleeping medications) or with tricyclic antidepressants can cause extreme drowsiness.

2. Phenobarbital and phenytoin can decrease the blood levels and effectiveness of clonazepam.

3. Concurrent use of clonazepam and valproic acid can lead to increased seizure activity.

4. Cimetidine and estrogen-containing drugs, such as oral contraceptives, may increase the blood levels of clonazepam.

Before you begin treatment with this medication, BE SURE TO TELL YOUR DOCTOR about any medications that you are currently taking, especially any of the medications that are listed above.

WARNINGS

• Notify your doctor about any unusual or allergic reactions you have had to any medications, especially to clonazepam or to other benzodiazepine tranquilizers (such as alprazolam, chlordiazepoxide, clorazepate, diazepam, flurazepam, halazepam, lorazepam, oxazepam, prazepam, temazepam, or triazolam).

• Tell your doctor if you now have or ever had glaucoma, kidney disease, liver disease, or lung disease.

• If this drug makes you dizzy or drowsy, do not take part in any activity that requires alertness, such as driving a car or operating potentially dangerous equipment. Children should be careful while playing.

• Do not abruptly stop taking this medication unless you first check with your doctor. If you have been taking this medication for several months or longer, suddenly stopping the medication could lead to a withdrawal reaction as well as a worsening of your condition. Your doctor may, therefore, want to reduce your dosage of this medication gradually.

• Be sure to tell your doctor if you are pregnant. Although no harmful effects have been reported from clonazepam use during pregnancy, extensive studies have not been conducted. The risks and benefits of clonazepam therapy during pregnancy should be discussed with your doctor. Also tell your doctor if you are breast-feeding an infant. Small amounts of clonazepam pass into breast milk and may cause excessive drowsiness in nursing infants.

clonidine

BRAND NAMES (Manufacturers)
Catapres (Boehringer Ingelheim)
Catapres-TTS (Boehringer Ingelheim)
clonidine hydrochloride (various manufacturers)
TYPE OF DRUG
Antihypertensive
INGREDIENT
clonidine hydrochloride
DOSAGE FORMS
Tablets (0.1 mg, 0.2 mg, and 0.3 mg)
Transdermal patch (2.5 mg, 5 mg, and 7.5 mg per patch; release rate of clonidine is 0.1 mg, 0.2 mg, and 0.3 mg per 24 hours, respectively)
STORAGE
Store tablets at room temperature in a tightly closed container. Do not remove a patch from its packaging until just before you apply it.

USES

This medication works on the central nervous system (brain and spinal cord) to prevent the release of chemicals that are responsible for maintaining high blood pressure. It has also been used to prevent hot flashes in women who are going through menopause and to help addicted patients during narcotic and nicotine withdrawal. This medication has also been used for many other conditions, including attention deficit hyperactivity disorder, ulcerative colitis, and restless legs syndrome.

TREATMENT

To avoid stomach irritation, take clonidine tablets with food or with a full glass of milk or water. To become accustomed to taking this medication, try to take it at the same time(s) every day.

Clonidine transdermal patches come with detailed patient instructions that should be carefully followed. Apply the patch to a hairless area of unbroken skin on the upper arm or chest. If the patch becomes loose before it is time to remove it (after seven days), apply adhesive tape over the patch to ensure good adhesion. To avoid skin irritation, apply each new patch to a different site on the skin. Do not cut the patch before applying, and be sure to keep the patch on your skin when showering, bathing, or swimming.

If you miss a dose of clonidine tablets, take the missed dose as soon as possible. However, if it is almost time for your next dose, do not take the missed dose at all; just return to your regular dosing schedule. Do not double the next dose. If you miss more than two doses of this medication, contact your doctor.

If you forget to remove the clonidine transdermal patch after seven days, remove the old patch and apply a new one immediately to a different site.

Clonidine does not cure high blood pressure, but it will help control the condition as long as you continue to use it.

SIDE EFFECTS

Minor. Anxiety, constipation, decreased sexual desire, dizziness, drowsiness, dry eyes, dry mouth, fatigue, headache, insomnia, jaw pain, loss of appetite, nasal congestion, nausea, nervousness, or vomiting. These side effects should disappear as your body adjusts to the medication.

The patches can also cause burning, inflammation, itching, rash, or increased or decreased pigmentation of the skin at the site of application. Be sure to TELL YOUR DOCTOR if the skin reactions persist or become bothersome.

To prevent constipation while taking this medication, increase the amount of fiber in your diet (fresh fruits and vegetables, salads, bran, and whole-grain breads), unless your doctor tells you not to do so.

To help relieve mouth dryness, suck on ice chips or a piece of hard candy or chew sugarless gum.

Eyedrops called "artificial tears," which are available without a prescription, may help relieve eye dryness.

To avoid dizziness or light-headedness when you stand, contract and relax the muscles of your legs for a few moments before rising. Do this by pushing one foot against the floor while raising the other foot slightly, alternating feet so that you are "pumping" your legs in a pedaling motion.

Major. Tell your doctor about any side effects that are persistent or particularly bothersome. IT IS ESPECIALLY IMPORTANT TO TELL YOUR DOCTOR about chest pain; cold fingertips or toes; depression; difficulty in breathing; difficulty in urinating; enlarged, painful breasts (in both sexes); hair loss; hives; impotence; itching; nightmares; rash; swelling of the hands or feet; weight gain; or yellowing of the eyes or skin.

INTERACTIONS

Clonidine interacts with several other types of medications:

1. Concurrent use of clonidine with other central nervous system depressants (such as alcohol, antihistamines, barbiturates, benzodiazepine tranquilizers, muscle relaxants, narcotics, pain medications, phenothiazine tranquilizers, and sleeping medications) or with tricyclic antidepressants can cause extreme drowsiness.

2. Concurrent use of tricyclic antidepressants, nonsteroidal anti-inflammatory agents such as indomethacin, some appetite suppressants, or prazosin may block the blood-pressure-lowering effects of clonidine.

3. The concurrent use of other antihypertensive agents with clonidine may cause blood pressure to be too low.

4. The effectiveness of the drug levodopa may be reduced if taken concurrently with clonidine.

5. Avoid the concurrent use of beta blockers and clonidine. These drugs antagonize (work against) each other. Also, dangerously high blood pressure may result if clonidine is stopped during treatment with a beta blocker.

Before you start to take this medication, BE SURE TO TELL YOUR DOCTOR about any medications you are currently taking, especially any of the medications that are listed above.

WARNINGS

• Tell your doctor about any unusual or allergic reactions you have had to medications, especially to clonidine.

• Tell your doctor if you have or have ever had heart disease, kidney disease, depression, Raynaud's disease, or a heart attack or stroke.

• Before having surgery or any other medical or dental treatment, be sure to tell your doctor or dentist that you are taking this medication.

• Do not take any over-the-counter (nonprescription) medications for weight control or for allergy, asthma, sinus problems, cough, or the common cold unless you first check with your doctor.

• If this drug makes you dizzy or drowsy, do not take part in any activity that requires alertness, such as driving a car or operating potentially dangerous equipment.

• Tolerance to this medication develops occasionally; consult your doctor if you feel that the drug is becoming less effective.

• Do not stop taking this medication without first consulting your doctor. If therapy with this drug is stopped abruptly, you may experience nervousness, agitation, headache, and a rise in blood pressure. Your doctor may therefore want to reduce your dosage of the drug gradually or start you on another medication immediately.

• Make sure you have enough medication on hand to last through weekends, vacations, and holidays.
• Drinking alcoholic beverages, standing for prolonged periods, exercising, and hot weather can each increase the blood-pressure-lowering effects of clonidine and can cause fainting or dizziness.
• Be sure to tell your doctor if you are pregnant. Although clonidine appears to be safe in animal pregnancy, extensive studies in humans during pregnancy have not been conducted. Also tell your doctor if you are breast-feeding an infant. Small amounts of clonidine pass into breast milk.

---

clopidogrel

BRAND NAME (Manufacturer)
Plavix (Sanofi)
TYPE OF DRUG
Antiplatelet agent
INGREDIENT
clopidogrel
DOSAGE FORM
Tablets (75 mg)
STORAGE
Store at room temperature in a tightly closed container. Do not store in the bathroom. Excess heat or moisture may cause this medicine to break down.

USES

Clopidogrel is used to decrease the risk of having a heart attack or stoke. It works by preventing red blood cells (platelets) from sticking or adhering to each other.

TREATMENT

This medication should be taken exactly as prescribed by your doctor. Using more than your doctor prescribed may increase the chance of bleeding or other side effects. To avoid stomach irritation, you can take clopidogrel with food or with a full glass of water (unless your doctor tells you to do otherwise).

If you miss a dose, take the missed dose as soon as possible. However, if it is almost time for the next dose, do not take the missed dose at all. Just return to your regular dosing schedule. Do not double the doses.

SIDE EFFECTS

Minor. Constipation, diarrhea, dizziness, headache, heartburn, itching, joint or back pain, leg cramps, muscle aches and fever, skin rash, stomach pain, tiredness. These side effects should disappear as your body adjusts to the medication.

To relieve constipation, increase the amount of fiber (fresh fruits and vegetables, salads, bran, and whole-grain breads) in your diet, exercise, and drink more water (unless your doctor directs you to do otherwise).

If this medication makes you dizzy, sit or lie down for a while; rise slowly from a sitting or reclining position; and use caution on stairs.

To avoid dizziness or light-headedness when you stand, contract and relax the muscles of your legs for a few moments before rising. Do this by pushing one foot against the floor while raising the other foot slightly, alternating feet so that you are "pumping" your legs in a pedaling motion.

Major. Tell your doctor about any side effects that are persistent or particularly bothersome. IT IS ESPECIALLY IMPORTANT TO TELL YOUR DOCTOR about black, tarry stools; blood in the urine or stool; chest pain; irregular heartbeats; purple or red spots on the skin; severe stomach pain; signs of infection (fever, chills, sore throat, or white spots in the mouth); sudden or severe headaches; unusual bleeding or bruising; or vomiting of blood or material that looks like coffee grounds.

INTERACTIONS

Clopidogrel may interact with a number of other drugs:

1. Aspirin or nonsteroidal anti-inflammatory agents (such as ibuprofen) may increase the risk of bleeding associated with clopidogrel.

2. Clopidogrel may increase the side effects of fluvastatin, phenytoin, tamoxifen, tolbutamide, or torsemide.

3. The concurrent use of warfarin (a blood thinner) and clopidogrel may increase the risk of bleeding.

WARNINGS

• Tell your doctor if you have ever had an allergic reaction to clopidogrel or to any other medication.

• Before starting this medication, be sure to tell your doctor if you have or ever had any major medical problems, especially bleeding problems, stomach or ulcer problems, or liver problems.

• Tell your doctor immediately if you notice any unusual bleeding while taking clopidogrel, including bleeding from the gums, nosebleeds, blood in the urine or stool, or vomiting of blood or material that looks like coffee grounds.

• Because of the risk of bleeding, be sure to tell your doctor or dentist that you are taking this medication before having any medical, dental, or surgical procedure. Your doctor may want you to stop taking this medication several days before surgery or dental procedures.

• Be sure to tell your doctor if you are pregnant. Although birth defects have not been documented in animals, it is unknown if clopidogrel is safe during human pregnancy. In addition, be sure to tell your doctor if you are breast-feeding an infant. It is not known if clopidogrel passes into human breast milk. Be sure to discuss the risks and benefits of using this medication while breast-feeding.

• If this medication makes you dizzy or drowsy, do not participate in any activity that requires alertness, such as driving an automobile or operating potentially dangerous equipment.

---

clotrimazole (topical)

BRAND NAMES (Manufacturers)
Lotrimin (Schering-Plough)
Lotrimin AF* (Schering-Plough)
Mycelex (Bayer)
Mycelex OTC* (Bayer)
*Available without a prescription in 1% cream, lotion, and solution.

TYPE OF DRUG
Antifungal

INGREDIENT
clotrimazole

DOSAGE FORMS
Topical cream (1%)
Topical lotion (1%)
Topical solution (1%)

STORAGE
Store at room temperature in tightly closed containers. This medication should never be frozen.

USES

This medication is used to treat superficial fungal infections of the skin. Clotrimazole is an antifungal medication that is active against a broad range of fungi and yeasts. The medication acts by preventing the growth and multiplication of these infecting organisms.

TREATMENT

Apply this medication in the morning and evening, unless your doctor directs you to do otherwise. Before applying clotrimazole, you should wash your hands. Then (unless otherwise directed) cleanse the affected area with soap and water. Pat the skin with a clean towel until it is almost dry. Gently massage a small amount of the cream, solution, or lotion over the entire area that is affected and the skin immediately surrounding this area. Do not bandage or cover the infected area after applying the medication unless your doctor instructs you to do so. Wash your hands again after you have finished applying the medication.

Improvement in your condition may not become apparent for as much as a week after you begin treatment with this drug. However, you should be sure to complete the full course of therapy. If you stop using this drug too soon, resistant fungi are given a chance to continue growing, and the infection could recur. If your condition has not improved after four weeks of treatment with this medication, however, CONTACT YOUR DOCTOR. Clotrimazole may not be effective against the organism that is causing your infection.

If you miss a dose of this medication, apply the missed dose as soon as possible. However, if it is almost time for the next dose, do not apply the missed dose at all; just return to your regular dosing schedule. Do not use a double dose of the medication at the next application.

SIDE EFFECTS

Minor. You may experience some burning, itching, stinging, or redness when this drug is applied to the skin. These side effects should disappear as your body adjusts to the medication.

Major. Tell your doctor about any side effects that are persistent or particularly bothersome. IT IS ESPECIALLY IMPORTANT TO TELL YOUR DOCTOR about blistering, irritation, peeling of the skin, or swelling.

INTERACTIONS

Clotrimazole should not interact with other medications as long as it is used according to directions.

WARNINGS

- Tell your doctor about any unusual or allergic reactions you have had to any medications, especially to clotrimazole.
- Clotrimazole should not be used in or around the eyes.
- This medication has been prescribed for your current infection only. Another infection may require a different medication. Therefore, you should not give your medicine to other people or use it for other infections, unless your doctor specifically directs you to do so.
- In order to avoid reinfection, keep the affected area clean and dry, wear freshly laundered clothes and undergarments, and avoid wearing anything tight-fitting.
- Be sure to tell your doctor if you are pregnant. Small amounts of clotrimazole may be absorbed through the skin. It should, therefore, be used cautiously, especially during the first three months of pregnancy. Also tell your doctor if you are breast-feeding an infant. It is not known whether clotrimazole passes into breast milk.

clotrimazole (vaginal)

BRAND NAMES (Manufacturers)
Femcare (Schering-Plough)*
Gyne-Lotrimin 3 (Schering-Plough)*
Gyne-Lotrimin 7 (Schering-Plough)*
Mycelex-G (Bayer)
Mycelex-7 (Bayer)*
*Available OTC in 1% cream or 100-mg, 200-mg, and 500-mg tablets.

TYPE OF DRUG
Antifungal

INGREDIENT
clotrimazole

DOSAGE FORMS
Vaginal cream (1%)
Vaginal tablets (100 mg, 200 mg, and 500 mg)

STORAGE
Store at room temperature in a tightly closed container. This medication should never be frozen.

USES

This medication is used to treat fungal infections of the vagina. Clotrimazole is an antifungal agent that prevents the growth and multiplication of a wide range of fungi and yeast, including Candida.

TREATMENT

Clotrimazole vaginal cream and tablets are packaged with detailed directions for use. Be sure to follow these instructions carefully. An applicator will probably be provided for inserting the cream or tablets into the vagina. Use this medication at bedtime, unless otherwise directed by your doctor.

Wash the area carefully before inserting the cream or tablet into the vagina.

If you begin to menstruate while being treated with clotrimazole, continue your regular dosing schedule.

If you miss a dose of this medication, insert the missed dose as soon as possible. However, if you do not remember until the following day, do not insert the missed dose at all; just return to your regular dosing schedule. Do not use a double dose of the medication at the next application.

It is important to continue to insert this medication for the entire time prescribed by your doctor (or if you are using the over-the-counter product, the entire time specified in the package directions)—even if your symptoms disappear before the end of that time. If you stop using the drug too soon, resistant fungus could be given a chance to continue growing, and it is possible that your infection could recur.

Contact your doctor if your symptoms of infection do not improve within three days of treatment or if symptoms have not been relieved after seven days of treatment.

SIDE EFFECTS

Minor. You may experience vaginal burning, itching, or irritation when this drug is inserted. This sensation should diminish or disappear as your body adjusts to the medication.

Do not treat any side effects that occur in the area of the infection unless you first consult your doctor.

Major. Tell your doctor about any side effects that are persistent or particularly bothersome. IT IS ESPECIALLY IMPORTANT TO TELL YOUR DOCTOR about abdominal cramps, blistering, bloating, excessive irritation in the vaginal area, painful urination, or peeling of the skin.

INTERACTIONS

Clotrimazole should not interact with any other medications if it is used according to directions.

WARNINGS

• Tell your doctor about any unusual or allergic reactions you have had to any medications, especially any reactions to clotrimazole.
• Tell your doctor if you have had other vaginal infections, especially if they have been resistant to treatment.
• To prevent reinfection, avoid sexual intercourse or ask your partner to use a condom until treatment is completed.
• There may be some vaginal drainage while using this medication; you may want to use a sanitary napkin or panty liner to prevent the staining of clothing. However, the use of tampons is not recommended since they may soak up too much of the medicine.
• Whenever possible, wear cotton panties rather than those made of nylon or other nonporous materials while being treated for a vaginal fungus infection. In order to better prevent reinfection, remember to always wear freshly laundered underclothes.
• If there is no improvement in your condition, or if irritation in the area continues after several days of treatment, CONTACT YOUR DOCTOR. This medication may be causing an allergic reaction, or it may not be effective against the organism causing your infection.
• The prescription form has been prescribed for your current infection only. Another infection that develops later on, or one that someone else has, may require a different medication. Therefore, you should not give your medication to other women or use it for other infections unless your doctor specifically directs you to do so.
• Tell your doctor if you are pregnant. Clotrimazole appears to be safe during pregnancy. However, extensive studies have not been conducted. In addition, your doctor may want to change the instructions on how you are to use this drug if you are pregnant. Also tell your doctor if you are breast-feeding an infant. It is not known whether this medication passes into breast milk.

---

clozapine

BRAND NAMES (Manufacturers)
clozapine (various manufacturers)
Clozaril (Novartis)
TYPE OF DRUG
Antipsychotic
INGREDIENT
clozapine
DOSAGE FORM
Tablets (25 mg and 100 mg)
STORAGE
Store at room temperature in the unit-dose packages provided by the manufacturer or in the original prescription vial.

USES

Clozapine is prescribed for the treatment of schizophrenia in patients who have not been helped by or could not tolerate other medications. The blood of patients taking this medication may be monitored weekly to prevent side effects that might affect their blood system.

TREATMENT

To avoid stomach irritation, take this medication with a meal or a glass of water or milk (unless your doctor directs you to do otherwise).

If you miss a dose of this medication, take the missed dose as soon as possible, then return to your regular dosing schedule. However, if it is almost time for the next dose, skip the one you missed and return to your regular schedule. Do not double the next dose of this medication (unless your doctor directs you to do so).

The full effects of this medication for the control of emotional or mental symptoms may not become apparent for two weeks after you start to take it.

SIDE EFFECTS

Minor. Abdominal discomfort, constipation, dizziness, drowsiness, dry mouth, headache, heartburn, increased saliva production, light-headedness, nausea, vomiting, or weight gain. As your body adjusts to the medication, these side effects should disappear.

If you are constipated, increase the amount of fiber in your diet (fresh fruits and vegetables, salads, bran, and whole-grain breads). You can also increase your exercise and drink more water (unless your doctor directs you to do otherwise).

Chew sugarless gum or suck on ice chips or a piece of hard candy to reduce mouth dryness.

To avoid dizziness or light-headedness when you stand, contract and relax the muscles of your legs for a few moments before rising. Do this by pushing one foot against the floor while raising the other foot slightly, alternating feet so that you are "pumping" your legs in a pedaling motion.

Major. Tell your doctor about any side effects that are persistent or particularly bothersome. IT IS ESPECIALLY IMPORTANT TO TELL YOUR DOCTOR about anxiety, blurred vision, chest pain, chills, confusion, convulsions, difficulty in urinating, fainting, fever, increased sweating, loss of bladder control, mouth sores, muscle stiffness, nightmares, rapid heart rate, rash, restlessness, severe headache, sore throat, tremor, trouble sleeping, or unusual bleeding or bruising.

INTERACTIONS

Clozapine antipsychotic medication interacts with several other types of medications:

1. This drug can cause extreme drowsiness when combined with alcohol or other central nervous system depressants, such as barbiturates, benzodiazepine tranquilizers, muscle relaxants, phenothiazine tranquilizers, narcotics, and pain medications, or with tricyclic antidepressants.

2. Lithium, cimetidine, and erythromycin may increase the side effects of this drug.

3. The effect of clozapine on blood cells may be increased by other drugs, such as antineoplastics (cancer medicine), antithyroid drugs, azathioprine, chloramphenicol, colchicine, flucytosine, interferon, and zidovudine.

4. The side effects of digoxin, phenytoin, and warfarin may be increased by this medication.

5. Certain antidepressants, such as fluvoxamine, fluoxetine, paroxetine, or sertraline may increase the side effects of clozapine.

Before starting to take clozapine, BE SURE TO TELL YOUR DOCTOR about any other medications you are currently taking, especially if they include any of those listed above.

WARNINGS

• Be sure to tell your doctor about unusual or allergic reactions you have had to any medications, especially clozapine.

• Tell your doctor if you have a history of alcoholism or if you now have or ever had blood disease, depression, enlarged prostate, gastrointestinal problems, glaucoma, heart or circulatory disease, liver disease, or seizures.

• To avoid oversedation, avoid drinking alcoholic beverages while taking this medication.
• If this medication makes you dizzy or drowsy, do not take part in any activity that requires alertness, such as driving an automobile or operating potentially dangerous equipment. Be careful when using stairs, and avoid getting up suddenly from a lying or sitting position.
• Do not stop taking this medication suddenly. Your doctor may want to gradually reduce the amount you are taking before stopping the drug. Be sure to consult your doctor before stopping this medication.
• It is very important that you have your blood tested weekly and that you have your doctor check your progress regularly. The results of your blood tests will assist your doctor in making safe dosage adjustments for you.
• Be sure to tell your doctor if you are pregnant. Although clozapine appears to be safe when used during animal pregnancy, extensive studies in human pregnancy have not been conducted. It is also very important that you tell your doctor if you are breast-feeding an infant. Small amounts of this medication pass into breast milk and may cause problems in the nursing infant.

---

codeine

BRAND NAMES (Manufacturers)
codeine phosphate (various manufacturers)
codeine sulfate (various manufacturers)
TYPE OF DRUG
Analgesic and cough suppressant
INGREDIENT
codeine
DOSAGE FORMS
Tablets (15 mg, 30 mg, and 60 mg)
Oral solution (15 mg per 5-mL spoonful)
STORAGE
Store at room temperature in a tightly closed, light-resistant container.

USES

Codeine is a narcotic analgesic that acts directly on the central nervous system (brain and spinal cord). It is used to relieve mild to moderate pain or to suppress coughing. It is also used to stop diarrhea.

TREATMENT

To avoid stomach upset, take codeine with food or milk.

This drug works best if you take it at the onset of pain, rather than waiting until the pain has already become intense.

Measure each dose of the solution carefully with a specially designed 5-mL measuring spoon. An ordinary kitchen teaspoon is not accurate enough.

If you are taking this medication on a regular schedule and miss a dose, take the missed dose as soon as possible. However, if it is almost time for your next dose, do not take the missed dose at all; just return to your regular dosing schedule. Do not double the next dose.

SIDE EFFECTS

Minor. Constipation, dizziness, drowsiness, dry mouth, false sense of well-being, flushing, light-headedness, loss of appetite, nausea, painful or difficult urination, or unusual sweating. These side effects should disappear as your body adjusts to the medication.

If you are constipated, increase the amount of fiber in your diet (fresh fruits and vegetables, salads, bran, and whole-grain breads), exercise, and drink more water (unless your doctor directs you to do otherwise).

Chew sugarless gum or suck on ice chips or hard candy to reduce mouth dryness.

If you feel dizzy, light-headed, or nauseated, sit or lie down for a while; get up from a sitting or lying position slowly; and be careful on stairs.

Major. Tell your doctor about any side effects that are persistent or particularly bothersome. IT IS ESPECIALLY IMPORTANT TO TELL YOUR DOCTOR about anxiety, breathing difficulties, excitation, fatigue, heart palpitations, rash, restlessness, sore throat and fever, tremors, or weakness.

INTERACTIONS

Codeine interacts with several other types of medications:

1. Concurrent use of this medication with other central nervous system depressants (such as alcohol, antihistamines, barbiturates, benzodiazepine tranquilizers, muscle relaxants, and phenothiazine tranquilizers) or with tricyclic antidepressants can cause extreme drowsiness.

2. A monoamine oxidase (MAO) inhibitor taken within 14 days of this medication can lead to unpredictable and severe side effects.

3. Cimetidine, combined with this medication, can cause confusion, disorientation, and shortness of breath.

4. Naloxone and naltrexone may reverse the effects of codeine and cause withdrawal symptoms in patients dependent on or taking high doses of codeine.

BE SURE TO TELL YOUR DOCTOR about any medications you are currently taking, especially any of those mentioned above.

WARNINGS

- Tell your doctor about unusual or allergic reactions you have had to medications, especially to codeine or to any other narcotic analgesics (such as hydrocodone, hydromorphone, meperidine, methadone, morphine, oxycodone, and propoxyphene).
- Tell your doctor if you now have or ever had acute abdominal conditions, asthma, brain disease, colitis, epilepsy, gallstones or gallbladder disease, head injuries, heart disease, kidney disease, liver disease, lung disease, mental illness, emotional disorders, prostate disease, thyroid disease, or urethral stricture.
- If this drug makes you dizzy or drowsy or blurs your vision, do not take part in any activity that requires mental alertness, such as driving a car, working with hazardous material, or operating potentially dangerous tools, equipment, or machinery.
- Before undergoing surgery or any other medical or dental treatment, tell your doctor or dentist you are taking this drug.
- Because this product contains codeine, it has the potential for abuse and must be used with caution. Usually, it should not be taken on a regular schedule for longer than ten days (unless your doctor directs you to do so). Tolerance develops quickly; do not increase the dosage or stop taking the drug abruptly unless you first consult your doctor. If you have been taking large amounts of this medication for long periods, you may experience a withdrawal reaction (muscle aches, diarrhea, gooseflesh, runny nose, nausea, vomiting, shivering, trembling, stomach cramps, sleep disorders, irritability, weakness, excessive yawning, or sweating) when you stop taking it. Your doctor may want to reduce the dosage gradually.
- Be sure to tell your doctor if you are pregnant. The effects of this medication during the early stages of pregnancy have not been thoroughly studied in humans. However, codeine, used regularly in large doses during the later stages of pregnancy, can result in addiction of the fetus, leading to withdrawal symptoms (irritability, excessive crying, tremors, fever, vomiting, diarrhea, sneezing, or excessive yawning) at birth. Also tell your doctor if you are breast-feeding an infant. Small amounts of this medication may pass into breast milk and cause excessive drowsiness in the nursing infant.

codeine and guaifenesin combination

BRAND NAMES (Manufacturers)
Cheracol (Roberts)
Guiatuss AC (various manufacturers)
Guiatussin with Codeine (Rugby)
Tussi-Organidin NR (Wallace)
TYPE OF DRUG
Cough suppressant and expectorant combination
INGREDIENT
codeine and guaifenesin
DOSAGE FORM
Oral syrup (10 mg codeine and 100 mg guaifenesin per 5-mL spoonful, with 3.5% or 4.75% alcohol; 2.5 mg codeine and 75 mg guaifenesin per 5-mL spoonful)
STORAGE
Store at room temperature in a tightly closed container.

USES

This combination medication is used to relieve coughs due to colds, infections, and inflammation of the upper respiratory tract. Guaifenesin is an expectorant that loosens bronchial secretions. Codeine is a narcotic cough suppressant that acts on the cough center in the brain.

TREATMENT

The syrup can be taken either on an empty stomach or, to avoid stomach irritation, with food or milk (as directed by your doctor).

Measure each dose carefully with a specially designed 5-mL measuring spoon. An ordinary kitchen teaspoon is not accurate enough.

To help loosen the mucus in the bronchi, drink a glass of water after each dose.

If you miss a dose of this medication, take it as soon as possible. However, if it is almost time for the next dose, do not take the missed dose at all; just return to your regular dosing schedule. Do not double the next dose.

SIDE EFFECTS

Minor. Constipation, dizziness, drowsiness, nausea, restlessness, stomach upset, vomiting, or weakness. These side effects should disappear over time as your body adjusts to the medication.

To relieve constipation, increase the amount of fiber in your diet (fresh fruits and vegetables, salads, bran, and whole-grain breads), exercise, and drink more water (unless your doctor directs you to do otherwise).

If you feel dizzy, sit or lie down for a while; stand up slowly from a sitting or reclining position; and be careful on stairs.

Major. Be sure to notify your doctor about any side effects that are persistent or particularly bothersome. IT IS ESPECIALLY IMPORTANT TO TELL YOUR DOCTOR about blurred vision; cold or clammy skin; confusion; difficulty in breathing; or fainting.

INTERACTIONS

This drug can interact with several other types of medications:

1. Concurrent use of this medication with other central nervous system depressants (such as alcohol, barbiturates, benzodiazepine tranquilizers, muscle relaxants, other narcotics, pain medications, phenothiazine tranquilizers, and sleeping medications) or with tricyclic antidepressants can lead to extreme drowsiness.

2. Use of a monoamine oxidase (MAO) inhibitor within 14 days of taking codeine and guaifenesin combination can lead to serious side effects.

3. Concurrent use of this medication and cimetidine can cause confusion, disorientation, and shortness of breath.

Before starting to take codeine and guaifenesin combination, BE SURE TO TELL YOUR DOCTOR about any medications you are currently taking.

WARNINGS

- Tell your doctor about unusual or allergic reactions you have had to any medications, especially to guaifenesin or codeine, or to other narcotics (such as hydrocodone, hydromorphone, meperidine, methadone, opium, oxycodone, propoxyphene, and pentazocine).
- Before starting to take this medication, be sure to notify your doctor if you now have or ever had any of the following: asthma, brain disease, enlarged prostate gland, gallstones or gallbladder disease, gastrointestinal diseases, heart disease, kidney disease, liver disease, lung disease, mental disorders, or thyroid disease.
- If this medication makes you dizzy or drowsy, do not take part in any activities that require alertness, such as driving a car or operating potentially dangerous equipment. Be careful on stairs, and avoid getting up suddenly from a lying or sitting position.
- While you are taking this medication, drink several glasses of water a day to help loosen bronchial secretions, unless your doctor specifically directs you to do otherwise.
- Because this product contains codeine, it has the potential for abuse and must be used with caution. Tolerance may develop quickly; you should not use it in higher doses or for longer periods than recommended by your doctor. If you have been taking it for longer than several weeks, do not stop taking it until you first check with your doctor. Stopping the drug abruptly can lead to a withdrawal reaction (body aches, diarrhea, gooseflesh, vomiting, restlessness, runny nose, sneezing, sweating, trembling, or excessive yawning). Your doctor may want to reduce your dosage gradually.
- Be sure to tell your doctor if you are pregnant. Large amounts of codeine taken during pregnancy can lead to addiction in the developing fetus, resulting in withdrawal reactions in the newborn infant. In addition, be sure to tell your doctor if you are breastfeeding an infant. Codeine may pass into breast milk and can cause extreme drowsiness in the nursing infant.

---

colchicine

BRAND NAMES (Manufacturers)
colchicine (various manufacturers)
Colchicine (Abbott)
TYPE OF DRUG
Antigout
INGREDIENT
colchicine
DOSAGE FORM
Tablets (0.5 mg and 0.6 mg)
STORAGE
Store at room temperature in a tightly closed, light-resistant container.

USES

Colchicine is used to relieve the symptoms of a gout attack and to prevent further attacks. Colchicine prevents the movement of uric acid crystals, which are responsible for the pain in the joints that occurs during an attack of gout.

TREATMENT

This drug can be taken on an empty stomach or with food or a full glass of water or milk (as directed by your doctor).

If you are taking colchicine to control a gout attack, it is important that you understand how to take it properly and when the medication should be stopped. CHECK WITH YOUR DOCTOR.

If you miss a dose of this medication, take the missed dose as soon as possible. However, if it is almost time for the next dose, do not take the missed dose at all; just return to your regular dosing schedule. Do not double the next dose.

SIDE EFFECTS

Minor. Abdominal pain, diarrhea, nausea, or vomiting. These side effects indicate that it is time for you to stop taking the medication. Be sure to contact your doctor when these side effects occur.

Major. Tell your doctor about any side effects that are persistent or particularly bothersome. IT IS ESPECIALLY IMPORTANT TO TELL YOUR DOCTOR about difficult or painful urination, fever, loss of hair, muscle pain, persistent diarrhea, skin rash, sore throat, tingling in the hands or feet, or unusual bleeding or bruising.

INTERACTIONS

Colchicine interacts with several other types of medications:

1. It can decrease absorption of vitamin B_{12}.

2. The action of colchicine can be blocked by vitamin C and enhanced by sodium bicarbonate or ammonium chloride.

3. Colchicine can increase the drowsiness commonly caused by central nervous system depressants.

BE SURE TO TELL YOUR DOCTOR about any medications that you are currently taking, including those mentioned above.

WARNINGS

• Tell your doctor about unusual or allergic reactions you have had to any medications, especially to colchicine.

• Tell your doctor if you now have or ever had blood disorders, gastrointestinal disorders, heart disease, kidney disease, or liver disease.

• Large amounts of alcohol can increase the blood levels of uric acid, which can decrease the effectiveness of colchicine. Alcohol ingestion should, therefore, be limited while you are taking this medication.

• Colchicine is not an analgesic (pain reliever) and does not relieve pain other than that of gout.

• Be sure to tell your doctor if you are pregnant. Colchicine is not recommended for use during pregnancy because it has been reported to cause birth defects in both animals and humans. In addition, be sure to tell your doctor if you are breast-feeding an infant. Colchicine passes into breast milk in small quantities.

---

cortisone (systemic)

BRAND NAMES (Manufacturers)

cortisone acetate (various manufacturers)
Cortone Acetate (Merck)

TYPE OF DRUG

Adrenocorticosteroid hormone

INGREDIENT

cortisone

DOSAGE FORM

Tablets (5 mg, 10 mg, and 25 mg)

STORAGE

Store this medication at room temperature in a tightly closed container.

USES

Your adrenal glands naturally produce certain cortisonelike chemicals. These chemicals are involved in various regulatory processes in the body (such as those involving fluid balance, temperature, and reaction to inflammation). Cortisone belongs to a group of drugs known as adrenocorticosteroids (or cortisonelike medications). It is used to treat a variety of disorders, including hormonal disorders; asthma; blood diseases; certain cancers; eye disorders; gastrointestinal disturbances, such as ulcerative colitis; respiratory diseases; and inflammations such as arthritis, dermatitis, and poison ivy. How this drug acts to relieve these disorders is not completely understood.

TREATMENT

To prevent stomach irritation, take cortisone with food or with milk.

If you are taking only one dose of this medication each day, try to take it before 9:00 in the morning.

It is important to try not to miss any doses of cortisone. However, if you do miss a dose of this medication, follow these guidelines:

If you are taking the medication more than once a day, take the missed dose as soon as possible and return to your regular schedule. If it is already time for the next dose, double the dose.

If you are taking the medication only once a day, take the dose that you missed as soon as possible, unless you don't remember until the next day. In that case, do not take the missed dose at all; just follow your regular dosing schedule. Do not double the next dose of the medication.

If you are taking this drug every other day, take it as soon as you remember. If you missed the scheduled time by a whole day, take it when you remember, then skip a day before you take the next dose. Do not double the dose.

If you miss more than one dose of cortisone, CONTACT YOUR DOCTOR.

SIDE EFFECTS

Minor. Dizziness, false sense of well-being, fatigue, increased appetite, increased sweating, indigestion, menstrual irregularities, muscle weakness, nausea, reddening of the skin on the face, restlessness, sleep disorders, thinning of the skin, or weight gain. These side effects should disappear as your body gets accustomed to the medication.

To help avoid potassium loss while using this drug, take your dose with a glass of fresh or frozen orange juice, or eat a banana each day. The use of a salt substitute also helps to prevent potassium loss. Do not change your diet or take a salt substitute, however, before discussing it with your doctor.

Major. Tell your doctor about any side effects that are persistent or particularly bothersome. IT IS ESPECIALLY IMPORTANT TO TELL YOUR DOCTOR about abdominal enlargement; acne or other skin problems; back or rib pain; bloody or black, tarry stools; blurred vision; convulsions; depression; eye pain; fever; glaucoma; growth impairment (in children); headaches; impaired healing of wounds; increased thirst and urination; mood changes; muscle wasting; nightmares; rapid weight gain (three to five pounds within a week); rash; severe abdominal pain; shortness of breath; sore throat; unusual bleeding or bruising; or unusual weakness.

INTERACTIONS

Cortisone interacts with several other types of medications:

1. Alcohol, aspirin, and nonsteroidal anti-inflammatory medications (such as diflunisal, ibuprofen, indomethacin, ketoprofen, mefenamic acid, meclofenamate, naproxen, piroxicam, sulindac, and tolmetin) aggravate the stomach problems that may occur with use of this medication.

2. The dosage of oral anticoagulants (blood thinners, such as warfarin) and oral antidiabetic drugs or insulin may need to be altered when you start or stop taking this medication.

3. The loss of potassium caused by cortisone can lead to serious side effects in individuals taking digoxin. Thiazide diuretics (water pills) and furosemide can increase the potassium loss caused by cortisone.
4. Phenobarbital, phenytoin, rifampin, and ephedrine can increase the elimination of cortisone from the body, thereby decreasing its effectiveness.
5. Oral contraceptives (birth control pills) and drugs that contain estrogen may decrease the elimination of this drug from the body, which can increase side effects.
6. Cortisone can increase elimination of aspirin and isoniazid from the body, decreasing their effectiveness.
7. Cholestyramine and colestipol can chemically bind this medication in the stomach and gastrointestinal tract, preventing its absorption.
8. Acetazolamide may increase the side effects of cortisone.

BE SURE TO TELL YOUR DOCTOR about any medications you are taking, especially any listed above.

WARNINGS

• Tell your doctor about unusual or allergic reactions you have had to any medications, especially to cortisone or other adrenocorticosteroids (such as betamethasone, dexamethasone, hydrocortisone, methylprednisolone, paramethasone, prednisolone, prednisone, or triamcinolone).

• Tell your doctor if you now have or ever had bone disease, diabetes mellitus, emotional instability, glaucoma, fungal infections, heart disease, high blood pressure, high cholesterol levels, myasthenia gravis, peptic ulcers, osteoporosis, thyroid disease, tuberculosis, ulcerative colitis, kidney disease, or liver disease.

• If you are using this medication for longer than a week, you may need to receive higher dosages if you are subjected to stress, such as serious infections, injury, or surgery. Discuss this with your doctor.

• If you have been taking this drug for more than a week, do not stop taking it suddenly. If it is stopped suddenly, you may experience abdominal or back pain, dizziness, extreme weakness, fainting, fever, muscle or joint pain, nausea, vomiting, or shortness of breath. Your doctor may, therefore, want to reduce the dosage gradually. Never increase the dose or take the drug for longer than the prescribed time unless you first consult your doctor.

• While you are taking this drug, you should not be vaccinated or immunized. This medication decreases the effectiveness of vaccines and can lead to infection if a live-virus vaccine is administered.

• Before having surgery or any other medical or dental treatment, be sure to tell your doctor or dentist that you are taking this medication.

• If you are taking this medication for prolonged periods of time, wear or carry an identification card, bracelet, or necklace indicating that you are taking an adrenocorticosteroid drug.

• Because this drug can cause glaucoma and cataracts with long-term use, your doctor may want you to have your eyes examined by an ophthalmologist from time to time during treatment.

• This medication can raise blood sugar levels in people who have diabetes, so blood sugar levels should be monitored carefully with blood or urine tests when this medication is being taken.

• Be sure to tell your doctor if you are pregnant. This medication crosses the placenta. Although studies of this drug in human pregnancy have not been conducted, birth defects have been observed in the offspring of animals that were given large doses of this type of drug during pregnancy. In addition, be sure to tell your doctor if you are breast-feeding an infant. Small amounts of this drug pass into breast milk and can cause growth suppression or a decrease in natural adrenocorticosteroid production in the nursing infant.

cromolyn sodium (inhalation)

BRAND NAME (Manufacturer)
Intal (Medeva)
TYPE OF DRUG
Antiallergic (antiasthmatic)
INGREDIENT
cromolyn
DOSAGE FORMS
Aerosol spray for inhalation only (800 mcg per spray)
Solution for inhalation only (20 mg per 2-mL ampule)
STORAGE
Store at room temperature in tightly closed, light-resistant containers. The container of the aerosol form is pressurized; it should never be punctured or broken. It should also be stored away from heat and direct sunlight.

USES

This medication is used to prevent asthma attacks. It is not effective in relieving asthma symptoms once an attack has begun. It works by preventing release of the body chemicals that are thought to be responsible for the symptoms of asthma or allergy.

TREATMENT

The solution should be used only with a power nebulizer equipped with a face mask. Never use the solution with a handheld nebulizer.

The aerosol comes packaged with instructions for use. Read the instructions carefully; if you have any questions, check with your doctor or pharmacist. Shake the aerosol wel just before each dose is sprayed, to disperse the medication and equalize the doses. The contents tend to settle on the bottom of the container. The 14.2 g container provides about 200 measured sprays, and the 8.1 g container provides about 112 measured sprays. The capsules for inhalation must not be swallowed.

This medication is most effective when therapy is started before contact with allergens (the suspected offending agents causing your allergy), so if you expect to be exposed to something to which you know you are allergic, it is a good idea to start taking your medication ahead of the exposure.

This medication will work most effectively when the level of medicine in your bloodstream is kept constant. It is best to take the doses at evenly spaced intervals throughout the day and night. For example, if you are to take four doses of this medication a day, the doses should be evenly spaced at six-hour intervals.

If you are using another inhaler to open up the lungs (a bronchodilator), it should be used 20 to 30 minutes before you use cromolyn sodium.

The full benefits of this medication may not become apparent for up to four weeks after you begin treatment.

If you inadvertently miss a dose of this medication but remember it within an hour or so, take the missed dose immediately. If more than an hour has passed, however, do not take the missed dose of medication at all; simply return to your regular dosing schedule. Do not double the next dose of this medication.

SIDE EFFECTS

Minor. Cough, dizziness, drowsiness, headache, increased urination, nasal congestion, nasal itching, nausea, sneezing, stomach irritation, or tearing. These side effects should disappear as your body adjusts to the medication.

If this medication makes you feel dizzy, sit or lie down for a while; get up slowly from a sitting or reclining position; and be careful on stairs.

This medication can cause mouth dryness, throat irritation, and hoarseness. Gargling and rinsing your mouth after each dose helps to prevent these effects.

Major. Tell your doctor about any side effects that are persistent or particularly bothersome. IT IS ESPECIALLY IMPORTANT TO TELL YOUR DOCTOR about burning sensation in the nose, itching, joint swelling or pain, nosebleeds, painful or increased urination, rash, swelling of the face or eyes, swollen glands, or wheezing.

INTERACTIONS

Cromolyn sodium should not interact with other medications if it is used according to directions.

WARNINGS

• Tell your doctor about unusual or allergic reactions you have had to any drugs.

• Before beginning treatment with this medication, tell your doctor if you now have or ever had kidney or liver disease.

• Do not stop taking this medication unless you first check with your doctor. Stopping the drug abruptly may lead to a worsening of your condition.

• Be sure to tell your doctor if you are pregnant. Extensive safety studies in human pregnancy have not been conducted. Also tell your doctor if you are breast-feeding an infant. Cromolyn passes into breast milk in very small quantities.

---

cromolyn sodium (nasal)

BRAND NAME (Manufacturer)

Nasalcrom (Medeva)*

*Available over the counter (without a prescription)

TYPE OF DRUG

Antiallergic

INGREDIENT

cromolyn

DOSAGE FORM

Nasal solution (each spray delivers 5.2 mg)

STORAGE

Store at room temperature in its original container.

USES

Cromolyn sodium nasal solution is used to prevent and treat allergic rhinitis (inflammation of the nasal passages resulting from allergies). Cromolyn sodium works by preventing the release of the body chemicals responsible for inflammation and swelling.

TREATMENT

This medication is for use within the nose only. The nasal passages should be cleared before administering the spray. Inhale through your nose as you spray the solution. Each 13-mL metered spray device provides approximately 100 sprays; each 26-mL metered spray device provides approximately 200 sprays.

This medication is most effective when therapy is started before contact with allergens (the suspected offending agents causing your allergy), so if you expect to be exposed to something to which you are certain you are allergic, it is always a good idea to start taking your medication ahead of the exposure.

This medication works best when the level of medicine in your bloodstream is kept constant. It is best to take the doses at evenly spaced intervals day and night. For example, if you are to take four doses a day, the doses should be spaced six hours apart.

The maximum benefits of this medication may not become fully apparent for as long as four weeks after you have started treatment.

If you miss a dose of this drug, take the missed dose as soon as possible. However, if it is almost time for the next dose, do not take the missed dose at all; just return to your regular dosing schedule. Do not double the next dose.

SIDE EFFECTS

Minor. Bad taste in the mouth, headaches, irritation or stinging, nasal burning, postnasal drip, or sneezing. These side effects should stop as your body adjusts to the drug.
Major. Tell your doctor about any side effects that are persistent or particularly bothersome. IT IS ESPECIALLY IMPORTANT TO TELL YOUR DOCTOR if you experience nosebleeds or skin rash.

INTERACTIONS

This drug should not interact with other medications if it is used according to directions.

WARNINGS

- Tell your doctor about unusual or allergic reactions you have had to any medication, especially to cromolyn sodium.
- Be sure to tell your doctor if you now have or if you have ever had kidney disease or liver disease.
- Do not stop taking this medication unless you first check with your doctor, even if the symptoms of your disorder disappear. Stopping the drug abruptly can lead to a worsening of your condition. Cromolyn sodium should be continued as long as you have contact with the substance causing your allergic symptoms.
- Be sure to tell your doctor if you are pregnant. Extensive safety studies in humans have not been conducted. Also tell your doctor if you are breast-feeding an infant. Cromolyn passes into breast milk in very small quantities.

---

cyclobenzaprine

BRAND NAMES (Manufacturers)
cyclobenzaprine (various manufacturers)
Flexeril (Merck)
TYPE OF DRUG
Muscle relaxant
INGREDIENT
cyclobenzaprine
DOSAGE FORM
Tablets (10 mg)
STORAGE
Store at room temperature in a tightly closed container.

USES

Cyclobenzaprine is prescribed to relieve muscle pain and stiffness caused by injuries such as sprains or strains. It is not clear how this drug works, but it may block reflexes involved in producing and maintaining muscle spasms. It does not act directly on tense muscles.

TREATMENT

To avoid stomach irritation, take cyclobenzaprine with food or with a full glass of water or milk.

If you miss a dose of this medication and remember within an hour, take the missed dose; then return to your regular dosing schedule. If more than an hour has passed, do not take the missed dose at all; just return to your dosing schedule. Do not double the next dose.

SIDE EFFECTS

Minor. Abdominal pain, black tongue, blurred vision, constipation, diarrhea, dizziness, drowsiness, dry mouth, fatigue, indigestion, insomnia, loss of appetite, muscle pain, nausea, nervousness, sweating, unpleasant taste in the mouth, vomiting, or weakness. These side effects should disappear as your body becomes accustomed to the medication.

If you are constipated, increase the amount of fiber in your diet (fresh fruits and vegetables, salads, bran, and whole-grain breads) and drink more water (unless your doctor directs you to do otherwise).

If you feel dizzy or light-headed, sit or lie down for a while; get up slowly from a sitting or reclining position; and be careful on stairs.

To relieve mouth dryness, chew sugarless gum, or suck on ice chips or a piece of hard candy.

Major. Tell your doctor about any side effects that are persistent or particularly bothersome. IT IS ESPECIALLY IMPORTANT TO TELL YOUR DOCTOR about confusion, depression, difficulty in urinating, disorientation, hallucinations, headache, itching, numbness in the fingers or toes, palpitations, rash, swelling of the face or tongue, tremors, or yellowing of your skin or eyes.

INTERACTIONS

Cyclobenzaprine interacts with several other types of drugs:

1. Concurrent use of cyclobenzaprine with other central nervous system depressants (such as alcohol, antihistamines, barbiturates, antianxiety medications, narcotics, pain medications, tranquilizers, and sleeping medications) or with tricyclic antidepressants can cause extreme drowsiness.

2. Cyclobenzaprine can block the blood-pressure-lowering effects of clonidine and guanethidine.

3. Use of this drug within 14 days of a monoamine oxidase (MAO) inhibitor (tranylcypromine, phenelzine, isocarboxazid, and pargyline) can lead to severe reactions and high blood pressure.

BE SURE TO TELL YOUR DOCTOR about any medications you are currently taking, especially those listed above.

WARNINGS

- Tell your doctor about any unusual or allergic reactions you have had to medications, especially to cyclobenzaprine or to tricyclic antidepressants (such as amitriptyline, amoxapine, desipramine, doxepin, imipramine, nortriptyline, protriptyline, and trimipramine).
- Tell your doctor if you have or if you have ever had blood clots, epilepsy, heart disease, a heart attack, narrow-angle glaucoma, thyroid disease, or urinary retention.
- Use of cyclobenzaprine for periods longer than two to three weeks is not recommended because there is no evidence of benefit with prolonged use and because muscle spasm caused by sprain or strain is generally of short duration.
- This medication should not be taken as a substitute for rest, physical therapy, or other measures recommended by your doctor to treat your condition.
- If this medication makes you dizzy or drowsy or blurs your vision, avoid any activity that requires alertness, such as driving a car or operating potentially dangerous equipment.
- If you have been taking large doses of this medication for prolonged periods, you may experience nausea, headache, or fatigue when you stop taking it until your body adjusts to the absence of the drug.
- Be sure to tell your doctor if you are pregnant. Although cyclobenzaprine appears to be safe during pregnancy, extensive studies in human pregnancy have not been conducted. Also tell your doctor if you are breast-feeding an infant. It is not known whether cyclobenzaprine passes into breast milk.

cyclosporine

BRAND NAMES (Manufacturers)
cyclosporin A (various manufacturers)
Neoral (Novartis)
Sandimmune (Novartis)
TYPE OF DRUG
Immunosuppressant
INGREDIENT
cyclosporine
DOSAGE FORMS
Oral solution (100 mg per mL, with 10.5% or 12.5% alcohol)
Oral solution for microemulsion (100 mg per mL, with 9.5% alcohol)
Soft-gelatin capsules (25 mg, 50 mg, and 100 mg)
Soft-gelatin capsules for microemulsion (25 mg and 100 mg)
STORAGE
Store in the original container at room temperature. This medication should never be refrigerated or frozen. Once the solution has been opened, it should be used within two months or discarded. At cooler (less than 68 degrees Fahrenheit) room temperatures, the Neoral solution may form a gel; in addition, particles or a slight sediment may be visible in the container. This change does not affect the stability or potency of the medication itself. These changes will disappear when the drug is allowed to warm to a higher room temperature.

USES

Cyclosporine is used to prevent organ rejection after kidney, liver, heart, or bone-marrow transplants. It is not clearly understood how cyclosporine works, but it appears to prevent the body's rejection of foreign tissue. Cyclosporine is also used to treat severe psoriasis and rheumatoid arthritis.

TREATMENT

To make it more palatable, dilute the solution with apple juice, orange juice, milk, or chocolate milk, preferably at room temperature. Neoral solution is best diluted in apple or orange juice. NEVER dilute cyclosporine solution in grapefruit juice. Measure the solution carefully with the dropper provided, and place it in one of the acceptable fluids listed above. Use a glass container (cyclosporine chemically binds to wax-lined and plastic surfaces). Stir well and drink at once—do not allow the mixture to stand before drinking. Refill the glass with the same beverage and drink this solution to ensure that the whole dose is taken. Wipe the outside of the dropper with a clean towel after use, and store it in its container. (If the dropper has to be cleaned, make sure it is completely dry before using it again.)

It is important not to miss any doses of this medication. If you do miss a dose, take the missed dose as soon as possible. However, if it is almost time for the next dose, do not take the missed dose at all; just return to your regular dosing schedule. Do not double the next dose. If you have any questions about a missed dose, contact your doctor immediately.

SIDE EFFECTS

Minor. Abdominal discomfort, diarrhea, flushing, headache, hiccups, leg cramps, loss of appetite, nausea, or vomiting. These side effects should disappear as your body adjusts to the medication.
Major. Tell your doctor about any side effects that are persistent or particularly bothersome. IT IS ESPECIALLY IMPORTANT TO TELL YOUR DOCTOR about acne; bleeding, tender, or enlarged gums; convulsions; difficult or painful urination; enlarged

and painful breasts (in both sexes); fever; hair growth; hearing loss; muscle pain; rapid weight gain (three to five pounds within a week); sore throat; tingling of the hands or feet; tremors; unusual bleeding or bruising; or yellowing of the eyes or skin.

INTERACTIONS

Cyclosporine interacts with several other types of drugs:

1. Carbamazepine, isoniazid, rifampin, phenytoin, phenobarbital, and trimethoprim/sulfamethoxazole can decrease the blood levels of cyclosporine, decreasing its effectiveness.

2. Allopurinol, bromocriptine, clarithromycin, cimetidine, danazol, diltiazem, erythromycin, estrogens, fluconazole, protease inhibitors, nefazodone, nicardipine, verapamil, ketoconazole, oral contraceptives, and amphotericin B can increase the blood levels of cyclosporine, which can lead to an increase in side effects.

3. Tell your doctor if you are currently taking corticosteroids, verapamil, or nonsteroidal anti-inflammatory drugs.

4. Grapefruit and grapefruit juice may increase blood levels of cyclosporine, increasing the risk of side effects.

5. Lovastatin and simvastatin may increase the side effects and the risk of kidney failure from cyclosporine.

6. Cyclosporine may increase the side effects of certain vaccines.

BE SURE TO TELL YOUR DOCTOR about these or any drugs you are taking.

WARNINGS

• Tell your doctor about unusual or allergic reactions you have had to any medications, especially to cyclosporine or to polyoxyethylated castor oil.

• Neoral and Sandimmune formulations of cyclosporine are not interchangeable. It is important to know the name of the formulation that has been prescribed for you.

• Before starting to take this medication, be sure to tell your doctor if you now have or ever had hypertension (high blood pressure) or gastrointestinal disorders.

• Repeated laboratory tests are necessary while you are taking cyclosporine to ensure that you are receiving the correct dosage and to avoid liver and kidney damage.

• Certain cancers have occurred in patients who received cyclosporine and other immunosuppressant medications after organ transplantation. No direct causal effect has been established, however.

• Do not stop taking this medication without first consulting your doctor. If the drug is stopped abruptly, organ rejection may occur. Your doctor may, therefore, want to reduce your dosage gradually or start you on another drug if this drug is to be discontinued.

• Be sure to tell your doctor if you are pregnant. Although extensive studies in human pregnancy have not been conducted, cyclosporine has caused fetal damage when administered to pregnant animals. Also tell your doctor if you are breast-feeding, because cyclosporine passes into breast milk.

---

darbepoetin

BRAND NAME (Manufacturer)
Aranesp (Amgen)
TYPE OF DRUG
Antianemia
INGREDIENT
darbepoetin
DOSAGE FORM
Injection (25 mcg, 40 mcg, 60 mcg, 100 mcg, and 200 mcg per 1-mL of solution with polysorbate; 25 mcg, 40 mcg, 60 mcg, 100 mcg, 150 mcg, 200 mcg, 300 mcg, and 500 mcg per 1-mL of solution with albumin)

STORAGE
Store in its original vial in the refrigerator and protect from light. Do not freeze or shake the vial.

USES
Darbepoetin is used to increase the number of red blood cells in the body in patients with anemia due to renal failure and dialysis or from chemotherapy for certain types of cancers. Darbepoetin stimulates the production of red blood cells in the body through a process called erythropoiesis. In patients with chronic renal failure or those receiving certain types of chemotherapy, this process of erythropoiesis is impaired. Darbepoetin is produced using recombinant technology, a method that does not involve the use of any human blood products.

TREATMENT
This medication should be taken exactly as prescribed by your doctor. Darbepoetin is given by injection, either directly into the vein or under the skin (subcutaneously), usually once a week. Complete instructions on using darbepoetin are included with the medication. Be sure to review those instructions before using darbepoetin. If you have any questions, be sure to contact your doctor or pharmacist. It is likely that you will be trained by a nurse or other health care specialist on how to inject this medication and how to monitor for side effects.

Since darbepoetin is given by injection, you will need a special container to dispose of used needles and syringes. Also, check the vial before using darbepoetin; the solution should be clear. Do not use the medication if there are floating particles or if the solution has a color. Do not mix darbepoetin with any other medications or dilute the solution. Do not shake the vial; this may inactivate the medication. Darbepoetin contains no preservatives; once the vial is opened with a syringe, it should be used immediately. The contents of an open vial should not be saved for later use.

SIDE EFFECTS
Minor. Diarrhea, dizziness, headache, itching, muscle aches and pains, nausea, pain at the site of injection, tiredness, or vomiting. These side effects should diminish or disappear as your body adjusts to the medication.

To avoid dizziness or light-headedness when you stand, contract and relax the muscles in your legs for a few moments before rising. Do this by pushing one foot against the floor while raising the other foot slightly, alternating feet so that you are "pumping" your legs in a pedaling motion.

If you feel dizzy or light-headed, sit or lie down for a while; get up from a sitting or lying position slowly; and be careful on stairs.

Major. Tell your doctor about any side effects you experience that are persistent or particularly bothersome. IT IS ESPECIALLY IMPORTANT TO TELL YOUR DOCTOR about chest pain; difficulty breathing or shortness of breath; feelings of warmth, pain, and swelling in the lower legs; palpitations; seizures; or swelling of the legs or hands.

INTERACTIONS
If used properly, darbepoetin should not interact with other drugs. However, before taking darbepoetin, BE SURE TO TELL YOUR DOCTOR about any medications you are taking.

WARNINGS
• Darbepoetin may cause an increase in blood pressure. Monitor your blood pressure regularly while taking this medication.

• To make sure this medication is working properly, it is important that blood tests are done to check for anemia.

• Tell your doctor about any unusual or allergic reactions you have ever had to any medications, especially to darbepoetin, to erythropoetin, or to any other injectable medication.
• Prior to having surgery or any other medical or dental treatment, be sure to tell your doctor or dentist that you are taking darbepoetin.
• Be sure to tell your doctor if you are pregnant. The effects of this medication during pregnancy have not been thoroughly studied in humans. It is also not known if darbepoetin passes into breast milk in humans, so be sure to tell your doctor if you are breast-feeding an infant.

---

delavirdine

BRAND NAME (Manufacturer)
Rescriptor (Agouron)
TYPE OF DRUG
Antiviral
INGREDIENT
delavirdine
DOSAGE FORM
Tablets (100 mg)
STORAGE
Store at room temperature in a tightly closed container. Do not store in the bathroom or expose to excess moisture or humidity.

USES

Delavirdine is used in the treatment of human immunodeficiency virus (HIV) infection. HIV is the virus that causes AIDS. Delavirdine works by inhibiting the reproduction, or growth, of the virus, which slows the progression of AIDS. Delavirdine does not cure HIV infection or AIDS, but it may delay onset of other infections and diseases caused by AIDS.

TREATMENT

This medication works best when the level of medicine in your bloodstream is kept constant. It is best to take the drug at evenly spaced intervals throughout the day. To avoid stomach irritation, you can take delavirdine with food or with a full glass of water (unless your doctor tells you to do otherwise). The tablets can be swallowed whole or dissolved in water (at least three ounces). If the tablets are dissolved in water, stir the mixture to keep the medication from settling to the bottom; take the mixture immediately. After taking the mixture, add more water to the glass to dissolve any remaining medication, and drink the water.

If your stomach does not secrete enough acid (a condition called achlorhydria), your doctor may want you to take delavirdine with an acidic beverage, such as orange juice or cranberry juice. Ask your doctor if this is necessary.

If you miss a dose of this medication, take it as soon as possible. However, if it is almost time for your next dose, skip the missed dose and go back to your regular dosing schedule. Do not double the doses.

SIDE EFFECTS

Minor. Diarrhea, fatigue, headache, nausea, or vomiting. These side effects should diminish or disappear as your body adjusts to the medication.
Major. Tell your doctor about any side effects that are persistent or particularly bothersome. IT IS ESPECIALLY IMPORTANT TO TELL YOUR DOCTOR about difficulty breathing, rash, eye inflammation, fever, mouth sores, muscle or joint aches, severe or itching skin rash, or swelling.

INTERACTIONS

Delavirdine may interact with a number of drugs:

1. Use of delavirdine with amphetamines, benzodiazepines, warfarin, calcium channel blockers, cisapride, or an ergot derivative may result in serious, life-threatening reactions.

2. Antacids or didanosine may block the absorption of delavirdine. At least one hour should separate the use of antacids or didanosine and delavirdine.

3. The effects of delavirdine may be reduced by carbamazepine, phenobarbital, phenytoin, rifabutin, rifampin, cimetidine, famotidine, nizatidine, or ranitidine.

4. The amount of clarithromycin or indinavir available in the body may be increased by delavirdine.

WARNINGS

• Tell your doctor if you have ever had an allergic reaction to delavirdine or to any other medication.

• Before starting this medication, be sure to tell your doctor what medications you are taking. Delavirdine may have serious interactions with other drugs.

• Before taking this medication, be sure to tell your doctor about any medical problems you may have, especially liver problems.

• Tell your doctor immediately if you notice any type of skin rash, especially if it is severe or itchy or is accompanied by blisters, eye inflammation, fever, muscle or joint aches, mouth ulcers, swelling, or difficulty breathing.

• Be sure to tell your doctor if you are pregnant. Although birth defects have not been documented in humans, delavirdine has been shown to cause birth defects in animals. It is unknown if delavirdine is safe during human pregnancy. It is not known if delavirdine passes into human breast milk. However, because of the risk of passing HIV to infants, it is recommended that mothers who have HIV infection NOT breastfeed their infants.

---

desipramine

BRAND NAMES (Manufacturers)
desipramine (various manufacturers)
Norpramin (Hoechst-Marion Roussel)
TYPE OF DRUG
Tricyclic antidepressant
INGREDIENT
desipramine
DOSAGE FORM
Tablets (10 mg, 25 mg, 50 mg, 75 mg, 100 mg, and 150 mg)
STORAGE
Store at room temperature in tightly closed containers; protect from excessive heat.

USES

Desipramine is used to relieve the symptoms of mental depression. This medication belongs to a group of drugs referred to as the tricyclic antidepressants. These medicines are thought to relieve depression by increasing the concentration of certain chemicals necessary for nerve transmission in the brain.

TREATMENT

This drug should be taken exactly as your doctor prescribes. To lessen stomach irritation, take it with food unless your doctor tells you otherwise.

If you miss a dose of this medication, take the missed dose as soon as possible, then return to your regular dosing schedule. If the dose you missed was a once-a-day bedtime dose, do not take that dose in the morning; check with your doctor instead. If the dose is taken in the morning, it may cause some unwanted side effects. Never double the dose.

The effects of therapy with this medication may not become apparent for several weeks; it may take four to six weeks to see full benefits.

SIDE EFFECTS

Minor. Agitation, anxiety, blurred vision, confusion, constipation, cramps, diarrhea, dizziness, drowsiness, dry mouth, fatigue, heartburn, insomnia, loss of appetite, nausea, peculiar tastes in the mouth, restlessness, sweating, vomiting, weakness, or weight gain or loss. As your body adjusts to the medication, these side effects should disappear.

This medication may increase your sensitivity to sunlight. You should therefore avoid prolonged exposure to sunlight and sunlamps. Wear protective clothing and sunglasses when out of doors, and use a sunscreen.

Dry mouth can be relieved by chewing sugarless gum or by sucking on ice chips or a piece of hard candy.

To relieve constipation, increase the amount of fiber in your diet (fresh fruits and vegetables, salads, bran, and whole-grain breads), exercise, and drink more water (unless your doctor directs you to do otherwise).

To avoid dizziness or light-headedness when you stand, contract and relax the muscles of your legs for a few moments before rising. Do this by pushing one foot against the floor while raising the other foot slightly, alternating feet so that you are "pumping" your legs in a pedaling motion.

Major. Tell your doctor about any side effects that are persistent or particularly bothersome. IT IS ESPECIALLY IMPORTANT TO TELL YOUR DOCTOR about chest pain, convulsions, difficulty in urinating, enlarged or painful breasts (in both sexes), fainting, fever, fluid retention, hair loss, hallucinations, headaches, impotence, mood changes, mouth sores, nervousness, nightmares, nosebleeds, numbness in the fingers or toes, palpitations, ringing in the ears, seizures, skin rash, sleep disorders, sore throat, tremors, uncoordinated movements or balance problems, unusual bleeding or bruising, or yellowing of the eyes or skin.

INTERACTIONS

Desipramine will interact with several other types of medications:

1. Extreme drowsiness can occur when this medicine is taken with central nervous system depressants (such as alcohol, antihistamines, barbiturates, benzodiazepine tranquilizers, muscle relaxants, narcotics, pain medications, phenothiazine tranquilizers, and medications to induce sleep) or with other antidepressants.

2. Desipramine may decrease the effectiveness of antiseizure medications.

3. It may block the blood-pressure-lowering effects of clonidine and guanethidine.

4. Concurrent use of cimetidine, venlafaxine, carbamazepine, bupropion, or fluoxetine can decrease the elimination of desipramine from the body, increasing the possibility of side effects.

5. Tricyclic antidepressants may increase the side effects of thyroid medication and of over-the-counter (nonprescription) cough, cold, allergy, asthma, sinus, and diet drugs.

6. The concurrent use of tricyclic antidepressants and monoamine oxidase (MAO) inhibitors should be avoided because the combination may result in fever, convulsions, or high blood pressure. At least 14 days should separate the use of this drug and the use of an MAO inhibitor.

BE SURE TO TELL YOUR DOCTOR about any drugs you are currently taking.

WARNINGS

• Tell your doctor if you have had unusual or allergic reactions to medications, especially to desipramine or any of the other tricyclic antidepressants (such as amitriptyline, imipramine, doxepin, trimipramine, amoxapine, protriptyline, maprotiline, and nortriptyline).

• Tell your doctor if you have a history of alcoholism or if you have or have had asthma, high blood pressure, liver disease, kidney disease, heart disease, a heart attack, circulatory disease, stomach problems, intestinal problems, difficulty in urinating, an enlarged prostate gland, epilepsy, seizures, glaucoma, thyroid disease, mental illness, or electroshock therapy.

• If this drug makes you dizzy or drowsy, do not take part in any activity that requires alertness, such as driving a car or operating potentially dangerous equipment.

• Before having surgery or other medical or dental treatment, tell your doctor or dentist about this drug.

• Do not stop taking this drug suddenly. Stopping it abruptly can cause nausea, headache, stomach upset, fatigue, or a worsening of your condition. Your doctor may want to reduce the dosage gradually.

• This medication may cause your urine to turn blue-green in color. This is an expected side effect that is harmless.

• The effects of this medication may last as long as seven days after you have stopped taking it, so continue to observe all precautions during that period.

• Be sure to tell your doctor if you are pregnant. Problems in humans have not been reported; however, studies in animals have shown that this medication can cause side effects in the fetus when given to the mother in large doses during pregnancy. Also tell your doctor if you are breast-feeding an infant. Small amounts of this drug can pass into breast milk, which may cause unwanted effects, such as irritability or sleeping problems, in the nursing infant.

---

desloratadine

BRAND NAME (Manufacturer)
Clarinex (Schering)
TYPE OF DRUG
Antihistamine
INGREDIENT
desloratadine
DOSAGE FORMS
Tablets (5 mg)
Tablets, rapidly disintegrating (5 mg)
STORAGE
Store at room temperature in a tightly closed, dry, light-resistant container.

USES

Desloratadine is a long-acting antihistamine. Antihistamines block the action of histamine, a chemical released from the body during an allergic reaction. This drug is used to provide symptomatic relief of seasonal allergic rhinitis, such as hay fever. It will reduce symptoms of an allergic response, including hives, sneezing, runny nose, itching, and tearing.

TREATMENT

The regular tablet form may be taken either on an empty stomach or with food or milk (unless your doctor directs you to do otherwise). The rapidly disintegrating tablet should be placed on the tongue; it will quickly dissolve and can be swallowed with or without water. Take this medication only as needed to control the symptoms of allergy. This medication will not cure the allergy, but it will help to relieve the symptoms that are associated with the condition.

If you miss a dose of this medication, take the missed dose as soon as possible. However, if it is almost time for your next dose, do not take the missed dose at all; just return to your regular dosing schedule. Do not double the next dose.

SIDE EFFECTS

Minor. Dry mouth, hoarseness, muscle aches, painful menses, sore throat, or unusual tiredness. These side effects should disappear as your body adjusts to the medication.

Dry mouth can be relieved by chewing sugarless gum or sucking on hard candy.

To avoid dizziness or light-headedness when you stand, contract and relax the muscles of your legs for a few moments before rising.

If you feel dizzy or light-headed, sit or lie down for a while; get up slowly from a sitting or lying position; and be careful on stairs.

Major. Tell your doctor about any side effects that are persistent or particularly bothersome. IT IS ESPECIALLY IMPORTANT TO TELL YOUR DOCTOR about anxiety; change in menstruation; clumsiness; depression; feeling faint; flushing of the face; hallucinations; migraines; palpitations; puffiness or swelling of eyelids or around the eyes, face, lip, or tongue; rash; seizures; shortness of breath; sleeping disorders; sore throat or fever; tightness in the chest or back; trouble breathing; unusual bleeding or bruising; unusual tiredness or weakness; urine discoloration; or yellowing of the eyes or the skin.

INTERACTIONS

This drug interacts with several other medications:

1. Concurrent use of this medication with other central nervous system depressants (such as alcohol, barbiturates, benzodiazepine tranquilizers, muscle relaxants, narcotics, pain medications, and phenothiazine tranquilizers) or with tricyclic antidepressants can cause extreme drowsiness.

2. Use of over-the-counter cough, cold, or allergy medications may increase the side effects of this medication and should be avoided.

3 Monoamine oxidase (MAO) inhibitors (such as selegiline, isocarboxazid, pargyline, phenelzine, and tranylcypromine) can be expected to increase the side effects of this medication.

BE SURE TO TELL YOUR DOCTOR about any medications that you are currently taking, especially any of those mentioned above.

WARNINGS

• Tell your doctor about unusual or allergic reactions you have had to any medications, especially to desloratadine, loratadine, cyproheptadine, azatadine, or any other antihistamines (such as astemizole, brompheniramine, carbinoxamine, cetirizine, chlorpheniramine, clemastine, dimenhydrinate, diphenhydramine, diphenylpyraline, doxylamine, fexofenadine, hydroxyzine, and terfenadine).

• Tell your doctor if you now have or have ever had asthma; blood-vessel disease; glaucoma; high blood pressure; kidney, liver, or thyroid disease; peptic ulcers; or an enlarged prostate.

• Because desloratadine is metabolized by the liver, patients who have liver disease or kidney disease will require a change in the dosing schedule. Discuss this with your doctor or pharmacist if you have either disease.

• Although desloratadine causes less drowsiness than many other medications in this class, your ability to perform tasks that require alertness, such as driving a car or operating potentially dangerous machinery, may be impaired.

• Be sure to tell your doctor if you are pregnant. The effects of using this medication during pregnancy have not been thoroughly studied in humans. Also be sure to tell your doctor if you are breast-feeding an infant. Desloratadine should not be used by nursing women.

dexamethasone, neomycin, and polymyxin B combination (ophthalmic)

BRAND NAMES (Manufacturers)
AK-Trol (Akorn)
Dexacidin (Ciba Vision)
dexamethasone, neomycin, and polymyxin B combination (various manufacturers)
Maxitrol (Alcon)
TYPE OF DRUG
Ophthalmic adrenocorticosteroid and antibiotic
INGREDIENTS
dexamethasone, neomycin, and polymyxin B
DOSAGE FORMS
Ophthalmic suspension (0.1% dexamethasone, 3.5 mg neomycin, and 10,000 units polymyxin B per mL)
Ophthalmic ointment (0.1% dexamethasone, 3.5 mg neomycin, and 10,000 units polymyxin B per gram)
STORAGE
Store at room temperature in tightly closed containers. Do not freeze. If the suspension or ointment changes color, don't use the medication. A change in color indicates a loss of effectiveness.

USES

This medication is used for the short-term treatment of bacterial infections and inflammation of the eyes.

Your adrenal glands naturally produce certain cortisonelike chemicals. These chemicals are involved in various regulatory processes in the body (such as those involving fluid balance, temperature, and the reaction to inflammation). Dexamethasone belongs to a group of drugs known as adrenocorticosteroids (or cortisonelike medications). It is used to relieve inflammation (redness, swelling, itching, and discomfort). How it does so is not completely understood.

Neomycin and polymyxin B are antibiotics, which act to prevent the growth and multiplication of infecting bacteria.

TREATMENT

Wash your hands with soap and water before using this medication.

If you are using the suspension, shake the bottle well before measuring out the drops to distribute the ingredients evenly and equalize the doses. The contents tend to settle on the bottom of the bottle.

To prevent contamination of the medicine, be careful not to touch the tube portion of the dropper, and do not let the dropper touch the eye.

Note that a new, unopened bottle of the eyedrops (ophthalmic suspension) is not completely full. This is normal and allows control of the number of drops used.

To apply the drops, tilt your head back and pull down the lower eyelid with one hand to make a pouch below the eyeball. Drop the medicine into the pouch and slowly close your eyes. Try not to blink. Place one finger at the corner of the eye next to your nose, applying slight pressure (to prevent loss of medication through the duct that drains fluid from the eye's surface into the nose and throat), and keep your eyes closed for a minute or two. If you think the drug did not get into your eye, repeat the process once. If you are using a second medication in the form of eyedrops, wait at least five minutes before administering the second type.

Follow the same general procedure for applying the ointment. Tilt your head back, pull down the lower eyelid, and squeeze the prescribed amount of ointment in a line along the pouch below the eyeball. Close your eyes, and place your finger at the corner of the eye near the nose for a minute or two. Do not rub your eyes. Wipe off excess ointment and the tip of the tube with clean tissues.

Since applying the medication is somewhat difficult to do, you may want someone else to apply it for you.

If you miss a dose of this drug, insert the drops or apply the ointment as soon as possible. However, if it is almost time for the next application, do not use the missed dose; just return to the regular dosing schedule.

Your doctor may advise you to reduce the number of times you are applying this medication when the inflammation and infection begin to improve. Continue to take this medication for the entire time prescribed by your doctor, even if the symptoms of infection disappear sooner. If you stop applying the drug too soon, bacteria are given a chance to continue growing, and the infection could recur.

SIDE EFFECTS

Minor. Blurred vision, burning, or stinging. These side effects should disappear as your body adjusts to the drug.

Major. Tell your doctor about any side effects that are persistent or particularly bothersome. IT IS ESPECIALLY IMPORTANT TO TELL YOUR DOCTOR about disturbed or reduced vision; eye pain, itching, or swelling; headache; rash; or severe irritation.

INTERACTIONS

This medication should not interact with any other medications as long as it is used according to directions.

WARNINGS

• Tell your doctor about any reactions you have had to medications, especially to dexamethasone or other adrenocorticosteroids (such as alclometasone, amcinonide, betamethasone, clobetasol, clocortolone, cortisone, desonide, desoximetasone, diflorasone, flumethasone, fluocinolone, fluorometholone, flurandrenolide, halcinonide, hydrocortisone, methylprednisolone, prednisolone, prednisone, and triamcinolone), to polymyxin B, to neomycin, or to any related antibiotic (amikacin, gentamicin, kanamycin, netilmicin, paromomycin, streptomycin, and tobramycin).

• Tell your doctor if you have ever had fungal or viral infections of the eye, inner-ear disease, kidney disease, or myasthenia gravis.

• If there is no change in your condition two or three days after starting to take this drug, contact your doctor. The drug may not be effective for your particular infection.

• Do not use this medication for longer than ten consecutive days unless your doctor directs you to do so. Prolonged use of this medication may result in glaucoma, secondary infection, cataracts, or eye damage. If you need to take this medication for several weeks, your doctor may want you to have your eyes examined by an ophthalmologist.

• This medication has been prescribed for your current infection only. Do not give this drug to other people or use it to treat other infections.

• Do not apply makeup to the affected eye.

• Be sure to tell your doctor if you are pregnant. When large amounts of dexamethasone are applied for prolonged periods, some of it is absorbed into the bloodstream. It may cross the placenta. Birth defects have been observed in the offspring of animals that were given large oral doses of this drug during pregnancy. Also tell your doctor if you are breast-feeding an infant. If absorbed through the eye, small amounts of dexamethasone can pass into breast milk and may cause growth suppression or a decrease in natural adrenocorticosteroid production in the nursing infant.

dexamethasone (systemic)

BRAND NAMES (Manufacturers)
Decadron (Merck Sharp & Dohme)
dexamethasone (various manufacturers)
Hexadrol (Organon)
TYPE OF DRUG
Adrenocorticosteroid hormone
INGREDIENT
dexamethasone
DOSAGE FORMS
Tablets (0.25 mg, 0.5 mg, 0.75 mg, 1 mg, 1.5 mg, 2 mg, 4 mg, and 6 mg)
Oral elixir (0.5 mg per 5-mL spoonful, with 5% alcohol)
Oral solution (0.5 mg per 5-mL spoonful)
Oral concentrate (0.5 mg per 0.5 mL, with 30% alcohol)
STORAGE
Store at room temperature in a tightly closed container.

USES

Your adrenal glands naturally produce certain cortisonelike chemicals. These chemicals are involved in various regulatory processes in the body (such as those involving fluid balance, temperature, and the reaction to inflammation). Dexamethasone belongs to a group of drugs known as adrenocorticosteroids (or cortisonelike medications). It is used to treat a variety of disorders, including endocrine and rheumatic disorders; asthma; blood diseases; certain cancers; eye disorders; gastrointestinal disturbances, such as ulcerative colitis; respiratory diseases; and inflammations such as arthritis, dermatitis, and poison ivy. How this medication acts to relieve these disorders is not completely understood.

TREATMENT

To prevent stomach irritation, take this medication with food or milk.

If you are taking only one dose of this medication each day, try to take it before 9:00 in the morning. This will mimic the body's normal production of this type of chemical.

Measure the elixir and solution with a specially designed 5-mL measuring spoon, not an ordinary kitchen teaspoon.

The concentrate may be diluted in juice, other liquids, or semisolid foods like applesauce.

It is important to not miss any doses of dexamethasone. If you do miss a dose, follow these guidelines:

1. If you are taking this medication more than once a day, take the missed dose as soon as possible and return to your regular schedule. If it is already time for the next dose of medication, double the dose.

2. If you are taking this medication once a day, take the dose you missed as soon as possible. However, if you don't remember until the next day, do not take the missed dose at all, just follow your regular dosing schedule. Do not double the next dose.

3. If you are taking this drug every other day, take it as soon as you remember. If you missed the scheduled time by a whole day, take it when you remember, then skip a day before you take the next dose. Do not double the next dose. If you miss more than one dose of dexamethasone, CONTACT YOUR DOCTOR.

SIDE EFFECTS

Minor. Dizziness, false sense of well-being, fatigue, increased appetite, increased sweating, indigestion, leg cramps, menstrual irregularities, muscle weakness, nausea, reddening of the skin on the face, restlessness, sleep disorders, thinning of the skin, or weight gain. These side effects should disappear as your body adjusts to the drug.

To help avoid potassium loss while using this drug, you can take your dose with a glass of fresh or frozen orange juice, or eat a banana each day. The use of a salt substitute also helps to prevent potassium loss. Check with your doctor before changing your diet or using a salt substitute.

Major. Tell your doctor about any side effects that are persistent or particularly bothersome. IT IS ESPECIALLY IMPORTANT TO TELL YOUR DOCTOR about abdominal enlargement or pain; acne or other skin problems; back or rib pain; bloody or black, tarry stools; blurred vision; convulsions; eye pain; fever and sore throat; growth impairment (in children); headaches; impaired healing of wounds; increased thirst and urination; mental depression; mood changes; muscle wasting; nightmares; peptic ulcers; rapid weight gain (three to five pounds within a week); rash; shortness of breath; unusual bleeding or bruising; or unusual weakness.

INTERACTIONS

This drug interacts with several other types of drugs:

1. Alcohol, aspirin, and anti-inflammatory medications (such as diclofenac, diflunisal, fenoprofen, flurbiprofen, ibuprofen, indomethacin, naproxen, piroxicam, sulindac, and tolmetin) aggravate the stomach problems that may occur with use of this medication.

2. The dosage of oral anticoagulants (blood thinners, such as warfarin), oral antidiabetic drugs, or insulin may need to be altered when this medication is started or stopped.

3. The loss of potassium caused by this medication can lead to serious side effects in individuals taking digoxin.

4. Thiazide diuretics (water pills) can increase the potassium loss caused by dexamethasone.

5. Phenobarbital, phenytoin, rifampin, and ephedrine can increase the elimination of dexamethasone from the body, thereby decreasing its effectiveness.

6. Oral contraceptives (birth control pills) and estrogen-containing drugs may decrease the elimination of this drug from the body, which can lead to an increase in side effects.

7. Dexamethasone can increase the elimination of aspirin and isoniazid from the body, thereby decreasing the effectiveness of these two medications.

8. Cholestyramine and colestipol can chemically bind this medication in the stomach and gastrointestinal tract, preventing its absorption.

BE SURE TO TELL YOUR DOCTOR about any medications you are currently taking, especially any of those listed above.

WARNINGS

• Tell your doctor about unusual or allergic reactions you have had to any medications, especially to dexamethasone or other adrenocorticosteroids (such as alclometasone, amcinonide, betamethasone, clobetasol, clocortolone, cortisone, desonide, desoximetasone, diflorasone, flumethasone, fluocinolone, fluocinonide, fluorometholone, flurandrenolide, halcinonide, hydrocortisone, methylprednisolone, paramethasone, prednisolone, prednisone, and triamcinolone).

• Tell your doctor if you now have or ever had bone disease of any sort, diabetes mellitus, emotional instability, glaucoma, fungal infections, heart disease, high blood pressure, high cholesterol levels, myasthenia gravis, peptic ulcers, osteoporosis, thyroid disease, tuberculosis, ulcerative colitis, kidney disease, or liver disease.

• If you are using this medication for longer than a week, you may need to receive higher doses if you are subjected to stress, such as serious infections, injury, or surgery. Discuss this with your doctor.

• If you have been taking this drug for more than one or two weeks, do not stop taking it suddenly. If it is stopped abruptly, you may experience abdominal or back pain, dizziness, extreme weakness, fainting, fever, muscle or joint pain, nausea, vomiting, or shortness of breath. Your doctor may, therefore, want to reduce the dosage gradually. Never increase the dosage or take the drug for longer than the prescribed time unless you first consult your doctor.

• While you are taking this drug, you should not be vaccinated or immunized. This medication decreases the effectiveness of vaccines and can lead to infection if a live-virus vaccine is administered.

• Before having surgery or other medical or dental treatment, tell your doctor or dentist you are taking this drug.

• Because this drug can cause glaucoma and cataracts when it is used long-term, your doctor may want to have your eyes examined periodically by an ophthalmologist during treatment.

• If you are taking this medication for prolonged periods, wear or carry an identification card, pendant, or bracelet stating that you are taking an adrenocorticosteroid.

• This drug can raise blood sugar levels in patients with diabetes. Blood sugar should be monitored carefully with blood or urine tests when this drug is being taken.

• Be sure to tell your doctor if you are pregnant. This drug crosses the placenta and may cause adverse effects in the fetus. Birth defects have been observed in the offspring of animals that were given large doses of this type of drug during pregnancy. In addition, be sure to tell your doctor if you are breast-feeding an infant. Small amounts of this medication pass into breast milk and may cause growth suppression or a decrease in natural adrenocorticosteroid production in the nursing infant.

---

diazepam

BRAND NAMES (Manufacturers)
Diastat (Elan)
diazepam (various manufacturers)
Diazepam Intensol (Roxane)
Valium (Roche)

TYPE OF DRUG
Sedative/hypnotic

INGREDIENT
diazepam

DOSAGE FORMS
Gel, rectal, adult (10 mg, 15 mg, and 20 mg)
Gel, rectal, pediatric (2.5 mg, 5 mg, and 10 mg)
Oral solution (5 mg per 5-mL spoonful)
Oral intensol solution (5 mg per mL)
Tablets (2 mg, 5 mg, and 10 mg)

STORAGE
Store at room temperature in a tightly closed, light-resistant container.

USES

Diazepam is prescribed to treat symptoms of anxiety and sometimes to treat muscle spasms, convulsions, seizures, or alcohol withdrawal. It is not clear exactly how this medicine works, but diazepam may relieve anxiety by acting as a depressant of the central nervous system (brain and spinal cord). It is currently used by many people to relieve nervousness. Diazepam is effective for this purpose for short periods, but it is also important to try to remove the underlying cause of the anxiety.

TREATMENT

The intensol solution should be mixed with a nonalcoholic liquid or semisolid food such as water, juice, soda or sodalike beverages, applesauce, or pudding. Use only the calibrated dropper provided. Stir the liquid or food gently for a few seconds after adding the intensol solution. The entire amount of the mixture should be consumed immediately. Do not store prepared mixtures for future use. The tablet form of this medication should be taken exactly as directed by your doctor. It can be taken with food or a full glass of water if stomach upset occurs. Do not take this medication with a dose of antacids, since they may slow its absorption.

If you are taking this drug regularly and you miss a dose but remember within an hour, take the missed dose immediately. If more than an hour has passed, skip the dose you missed and wait for the next scheduled dose. Do not double the next dose.

The rectal form of diazepam is reserved for patients whose epilepsy is difficult to control. Your doctor will provide you with specific recommendations about how and when to use rectal diazepam.

SIDE EFFECTS

Minor. Bitter taste in the mouth, constipation, depression, diarrhea, dizziness, drowsiness (after a night's sleep), dry mouth, excessive salivation, fatigue, flushing, headache, heartburn, loss of appetite, nausea, nervousness, sweating, or vomiting. These side effects may disappear once your body gets accustomed to the medication.

To relieve constipation, increase the amount of fiber in your diet (fresh fruits and vegetables, salads, bran, and whole-grain breads), exercise, and drink more water (unless your doctor directs you to do otherwise).

Dry mouth can be relieved by chewing sugarless gum or by sucking on ice chips or hard candy.

If you feel dizzy, sit or lie down for a while; get up slowly from a sitting or reclining position; and be careful on stairs.

Major. Tell your doctor about any side effects that are persistent or particularly bothersome. IT IS ESPECIALLY IMPORTANT TO TELL YOUR DOCTOR about blurred or double vision, chest pain, difficulty in urinating, fainting, falling, fever, joint pain, hallucinations, mouth sores, nightmares, palpitations, rash, severe depression, shortness of breath, slurred speech, sore throat, uncoordinated movements, unusual excitement, unusual tiredness, or yellowing of the eyes or skin.

INTERACTIONS

This medication interacts with several other types of medications:

1. To prevent oversedation, this medication should not be taken with alcohol, with other sedative medications or central nervous system depressants (such as antihistamines, barbiturates, muscle relaxants, pain medicines, narcotics, medicines for seizures, and tranquilizers), or with antidepressant medications.

2. This medication may decrease the effectiveness of carbamazepine, levodopa, and oral anticoagulants (blood thinners) and may increase the effects of phenytoin.

3. Disulfiram, birth control pills, isoniazid, fluoxetine, valproic acid, propranolol, metoprolol, ketoconazole, and cimetidine can increase the blood levels of diazepam, which can lead to toxic effects.

4. Concurrent use of rifampin may decrease the effectiveness of diazepam.

BE SURE TO TELL YOUR DOCTOR about any medications you are currently taking, especially any of those listed above.

WARNINGS

• Tell your doctor about unusual or allergic reactions you have had to any medications, especially to diazepam or other benzodiazepine tranquilizers (such as alprazolam, flurazepam, halazepam, lorazepam, oxazepam, prazepam, temazepam, and triazolam).

• Be sure to tell your doctor if you now have or have ever had liver disease, kidney disease, epilepsy, lung disease, myasthenia gravis, porphyria, mental depression, or any other type of mental illness.

• This medicine can cause drowsiness. Avoid tasks that require alertness, such as driving a car or operating potentially dangerous machinery.
• This medication has the potential for abuse and must be used with caution. Tolerance may develop quickly; do not increase your dosage of the drug without first consulting your doctor. It is also important not to stop taking this drug suddenly if you have been taking it in large amounts or if you have used it for several weeks. Your doctor may want to reduce your dosage gradually.
• This is a safe drug when used properly. When it is combined with other sedative drugs or alcohol, however, serious side effects can develop.
• Be sure to tell your doctor if you are pregnant. This medicine may increase the chance of birth defects if it is taken during the first three months of pregnancy. In addition, too much use of this medicine during the last six months of pregnancy may cause the baby to become dependent on it, resulting in withdrawal side effects in the newborn. Use of diazepam during the last weeks of pregnancy may cause excessive drowsiness, slowed heartbeat, and breathing difficulties in the infant. Tell your doctor if you are breast-feeding an infant. This drug can pass into breast milk and cause excessive drowsiness, slowed heartbeat, and breathing difficulties in nursing infants.

---

diclofenac

BRAND NAMES (Manufacturers)
Cataflam (Novartis)
diclofenac (various manufacturers)
Voltaren (Novartis)
Voltaren-XR (Novartis)
TYPE OF DRUG
Nonsteroidal anti-inflammatory analgesic
INGREDIENT
diclofenac
DOSAGE FORMS
Tablets (50 mg)
Delayed-release tablets (25 mg, 50 mg, and 75 mg)
Extended-release tablets (100 mg)
STORAGE
Store in a tightly closed container at room temperature away from heat and direct sunlight.

USES

Diclofenac is used to treat the inflammation (pain, swelling, and stiffness) of arthritis and ankylosing spondylitis. It is also used for relief of mild to moderate pain. Diclofenac has been shown to block the production of certain body chemicals, called prostaglandins, that may trigger pain. However, it is not yet fully understood how diclofenac works.

TREATMENT

You may take this medication with or without food. To decrease stomach irritation, your doctor may want you to take this medication with food or antacids.

Do not break, crush, or chew the tablets before swallowing them. They should be swallowed whole to lessen any side effects.

It may take two weeks before you feel the full effects of this medication. Diclofenac does not cure arthritis or ankylosing spondylitis, but it will help to control the condition as long as you continue to take it.

It is important that you take diclofenac on schedule and do not miss any doses. If you do miss a dose, take it as soon as possible. However, if it is almost time for your next dose, do not take the missed dose at all; just return to your regular dosing schedule. Do not double the next dose.

SIDE EFFECTS

Minor. Abdominal cramps, constipation, diarrhea, dizziness, headache, indigestion, or nausea. As your body adjusts to the drug, these side effects should disappear.

To relieve constipation, increase the amount of fiber in your diet (fresh fruits and vegetables, salads, bran, and whole-grain breads), exercise, and drink more water (unless your doctor directs you to do otherwise).

If you become dizzy, sit or lie down for a while; get up slowly from a sitting or reclining position; and be careful when on stairs.

Major. Tell your doctor about any side effects that are persistent or particularly bothersome. IT IS ESPECIALLY IMPORTANT TO TELL YOUR DOCTOR about bloody or black, tarry stools; blurred vision; confusion; difficult or painful urination; palpitations; a problem with hearing, or ringing or buzzing in your ears; skin rash, hives, or itching; soreness of the tongue or mouth; stomach pain; swelling of the feet or hands; tightness in the chest; unexplained sore throat and fever; unusual fatigue or weakness; unusual weight gain; wheezing or difficulty in breathing; or yellowish discoloration of the eyes or skin.

INTERACTIONS

Diclofenac interacts with several other types of medications:

1. Anticoagulants (blood thinners, such as warfarin) can lead to an increase in bleeding complications.

2. Aspirin, other salicylates, and other anti-inflammatory medications can increase stomach irritation. Aspirin may also decrease the effectiveness of diclofenac. Therefore, aspirin should not be used concurrently with this medication.

3. Diclofenac can decrease the elimination of digoxin, methotrexate, and lithium from the body, which can lead to serious side effects.

4. The activity of diuretics (water pills) and drugs to lower blood pressure may be inhibited by diclofenac.

5. Diclofenac may alter a diabetic patient's response to insulin, oral hypoglycemic agents, or antiseizure medication (phenytoin).

Before starting to take diclofenac, BE SURE TO TELL YOUR DOCTOR about any medications you are taking, especially any of those listed above.

WARNINGS

• Before you start to take this medication, it is important to tell your doctor if you have ever had unusual or allergic reactions to diclofenac or to any of the other chemically related drugs (aspirin, other salicylates, diflunisal, fenoprofen, flurbiprofen, indomethacin, ketoprofen, meclofenamate, mefenamic acid, naproxen, oxyphenbutazone, phenylbutazone, piroxicam, sulindac, or tolmetin).

• Tell your doctor if you now have or ever had asthma, bleeding problems, colitis, stomach ulcers or other stomach problems, epilepsy, heart disease, high blood pressure, kidney disease, liver disease, mental illness, or Parkinson's disease.

• If diclofenac makes you dizzy or drowsy, do not take part in any activity that requires alertness, such as driving a car or operating potentially dangerous machinery.

• Because this drug can prolong your bleeding time, it is important to tell your doctor or dentist that you are taking this drug before having surgery or any other medical or dental treatment.

• Stomach problems are more likely to occur if you take aspirin regularly or drink alcohol while being treated with this medication.

• Be sure to tell your doctor if you are pregnant or planning to become pregnant. This medication can cause unwanted effects on the heart or blood flow of the fetus. Studies in animals have also shown that this medicine, if taken late in pregnancy, may increase the length of pregnancy, prolong labor, or cause other problems during delivery. Also tell your doctor if you are breast-feeding an infant. Small amounts of diclofenac can pass into breast milk.

dicloxacillin

BRAND NAMES (Manufacturers)
dicloxacillin sodium (various manufacturers)
Pathocil (Wyeth)
TYPE OF DRUG
Penicillin antibiotic
INGREDIENT
dicloxacillin
DOSAGE FORM
Capsules (125 mg, 250 mg, and 500 mg)
STORAGE
Store this medication at room temperature in a tightly closed container.

USES

Dicloxacillin is used to treat a wide variety of bacterial infections, especially those caused by staphylococcus bacteria. It acts by severely injuring the cell membranes of the infecting bacteria, thereby preventing them from growing and multiplying. Dicloxacillin kills susceptible bacteria, but it is not effective against viruses, parasites, or fungi.

TREATMENT

Take this medication on an empty stomach or with a glass of water, one hour before or two hours after a meal. This drug should never be taken with fruit juices or carbonated beverages because the acidity of these drinks destroys the drug in the stomach.

Dicloxacillin works best when the level of medicine in your bloodstream is kept constant. It is best to take the doses at evenly spaced intervals day and night. For example, if you are taking four doses a day, the doses should be spaced six hours apart.

If you miss a dose of this medication, take the missed dose immediately. However, if you do not remember to take the missed dose until it is almost time for your next dose, take it; space the following dose about halfway through the regular interval between doses; then return to your regular schedule. Try not to skip any doses.

It is important for you to continue to take this medication for the entire time prescribed by your doctor (usually 7 to 14 days), even if the symptoms of your infection disappear before the end of that period. If you stop taking the drug too soon, bacteria are given a chance to continue growing, and the infection could recur.

SIDE EFFECTS

Minor. Diarrhea, heartburn, nausea, or vomiting. These side effects should disappear over time as your body adjusts to this medication.

Major. Tell your doctor about any side effects that are persistent or particularly bothersome. IT IS ESPECIALLY IMPORTANT TO TELL YOUR DOCTOR about bloating, chills, cough, darkened tongue, difficulty in breathing, fever, irritation of the mouth, muscle aches, rash, rectal or vaginal itching, severe diarrhea, or sore throat. In addition, if the symptoms of your infection seem to be getting worse rather than improving, you should contact your doctor.

INTERACTIONS

Dicloxacillin interacts with other types of medications:

1. Probenecid can increase blood concentrations and side effects of this medication.

2. Dicloxacillin may decrease the effectiveness of oral contraceptive medications (birth control pills), and pregnancy could result. You should, therefore, use a different or additional form of birth control while you are taking this medication. Discuss this with your doctor.

BE SURE TO TELL YOUR DOCTOR about any medications you are currently taking, especially any of the medications that are listed above.

WARNINGS

- Tell your doctor about unusual or allergic reactions you have had to any medications, especially to dicloxacillin or penicillins or to cephalosporin antibiotics, penicillamine, or griseofulvin.
- Tell your doctor if you now have or ever had kidney disease, asthma, or allergies.
- This medication has been prescribed for your current infection only. Another infection that you develop later on, or one that someone else has, may require a different medicine. You should not give your medicine to other people or use it for other infections unless your doctor specifically directs you to do so.
- People with diabetes should know that dicloxacillin can cause interference with a Clinitest urine glucose test. To avoid this problem, they should switch to Clinistix or Tes-Tape to test their urine for sugar.
- Be sure to tell your doctor if you are pregnant. Although dicloxacillin appears to be safe when taken during pregnancy, extensive studies in humans have not been conducted. In addition, be sure to tell your doctor if you are breast-feeding an infant. Small amounts of this medication pass into breast milk and may temporarily alter the natural bacterial balance in the intestinal tract of the nursing infant, resulting in episodes of diarrhea.

---

didanosine

BRAND NAMES
Videx (Bristol-Myers Squibb)
Videx EC (Bristol-Myers Squibb)
TYPE OF DRUG
Antiretroviral
INGREDIENT
didanosine
DOSAGE FORMS
Tablets, buffered; chewable/dispersible (25 mg, 50 mg, 100 mg, 150 mg, and 200 mg)
Capsules, delayed release (125 mg, 200 mg, 250 mg, and 400 mg)
Powder packets for oral solution (100 mg, 167 mg, and 250 mg in single-dose packets)
Powder for oral solution, pediatric (2 g per 120 mL and 4 g per 240 mL)
STORAGE
Store tablets and powder for oral solution at room temperature in a tightly closed container. Do not store in the bathroom or expose to excess moisture or heat. Once a solution has been prepared from the powder packets for oral solution, it may be kept at room temperature for up to four hours. The pediatric powder for oral solution should be stored in the refrigerator for up to 30 days. After 30 days, any unused solution should be discarded.

USES

Didanosine is used in the treatment of human immunodeficiency virus (HIV) infection. HIV is the virus that causes AIDS. Didanosine works by inhibiting the reproduction, or growth, of the virus, which slows down the progression of AIDS. Didanosine

... not cure HIV infection or AIDS, but it may delay the onset of other infections and diseases caused by AIDS.

TREATMENT

This medication works best when the level of medicine in your bloodstream is kept constant. It is best to take the drug at evenly spaced intervals throughout the day. Didanosine should be taken without food, on an empty stomach (unless your doctor tells you to do otherwise). The tablets should be chewed before swallowing or dissolved in at least one ounce of water (for every two tablets). If the tablets are dissolved in water, the mixture should be stirred to keep the medication from settling to the bottom; it should be taken immediately. The powder packets for oral solution should be dissolved in four ounces of water. Do not use fruit juice or any acidic beverages to dissolve the powder or tablets.

If you miss a dose of this medication, take it as soon as possible after you remember. However, if it is almost time for your next dose of the medication, do not take the missed dose at all; simply return to your regular dosing schedule. Do not double the next dose.

SIDE EFFECTS

Minor. Anxiety, diarrhea, dry mouth, headache, insomnia, nausea, or stomach pain. These side effects should diminish or disappear as your body becomes accustomed to this medication.

Dry mouth can be relieved by chewing sugarless gum or sucking on ice chips or a piece of hard candy.

Major. Tell your doctor about any side effects that are persistent or particularly bothersome. IT IS ESPECIALLY IMPORTANT TO TELL YOUR DOCTOR about abdominal pain; fever and chills; itchy skin rash; nausea and vomiting; seizures (convulsions); shortness of breath; sore throat; swelling; tingling, burning, numbness, or pain in the hands or feet; unusual bleeding or bruising; unusual tiredness; vision problems; or yellowing of the skin or eyes.

INTERACTIONS

Didanosine may interact with a number of other drugs:

1. Antacids, delavirdine, and indinavir should not be taken at the same time as didanosine. Talk to your doctor and pharmacist about the potential interactions between these medicines and didanosine before taking them.

2. Didanosine may reduce the amount of tetracycline, doxycycline, fluoroquinolones (ciprofloxacin, enoxacin, lomefloxacin, norfloxacin, sparfloxacin, levofloxacin, grepafloxacin, or ofloxacin), and antifungals absorbed by the body.

3. Do not take stavudine with didanosine; increased toxicity may occur.

WARNINGS

- Tell your doctor if you have ever had an allergic reaction to didanosine or to any other medication.
- Before taking this medication, be sure to tell your doctor about any medical problems you may have, especially problems with the pancreas.
- Tell your doctor immediately if you notice any tingling, burning, pain, or numbness in your hands or feet or if you develop abdominal pain, nausea, and vomiting.
- Be sure to tell your doctor if you are pregnant. Although birth defects have not been documented in animals, didanosine does cross the placenta in humans. It is unknown if didanosine is safe for use during human pregnancy. It is not known if didanosine passes into human breast milk. However, because of the risk of passing HIV to her infant, it is recommended that a mother who has HIV infection or AIDS NOT breastfeed her infant.

digoxin

BRAND NAMES (Manufacturers)
digoxin (various manufacturers)
Digitek (Bertek Pharmaceuticals)
Lanoxicaps (GlaxoWellcome)
Lanoxin (GlaxoWellcome)
TYPE OF DRUG
Cardiac glycoside
INGREDIENT
digoxin
DOSAGE FORMS
Tablets (0.125 mg and 0.25 mg)
Capsules (0.05 mg, 0.1 mg, and 0.2 mg)
Pediatric elixir (0.05 mg per mL, with 10% alcohol)
STORAGE
Store at room temperature in tightly closed, light-resistant containers. Do not freeze.

USES

Digoxin is used to treat heart arrhythmias and congestive heart failure. It works directly on the muscle of the heart to strengthen the heartbeat and improve heart rhythm and contraction.

TREATMENT

To avoid stomach irritation, take digoxin with water or with food. Try to take it at the same time every day.

Measure the dose of the pediatric elixir carefully with the dropper provided. An ordinary kitchen teaspoon is not accurate enough.

Try not to miss any doses of this medication. If you do miss a dose, take the missed dose as soon as possible. However, if it is almost time for the next dose, do not take the missed dose at all; just return to your regular schedule. Do not double the next dose. If you miss more than two doses of digoxin, contact your doctor.

Digoxin does not cure congestive heart failure, but it will help to control the condition as long as you continue to take the medication.

SIDE EFFECTS

Minor. Apathy, diarrhea, drowsiness, headache, muscle weakness, or tiredness. These side effects should disappear as your body adjusts to the medication.
Major. Tell your doctor about any side effects that are persistent or particularly bothersome. IT IS ESPECIALLY IMPORTANT TO TELL YOUR DOCTOR about disorientation, enlarged and painful breasts (in both sexes), hallucinations, loss of appetite, mental depression, nausea, palpitations, severe abdominal pain, slowed heart rate, visual disturbances (such as blurred or yellow vision), or vomiting.

INTERACTIONS

Digoxin interacts with several other types of medications (interactions may vary depending upon the dose of digoxin being used):
1. Erythromycin, clarithromycin, amiodarone, benzodiazepine tranquilizers, tetracycline, verapamil, nifedipine, diltiazem, quinidine, quinine, cyclosporin, bepridil, propafenone, itraconazole, and spironolactone can increase the blood levels of digoxin, which can lead to an increase in side effects.
2. Thyroid hormone, propylthiouracil, and methimazole can change the dosage requirements of digoxin.

...ds, kaolin with pectin, sulfasalazine, aminosalicylic acid, metoclopramide, anticancer drugs, neomycin, colestipol, and cholestyramine can decrease the absorption of digoxin from the gastrointestinal tract, decreasing its effectiveness.

4. Diuretics (water pills) and adrenocorticosteroids (cortisonelike medications) can cause hypokalemia (low blood levels of potassium), and hypokalemia can increase the side effects of digoxin.

BE SURE TO TELL YOUR DOCTOR about any medications that you are currently taking—including over-the-counter products—especially any of those listed above.

WARNINGS

- Tell your doctor about unusual or allergic reactions you have had to any medications, especially to digoxin, digitoxin, or any other digitalis glycoside.
- Tell your doctor if you now have or ever had kidney disease, lung disease, thyroid disease, hypokalemia (low blood levels of potassium), or hypercalcemia (high blood levels of calcium).
- The pharmacologic activity of the different brands of this drug varies widely—the tablets dissolve in the stomach and bowel at different rates and to varying degrees. Because of this variability, it is important not to change brands of the drug without consulting your doctor.
- Meals high in bran fiber may reduce the absorption of digoxin from the gastrointestinal tract. Avoid these types of meals when taking your dose of medication.
- Your doctor may want you to take your pulse daily while you are using digoxin. Contact your doctor if your pulse becomes slower than what your doctor tells you is normal, or if it drops below 50 beats per minute.
- Before having surgery or any other medical or dental treatment, tell your doctor or dentist you are taking this drug.
- Before taking any over-the-counter (nonprescription) asthma, allergy, cough, cold, sinus, or diet product, be sure to check with your doctor or pharmacist. Some of these drugs can increase the side effects of digoxin.
- Be sure to tell your doctor if you are pregnant. Although this drug appears to be safe during pregnancy, extensive studies in humans have not been conducted. In addition, the dosage of digoxin required to control your symptoms may change during pregnancy. Also tell your doctor if you are breast-feeding an infant. Small amounts of digoxin pass into breast milk.

---

diltiazem

BRAND NAMES (Manufacturers)

Cardizem (Biovail)
Cardizem CD (Biovail)
Cardizem SR (Biovail)
Dilacor XR (Watson)
diltiazem (various manufacturers)
Tiazac (Forest)
Tiazac ER (Forest)

TYPE OF DRUG

Antianginal and antihypertensive

INGREDIENT

diltiazem

DOSAGE FORMS

Extended-release capsules (120 mg, 180 mg, 240 mg, 300 mg, 360 mg, and 420 mg)
Tablets (30 mg, 60 mg, 90 mg, and 120 mg)
Sustained-release capsules (60 mg, 90 mg, and 120 mg)

STORAGE

Each of the various forms of this medication should be stored at room temperature in a tightly closed container.

USES

This medication is used to prevent the symptoms of angina (chest pain). It belongs to a group of drugs known as calcium channel blockers. It is unclear exactly how it does so, but diltiazem dilates the blood vessels of the heart and increases the amount of oxygen that reaches the heart muscle. This drug is also prescribed to lower blood pressure in patients who have a history of hypertension.

TREATMENT

If stomach irritation occurs, diltiazem can be taken on an empty stomach or with meals, as directed by your doctor.

Swallow the sustained-release and extended-release capsules whole; chewing, crushing, or crumbling them destroys their controlled-release activity and possibly increases the side effects.

To become accustomed to taking this medication, try to take it at the same times each day.

Although diltiazem does not relieve chest pain once the pain has begun, this medication can be used to prevent angina attacks.

If you miss a dose of this medication, take the missed dose as soon as possible, unless it is within four hours of the next scheduled dose. In that case, do not take the missed dose at all; just return to your regular dosing schedule. Do not double the next dose.

This medication does not cure angina or hypertension, but it will help to control the condition as long as you continue to take it.

SIDE EFFECTS

Minor. Constipation, diarrhea, dizziness, drowsiness, headache, insomnia, light-headedness, nausea, nervousness, stomach upset, or vomiting. These side effects should disappear as your body adjusts to the medication.

This drug can increase your sensitivity to sunlight. Therefore, avoid prolonged exposure to sunlight and sunlamps. Wear protective clothing and sunglasses, and use an effective sunscreen.

If you feel dizzy or light-headed, sit or lie down for a while; get up slowly from a sitting or reclining position; and be careful on stairs. To avoid dizziness when you stand, relax and contract the muscles of your legs for a few moments before rising. Do this by pushing one foot against the floor while raising the other foot slightly, alternating feet so that you are "pumping" your legs in a pedaling motion.

To relieve constipation, increase the amount of fiber in your diet (fresh fruits and vegetables, salads, bran, and whole-grain breads), exercise, and drink more water (unless your doctor directs you to do otherwise).

Major. Tell your doctor about any side effects that are persistent or particularly bothersome. IT IS ESPECIALLY IMPORTANT TO TELL YOUR DOCTOR about confusion, depression, fainting, fatigue, flushing of the face, hallucinations, palpitations, skin rash, swelling of the hands and feet, tingling in the fingers or toes, unusual weakness, or yellowing of the eyes or skin.

INTERACTIONS

Diltiazem can interact with several other medications:

1. Diltiazem should be used cautiously with beta blockers (acebutolol, atenolol, betaxolol, carteolol, esmolol, labetalol, metoprolol, nadolol, penbutolol, propranolol, pindolol, and timolol), digitoxin, digoxin, or disopyramide. Side effects on the heart may be increased by the concurrent use of these medications.

2. Cimetidine can reduce the elimination of diltiazem from the body, increasing the risk of side effects.
3. Diltiazem can increase the blood concentrations of carbamazepine and cyclosporine, which can increase the risk of side effects.
4. Varying effects have been reported when this medication is taken concurrently with lithium; tell your doctor if you are taking both lithium and diltiazem.

BE SURE TO TELL YOUR DOCTOR about any medications you are currently taking, especially any listed above.

WARNINGS

- Tell your doctor about unusual or allergic reactions you have had to any medications, especially to diltiazem.
- Be sure to tell your doctor if you now have or ever had bradycardia (slow heartbeat), heart block, heart failure, kidney disease, liver disease, low blood pressure, or sick sinus syndrome.
- If this medication makes you dizzy or drowsy, avoid taking part in any activity that requires alertness, such as driving an automobile or operating potentially dangerous equipment.
- To prevent fainting while taking this drug, avoid drinking large amounts of alcohol. Also avoid prolonged standing and strenuous exercise in hot weather.
- Be sure to tell your doctor if you are pregnant. Extensive studies in pregnant women have not been conducted, but birth defects have been reported in the offspring of animals that received large doses of diltiazem during pregnancy. It is also known that diltiazem passes into breast milk. If you are breast-feeding an infant while being treated with this medication, tell your doctor.

---

diphenhydramine

BRAND NAMES (Manufacturers)
AllerMax* (Pfeiffer)
Benadryl* (Pfizer)
Benadryl Dye-Free Allergy LiquiGels* (Pfizer)
Benadryl Kapseals (Pfizer)
diphenhydramine hydrochloride (various manufacturers)
Nervine Nighttime Sleep Aid* (Miles)
Nytol* (Block)
Sominex (SmithKline Beecham)
Twilite* (Pfeiffer)
Unisom Nighttime Sleep Aid* (Pfizer)
*Available over the counter (without a prescription)

TYPE OF DRUG
Antihistamine and sedative/hypnotic

INGREDIENT
diphenhydramine

DOSAGE FORMS
Chewable tablets (12.5 mg)
Tablets (25 mg and 50 mg)
Capsules (25 mg and 50 mg)
Elixir (12.5 mg per 5-mL spoonful, with 0%, 0.5%, 5.6%, or 14% alcohol)
Oral syrup (12.5 mg per 5-mL spoonful, with 5% alcohol)

STORAGE
Store at room temperature in a tightly closed container, away from heat and direct sunlight.

USES

Diphenhydramine belongs to a group of drugs known as antihistamines (antihistamines block the action of histamine, a chemical that is released by the body during an allergic reaction). It is therefore used to treat or prevent symptoms of allergy. It is also used to treat motion sickness and Parkinson's disease, as a nighttime sleeping aid, and as a nonnarcotic cough suppressant.

TREATMENT

To avoid stomach upset, take diphenhydramine with food, milk, or water (unless your doctor directs you otherwise).

Measure the elixir and syrup carefully with a specially designed 5-mL measuring spoon. An ordinary teaspoon is not accurate enough for medical purposes.

If you miss a dose of this medication, take the missed dose as soon as possible. However, if it is almost time for your next dose, do not take the missed dose at all; just return to your regular dosing schedule. Do not double the next dose.

SIDE EFFECTS

Minor. Blurred vision; confusion; constipation; diarrhea; dizziness; dry mouth, throat, or nose; headache; irritability; loss of appetite; nausea; restlessness; stomach upset; or unusual increase in sweating. These side effects should disappear as your body adjusts to the medication.

This medication can cause increased sensitivity to sunlight. It is important to avoid prolonged exposure to sunlight and sunlamps. Wear protective clothing and sunglasses, and use an effective sunscreen.

If you are constipated, increase the amount of fiber in your diet (fresh fruits and vegetables, salads, bran, and whole-grain breads), exercise, and drink more water (unless your doctor tells you not to do so).

To reduce mouth dryness, chew sugarless gum or suck on ice chips or a piece of hard candy.

If you feel dizzy or light-headed, sit or lie down for a while; get up slowly from a sitting or reclining position; and be careful on stairs.

Major. Tell your doctor about any side effects that are persistent or particularly bothersome. IT IS ESPECIALLY IMPORTANT TO TELL YOUR DOCTOR about changes in menstruation, clumsiness, difficult or painful urination, feeling faint, flushing of the face, hallucinations, palpitations, rash, ringing or buzzing in the ears, seizures, shortness of breath, sleeping disorders, sore throat or fever, tightness in the chest, unusual bleeding or bruising, or unusual tiredness or weakness.

INTERACTIONS

Diphenhydramine interacts with several other types of medications:

1. Concurrent use of diphenhydramine with other central nervous system depressants (for example, alcohol, barbiturates, benzodiazepine tranquilizers, muscle relaxants, narcotics, pain medications, and phenothiazine tranquilizers) or with tricyclic antidepressants can cause extreme fatigue or drowsiness.

2. Monoamine oxidase (MAO) inhibitors (isocarboxazid, pargyline, phenelzine, and tranylcypromine) can increase the side effects of this medication. At least 14 days should separate the use of this drug and the use of an MAO inhibitor.

BE SURE TO TELL YOUR DOCTOR about any medications you are currently taking, especially any of those listed above.

WARNINGS

• Be sure to tell your doctor about unusual or allergic reactions you have had to any medications, especially to diphenhydramine or to any other antihistamine (such as astemizole, azatadine, brompheniramine, carbinoxamine, chlorpheniramine, clemastine, cyproheptadine, dexchlorpheniramine, dimenhydrinate, doxylamine, hydrox-

yzine, phenindamine, promethazine, pyrilamine, terfenadine, trimeprazine, tripelennamine, and triprolidine).
• Tell your doctor if you now have or ever had asthma, blood vessel disease, glaucoma, high blood pressure, kidney disease, peptic ulcers, enlarged prostate gland, or thyroid disease.
• Diphenhydramine can cause drowsiness or dizziness. Your ability to perform tasks that require alertness, such as driving an automobile or operating potentially dangerous equipment or machinery, may be decreased. Appropriate caution should, therefore, be taken.
• Diphenhydramine is highly sedating and has other adverse effects that may be especially detrimental to elderly patients. This medication, therefore, is not recommended for long-term use by elderly patients.
• Be sure to tell your doctor if you are pregnant. The effects of this medication during pregnancy have not been thoroughly studied in humans. Also be sure that you consult with your doctor if you are breast-feeding an infant. Small amounts of diphenhydramine pass into breast milk and may cause unusual excitement or irritability in nursing infants.

diphenoxylate and atropine combination

BRAND NAMES (Manufacturers)
diphenoxylate hydrochloride with atropine sulfate (various manufacturers)
Lomotil (Pharmacia)
Lonox (Geneva)
TYPE OF DRUG
Antidiarrheal (antispasmodic and anticholinergic)
INGREDIENTS
diphenoxylate and atropine
DOSAGE FORMS
Tablets (2.5 mg diphenoxylate and 0.025 mg atropine)
Oral liquid (2.5 mg diphenoxylate and 0.025 mg atropine per 5-mL spoonful, with 15% alcohol)
STORAGE
Store at room temperature in tightly closed, light-resistant containers. Do not freeze.

USES

Diphenoxylate and atropine combination is used to treat severe diarrhea. Diphenoxylate is related to the narcotic analgesics and acts by slowing the movement of the gastrointestinal tract. Small amounts of atropine are added to this medication to prevent abuse of the narcotic diphenoxylate.

TREATMENT

To avoid getting an upset stomach, take this medication with food or with a full glass of water or milk.

Measure the liquid carefully using a specially designed 5-mL measuring spoon. An ordinary kitchen teaspoon is not accurate enough.

If you miss a dose of this medication, do not take the missed dose at all; just return to your regular dosing schedule. Do not double the next dose.

SIDE EFFECTS

Minor. Blurred vision, constipation, dizziness, drowsiness, dry mouth, flushing, headache, loss of appetite, nervousness, sweating, or swollen gums. These side effects should disappear as your body adjusts to the medication.

To relieve mouth dryness, chew sugarless gum or suck on ice chips or a piece of hard candy.

If you feel dizzy or light-headed, sit or lie down for a while; get up slowly from a sitting or reclining position; and be careful on stairs.

Major. Tell your doctor about any side effects that are persistent or particularly bothersome. IT IS ESPECIALLY IMPORTANT TO TELL YOUR DOCTOR about abdominal pain, bloating, breathing difficulties, depression, difficult or painful urination, false sense of well-being, fever, hives, itching, numbness in the fingers or toes, palpitations, rash, severe nausea, vomiting, or weakness.

INTERACTIONS

This drug combination interacts with several other types of medications:

1. Concurrent use of this medication with central nervous system depressants (such as alcohol, antihistamines, barbiturates, benzodiazepine tranquilizers, muscle relaxants, narcotics, pain medications, and phenothiazine tranquilizers) or with tricyclic antidepressant medications can cause extreme drowsiness.

2. A monoamine oxidase (MAO) inhibitor (tranylcypromine, phenelzine, isocarboxazid, and pargyline) taken within 14 days of this medication can lead to unpredictable and severe side effects.

3. The side effects of the atropine component of this medication may be increased if amantadine, haloperidol, phenothiazine tranquilizers, procainamide, or quinidine is taken concurrently.

BE SURE TO TELL YOUR DOCTOR about any medications you are currently taking, especially any of those listed above.

WARNINGS

• Tell your doctor about unusual or allergic reactions you have had to medications, especially to diphenoxylate or to atropine.

• Tell your doctor if you now have or ever had drug-induced diarrhea, gallstones or gallbladder disease, glaucoma, heart disease, hiatal hernia, high blood pressure, kidney disease, liver disease, lung disease, myasthenia gravis, enlarged prostate gland, thyroid disease, or ulcerative colitis.

• If this medication makes you dizzy or drowsy, you should avoid taking part in any activity that requires alertness, such as driving a car or operating any potentially dangerous equipment.

• Before having surgery or any other medical or dental treatment, be sure to tell your doctor or dentist that you are taking this medication.

• Because this product contains diphenoxylate, it has the potential for abuse and must be used with caution. Tolerance develops quickly; do not increase the dosage or stop taking the drug unless you first consult your doctor. If you have been taking large amounts of this medication for long periods and then stop abruptly, you may experience a withdrawal reaction (muscle aches, diarrhea, gooseflesh, runny nose, nausea, vomiting, shivering, trembling, stomach cramps, sleep disorders, irritability, weakness, excessive yawning, or sweating). Your doctor may, therefore, want to reduce the dosage gradually.

• Check with your doctor if your diarrhea does not subside within two to three days. Unless your doctor specifically directs otherwise, you should not take this medication for more than ten days.

• While taking this medication, be sure to drink lots of fluids to replace those lost due to diarrhea.

• Be sure to tell your doctor if you are pregnant. Although this medication has been shown to be safe in animals, its effects in humans during pregnancy have not been thoroughly studied. Also tell your doctor if you are breast-feeding an infant. Small amounts of this medication may pass into breast milk and cause excessive drowsiness in nursing infants.

dipyridamole

BRAND NAMES (Manufacturers)
dipyridamole (various manufacturers)
Persantine (Boehringer Ingelheim)
TYPE OF DRUG
Antiplatelet agent
INGREDIENT
dipyridamole
DOSAGE FORM
Tablets (25 mg, 50 mg, and 75 mg)
STORAGE
Store at room temperature in a tightly closed container.

USES

Dipyridamole is primarily used to prevent blood-clot formation, especially in patients who have artificial heart valves and are taking the blood thinner warfarin. Dipyridamole has also been used to prevent chronic chest pain (angina) due to heart disease, although this medication has not been found to be highly effective for the treatment of angina.

TREATMENT

Take this medication on an empty stomach with a full glass of water one hour before or two hours after a meal. If this drug upsets your stomach, check with your doctor to see if you can take it with food.

The full benefits of this medication may not become apparent for up to two to three months.

If you miss a dose of this medication, take the missed dose as soon as possible. However, if it is within four hours of your next scheduled dose, do not take the missed dose at all; just return to your regular dosing schedule. Do not double the next dose.

SIDE EFFECTS

Minor. Dizziness, fatigue, flushing, headache, nausea, stomach cramps, or weakness. These side effects should disappear as your body adjusts to the medication.

To avoid dizziness or light-headedness when you stand, contract and relax the muscles of your legs for a few moments before rising. Do this by pushing one foot against the floor while raising the other foot slightly, alternating feet so that you are "pumping" your legs in a pedaling motion.

Major. Tell your doctor about any side effects that are persistent or particularly bothersome. IT IS ESPECIALLY IMPORTANT TO TELL YOUR DOCTOR about fainting, skin rash, or a worsening of your chest pain.

INTERACTIONS

Dipyridamole interacts with certain types of medications: Aspirin-containing products should not be taken concurrently with dipyridamole and blood thinners such as warfarin. This combination may lead to bleeding problems.

BE SURE TO TELL YOUR DOCTOR about any medications you are currently taking, especially any of those listed above.

WARNINGS

- Tell your doctor about unusual or allergic reactions you have had to any medications, especially to dipyridamole.
- Tell your doctor if you have ever had low blood pressure.

• The effectiveness of dipyridamole in controlling chronic angina is controversial. At one time, dipyridamole was indicated as "possibly effective" for long-term therapy of chronic angina, but the Food and Drug Administration (FDA) withdrew its approval for this specific use. Today, this medication is more frequently prescribed with blood-thinner medications (warfarin) to prevent blood-clot formation after heart valve replacement.
• This drug does not stop chest pain from angina that has already begun. It is used only to prevent such pain.
• If this medication makes you dizzy, do not take part in any activity that requires alertness, such as driving an automobile or operating potentially dangerous equipment or machinery.
• Before having any surgery or other medical or dental treatment, be sure to tell your doctor or dentist that you are taking this medication.
• Be sure to tell your doctor if you are pregnant. Although this drug appears to be safe, extensive studies in humans during pregnancy have not been conducted. Also consult with your doctor if you are breast-feeding an infant. Small amounts of dipyridamole have been known to pass into breast milk, so caution is warranted.

---

dolasetron

BRAND NAME (Manufacturer)
Anzemet (Hoechst-Marion Roussel)
TYPE OF DRUG
Antiemetic
INGREDIENT
dolasetron
DOSAGE FORM
Tablets (50 mg and 100 mg)
STORAGE
Store at room temperature and protected from light.

USES

Dolasetron is used to prevent the nausea, vomiting, and retching associated with cancer chemotherapy. Dolasetron is also used to prevent the nausea and vomiting that occur following surgery. Although it is unclear precisely how dolasetron acts, it appears to work by blocking the release of certain chemicals in the brain that stimulate the impulse to vomit.

TREATMENT

Take exactly as prescribed by your physician. Dolasetron's effectiveness is thought to be related to keeping a steady level of it in the bloodstream. It is very important not to skip any doses of this medication.

SIDE EFFECTS

Minor. Constipation, diarrhea, dizziness, drowsiness, fatigue, fever or chills, headache, low blood pressure, skin rash, or slow heartbeat. These side effects should diminish or disappear as your body adjusts to the medication.

If you feel dizzy or light-headed, sit or lie down for a while, stand up slowly, and be careful on stairs.

To relieve constipation, increase the amount of fiber (fresh fruits and vegetables, salads, bran, and whole-grain breads) in your diet and drink more water (unless your doctor directs you to do otherwise).

Major. Tell your doctor about any side effects that are persistent or particularly bothersome. IT IS ESPECIALLY IMPORTANT TO NOTIFY YOUR DOCTOR about irregular heartbeat, shortness of breath, skin rash, tightness of the chest, troubled breathing, or wheezing.

INTERACTIONS

Dolasetron can cause electrocardiogram (ECG) interval changes. It should be used with caution in individuals who are taking drugs that can change the ECG intervals. It is important to discuss all medications that you are taking with your physician prior to beginning treatment with dolasetron.

Cimetidine and atenolol, when taken with dolasetron, may result in higher dolasetron blood levels and possible toxicity.

Before starting dolasetron, BE SURE TO TELL YOUR DOCTOR about any medication you are taking.

WARNINGS

• Tell your doctor about unusual or allergic reactions you have had to any medications, especially to dolasetron, granisetron, or ondansetron.
• Dolasetron should not be taken together with other drugs from the same class (such as granisetron or ondansetron).
• Before starting to take dolasetron, tell your doctor if you now have or ever had heart disease or irregularities in your heartbeat. Be sure to tell your physician if you are taking antiarrhythmic drugs or diuretics (water pills).
• If this medication makes you dizzy or drowsy, do not participate in any activities that require mental alertness, such as driving an automobile or operating potentially dangerous machinery or equipment.
• Be sure to tell your doctor if you are pregnant. Adequate studies have not been conducted in human pregnancy. Be sure to tell your doctor if you are breast-feeding an infant. It is not known if dolasetron passes into breast milk.

---

donepezil

BRAND NAME (Manufacturer)
Aricept (Eisai/Pfizer)
TYPE OF DRUG
Alzheimer's disease medication, cholinesterase inhibitor
INGREDIENT
donepezil
DOSAGE FORM
Tablets (5 mg and 10 mg)
STORAGE
Store at room temperature in a tightly closed container. Do not store in the bathroom. Excessive heat or moisture may cause this medication to break down.

USES

Donepezil is used for patients with Alzheimer's disease. Although this medication helps to reduce the symptoms associated with the disease, it will not cure it. Some research has shown that this medication can help improve thinking ability in some patients.

TREATMENT

Donepezil tablets may be taken either on an empty stomach or with food or milk (unless your doctor directs you to do otherwise). The medication is usually taken at bedtime, unless your doctor directs you to take it differently. Donepezil should be taken as directed.

If you miss a dose of this medication, take the missed dose as soon as possible after you remember. However, if it is almost time for your next dose of the medication, do not take the missed dose at all; just return to your regular dosing schedule. Do not double the next dose.

SIDE EFFECTS

Minor. Constipation, diarrhea, dizziness, drowsiness, fainting, frequent urination, headache, loss of appetite, mental depression, muscle cramps, nausea, strange dreams, trouble sleeping, unusual bleeding or bruising, unusual tiredness or weakness, vomiting, or weight loss. These minor side effects should diminish or disappear as your body adjusts to this medication.

To avoid dizziness or light-headedness when you stand, contract and relax the muscles of your legs for a few moments before rising. Do this by pressing one foot against the floor while raising the other foot slightly so that you are "pumping" your legs in a pedaling motion.

If you feel dizzy or light-headed, sit or lie down for a while, get up slowly from a sitting or lying position, and be careful on stairs.

Major. Tell your doctor about any side effects that are persistent or particularly bothersome. IT IS ESPECIALLY IMPORTANT TO TELL YOUR DOCTOR about anxiety; black or tarry stools; cloudy urine; clumsiness; decreased urination; depression; dry mouth; feeling faint; flushing of the face; hallucinations; hot flashes; increased heart rate; loss of bowel or bladder control; migraines; palpitations; puffiness or swelling of the eyelids, eye area, face, lips, or tongue; rash; seizures; shortness of breath; sleeping disorders; sore throat or fever; tightness in the chest or back; trouble breathing; unusual bleeding or bruising; unusual tiredness or weakness; or yellowing of the eyes or skin.

INTERACTIONS

The use of this medication with nonsteroidal anti-inflammatory drugs (including ibuprofen and naproxen) may increase the risk of stomach problems or peptic ulcer disease. Discuss this with your doctor or pharmacist.

BE SURE TO TELL YOUR DOCTOR about any medications that you are currently taking, especially any of the type mentioned above.

WARNINGS

- Tell your doctor about unusual or allergic reactions you have had to any medications, especially to donepezil, biperiden, bupivacaine, methylphenidate, paroxetine, rifabutin, or trihexyphenidyl.
- Tell your doctor if you now have or if you have ever had asthma, lung disease, seizures, blood-vessel disease, glaucoma, high blood pressure, any heart problems, kidney disease, liver disease, peptic ulcers, enlarged prostate gland, urinary tract problems, or thyroid disease.
- This medication may cause you to be unusually drowsy. As a result, your ability to perform tasks that require alertness, such as driving a car or operating potentially dangerous machinery, may be impaired.
- Do not take any over-the-counter medications for weight control or for asthma, sinus problems, cough, cold, or allergies unless you first discuss it with your doctor or pharmacist.
- Before having any surgery or medical or dental treatment, be sure the doctor or dentist is informed that you are taking this medication. This very important step will help to prevent unwanted drug interactions and side effects.
- Be sure to tell your doctor if you are pregnant. The effects of using this medication during pregnancy have not been thoroughly studied in humans. Also, be sure to tell your doctor if you are breast-feeding an infant. Donepezil may cause unwanted effects in the nursing infant and should not be taken by nursing women.

dorzolamide

BRAND NAME (Manufacturer)
Trusopt (Merck)
TYPE OF DRUG
Carbonic anhydrase inhibitor
INGREDIENT
dorzolamide
DOSAGE FORM
Ophthalmic solution 2%
STORAGE
Store at room temperature in a tightly closed, light-resistant container. Do not freeze. Be sure to discard any outdated or unneeded medication, and store all drugs out of the reach of children and pets.

USES

Dorzolamide is used in the treatment of glaucoma and ocular hypertension.

TREATMENT

Wash your hands with soap and water before applying this medication. To avoid contaminating the eyedrop solution, be careful not to touch the tube portion of the dropper or to let the tube touch your eye; and DO NOT wipe off or rinse the dropper after each use.

To apply the eyedrops, tilt your head back and pull down your lower eyelid with your finger to make a pouch below the eye. Drop the prescribed amount of medicine into this pouch and slowly close your eyes. Try not to blink. Keep your eyes closed, and place one finger at the corner of the eye next to your nose for a minute or two, applying slight pressure (this is done to prevent loss of the medication through the duct that drains fluid from the surface of the eye into the nose and throat). Then wipe away any excess with a clean tissue. Since the drops are somewhat difficult to apply, you may want someone else to apply them for you.

If more than one type of eyedrop has been prescribed for you, wait at least ten minutes before applying the second eye medication.

If you miss a dose of dorzolamide, apply the missed dose as soon as possible. However, if it is almost time for the next dose, do not attempt to administer the missed dose at all; just return to your regular dosing schedule. Do not double the next dose.

SIDE EFFECTS

Minor. Blurred vision, burning sensation in the eyes, headache, or stinging or bitter taste in the mouth immediately following application. These side effects should lessen as your body adjusts to the medication.

Major. Tell your doctor about any side effects that are persistent or particularly bothersome. IT IS ESPECIALLY IMPORTANT TO TELL YOUR DOCTOR about allergic reactions, blurred vision, eye pain, fatigue, fever, muscle cramps, severe itching of the eyes, skin rash, unusual bleeding or bruising, or yellowing of the eyes or skin.

INTERACTIONS

Although no significant interactions have been seen with dorzolamide, other drugs of this type interact with other medications. Specifically, high doses of salicylates (aspirin, methyl salicylate) may increase the side effects of carbonic anhydrase inhibitors.

BE SURE TO TELL YOUR DOCTOR about any medications you are taking, especially any of those listed above.

WARNINGS

• Tell your doctor about any unusual or allergic reactions you have had to any medications, especially to dorzolamide, acetazolamide, methazolamide, sulfonamide antibiotics, diuretics (water pills), oral antidiabetics, dapsone, sulfone, or sulfoxone.
• Before starting this medication, be sure to tell your doctor if you now have or ever had Addison's disease (underactive adrenal gland), chronic lung disease, diabetes mellitus, electrolyte disorders, gout, kidney disease, or liver disease.
• If this medication blurs your vision, try to avoid activities that require visual acuity, such as driving a car or operating potentially dangerous equipment.
• Do not use this medication while wearing soft contact lenses. The preservative in dorzolamide (benzalkonium chloride) may be absorbed by soft contact lenses.
• Be sure to tell your doctor if you are pregnant. Although extensive studies of dorzolamide in human pregnancy have not been conducted, dorzolamide has been shown to cause side effects in the fetuses of animals that received large doses of the drug during pregnancy. Also tell your doctor if you are breast-feeding an infant. It is not known if this medication passes into breast milk.

---

doxazosin

BRAND NAMES (Manufacturers)
doxazosin (various manufacturers)
Cardura (Pfizer)
TYPE OF DRUG
Antihypertensive
INGREDIENT
doxazosin
DOSAGE FORM
Tablets (1 mg, 2 mg, 4 mg, and 8 mg)
STORAGE
Store at room temperature in a tightly closed container.

USES

Doxazosin mesylate is used to treat high blood pressure. It relaxes the muscle tissue of the blood vessels, which in turn lowers blood pressure. Doxazosin is also used to reduce urinary obstruction and relieve associated symptoms of benign prostatic hypertrophy (BPH).

TREATMENT

Doxazosin may be taken before or after meals, as directed by your doctor.

The first dose of this medication may cause very low blood pressure, especially in the elderly, when treatment is first started. This effect is particularly strong in some people two to six hours after the first dose.

If you miss a dose of this medication, take it as soon as possible. However, if it is almost time for your next dose, do not take the missed dose at all; just wait until the next scheduled dose. Do not double the dose.

This medication does not cure high blood pressure or benign prostatic hypertrophy, but it will help to control the condition as long as you continue to take it. In order to become accustomed to taking this medication, try to take it at the same time(s) each day.

SIDE EFFECTS

Minor. Breast pain, constipation, diarrhea, dizziness, drowsiness, edema, frequent urination, headache, itching, lack of energy, malaise, nasal congestion, nausea, nervousness, rash, sweating, or weight gain. These side effects should disappear as your body adjusts to the medication. TELL YOUR DOCTOR if skin reactions or other side effects persist or become bothersome.

To prevent constipation, increase the amount of fiber in your diet (fresh fruits and vegetables, salads, bran, and whole-grain breads), unless your doctor tells you otherwise.

To avoid dizziness or light-headedness when you stand, contract and relax the muscles of your legs for a few moments before rising. Do this by pushing one foot against the floor while raising the other foot slightly, alternating feet so that you are "pumping" your legs in a pedaling motion.

Major. Tell your doctor about any side effects that are persistent or particularly bothersome. IT IS ESPECIALLY IMPORTANT TO TELL YOUR DOCTOR about blurred vision; chest pain; difficulty breathing; difficulty urinating; dizziness or light-headedness (severe or persistent); edema; fainting; fever; flulike symptoms; heart rate disturbance; nosebleeds; palpitations; persistent malaise/fatigue; persistent, painful erection; or ringing in the ears.

INTERACTIONS

Doxazosin has been known to interact with other types of medications:

1. The combination of doxazosin and alcohol or verapamil can bring about a severe drop in blood pressure and cause fainting.

2. The antihypertensive effects of clonidine may be reduced during therapy with doxazosin.

BE SURE TO TELL YOUR DOCTOR about any medications you are currently taking, especially those listed above.

WARNINGS

- Tell your doctor about unusual or allergic reactions you have had to any medications, especially to doxazosin, prazosin, or terazosin.
- Before starting to take this medication, be sure to tell your doctor if you now have or ever had angina (chest pain) or any kind of kidney disease or liver disease.
- Because initial therapy with this drug may cause dizziness or fainting, your doctor will probably start you on a low dosage and increase the dosage gradually.
- If this drug makes you dizzy or drowsy or blurs your vision, do not take part in any activity that requires alertness, such as driving an automobile or operating potentially dangerous machinery.
- To avoid dizziness or fainting while taking this drug, try not to stand for long periods of time, avoid drinking excess amounts of alcohol, and try not to get overheated (avoid exercising strenuously in hot weather and taking hot baths, showers, and saunas).
- Before taking any over-the-counter (nonprescription) sinus, allergy, asthma, cough, cold, or diet preparations, check with your doctor or pharmacist. Some of these products can cause an increase in blood pressure.
- Do not stop taking this medication unless you first check with your doctor. If you stop taking this drug, you may experience a rise in blood pressure. Your doctor may want to decrease your dose gradually.
- Be sure to tell your doctor if you are pregnant. Although the drug appears to be safe, only limited studies have been conducted with pregnant women. Also tell your doctor if you are breast-feeding an infant. Doxazosin should be used with caution in nursing women.

---

doxepin

BRAND NAMES (Manufacturers)

doxepin (various manufacturers)
Sinequan (Roerig)

TYPE OF DRUG
Tricyclic antidepressant
INGREDIENT
doxepin
DOSAGE FORMS
Capsules (10 mg, 25 mg, 50 mg, 75 mg, 100 mg, and 150 mg)
Oral concentrate (10 mg per mL)
STORAGE
Store at room temperature in tightly closed containers. Do not freeze.

USES

Doxepin is used to relieve the symptoms of mental depression and anxiety. This medication belongs to a group of drugs referred to as tricyclic antidepressants. These medicines are thought to relieve depression by increasing the concentration of certain chemicals necessary for nerve transmission in the brain.

TREATMENT

This medication should be taken exactly as your doctor prescribes. You can take it with food to lessen the chance of stomach irritation (unless your doctor tells you to do otherwise).

Dilute each dose of the oral concentrate in at least four ounces (half a glass) of water, milk, or fruit juice just prior to administration. Measure the correct amount carefully with the dropper provided. DO NOT mix the medication with grape juice or with carbonated beverages, since they may decrease the medicine's effectiveness.

If you miss a dose of this medication, take the missed dose as soon as possible, then return to your regular dosing schedule. If the dose you missed was a once-a-day bedtime dose, do not take that dose in the morning; check with your doctor instead. If the dose is taken in the morning, it may cause some unwanted side effects. Never double the dose.

The antidepressant effects of therapy with this medication may not become apparent for four to six weeks; however, the antianxiety effects should become apparent within days.

SIDE EFFECTS

Minor. Blurred vision, constipation, cramps, diarrhea, dizziness, drowsiness, dry mouth, fatigue, indigestion, insomnia, loss of appetite, nausea, peculiar tastes in the mouth, restlessness, sweating, vomiting, weakness, or weight gain or loss. As your body adjusts to the medication, these side effects should disappear.

This drug may cause increased sensitivity to sunlight. Therefore, avoid prolonged exposure to sunlight and sunlamps. Wear protective clothing and use an effective sunscreen.

Dry mouth can be relieved by chewing sugarless gum or by sucking on ice chips or a piece of hard candy.

To relieve constipation, increase the amount of fiber in your diet (fresh fruits and vegetables, salads, bran, and whole-grain breads), exercise, and drink more water (unless your doctor directs you to do otherwise).

To avoid dizziness or light-headedness when you stand, contract and relax the muscles of your legs for a few moments before rising. Do this by pushing one foot against the floor while raising the other foot slightly, alternating feet so that you are "pumping" your legs in a pedaling motion.

Major. Tell your doctor about any side effects that are persistent or particularly bothersome. IT IS ESPECIALLY IMPORTANT TO TELL YOUR DOCTOR about agitation, anxiety, chest pain, confusion, convulsions, difficulty in urinating, enlarged or painful breasts (in both sexes), fainting, fever, fluid retention, hair loss, hallucinations, headaches, impotence, mood changes, mouth sores, nervousness, nightmares, numbness in the fingers or toes, palpitations, ringing in the ears, seizures, skin rash, sleep disorders, sore throat, a tendency to bleed or bruise, tremors, uncoordinated movements or balance problems, or yellowing of the eyes or skin.

INTERACTIONS

Doxepin interacts with a number of other types of medications:
1. Extreme drowsiness can occur when this medicine is taken with central nervous system depressants (such as alcohol, antihistamines, barbiturates, benzodiazepine tranquilizers, muscle relaxants, narcotics, pain medications, phenothiazine tranquilizers, and medications to induce sleep) or with other antidepressants.
2. Doxepin may decrease the effectiveness of antiseizure medications and may block the blood-pressure-lowering effects of clonidine and guanethidine.
3. Birth control pills and estrogen-containing drugs can increase the side effects and reduce the effectiveness of doxepin.
4. Cimetidine can decrease the elimination of doxepin from the body, which can increase the possibility that side effects will occur.
5. Doxepin may increase the side effects of thyroid medications and over-the-counter (nonprescription) cough, cold, allergy, asthma, sinus, and diet medications if it is used concurrently with any of these.
6. The concurrent use of this drug and monoamine oxidase (MAO) inhibitors should be avoided, because the combination may result in fever, convulsions, or high blood pressure. At least 14 days should separate the use of this drug and the use of an MAO inhibitor.

BE SURE TO TELL YOUR DOCTOR about any medications you are currently taking, especially any of those listed above.

WARNINGS

• Tell your doctor if you have had unusual or allergic reactions to any medications, especially to doxepin or any of the other tricyclic antidepressants (amitriptyline, imipramine, trimipramine, amoxapine, protriptyline, desipramine, maprotiline, and nortriptyline).
• Be sure to tell your doctor if you have a history of alcoholism or if you have ever had asthma, high blood pressure, liver or kidney disease, heart disease, a heart attack, circulatory disease, stomach problems, intestinal problems, difficulty in urinating, enlarged prostate gland, epilepsy, glaucoma, thyroid disease, mental illness, or electroshock therapy.
• If this medication makes you feel dizzy or drowsy, do not take part in any activity that requires alertness, such as driving an automobile or operating potentially dangerous equipment.
• Before having surgery or any other medical or dental treatment, be sure to tell your doctor or dentist that you are taking this medication.
• Do not stop taking this drug suddenly. Abruptly stopping it can cause nausea, headache, stomach upset, fatigue, or a worsening of your condition. Your doctor may want to reduce the dosage gradually.
• The effects of this medication may last as long as seven days after you have stopped taking it, so continue to observe all precautions during that period.
• Be sure to tell your doctor if you are pregnant. The effects of this drug during pregnancy have not been thoroughly studied in humans. Studies in animals have shown that this medication can cause side effects to the fetus if given to the mother in large doses during pregnancy. Also tell your doctor if you are breast-feeding an infant. Small amounts of this drug can pass into breast milk and may cause unwanted effects in the nursing infant.

doxycycline

BRAND NAMES (Manufacturers)
Adoxa (Bioglan)
Doryx (Warner-Chilcott)
doxycycline (various manufacturers)
Monodox (Oclassen)
Vibramycin (Pfizer)
Vibra Tabs (Pfizer)
TYPE OF DRUG
Tetracycline antibiotic
INGREDIENT
doxycycline
DOSAGE FORMS
Tablets (50 mg, 75 mg, and 100 mg)
Capsules (50 mg and 100 mg)
Capsules, coated pellets (75 mg and 100 mg)
Oral suspension (25 mg per 5-mL spoonful)
Oral syrup (50 mg per 5-mL spoonful)
STORAGE
Store at room temperature in tightly closed, light-resistant containers. Discard any unused portion of the suspension after 14 days because the suspension loses potency after that period. This medication should never be frozen.

USES

Doxycycline is used to treat a wide variety of bacterial infections and to prevent or treat traveler's diarrhea. It acts by inhibiting the growth of bacteria.

Doxycycline kills susceptible bacteria, but it is not effective against viruses or fungi.

TREATMENT

To avoid stomach upset, you can take this drug with food (unless your doctor directs you to do otherwise).

Shake the suspension well just before measuring each dose to distribute the ingredients evenly and equalize the doses. The contents tend to settle on the bottom of the bottle. Measure each dose of the suspension or syrup carefully with a specially designed 5-mL measuring spoon. An ordinary kitchen teaspoon is not accurate enough for this purpose.

Do not mix the oral syrup form of this drug with other substances unless directed to do so by your doctor.

Doxycycline works best when the level of medicine in your bloodstream is kept constant. It is best to take the doses at evenly spaced intervals day and night. For example, if you are to take two doses a day, the doses should be spaced 12 hours apart.

If you miss a dose of this medication, take the missed dose immediately. However, if you do not remember to take the missed dose until it is almost time for your next dose, take it; space the following dose about halfway through the regular interval between doses; then return to your regular dosing schedule. Try not to skip any doses.

It is very important that you take this drug for the entire time prescribed, even if the symptoms disappear before the end of that period. If you stop taking the drug too soon, resistant bacteria can continue to grow, and the infection could recur.

SIDE EFFECTS

Minor. Diarrhea, discoloration of the nails, dizziness, loss of appetite, nausea, stomach cramps and upset, or vomiting. These side effects should disappear as your body adjusts to the medication.

Doxycycline can increase your sensitivity to sunlight. You should try to avoid prolonged exposure to sunlight and sunlamps. Wear protective clothing and sunglasses, and use an effective sunscreen.

Major. Tell your doctor about any side effects that are persistent or particularly bothersome. IT IS ESPECIALLY IMPORTANT TO TELL YOUR DOCTOR about darkened tongue, difficulty in breathing, joint pain, mouth irritation, rash, rectal or vaginal itching, sore throat and fever, unusual bleeding or bruising, or yellowing of the eyes or skin. If your symptoms of infection seem to be getting worse rather than improving, you should contact your doctor.

INTERACTIONS

Doxycycline interacts with other types of medications:

1. It can increase the absorption of digoxin, which may lead to digoxin toxicity.

2. The gastrointestinal side effects (nausea, vomiting, stomach upset) of theophylline may be increased by doxycycline.

3. The dosage of oral anticoagulants (blood thinners, such as warfarin) may need to be adjusted when this medication is started.

4. Doxycycline may decrease the effectiveness of oral contraceptives (birth control pills), and pregnancy could result. You should, therefore, use a different or additional form of birth control during treatment with doxycycline. Discuss this with your doctor.

5. Barbiturates, carbamazepine, phenytoin, and antacids can lower the levels of doxycycline in the blood, thus decreasing its effectiveness.

6. Iron can bind to doxycycline in the gastrointestinal tract, which can decrease its absorption and, therefore, its effectiveness.

BE SURE TO TELL YOUR DOCTOR about any medications you are currently taking, especially any of those listed above.

WARNINGS

• Tell your doctor about any unusual or allergic reactions you have ever had to any medications, especially to doxycycline, oxytetracycline, tetracycline, or minocycline.

• Tell your doctor if you now have or ever had kidney or liver disease.

• Make sure that your prescription for this medication is marked with the drug's expiration date. The drug should be discarded after the expiration date. If doxycycline is used after it has expired, serious side effects (especially to the kidneys) could result.

• This medication has been prescribed for your current infection only. Another infection later on, or one that someone else has, may require a different medicine. You should not give your medicine to other people or use it for other infections, unless your doctor specifically directs you to do so.

• Be sure to tell your doctor if you are pregnant or if you are breast-feeding an infant. Doxycycline should not be used during pregnancy and breast-feeding. It crosses the placenta and passes into breast milk. This drug can cause permanent discoloration of the teeth and can inhibit tooth and bone growth if used during their development. This drug should not be used by children less than eight years of age.

---

efavirenz

BRAND NAME (Manufacturer)

Sustiva (Bristol-Myers Squibb)

TYPE OF DRUG

Antiretroviral

INGREDIENT

efavirenz

DOSAGE FORMS

Capsules (50 mg, 100 mg, and 200 mg)
Tablets (600 mg)

STORAGE

Store at room temperature in a tightly closed container. Do not expose to excess heat.

USES

Efavirenz is used in the treatment of human immunodeficiency virus (HIV) infection. HIV is the virus that causes AIDS. Efavirenz works by inhibiting the reproduction, or growth, of the virus, which slows down the progression of AIDS. Efavirenz does not cure HIV infection or AIDS, but it may delay the onset of other infections and diseases caused by AIDS.

TREATMENT

This medication works best when the level of medicine in your bloodstream is kept constant. It is best to take the drug at evenly spaced intervals throughout the day. To avoid stomach irritation, you can take efavirenz with food or with a full glass of water (unless your doctor tells you to do otherwise). However, efavirenz should NOT be taken with a high-fat meal. Bedtime dosing is often recommended.

If you miss a dose of this medication, take it as soon as possible. However, if it is almost time for your next dose, skip the missed dose and go back to your regular dosing schedule. Do not double the doses.

SIDE EFFECTS

Minor. Abnormal dreams, diarrhea, difficulty concentrating, dizziness, headache, insomnia, muscle aches or pains, nausea, rash, or vomiting. These side effects should diminish or disappear as your body adjusts to the medication.

To avoid dizziness or light-headedness when you stand, contract and relax the muscles of your legs for a few moments before rising.

Major. Tell your doctor about any side effects that are persistent or particularly bothersome. IT IS ESPECIALLY IMPORTANT TO TELL YOUR DOCTOR about anxiety, changes in the position or location of body fat, confusion, drowsiness, hallucinations, mood changes, severe skin rash with blistering or fever, or yellowing of the skin or the eyes.

INTERACTIONS

Efavirenz may interact with a number of medications.

1. Concurrent use of alcohol or other central nervous system depressants (antihistamines, barbiturates, benzodiazepines, muscle relaxants, or antidepressants) with efavirenz may cause extreme drowsiness.

2. Efavirenz should not be given together with benzodiazepines (including diazepam, midazolam, and triazolam) or ergot derivatives, since these combinations may cause serious, life-threatening reactions.

3. Efavirenz may interfere with the actions of warfarin (a blood thinner).

4. The effects of indinavir, saquinavir, and clarithromycin may be reduced by efavirenz.

5. Efavirenz may increase the side effects of ritonavir.

BE SURE TO TELL YOUR DOCTOR about any medications you are currently taking, especially any of those listed above.

WARNINGS

• Tell your doctor if you have ever had an allergic reaction to efavirenz or to any other medication.

• Before taking this medication, be sure to tell your doctor about any medical problems you may have, especially liver problems.

• Tell your doctor immediately if you notice any type of skin rash, especially if it is severe or if it is accompanied by blisters or fever.
• If this drug makes you dizzy or drowsy, do not participate in any activity that requires alertness, such as driving a car or operating potentially dangerous equipment.
• Efavirenz may cause some nervous system effects. For some patients, these may be severe. Talk to your doctor if you have persistent difficulty sleeping or abnormal dreams or you become confused, have loss of memory, become nervous or agitated, or experience hallucinations.
• Be sure to tell your doctor if you are pregnant. Although birth defects have not been documented in humans, efavirenz has been shown to cause birth defects in animals when given at the same doses used in humans. Because of this, it is likely that efavirenz would be harmful during a human pregnancy. It is important that women use two methods of birth control while taking efavirenz. It is not known if efavirenz passes into human breast milk. However, because of the risk of passing HIV to infants, it is recommended that mothers who have HIV infection NOT breast-feed their infants.

---

enalapril

BRAND NAME (Manufacturer)
Vasotec (Merck Sharp & Dohme)
TYPE OF DRUG
Antihypertensive
INGREDIENT
enalapril
DOSAGE FORM
Tablets (2.5 mg, 5 mg, 10 mg, and 20 mg)
STORAGE
Store at room temperature in a tightly closed container and protected from moisture and humidity.

USES

Enalapril is in a class of drugs called angiotensin-converting enzyme inhibitors. It is most commonly used to treat high blood pressure and congestive heart failure. It is a vasodilator (it widens the blood vessels) that acts by blocking the production of chemicals that may be responsible for constricting, or narrowing, the blood vessels.

TREATMENT

Enalapril can be taken either on an empty stomach or with food if it causes stomach irritation (unless your doctor directs otherwise). To become accustomed to taking this medication, try to take it at the same time(s) every day.

It may be several weeks before you notice the full effects of this medication.

If you miss a dose, take the missed dose as soon as possible. However, if it is almost time for the next dose, do not take the missed dose at all; just wait until the next scheduled dose. Do not double the dose.

Enalapril does not cure high blood pressure or heart failure, but it will help to control the condition as long as you continue to take it.

SIDE EFFECTS

Minor. Abdominal pain, diarrhea, dizziness, drowsiness, fatigue, headache, heartburn, insomnia, nausea, nervousness, sweating, or vomiting. These side effects should disappear as your body adjusts to the medication.

To avoid dizziness when you stand, contract and relax the muscles of your legs for a few moments before rising. Do this by alternately pushing one foot against the floor while lifting the other foot slightly in a pedaling motion.

Major. Tell your doctor about any side effects that are persistent or particularly bothersome. IT IS ESPECIALLY IMPORTANT TO TELL YOUR DOCTOR about change in your taste perception; chest pain; difficulty in breathing; fainting; fever; itching; lightheadedness (especially during the first few days); muscle cramps; palpitations; rash; sore throat; swelling of the face, eyes, lips, or tongue; tingling in the fingers or toes; or yellowing of the eyes or skin.

INTERACTIONS

Enalapril interacts with several other types of medications:

1. Diuretics (water pills) and other antihypertensive medications can cause an excessive drop in blood pressure when combined with enalapril (especially with the first dose).

2. The combination of enalapril with spironolactone, triamterene, amiloride, potassium supplements, or salt substitutes can lead to hyperkalemia (dangerously high levels of potassium in the bloodstream).

3. Antacids containing aluminum or magnesium may decrease the efficacy of enalapril. Take antacids one hour before or two hours after your dose of enalapril.

4. The concurrent use of enalapril with probenecid, rifampin, lithium, digoxin, capsaicin, or allopurinol may result in an adverse drug interaction. Be sure to tell your doctor if enalapril has been prescribed for you and you are taking any of these other medications.

5. Nonsteroidal anti-inflammatory agents (including ibuprofen, indomethacin, and naproxen) may reduce the effectiveness of this medication.

Before starting to take enalapril, BE SURE TO TELL YOUR DOCTOR about any medications you are currently taking, especially any of those listed above.

WARNINGS

- Tell your doctor about unusual or allergic reactions you have had to any medications, especially to enalapril.
- Tell your doctor if you now have or ever had blood disorders, heart failure, renal disease, or systemic lupus erythematosus.
- Excessive perspiration, dehydration, or prolonged vomiting or diarrhea can lead to an excessive drop in blood pressure while you are taking this medication. Contact your doctor if you have any of these symptoms.
- Before having surgery or other medical or dental treatment, tell your doctor or dentist you are taking this drug.
- If this drug makes you dizzy or drowsy, do not take part in any activity that requires alertness, such as driving an automobile or operating potentially dangerous tools, machinery, or other equipment.
- If you have high blood pressure, do not take any over-the-counter (nonprescription) medications for weight control or for asthma, sinus, cough, cold, or allergy problems unless you first check with your doctor.
- Be sure to tell your doctor if you are pregnant. Drugs in the same class as enalapril have been shown to cause birth defects, including kidney damage, low blood pressure, improper skull development, and death, when taken in the second and third trimesters. Also tell your doctor if you are breast-feeding an infant. This drug should not be given to nursing women.

---

enfuvirtide

BRAND NAME (Manufacturer)

Fuzeon (Hoffman-La Roche)

TYPE OF DRUG

Fusion inhibitor antiretroviral agent

INGREDIENT
enfuvirtide
DOSAGE FORM
Injection (90 mg per ml)
STORAGE
Vials of this medication may be stored at room temperature. However, after the addition of sterile water for injection, this medication must be refrigerated and used within 24 hours. When the vial is removed from the refrigerator for a subsequent dose, the medication must be brought to room temperature before it is put into a syringe for administration. Before injecting the mixture into the body, it is also important that you check the mixture to make sure that it is clear and colorless.

USES

Enfuvirtide is used in the treatment of human immunodeficiency virus (HIV) infection. HIV is the virus that causes AIDS. This medication works by inhibiting the reproduction, or growth, of the virus, which slows down the progression of AIDS. Enfuvirtide does not cure HIV infection or AIDS, but it may delay the onset of other infections and diseases caused by AIDS. Enfuvirtide comes in injectable form and is given as a shot under the skin (subcutaneously), usually in the upper arm, thigh, or abdomen, two times each day.

TREATMENT

This medication works best when the level of medicine in your bloodstream is kept constant. It is best to administer this medication at the exact, evenly spaced interval directed by your doctor. This medication will not cure HIV disease but may help control the symptoms associated with the condition in some patients.

Complete instructions on using this medication should be included with the prescription. Be sure to review those instructions before using enfuvirtide. If you have any questions, be sure to contact your doctor or pharmacist. In many cases, you will be trained by a nurse or other health care specialist on how to inject this medication properly and how to monitor for side effects.

Since enfuvirtide is given by injection, you will need a special container to dispose of used needles and syringes. Also, check the vial before using enfuvirtide; the solution should be clear. Do not use the medication if there are floating particles or if the solution has a color. Do not mix enfuvirtide with any other medications or dilute the solution.

Be sure to ask your doctor what you should do if you inadvertently miss a dose of this medication. Do not double the next dose, and never take more of this medication than your doctor prescribes.

SIDE EFFECTS

Minor. Bad taste in the mouth; bruising, cysts, nodules, pain, rash, and a depression in the skin where the shot was given; constipation; cough; depression; diarrhea; extreme tiredness; eye infection; flu-like symptoms; itchy rash; loss of appetite; nausea; nervousness; pain and tingling in the hands and feet; skin warts; stomach pain; trouble sleeping; or weight loss. These side effects should become less bothersome as your body adjusts to the medication; contact your doctor, however, if any of these side effects continue.

Major. Remember to tell your doctor about any side effects that are persistent or particularly bothersome. IT IS ESPECIALLY IMPORTANT TO TELL YOUR DOCTOR about chills, fever, inability to move, kidney problems, low blood pressure, nausea and vomiting, rapid breathing, severe rash, shortness of breath, or trouble breathing. Pneumonia (lung infection) and severe infections at body sites where the shots were given have been reported with this medication.

INTERACTIONS

Although no important drug interactions have been reported with this medication at this time, BE SURE TO TELL YOUR DOCTOR about all of the medications, prescription and nonprescription, you are currently taking.

WARNINGS

• Tell your doctor about unusual or allergic reactions you have had to any medications, especially to enfuvirtide or any other medication.
• Tell your doctor if you now have or if you have ever had asthma, lung disease, seizures, blood-vessel disease, glaucoma, high blood pressure, any heart problems, kidney disease, liver disease, peptic ulcers, enlarged prostate gland, urinary tract problems, or thyroid disease.
• This medication may cause you to be unusually drowsy. Therefore, your ability to perform tasks that require alertness, such as driving an automobile or operating potentially dangerous machinery, may be impaired.
• To avoid dizziness or light-headedness when you stand, contract and relax the muscles of your legs for a few moments before rising. Do this by pushing one foot into the floor while raising the other foot slightly, alternating feet so that you are "pumping" your legs in a pedaling motion.
• If you feel dizzy or light-headed, sit or lie down for a while; get up from a sitting or lying position slowly, and be careful on stairs.
• Do not take any over-the-counter (nonprescription) medications for weight control or for asthma, sinus, cough, cold, or allergy problems unless you first check with a doctor or pharmacist.
• This medication is never used alone for the treatment of HIV infection; it is always used in conjunction with other antiretroviral agents.
• It is very important to monitor your skin at the injection sites and to tell your doctor about any pain or signs of infection (redness, swelling, fever) that may appear. Never give two injections into the same location on your body in the same day, and never inject the medicine into a mole, scar, or bruise or into your navel.
• Be sure to tell your doctor if you are pregnant. Although birth defects have not been reported in humans, it is unknown if enfuvirtide is safe during human pregnancy. It is not known if this medication passes into human breast milk. However, because of the risk of passing HIV to infants, it is recommended that mothers who have HIV infection NOT breast-feed their infants.

---

enoxaparin

BRAND NAME (Manufacturer)
Lovenox (Aventis)
TYPE OF DRUG
Anticoagulant (blood thinner)
INGREDIENT
enoxaparin
DOSAGE FORM
Injection (prefilled syringes of 30 mg, 40 mg, 60 mg, 80 mg, 90 mg, 100 mg, 120 mg, and 150 mg)
STORAGE
Store this medication at room temperature, away from light and heat.

USES

Enoxaparin is an anticoagulant (blood thinner) used to prevent or treat blood clots in your body. It is commonly used in the prevention or treatment of deep vein thrombosis, a medical condition in which harmful blood clots form in the large veins of the legs. This condition can sometimes occur after hip or knee replacement surgery or abdominal surgery, because of the patient's temporary inability to walk and circulate the blood properly. This drug can also be used to prevent blood clots from forming in the arteries of your heart and may be used for certain types of heart disease.

Enoxaparin comes in injectable form and is given as a shot under the skin (subcutaneously), usually in the upper thigh, around the navel, or in the buttocks, one or two times each day. Your exact dose and length of treatment with enoxaparin can only be determined by your doctor.

TREATMENT

Enoxaparin works best when the level of medicine in your bloodstream is kept constant. It is best to administer this medication at exact, evenly spaced intervals as directed by your doctor. When used exactly as directed by your doctor, this medication will help control the development of blood clots associated with several different medical conditions.

Complete instructions on using enoxaparin should be included with the medication. Be sure to review those instructions before using enoxaparin. If you have any questions, be sure to contact your doctor or pharmacist. In many cases, you will be trained by a nurse or other health care specialist on how to inject this medication and how to monitor for side effects.

Since this medication is given by injection, you will need a special container to dispose of used needles and syringes. Also, check the vial before using; the solution should be clear. Do not use the medication if there are floating particles or if the solution has a color. Do not mix enoxaparin with any other medications or dilute the solution. The contents of an open vial should not be saved for later use.

If you miss a dose of this medication, use it as soon as possible. However, if it is almost time for your next dose, do not take the missed dose at all; just return to your regular dosing schedule. Do not double the next dose.

SIDE EFFECTS

Minor. Increased menstrual bleeding; irritation, pain, or redness at the site of injection; nausea; or vomiting. These side effects should become less bothersome as your body adjusts to the medication; contact your doctor if any of these side effects continues.

Major. Remember to tell your doctor about any side effects that are persistent or particularly bothersome. IT IS ESPECIALLY IMPORTANT TO TELL YOUR DOCTOR about bleeding from your nose or mouth or from a surgical wound; blood in the urine; bloody or black, tarry stools; collection of blood under the skin, coughing up blood; fever; headache; inability to move; irritability; kidney problems; low blood pressure; moderate to severe pain or numbness in the arms; shortness of breath; rapid breathing; severe rash; trouble breathing; unusual tiredness or weakness; or vomiting of blood or material that looks like coffee grounds.

INTERACTIONS

Enoxaparin interacts with other types of medications. The use of enoxaparin with certain other medicines may increase your risk of bleeding from the enoxaparin. While taking enoxaparin, do not use aspirin, valproic acid, nonsteroidal anti-inflammatory agents (including pain relievers such as ibuprofen or naproxen), ticlopidine, plicamycin, or other medicines unless you first discuss potential drug interactions with your doctor or pharmacist.

BE SURE TO TELL YOUR DOCTOR about any drugs you are currently taking.

WARNINGS

• Tell your doctor about unusual or allergic reactions you have had to any medications, especially to enoxaparin, heparin, warfarin, dalteparin, tinzaparin, or any other medication. It is especially important to tell your doctor if you have ever had thrombocytopenia (low blood platelets).

• Tell your doctor if you now have or ever had blood-vessel disease or bleeding problems, septic shock, seizures, high blood pressure, kidney disease, liver disease, peptic ulcers, heart disease, intestinal problems, or miscarriage.

• It is important to notify your doctor if you have recently given birth, fallen, or suffered an injury to your head or other part of your body. In addition, tell your doctor if you have had recent medical or dental surgery. These events may increase your chance of bleeding and other side effects from the enoxaparin.

• If excessive bruising occurs during injection of this medication, it may be reduced by preapplying an ice-cube massage to the site where the next injection will be given.

• Be sure to tell your doctor if you are pregnant. The effects of using this medication during pregnancy have not been thoroughly studied in humans. Also be sure to tell your doctor if you are breast-feeding an infant. Mothers who are using enoxaparin and who wish to continue to breast-feed their infants should discuss the potential risks with their doctor.

---

ergotamine

BRAND NAME (Manufacturer)
Ergomar (Lotus)
TYPE OF DRUG
Antimigraine (vasoconstrictor)
INGREDIENT
ergotamine
DOSAGE FORM
Sublingual tablets (2 mg)
STORAGE
Store this medication at room temperature in a tightly closed, light-resistant container. Do not freeze it.

USES

This medication is used to treat migraine headaches and cluster headaches. Both types of headaches are thought to be caused by an increase in the diameter of the blood vessels in the head, which results in more blood flow, increased pressure on nearby tissues, and pain. Ergotamine is a vasoconstrictor; it acts by constricting (narrowing) the blood vessels.

TREATMENT

Take this medication as soon as you notice your migraine headache symptoms. If you wait until the headache is severe, the drug takes longer to work and may not be as effective.

After you take ergotamine, you should try to lie down in a quiet, dark room for at least two hours (in order to help the medication work). The drug usually takes effect in 30 to 60 minutes.

It is very important that you understand how often you can repeat a dose of this medication during an attack (usually every 30 to 60 minutes) and the maximum amount of medication you can take per day (usually three tablets). Five is generally the maximum number of tablets that can be taken in any one-week period. CHECK WITH YOUR DOCTOR if you have any questions.

The sublingual tablets should be placed under your tongue. DO NOT swallow these tablets—they are more efficiently absorbed through the lining of the mouth than from the gastrointestinal tract. Try not to eat, drink, chew, or smoke while the tablet is dissolving.

SIDE EFFECTS

Minor. Diarrhea, dizziness, headache, nausea, sensation of cold hands and feet with MILD numbness or tingling, or vomiting. These side effects should disappear as your body adjusts to the medication.

Major. Tell your doctor about any side effects that are persistent or particularly bothersome. IT IS ESPECIALLY IMPORTANT TO TELL YOUR DOCTOR about chest pain; coldness, numbness, pain, tingling, or dark discoloration of the fingers or toes; confusion; fluid retention; itching; localized swelling; muscle pain; severe abdominal pain and swelling; or unusual weakness.

INTERACTIONS

Ergotamine interacts with several other types of medications:

1. Ergotamine interacts with amphetamines, ephedrine, epinephrine (adrenaline), pseudoephedrine, erythromycin, clarithromycin, beta blockers, protease inhibitors, and antifungal agents. Such combinations can lead to increases in blood pressure or increased risk of adverse reactions to ergotamine.

2. Do not drink alcoholic beverages while you are taking this medication. Since alcohol dilates (widens) the blood vessels (which are already dilated during migraine headaches), drinking will only make your headache worse.

3. Nicotine and cocaine may increase the risk of serious adverse reactions to ergotamine, since these substances also cause a constriction, or narrowing, of blood vessels throughout the body.

4. The caffeine in tea, coffee, and cola drinks may increase the amount of ergotamine absorbed by the body.

5. Do not take this medication in the same 24-hour period with the following migraine drugs: sumatriptan, frovatriptan, naratriptan, rizatriptan, zolmitriptan, almotriptan, and eletriptan. Severe and dangerous effects may result.

6. Do not take sibutramine with this medication.

BE SURE TO TELL YOUR DOCTOR about any medications you are currently taking, especially any of those listed above.

WARNINGS

• Tell your doctor about unusual or allergic reactions you have had to any medications, especially to ergotamine or other ergot alkaloids (such as ergonovine or bromocriptine).

• Before starting to take this medication, be sure to tell your doctor if you now have or ever had heart or blood-vessel disease, high blood pressure, infections, kidney disease, liver disease, or thyroid disease.

• Avoid any foods to which you are allergic or sensitive.

• If this drug makes you dizzy or drowsy, do not take part in any activity that requires alertness, such as driving an automobile or operating potentially dangerous tools, machinery, or other equipment.

• Try to avoid exposure to cold. Since this drug acts by constricting blood vessels throughout the body, your fingers and toes may become especially sensitive to it.

• Elderly patients are more sensitive to the effects of ergotamine. Consult your doctor if the side effects become particularly bothersome.

• This medication should not be taken for longer periods or in higher doses than recommended by your doctor. Extended use of this drug can lead to serious side effects. In addition, tolerance can develop—higher doses would be required to obtain the same beneficial effects (at the same time increasing the risk of side effects).

• Be sure to tell your doctor if you are pregnant. Ergotamine can cause contractions of the uterus, which can harm the developing fetus. This drug should not be used during pregnancy. Also tell your doctor if you are breast-feeding an infant. Ergotamine passes into breast milk and is not recommended for nursing women.

ergotamine and caffeine combination

BRAND NAMES (Manufacturers)
Cafatine (Major)
Cafergot (Novartis)
Cafetrate (Schein)
Ercaf (Geneva Marsam)
Wigraine (Organon)
TYPE OF DRUG
Antimigraine (vasoconstrictor)
INGREDIENTS
ergotamine and caffeine
DOSAGE FORMS
Tablets (1 mg ergotamine, 100 mg caffeine)
Suppositories (2 mg ergotamine, 100 mg caffeine)
STORAGE
Store the tablets at room temperature in a tightly closed, light-resistant container, away from heat and direct sunlight. Keep the suppositories in the refrigerator in a closed container. This medication should never be frozen.

USES

This medication is used to treat migraine and cluster headaches. These headaches are thought to be caused by an increase in the diameter of the blood vessels in the head, which results in increased blood flow, increased pressure on nearby tissues, and pain. Ergotamine is a vasoconstrictor: It acts by constricting (narrowing) the blood vessels. Caffeine helps in both the absorption of the drug from the gastrointestinal tract and in constricting blood vessels.

TREATMENT

It is best to take this medication as soon as you notice your migraine headache symptoms. If you wait until the headache becomes severe, the drug takes longer to work and may not be as effective.

After you take this medication, you should try to lie down in a quiet, dark room for at least two hours (in order to help the medication work). The drug usually takes effect within 30 to 60 minutes.

It is very important that you understand how often you can repeat a dose of this medication during an attack (usually every 30 to 60 minutes) and the maximum amount of medication you can take per day (usually six tablets or two suppositories). Ten is generally the maximum number of tablets and four is the maximum number of suppositories that can be taken in any one-week period. CHECK WITH YOUR DOCTOR if you have any questions.

To use the suppository form of this medication, first unwrap it and moisten it slightly with water (if the suppository is too soft to insert, run cold water over it or refrigerate it for 30 minutes before you unwrap it). Lie down on your left side, with your right knee bent. Push the suppository well into the rectum with your finger. Try to avoid having a bowel movement for at least an hour to give the medication time to be absorbed. Insert one suppository when you first notice your migraine symptoms. If necessary, insert a second suppository one hour later for full relief of your migraine headache.

If you are on prolonged treatment with this drug and you miss a dose, take it as soon as you remember. Wait four hours to take the next dose. It is very important that you consult your doctor before you discontinue using ergotamine and caffeine combination. Your doctor may want to reduce your dosage gradually.

SIDE EFFECTS

Minor. Diarrhea, dizziness, headache, nausea, nervousness or jitters, sensation of cold hands and feet with MILD numbness or tingling, or vomiting. These side effects should disappear as your body gets accustomed to the medication.

Major. Tell your doctor about any side effects that are persistent or particularly bothersome. IT IS ESPECIALLY IMPORTANT TO TELL YOUR DOCTOR about chest pain; coldness, numbness, pain, tingling, or dark discoloration of the fingers or toes; confusion; fluid retention; itching; localized swelling; muscle pain; severe abdominal pain and swelling; severe nausea or vomiting; or unusual weakness.

INTERACTIONS

Ergotamine and caffeine combination interacts with several other types of medications:

1. Ergotamine interacts with amphetamines, ephedrine, epinephrine (adrenaline), pseudoephedrine, erythromycin, clarithromycin, beta blockers, protease inhibitors, and antifungal agents. Such combinations can lead to increases in blood pressure or increased risk of adverse reactions to ergotamine.

2. Do not drink alcoholic beverages while you are taking this medication. Since alcohol dilates (widens) the blood vessels, drinking will only make your headache worse.

3. Nicotine and cocaine may increase the risk of serious adverse reactions to ergotamine, because these agents may also constrict (narrow) blood vessels throughout the body.

4. Taking this medication with tea, coffee, or cola drinks may increase the side effects from caffeine, since these drinks also contain caffeine.

5. Concurrent use of caffeine, including the caffeine in this medication, with monoamine oxidase (MAO) inhibitors can lead to serious side effects. At least 21 days should separate ingestion of caffeine and the use of MAO inhibitors.

6. Do not take this medication in the same 24-hour period with the following migraine drugs: sumatriptan, frovatriptan, naratriptan, rizatriptan, zolmitriptan, almotriptan, or eletriptan. Severe effects may result.

7. Do not take this medication with sibutramine.

BE SURE TO TELL YOUR DOCTOR about any medications or substances you are currently taking or using, especially any of those listed above.

WARNINGS

• Tell your doctor about unusual or allergic reactions you have had to medications, especially to ergotamine, caffeine, or any ergot alkaloid (ergonovine, ergoloid mesylates, and bromocriptine).

• Before starting to take ergotamine and caffeine combination, be sure to tell your doctor if you now have or ever had heart or blood-vessel disease, high blood pressure, infections, kidney disease, liver disease, or thyroid disease.

• Avoid any foods to which you are allergic or sensitive—they may make your headache worse.

• If this drug makes you dizzy or drowsy, do not take part in any activity that requires alertness, such as driving a car or operating potentially dangerous equipment.

• Since this drug acts by constricting blood vessels throughout the body (not just in the head), your fingers and toes may become especially sensitive to the cold.

• Elderly patients are more sensitive to the effects of ergotamine. Consult your doctor if you find the side effects particularly bothersome.

• This medication should not be taken for longer periods or in higher doses than recommended by your doctor. Extended use of this medication can lead to serious side effects. In addition, your body can develop a tolerance to this medication—higher doses would be required to obtain the same beneficial effects and, at the same time, the risk of side effects would be increased.

• Be sure to tell your doctor if you are pregnant. Ergotamine can cause contractions of the uterus, which can harm the developing fetus. This drug should not be used during pregnancy. Also tell your doctor if you are breast-feeding an infant. Ergotamine and caffeine combination passes into breast milk and is not recommended for nursing women.

---

erythromycin

BRAND NAMES (Manufacturers)
E.E.S. (Abbott)
E-Mycin (Knoll)
Eryc (Warner-Chilcott)
EryPed (Abbott)
Ery-Tab (Abbott)
Erythrocin Stearate (Abbott)
erythromycin base (various manufacturers)
erythromycin estolate (various manufacturers)
erythromycin ethylsuccinate (various manufacturers)
Erythromycin Filmtabs (Abbott)
erythromycin stearate (various manufacturers)
Ilosone (Lilly)
Ilosone Pulvules (Lilly)
PCE Dispertab (Abbott)
TYPE OF DRUG
Antibiotic
INGREDIENT
erythromycin
DOSAGE FORMS
Tablets (250 mg, 333 mg, 400 mg, and 500 mg)
Chewable tablets (200 mg)
Enteric-coated tablets (250 mg, 333 mg, and 500 mg)
Film-coated tablets (250 mg and 500 mg)
Polymer-coated tablets (333 mg)
Capsules (250 mg)
Oral drops (100 mg per 2.5 mL)
Oral suspension (125 mg, 200 mg, 250 mg, and 400 mg per 5-mL spoonful)
STORAGE
Store tablets and capsules at room temperature in tightly closed, light-resistant containers. Keep oral drops and oral suspension in the refrigerator in tightly closed, light-resistant containers. Discard any unused portion of the liquid forms after 14 days. Erythromycin ethylsuccinate liquid does not need to be refrigerated; however, refrigeration helps to preserve the taste. This medication should never be frozen.

USES

Erythromycin is used to treat a wide variety of bacterial infections, including infections of the middle ear and the respiratory tract. It is also used to treat infections in persons who are allergic to penicillin. It acts by preventing the bacteria from growing. It is not effective against viruses, parasites, or fungi.

TREATMENT

To prevent stomach upset, erythromycin coated tablets and erythromycin estolate or ethylsuccinate can be taken with food or milk. Other erythromycin products should be taken with a full glass of water, preferably on an empty stomach, one hour before or two hours after a meal.

Do not dilute the liquid forms of this medication; use them full strength.

Measure each dose of the oral drops carefully with the dropper provided.

Shake the oral suspension well just before measuring each dose to distribute the ingredients evenly and equalize the doses. The contents tend to settle on the bottom of the bottle. Measure each dose carefully with a specially designed 5-mL measuring spoon. An ordinary kitchen teaspoon is not accurate enough.

To prevent gastrointestinal side effects, swallow the coated tablets and capsules whole; do not break, chew, or crush these products.

Erythromycin works best when the level of medicine in your bloodstream is kept constant. It is best to take the doses at evenly spaced intervals day and night. For example, if you are to take four doses a day, the doses should be spaced six hours apart.

If you miss a dose of this medication, take the missed dose immediately. However, if you do not remember to take the missed dose until it is almost time for your next dose, take it; space the following dose about halfway through the regular interval between doses; then return to your regular schedule. Try not to skip any doses.

It is important to continue to take this medication for the entire time prescribed by your doctor (usually 7 to 14 days), even if the symptoms disappear before the end of that period. If you stop taking this drug too soon, resistant bacteria continue growing, and the infection could recur.

SIDE EFFECTS

Minor. Abdominal cramps, diarrhea, fatigue, irritation of the mouth, loss of appetite, nausea, sore tongue, or vomiting. These side effects should disappear as your body adjusts to the medication.

Major. Tell your doctor about any side effects that are persistent or particularly bothersome. IT IS ESPECIALLY IMPORTANT TO TELL YOUR DOCTOR about fever, hearing loss, hives, rash, rectal or vaginal itching, or yellowing of the eyes or skin. If your symptoms of infection seem to be getting worse rather than improving, contact your doctor.

INTERACTIONS

This medication interacts with several other drugs:

1. Erythromycin can decrease the elimination of aminophylline, oxtriphylline, theophylline, digoxin, oral anticoagulants (blood thinners, such as warfarin), carbamazepine, valproic acid, triazolam, and cyclosporine from the body, which can lead to serious side effects.

2. Therapy with erythromycin may increase the effects of methylprednisolone.

3. Erythromycin should not be used with grepafloxacin or sparfloxacin because of the risk of serious, even life-threatening, reactions.

4. Benzodiazepines (including diazepam, alprazolam, and triazolam), felodipine, ergot alkaloids, buspirone, bromocriptine, birth control pills, and certain drugs for high cholesterol (including lovastatin, simvastatin, and pravastatin) can interact with erythromycin. Discuss this with your doctor or pharmacist.

BE SURE TO TELL YOUR DOCTOR about any medications you are currently taking, especially any listed above.

WARNINGS

• Tell your doctor about unusual or allergic reactions you have had to any medications, especially to erythromycin.

• Be sure to tell your doctor if you now have or have ever had liver disease.

• This drug has been prescribed for your current infection only. Another infection later on, or one that someone else has, may require a different medication altogether. Do not give your medicine to other people or use it for other infections unless your doctor specifically directs you to.

• Before having surgery or any other medical or dental treatment, be sure to tell your doctor or dentist that you are taking erythromycin.

• Not all erythromycin products are chemically equivalent. However, they all produce the same therapeutic effect. Discuss with your doctor or pharmacist which forms of erythromycin are appropriate for you, and then choose the least expensive product among those recommended.
• Be sure to tell your doctor if you are pregnant. Although erythromycin appears to be safe during pregnancy, extensive studies in humans have not been conducted. Also tell your doctor if you are breast-feeding an infant. Small amounts of this medication pass into breast milk and may temporarily alter the bacterial balance in the intestinal tract of the nursing infant, resulting in diarrhea.

erythromycin and sulfisoxazole combination

BRAND NAMES (Manufacturers)
erythromycin and sulfisoxazole (various manufacturers)
Eryzole (Alra)
Pediazole (Ross)
TYPE OF DRUG
Antibiotic
INGREDIENTS
erythromycin and sulfisoxazole
DOSAGE FORM
Oral suspension (200 mg erythromycin and 600 mg sulfisoxazole per 5-mL spoonful)
STORAGE
Store in the refrigerator in a tightly closed container. Do not freeze. Discard any unused portion after the expiration date (usually after 14 days) because the suspension loses potency after that time.

USES

Erythromycin and sulfisoxazole combination is used to treat acute otitis media (middle ear infection) in children. Erythromycin acts by preventing the bacteria from manufacturing protein, thereby preventing their growth. Sulfisoxazole also acts by preventing production of nutrients that are required for growth of the infecting bacteria. Erythromycin and sulfisoxazole combination kills a wide range of susceptible bacteria, but it is not effective against viruses, parasites, or fungi.

TREATMENT

To avoid stomach upset, you can take this medication either with food or with a full glass of water or milk. You can also take it on an empty stomach.

Shake the suspension well just before measuring each dose to distribute the ingredients evenly and equalize the doses. The contents tend to settle on the bottom of the bottle. Measure each dose carefully with a specially designed 5-mL measuring spoon. An ordinary kitchen teaspoon is not accurate enough.

This medication works best when the level of medicine in the bloodstream is kept constant. It is best to take the doses at evenly spaced intervals day and night. For example, if you are to take four doses a day, the doses should be spaced six hours apart.

If you miss a dose of this medication, take the missed dose immediately. However, if you do not remember to take the missed dose until it is almost time for your next dose, take it; space the following dose about halfway through the regular interval between doses; then return to your regular schedule. Try not to skip any doses.

It is important to continue to take this medication for the entire time prescribed by your doctor (usually 7 to 14 days), even if the symptoms disappear before the end of that period. If you stop taking the drug too soon, resistant bacteria are given a chance to continue growing, and the infection could recur.

SIDE EFFECTS

Minor. Diarrhea, dizziness, headache, loss of appetite, nausea, sleep disorders, sore mouth or tongue, or vomiting. These side effects should disappear over time as your body adjusts to the medication.

This medication can cause increased sensitivity to sunlight. It is important to avoid prolonged exposure to sunlight and sunlamps. Wear protective clothing and sunglasses, and use an effective sunscreen.

If you feel dizzy, sit or lie down for a while; get up slowly from a sitting or reclining position; and be careful on stairs.

Major. Tell your doctor about any side effects that are persistent or particularly bothersome. IT IS ESPECIALLY IMPORTANT TO TELL YOUR DOCTOR about aching or painful joints and muscles; convulsions; difficult or painful urination; difficulty swallowing; hallucinations; loss of hearing; mental depression; peeling, itching, redness, or blistering of the skin; itching; rash; sore throat and fever; uncoordinated movements; unusual bleeding or bruising; unusual tiredness; or yellowing of the eyes or skin. If the symptoms of infection seem to be getting worse, contact your doctor.

INTERACTIONS

This medication interacts with several other types of drugs:

1. Erythromycin can decrease the elimination of aminophylline, oxtriphylline, theophylline, digoxin, oral anticoagulants (blood thinners, such as warfarin), carbamazepine, valproic acid, and cyclosporine from the body, which can lead to serious side effects.

2. Sulfisoxazole can increase the active blood levels of oral anticoagulants (blood thinners, such as warfarin), oral antidiabetic agents, methotrexate, oxyphenbutazone, phenylbutazone, and phenytoin, which can lead to serious side effects.

3. Erythromycin may increase the effects of methylprednisolone.

4. Erythromycin should not be used with grepafloxacin or sparfloxacin because of the risk of serious, even life-threatening reactions.

5. Benzodiazepines (including diazepam, alprazolam, and triazolam), felodipine, ergot alkaloids, buspirone, bromocriptine, birth control pills, and certain drugs for high cholesterol (including lovastatin, simvastatin, and pravastatin) can interact with erythromycin. Discuss this with your doctor or pharmacist.

Before starting to take this medication, BE SURE TO TELL YOUR DOCTOR about any medications you are currently taking, especially any of the drugs listed above.

WARNINGS

• Tell your doctor about unusual or allergic reactions you have ever had to any medications, especially to erythromycin, sulfisoxazole, any other sulfa medications (such as sulfonamide antibiotics, diuretics, dapsone, sulfoxone, oral antidiabetic medicines) or acetazolamide.

• Tell your doctor if you now have or ever had glucose–6-phosphate dehydrogenase (G6PD) deficiency, kidney disease, liver disease, or porphyria.

• This medication has been prescribed for your current infection only. Another infection later on, or one that someone else has, may require a different medicine. You should not give your medicine to other people, nor should you use it yourself for other infections, unless your doctor specifically directs you to do so.

• Be sure to tell your doctor if you are pregnant. Small amounts of erythromycin and sulfisoxazole cross the placenta. Although these antibiotics appear to be safe during pregnancy, extensive studies in humans have not been conducted. Also tell your doctor if you are breast-feeding an infant. Small amounts of this medication pass into breast milk and may temporarily alter the bacterial balance in the intestinal tract of the infant, resulting in diarrhea. This medication should not be used in an infant less than two months of age in order to avoid side effects involving the liver.

erythropoietin

BRAND NAMES (Manufacturers)
Epogen (Amgen)
Procrit (Amgen, Ortho-Biotech)
TYPE OF DRUG
Antianemia
INGREDIENT
erythropoietin
DOSAGE FORM
Injection (2,000 units, 3,000 units, 4,000 units, 10,000 units, 20,000 units, or 40,000 units per 1-mL of solution with albumin)
STORAGE
Store in the refrigerator in the original vial, and protect from light. Do not freeze or shake the vial.

USES

Erythropoietin is used to increase the number of red blood cells in the body in patients with anemia due to renal failure and dialysis or from chemotherapy for certain types of cancers. This drug stimulates the production of red blood cells in the body through a process called erythropoiesis. In patients with chronic renal failure or those receiving certain types of chemotherapy, the process of erythropoiesis is impaired. Erythropoietin is produced using recombinant technology, a method that does not involve the use of any human blood products.

TREATMENT

This medication should be taken exactly as prescribed by your doctor. Erythropoietin is given by injection, either directly into the vein or under the skin (subcutaneously), usually several times throughout the week. The exact dose and length of treatment can only be determined by your doctor.

Complete instructions should be included with the medication. Be sure to review those instructions before using erythropoietin. If you have any questions, contact your doctor or pharmacist. In many cases, you will be trained by a nurse or other health care specialist on how to inject this medication and how to monitor for side effects.

Since erythropoietin is given by injection, you will need a special container to dispose of used needles and syringes. Do not use the medication if there are floating particles or if the solution has a color. Do not mix erythropoietin with any other medications or dilute the solution.

If you miss a dose of this medication, take it as soon as possible. However, if it is almost time for your next dose, do not take the missed dose at all; just return to your regular dosing schedule. Do not double the next dose.

SIDE EFFECTS

Minor. Diarrhea, dizziness, headache, itching, muscle aches and pains, nausea, pain at the site of injection, tiredness, or vomiting. These side effects should diminish or disappear as your body adjusts to the medication.

To avoid dizziness when you stand, contract and relax the muscles in your legs for a few moments before rising. Do this by pushing one foot against the floor while raising the other foot slightly, alternating feet so that you are "pumping" your legs in a pedaling motion.

Major. Tell your doctor about any side effects that are persistent or particularly bothersome. IT IS ESPECIALLY IMPORTANT TO TELL YOUR DOCTOR about chest pain; difficulty breathing or shortness of breath; feelings of warmth, pain, or swelling in the legs or hands; palpitations; or seizures.

INTERACTIONS

If used properly, erythropoietin should not interact with other medications.

However, BE SURE TO TELL YOUR DOCTOR about any medication you are currently taking.

WARNINGS

- Erythropoietin may increase your blood pressure. Monitor your blood pressure regularly while taking this medication.
- To make sure this medication is working properly, it is important that blood tests are done to check for anemia while you are being treated with the drug.
- Tell your doctor about any unusual or allergic reactions you have had to any medications, especially to erythropoietin, darbepoetin, or any other medication.
- Before having surgery or any other medical or dental treatment, be sure to tell your doctor or dentist that you are taking this medication.
- Be sure to tell your doctor if you are pregnant. The effects of this medication during pregnancy have not been thoroughly studied in humans. It is also not known if erythropoietin passes into breast milk in humans, so be sure to tell your doctor if you are breast-feeding an infant.

---

escitalopram

BRAND NAME (Manufacturer)
Lexapro (Forest)
TYPE OF DRUG
Selective serotonin reuptake inhibitor (SSRI) antidepressant
INGREDIENT
escitalopram
DOSAGE FORMS
Tablets (10 mg and 20 mg)
Oral solution (5 mg per 5 mL spoonful)
STORAGE
Store at room temperature in a tightly closed container. Do not store in the bathroom. Excessive heat or moisture may cause this medication to break down.

USES

Escitalopram is used to treat the symptoms of mental depression. It increases the concentration of a certain chemical (serotonin) necessary for nerve transmission in the brain. It belongs to a group of medications known as the selective serotonin reuptake inhibitor (SSRI) antidepressants, which also includes medicines such as fluoxetine, paroxetine, sertraline, and citalopram.

TREATMENT

This medication should be taken exactly as prescribed by your doctor. It may be taken either on an empty stomach or with food or milk (unless your doctor directs you otherwise).

The full effects of this medication may not be apparent for four to six weeks.

If you miss a dose of this medication, ask your doctor for instructions. Do not double the doses or take more than your doctor prescribes.

SIDE EFFECTS

Minor. Changes in the sense of taste, diarrhea, dizziness, drowsiness, dry mouth, increased sweating, increased yawning, insomnia, loss of appetite, muscle or joint pain, nausea, nervousness, stomach cramps, stuffy nose, vomiting, watering of the mouth, or weight loss or gain. Most of these effects should disappear as your body adjusts to the medication.

Dry mouth can be relieved by chewing sugarless gum or sucking on hard candy.

To avoid dizziness or light-headedness when you stand, contract and relax the muscles of your legs for a few moments before rising.

If you feel dizzy or light-headed, sit or lie down for a while. Get up from a sitting or lying position slowly, and be careful on stairs.

Major. Tell your doctor about any side effects that are persistent or particularly bothersome. IT IS ESPECIALLY IMPORTANT TO TELL YOUR DOCTOR about abnormal bleeding, anxiety, blurred vision, breast enlargement or tenderness (in both men and women), chills or fever, fainting, irregular heartbeat, memory loss, mood changes, pain or difficulty in urinating, sexual problems, or skin rash.

INTERACTIONS

Escitalopram may interact with a number of other types of medication:

1. Concurrent use of this medication with other central nervous system depressants (such as alcohol, barbiturates, benzodiazepine tranquilizers, muscle relaxants, narcotics, pain medications, and phenothiazine tranquilizers) or with tricyclic antidepressants can cause extreme drowsiness.

2. Use of over-the-counter (nonprescription) cough, cold, or allergy medications may increase the side effects of this medication and should be avoided.

3. Monoamine oxidase (MAO) inhibitors (such as isocarboxazid, pargyline, phenelzine, selegiline, and tranylcypromine) can be expected to increase the side effects of this medication. They should never be administered at the same time as escitalopram or within 14 days of each other.

4. Ketoconazole, itraconazole, fluconazole, erythromycin, cimetidine, and omeprazole may increase the amount of escitalopram in the body and increase the risk of side effects.

5. Escitalopram may increase the risk of side effects from other antidepressants and from some antimigraine agents, including sumatriptan.

BE SURE TO TELL YOUR DOCTOR about any medications that you are currently taking, including any of those mentioned above.

WARNINGS

• Tell your doctor immediately if you develop a skin rash or hives while taking this medication or if you have ever had an allergic reaction to this medication or other medicines in this class (including fluoxetine, paroxetine, sertraline, and citalopram).

• Tell your doctor if you now have or if you have ever had asthma, blood-vessel disease, glaucoma, mania or hypomania, seizures, high blood pressure, kidney disease, liver disease, peptic ulcers, enlarged prostate gland, difficulty urinating, electroshock therapy, heart disease, intestinal problems, or thyroid disease.

• Because escitalopram is metabolized by the liver, elderly patients, patients with liver disease, and patients with severe kidney disease may require a change in the dose or dosing schedule. Discuss this with your doctor or pharmacist.

• While taking this medication, your ability to perform tasks that require alertness, such as driving a car or operating potentially dangerous machinery, may be impaired.

• Although you may notice improvement in your condition in one to four weeks, it is important to continue taking this medication as directed by your doctor.

• Be sure to tell your doctor if you are pregnant. Although birth defects have not been documented in humans, in animal studies escitalopram caused decreased survival rates and slowed growth in offspring. It is not known if escitalopram is safe during human pregnancy. Escitalopram can also pass into human breast milk, causing drowsiness, decreased feeding, and weight loss in infants. Be sure to tell your doctor if you are breast-feeding an infant and discuss the risks and benefits of this medication.

esomeprazole

BRAND NAME (Manufacturer)
Nexium (Astra Zeneca)
TYPE OF DRUG
Gastric acid secretion inhibitor
INGREDIENT
esomeprazole
DOSAGE FORM
Capsules (20 mg and 40 mg)
STORAGE
Store at room temperature in a tightly closed container. Do not expose to extreme temperatures.

USES

Esomeprazole is prescribed to treat peptic ulcer disease, gastroesophageal reflux disease (GERD), and hypersecretory syndromes. It suppresses stomach acid secretion.

TREATMENT

This medication should be taken at least one hour before meals, unless your doctor directs you to do otherwise. Swallow the capsules whole; do not chew or crush them. If you cannot swallow the capsule whole, open it up and carefully mix the contents with a small amount of applesauce. (If you prefer, you can mix the contents with water, orange juice, apple juice, or yogurt instead.) Take the mixture immediately, swallowing it without chewing. Do not save the mixture for later use.

If you miss a dose of this medication, take it as soon as you remember. However, if it's almost time for your next dose, skip the missed dose and return to your regular dosing schedule. Do not double the next dose.

It is important to take this medication for as long as prescribed by your doctor.

SIDE EFFECTS

Minor. Abdominal pain, burning sensation in mouth, constipation, diarrhea, dizziness, dry mouth, fatigue, headache, or palpitations. These side effects should diminish or disappear as your body adjusts to the medication.

Dry mouth can be relieved by chewing sugarless gum or sucking on hard candy.

To avoid dizziness or light-headedness when you stand, contract and relax the muscles of your legs for a few moments before rising.

If you feel dizzy or light-headed, sit or lie down for a while. Get up slowly from a sitting or lying position, and be careful on stairs.

To relieve constipation, increase the amount of fiber in your diet (fresh fruits and vegetables, salads, bran, and whole-grain breads), exercise, and drink more water (unless your doctor directs you to do otherwise).

Major. Tell your doctor about any side effects that are persistent or particularly bothersome. IT IS ESPECIALLY IMPORTANT TO TELL YOUR DOCTOR about itching, rash, tingling of the fingers or toes, unusual tiredness, or yellowish discoloration of the eyes and skin.

INTERACTIONS

Esomeprazole may interact with a number of other types of medications:

1. Use of esomeprazole with ketoconazole, itraconazole, digoxin, some forms of penicillin, or iron supplements alters the absorption of these medications and can either reduce or increase their effectiveness.

2. Esomeprazole may increase the effects and side effects of diazepam and warfarin (a blood thinner).

BE SURE TO TELL YOUR DOCTOR about these or any other medications you are currently taking.

WARNINGS

• Tell your doctor about any unusual reactions you have had to any medication, especially reactions to esomeprazole, omeprazole, or any other medication used for ulcers or acid reflux (GERD).
• Tell your doctor if you now have or ever had thyroid disease, liver disease, Addison's disease, or Cushing's disease.
• While taking this medication, your ability to perform tasks that require alertness, such as driving a car or operating potentially dangerous machinery, may be impaired.
• Long-term and high-dose treatment with medications similar to esomeprazole have been associated with a higher incidence of gastric tumors. Discuss this potential risk with your doctor if you need to take high doses of this medication for a long time.
• Be sure to tell your doctor if you are pregnant. There have not been adequate human studies conducted with esomeprazole to determine its safety when used during pregnancy. In addition, be sure to tell your doctor if you are breast-feeding an infant. It is not known if esomeprazole will pass into breast milk, but similar medications have been found in breast milk. Discuss the risks with your doctor.

---

estradiol (transdermal)

BRAND NAMES (Manufacturers)
Alora (Procter & Gamble)
Climara (Berlex)
Esclim (Women First Healthcare)
Estraderm (Novartis)
FemPatch (Parke-Davis)
Vivelle (Novartis)
TYPE OF DRUG
estrogen
INGREDIENT
estradiol
DOSAGE FORM
Transdermal patch (delivers 0.025 mg, 0.0375 mg, 0.05 mg, 0.075 mg, or 0.1 mg per 24 hours)
STORAGE
Store at room temperature in the original packages.

USES

Estradiol is a synthetic estrogen that is used to treat menopausal symptoms or other conditions associated with estrogen deficiency.

TREATMENT

Your prescription for estradiol will come with patient instructions. It is important that you read and follow the directions carefully.

Wash and dry your hands before and after applying the patch. Apply the patch to a clean, dry, hairless area of the skin on the trunk of the body or on the abdomen. Do not apply to the breasts. Avoid applying the patch over a cut or to any area of the body where tight clothes might rub against the patch and cause it to loosen. Apply the patch immediately after opening the packet and removing the protective liner. Press the patch firmly to the skin with the palm of your hand for about ten seconds. Make sure there is good contact of the patch to the skin, especially around the edges. Rotate the application sites on the skin, waiting at least one week before applying to the same site.

If the patch becomes loose or falls off, the same one can be reapplied. If necessary, however, a new patch can be applied. In either case, continue with your original treatment schedule.

If you miss an application of this medication, apply a new patch as soon as possible. However, if it is almost time for the next application, return to your regular schedule. Do not apply a double dose.

SIDE EFFECTS

Minor. Abdominal cramping, abnormal vaginal bleeding, acne, bloating, breast tenderness, change in sexual desire, darkening of the skin, diarrhea, dizziness, fluid retention, frequent or painful urination, hair loss, headache, nausea, nervousness, skin irritation at patch site, vomiting, or weight gain. These side effects should disappear as your body adjusts to the drug.

If you feel dizzy, sit or lie down for a while; get up slowly from a sitting or reclining position; and be careful on stairs.

Eating a full breakfast or having a midmorning snack may help to relieve the nausea and vomiting.

This medication can increase your sensitivity to sunlight. You should try to avoid prolonged exposure to sunlight and sunlamps. Wear protective clothing and sunglasses, and use an effective sunscreen.

Major. Tell your doctor about any side effects that are persistent or particularly bothersome. IT IS ESPECIALLY IMPORTANT TO TELL YOUR DOCTOR about blurred vision, chest pain, convulsions, depression, itching, loss of coordination, pain or inflammation of the calves or thighs, shortness of breath, skin rash, slurred speech, or yellowish discoloration of the eyes or skin.

INTERACTIONS

Estradiol interacts with several other types of medications:

1. It can decrease the effectiveness of oral anticoagulants (blood thinners, such as warfarin).

2. Carbamazepine, phenobarbital, phenytoin, protease inhibitors, primidone, and rifampin can reduce the effectiveness of estradiol.

3. Estradiol can increase the side effects and decrease the effectiveness of tricyclic antidepressants.

4. Estrogens may interfere with the breakdown of cyclosporine, increasing cyclosporine's toxic effects.

BE SURE TO TELL YOUR DOCTOR about any medications you are currently taking, especially any of those mentioned above.

WARNINGS

• Estrogens can change your blood's clotting ability, so be especially careful to avoid injuries.

• Tell your doctor about any unusual or allergic reactions you have had to any medications, especially to estradiol, to other estrogens, or to oral contraceptives (birth control pills).

• Tell your doctor if you now have or ever had asthma, blood clot disorders, breast disease, depression, diabetes mellitus, epilepsy, endometriosis, gallstones or gallbladder disease, heart disease, high blood pressure, kidney disease, liver disease, migraine headaches, porphyria, or uterine tumors.

• Estrogens may cause a change in glucose tolerance in people with diabetes. Be sure to tell your doctor if you notice any abnormalities in your glucose levels.

• Although it is not known if estrogens can increase the risk of breast cancer, it is important that you examine your breasts regularly for lumps or discharge.

• If you notice tenderness, swelling, or bleeding of your gums, consult your doctor or dentist.

• Your doctor may schedule regular office visits to be sure your medication is working properly and to monitor for side effects of estrogen therapy.
• Before having surgery or any other medical or dental treatment, be sure to tell your doctor or dentist that you are taking this medication.
• Studies have shown that estrogen may increase the risk of certain types of cancer. Ask your pharmacist for the brochure "Information for the Patient." It is important that you understand the possible risks and benefits of this medication. If you have any questions, talk to your doctor or pharmacist.
• Cigarette smoking can greatly increase the risk of developing disorders of the heart or blood vessels while taking this medication. The risk increases with the amount of smoking and the age of the smoker.
• Be sure to tell your doctor if you are pregnant. If you suspect you are pregnant, discontinue use of the medication immediately. Estrogens have been shown to cause birth defects in the offspring of women who received these medications during pregnancy. Also tell your doctor if you are breast-feeding an infant. Small amounts of estrogen pass into breast milk, so caution is warranted. Estradiol can also decrease milk production.

---

estrogens, conjugated

BRAND NAMES (Manufacturers)
conjugated estrogens (various manufacturers)
Premarin (Wyeth-Ayerst)
TYPE OF DRUG
Estrogen
INGREDIENTS
conjugated estrogens
DOSAGE FORM
Tablets (0.3 mg, 0.625 mg, 0.9 mg, 1.25 mg, and 2.5 mg)
STORAGE
Store at room temperature in a tightly closed container.

USES

Conjugated estrogens are a group of estrogenlike products obtained from natural sources (the urine of pregnant mares). They are used to treat menopausal symptoms, prostatic cancer, uterine bleeding, and some cases of breast cancer. They can also be used in hormone replacement therapy for women who do not produce enough estrogen of their own.

TREATMENT

To avoid stomach irritation, you can take conjugated estrogens with food or immediately after a meal.

Follow your doctor's instructions carefully when you take this medication. Often, conjugated estrogens are prescribed to be taken for three-week periods, with one week off (in order to reduce potential side effects).

If you miss a scheduled dose of this medication, take the missed dose as soon as possible after you remember. However, if it is almost time for the next dose, do not take the missed dose at all; just return to your regular dosing schedule. Do not double the next dose.

SIDE EFFECTS

Minor. Bloating, change in sexual desire, depression, diarrhea, dizziness, headache, loss of appetite, nausea, or vomiting. These side effects should disappear as your body adjusts to the medication.

This medication can increase your sensitivity to sunlight. You should try to avoid prolonged exposure to sunlight and sunlamps. Wear protective clothing and sunglasses, and use an effective sunscreen.

If you feel dizzy or light-headed, sit or lie down for a while; get up slowly from a sitting or reclining position; and be careful on stairs.

Major. Tell your doctor about side effects that are persistent or particularly bothersome. IT IS ESPECIALLY IMPORTANT TO TELL YOUR DOCTOR about changes in menstrual patterns; chest pain; difficulty in breathing; eye pain; loss of coordination; lumps in the breast; painful urination; pain in the calves; skin color changes; slurred speech; sudden, severe headache; swelling of the feet or ankles; vision changes; weight gain or loss; or yellowing of the eyes or skin.

INTERACTIONS

Conjugated estrogens will interact with several other medications:

1. Estrogens can decrease the effectiveness of oral anticoagulants (blood thinners, such as warfarin).

2. Carbamazepine, phenobarbital, phenytoin, primidone, protease inhibitors, and rifampin can increase the elimination of estrogen from the body, thus decreasing its effectiveness.

3. Estrogens can increase the side effects and decrease the effectiveness of the tricyclic antidepressants.

4. Estrogens may interfere with the breakdown of cyclosporine, increasing cyclosporine's toxic effects.

BE SURE TO TELL YOUR DOCTOR about any medications you are currently taking, especially those listed above.

WARNINGS

• Tell your doctor about unusual or allergic reactions you have had to any medications, especially to conjugated estrogens, to oral contraceptives (birth control pills), or to any other estrogen product.

• Before starting to take this drug, tell your doctor if you have ever had asthma, blood clot disorders, breast cancer, diabetes mellitus, endometriosis, epilepsy, gallbladder disease, heart disease, high blood pressure, hypercalcemia, kidney disease, liver disease, migraines, porphyria, uterine fibroid tumors, vaginal bleeding, or depression.

• Studies have shown that estrogens increase the risk of certain types of cancer. Ask your pharmacist for the brochure "Information for the Patient." It is important that you understand the possible risks and benefits of this medication. If you have questions, check with your doctor or pharmacist.

• Although it is not known if estrogens can increase the risk of breast cancer, it is important that you examine your breasts regularly for lumps or discharge.

• If you notice tenderness, swelling, or bleeding of your gums, consult your doctor or dentist.

• Estrogens can cause a change in glucose tolerance in diabetic patients. If you have diabetes, be sure to tell your doctor if you notice any abnormalities in your glucose levels.

• Do not change your brand of medication without the consent of your doctor. If your refill does not look the same, consult your doctor or pharmacist.

• Cigarette smoking increases the risk of serious side effects from estrogens. The risk increases with both age and the amount of smoking.

• If this medication makes you dizzy or light-headed, do not take part in any activity that requires alertness, such as driving an automobile or operating potentially dangerous equipment or machinery.

• Estrogens can change your blood's clotting ability, so be especially careful to avoid injuries.

• Before having surgery or any other medical or dental treatment, be sure to tell your doctor or dentist that you are taking this medication.
• Be sure to tell your doctor if you are pregnant. If you suspect that you are pregnant, discontinue the use of this medication immediately. Several studies have shown that estrogens taken during pregnancy can cause birth defects in the child. Also be sure to notify your doctor if you are breast-feeding an infant. Estrogens have been known to pass into breast milk.

---

etanercept

BRAND NAME (Manufacturer)
Enbrel (Immunex)
TYPE OF DRUG
Antiarthritic
INGREDIENT
etanercept
DOSAGE FORM
Injection (25 mg per vial)
STORAGE
Store this medication in the refrigerator and protect it from light. Do not freeze the medication.

USES

Etanercept is used to treat the symptoms of rheumatoid arthritis, such as pain and swelling of the joints, in both adults and children. This medication may also help prevent further damage to the bones and joints. Etanercept is also used for a condition known as ankylosing spondylitis (a form of arthritis of the spine).

Etanercept is in a new class of medication for arthritis called TNF blockers. It works by blocking the effects of a chemical called TNF-alpha, which is part of your body's immune system. People with rheumatoid arthritis have too much TNF-alpha. Although TNF-alpha is an important part of your body's defense mechanism, helping to fight off infections, too much TNF-alpha can cause healthy tissues (especially tissues in the bones and joints) to become inflamed and painful. However, blocking TNF-alpha may make you more susceptible to infections.

TREATMENT

Take this medication exactly as prescribed by your doctor. Etanercept is given by injection under the skin (subcutaneously), twice a week. Complete instructions on using etanercept should be included with the medication and should be reviewed before use. If you have any questions, be sure to contact your doctor or pharmacist. In many cases, you will be trained by a nurse or other health care specialist on how to inject this medication properly and how to monitor for side effects.

Since etanercept is given by injection, you will need a special container to dispose of used needles and syringes. Also, etanercept comes as a powder that has to be mixed with a special solution before using. When mixing etanercept, do not shake the vial. After mixing, check the vial before using it; the solution should be clear. Do not use the medication if there are floating particles or if the solution has a color. Do not mix etanercept with any other medications or dilute the solution any more than directed. Etanercept contains no preservatives and should be used immediately after mixing. If it is necessary to wait before injecting the medication, you may store the mixed vial of etanercept in the refrigerator for up to six hours. Any portion of etanercept solution that is not used should be discarded. The contents of a used syringe should not be saved for later use.

If you miss a dose, take the missed dose as soon as possible. However, if it is almost time for your next dose, do not take the missed dose; just return to your regular dosing schedule. Do not double the next dose.

SIDE EFFECTS

Minor. Headache; nausea; redness, rash, swelling, itching, or bruising at the injection site; or sinus infections. These side effects should diminish or disappear as your body adjusts to the medication.

The swelling, rash, and redness at the injection site should go away in a few days. Applying a cold towel may help relieve some of the discomfort. If the swelling, redness, and rash persist for more than a few days, contact your doctor.

Major. Tell your doctor about any side effects you experience that are persistent or particularly bothersome. IT IS ESPECIALLY IMPORTANT TO TELL YOUR DOCTOR about chest pains, dizziness, infection, joint pain, numbness or tingling, rash on the chest or face, vision problems, or weakness in the legs.

INTERACTIONS

If taken as directed, etanercept is unlikely to interact with any other medications.

However, before starting to take this medication, BE SURE TO TELL YOUR DOCTOR about any medications you are currently taking, including natural or herbal products or over-the-counter medications.

WARNINGS

- Tell your doctor if you have a history of infections that keep returning, any conditions that may increase your risk of getting an infection, tuberculosis, any type of disorder or disease of the nervous system, or lupus or lupuslike symptoms. Also be sure to tell your doctor if you are scheduled to have any type of surgery or receive any type of vaccination.
- Tell your doctor about unusual or allergic reactions you now have or have had to any medications, especially to etanercept or other agents used to treat arthritis.
- Etanercept may increase your risk of getting a serious infection, including tuberculosis and life-threatening fungal or bacterial infections. Your doctor may want to test you for tuberculosis before beginning treatment with etanercept.
- Some patients with rheumatoid arthritis have an increased risk of getting certain types of cancers, including lymphoma, a cancer that can affect your lymph system. Discuss your risk of cancer with your doctor before beginning etanercept.
- The risk of a condition known as lupus may be increased with etanercept. Symptoms include joint pain, a rash across the cheeks of the face or arms that is sensitive to sunlight, and shortness of breath. If you experience these symptoms, call your doctor. It may be necessary to stop treatment with etanercept.
- If you develop a severe rash, swelling of the face, or difficulty in breathing after taking etanercept, call your doctor immediately.
- Before having surgery or any other type of medical or dental treatment, be sure to tell your doctor that you are taking this medication.
- Be sure to tell your doctor if you are pregnant. Effects of this drug during pregnancy have not been thoroughly studied in either humans or animals. Also tell your doctor if you are breast-feeding an infant. It is unknown if etanercept passes into breast milk or what the effects of etanercept would be on an infant.

---

ethinyl estradiol

BRAND NAMES (Manufacturers)
Estinyl (Schering)
Feminone (Pharmacia)

TYPE OF DRUG
Estrogen
INGREDIENT
ethinyl estradiol
DOSAGE FORM
Tablets (0.02 mg, 0.05 mg, and 0.5 mg)
STORAGE
Store at room temperature in a tightly closed container. Do not refrigerate.

USES

Ethinyl estradiol is a synthetic estrogen that is used to treat symptoms of menopause, certain types of breast cancer, and prostate cancer.

TREATMENT

To avoid stomach irritation from this medication, take ethinyl estradiol with food, milk, or water (unless your doctor directs you to do otherwise).

If you miss a dose of this medication, take the missed dose as soon as possible. However, if it is almost time for the next scheduled dose, do not take the missed dose at all; instead, return to your regular dosing schedule. Do not double the next dose of this medication.

SIDE EFFECTS

Minor. Abdominal cramping, abnormal vaginal bleeding, bloating, breast tenderness, darkening of the skin, diarrhea, dizziness, fluid retention, frequent or painful urination, headache, nausea, vomiting, or weight gain. These side effects should disappear over time as your body adjusts to the medication.

This medication can increase your sensitivity to sunlight. You should try to avoid prolonged exposure to sunlight and sunlamps. Wear protective clothing and sunglasses, and use an effective sunscreen.

If you feel dizzy, sit or lie down for a while; get up slowly from a sitting or reclining position; and be careful on stairs.

Eating a full breakfast or having a midmorning snack may help to relieve the nausea and vomiting.

Major. Tell your doctor about any side effects that are persistent or particularly bothersome. IT IS ESPECIALLY IMPORTANT TO TELL YOUR DOCTOR about blurred vision, chest pain, convulsions, depression, hair loss, itching, pain or inflammation of the calves or thighs, shortness of breath, skin rash, or yellowing of the eyes or skin.

INTERACTIONS

Ethinyl estradiol interacts with other types of medications:

1. It can decrease the effectiveness of oral anticoagulants (blood thinners, such as warfarin).

2. Protease inhibitors, carbamazepine, phenobarbital, phenytoin, primidone, and rifampin can reduce the effectiveness of ethinyl estradiol.

3. Ethinyl estradiol can increase the side effects and decrease the effectiveness of tricyclic antidepressants.

4. Estrogens may interfere with the breakdown of cyclosporine, increasing cyclosporine's toxic effects.

BE SURE TO TELL YOUR DOCTOR about any medications you are currently taking, especially any listed above.

WARNINGS

• Tell your doctor about unusual or allergic reactions you have had to any medications, especially to ethinyl estradiol or other estrogens or to oral contraceptive medications (birth control pills).

• Tell your doctor if you now have or ever had asthma, blood-clot disorders, breast disease, depression, diabetes mellitus, epilepsy, endometriosis, gallstones or gallbladder disease, heart disease, high blood pressure, kidney disease, liver disease, migraine headaches, porphyria, or uterine tumors.
• Some of these products contain the color additive FD&C Yellow No. 5 (tartrazine), which can cause allergic-type reactions (shortness of breath, fainting, rash) in certain susceptible individuals.
• Estrogens can change your blood's clotting ability, so be especially careful to avoid injuries.
• Estrogens can cause a change in glucose tolerance in people with diabetes. Be sure to tell your doctor if you notice any abnormalities in your glucose levels.
• Before having surgery or any other medical or dental treatment, be sure to tell your doctor or dentist that you are taking this medication.
• Studies have shown that estrogens may increase the risk of certain types of cancer.
• A package insert titled "Information for the Patient" should be dispensed with your prescription. It is important that you understand the possible risks and benefits of this medication. If you have any questions, discuss them with your doctor or pharmacist.
• Although it is not known if estrogens increase the risk of breast cancer, it is important that you examine your breasts regularly for lumps or discharge.
• Cigarette smoking can greatly increase the risk of developing disorders of the heart or blood vessels while taking this medication. The risk increases with the amount of smoking and the age of the smoker.
• Be sure to tell your doctor if you are pregnant. If you suspect you are pregnant, discontinue use of this medication immediately. Estrogens have caused birth defects in the offspring of women who received these medications during pregnancy. Also tell your doctor if you are breast-feeding an infant. Small amounts of estrogen pass into breast milk. Ethinyl estradiol can also decrease milk production.

---

etodolac

BRAND NAMES (Manufacturers)
Lodine (Wyeth-Ayerst)
Lodine XL (Wyeth-Ayerst)
TYPE OF DRUG
Nonsteroidal anti-inflammatory analgesic
INGREDIENT
etodolac
DOSAGE FORMS
Capsules (200 mg and 300 mg)
Tablets (400 mg)
STORAGE
Store in a tightly closed, light-resistant container at room temperature. This medication should never be frozen.

USES

Etodolac is used to treat the pain and inflammation (swelling, stiffness) of acute and chronic osteoarthritis. It is also used for the relief of pain. Etodolac is not recommended for treating the symptoms of rheumatoid arthritis.

TREATMENT

Take with meals or an antacid to decrease stomach irritation. However, if you are taking this medication for acute pain (not osteoarthritis), the first one or two doses may be taken on an empty stomach (30 to 60 minutes before or 2 hours after meals) so that the medication can reach your bloodstream more quickly.

If etodolac is being taken to relieve arthritis, you must take it regularly as directed by your doctor. Etodolac does not cure osteoarthritis, but it will help to control the condition as long as you continue to take it.

It is important to take etodolac on schedule and not to miss any doses. If you do miss a dose, take it as soon as possible. However, if it is almost time for your next dose, don't take the missed dose at all; just return to your regular dosing schedule. Do not double the next dose.

SIDE EFFECTS

Minor. Constipation, diarrhea, dizziness, drowsiness, excessive thirst, feeling of fullness, flatulence, headache, heartburn, increased appetite, indigestion, nausea, or nervousness. As your body adjusts to the drug, these side effects should disappear.

To relieve constipation, increase the amount of fiber in your diet (fresh fruits and vegetables, salads, bran, and whole-grain breads), exercise, and drink more water, unless your doctor directs you to do otherwise.

If you become dizzy or light-headed, sit or lie down for a while; get up slowly from a sitting or reclining position; and be careful on stairs.

Major. If any side effects are persistent or particularly bothersome, you should report them to your doctor. IT IS ESPECIALLY IMPORTANT TO TELL YOUR DOCTOR about bloody or black tarry stools; blurred vision; confusion; depression; difficulty breathing; difficult or painful urination; fever; palpitations; problems with hearing; ringing or buzzing in your ears; seizures; skin rash, hives, or itching; stomach pain; swelling; tremors; unusual bleeding or bruising; unusual fatigue or weakness; unusual weight gain; or yellowing of the eyes or skin.

INTERACTIONS

Etodolac interacts with several other types of medications:

1. Concurrent use of etodolac and anticoagulants (blood thinners, such as warfarin) or valproic acid can lead to an increase in bleeding complications.

2. Concurrent use of etodolac and aspirin, other salicylates, or other anti-inflammatory medications can increase stomach irritation.

3. Etodolac can reduce the effects of diuretics (water pills) and other medications for high blood pressure.

4. Probenecid may increase the blood levels of etodolac, which may increase the risk of side effects.

5. The action of beta blockers may be decreased by this drug.

6. This drug may increase the amount of methotrexate in the body, increasing the risk of toxicity from methotrexate. Do not use etodolac with methotrexate.

7. Etodolac may increase the amount of lithium and cyclosporine in the body, increasing their side effects.

BE SURE TO TELL YOUR DOCTOR about any medications you are currently taking, especially any listed above.

WARNINGS

• Before you start to take this medication, it is important to tell your doctor if you have ever had unusual or allergic reactions to etodolac or to any of the other chemically related drugs (aspirin, other salicylates, diclofenac, diflunisal, fenoprofen, flurbiprofen, ibuprofen, indomethacin, ketorolac, meclofenamate, mefenamic acid, nabumetone, naproxen, oxaprozin, oxyphenbutazone, phenylbutazone, piroxicam, sulindac, tenoxicam, tiaprofenic acid, or tolmetin).

• Tell your doctor if you now have or ever had asthma, bleeding problems, colitis, epilepsy, heart disease, high blood pressure, kidney disease, liver disease, mental illness, stomach ulcers or other stomach problems, or Parkinson's disease.

• If etodolac makes you dizzy or drowsy, do not take part in any activity that requires alertness, such as driving or operating dangerous machinery.

• Because etodolac can prolong bleeding time, be certain to tell your doctor that you are taking this drug before having surgery or any other medical or dental treatment.
• Stomach problems are more likely to occur if you take aspirin regularly or if you drink alcohol while being treated with etodolac. These should be avoided (unless your doctor directs you to do otherwise).
• The elderly may be at increased risk for experiencing side effects from this drug.
• Be sure to tell your doctor if you are pregnant. This type of medication can cause unwanted effects to the heart or to the blood flow of the fetus. Studies in animals have shown that this type of medication, if taken late in pregnancy, can prolong labor or cause other problems during delivery. Also tell your doctor if you are breast-feeding an infant. Small amounts of etodolac can pass into the breast milk.

---

famciclovir

BRAND NAME (Manufacturer)
Famvir (GlaxoSmithKline)
TYPE OF DRUG
Antiviral
INGREDIENT
famciclovir
DOSAGE FORM
Tablets (125 mg, 250 mg, and 500 mg)
STORAGE
Store at room temperature in a tightly closed container. Do not expose to excess heat.

USES

Famciclovir is used to treat genital herpes and herpes zoster (shingles) infections of the skin. Famciclovir prevents the growth and multiplication of the herpes virus. This medication does not cure the herpes infection, but it may relieve the pain associated with the viral infection and may shorten the duration of an outbreak.

TREATMENT

To lessen stomach upset, take this medication with food (unless your doctor tells you to do otherwise).

Take famciclovir as soon as possible after the symptoms of a herpes virus infection appear. This medication works best when it is started within 48 hours of the onset of the rash that appears with shingles or within 6 hours of the onset of the symptoms of genital herpes.

Complete the full course of therapy, even if your symptoms disappear sooner. The full course usually lasts five to seven days.

If you miss a dose of this medication, take it as soon as possible. However, if it is almost time for your next dose, do not take the missed dose at all; just return to your regular dosing schedule. Do not double the doses.

SIDE EFFECTS

Minor. Diarrhea, dizziness, headache, nausea, unusual tiredness or weakness, or vomiting. These side effects should diminish or disappear as your body adjusts to the medication.

To avoid dizziness or light-headedness when you stand, contract and relax the muscles of your legs for a few moments before rising. Do this by pressing one foot against the floor while raising the other foot slightly, alternating feet so that you are "pumping" your legs in a pedaling motion.

Major. Tell your doctor about any side effects that are persistent or bothersome.

INTERACTIONS

Probenecid may increase the amount of famciclovir in the body.

WARNINGS

• Be sure to tell your doctor about any unusual or allergic reactions you have had to famciclovir or to any other medication, including antiviral medications.
• Before starting this medication, tell your doctor if you have any other medical problems, especially kidney problems.
• If this medication makes you feel dizzy, do not take part in any activity that requires alertness, such as driving an automobile or operating potentially dangerous equipment or machinery.
• Avoid sexual activity while you have signs or symptoms of genital herpes. This medication does not prevent transmission of the herpes virus to sexual partners nor does it prevent recurrence of outbreaks.
• This medication has been prescribed for your current infection only. An infection that someone else has may require a different medication. Do not give your medication to someone else, and do not use it to treat other types of infections unless your doctor directs you to do so.
• Be sure to tell your doctor if you are pregnant. Although this medication appears to be safe in animals, there is no information on its use in humans during pregnancy. Also tell your doctor if you are breast-feeding an infant. Famciclovir is not considered safe to use during breast-feeding.

---

famotidine

BRAND NAMES (Manufacturers)
Pepcid (Merck)
Pepcid AC Acid Controller* (J & J Merck)
Pepcid AC Chewable* (J & J Merck)
Pepcid RPD (Merck)
*Available over the counter (without a prescription) in 10-mg strength.
TYPE OF DRUG
Gastric-acid-secretion inhibitor (decreases stomach acid)
INGREDIENT
famotidine
DOSAGE FORMS
Tablets (10 mg, 20 mg, and 40 mg)
Tablets, chewable (10 mg)
Tablets, orally disintegrating (20 mg and 40 mg)
Oral suspension (40 mg per 5-mL spoonful)
STORAGE
Store at room temperature in a tightly closed container. Do not freeze, and do not expose to high temperatures. Discard any unused oral suspension after 30 days.

USES

Famotidine is used to treat active duodenal ulcers. It is also used in the long-term treatment of excessive stomach acid secretion (Zollinger-Ellison syndrome) and in the prevention of recurrent ulcers. Famotidine reduces stomach acid secretions by blocking the effects of histamine in the stomach.

TREATMENT

If you are taking a single daily dose of famotidine, it is best to take the dose at bedtime to obtain the maximum benefits from it. Antacids will not affect the activity of famotidine. Check with your doctor to see if you should be taking antacids as part of your ulcer treatment.

Measure the suspension carefully with a specially designed 5-mL measuring spoon. An ordinary kitchen teaspoon is not accurate enough to ensure that the proper dose will be taken.

The RPD (orally disintegrating) tablet is made to dissolve in the mouth. Remove it from the foil package with dry hands, and place it on the tongue to dissolve. Swallow with saliva.

If you miss a dose of famotidine, take the missed dose as soon as possible. However, if it is almost time for the next dose, do not take the missed dose at all; just return to your regular dosing schedule. Do not double the next dose.

SIDE EFFECTS

Minor. Abdominal pain, acne, change in taste, constipation, diarrhea, dizziness, dry mouth, dry skin, fatigue, flushing, headache, insomnia, loss of appetite, nausea, or vomiting. These side effects should disappear as your body adjusts to this drug.

If you are constipated, increase the amount of fiber in your diet (fresh fruits and vegetables, salads, bran, and whole-grain breads), exercise, and drink more water (unless your doctor tells you not to do so).

To reduce mouth dryness, chew sugarless gum or suck on ice chips or hard candy.

If you feel dizzy or light-headed, sit or lie down for a while; get up slowly from a sitting or reclining position; and be careful on stairs.

Major. Tell your doctor about any side effects you are experiencing that are persistent or particularly bothersome. IT IS ESPECIALLY IMPORTANT TO TELL YOUR DOCTOR about anxiety, confusion, depression, fever, hair loss, hallucinations, itching, muscle or joint pain, palpitations, ringing in the ears, seizures, shortness of breath, tingling in the fingers or toes, or yellowing of the eyes or skin.

INTERACTIONS

Famotidine may interact with other medications. It is very important to tell your doctor about all the medications you are taking before starting famotidine.

1. Famotidine may decrease the absorption of ketoconazole or itraconazole, reducing their effects. Take famotidine at least two hours after these other medications.

2. Sucralfate may decrease the absorption of famotidine. This medication should be taken at least two hours before you take a dose of sucralfate.

WARNINGS

• Tell your doctor about any unusual or allergic reactions you have had to any medications, especially to famotidine or to the other gastric-acid-secretion inhibitors (cimetidine, ranitidine, or nizatidine).

• Before starting treatment with famotidine, tell your doctor if you now have or ever had kidney disease.

• Famotidine should be taken continuously for as long as your doctor prescribes. Stopping therapy early may be a cause of ineffective treatment.

• Cigarette smoking may interfere with the beneficial effects of famotidine.

• Aspirin, foods known to cause stomach upset, and certain beverages (such as those containing caffeine) may worsen your stomach irritation.

• If this drug makes you dizzy or drowsy, do not take part in any activity that requires alertness, such as driving a car or operating potentially dangerous equipment.

• The chewable tablets and the RPD tablets contain aspartame, which the body changes to phenylalanine. Patients with phenylketonuria should use these dosage forms with caution.

• Be sure to tell your doctor if you are pregnant. Extensive studies in pregnant women have not yet been conducted. Also tell your doctor if you are breast-feeding an infant. Small amounts of famotidine may pass into breast milk.

felodipine

BRAND NAME (Manufacturer)
Plendil (Astra-Merck)
TYPE OF DRUG
Antihypertensive and antianginal
INGREDIENT
felodipine
DOSAGE FORM
Extended-release tablets (2.5 mg, 5 mg, and 10 mg)
STORAGE
Store in a tightly closed container at room temperature, away from heat and direct sunlight. Do not refrigerate or freeze.

USES

This medication is used to treat various types of angina (chest pain) and hypertension (high blood pressure). This medication belongs to a class of drugs called calcium channel blockers. By blocking calcium, this medicine relaxes and prevents spasms of the blood vessels of the heart and reduces the heart's oxygen needs.

TREATMENT

This medication should be taken exactly as prescribed by your doctor. Felodipine can be taken either on an empty stomach or with a meal; however, you should avoid taking this medication with grapefruit juice. It is very important that this medication NOT be crushed or chewed. The tablets should be swallowed whole for maximum benefit. While using this medication, try to develop a set schedule for taking it. If you miss a dose and remember within a few hours, take the missed dose and resume your regular schedule. If many hours have passed, skip the dose you missed and then take your next dose as scheduled. Do not double the dose. Felodipine does not cure high blood pressure, but it will help to control the condition as long as you continue to take it. It may be several weeks before you notice the full effect of this medication.

SIDE EFFECTS

Minor. Bloating, constipation, cough, diarrhea, dizziness, flushing, gas, giddiness, headache, heartburn, heat sensation, nasal congestion, nausea, nervousness, sleep disturbances, sweating, or weakness. These side effects should disappear as your body adjusts to the medication.

To avoid dizziness when you stand, contract and relax the muscles of your legs for a few moments before rising. Do this by alternately pushing one foot against the floor while lifting the other foot slightly. It may be helpful to sit or lie down for a while, to get up slowly from a sitting or reclining position, and to be careful on stairs.

Major. Tell your doctor about any side effects that are persistent or particularly bothersome. IT IS ESPECIALLY IMPORTANT TO TELL YOUR DOCTOR about blurred vision, chills, confusion, difficulty breathing, dizziness (persistent), fainting, fever, fluid retention (swelling of the feet, legs, or hands), impotence, mood changes, muscle cramps, palpitations, rash, sore throat, or tremors.

INTERACTIONS

Felodipine interacts with several other types of medications:

1. The combination of this medication with beta blockers can lead to a severe drop in blood pressure. However, for some patients, this combination of medications may have beneficial effects.

2. Cimetidine and ranitidine can cause an increase in the blood levels and adverse effects of felodipine.

3. Erythromycin and itraconazole may increase the blood levels and adverse effects of felodipine.
4. Concurrent use of carbamazepine and this medication can lead to decreased blood levels of felodipine and a decrease in its effectiveness.
5. This medication can delay the body's elimination of digoxin and increase digoxin's adverse effects.
6. Concurrent administration of this medication with theophylline or cyclosporine can lead either to increased or decreased blood levels and therefore to adverse effects from these medications.
7. Procainamide and quinidine may increase the side effects of felodipine.

Before starting to take felodipine, BE SURE TO TELL YOUR DOCTOR about any medications you are taking, especially those listed above.

WARNINGS

• Tell your doctor about any unusual or allergic reactions you have had to any medications, especially to calcium channel blockers (including verapamil, diltiazem, nifedipine, bepridil, isradipine, nicardipine, nimodipine, or nisoldipine) or to this medication.
• Be sure to tell your doctor if you have or ever had a heart attack, stroke, blood disorders, kidney or liver disease, or low blood pressure.
• Before having surgery or other medical or dental treatment, tell your doctor or dentist you are taking this medication.
• If this drug makes you dizzy or drowsy (sometimes this effect is seen after the first few doses), try to avoid sudden changes in posture. Also avoid tasks requiring alertness, such as driving a car or operating dangerous equipment.
• Do not take any over-the-counter (nonprescription) medications for weight control or for asthma, sinus, cough, cold, or allergy problems unless you first check with your doctor.
• This medication may cause excessively low blood pressure in elderly patients. Therefore, lower beginning doses may be necessary to avoid this adverse effect in older adults.
• Do not stop taking this medication unless you first consult your doctor. Stopping this drug abruptly may lead to a rise in blood pressure.
• Mild gum disease has been noticed in some people who take this medication. To avoid this adverse effect, it is very important to maintain good oral hygiene.
• Be sure to tell your doctor if you are pregnant. This medication and other drugs in the class called calcium channel blockers have been shown to cause birth defects in the offspring of animals that received large doses of such medications during pregnancy. Also tell your doctor if you are breast-feeding an infant. It is not known if this medication passes into breast milk.

---

fenoprofen

BRAND NAMES (Manufacturers)
fenoprofen (various manufacturers)
Nalfon (Dista)
TYPE OF DRUG
Nonsteroidal anti-inflammatory analgesic
INGREDIENT
fenoprofen
DOSAGE FORMS
Capsules (200 mg and 300 mg)
Tablets (600 mg)

STORAGE

Store in tightly closed containers at room temperature, away from heat and direct sunlight.

USES

Fenoprofen is used to treat inflammation (pain, swelling, and stiffness) that is associated with certain types of arthritis, bursitis, gout, and tendinitis. Fenoprofen has been shown to block the production of certain body chemicals, called prostaglandins, that are known to trigger pain. However, it is not yet fully understood how fenoprofen works.

TREATMENT

Take this medication with meals or milk to avoid stomach irritation. However, if you are taking this medication for acute pain, the first one or two doses may be taken on an empty stomach (30 to 60 minutes before or 2 hours after a meal) so that it reaches your bloodstream quickly.

If you are taking fenoprofen to relieve arthritis, you must take it regularly as directed by your doctor. It may take up to three weeks before you feel its full benefits. This medication does not cure arthritis, but it will help to control the condition as long as you continue to take it.

It is important to take fenoprofen on schedule and not to miss any doses. If you do miss a dose, take the missed dose as soon as possible. However, if it is almost time for your next dose, do not take the missed dose at all; just return to your regular dosing schedule. Do not double the next dose of medication.

SIDE EFFECTS

Minor. Bloating, constipation, diarrhea, difficulty in sleeping, dizziness, drowsiness, headache, heartburn, indigestion, light-headedness, loss of appetite, nausea, nervousness, soreness of the mouth, unusual sweating, or vomiting. As your body adjusts to the drug, these side effects should disappear.

To relieve constipation, increase the amount of fiber in your diet (fresh fruits and vegetables, salads, bran, and whole-grain breads), exercise, and drink more water (unless your doctor directs you to do otherwise).

If you become dizzy, sit or lie down for a while; get up slowly from a sitting or reclining position; and be careful when on stairs.

Major. If any side effects are persistent or particularly bothersome, you should report them to your doctor. IT IS ESPECIALLY IMPORTANT TO TELL YOUR DOCTOR about bloody or black, tarry stools; blurred vision; confusion; depression; difficult or painful urination; difficulty in breathing; hearing difficulties; palpitations; ringing or buzzing in the ears; skin rash, hives, or itching; stomach pain; swelling of the feet; tightness in the chest; unexplained sore throat and fever; unusual bleeding or bruising; unusual fatigue or weakness; unusual weight gain; or yellowing of the eyes or skin.

INTERACTIONS

Fenoprofen interacts with several types of medications:

1. Concurrent use with anticoagulants (blood thinners, such as warfarin) or valproic acid can lead to an increase in bleeding complications.

2. Aspirin, salicylates, and other anti-inflammatory medications can lead to an increase in stomach irritation caused by fenoprofen.

3. Fenoprofen levels may be affected by concurrent use of phenobarbital.

4. Probenecid may increase blood levels of fenoprofen, which may increase the risk of side effects.

5. The action of beta blockers or diuretics may be decreased when used concurrently with this medication.

6. Concurrent use of this drug and methotrexate may increase the amount of methotrexate in the body, increasing the risk of toxicity from methotrexate. Do not take this medication with methotrexate.
7. Fenoprofen may increase the amount of lithium and cyclosporine in the body, increasing their side effects.

BE SURE TO TELL YOUR DOCTOR about any medications you are currently taking, especially any of those listed above.

WARNINGS

- Tell your doctor if you have ever had unusual or allergic reactions to medications, especially to fenoprofen or any chemically related drug (such as aspirin or other salicylates, diclofenac, diflunisal, flurbiprofen, indomethacin, ibuprofen, oxyphenbutazone, piroxicam, sulindac, tolmetin, etodolac, ketorolac, meclofenamate, mefenamic acid, nabumetone, naproxen, oxaprozin, tenoxicam, and tiaprofenic acid).
- Tell your doctor if you have ever had bleeding problems, colitis, ulcers or other stomach problems, epilepsy, heart disease, high blood pressure, asthma, kidney disease, liver disease, mental illness, or Parkinson's disease.
- If this drug makes you dizzy or drowsy, do not take part in any activity that requires alertness, such as driving a car or operating potentially dangerous equipment.
- Before having surgery or other medical or dental treatment, tell your doctor or dentist about this drug.
- Stomach problems are more likely to occur if you take aspirin regularly or drink alcohol while being treated with this medication. These should, therefore, be avoided (unless your doctor directs you to do otherwise).
- Be sure to tell your doctor if you are pregnant. Although studies in humans have not been conducted, unwanted heart side effects have been reported in the offspring of animals that received fenoprofen during pregnancy. Also tell your doctor if you are breast-feeding an infant. Small amounts of this medication have been known to pass into breast milk.

---

fexofenadine

BRAND NAME (Manufacturer)
Allegra (Hoechst-Marion Roussell)
TYPE OF DRUG
Antihistamine
INGREDIENT
fexofenadine
DOSAGE FORMS
Capsules (60 mg)
Tablets (30 mg, 60 mg, and 180 mg)
STORAGE
Store at room temperature in a tightly closed container. Do not expose to excess heat or moisture, and do not store in the bathroom.

USES

Fexofenadine is used to treat the symptoms of an allergic response, including sneezing, runny nose, itching, and watery eyes. This medication belongs to a group of drugs known as antihistamines, which act by blocking the action of histamine, a chemical that is released by the body during an allergic reaction.

TREATMENT

Take either on an empty stomach or with food or milk (unless your doctor directs you to do otherwise). Fexofenadine should be taken only as needed to control the symptoms of allergy. If you miss a dose of this medication, take it as soon as you remember. However, if it is almost time for the next dose, do not take the missed dose at all; just return to your regular dosing schedule. Do not double the dose.

SIDE EFFECTS

Minor. Drowsiness, dry mouth, painful menses, stomach upset, or unusual tiredness. These side effects should diminish or disappear as your body adjusts to the medication.

Dry mouth can be relieved by chewing sugarless gum or sucking on hard candy.

Major. Tell your doctor about any side effects that are persistent or particularly bothersome. IT IS ESPECIALLY IMPORTANT TO TELL YOUR DOCTOR about flulike symptoms or unusual tiredness.

INTERACTIONS

Fexofenadine may interact with a number of other types of medications:

1. Erythromycin, clarithromycin, ketoconazole, or itraconazole may increase the amount of fexofenadine in the body, increasing the risk of side effects.

2. Use of over-the-counter (nonprescription) cough, cold, or allergy medications may increase the side effects of this medication and should be avoided.

3. Antacids may decrease the amount of fexofenadine absorbed by the body, reducing its effect.

WARNINGS

- Be sure to tell your doctor about any unusual or allergic reactions you have had to any medications, including fexofenadine, terfenadine, or other antihistamines.
- Tell your doctor about any medical problems you may have, especially kidney problems, glaucoma, enlarged prostate, or difficulty urinating.
- Before starting fexofenadine, tell your doctor if you now have or ever had asthma.
- Fexofenadine causes less drowsiness than other antihistamines. However, until you see how it affects you, be cautious about performing tasks that require alertness, such as driving a car or operating potentially dangerous machinery.
- Be sure to tell your doctor if you are pregnant. It is not known if fexofenadine is safe during pregnancy. It is not known if fexofenadine can pass into human breast milk. Discuss the risks and benefits of this medication with your doctor if you are breast-feeding an infant.

---

fexofenadine and pseudoephedrine combination

BRAND NAME (Manufacturer)
Allegra-D (Hoechst-Marion Roussell)
TYPE OF DRUG
Antihistamine and decongestant combination
INGREDIENTS
fexofenadine and pseudoephedrine
DOSAGE FORM
Extended-release capsules (fexofenadine 60 mg and pseudoephedrine 120 mg)
STORAGE
Store at room temperature in a tightly closed, light-resistant container. Do not expose to excess heat or moisture, and do not store in the bathroom.

USES

This medication is used to treat the symptoms of an allergic response, including sneezing, runny nose, itching, and tearing. Fexofenadine belongs to a group of drugs known as antihistamines, which act by blocking the action of histamine, a chemical that is released by the body during an allergic reaction. Pseudoephedrine belongs to a group of drugs known as adrenergic agents (decongestants). They act by constricting (narrowing) blood vessels in the nasal passages to reduce swelling and congestion.

TREATMENT

This medication should be taken on an empty stomach. However, to avoid stomach irritation, you may take this medication with food or milk (unless your doctor directs you to do otherwise). Fexofenadine and pseudoephedrine should be taken only as needed to control the symptoms of allergy. The capsules are designed to release the drug slowly and should be swallowed whole, not crushed, broken, or chewed. If you miss a dose of this medication, take it as soon as you remember, unless it is almost time for the next dose. In that case, do not take the missed dose at all; just return to your regular dosing schedule. Do not double the next dose.

SIDE EFFECTS

Minor. Anxiety, back pain, drowsiness, dry mouth, headache, heartburn, nausea, painful menstruation, sore throat, stomach pain, stomach upset, or unusual tiredness. These side effects should diminish or disappear as your body adjusts to the medication.

Dry mouth can be relieved by chewing sugarless gum or sucking on hard candy.

Major. Tell your doctor about any side effects that are persistent or particularly bothersome. IT IS ESPECIALLY IMPORTANT TO TELL YOUR DOCTOR about cough, difficulty sleeping, irregular heartbeat, nervousness, or sore throat.

INTERACTIONS

This medication may interact with a number of other drugs:

1. The medication may interfere with the blood-pressure-lowering effects of reserpine and methyldopa.

2. This medication may decrease the actions of digoxin or of digitalis.

3. Erythromycin, clarithromycin, ketoconazole, or itraconazole may increase the amount of fexofenadine (an ingredient in this medication) in the body, increasing the risk of side effects from it.

4. Serious side effects may occur if a monoamine oxidase (MAO) inhibitor (such as furazolidone, isocarboxazid, pargyline, phenelzine, procarbazine, or tranylcypromine) is taken with this medication. At least 14 days should separate the use of this medication and the use of an MAO inhibitor.

5. Use of over-the-counter (nonprescription) cough, cold, or allergy medications may increase the side effects of this medication and should be avoided.

WARNINGS

• Be sure to tell your doctor about any unusual or allergic reactions you have had to any medications, including fexofenadine, terfenadine, pseudoephedrine, other antihistamines, decongestants, or diet pills.

• Tell your doctor about any medical problems you may have, especially heart disease, kidney problems, glaucoma, high blood pressure, diabetes, thyroid problems, enlarged prostate, or difficulty urinating.

• Before starting this medication, tell your doctor if you now have or ever had asthma.

• Fexofenadine, an ingredient in this medication, causes less drowsiness than other antihistamines. However, until you see how it affects you, be cautious about performing tasks that require alertness, such as driving a car or operating potentially dangerous machinery.

• Be sure to tell your doctor if you are pregnant. It is not known if this medication is safe during pregnancy. It is not known if this medication can pass into human breast milk. You should discuss with your doctor the risks and benefits of this medication if you are breast-feeding an infant.

fluconazole

BRAND NAME (Manufacturer)
Diflucan (Roerig)
TYPE OF DRUG
Antifungal agent
INGREDIENT
fluconazole
DOSAGE FORMS
Tablets (50 mg, 100 mg, 150 mg, and 200 mg)
Oral suspension (50 mg and 200 mg per 5-mL spoonful)
STORAGE
Store the tablets in a tightly closed container at room temperature, away from heat and direct sunlight. Store the suspension in the refrigerator or at room temperature, away from heat. Discard any unused portion of the suspension after 14 days because it loses its potency after that time. Do not freeze.

USES

Fluconazole is used to treat fungal infections of the mouth, throat, urinary tract, vagina, kidney, and liver. It is also used to treat pneumonia or meningitis caused by fungi. This medication acts by severely injuring the cell walls of the infecting fungus, thereby preventing it from growing and multiplying. Fluconazole is effective against susceptible fungi but does not kill bacteria, viruses, or parasites.

TREATMENT

Take this medication exactly as prescribed by your doctor, even if your symptoms improve. If you stop taking this medication too soon, resistant fungi are given a chance to grow and the infection may recur. You may have to take fluconazole for an extended period of time to completely cure the infection.

Shake the suspension well just before measuring each dose to distribute the ingredients evenly and equalize the doses. The contents tend to settle on the bottom of the bottle. Measure each dose carefully using a specially designed 5-mL measuring spoon. An ordinary kitchen teaspoon is not accurate enough.

If you miss a dose and remember within a few hours, take the missed dose and resume your regular schedule. If many hours have passed, take the missed dose as soon as you remember. Space the following dose halfway through the regular interval between doses, then return to your regular schedule. Try not to skip any doses.

SIDE EFFECTS

Minor. Abdominal pain or cramps, diarrhea, dizziness, headache, nausea, skin rash or itching, or vomiting. These side effects should diminish or disappear as your body adjusts to the medication.

If you feel dizzy, sit or lie down for a while, get up slowly from a sitting or reclining position, and be careful on stairs.

To avoid dizziness when you stand, contract and relax the muscles of your legs for a few moments before rising. Do this by alternately pushing one foot against the floor while lifting the other foot slightly, so you are pumping your legs in a pedaling motion.

Major. Tell your doctor about any side effects that are persistent or particularly bothersome to you. IT IS ESPECIALLY IMPORTANT TO TELL YOUR DOCTOR if you notice paler-than-normal stools, urine that is darker than normal, or yellowing of the skin or the whites of the eyes.

INTERACTIONS

Fluconazole interacts with several other types of drugs:

1. Fluconazole may increase the effectiveness of oral anticoagulants (blood thinners, such as warfarin), phenytoin, cyclosporine, and oral antidiabetic agents.
2. Rifampin and isoniazid may decrease the effectiveness of fluconazole.
3. Fluconazole may increase the amount of some diabetes medications in the body. This may increase the risk of side effects, such as low blood sugar, from these drugs.
4. Fluconazole may increase the blood levels of cyclosporine and tacrolimus, potentially increasing side effects from these medications.

BE SURE TO TELL YOUR DOCTOR about any medications you are currently taking, especially any of those listed above.

WARNINGS

• Tell your doctor about any unusual or allergic reactions you have had to any medications, especially to fluconazole, itraconazole, or ketoconazole.
• Tell your doctor if you now have or if you ever had liver disease.
• This drug should not be taken if you are pregnant or breast-feeding an infant. Be sure to tell your doctor if you are pregnant or breast-feeding.

---

flunisolide (inhalation)

BRAND NAMES (Manufacturers)
AeroBid (Forest)
AeroBid-M (Forest)
TYPE OF DRUG
Corticosteroid inhalant (antiasthmatic)
INGREDIENT
flunisolide
DOSAGE FORM
Inhalation aerosol (250 mcg per spray)
STORAGE
Store at room temperature, away from excessive heat; the contents are pressurized and can explode if heated. Do not puncture the container. Do not refrigerate or freeze.

USES

Inhalation corticosteroids are cortisonelike medicines. They are used to help prevent the symptoms of asthma. When used regularly every day, inhalation corticosteroids decrease the number and severity of asthma attacks. However, they will not relieve an asthma attack that has already started. This medicine works by preventing certain cells in the lungs and breathing passages from releasing substances that cause asthma symptoms.

TREATMENT

This medication should be packaged with an instruction sheet. Read the directions carefully before using this medication. You may wish to consult your doctor or pharmacist about the proper administration of this drug. The container should be shaken well just before each use. The contents tend to settle on the bottom, so it is necessary to shake the bottle in order to distribute the ingredients evenly and equalize the doses. If more than one inhalation is necessary, wait at least a full minute between doses, in order to receive the full benefit of the first dose.

Take this medication exactly as prescribed by your doctor. Do not use more of it and do not use it more often than recommended by your doctor. Doing so may increase the chance of side effects. While using this medication, try to develop a set schedule for taking it. If you miss a dose and remember within a few hours, take the missed dose and use any remaining doses for that day at regularly spaced times. Do not double the dose. This medication does not cure asthma, but it will help to control the condition as long as you take it. It may be several weeks before you notice the full effect of this medication.

SIDE EFFECTS

Minor. Cough, dry mouth, hoarseness or other voice changes, sore throat, or unpleasant taste. These side effects should diminish or disappear as your body adjusts to the medication.

Chew sugarless gum or suck on ice chips or a piece of hard candy to relieve mouth or throat dryness.

To prevent dryness, irritation, or infection of the mouth and throat, rinse your mouth or gargle with water after each dose of this medication. DO NOT SWALLOW the water after rinsing your mouth.

Major. Tell your doctor about any side effects that are persistent or particularly bothersome. IT IS ESPECIALLY IMPORTANT TO TELL YOUR DOCTOR about behavior changes; creamy, curdlike patches in the mouth or throat and/or pain when eating or swallowing; difficulty breathing; mental depression; nervousness; pain or burning in the chest; restlessness; tightness in the chest; or wheezing.

INTERACTIONS

This medication should not interact with other medications when used according to directions. Before starting to take this medication, BE SURE TO TELL YOUR DOCTOR about any medications you are taking.

WARNINGS

• Tell your doctor about unusual or allergic reactions you have had to any cortisone-like medications, especially to this medication.
• Be sure to tell your doctor if you have ever had bone disease of any sort (including osteoporosis), diabetes mellitus, emotional instability, glaucoma, fungal infections, heart disease, high blood pressure, high cholesterol levels, myasthenia gravis, ulcerative colitis, peptic ulcers, kidney disease, liver disease, or tuberculosis.
• Before having surgery or other medical or dental treatment, tell your doctor or dentist that you are taking this medication. Depending on how long you have been taking this medication, you may need to receive higher doses if you are exposed to stress, such as serious infections, injury, or surgery. Discuss this with your doctor or dentist.
• Avoid getting this medication in your eyes.
• Do not puncture, break, or burn the aerosol container. The contents are under pressure and may explode. In addition, avoid exposing this medication to cold or freezing temperatures. This medication may be less effective if it is cold when you use it.
• Do not stop taking this medication without first checking with your doctor. Your doctor may want to gradually reduce the amount of medicine you are taking before completely stopping it. Make sure that you have enough medicine on hand to last through vacations, holidays, and weekends.
• Do not take any over-the-counter (nonprescription) medications for weight control or for asthma, sinus, cough, cold, or allergy problems unless you first check with your pharmacist or doctor.
• Your doctor may want you to carry a medical identification card stating that you are using this medicine and that you may need additional medicine during times of emergency, stress, severe asthma attack, or other illness.
• If you are using a bronchodilator, such as albuterol, by inhalation, you must use the bronchodilator several minutes BEFORE this medication (corticosteroid inhaler). Discuss this with your doctor or pharmacist.
• Notify your doctor immediately if you are exposed to any person with chicken pox or the measles.
• This medication is for preventative therapy only. DO NOT use it to treat an acute asthma attack. This medication should be used at regularly scheduled intervals through-

out the day as prescribed by your doctor, even if you are not having any symptoms of asthma.

• Be sure to tell your doctor if you are pregnant. This medication has been shown to cause birth defects in the offspring of animals that received large doses of it during pregnancy. Adequate studies have not been done in humans. Also tell your doctor if you are breast-feeding an infant. Small amounts of this medication pass into breast milk and may cause growth suppression or a decrease in natural corticosteroid production in the nursing infant.

flunisolide (nasal)

BRAND NAMES (Manufacturers)
Nasalide (Dura)
Nasarel (Dura)
TYPE OF DRUG
Nasal adrenocorticosteroid hormone
INGREDIENT
flunisolide
DOSAGE FORM
Nasal solution (25 mcg flunisolide per spray)
STORAGE
Store at room temperature in a tightly closed container. Opened containers of this medication should be discarded after three months.

USES

Flunisolide nasal solution is used to relieve symptoms of rhinitis (inflammation of the nasal passages). How this drug acts to relieve these symptoms is not completely understood. Your adrenal glands naturally produce certain cortisonelike chemicals. These chemicals are involved in various regulatory processes in the body (such as those involving fluid balance, temperature, and reaction to inflammation). Flunisolide belongs to a group of medications known as adrenocorticosteroids (or cortisonelike medications).

TREATMENT

Just before applying flunisolide nasal solution, clear your nasal passages of all secretions. Then carefully follow the patient instructions, which you should receive when your prescription is dispensed. The instructions will explain how to properly apply this medication. Do not increase the dose of flunisolide or increase the number of applications per day without first checking with your doctor.

If your doctor recommends that you use a nasal decongestant to clear your nasal passages, use the decongestant just before you apply flunisolide.

Relief from the symptoms of inflammation may not become apparent for up to three weeks after starting flunisolide. This drug does not cure the cause of inflammation, but it may help relieve the symptoms as long as you continue to use it. Therefore, its effectiveness depends on regular use while the condition is present. Your doctor may then recommend that you gradually decrease the number of daily doses as your condition improves.

If there is no improvement in your condition within three weeks after starting flunisolide, check with your doctor. He or she may want you to stop the medication.

Try not to miss any doses of this medication. If you do miss a dose, apply the dose as soon as possible. However, if it is almost time for the next dose, do not apply the missed dose; just return to your regular dosing schedule. Never double the next dose of the medication.

SIDE EFFECTS

Minor. Drying of nasal passages, headache, loss of smell or taste, nasal congestion, nasal irritation, nausea, nosebleeds, sneezing, sore throat, vomiting, or watery eyes. These side effects should disappear as your body adjusts to this medication. A mild, temporary burning or stinging sensation may occur after this medication is applied.
Major. Tell your doctor about any side effects that are persistent or particularly bothersome. IT IS ESPECIALLY IMPORTANT TO TELL YOUR DOCTOR about burning or stinging that persists after application.

INTERACTIONS

This medication should not interact with any other medications as long as it is used according to directions.

WARNINGS

• Tell your doctor about unusual or allergic reactions you have had to any medications, especially to flunisolide or other adrenocorticosteroids (such as amcinonide, beclomethasone, betamethasone, clocortolone, cortisone, desonide, desoximetasone, dexamethasone, diflorasone, flumethasone, fluocinolone, fluocinonide, fluorometholone, flurandrenolide, halcinonide, hydrocortisone, methylprednisolone, paramethasone, prednisolone, prednisone, and triamcinolone).
• Before starting flunisolide, tell your doctor if you now have or ever had chicken pox, diabetes mellitus, or tuberculosis.
• Flunisolide can slow the healing of wounds. Therefore, tell your doctor about recent nasal surgery or injury, recurrent nosebleeds, or nasal ulcers.
• Tell your doctor if you are pregnant. Birth defects have been observed in the offspring of animals that were given large doses of this drug during pregnancy. Tell your doctor if you are breast-feeding. Small amounts of adrenocorticosteroids do pass into breast milk and may cause growth suppression or a decrease in natural adrenocorticosteroid production in the nursing infant.

---

fluocinolone (topical)

BRAND NAMES (Manufacturers)
fluocinolone acetonide (various manufacturers)
Fluonid (Herbert)
Flurosyn (Rugby)
Synalar (Roche)
Synalar-HP (Roche)
TYPE OF DRUG
Adrenocorticosteroid hormone
INGREDIENT
fluocinolone
DOSAGE FORMS
Cream (0.01%, 0.025%, and 0.2%)
Ointment (0.025%)
Solution (0.01%)
STORAGE
Store at room temperature in a tightly closed container. This medication should never be frozen.

USES

Your adrenal glands naturally produce certain cortisonelike chemicals. These chemicals are involved in various regulatory processes in the body (such as those involving fluid balance, temperature, and reaction to inflammation). Fluocinolone belongs to a group of drugs known as adrenocorticosteroids (or cortisonelike medications). It is used to relieve the skin inflammation (redness, swelling, itching, and discomfort) associated with conditions such as dermatitis, eczema, and poison ivy. Exactly how this medication works is not completely understood.

TREATMENT

Before applying this medication, wash your hands. Then, unless your doctor gives you different instructions, gently wash the area of the skin where the medication is to be applied. With a clean towel, pat the area until it is almost dry; it should be slightly damp when you apply the medicine.

Apply a small amount of fluocinolone to the affected area in a thin layer. Do not bandage the area unless your doctor specifically directs you to do so. If you have been directed to apply an occlusive dressing (such as kitchen plastic wrap) to cover the area, be sure to ask for instructions. Wash your hands again after application.

If you miss a dose of this medication, apply the missed dose as soon as possible. However, if it is almost time for the next application, do not apply the missed dose at all; just return to your regular schedule. Do not put twice as much of the medication on your skin at the next application.

SIDE EFFECTS

Minor. Acne, burning, itching, rash, or skin dryness.

If the affected area is extremely dry or scaling, the skin may be moistened before applying the medication by soaking in water or by applying water with a clean cloth. The ointment form is probably better for dry skin.

A mild, temporary stinging sensation may occur after this medication is applied. If this persists, contact your doctor.

Major. Tell your doctor about any side effects that are persistent or particularly bothersome. IT IS ESPECIALLY IMPORTANT TO TELL YOUR DOCTOR about blistering, increased hair growth, irritation of the affected area, loss of skin color, secondary infection in the area being treated, or thinning of the skin with easy bruising.

INTERACTIONS

This medication should not interact with other medications as long as it is used according to directions.

WARNINGS

• Tell your doctor about unusual or allergic reactions you have had to any medications, especially to fluocinolone or to any other adrenocorticosteroid (such as amcinonide, beclomethasone, betamethasone, clocortolone, cortisone, desonide, desoximetasone, dexamethasone, diflorasone, flumethasone, fluocinonide, fluorometholone, flurandrenolide, halcinonide, hydrocortisone, methylprednisolone, paramethasone, prednisolone, prednisone, and triamcinolone).

• Tell your doctor if you now have or ever had blood-vessel disease, cataracts, chicken pox, diabetes mellitus, fungal infection, glaucoma, shingles, thinning of the skin (skin atrophy), tuberculosis, or any other type of infection, especially at the site currently being treated.

• If irritation develops while using this drug, immediately discontinue its use and notify your doctor.

• This product is not for use in the eyes, nose, or mouth; inproper use of the medication may result in side effects.

• Do not use this product with an occlusive wrap unless your doctor directs you to do so. Systemic absorption of this drug is increased if large areas of the body are treated, particularly if occlusive bandages are used. If it is necessary for you to use this drug under a wrap, follow your doctor's instructions exactly; do not leave the wrap in place longer than specified.

• If you are using fluocinolone on a child's diaper area, do not put tight-fitting diapers or plastic pants on the child. This could lead to increased systemic absorption of the drug and a possible increase in side effects.
• Be sure to tell your doctor if you are pregnant. If large amounts of this drug are applied for prolonged periods, some of it will be absorbed and may cross the placenta. Although studies in humans have not been conducted, birth defects have been observed in the offspring of animals that were given large oral doses of this type of drug during pregnancy. Also tell your doctor if you are breast-feeding an infant. If absorbed through the skin, small amounts of this medication pass into breast milk and may cause growth suppression or a decrease in natural adrenocorticosteroid hormone production in the nursing infant.

---

fluocinonide (topical)

BRAND NAMES (Manufacturers)
fluocinonide (various manufacturers)
Fluonex (Astra Zeneca)
Lidex (Roche)
Lidex-E (Roche)
TYPE OF DRUG
Adrenocorticosteroid hormone
INGREDIENT
fluocinonide
DOSAGE FORMS
Ointment (0.05%)
Cream (0.05%)
Gel (0.05%)
Solution (0.05% with 35% alcohol)
STORAGE
Store all forms at room temperature in tightly closed containers. This medication should not be refrigerated, and it should never be frozen.

USES

Your adrenal glands naturally produce certain cortisonelike chemicals. These chemicals are involved in various regulatory processes in the body (such as those involving fluid balance, temperature, and reaction to inflammation). Fluocinonide belongs to a group of drugs known as adrenocorticosteroids (or cortisonelike medications). It is used to relieve the skin inflammation (redness, swelling, itching, and discomfort) associated with conditions such as dermatitis, eczema, and poison ivy. Exactly how this medication works is not completely understood.

TREATMENT

Before applying this medication, wash your hands. Then, unless your doctor gives you different instructions, gently wash the area of the skin where the medication is to be applied. With a clean towel, pat the area almost dry; it should be slightly damp when you apply the medicine.

Apply a small amount of fluocinonide to the affected area in a thin layer. Do not bandage the area unless your doctor tells you to do so. If you are to apply an occlusive dressing (like kitchen plastic wrap), be sure you understand the instructions. Wash your hands again after application.

If you miss a dose of this medication, apply the missed dose as soon as possible after you remember it. However, if it is almost time for the next application, do not apply the missed dose at all; just return to your regular schedule. Do not double the next dose of medication.

SIDE EFFECTS

Minor. Acne, burning sensation, dry skin, itching, or rash.

If the affected area is extremely dry or scaling, the skin may be moistened before applying the medication by soaking in water or by applying water with a clean cloth. The ointment form is probably better for dry skin.

A mild, temporary stinging sensation may occur after this medication is applied. If this sensation persists, contact your doctor.

Major. Tell your doctor about any side effects that are persistent or particularly bothersome. IT IS ESPECIALLY IMPORTANT TO TELL YOUR DOCTOR about blistering, increased hair growth, irritation of the affected area, loss of skin color, secondary infection in the area being treated, or thinning of the skin with easy bruising.

INTERACTIONS

This medication should not interact with any other medications as long as it is used according to directions.

WARNINGS

- Tell your doctor about unusual or allergic reactions you have had to any medications, especially to fluocinonide or any other adrenocorticosteroid (such as amcinonide, betamethasone, clocortolone, cortisone, desonide, desoximetasone, dexamethasone, diflorasone, flumethasone, fluocinolone, fluorometholone, flurandrenolide, halcinonide, hydrocortisone, methylprednisolone, paramethasone, prednisolone, prednisone, and triamcinolone).
- Tell your doctor if you have or ever had blood-vessel disease, cataracts, chicken pox, diabetes, fungal infection, glaucoma, shingles, thinning skin (skin atrophy), tuberculosis, or any other type of infection, especially at the site being treated.
- If any type of irritation develops while using this medication, immediately discontinue use and notify your doctor.
- Fluocinonide is a topical medication. It is meant for use on the skin only. This product is not for use in the eyes, nose, or mouth; contact may result in side effects.
- Do not use this product with an occlusive wrap or covering, unless your doctor directs you to do so. Systemic absorption of this drug is increased if large areas of the body are treated, particularly if occlusive bandages are used. If it is necessary for you to use this medication under a wrap, follow your doctor's instructions exactly; do not leave the wrap in place longer than specified.
- If you are using fluocinonide on a child's diaper area, do not put tight-fitting diapers or plastic pants on the child. This may lead to increased systemic absorption of the drug and a possible increase in side effects.
- Be sure to tell your doctor if you are pregnant. If large amounts of this drug are applied for prolonged periods, some of it will be absorbed and may cross the placenta. Although studies in humans have not been conducted, birth defects have been observed in the offspring of animals that were given large oral doses of this type of drug during pregnancy. Also tell your doctor if you are breast-feeding an infant. If absorbed through the skin, small amounts of fluocinonide pass into breast milk and may cause growth suppression or a decrease in natural adrenocorticosteroid hormone production in the nursing infant.

---

fluoxetine

BRAND NAMES (Manufacturers)

fluoxetine (various manufacturers)
Prozac (Eli Lilly)
Prozac Weekly (Eli Lilly)
Sarafem (Eli Lilly)

TYPE OF DRUG
Cyclic antidepressant
INGREDIENT
fluoxetine
DOSAGE FORMS
Capsules (10 mg, 20 mg, 40 mg, 90 mg)
Tablets (10 mg)
Liquid (20 mg per 5 mL spoonful)
STORAGE
Store at room temperature in a tightly closed, light-resistant container. Do not store in the bathroom. Heat or moisture can cause this medicine to break down. Do not freeze the liquid form of the medication.

USES

Fluoxetine is used to treat the symptoms of mental depression. It increases the concentration of certain chemicals necessary for nerve transmission in the brain. Fluoxetine is also used in the management of obsessive-compulsive disorder and in the treatment of premenstrual symptoms.

TREATMENT

Take this medication exactly as prescribed by your doctor. To avoid stomach irritation, you can take fluoxetine with food or with a full glass of water (unless your doctor directs you to do otherwise).

The effects of therapy with this medication may not become apparent for one to three weeks.

If you miss a dose, it is not necessary to make up the missed dose. Skip that dose and continue with your regular dosing schedule. You should never take a double dose of the medication to make up for one you missed. If you are taking this medication once a week, take the missed dose as soon as you remember, and continue with the regular dosing schedule by taking the next dose in one week.

SIDE EFFECTS

Minor. Agitation, change in vision, changes in sense of taste, constipation, decreased appetite, decreased mental concentration, decreased sex drive, diarrhea, dizziness, drowsiness, dry mouth, flushing, frequent urination, headache, increased sweating, insomnia, nausea, nervousness, rapid heartbeat, stomach cramps, stuffy nose, vomiting, or weight gain or loss. These side effects should diminish or disappear as your body adjusts to the medication.

Dry mouth can be relieved by chewing sugarless gum or sucking on ice chips or a piece of hard candy.

To relieve constipation, increase the amount of fiber in your diet (fresh fruits and vegetables, salads, bran, and whole-grain breads), exercise, and drink more water (unless your doctor directs you to do otherwise).

To avoid dizziness or light-headedness when you stand, contract and relax the muscles of your legs for a few moments before rising.

Major. Tell your doctor about any side effects that are persistent or particularly bothersome. IT IS ESPECIALLY IMPORTANT TO TELL YOUR DOCTOR about anxiety, chills or fever, convulsions (seizures), difficulty in breathing, enlarged lymph glands (swelling under the jaw, in the armpits, or in the groin area), joint or muscle pain, skin rash or hives, or swelling of the feet or lower legs.

INTERACTIONS

Fluoxetine interacts with a number of other types of drugs:

1. Extreme drowsiness can occur when this medicine is taken with central nervous system depressants (such as alcohol, antihistamines, barbiturates, benzodiazepine

tranquilizers, muscle relaxants, narcotics, pain medications, phenothiazine tranquilizers, and medications to induce sleep) or with other antidepressants.
2. Fluoxetine may increase the effects of anticoagulants (blood thinners, such as warfarin), certain heart medications (such as digitoxin), tricyclic antidepressants, and lithium.
3. Serious side effects may occur if a monoamine oxidase (MAO) inhibitor (such as furazolidone, isocarboxazid, pargyline, phenelzine, procarbazine, or tranylcypromine) is taken with fluoxetine. At least 14 days should separate the use of fluoxetine and the use of an MAO inhibitor.
4. Fluoxetine can increase agitation, restlessness, and stomach irritation when taken along with tryptophan.
5. Concurrent use of fluoxetine and phenytoin may increase the amount of phenytoin in the body, increasing phenytoin's side effects.
6. Fluoxetine may increase the toxic effects of some antimigraine medicines, such as sumatriptan, naratriptan, frovatriptan, rizatriptan, zolmitriptan, or almotriptan.
7. The use of fluoxetine with tramadol may increase the risk of seizures.
8. Fluoxetine should not be used with other antidepressants, such as nefazodone, venlafaxine, or clomipramine, because of the increased risk of side effects.

Before starting to take fluoxetine, BE SURE TO TELL YOUR DOCTOR about any medications you are currently taking, especially any of those listed above.

WARNINGS

• Tell your doctor immediately if you develop a rash or hives while taking this medication or if you have ever had an allergic reaction to fluoxetine or any other antidepressant.
• Tell your doctor if you have allergies to any substance such as foods, sulfites, or other preservatives or dyes.
• Before starting to take this medication, be sure to tell your doctor if you have a history of alcoholism or if you have ever had a heart attack, asthma, circulatory disease, difficulty in urinating, electroshock therapy, enlarged prostate gland, epilepsy, glaucoma, high blood pressure, intestinal problems, liver or kidney disease, mental illness, stomach problems, or thyroid disease.
• If this drug makes you dizzy or drowsy, do not take part in any activity that requires alertness, such as driving a car or operating potentially dangerous equipment.
• Do not stop taking this drug suddenly. Abruptly stopping it can cause nausea, headache, stomach upset, or a worsening of your condition. Your doctor may want to reduce the dosage gradually.
• The elderly may be at increased risk for side effects. Use this drug cautiously, and report any mental status changes to your doctor immediately.
• The effects of this medication may persist for as long as five weeks after you stop taking it, so continue to observe all precautions during that period.
• Be sure to tell your doctor if you are pregnant. Although birth defects have not been documented in animal studies, it is not known if fluoxetine is safe during human pregnancy. It is also not known if fluoxetine passes into breast milk, so be sure to tell your doctor if you are breast-feeding an infant.

---

fluphenazine

BRAND NAMES (Manufacturers)
fluphenazine (various manufacturers)
Permitil (Schering-Plough)
Prolixin (Apothecon)
TYPE OF DRUG
Phenothiazine tranquilizer

INGREDIENT
fluphenazine
DOSAGE FORMS
Tablets (1 mg, 2.5 mg, 5 mg, and 10 mg)
Oral concentrate (5 mg per mL, with 1% or 14% alcohol)
Oral elixir (2.5 mg per 5-mL spoonful, with 14% alcohol)
STORAGE
Store the tablets, concentrate, and elixir at room temperature in a tightly closed, light-resistant container. If the concentrate or elixir turns slightly yellow, the medicine is still effective and can be used. However, do not use it if it changes color markedly or has particles floating in it; discard it down the sink. This drug should never be frozen.

USES

Fluphenazine is prescribed to treat the symptoms of certain types of mental illness, such as emotional symptoms of psychosis, the manic phase of manic-depressive illness, and severe behavioral problems in children and adults. This medication is thought to relieve the symptoms of mental illness by blocking certain chemicals involved with nerve transmission in the brain.

TREATMENT

To avoid stomach irritation, you can take the tablet or elixir form of this medication with a meal or with a glass of water or milk (unless your doctor directs you to do otherwise).

Measure the elixir carefully with a specially designed 5-mL measuring spoon. An ordinary kitchen teaspoon is not accurate enough for medical purposes.

Immediately prior to administration, measure the oral concentrate carefully with the dropper provided, then add it to four ounces (½ cup) or more of water, milk, applesauce, pudding, or a cola-free, caffeine-free carbonated beverage. To prevent possible loss of effectiveness, the medication should not be diluted in tea, coffee, or apple juice.

Antacids and antidiarrheal medicines may decrease the absorption of this medication from the gastrointestinal tract. Therefore, at least one hour should separate doses of one of these medicines and fluphenazine.

The full effects of this medication for the control of emotional or mental symptoms may not become apparent until two weeks after the date that you begin taking the medication.

If you miss a dose of this medication, take the missed dose as soon as possible and return to your regular dosing schedule. However, if it is almost time for the next dose, skip the one you missed and return to your regular schedule. Do not double the dose (unless your doctor directs you to do so).

SIDE EFFECTS

Minor. Blurred vision, constipation, decreased sweating, diarrhea, dizziness, drooling, drowsiness, dry mouth, fatigue, jitteriness, menstrual irregularities, nasal congestion, restlessness, vomiting, or weight gain. As your body adjusts to this medication, these side effects should disappear.

Fluphenazine can also cause discoloration of the urine to red, pink, or red-brown. This is a harmless effect.

This drug can cause increased sensitivity to sunlight. Avoid prolonged exposure to sunlight and sunlamps. Wear protective clothing and use an effective sunscreen when outdoors during daylight hours.

If you are constipated, increase the amount of fiber in your diet (fresh fruits and vegetables, salads, bran, and whole-grain breads) and drink more water (unless your doctor directs you to do otherwise).

Chew sugarless gum or suck on ice chips or a piece of hard candy to help reduce the mouth dryness that may be caused by this medication.

To avoid dizziness or light-headedness when you stand, contract and relax the muscles of your legs for a few moments before rising. Do this by pushing one foot against the floor while raising the other foot slightly, alternating feet so that you are "pumping" your legs in a pedaling motion.

Major. Tell your doctor about any side effects that are persistent or particularly bothersome. IT IS ESPECIALLY IMPORTANT TO TELL YOUR DOCTOR about breast enlargement (in both sexes); chest pain; convulsions; darkened skin; difficulty in swallowing or breathing; fainting; fever; impotence; involuntary movements of the face, mouth, jaw, tongue, or limbs; palpitations; rash; sleep disorders; sore throat; tremors; uncoordinated movements; unusual bleeding or bruising; visual disturbances; or yellowing of the eyes or skin. Also tell your doctor if your original symptoms worsen or change after you begin taking fluphenazine.

INTERACTIONS

Fluphenazine interacts with several other types of drugs:

1. Fluphenazine can cause extreme drowsiness when combined with alcohol or other central nervous system depressants (such as antihistamines, barbiturates, benzodiazepine tranquilizers, muscle relaxants, narcotics, and pain medications) or with tricyclic antidepressants.

2. Fluphenazine can decrease the effectiveness of amphetamines, guanethidine, anticonvulsants, and levodopa.

3. The side effects of epinephrine, monoamine oxidase (MAO) inhibitors, propranolol, phenytoin, and tricyclic antidepressants may be increased by this medication. At least 14 days should separate the use of this drug and the use of an MAO inhibitor.

4. Lithium, when used concurrently, may increase the side effects and decrease the effectiveness of this medication.

5. Do not use pimozide, disopyramine, erythromycin, procainamide, quinidine, or probucol with fluphenazine. The risk of serious side effects may be increased.

Before starting to take fluphenazine, BE SURE TO TELL YOUR DOCTOR about any medications you are currently taking, especially any of those listed above.

WARNINGS

• Tell your doctor about unusual or allergic reactions you have had to medications, especially to fluphenazine or any other phenothiazine tranquilizers (such as chlorpromazine, mesoridazine, perphenazine, prochlorperazine, promazine, thioridazine, and triflupromazine) or to loxapine.

• Tell your doctor if you have a history of alcoholism, blood disease, bone marrow disease, brain disease, breast cancer, blockage of the urinary or digestive tract, drug-induced depression, epilepsy, high or low blood pressure, diabetes mellitus, glaucoma, heart or circulatory disease, liver disease, lung disease, Parkinson's disease, peptic ulcers, or an enlarged prostate gland.

• Tell your doctor about any recent exposure to a pesticide or an insecticide. Fluphenazine may increase the side effects from the exposure.

• To prevent oversedation, avoid drinking alcoholic beverages while you are taking this medication.

• If this drug makes you dizzy or drowsy, do not take part in any activity that requires alertness, such as driving a car. Be careful on stairs, and avoid getting up suddenly from a lying or sitting position.

• Prior to having surgery or any other medical or dental treatment, be sure to tell your doctor or dentist that you are taking this medication.

• Some of the side effects of this medication can be prevented by taking an antiparkinsonism drug. Discuss this with your physician.

• This medication can decrease sweating and heat release from the body. You should, therefore, avoid getting overheated by strenuous exercise in hot weather and should avoid hot baths, showers, and saunas.
• Do not stop taking this medication suddenly. If the drug is stopped abruptly, you may experience nausea, vomiting, stomach upset, headache, increased heart rate, insomnia, tremors, or a worsening of your condition. Your doctor may want to reduce the dosage gradually.
• If you are planning to have a myelogram, or any other procedure in which dye will be injected into your spinal cord, tell your doctor that you are taking this medication.
• Avoid spilling the oral concentrate or elixir form of this medication on your skin or clothing; it may cause redness and irritation of the skin.
• While taking this medication, do not take any over-the-counter (nonprescription) medications for weight control or for cough, cold, allergy, asthma, or sinus problems without first checking with your doctor. The combination of these medications may cause high blood pressure.
• Some of these products contain the color additive FD&C Yellow No. 5 (tartrazine), which can cause allergic-type reactions (shortness of breath, rash, fainting) in certain susceptible individuals.
• A potentially permanent movement disorder called tardive dyskinesia may develop with the use of this medication. It is important to discuss this with your doctor and to report any unusual or uncontrolled movements.
• The elderly may be at greater risk for adverse effects when using this drug.
• Be sure to tell your doctor if you are pregnant. Small amounts of this medication cross the placenta. Although there are reports of safe use of this drug during pregnancy, there are also reports of liver disease and tremors in newborn infants whose mothers received this type of medication close to term. Also tell your doctor if you are breast-feeding an infant. Small amounts of this medication pass into breast milk and may cause unwanted effects in the nursing infant.

---

flurbiprofen

BRAND NAMES (Manufacturers)
Ansaid (Pharmacia)
flurbiprofen (various manufacturers)
TYPE OF DRUG
Nonsteroidal anti-inflammatory agent
INGREDIENT
flurbiprofen
DOSAGE FORM
Tablets (50 mg and 100 mg)
STORAGE
Store at room temperature in a light-resistant container.

USES

Flurbiprofen is used to treat the inflammation (pain, swelling, and stiffness) of arthritis, especially osteoarthritis. Flurbiprofen has been shown to block the production of certain body chemicals, called prostaglandins, that may trigger pain.

TREATMENT

If you are taking this medication for acute pain, take the first one or two doses on an empty stomach (30 to 60 minutes before meals or 2 hours after meals), so that it gets into your bloodstream quickly. However, to decrease stomach irritation, take this medication with food or antacids.

To relieve arthritis symptoms, you must take flurbiprofen regulary as directed by your doctor. It may take up to two weeks before you feel the full effects of this medication. Flurbiprofen does not cure arthritis, but it will help to control the condition as long as you continue to take it.

It is important to take flurbiprofen on schedule and not to miss any doses. If you do miss a dose, take it as soon as possible. However, if it is almost time for your next dose, do not take the missed dose at all; just return to your regular dosing schedule. Do not double the next dose.

SIDE EFFECTS

Minor. Bloating, constipation, diarrhea, difficulty in sleeping, dizziness, drowsiness, headache, heartburn, indigestion, light-headedness, loss of appetite, nausea, nervousness, soreness of the mouth, unusual sweating, or vomiting. As your body adjusts to the medication, these side effects should diminish or disappear.

To relieve constipation, increase the amount of fiber in your diet (fresh fruits and vegetables, salads, bran, and whole-grain breads). You can also exercise more and drink more water (unless your doctor directs you to do otherwise).

If you become dizzy or light-headed, sit or lie down for a while; get up slowly from a sitting or reclining position; and be careful on stairs.

Major. Tell your doctor about any side effects that are persistent or particularly bothersome. IT IS ESPECIALLY IMPORTANT TO TELL YOUR DOCTOR about bloody or black, tarry stools; blurred vision; confusion; depression; difficult or painful urination; palpitations; a problem with hearing, or ringing or buzzing in your ears; skin rash, hives, or itching; stomach pain; swelling of the feet or hands; tightness in the chest; unexplained sore throat and fever; unusual bleeding or bruising; unusual fatigue or weakness; unusual weight gain; wheezing or difficulty in breathing; or yellowing of the skin or the whites of the eyes.

INTERACTIONS

Flurbiprofen interacts with several other medications:

1. Anticoagulants (blood thinners, such as warfarin) and valproic acid taken in conjunction with flurbiprofen can lead to an increase in bleeding complications.

2. Aspirin, other salicylates, and other anti-inflammatory medications can increase stomach irritation. Aspirin may also decrease the effectiveness of flurbiprofen.

3. Flurbiprofen can interact with diuretics (water pills).

4. Probenecid can increase blood levels of flurbiprofen, which may increase the risk of side effects.

5. The action of beta blockers may be decreased by the use of flurbiprofen.

6. Do not take methotrexate with this drug. Flurbiprofen may increase the amount of methotrexate in the body, increasing the risk of toxicity from methotrexate.

7. Flurbiprofen may increase the amount of lithium and cyclosporine in the body and increase the side effects from these medications.

Before starting to take flurbiprofen, BE SURE TO TELL YOUR DOCTOR about any medications you are currently taking, especially any of those listed above.

WARNINGS

• Before taking this medication, tell your doctor if you have ever had unusual or allergic reactions to flurbiprofen or to any of the other chemically related drugs (aspirin, other salicylates, diclofenac, diflunisal, etodolac, fenoprofen, ibuprofen, indomethacin, ketoprofen, ketorolac, meclofenamate, mefenamic acid, nabumetone, naproxen, oxaprozin, oxyphenbutazone, phenylbutazone, piroxicam, sulindac, tenoxicam, tiaprofenic acid, or tolmetin).

• Tell your doctor if you now have or ever had asthma, bleeding problems, colitis, epilepsy, heart disease, high blood pressure, kidney disease, liver disease, mental illness, Parkinson's disease, or stomach ulcers or other stomach problems.

• If flurbiprofen makes you dizzy or drowsy, do not take part in any activity that requires alertness, such as driving a car or operating potentially dangerous machinery.
• Because this drug can prolong your bleeding time, it is important to tell your doctor or dentist that you are taking flurbiprofen before having surgery or any other medical or dental treatment.
• Stomach problems are more likely to occur if you take aspirin regularly or if you drink alcoholic beverages while being treated with this medication. These should, therefore, be avoided during treatment with flurbiprofen (unless your doctor directs you to do otherwise).
• The elderly may experience more side effects from this medication.
• Be sure to tell your doctor if you are pregnant or if you are planning to become pregnant. This medication can cause unwanted effects on the fetal heart or on the blood flow to the fetus. Studies in animals have also shown that this medication, if taken late in pregnancy, may increase the length of pregnancy, prolong labor, or cause other problems during delivery. Also tell your doctor if you are breast-feeding an infant. Small amounts of flurbiprofen can pass into breast milk.

---

fluticasone

BRAND NAMES (Manufacturers)
Flovent (GlaxoSmithKline)
Flovent Rotadisk (GlaxoSmithKline)
TYPE OF DRUG
Corticosteroid inhalant (antiasthmatic)
INGREDIENT
fluticasone
DOSAGE FORMS
Inhalation aerosol (44 mcg, 110 mcg, or 220 mcg per actuation)
Inhalation powder (50 mcg, 100 mcg, or 250 mcg)
STORAGE
Store at room temperature. Keep aerosol away from excessive heat, as the contents are pressurized and can explode if heated; do not puncture the container. Do not refrigerate or freeze. Store aerosol container with nozzle end down.

USES

Inhalation corticosteroids are cortisonelike medicines. They are used to help prevent the symptoms of asthma. When used regularly every day, inhalation corticosteroids decrease the number and severity of asthma attacks. However, they will not relieve an asthma attack that has already started. This medicine works by preventing certain cells in the lungs and breathing passages from releasing substances that cause asthma symptoms.

TREATMENT

This medication should be packaged with an instruction sheet. Read the directions carefully before using this medication. You may wish to consult your doctor or pharmacist about the proper administration of this drug. Shake the container well just before each use to distribute the ingredients evenly and equalize the doses, as the contents tend to settle on the bottom. If more than one inhalation is necessary, wait at least one full minute between doses to receive the full benefit of the first dose.

Take this medication exactly as prescribed by your doctor. Do not use more of it and do not use it more often than recommended by your doctor; to do so may increase the chance of side effects. While using this medication, try to develop a set schedule for taking it. If you miss a dose and remember within a few hours, take the missed dose and space any remaining doses for that day at regular intervals. Do not double the dose. This medication does not cure asthma, but it will help to control the condition as long as you continue to take it. It may be several weeks before you notice the full effect of this medication.

SIDE EFFECTS

Minor. Cough, dry mouth, hoarseness or other voice changes, sore throat, or unpleasant taste in the mouth. These side effects should disappear as your body adjusts to the medication.

Chew sugarless gum or suck on ice chips or a piece of hard candy to relieve mouth or throat dryness.

To prevent dryness, irritation, or infection of the mouth or throat, rinse your mouth or gargle with water after each dose. DO NOT SWALLOW the water after rinsing.

Major. Tell your doctor about any side effects that are persistent or particularly bothersome. IT IS ESPECIALLY IMPORTANT TO TELL YOUR DOCTOR about behavior changes; creamy white, curdlike patches in the mouth or throat and/or pain when eating or swallowing; difficulty breathing; mental depression; nervousness; pain or burning in the chest; restlessness; tightness in the chest; or wheezing.

INTERACTIONS

This medication should not interact with other medications when it is used according to directions.

Before starting to take this medication, BE SURE TO TELL YOUR DOCTOR about any medications you are taking.

WARNINGS

• Tell your doctor about unusual or allergic reactions you have had to any cortisone-like medications, especially to this medication.

• Be sure to tell your doctor if you have or ever had bone disease of any sort (including osteoporosis), diabetes mellitus, emotional instability, glaucoma, fungal infections, heart disease, high blood pressure, high cholesterol levels, myasthenia gravis, ulcerative colitis, peptic ulcers, kidney disease, liver disease, or tuberculosis.

• Before having surgery or other medical or dental treatment, tell your doctor or dentist you are taking this medication. Depending on how long you have been taking this medication, you may need to receive higher doses if you are exposed to stress, such as serious infections, injury, or surgery. Discuss this with your doctor or dentist.

• Avoid getting the medication in your eyes.

• Do not puncture, break, or burn the aerosol container. The contents are under pressure and may explode. In addition, avoid exposure of this medication to cold or freezing temperatures. This medication may be less effective if it is cold when you use it.

• Do not stop taking this medication without first checking with your doctor. Your doctor may want to gradually reduce the amount of medicine you are taking before completely stopping it. Make sure that you have enough medicine on hand to last through vacations, holidays, and weekends.

• Do not take any over-the-counter (nonprescription) medications for weight control or for asthma, sinus, cough, cold, or allergy problems unless you first check with your pharmacist or doctor.

• Your doctor may want you to carry a medical identification card stating that you are using this medicine and that you may need additional medicine during times of emergency, stress, severe asthma attack, or other illness.

• If you are using a bronchodilator (such as albuterol) by inhalation, you must use the bronchodilator several minutes BEFORE taking fluticasone. Discuss this with your doctor or pharmacist.

• Notify your doctor immediately if you are exposed to any person with chicken pox or the measles.

• This medication is for preventative therapy only; DO NOT use it to treat an acute asthmatic attack. This medication should be used at regularly scheduled intervals throughout the day as prescribed by your doctor, even if you are not having any asthma symptoms.
• Be sure to tell your doctor if you are pregnant. This medication has been shown to cause birth defects in the offspring of animals that received large doses of it during pregnancy. Adequate studies have not been done in humans. Also tell your doctor if you are breast-feeding an infant. Small amounts of this medication pass into breast milk and may cause growth suppression or a decrease in natural corticosteroid production in the nursing infant.

---

fluvastatin

BRAND NAME (Manufacturer)
Lescol (Novartis)
TYPE OF DRUG
Antihyperlipidemic (lipid-lowering drug)
INGREDIENT
fluvastatin
DOSAGE FORM
Capsules (20 mg and 40 mg)
STORAGE
Store at room temperature in a tightly closed container away from heat and direct sunlight.

USES

Fluvastatin is used to treat hyperlipidemia (high blood fat levels). It may be prescribed with nondrug therapies such as diet control and exercise in an attempt to regulate lipid and cholesterol levels. Fluvastatin chemically interferes with an enzyme in the body that is responsible for synthesizing cholesterol. This enzyme blockade decreases the LDL (low-density lipoprotein) type of cholesterol. This type of cholesterol has been associated with coronary artery disease and atherosclerosis.

TREATMENT

Take this medication exactly as prescribed by your doctor. If you are to take the drug once a day, it is best to take the drug in the evening. Fluvastatin can be taken with meals or with a full glass of water if stomach upset occurs.

While taking this medication, try to develop a set schedule for taking it. If you miss a dose and remember within a few hours, take the missed dose and resume your regular schedule. If many hours have passed, skip the dose you missed and then take your next dose as scheduled. Do not double the next dose of this medication.

SIDE EFFECTS

Minor. Abdominal pain or cramps, constipation, diarrhea, gas, nausea, or stomach pain. These effects may be relieved by taking fluvastatin with a meal. They may also diminish or disappear as your body adjusts to the medication.

To relieve constipation, increase the amount of fiber (fresh fruits and vegetables, salads, bran, and whole-grain breads) in your diet, exercise, and drink plenty of water (unless your doctor directs you otherwise).

Major. Tell your doctor about any side effects that are persistent or particularly bothersome. IT IS ESPECIALLY IMPORTANT TO TELL YOUR DOCTOR about blurred vision (or any other visual changes or difficulties) or about muscle pain or tenderness, especially when accompanied by malaise or fever.

INTERACTIONS

Fluvastatin interacts with several other types of drugs:

1. Fluvastatin may increase the blood levels of oral anticoagulants (blood thinners, such as warfarin) and digoxin, increasing the risk of toxicity of these agents.

2. Because of the risk of severe myopathy (muscle weakness), the combined use of fluvastatin with gemfibrozil or clofibrate should generally be avoided.

3. Cyclosporine, erythromycin, clarithromycin, fluconazole, itraconazole, nicotinic acid, or niacin may increase the side effects of fluvastatin and should be used with extreme caution.

4. The amount of fluvastatin absorbed by the body may be decreased if it is used concurrently with cholestyramine or colestipol. Fluvastatin, therefore, should be taken four hours after a dose of one of these medicines.

5. Cimetidine, omeprazole, and ranitidine may increase the amount of fluvastatin in the body and may therefore increase its side effects.

Be sure to tell your doctor about any medications you are currently taking, especially any of those listed above.

WARNINGS

- Tell your doctor about unusual or allergic reactions you have ever had to any medications, especially to fluvastatin.
- Tell your doctor if you have ever had liver disease, heart disease, stroke, or disorders of the digestive tract.
- Patients taking another drug in this same class developed eye-related problems during treatment. It is, therefore, advisable to have regular checkups with your ophthalmologist, who should be informed about your use of this drug.
- Do not take this drug if you are pregnant. Serious side effects have been reported in the offspring of animals that were given this drug during pregnancy. Also be sure to tell your doctor if you are breast-feeding an infant. This medication should not be used while breast-feeding.

---

fluvoxamine

BRAND NAME (Manufacturer)
Luvox (Solvay)
TYPE OF DRUG
Antidepressant
INGREDIENT
fluvoxamine
DOSAGE FORM
Tablets (25 mg, 50 mg, and 100 mg)
STORAGE
Store in a tightly closed container at room temperature, away from heat and direct sunlight. Do not store in the bathroom.

USES

Fluvoxamine is used to treat the symptoms of obsessive-compulsive disorder, a mental condition. It works by increasing the concentration of certain chemicals that are necessary for nerve transmission in the brain.

TREATMENT

This medication should be taken exactly as prescribed by your doctor. To avoid stomach irritation, you can take fluvoxamine with food or a full glass of water (unless your doctor directs you to do otherwise).

The effects of treatment with fluvoxamine may not become apparent for one to four weeks after the start of therapy.

If you are taking this medication once a day and you miss a dose, take the missed dose as soon as possible and return to your regular dosing schedule. Do not double the next dose. If you are taking this medication more than once a day and you miss a dose, do not take the missed dose at all; just return to your regular dosing schedule. Again, do not double the dose of medication.

SIDE EFFECTS

Minor. Changes in taste, constipation, decreased appetite, decreased sex drive, dizziness, drowsiness, dry mouth, frequent urination, headache, heartburn, increased sweating, insomnia, nausea, nervousness, runny nose, twitching, unusual tiredness or weakness, or weight loss. These side effects should diminish or disappear as your body adjusts to the medication.

To relieve constipation, increase the amount of fiber in your diet (fresh fruits and vegetables, salads, bran, and whole-grain breads), exercise, and drink more water (unless your doctor directs you to do otherwise).

To avoid dizziness when you stand, contract and relax the muscles in your legs for a few moments before rising.

Dry mouth can be relieved by chewing sugarless gum or sucking on ice chips or a piece of hard candy.

Major. Tell your doctor about any side effects that are persistent or especially bothersome. IT IS ESPECIALLY IMPORTANT TO TELL YOUR DOCTOR about anxiety, chills or fever, difficulty in breathing, easy bruising, enlarged lymph glands (swelling under the jaw, in the armpits, or in the groin area), eye problems, joint or muscle pain, mood or mental changes, seizures (convulsions), skin rash or hives, swelling in the feet or lower legs, or unusual tiredness or weakness.

INTERACTIONS

Fluvoxamine interacts with several medications:

1. Fluvoxamine may interfere with the elimination of alprazolam, midazolam, or triazolam from your body, increasing the toxicity of these drugs.

2. The combination of fluvoxamine and medications that increase serotonin (a chemical in the body), such as certain antimigraine medications, antidepressants, and medications used for nausea and vomiting, should be avoided.

3. The toxicity of amitriptyline, carbamazepine, cisapride, clomipramine, clozapine, imipramine, lithium, methadone, metoprolol, propranolol, theophylline, tryptophan, or warfarin may be increased if taken with fluvoxamine.

4. The combination of fluvoxamine and MAO inhibitors (including selegiline, procarbazine, furazolidone, isocarboxazid, pargyline, phenelzine, and tranylcypromine) may result in serious toxic effects. You should wait at least 14 days between stopping treatment with fluvoxamine and starting treatment with an MAO inhibitor.

WARNINGS

• Tell your doctor immediately if you develop a skin rash or have hives while taking this medication or if you have ever had a reaction in the past to fluvoxamine or to any other medication.

• Be sure to tell your doctor if you have a history of alcohol or drug abuse or if you currently have or ever had a heart attack, asthma, circulatory disease, difficulty in urinating, electroshock therapy, enlarged prostate gland, seizures or epilepsy, glaucoma, high blood pressure, intestinal problems, liver disease, kidney disease, any type of mental illness, or thyroid disease.

• If this medication makes you drowsy or dizzy, do not take part in any activity that requires mental alertness, such as driving a car or operating dangerous equipment.

• Do not stop taking this medication abruptly. Stopping it suddenly can cause nausea, headache, stomach upset, or worsening of your condition. Your doctor may want to reduce the dose gradually.
• Elderly individuals may be at greater risk of experiencing unwanted or otherwise bothersome side effects. Use this drug cautiously and report any changes in mental status to your doctor immediately.
• The effects of this medication may be present for several weeks after you stop taking it. Therefore, it is especially important that you continue to observe all precautions during this period.
• Be sure to tell your doctor if you are pregnant or plan to become pregnant. It is not known if fluvoxamine is safe to take during pregnancy. Also be sure to tell your doctor if you are breast-feeding an infant. Small amounts of fluvoxamine pass into breast milk.

---

fosinopril

BRAND NAME (Manufacturer)
Monopril (Mead Johnson)
TYPE OF DRUG
Antihypertensive
INGREDIENT
fosinopril
DOSAGE FORM
Tablets (10 mg, 20 mg, and 40 mg)
STORAGE
Store in a tightly closed container at room temperature, away from heat and direct sunlight. Do not refrigerate or freeze.

USES

Fosinopril is used to treat high blood pressure and congestive heart failure. It is a vasodilator (it widens blood vessels) that acts by blocking the production of chemicals that may be responsible for constricting or narrowing blood vessels. It is a medication in a class of drugs called the angiotensin-converting enzyme (ACE) inhibitors.

TREATMENT

Take this medication exactly as prescribed by your doctor. Fosinopril can be taken either on an empty stomach or with a meal. While using this medication, try to develop a set schedule for taking it. If you miss a dose and remember within a few hours, take the missed dose and resume your regular schedule. If many hours have passed, skip the dose you missed and then take your next dose as scheduled. Do not double the dose. Fosinopril does not cure high blood pressure, but it will help to control the condition as long as you continue to take it. It may be several weeks before you notice the full effect of this medication.

SIDE EFFECTS

Minor. Abdominal pain, cough, diarrhea, dizziness, drowsiness, fatigue, headache, insomnia, nausea, nervousness, sweating, or vomiting. These side effects should disappear as your body adjusts to the medication.

To avoid dizziness when you stand, contract and relax the muscles of your legs for a few moments before rising. Do this by alternately pushing one foot against the floor while lifting the other foot slightly.

This medication can cause increased sensitivity to sunlight. Avoid prolonged exposure to sunlight and sunlamps, wear protective clothing and sunglasses, and use an effective sunscreen.

Major. Tell your doctor about any side effects that are persistent or particularly bothersome. IT IS ESPECIALLY IMPORTANT TO TELL YOUR DOCTOR about chest pain; difficulty breathing; excessive perspiration; fainting; fever; impaired taste perception; irregular heartbeat; itching; light-headedness (especially during the first few days); muscle cramps; rash; sore throat; swelling of the face, eyes, lips, or tongue; tingling in the fingers and toes; or yellowing of the eyes or skin.

INTERACTIONS

Fosinopril interacts with several other types of medications:

1. Diuretics and other antihypertensive medications can cause an excessive drop in blood pressure when they are combined with this medication (especially the first dose).

2. The combination of this medication with amiloride, potassium supplements, salt substitutes, spironolactone, or triamterene can lead to hyperkalemia (dangerously high levels of potassium in the bloodstream).

3. Nonsteroidal anti-inflammatory agents (including ibuprofen, indomethacin, and naproxen) may reduce the effectiveness of this medication.

4. Concurrent use of antacids with this medication may result in decreased effectiveness of fosinopril. To avoid this drug interaction, it is recommended that this medication be taken either one hour before or two hours after taking antacids.

5. Phenothiazine tranquilizers or probenecid may increase the blood level and adverse effects of fosinopril.

6. Concurrent use of this medication and allopurinol can increase the risk of developing an allergic reaction to these medications.

7. This medication can delay the body's elimination of lithium and increase lithium's adverse effects.

8. Concurrent administration of this medication with digoxin can lead to increased blood levels and adverse effects from digoxin.

Before starting to take fosinopril, BE SURE TO TELL YOUR DOCTOR about any medications you are taking, especially those listed above.

WARNINGS

• Tell your doctor about any unusual or allergic reactions you have had to any medications, especially to angiotensin-converting enzyme (ACE) inhibitors (including captopril, enalapril, lisinopril, moexipril, quinapril, ramipril, trandolapril, and benazepril) or to this medication.

• Be sure to tell your doctor if you have ever had aortic stenosis, heart attack, stroke, blood disorders, kidney or liver disease, kidney transplant, or systemic lupus erythematosus.

• A persistent dry cough may occur and usually does not subside unless this medication is stopped. If this effect is bothersome, consult your doctor,

• Excessive perspiration, dehydration, or prolonged vomiting or diarrhea can lead to an excessive drop in blood pressure while you are taking this medication. Contact your doctor if you have any of these symptoms.

• Before having surgery or other medical or dental treatment, be sure to tell your doctor or dentist that you are taking this medication.

• If this drug makes you dizzy or drowsy (sometimes this effect is seen after the first few doses), try to avoid any sudden changes in posture.

• Do not take any over-the-counter (nonprescription) medications for weight control or for asthma, sinus, cough, cold, or allergy problems unless you first check with your doctor.

• Do not stop taking this medication unless you first consult your doctor. Stopping this drug abruptly may lead to a rise in blood pressure.

• Be sure to tell your doctor if you are pregnant. This medication and other drugs in the class called ACE inhibitors (including captopril, enalapril, lisinopril, moexipril, quinapril, ramipril, trandolapril, and benazepril) have been shown to cause birth defects (including kidney damage, low blood pressure, improper skull development) and fetal death when taken in the second and third trimesters. Also tell your doctor if you are breast-feeding an infant. This medication may pass into breast milk and should not be taken by a nursing mother.

---

furosemide

BRAND NAMES (Manufacturers)
furosemide (various manufacturers)
Lasix (Hoechst)
TYPE OF DRUG
Diuretic (water pill) and antihypertensive
INGREDIENT
furosemide
DOSAGE FORMS
Tablets (20 mg, 40 mg, and 80 mg)
Oral solution (10 mg per mL and 40 mg per 5 mL, with 11.5% alcohol)
STORAGE
Store at room temperature in a tightly closed, light-resistant container. Do not freeze.

USES

Furosemide is prescribed to treat high blood pressure. It is also used to reduce fluid accumulation in the body caused by conditions such as heart failure, cirrhosis of the liver, kidney disease, and the long-term use of some medications. Furosemide reduces fluid accumulation by increasing the elimination of sodium and water through the kidneys.

TREATMENT

To decrease stomach irritation, take furosemide with a glass of milk or with a meal (unless your doctor directs you to do otherwise). Try to take it at the same time every day. Avoid taking a dose after 6:00 in the evening; this will prevent you from having to get up during the night to urinate.

Measure each dose of the solution with a specially designed 5-mL measuring spoon or dropper. An ordinary kitchen teaspoon is not accurate enough.

This medication does not cure high blood pressure, but it will help to control the condition for as long as you continue to take it.

If you miss a dose of furosemide, take it as soon as possible. However, if it is almost time for the next dose, do not take the missed dose at all; just wait until the next scheduled dose. Do not double the dose.

SIDE EFFECTS

Minor. Blurred vision, constipation, cramping, diarrhea, dizziness, headache, itching, loss of appetite, muscle spasms, nausea, sore mouth, stomach upset, vomiting, or weakness. As your body adjusts to the drug, these side effects should disappear.

To relieve constipation, increase the amount of fiber in your diet (including fresh fruit and vegetables, bran, and whole-grain bread), exercise, and drink more water, unless your doctor directs you to do otherwise.

This medication will cause an increase in the amount of urine or in your frequency of urination when you first begin to take it. It may also cause you to have an unusual feeling of tiredness. These effects should subside after several days.

Furosemide can cause increased sensitivity to sunlight. It is therefore important to avoid prolonged exposure to sunlight and sunlamps. Wear protective clothing and use an effective sunscreen.

To avoid dizziness and light-headedness when you stand, contract and relax the muscles of your legs for a few moments before rising. Do this by pushing one foot against the floor while raising the other foot slightly, alternating feet so that you are "pumping" your legs in a pedaling motion.

Major. Tell your doctor about any side effects that are persistent or bothersome. IT IS ESPECIALLY IMPORTANT TO TELL YOUR DOCTOR about confusion, difficulty in breathing, dry mouth, fainting, increased thirst, joint pains, loss of appetite, mood changes, muscle cramps, palpitations, rash, ringing in the ears, severe abdominal pain, sore throat, tingling in the fingers or toes, unusual bleeding or bruising, or yellowing of the eyes or skin.

INTERACTIONS

Furosemide interacts with several other drugs:

1. It can increase the side effects of alcohol, barbiturates, narcotics, cortisonelike steroids (such as cortisone, dexamethasone, hydrocortisone, prednisone, and prednisolone), digoxin, digitalis, and lithium.

2. The effectiveness of antigout medications, insulin, and oral antidiabetic medications may be decreased by the use of furosemide.

3. Phenytoin can decrease the absorption and effectiveness of furosemide.

4. Indomethacin and other nonsteroidal anti-inflammatory agents can decrease the diuretic effects of furosemide.

5. Furosemide may interfere with the actions of anticoagulants (blood thinners) and theophylline.

6. Clofibrate, thiazide diuretics, and probenecid may increase the side effects of furosemide.

Before taking furosemide, BE SURE TO TELL YOUR DOCTOR if you are taking any of the medicines listed above.

WARNINGS

• Tell your doctor about any unusual or allergic reactions you have had to furosemide or any medications, especially to diuretics, oral antidiabetic medicines, or sulfonamide antibiotics.

• Tell your doctor if you now have or ever had kidney disease or problems with urination, diabetes mellitus, gout, liver disease, asthma, pancreatic disease, or systemic lupus erythematosus (SLE).

• Furosemide can cause potassium loss. Signs of potassium loss include dry mouth, thirst, weakness, muscle pain or cramps, nausea, and vomiting. If you experience any of these symptoms, call your doctor. Your doctor may want to have blood tests performed periodically in order to monitor your blood potassium levels. To help avoid potassium loss, take this medication with a glass of fresh or frozen orange juice or cranberry juice, or eat a banana every day. The use of a salt substitute also helps to prevent potassium loss. Do not change your diet, however, before discussing it with your doctor. Too much potassium may also be dangerous.

• Before having any kind of surgery or other medical or dental treatment, be sure to tell your doctor or dentist that you are taking furosemide.

• To avoid dizziness, light-headedness, or fainting, get up from a sitting or lying position slowly, and avoid standing for long periods of time. You should also avoid strenuous exercise and prolonged exposure to hot weather.

• While taking this medication, limit your intake of alcoholic beverages to prevent dizziness and light-headedness.

• If you have high blood pressure, do not take any over-the-counter (nonprescription) medications for weight control or for cough, cold, asthma, allergy, or sinus problems unless you first check with your doctor.

• To prevent severe water loss (dehydration) while taking this drug, check with your doctor if you have any illness that causes severe nausea, vomiting, or diarrhea.

• This medication can raise blood-sugar levels in people who have diabetes. Blood sugar should be monitored carefully with blood or urine tests when treatment with this medication is started.
• Be sure to tell your doctor if you are pregnant. This drug crosses the placenta. Although studies in humans have not been completed, adverse effects have been observed in the fetuses of animals who received large doses of this drug during pregnancy. Also be sure to tell your doctor if you are breast-feeding an infant. Small amounts of furosemide pass into breast milk.

---

gabapentin

BRAND NAME (Manufacturer)
Neurontin (Parke-Davis)
TYPE OF DRUG
Anticonvulsant
INGREDIENT
gabapentin
DOSAGE FORMS
Tablets (600 mg and 800 mg)
Capsules (100 mg, 300 mg, and 400 mg)
Oral solution (50 mg per mL)
STORAGE
Store capsules and tablets at room temperature in tightly closed, light-resistant containers. Keep the solution in the refrigerator. Do not freeze this medication.

USES

Gabapentin is used in conjunction with other anticonvulsants for the treatment of seizure disorders. The mechanism of action of gabapentin is not related to that of any other anticonvulsant and is not well understood. Gapapentin has also been used to control certain types of pain, especially pain caused by nerve damage.

TREATMENT

If stomach upset occurs, gabapentin may be taken with food, unless your doctor instructs you to do otherwise.

Measure each dose of the solution carefully using a specially designed 5-mL measuring spoon or dropper. An ordinary kitchen teaspoon is not accurate enough.

Routine monitoring of the level of gabapentin in your bloodstream is not necessary. Doses should be administered at evenly spaced intervals day or night, depending on the specific dosage recommended by your doctor. For example, if you take three doses a day, the doses should be spaced eight hours apart.

Try not to miss any doses of this medication. If you do miss a dose, take the missed dose as soon as possible. However, if it is almost time for your next dose, do not take the missed dose at all; just return to your regular dosing schedule. Do not double the next dose unless your doctor directs you to do so. If you miss two or more doses in a row, be sure to contact your doctor.

SIDE EFFECTS

Minor. Constipation, dizziness, drowsiness, headache, nausea, rash, or vomiting. These side effects should disappear over time as your body adjusts to the medication.

This medication can increase your sensitivity to sunlight. It is important to avoid prolonged exposure to sunlight or sunlamps. Wear protective clothing and sunglasses, and use an effective sunscreen.

To prevent constipation, increase the amount of fiber in your diet (fresh fruits and vegetables, salads, bran, whole-grain breads), exercise, and drink more water (unless your doctor tells you not to do so).

If you feel dizzy or light-headed, sit or lie down for a while; get up slowly from a sitting or reclining position; and be careful when climbing stairs.

Major. Tell your doctor about any side effects that are persistent or particularly bothersome. IT IS ESPECIALLY IMPORTANT TO TELL YOUR DOCTOR about abnormal balance, abnormal dreaming/hallucinations, blurred vision, chest pain, depression, difficulty breathing, difficulty walking, difficulty with urination, double vision, elevated blood pressure, fever, forgetfulness, numbness or tingling in the hands or feet, palpitations, severe rash, skin discoloration, or tremor.

INTERACTIONS

Gabapentin interacts with several other types of medications:

1. Concurrent use of gabapentin with central nervous system depressants (such as alcohol, antihistamines, barbiturates, benzodiazepine tranquilizers, muscle relaxants, narcotics, pain medications, and phenothiazine tranquilizers) or with tricyclic antidepressants can cause extreme drowsiness.

2. Use of antacids with gabapentin can reduce the level of gabapentin in the blood, which may decrease the effectiveness of gabapentin. It is recommended that gabapentin be taken at least two hours after a dose of antacid.

Before you start gabapentin, BE SURE TO TELL YOUR DOCTOR about any medications you are currently taking, especially any of those listed above.

WARNINGS

- Tell your doctor about any unusual or allergic reactions you have had to any medications, especially to gabapentin or any other anticonvulsant medication.
- Before having surgery or any other medical or dental procedure, be sure to tell your doctor or dentist that you are taking this medication.
- If this medication makes you dizzy or drowsy, do not take part in any activity that requires alertness, such as driving a car or operating potentially dangerous equipment.
- Do not stop taking this medication suddenly. If you stop abruptly, you may experience an uncontrollable seizure.
- Be sure to tell your doctor if you now have or have ever had blood disorders, urinary tract infections, urinary incontinence, glaucoma, heart disease, kidney disease, or liver disease.
- Be sure to tell your doctor if you are pregnant. Although extensive studies of gabapentin in humans have not been conducted, gabapentin has been shown to cause side effects in the fetuses of animals that received large doses during pregnancy. Also be sure to tell your doctor if you are breast-feeding an infant. It is not known if this medication passes into breast milk.
- This medication has not been shown to be safe and effective in children under 12 years of age.

---

galantamine

BRAND NAME (Manufacturer)
Reminyl (Janssen)
TYPE OF DRUG
Acetylcholinesterase inhibitor
INGREDIENT
galantamine
DOSAGE FORM
Tablets (4 mg, 8 mg, and 12 mg)

STORAGE

Store the tablets at room temperature in a tightly closed container. Do not expose to extreme temperatures.

USES

Galantamine is used to treat Alzheimer's disease. This medication works by preventing the breakdown of a certain chemical in the brain, called acetylcholine. Acetylcholine is important in maintaining thinking and other cognitive abilities. In patients with Alzheimer's disease, there is less acetylcholine present in the brain than normal. Galantamine helps to increase the amount of this chemical in the brain. Galantamine will not cure Alzheimer's, but it may slow its progression, especially when used in the early stages of the disease.

TREATMENT

Take this medication exactly as prescribed by your doctor. It is best to take galantamine at regular intervals, with meals if possible. Usually, galantamine is started at a low dose and gradually increased over several weeks. If for any reason this medication is stopped for more than several days, it may be necessary to start at a low dose again and gradually increase it; check with your doctor.

If you miss a dose of this medication, take it as soon as you remember. However, if it is almost time for your next dose, do not take the missed dose at all; just return to your regular dosing schedule. Do not double the next dose.

SIDE EFFECTS

Minor. Diarrhea, dizziness, fatigue, headache, insomnia, loss of appetite, nausea, tremor, vomiting, or weight loss. These side effects should diminish or disappear as your body adjusts to the medication.

To avoid dizziness or light-headedness when you stand, contract and relax the muscles of your legs for a few moments before rising.

If you feel dizzy or light-headed, sit or lie down for a while. Get up from a sitting or lying position slowly, and be careful on stairs.

Major. Tell your doctor about any side effects that are persistent or particularly bothersome. IT IS ESPECIALLY IMPORTANT TO TELL YOUR DOCTOR about abdominal pain, difficulty breathing, difficulty urinating, fainting, seizures, slow or irregular heartbeat, or very low blood pressure.

INTERACTIONS

This medication may interact with a number of other medications:

1. Use of galantamine with bethanechol may increase the side effects of both medications.

2. Cimetidine, erythromycin, ketoconazole, itraconazole, or paroxetine may increase the amount of galantamine in the body and increase its effects and toxicities.

3. Taking galantamine with a nonsteroidal anti-inflammatory agent (such as ibuprofen) may increase stomach irritation and the risk of stomach ulcers.

BE SURE TO TELL YOUR DOCTOR about any medications you are currently taking, especially any of those mentioned above.

WARNINGS

• Tell your doctor about any unusual reactions you have had to any medication, especially galantamine or other medications used for Alzheimer's disease.

• Tell your doctor if you now have or have ever had asthma, heart disease or problems with too slow a heart rate, low blood pressure, seizures or epilepsy, stomach ulcers, or urinary problems.

• If you are having surgery or undergoing any type of dental procedure, be sure to tell your doctor or dentist that you are taking galantamine.

• While taking this medication, your ability to perform tasks that require alertness, such as driving a car or operating potentially dangerous machinery, may be impaired.
• Be sure to tell your doctor if you are pregnant. Adequate human studies have not been conducted with galantamine. This medication should not be used by women who are breast-feeding an infant.

---

gatifloxacin

BRAND NAME (Manufacturer)
Tequin (Bristol-Myers Squibb)
TYPE OF DRUG
Quinolone antibiotic
INGREDIENT
gatifloxacin
DOSAGE FORM
Tablets (200 mg and 400 mg)
STORAGE
Store at room temperature in a tightly closed container.

USES

Gatifloxacin is an antibiotic that is used to treat a wide variety of bacterial infections, including pneumonia, urinary tract infections, sinusitis, and acute attacks of bronchitis. It acts by severely injuring the cell walls of infecting bacteria, preventing them from growing and multiplying. This medication kills susceptible bacteria, but it is not effective against viruses, parasites, or fungi.

TREATMENT

Take this medication exactly as prescribed by your doctor—usually for 7 to 14 days—even if your symptoms improve. If you stop taking this medication too soon, resistant bacteria are given a chance to continue growing, and the infection could recur.

Gatifloxacin may be taken with food or on an empty stomach. Drink several additional glasses of water every day when you are taking this medication, unless your doctor tells you otherwise. Drinking water will help to prevent unwanted effects from this medication.

It is very important that you do not miss a dose of this medication. If you miss a dose of this medication, take the missed dose immediately. However, if you do not remember to take the missed dose until it is almost time for your next dose, take it and space the following dose halfway through the regular interval between doses; then return to your regular dosing schedule. It is important that you try not to skip any doses of this medication.

SIDE EFFECTS

Minor. Abdominal pain, diarrhea, dizziness, insomnia, light-headedness, nausea, or vomiting. These side effects usually go away during treatment, as your body adjusts to the medicine.

Gatifloxacin may increase your sensitivity to sunlight. Be cautious during exposure to the sun. Use an effective sunscreen and avoid exposure to sunlamps.

To avoid dizziness or light-headedness when you stand, contract and relax the muscles of your legs for a few moments before rising.

If you feel dizzy or light-headed, sit or lie down for a while. Get up slowly from a sitting or lying position, and be careful on stairs.

Major. Notify your doctor if any side effects are persistent or particularly bothersome. IT IS ESPECIALLY IMPORTANT TO TELL YOUR DOCTOR about agitation, change in your vision, confusion, difficulty breathing, difficulty urinating, headache, muscle or joint pain, restlessness, severe diarrhea (which can be watery or contain pus or blood), skin rash, or swelling of the face. If your symptoms of infection seem to be getting worse rather than improving, contact your doctor immediately.

INTERACTIONS

Gatifloxacin interacts with a number of other medications:

1. Antacids with aluminum or magnesium, vitamins with iron, or sucralfate should not be taken within four hours after taking gatifloxacin, since these medications may reduce the effectiveness of gatifloxacin.

2. Gatifloxacin should not be taken with quinidine, procainamide, amiodarone, or sotalol. These medications may increase the risk of side effects on the heart.

3. The effects of phenytoin may be reduced if given together with gatifloxacin, increasing the risk of having a seizure.

4. Regular consumption of large quantities of caffeine-containing beverages, such as coffee, tea, or colas, with this medication may lead to exaggerated or prolonged effects of caffeine. Your doctor may ask you to restrict your intake of caffeine during therapy with this medication.

5. Gatifloxacin may increase the actions and adverse effects of warfarin, cyclosporine, digoxin, and theophylline.

6. Probenecid can increase the blood levels and adverse effects of gatifloxacin.

BE SURE TO TELL YOUR DOCTOR if you are already taking any of the medications listed above or about any other medications you are taking.

WARNINGS

- It is important to tell your doctor if you have ever had any unusual or allergic reaction to gatifloxacin, any other quinolone antibiotic (including ciprofloxacin, levofloxacin, ofloxacin, sparfloxacin, enoxacin, norfloxacin, cinoxacin, or nalidixic acid), or any other medication.
- It is important to tell your doctor if you now have or ever had brain or spinal cord disease, epilepsy, kidney disease, or liver disease.
- To decrease the potential for harmful effects on your kidneys, increase your intake of fluids (nonalcoholic) unless your doctor directs you to do otherwise.
- If you are having surgery or undergoing any type of dental procedure, be sure to tell your doctor or dentist that you are taking gatifloxacin.
- While taking this medication, your ability to perform tasks that require alertness, such as driving a car or operating potentially dangerous machinery, may be impaired.
- This medication has been prescribed for your current infection only. Another infection later on, or one that someone else has, may require a different medicine. You should not give your medication to other people or use it for other infections, unless your doctor specifically directs you to do so.
- Be sure to call your doctor immediately if you experience rash, swelling of the face, or difficulty breathing after you take this medication.
- This medication should not be used in young children.
- Be sure to tell your doctor if you are pregnant. This medication and other quinolone antibiotics have been shown to cause serious adverse effects in the developing fetus. Also tell your doctor if you are breast-feeding an infant. This medication may pass into breast milk and should not be taken by a nursing mother.

---

gemfibrozil

BRAND NAMES (Manufacturers)

gemfibrozil (various manufacturers)
Lopid (Parke-Davis)

TYPE OF DRUG
Antihyperlipidemic (lipid-lowering drug)
INGREDIENT
gemfibrozil
DOSAGE FORM
Tablets (600 mg)
STORAGE
Store at room temperature in a tightly closed container.

USES

Gemfibrozil is used to treat hyperlipidemia (high blood fat levels) in patients who have not responded to diet, weight reduction, exercise, and control of blood sugar. It is not clear how gemfibrozil lowers blood lipid levels, but it is thought to decrease the body's production of certain fats.

TREATMENT

To maximize its effectiveness, gemfibrozil should be taken 30 minutes before meals.

If you miss a dose of this medication, take the missed dose as soon as possible. However, if it is almost time for the next dose, do not take the missed dose; just return to your regular dosing schedule. Do not double the dose.

SIDE EFFECTS

Minor. Constipation, diarrhea, dizziness, dry mouth, gas, headache, insomnia, loss of appetite, nausea, or stomach upset. These side effects should disappear in several days, as your body adjusts to the medication.

To relieve constipation, increase the amount of fiber in your diet (bran, salads, fresh fruits and vegetables, and whole-grain breads), exercise, and drink more water (unless your doctor directs you to do otherwise).

If you feel dizzy, sit or lie down a while; get up slowly from a sitting or lying position; and be careful on stairs.

To help relieve mouth dryness, chew sugarless gum or suck on ice chips.

Major. Tell your doctor about any side effects that are persistent or particularly bothersome. IT IS ESPECIALLY IMPORTANT TO TELL YOUR DOCTOR about back pain, blurred vision, fatigue, muscle cramps, rash, swollen or painful joints, tingling sensations, or yellowing of the eyes or skin.

INTERACTIONS

Gemfibrozil interacts with certain other types of medications:

1. Gemfibrozil can increase the effects of oral anticoagulants (blood thinners, such as warfarin), which can lead to bleeding complications.

2. Use of gemfibrozil with lovastatin and similar agents may increase the risk of severe myopathy (muscle weakness).

Before you start gemfibrozil, BE SURE TO TELL YOUR DOCTOR about any medications you are currently taking, especially any of those listed above.

WARNINGS

- Tell your doctor about unusual or allergic reactions you have had to any medications, especially to gemfibrozil.
- Before starting this medication, be sure to tell your doctor if you now have or ever had biliary disorders, gallstones or gallbladder disease, kidney disease, or liver disease.
- If this drug makes you dizzy or otherwise interferes with your vision, do not take part in activities that require mental alertness, such as driving an automobile or operating any potentially dangerous machinery or equipment.

• Do not stop taking this medication unless you first check with your doctor. Stopping the drug abruptly may lead to a rapid increase in blood lipid (fats) and cholesterol levels. Your doctor may therefore want to start you on a special diet or another medication when gemfibrozil is discontinued.

• Large doses of gemfibrozil administered to animals for prolonged periods of time have been associated with benign and malignant tumors. This association has not been observed in humans.

• Be sure to tell your doctor if you are pregnant. Although gemfibrozil appears to be safe during pregnancy, extensive studies in humans have not yet been completed. Also tell your doctor if you are breast-feeding an infant. It is not known whether or not gemfibrozil passes into breast milk.

---

glimepiride

BRAND NAME (Manufacturer)
Amaryl (Hoechst Roussel)
TYPE OF DRUG
Oral antidiabetic
INGREDIENT
glimepiride
DOSAGE FORM
Tablets (1 mg, 2 mg, and 4 mg)
STORAGE
Store at room temperature in a tightly closed container.

USES

Glimepiride is used for the treatment of diabetes mellitus that appears in adulthood (this type of diabetes is known as type 2 diabetes, sometimes called adult-onset or non–insulin-dependent diabetes) and cannot be successfully managed through dietary therapy alone. Glimepiride lowers the blood sugar levels by increasing the release of insulin from the pancreas.

TREATMENT

Take this medication with breakfast or the first main meal of the day (unless your doctor directs you to do otherwise).

It is important to try not to miss any doses of this medication. If you do miss a dose, take it as soon as possible. However, if it is almost time for the next dose, do not take the missed dose at all; just return to your regular dosing schedule. Do not double the next dose. Tell your doctor if you feel any side effects from missing a dose of this drug.

SIDE EFFECTS

Minor. Diarrhea, headache, heartburn, loss of appetite, nausea, stomach discomfort, stomach pain, or vomiting. These side effects usually go away during treatment as your body adjusts to the medicine.

Glimepiride may increase your sensitivity to sunlight. It is therefore important to use caution during exposure to the sun. Wear protective clothing and use an effective sunscreen when you are outdoors during the day, and do not expose your skin to sunlamps.

Major. Notify your doctor if any side effects are persistent or particularly bothersome to you. IT IS ESPECIALLY IMPORTANT TO TELL YOUR DOCTOR about dark urine, fatigue, itching of the skin, light-colored stools, rash, sore throat and fever, unusual bleeding or bruising, weight gain, or yellowing of the eyes or skin.

INTERACTIONS

Glimepiride interacts with a number of other medications:
1. Glimepiride can lower blood sugar levels, sometimes dangerously so, when it is combined with cimetidine, ranitidine, ciprofloxacin, guanethidine, monoamine oxidase (MAO) inhibitors, quinidine, quinine, salicylates, chloramphenicol, and antifungal agents (such as fluconazole).
2. Thyroid hormones, albuterol, dextrothyroxine, epinephrine, lithium, phenytoin, thiazide diuretics (water pills), furosemide, calcium channel blocking agents (such as verapamil or nifedipine), protease inhibitors (such as ritonavir or indinavir), and cortisonelike medications (such as dexamethasone, hydrocortisone, and prednisone) can actually increase blood sugar levels when any of these medications are combined with glimepiride—which is exactly what you are trying to avoid.
3. Antidiabetic medications can increase the effects of warfarin, which can lead to bleeding complications.
4. Beta-blocking medications (atenolol, metoprolol, nadolol, pindolol, propranolol, and timolol) combined with glimepiride can result in either high or low blood sugar levels. Beta blockers can also mask the symptoms of low blood sugar, which can be dangerous.

BE SURE TO TELL YOUR DOCTOR if you are already taking any of the medications listed above.

WARNINGS

• It is important to tell your doctor if you have ever had any unusual or allergic reaction to glimepiride or any other oral antidiabetics or to any sulfa medication, including sulfonamide antibiotics or diuretics (water pills).
• It is also important to tell your doctor if you now have or ever had kidney disease, liver disease, severe infection, or thyroid disease.
• Avoid drinking alcoholic beverages while taking this medication (unless directed otherwise by your doctor). Some patients who take this medicine experience nausea, vomiting, dizziness, stomach pain, pounding headache, sweating, or redness of the face and skin when they drink alcohol, and large amounts of alcohol can decrease blood sugar to dangerously low levels.
• Follow the special diet that your doctor gave you. This is an important part of controlling your blood sugar and is necessary for this medicine to work properly.
• Be sure to tell your doctor or dentist that you are taking this medicine before having any kind of surgery or other medical or dental treatment.
• Test for sugar in your blood or urine as directed by your doctor. It is a convenient way to determine if your diabetes is being controlled by this medicine.
• Eat or drink something containing sugar right away if you experience any symptoms of low blood sugar (such as anxiety, chills, cold sweats, cool or pale skin, drowsiness, excessive hunger, headache, nausea, nervousness, rapid heartbeat, shakiness, or unusual tiredness or weakness). It is important that your family and friends know the symptoms of low blood sugar and what to do if they recognize any of these symptoms in you. Also, check with your doctor as soon as possible, even if these symptoms are corrected by the sugar. The blood-sugar-lowering effects of this medicine can last for hours, and the symptoms may return during this period. Good sources of sugar are orange juice, corn syrup, honey, sugar cubes, and table sugar. You are at greatest risk of developing low blood sugar if you skip or delay meals, exercise more than you usually do, cannot eat because of nausea or vomiting, or drink large amounts of alcohol.
• Be sure to tell your doctor if you are pregnant. Studies have not yet been completed in humans during pregnancy, but studies in animal pregnancies have shown that this medicine can cause birth defects. Also tell your doctor if you are breast-feeding an infant. Small amounts of glimepiride pass into breast milk.

glipizide

BRAND NAMES (Manufacturers)
glipizide (various manufacturers)
Glucotrol (Pfizer)
Glucotrol XL (Pfizer)
TYPE OF DRUG
Oral antidiabetic
INGREDIENT
glipizide
DOSAGE FORMS
Tablets (5 mg and 10 mg)
Tablets, XL (2.5 mg, 5 mg, and 10 mg)
STORAGE
Store at room temperature in a tightly closed container.

USES

Glipizide is used in the treatment of type 2 diabetes mellitus (sometimes called non–insulin-dependent, or adult-onset, diabetes) that cannot be managed by control of diet alone. Glipizide lowers blood sugar levels by increasing the release of insulin from the pancreas.

TREATMENT

This medication should be taken on an empty stomach 30 minutes before a meal, unless your doctor directs you to do otherwise.

Swallow the XL tablets whole; do not chew or crush them.

It is important to try not to miss any doses of this medication. If you do miss a dose, take it as soon as possible. However, if it is almost time for the next dose, do not take the missed dose at all; just return to your regular dosing schedule. Do not double the next dose. Tell your doctor if you feel any side effects from missing a dose of this drug.

People with diabetes who are taking oral antidiabetic medication may need to be switched to insulin if they develop diabetic coma, have a severe infection, are scheduled for major surgery, or become pregnant.

SIDE EFFECTS

Minor. Diarrhea, headache, heartburn, loss of appetite, nausea, stomach discomfort, stomach pain, or vomiting. These side effects usually go away during treatment, as your body adjusts to the medicine.

Glipizide may increase your sensitivity to sunlight. It is therefore important to use caution during exposure to the sun. Wear protective clothing and use an effective sunscreen outdoors during the day, and avoid exposure to sunlamps.

Major. If any side effects are persistent or particularly bothersome, it is important to notify your doctor. IT IS ESPECIALLY IMPORTANT TO TELL YOUR DOCTOR about dark urine, fatigue, itching of the skin, light-colored stools, rash, sore throat and fever, unusual bleeding or bruising, or yellowing of the eyes or skin.

INTERACTIONS

Glipizide interacts with a number of other medications:

1. Glipizide can lower blood sugar levels, sometimes dangerously so, when it is combined with cimetidine, ranitidine, ciprofloxacin, guanethidine, monoamine oxidase (MAO) inhibitors, quinidine, quinine, salicylates, chloramphenicol, and antifungal agents (such as fluconazole).

2. Thyroid hormones; dextrothyroxine; epinephrine; lithium; phenytoin; thiazide diuretics (water pills); and cortisonelike medications (such as dexamethasone, hydro-

cortisone, prednisone), combined with glipizide, can actually increase blood sugar levels—just what you are trying to avoid.
3. Antidiabetic medications can increase the effects of warfarin, which can lead to bleeding complications.
4. Beta-blocking medications (atenolol, metoprolol, nadolol, pindolol, propranolol, and timolol), combined with glipizide, can result in either high or low blood sugar levels. Beta blockers can also mask the symptoms of low blood sugar, which can be dangerous.
5. Glipizide can increase the blood levels of cyclosporine, increasing the risk of side effects from cyclosporine.

BE SURE TO TELL YOUR DOCTOR if you are already taking any of the medications listed above.

WARNINGS

• It is important to tell your doctor if you have ever had any unusual or allergic reaction to this medicine or to any sulfa medication, including sulfonamide antibiotics, diuretics (water pills), or other oral antidiabetics.
• It is also important to tell your doctor if you now have or ever had kidney disease, liver disease, severe infection, or thyroid disease.
• Avoid drinking alcoholic beverages while taking this medication (unless directed otherwise by your doctor). Some patients who take this medicine experience nausea, vomiting, dizziness, stomach pain, pounding headache, sweating, and redness of the face and skin when they drink alcohol, and large amounts of alcohol can lower blood sugar to dangerously low levels.
• Follow the special diet that your doctor gave you. This is an important part of controlling your blood sugar and is necessary for this medicine to work properly.
• Be sure to tell your doctor or dentist that you are taking this medicine before having any kind of surgery or other medical or dental treatment.
• Test for sugar in your urine as directed by your doctor. It is a convenient way to determine whether or not your diabetes is being controlled by this medicine.
• Eat or drink something containing sugar right away if you experience any symptoms of low blood sugar (such as anxiety, chills, cold sweats, cool or pale skin, drowsiness, excessive hunger, headache, nausea, nervousness, rapid heartbeat, shakiness, or unusual tiredness or weakness). It is important that your family and friends know the symptoms of low blood sugar and what to do if they recognize any of these symptoms in you. Also, check with your doctor as soon as possible—even if these symptoms are corrected by the sugar. The blood-sugar-lowering effects of this medicine can last for hours, and the symptoms may return during this period. Good sources of sugar are orange juice, corn syrup, honey, sugar cubes, and table sugar. You are at greatest risk of developing low blood sugar if you skip or delay meals, exercise more than usual, cannot eat because of nausea or vomiting, or drink large amounts of alcohol.
• Be sure to tell your doctor if you are pregnant. Studies have not yet been completed in humans, but studies in animals have shown that this medicine can cause birth defects. Also tell your doctor if you are breast-feeding an infant. Small amounts of glipizide pass into breast milk.

---

glyburide

BRAND NAMES (Manufacturers)
DiaBeta (Hoechst)
glyburide (various manufacturers)
Glynase Prestabs (Pharmacia)
Micronase (Pharmacia)
micronized glyburide (various manufacturers)

TYPE OF DRUG
Oral antidiabetic
INGREDIENT
glyburide
DOSAGE FORMS
Tablets (1.25 mg, 2.5 mg, and 5 mg)
Tablets, micronized (1.5 mg, 3 mg, and 6 mg)
STORAGE
Store this medication at room temperature in a tightly closed container.

USES

Glyburide is used for the treatment of diabetes mellitus that usually appears in adulthood—this type of diabetes is referred to as type 2, or non–insulin-dependent, diabetes—that cannot be managed by control of diet alone. Glyburide lowers blood sugar levels by increasing the release of insulin from the pancreas.

TREATMENT

Take this medication with a meal, usually breakfast or the first main meal of the day.

For glyburide to work correctly, it must be taken as directed by your doctor. To maintain a constant blood sugar level, it is best to take this medication at the same time(s) each day. It is therefore important to try not to miss any doses of this medication. If you do miss a dose, take it as soon as possible. However, if it is almost time for the next dose, do not take the missed dose at all; just return to your regular dosing schedule. Do not double the next dose. Tell your doctor if you feel any side effects from missing a dose of this medication.

People with diabetes who are taking oral antidiabetic medication may need to be switched to insulin if they develop diabetic coma, have a severe infection, are scheduled for major surgery, or become pregnant.

SIDE EFFECTS

Minor. Diarrhea, headache, heartburn, loss of appetite, nausea, stomach discomfort, stomach pain, or vomiting. The side effects from glyburide will most likely disappear during treatment as your body adjusts to the medicine.

Glyburide may increase your sensitivity to sunlight. It is therefore important to use caution during exposure to the sun. You may want to wear protective clothing and sunglasses. Use an effective sunscreen, and avoid exposure to sunlamps.

Major. Notify your doctor if any side effects are persistent or particularly bothersome. IT IS ESPECIALLY IMPORTANT TO TELL YOUR DOCTOR about dark urine, fatigue, itching of the skin, light-colored stools, rash, sore throat and fever, unusual bleeding or bruising, or yellowing of the eyes or skin.

INTERACTIONS

Glyburide interacts with a number of other medications:

1. Glyburide can lower blood sugar levels, sometimes dangerously so, when it is combined with cimetidine, ranitidine, ciprofloxacin, guanethidine, monoamine oxidase (MAO) inhibitors, quinidine, quinine, salicylates, chloramphenicol, and antifungal agents (such as fluconazole).

2. Thyroid hormones, dextrothyroxine, epinephrine, lithium, phenytoin, thiazide diuretics (water pills), and cortisonelike medications (such as dexamethasone, hydrocortisone, prednisone), combined with glyburide, can actually increase blood sugar levels.

3. Antidiabetic medications can increase the effects of warfarin, which can lead to bleeding complications.

4. Beta-blocking medications (such as atenolol, metoprolol, nadolol, pindolol, propranolol, and timolol), combined with glyburide, can result in either high or low

blood sugar levels. Beta blockers can also mask the symptoms of low blood sugar, which can be dangerous.
5. Blood levels of cyclosporine may be increased with glyburide, increasing the risk of side effects from cyclosporine.

BE SURE TO TELL YOUR DOCTOR if you are already taking any of the medications listed above.

WARNINGS

• Tell your doctor if you have ever had unusual or allergic reactions to medications, especially to glyburide or to any sulfa medication, including sulfonamide antibiotics, diuretics (water pills), or other oral antidiabetics.
• Tell your doctor if you now have or ever had kidney disease, liver disease, thyroid disease, or a severe infection.
• Follow the special dietary instructions that your doctor gave you. This is an important part of controlling your blood sugar levels and is necessary for this medicine to work properly.
• Avoid drinking alcoholic beverages while taking this medication (unless otherwise directed by your doctor). Some patients who take this medicine experience nausea, vomiting, dizziness, stomach pain, pounding headache, sweating, and redness of the face and skin when they drink alcohol, and large amounts of alcohol can lower blood sugar to dangerously low levels.
• Be sure to tell your doctor or dentist that you are taking this medication before having any kind of surgery or other medical or dental treatment.
• Test for sugar in your urine as directed by your doctor. It is a convenient way to determine whether or not your diabetes is being controlled by this medicine.
• Eat or drink something containing sugar right away if you experience any symptoms of low blood sugar (such as anxiety, chills, cold sweats, cool or pale skin, drowsiness, excessive hunger, headache, nausea, nervousness, rapid heartbeat, shakiness, or unusual tiredness or weakness). It is also important that your family and friends recognize the symptoms of low blood sugar and know what to do if they observe any of these symptoms in you. Also, check with your doctor as soon as possible—even if these symptoms are corrected by the sugar. The blood-sugar-lowering effects of this medicine can last for hours, and the symptoms may return during this period. Good sources of sugar are orange juice, corn syrup, honey, sugar cubes, and table sugar. You are at greatest risk of developing low blood sugar if you skip or delay meals, exercise more than usual, cannot eat because of nausea or vomiting, or drink large amounts of alcohol.
• Be sure to tell your doctor if you are pregnant. Studies of this drug taken in human pregnancy have not yet been completed, but studies in animals have shown it can cause birth defects. Consult your doctor if you are nursing an infant.

---

griseofulvin

BRAND NAMES (Manufacturers)
Fulvicin P/G (Schering)
Fulvicin U/F (Schering)
Grifulvin V (Ortho Derm)
Grisactin Ultra (Wyeth-Ayerst)
griseofulvin (various manufacturers)
Gris-PEG (Herbert)
TYPE OF DRUG
Antifungal
INGREDIENT
griseofulvin

DOSAGE FORMS

Tablets (125 mg, 165 mg, 250 mg, 330 mg, and 500 mg)
Capsules (125 mg and 250 mg)
Oral suspension (125 mg per 5-mL teaspoonful, with 0.2% alcohol)

STORAGE

Store all forms of this medication at room temperature in tightly closed containers. Do not freeze.

USES

This medication is used to treat certain fungal infections of the skin and nails. Griseofulvin prevents the multiplication of susceptible fungi. It also enters the cells of skin, hair, and nails and protects them from fungal invasion.

TREATMENT

To avoid stomach irritation from this medication, take each dose of griseofulvin with food or milk.

Shake the suspension well just before measuring each dose to evenly distribute the ingredients and equalize the doses. The contents tend to settle on the bottom of the bottle. Measure each dose carefully with a specially designed 5-mL measuring spoon. An ordinary kitchen teaspoon is not accurate enough.

If you miss a dose of this medication, take the missed dose as soon as possible after you remember. However, if it is almost time for the next dose of the medication, do not take the missed dose at all; just return to your regular dosing schedule. Do not double the next dose.

It is important to continue to take this medication for the entire time prescribed by your doctor (perhaps six months or more), even if the symptoms disappear before the end of that period. If you stop taking this drug too soon, resistant fungi are given a chance to continue growing, and your infection could recur.

SIDE EFFECTS

Minor. Diarrhea, dizziness, fatigue, headache, insomnia, nausea, stomach upset, or vomiting. These side effects should disappear in several days, as your body adjusts to the medication.

If you feel dizzy, sit or lie down a while; get up slowly from a sitting or lying position; and be careful on stairs.

This medication can increase your sensitivity to sunlight. You should therefore avoid prolonged exposure to sunlight and sunlamps. Wear protective clothing and sunglasses, and use an effective sunscreen.

Major. Tell your doctor about any side effects that are persistent or particularly bothersome. IT IS ESPECIALLY IMPORTANT TO TELL YOUR DOCTOR about confusion, itching, skin rash, sore throat, or tingling of the hands or feet.

INTERACTIONS

Griseofulvin interacts with other types of medications:

1. Griseofulvin can increase the effects of alcohol, resulting in flushing and an increased heart rate.

2. Barbiturates or primidone used concurrently with this medication can cause a decrease in the effectiveness of griseofulvin.

3. Griseofulvin can decrease the effectiveness of oral anticoagulants (blood thinners, such as warfarin).

4. Griseofulvin can reduce the effectiveness of oral contraceptives (birth control pills). An additional form of birth control should be used during and for one month after treatment with griseofulvin.

Before starting to take griseofulvin, BE SURE TO TELL YOUR DOCTOR if you are already taking any of these medications.

WARNINGS

• Tell your doctor about unusual or allergic reactions you have had to any medications, especially to griseofulvin, penicillin antibiotics, cephalosporin antibiotics, or penicillamine.
• Before starting to take griseofulvin, be sure to tell your doctor if you now have, or if you have ever had, liver disease, porphyria, or systemic lupus erythematosus.
• If this drug makes you dizzy, do not take part in any activity that requires alertness, such as driving a car or operating potentially dangerous equipment.
• Observe good hygiene to control the source of infection and to prevent reinfection.
• Use of an appropriate topical antifungal medication during your therapy with griseofulvin may be necessary to help clear the infection.
• Be sure to tell your doctor if you are pregnant. Extensive studies in pregnant women have not yet been completed, but birth defects have been reported in animals whose mothers received large doses of griseofulvin during pregnancy. Also be sure to tell your doctor if you are breast-feeding an infant. It is not known whether or not griseofulvin passes into breast milk.

---

haloperidol

BRAND NAMES (Manufacturers)
Haldol (Ortho McNeil)
haloperidol (various manufacturers)
TYPE OF DRUG
Antipsychotic
INGREDIENT
haloperidol
DOSAGE FORMS
Tablets (0.5 mg, 1 mg, 2 mg, 5 mg, 10 mg, and 20 mg)
Oral concentrate (2 mg per mL)
STORAGE
Store at room temperature in a tightly closed, light-resistant container. Do not refrigerate or freeze.

USES

Haloperidol is prescribed to treat the symptoms of certain types of mental illness, such as the emotional symptoms of psychosis, the manic phase of manic-depressive illness, Tourette's syndrome, and severe behavioral problems in children. This drug is thought to relieve symptoms of mental illness by blocking certain chemicals involved with nerve transmission in the brain.

TREATMENT

To avoid stomach irritation, take the tablets with a meal or with a glass of water or milk (unless your doctor directs you to do otherwise).

Immediately prior to administration, carefully measure the concentrate with the dropper provided, then add to four ounces (½ cup) or more of water, milk, applesauce, pudding, or a cola-free, caffeine-free carbonated beverage. To prevent possible loss of effectiveness, do not dilute the medication in tea, coffee, other caffeine-containing beverages, or apple juice.

If you miss a dose of this medication and remember within six hours, take the missed dose as soon as possible, then return to your regular schedule. If more than six hours have passed, however, skip the missed dose and return to your regular dosing schedule. Do not double the next dose unless your doctor directs you to do so.

The full effects of haloperidol may not become apparent for two weeks after you start to take it.

SIDE EFFECTS

Minor. Blurred vision, constipation, decreased or increased sweating, diarrhea, dizziness, drooling, drowsiness, dry mouth, fatigue, headache, heartburn, jitteriness, loss of appetite, menstrual irregularities, nausea, restlessness, sleep disorders, vomiting, or weakness. As your body adjusts to the drug, these side effects should disappear.

This medication can cause increased sensitivity to sunlight. It is, therefore, important to avoid prolonged exposure to sunlight and sunlamps. Wear protective clothing and use an effective sunscreen.

If you are constipated, increase the amount of fiber in your diet (fresh fruits and vegetables, salads, bran, and whole-grain breads), exercise, and drink more water (unless your doctor directs you to do otherwise).

To reduce mouth dryness, chew sugarless gum or suck on ice chips or a piece of hard candy.

To avoid dizziness or light-headedness when you stand, contract and relax the muscles of your legs for a few moments before rising. Do this by pushing one foot against the floor while raising the other foot slightly, alternating feet so that you are "pumping" your legs in a pedaling motion.

Major. Tell your doctor about any side effects that are persistent or particularly bothersome. IT IS ESPECIALLY IMPORTANT TO TELL YOUR DOCTOR about aching joints and muscles; breast enlargement (in both sexes); chest pain; confusion; convulsions; difficulty in breathing or swallowing; difficulty in urinating; fainting; fever; fluid retention; hair loss; hallucinations; impotence; involuntary movements of the mouth, face, neck, tongue, or limbs; mouth sores; palpitations; skin darkening; skin rash; sore throat; tremors; unusual bleeding or bruising; visual disturbances; or yellowish discoloration of the eyes or skin.

INTERACTIONS

Haloperidol interacts with several other drugs:

1. Haloperidol can cause extreme drowsiness when combined with alcohol or other central nervous system depressants (such as antihistamines, barbiturates, benzodiazepine tranquilizers, muscle relaxants, narcotics, and pain medications) or with tricyclic antidepressants.

2. This drug can alter the effects of guanethidine, anticonvulsants (antiseizure medications), anticoagulants (blood thinners), levodopa, and pergolide.

3. Haloperidol may increase the side effects of bupropion, epinephrine, fluoxetine, lithium, methyldopa, trazodone, MAO inhibitors, and tricyclic antidepressants.

Before starting to take haloperidol, BE SURE TO TELL YOUR DOCTOR about any medications you are currently taking, especially any of those listed above.

WARNINGS

• Tell your doctor about unusual or allergic reactions you have had to any medications, especially to haloperidol or to any other medications that are used to treat mental illness.

• Tell your doctor if you now have or ever had any blood disorders, blockage of the urinary tract, depression induced by drugs, enlarged prostate gland, epilepsy, glaucoma, heart or circulatory disease, kidney disease, liver disease, lung disease, mental depression, Parkinson's disease, peptic ulcers, or thyroid disease.

• To prevent oversedation, avoid drinking alcoholic beverages while you are taking this medication.

• If this medication makes you dizzy or drowsy, do not take part in any activity that requires alertness, such as driving a car or operating potentially dangerous machinery. Be careful on stairs, and avoid getting up suddenly from a lying or sitting position.

• This medication can decrease sweating and heat release from the body. You should, therefore, avoid getting overheated by strenuous exercise in hot weather and should avoid taking hot baths, showers, and saunas.

• Prior to having surgery or any other medical or dental treatment, be sure to tell your doctor or dentist that you are taking this medication.
• Some of the side effects caused by this drug can be prevented by taking an antiparkinsonism drug. Discuss this with your doctor.
• Do not stop taking this drug suddenly. Doing so may cause nausea, vomiting, stomach upset, headache, increased heart rate, insomnia, tremors, or a worsening of your condition. Your doctor may want to reduce the dosage gradually.
• The elderly may be at increased risk for side effects. Watch closely for side effects and for any other changes—especially in mental status—after taking haloperidol, and report them to your doctor.
• If you are planning to have a myelogram or any other procedure in which dye is injected into the spinal cord, tell your doctor that you are taking this medication.
• Avoid spilling the oral-concentrate form of this medication on your skin or clothing; it can cause redness and irritation of the skin.
• While taking haloperidol, do not take any over-the-counter (nonprescription) medications for weight control or for cough, cold, allergy, asthma, or sinus problems unless you first check with your doctor. The combination of these medications may cause high blood pressure.
• Haloperidol has the potential to cause a permanent movement disorder called tardive dyskinesia. It is important to discuss this with your doctor and to report any unusual or uncontrolled body movements.
• Some haloperidol formulations contain the color additive FD&C Yellow No. 5 (tartrazine), which can cause allergic-type reactions (rash, shortness of breath, fainting) in certain susceptible individuals.
• Be sure to tell your doctor if you are pregnant. A few cases of limb malformations have occurred in infants whose mothers had received haloperidol in combination with several other drugs during the first three months of pregnancy. Whether haloperidol was the cause is still not known. Also tell your doctor if you are breast-feeding an infant. Small amounts of haloperidol pass into breast milk.

---

hydrochlorothiazide

BRAND NAMES (Manufacturers)
Esidrix (Novartis)
hydrochlorothiazide (various manufacturers)
HydroDIURIL (Merck)
Microzide (Watson)
Oretic (Abbott)
TYPE OF DRUG
Diuretic and antihypertensive
INGREDIENT
hydrochlorothiazide
DOSAGE FORMS
Capsules (12.5 mg)
Tablets (25 mg, 50 mg, and 100 mg)
Oral solution (50 mg per 5-mL spoonful)
Intensol oral solution (100 mg per mL)
STORAGE
Store at room temperature in a tightly closed container. Do not freeze the solution.

USES

Hydrochlorothiazide is prescribed to treat high blood pressure (hypertension). It is also used to reduce fluid accumulation in the body caused by conditions such as heart failure, cirrhosis of the liver, kidney disease, and the long-term use of some medications. This medication reduces body fluid accumulation by increasing the elimination of salt and water through the kidneys.

TREATMENT

To decrease stomach irritation, take this medication with a glass of milk or with a meal (unless your doctor directs you to do otherwise). Each dose of the oral solution should be measured carefully with the dropper provided (Intensol solution) or a specially designed 5-mL measuring spoon. An ordinary kitchen teaspoon is not accurate enough. Try to take it at the same time every day. Avoid taking a dose after 6:00 in the evening; otherwise, you may have to get up during the night to urinate.

If you miss a dose of this medication, take the missed dose as soon as possible. However, if it is almost time for the next dose, do not take the missed dose at all; just wait until the next scheduled dose. Do not double the dose.

This medication does not cure high blood pressure but can help control it, so it is important to take the drug on a regular schedule as directed by your doctor.

SIDE EFFECTS

Minor. Constipation, cramps, diarrhea, dizziness, drowsiness, headache, heartburn, loss of appetite, restlessness, or upset stomach. As your body adjusts to the medication, these side effects should disappear.

This drug can cause increased sensitivity to sunlight. Therefore, avoid prolonged exposure to sunlight and sunlamps. Wear protective clothing and use an effective sunscreen.

To relieve constipation, increase the amount of fiber in your diet (fresh fruits and vegetables, salads, bran, and whole-grain breads) and exercise more (unless your doctor directs you to do otherwise).

To avoid dizziness or light-headedness when you stand, contract and relax the muscles of your legs for a few moments before rising. Do this by pushing one foot against the floor while raising the other foot slightly, alternating feet so that you are "pumping" your legs in a pedaling motion.

Major. Tell your doctor about any side effects that are persistent or particularly bothersome. IT IS ESPECIALLY IMPORTANT TO TELL YOUR DOCTOR about blurred vision, confusion, difficulty in breathing, dry mouth, excessive thirst, excessive weakness, fever, itching, joint pain, mood changes, muscle pain or spasms, nausea, palpitations, skin rash, sore throat, tingling in the fingers or toes, vomiting, or yellowing of the skin or of the whites of the eyes.

INTERACTIONS

Hydrochlorothiazide interacts with certain other drugs:

1. It can decrease the effectiveness of oral anticoagulants, antigout medications, insulin, oral antidiabetic medicines, and methenamine.

2. Sympathomimetics (stimulants) can decrease the blood-pressure-lowering effects of hydrochlorothiazide (which can be dangerous).

3. Indomethacin and other nonsteroidal anti-inflammatory agents can counteract the desired blood-pressure-lowering effects of hydrochlorothiazide.

4. Cholestyramine and colestipol decrease the absorption of this medication from the gastrointestinal tract. Hydrochlorothiazide should, therefore, be taken one hour before or four hours after a dose of cholestyramine or colestipol (if you have also been prescribed one of these medications).

5. Cortisone and cortisonelike steroids, laxatives (when overused), and furosemide may increase the amount of potassium lost from the body with hydrochlorothiazide.

6. Hydrochlorothiazide may increase the side effects of lithium, digoxin, and digitalis if used concurrently with any of these medications.

BE SURE TO TELL YOUR DOCTOR about any medications you are currently taking, especially any of those listed above.

WARNINGS

- Be sure to tell your doctor about unusual or allergic reactions you have had to any medications, especially to hydrochlorothiazide or other sulfa medications, including other diuretics, oral antidiabetic medications, and sulfonamide antibiotics.
- Be sure to tell your doctor if you now have or ever had kidney disease or problems with urination, diabetes mellitus, gout, liver disease, asthma, pancreatic disease, or systemic lupus erythematosus.
- Hydrochlorothiazide can cause potassium loss. Signs of potassium loss include dry mouth, thirst, weakness, muscle pain or cramps, nausea, and vomiting. If you experience any of these symptoms, it is important that you call your doctor. To help avoid potassium loss, take this medication with a glass of fresh or frozen orange or cranberry juice, or eat a banana every day. The use of a salt substitute also helps to prevent potassium loss. Do not change your diet or use a salt substitute, however, before discussing it with your doctor. Too much potassium can also be dangerous. Your doctor may want you to have blood tests performed periodically in order to monitor your potassium levels while you are being treated with this medication.
- To prevent dizziness and light-headedness, limit your intake of alcoholic beverages while taking this medication.
- Becoming overheated can be hazardous while you are taking this medication. Avoid strenuous exercise in hot weather and do not take hot baths, showers, or saunas.
- If you have high blood pressure, do not take any over-the-counter (nonprescription) medications for weight control or for allergy, asthma, cough, cold, or sinus problems unless your doctor directs you to do so.
- To prevent dehydration (severe water loss) while taking this drug, contact your doctor if you have an illness that causes severe or continuous nausea, vomiting, or diarrhea.
- This drug can raise blood sugar levels in people with diabetes. Therefore, blood sugar should be carefully monitored when this medication is being taken.
- Before having surgery or any other medical or dental treatment, be sure to tell your doctor or dentist that you are taking this medication.
- Be certain to inform your doctor if you are pregnant. Hydrochlorothiazide can cross the placenta and may cause adverse effects on the developing fetus. Also tell your doctor if you are breast-feeding an infant. Although problems in humans have not been reported, small amounts of this medication can pass into breast milk, so caution is warranted.

---

hydrocortisone, polymyxin B, and neomycin combination (otic)

BRAND NAMES (Manufacturers)
Cortatrigen Modified Ear Drops (Ivax)
Cortisporin Otic (Monarch)
hydrocortisone, polymyxin B, and neomycin (various manufacturers)
Otocort (Teva)

TYPE OF DRUG
Otic adrenocorticosteroid and antibiotic

INGREDIENTS
hydrocortisone, polymyxin B, and neomycin

DOSAGE FORMS
Otic solution (1% hydrocortisone, 10,000 units polymyxin B, and 5 mg neomycin sulfate per mL)
Otic suspension (1% hydrocortisone, 10,000 units polymyxin B, and 5 mg neomycin sulfate per mL)

STORAGE

Store at room temperature in tightly closed, light-resistant containers. Do not refrigerate or freeze.

USES

This medication is used to treat superficial bacterial infections of the outer ear. Your adrenal glands naturally produce certain cortisonelike chemicals. These chemicals are involved in various regulatory processes in the body (such as those involving fluid balance, temperature, and reaction to inflammation). Hydrocortisone belongs to a group of drugs known as adrenocorticosteroids (or cortisonelike medications). It is used to relieve inflammation (redness, swelling, itching, pain). Polymyxin B and neomycin are antibiotics, which act to prevent the growth and multiplication of the infecting bacteria.

TREATMENT

To warm the drops before administration, roll the bottle back and forth between your hands. DO NOT place the bottle in boiling water or expose to excess heat; high temperatures destroy the medication.

Before applying the suspension form of this medication, shake the bottle well to distribute the ingredients evenly and equalize the doses. The contents tend to settle on the bottom of the bottle.

For accuracy and to avoid contamination, another person should insert the eardrops if possible. To administer the eardrops, tilt the head to one side, with the affected ear turned upward. Grasp the earlobe and gently pull it upward and back to straighten the ear canal. (If administering eardrops to a child, gently pull the earlobe downward and back.) Fill the dropper and place the prescribed number of drops into the ear. Be careful not to touch the dropper to the ear canal, since the dropper can easily become contaminated. Keep the ear tilted upward for about five minutes. Your doctor may want you to put a piece of cotton soaked with the medication into your ear to keep the medicine from leaking back out. To avoid contamination, DO NOT wash or wipe the dropper after you use it.

If you miss a dose of this medication, administer it as soon as possible. However, if it is almost time for the next dose, don't use the missed dose at all; simply return to the regular dosing schedule.

It is important to continue to take this medication for the entire time prescribed by your doctor, even if the symptoms of infection disappear before the end of that period. If you stop using the drug too soon, resistant bacteria are given a chance to continue growing, and the infection could recur.

SIDE EFFECTS

Minor. Burning sensation upon application. The burning should disappear as your body adjusts to the medication.

Major. Tell your doctor about any side effects that are persistent or particularly bothersome. IT IS ESPECIALLY IMPORTANT TO TELL YOUR DOCTOR about itching, rash, redness, or swelling at the site of application.

INTERACTIONS

This medication should not interact with any other medications as long as it is used according to directions from your doctor or pharmacist.

WARNINGS

• Tell your doctor about unusual or allergic reactions you have had to medications, especially to hydrocortisone or any other adrenocorticosteroids (such as amcinonide, betamethasone, clocortolone, cortisone, desonide, desoximetasone, dexamethasone, diflorasone, flumethasone, fluocinolone, fluocinonide, fluorometholone, flurandrenolide, halcinonide, methylprednisolone, prednisolone, prednisone, and triamcinolone), to polymyxin B, or to neomycin or any related antibiotic (such as amikacin, colistimethate, colistin, gentamicin, kanamycin, netilmicin, paromycin, streptomycin, or tobramycin).

• Tell your doctor if you now have or ever had viral or fungal infections of the ear, a punctured eardrum, myasthenia gravis, or kidney disease.

• Do not use this medication for longer than ten consecutive days, unless your doctor directs you to do so. If there is no change in your condition within two or three days after you start treatment with this medication, contact your doctor. The medication may not be effective for the type of infection you have.

• This drug has been prescribed for your current infection only. Another infection later on, or one that someone else has, may require a different medicine. You should not give your medicine to other people or use it for other infections, unless your doctor directs you to do so.

• Be sure to tell your doctor if you are pregnant. If large amounts of hydrocortisone are applied for long periods, some will be absorbed and may cross the placenta. Studies in human pregnancy have not been conducted, but birth defects have been observed in the offspring of animals given large oral doses during pregnancy. Also tell your doctor if you are breast-feeding an infant. If absorbed through the skin, small amounts of the drug pass into breast milk and may cause growth suppression or a decrease in natural adrenocorticosteroid hormone production in the infant.

---

hydrocortisone, polymyxin B, neomycin, and bacitracin combination (ophthalmic)

BRAND NAMES (Manufacturers)

Cortisporin Ophthalmic (Monarch)
Triple Antibiotic with HC (various manufacturers)

TYPE OF DRUG

Ophthalmic adrenocorticosteroid and antibiotic

INGREDIENTS

hydrocortisone, polymyxin B, neomycin, and bacitracin* (*ointment only)

DOSAGE FORMS

Ophthalmic drops (1% hydrocortisone; 10,000 units polymyxin B; 0.5% neomycin; and 0.001% thimerosal per mL)
Ophthalmic ointment (1% hydrocortisone; 10,000 units polymyxin B; 0.5% neomycin; 400 units bacitracin)

STORAGE

Store at room temperature in tightly closed containers. Do not freeze. If the drops or ointment change color, do not use the medication. A change in color signifies that the drug has lost its therapeutic effectiveness.

USES

This medication is used for the short-term treatment of bacterial infections of the eyes.

Your adrenal glands naturally produce certain cortisonelike chemicals. These chemicals are involved in various regulatory processes in the body (such as those involving fluid balance, temperature, and reaction to inflammation). Hydrocortisone belongs to a group of drugs known as adrenocorticosteroids (or cortisonelike medications). It is used to relieve inflammation (redness, swelling, itching, and discomfort). How it does so is not completely understood.

Polymyxin B, neomycin, and bacitracin are antibiotics, which act to prevent the growth and multiplication of infecting bacteria. Thimerosal is a preservative.

TREATMENT

Wash your hands with soap and water before using this medication. If you are using the drops, shake the bottle well before measuring out the drops. The contents tend to settle on the bottom of the bottle, so it is necessary to shake the container to distribute the ingredients evenly and to equalize the doses.

To prevent contamination of the medicine, do not touch the tube portion of the dropper or let it touch the eye.

Note that the bottle of the eyedrops is not completely full. This is to allow control of the number of drops used when administering the medication.

To apply the drops, tilt your head back and pull down the lower eyelid with one hand to make a pouch below the eye. Drop the prescribed amount of medicine into the pouch and slowly close your eyes. Try not to blink. Keep your eyes closed, and place one finger at the corner of the eye next to your nose for a minute or two, applying a slight pressure (this is done to prevent loss of medication through the duct that drains fluid from the surface of the eye into the nose and throat). Then wipe away any excess with a clean tissue. If you don't think the medicine got into your eye, repeat the process once. If you are using more than one type of eyedrop, wait at least five minutes between doses of the two types of medication.

Follow the same general procedure for applying the ointment. Tilt your head back, pull down the lower eyelid, and squeeze the ointment in a line along the pouch below the eye. Close your eyes, and place your finger at the corner of the eye near the nose for a minute or two. Do not rub your eyes. Wipe off excess ointment. With a clean tissue, wipe the tip of the tube.

Since applying the medication is somewhat difficult to do, you may want someone else to apply it for you.

If you miss a dose of this medication, insert the drops or apply the ointment as soon as possible. However, if it is almost time for the next application, do not use the missed dose at all; just wait until the next scheduled dose.

It is important to continue to take this medication for the entire time prescribed by your doctor, even if the symptoms of infection disappear before the end of that period. If you stop applying the drug too soon, resistant bacteria are given a chance to continue growing, and the infection could recur.

SIDE EFFECTS

Minor. Blurred vision, burning, or stinging. These side effects should disappear as your body adjusts to the medication.

Major. Tell your doctor about any side effects that are persistent or particularly bothersome. IT IS ESPECIALLY IMPORTANT TO TELL YOUR DOCTOR about continued burning; disturbed or reduced vision, eye pain, itching, or swelling; headache; rash; or severe irritation.

INTERACTIONS

This medication should not interact with other medications as long as it is used according to the directions given to you by your doctor or pharmacist.

WARNINGS

• Tell your doctor about unusual or allergic reactions you have had to any medications, especially to hydrocortisone or other adrenocorticosteroids (such as amcinonide, betamethasone, clocortolone, cortisone, desonide, desoximetasone, dexamethasone, diflorasone, flumethasone, fluocinolone, fluorometholone, flurandrenolide, halcino-nide, methylprednisolone, prednisolone, prednisone, and triamcinolone) or to polymyxin B, neomycin, bacitracin, or any related antibiotic (amikacin, colistimethate, colistin, gentamicin, kanamycin, neomycin, netilmicin, paromycin, streptomycin, or tobramycin) or to thimerosal or other mercury compounds.

• Tell your doctor if you now have or have ever had fungal or viral infections of the eye, cataracts, glaucoma, inner ear disease, kidney disease, or myasthenia gravis.
• Tell your doctor if you wear contact lenses. Your doctor may suggest that you wear eyeglasses instead of contacts until the infection is gone.
• If there is no change in your condition within two or three days after you start taking this medication, contact your doctor. This medication may not be effective for the particular infection you have.
• Do not use this eye medication for longer than ten consecutive days, unless your doctor directs you to. Prolonged use of this medication may result in glaucoma, secondary infection, cataracts, or eye damage. If you need to take this medication for as long as six weeks, your doctor may want you to have an eye examination by an ophthalmologist.
• This medication has been prescribed for your current infection only. Another infection you develop later on, or one that a family member or friend has, may require a different medicine. You should not give your medicine to other people or use it for other infections, unless your doctor specifically directs you to do so.
• In order to allow your eye infection to clear, you should not apply makeup to the affected eye during treatment with this medication.
• Be sure to tell your doctor if you are pregnant. When large amounts of hydrocortisone are applied for prolonged periods, some of it is absorbed into the bloodstream. It may cross the placenta. Studies in human pregnancy have not been conducted, but birth defects have been observed in the offspring of animals that were given large oral doses of hydrocortisone during pregnancy. Also tell your doctor if you are breast-feeding. If absorbed through the skin, small amounts of hydrocortisone pass into breast milk and may cause growth suppression or a decrease in natural adrenocorticosteroid hormone production in the nursing infant.

---

hydrocortisone (topical)

BRAND NAMES (Manufacturers)
Acticort Lotion 100 (Baker Norton)
CaldeCort Anti-Itch* (Novartis Consumer)
Cetacort (Galderma)
Cortaid* (Pharmacia)
Cort-Dome* (Bayer)
Cortef* (Pharmacia)
Cortifoam* (Schwarz Pharma)
Cortizone* (Pfizer Consumer)
Dermacort (Solvay)
Hycort (Everett)
hydrocortisone acetate (various manufacturers)
Hytone (Dermik)
LactiCare-HC (Stiefel)
Lanacort* (Combe)
Proctocort (Solvay)
ProctoCream-HC (Schwarz Pharma)
Texacort (Rydelle)
Westcort (Westwood-Squibb)
*Available over the counter (without a prescription) in concentrations of 0.5% or less.

TYPE OF DRUG
Adrenocorticosteroid hormone

INGREDIENT
hydrocortisone

DOSAGE FORMS

Cream (0.1%, 0.2%, 0.25%, 0.5%, 1%, and 2.5%)
Ointment (0.1%, 0.2%, 0.5%, 1%, and 2.5%)
Lotion (0.25%, 0.5%, 1%, 2%, and 2.5%)
Gel (0.5% and 1%)
Pump spray (0.5% and 1%)
Aerosol (0.5%)

STORAGE

Store all forms at room temperature in tightly closed containers. Do not freeze.

The aerosol form is packaged under pressure. Do not store near heat or an open flame or in direct sunlight, and do not puncture the container.

USES

Your adrenal glands naturally produce certain cortisonelike chemicals. These chemicals are involved in various regulatory processes in the body (such as fluid balance, temperature, and reaction to inflammation). Hydrocortisone belongs to a group of drugs known as adrenocorticosteroids (or cortisonelike medications). It is used to relieve the skin inflammation (redness, swelling, itching, and discomfort) that is associated with conditions such as dermatitis, eczema, psoriasis, and poison ivy.

TREATMENT

Before applying this medication, wash your hands. Then, unless your doctor gives you different instructions, gently wash the area of the skin where the medication is to be applied. With a clean towel, pat the area almost dry; it should be slightly damp when you put the medicine on.

Apply a small amount of the medication to the affected area in a thin layer. Do not bandage the area unless your doctor tells you to do so. If you are to apply an occlusive dressing (such as kitchen plastic wrap), be sure that you understand the instructions for using it. Wash your hands again after application.

If you are using the aerosol form of this medication, shake the can well in order to disperse the medication evenly. Hold the can upright approximately six to eight inches from the area to be sprayed, and spray the area for one to three seconds. DO NOT SMOKE while you are using the aerosol; the contents of the can are under pressure and may explode if exposed to heat or flames.

If you miss a dose of this medication, apply the dose as soon as possible. However, if it is almost time for the next application, do not apply the missed dose at all; just return to your regular dosing schedule. Do not double the next dose of the medication.

SIDE EFFECTS

Minor. Acne, burning sensation, itching, rash, or skin dryness. These side effects should diminish or disappear as your body adjusts to the medication.

If the affected area is extremely dry or scaling, the skin may be moistened before applying the medication by soaking in water or by applying water with a clean cloth. The ointment form is probably most suitable for dry skin.

A mild stinging sensation may occur after this medication is applied. If this sensation persists, contact your doctor.

Major. Tell your doctor about any side effects that are persistent or particularly bothersome. IT IS ESPECIALLY IMPORTANT TO TELL YOUR DOCTOR about blistering, increased hair growth, irritation of the affected area, loss of skin color, secondary infection in the area being treated, or thinning of the skin with easy bruising.

INTERACTIONS

This medication should not interact with other medications as long as it is used according to the directions given to you by your doctor or pharmacist.

WARNINGS

- Tell your doctor about unusual or allergic reactions you have had to any medications, especially to hydrocortisone or other adrenocorticosteroids (such as amcinonide, betamethasone, clocortolone, cortisone, desonide, desoximetasone, dexamethasone, diflorasone, flumethasone, fluocinolone, fluocinonide, flurandrenolide, halcinonide, methylprednisolone, paramethasone, prednisolone, prednisone, and triamcinolone).
- Tell your doctor if you now have or ever had blood-vessel disease, cataracts, chicken pox, diabetes mellitus, fungal infections, glaucoma, shingles, skin atrophy (thinning of the skin), tuberculosis, or any other type of infection, especially at the site currently being treated.
- If any irritation develops while using hydrocortisone, immediately discontinue its use and notify your doctor.
- This product is not for use in the eyes, nose, or mouth; contact may result in side effects.
- Do not use this product with an occlusive wrap unless your doctor directs you to do so. Systemic absorption of hydrocortisone is increased if large areas of the body are treated, particularly if occlusive bandages are used. If it is necessary for you to use this drug under a wrap, follow your doctor's instructions exactly; do not leave the wrap in place longer than specified.
- If you are using this medication on a child's diaper area, do not put tight-fitting diapers or plastic pants on the child. This may lead to increased systemic absorption of the drug and a possible increase in side effects.
- To avoid freezing skin tissue when using the aerosol or pump spray form of hydrocortisone, make sure that you do not spray for more than three seconds; and hold the container at least six inches away from the skin as you spray.
- When using the aerosol or pump spray form of this medication near the face, cover your eyes, and do not inhale the spray (in order to avoid side effects).
- Be sure to tell your doctor if you are pregnant. If large amounts of this drug are applied for prolonged periods, some of it will be absorbed and may cross the placenta. Although studies in human pregnancy have not been conducted, birth defects have been observed in the offspring of animals that were given large oral doses of this drug during pregnancy. Also tell your doctor if you are breast-feeding an infant. If hydrocortisone is absorbed through the skin, small amounts of it are known to pass into breast milk and may cause growth suppression or a decrease in natural adrenocorticosteroid production in the nursing infant.

---

hydroxyzine

BRAND NAMES (Manufacturers)
Atarax (Pfizer)
hydroxyzine hydrochloride (various manufacturers)
hydroxyzine pamoate (various manufacturers)
Vistaril (Pfizer)

TYPE OF DRUG
Antihistamine and sedative/hypnotic

INGREDIENT
hydroxyzine

DOSAGE FORMS
Tablets (10 mg, 25 mg, 50 mg, and 100 mg)
Capsules (25 mg, 50 mg, and 100 mg)
Oral solution (10 mg per 5-mL spoonful, with 0.5% alcohol)
Oral suspension (25 mg per 5-mL spoonful)

STORAGE
Store all forms at room temperature in tightly closed, light-resistant containers. Do not freeze.

USES
Hydroxyzine belongs to a group of medications that are known as antihistamines (antihistamines block the action of histamine, which is a chemical that is released by the body during an allergic reaction). This medication is used to treat or prevent symptoms of allergy. It is also used as a sleeping aid and to relieve the symptoms of anxiety and tension.

TREATMENT
To avoid stomach upset, you can take hydroxyzine with food or with a full glass of milk or water (unless your doctor directs you to do otherwise).

Shake the oral suspension well just before measuring each dose to distribute the ingredients evenly and equalize the doses. Carefully measure each dose of the solution or suspension with a specially designed 5-mL measuring spoon. An ordinary kitchen teaspoon is not accurate enough for medical purposes.

If you miss a dose of this medication, take the missed dose as soon as possible. However, if it is almost time for your next dose, don't take the missed dose at all; just return to your regular dosing schedule. Do not double the next dose of this medication.

SIDE EFFECTS
Minor. Drowsiness or dry mouth. These side effects should disappear as your body gets accustomed to the medication.

Dry mouth can be relieved by chewing sugarless gum or by sucking on ice chips or a piece of hard candy.

Major. Tell your doctor about any side effects that are persistent or particularly bothersome. IT IS ESPECIALLY IMPORTANT TO TELL YOUR DOCTOR about convulsions, feeling faint, irritability, mental confusion, rash, or trembling or shakiness.

INTERACTIONS
Hydroxyzine can interact with other types of drugs: Concurrent use of it with other central nervous system depressants (such as alcohol, barbiturates, benzodiazepine tranquilizers, muscle relaxants, narcotics, pain medications, and phenothiazine tranquilizers) or with tricyclic antidepressants can cause extreme drowsiness.

BE SURE TO TELL YOUR DOCTOR about any medications that you are currently taking, especially any of the medications that are listed above.

WARNINGS
- Tell your doctor about allergic or unusual reactions you have had to drugs, especially to hydroxyzine or other antihistamines (such as azatadine, brompheniramine, carbinoxamine, chlorpheniramine, clemastine, cyproheptadine, dexchlorpheniramine, dimenhydrinate, dimethindene, diphenhydramine, diphenylpyraline, doxylamine, promethazine, pyrilamine, trimeprazine, tripelennamine, and triprolidine).
- Hydroxyzine can cause drowsiness or dizziness. Your ability to perform tasks that require alertness, such as driving an automobile or operating potentially dangerous machinery, may be decreased. Appropriate caution should, therefore, be taken.
- Elderly patients may be more sensitive to side effects, especially drowsiness, confusion, and irritability. Report any such effects to your doctor.
- Be sure to tell your doctor if you are pregnant. The effects of using this medication during pregnancy have not been thoroughly studied in humans. Also be sure to tell your doctor if you are breast-feeding an infant. Small amounts of hydroxyzine pass into breast milk.

ibuprofen

BRAND NAMES (Manufacturers)
Advil* (Whitehall-Robins)
Advil, Children's (Whitehall-Robins)
Bayer Select Pain Relief Formula* (Bayer)
Dynafed IB* (BDI)
Genpril* (Ivax)
Haltran* (Lee Pharmaceuticals)
ibuprofen* (various manufacturers)
Menadol* (Rugby)
Midol 200* (Glenbrook)
Motrin (Pharmacia)
Motrin IB* (McNeil CPC)
Nuprin* (Bristol-Myers Squibb)
Saleto* (Roberts Med)
*Available over the counter (without a prescription) as 200-mg tablets.

TYPE OF DRUG
Nonsteroidal anti-inflammatory analgesic

INGREDIENT
ibuprofen

DOSAGE FORMS
Caplets (100 mg)
Chewable tablets (50 mg and 100 mg)
Tablets (200 mg, 300 mg, 400 mg, 600 mg, and 800 mg)
Oral drops (40 mg per 1 mL)
Oral suspension (100 mg per 5-mL spoonful)

STORAGE
Store in a tightly closed, light-resistant container at room temperature. Do not freeze.

USES

Ibuprofen is used to treat the inflammation (pain, swelling, stiffness) of certain types of arthritis, gout, bursitis, and tendinitis. It is also used to treat painful menstruation and fever. Ibuprofen has been shown to block production of prostaglandins, which may trigger pain.

TREATMENT

If you are taking this medication for acute pain, take the first one or two doses on an empty stomach (30 to 60 minutes before meals or 2 hours after meals) so it gets into your bloodstream quickly. However, if you experience stomach irritation, take the medication with food or antacids.

Shake the suspension well just before measuring each dose to distribute the ingredients evenly and equalize the doses. The contents tend to settle on the bottom of the bottle. Measure each dose of the syrup or suspension carefully with a specially designed 5-mL measuring spoon. An ordinary kitchen teaspoon is not accurate enough. The oral drops should be measured only with the dropper supplied.

If you are taking ibuprofen to relieve arthritis, you must take it regularly as directed by your doctor. It may take up to two weeks before you feel the full effects of this medication. Ibuprofen does not cure arthritis, but it will help to control the condition as long as you continue to take it.

It is important to take ibuprofen on schedule and not to miss any doses. If you do miss a dose, take it as soon as possible. However, if it is almost time for your next dose, don't take the missed dose at all; just return to your regular dosing schedule. Do not double the next dose.

SIDE EFFECTS

Minor. Bloating, constipation, diarrhea, difficulty in sleeping, dizziness, drowsiness, headache, heartburn, indigestion, light-headedness, loss of appetite, nausea, nervousness, soreness of the mouth, unusual sweating, or vomiting. As your body adjusts to the drug, these side effects should disappear.

To relieve constipation, increase the amount of fiber in your diet (fresh fruits and vegetables, salads, bran, and whole-grain breads), exercise, and drink more water (unless your doctor directs you to do otherwise).

If you become dizzy or light-headed, sit or lie down for a while; get up slowly from a sitting or reclining position; and be careful on stairs.

Major. If you experience any side effects that are persistent or particularly bothersome, you should report them to your doctor. IT IS ESPECIALLY IMPORTANT TO TELL YOUR DOCTOR about bloody or black, tarry stools; blurred vision; confusion; depression; difficult or painful urination; palpitations; problems with hearing; ringing or buzzing in your ears; skin rash, hives, or itching; stomach pain; swelling of the feet; tightness in the chest; unexplained sore throat and fever; unusual bleeding or bruising; unusual fatigue or weakness; unusual weight gain; wheezing or difficulty in breathing; or yellowing of the eyes or skin.

INTERACTIONS

Ibuprofen interacts with several other types of medications:

1. Anticoagulants (blood thinners) used with ibuprofen can increase the risk of bleeding complications.

2. Aspirin, other salicylates, and other anti-inflammatory drugs can increase stomach irritation from ibuprofen. Aspirin may also decrease the effectiveness of ibuprofen.

3. Ibuprofen can interact with diuretics (water pills).

4. Probenecid may increase blood levels of ibuprofen, which may increase the risk of side effects.

5. The action of beta blockers may be decreased by the use of ibuprofen.

6. Do not take methotrexate with this drug. Ibuprofen may increase the amount of methotrexate in the body, increasing the risk of toxicity.

7. Ibuprofen may increase the amount of cyclosporine or lithium in the body, increasing the side effects of these medications.

BE SURE TO TELL YOUR DOCTOR about any medications you are currently taking, especially any listed above.

WARNINGS

• Before you start to take this medication, it is important to tell your doctor if you have ever had unusual or allergic reactions to ibuprofen or to any of the other chemically related medications, such as aspirin, other salicylates, diclofenac, diflunisal, etodolac, fenoprofen, flurbiprofen, indomethacin, ketoprofen, ketorolac, meclofenamate, mefenamic acid, nabumetone, naproxen, oxaprozin, oxyphenbutazone, phenylbutazone, piroxicam, sulindac, tenoxicam, tiaprofenic acid, or tolmetin.

• Tell your doctor if you now have or ever had bleeding problems, colitis, stomach ulcers or other stomach problems, epilepsy, heart disease, high blood pressure, asthma, kidney disease, liver disease, mental illness, or Parkinson's disease.

• If ibuprofen makes you dizzy or drowsy, do not take part in any activity that requires alertness.

• Because this drug can prolong bleeding time, tell your doctor or dentist you are taking this drug before having surgery or other medical or dental treatment.

• Stomach problems are more likely to occur if you take aspirin regularly or drink alcohol while being treated with this medication. These should, therefore, be avoided (unless your doctor directs you to do otherwise).

• The elderly may be at increased risk for experiencing side effects of this drug.

• Be sure to tell your doctor if you are pregnant. This type of medication can cause unwanted effects to the heart or blood flow of the fetus. Studies in animals have also shown that this type of medicine, if taken late in pregnancy, may increase the length of pregnancy, prolong labor, or cause other problems during delivery. Also be sure to tell your doctor if you are breast-feeding an infant. Small amounts of ibuprofen can pass into breast milk.

---

imipramine

BRAND NAMES (Manufacturers)
imipramine hydrochloride (various manufacturers)
Tofranil (Novartis)
Tofranil-PM (Novartis)
TYPE OF DRUG
Tricyclic antidepressant
INGREDIENT
imipramine
DOSAGE FORMS
Tablets (10 mg, 25 mg, and 50 mg)
Capsules (75 mg, 100 mg, 125 mg, and 150 mg)
STORAGE
Store at room temperature in a tightly closed container.

USES

Imipramine is used to relieve the symptoms of mental depression. This medication belongs to a group of drugs referred to as tricyclic antidepressants. These medicines are thought to relieve depression by increasing the concentration of certain chemicals necessary for nerve transmission in the brain. This medication is also used to treat enuresis (bed-wetting) in children 6 to 12 years of age.

TREATMENT

Take this medication exactly as your doctor prescribes. Imipramine can be taken with water or with food to lessen the chance of stomach irritation, unless your doctor directs you to do otherwise.

If you miss a dose of this medication, take the missed dose as soon as possible, then return to your regular dosing schedule. If the dose you missed was a once-a-day bedtime dose, do not take that dose in the morning; check with your doctor instead. If the dose is taken in the morning, it may cause unwanted side effects.

The effects of therapy with this medication may not become apparent for two or three weeks.

SIDE EFFECTS

Minor. Agitation, anxiety, blurred vision, confusion, constipation, cramps, diarrhea, dizziness, drowsiness, dry mouth, fatigue, heartburn, insomnia, loss of appetite, nausea, peculiar tastes in the mouth, restlessness, sweating, vomiting, weakness, or weight gain or loss. As your body adjusts to the medication, these side effects should disappear.

This drug may cause increased sensitivity to sunlight. Therefore, avoid prolonged exposure to sunlight and do not expose your skin to sunlamps. When you are outdoors during daylight hours, wear protective clothing, and use an effective sunscreen.

Dry mouth caused by therapy with this medication can be relieved by chewing sugarless gum or by sucking on ice chips or a piece of hard candy.

To relieve constipation, increase the amount of fiber in your diet (fresh fruits and vegetables, salads, bran, and whole-grain breads). You can also increase your exercise and drink more water (unless your doctor directs you to do otherwise).

To avoid dizziness or light-headedness when you stand, contract and relax the muscles of your legs for a few moments before rising. Do this by pushing one foot against the floor while raising the other foot slightly, alternating feet so that you are "pumping" your legs in a pedaling motion.

Major. Tell your doctor about any side effects that are persistent or particularly bothersome. IT IS ESPECIALLY IMPORTANT TO TELL YOUR DOCTOR about chest pains, convulsions, difficulty in urinating, enlarged or painful breasts (in both sexes), fainting, fever, fluid retention, hair loss, hallucinations, headaches, impotence, mood changes, mouth sores, nervousness, nightmares, numbness in the fingers or toes, palpitations, ringing in the ears, seizures, skin rash, sleep disorders, sore throat, tremors, uncoordinated movements or balance problems, unusual bleeding or bruising, or yellowing of the eyes or skin.

INTERACTIONS

Imipramine interacts with a number of other types of medications:

1. Extreme drowsiness can occur when this medicine is taken with central nervous system depressants (such as alcohol, antihistamines, barbiturates, benzodiazepine tranquilizers, muscle relaxants, narcotics, pain medications, phenothiazine tranquilizers, and sleeping medications) or with other tricyclic antidepressants.

2. Imipramine may decrease the effectiveness of antiseizure medications if taken concurrently with them. Imipramine may also possibly block the blood-pressure-lowering effects of clonidine and guanethidine.

3. Oral contraceptives (birth control pills) and drugs that contain estrogen can increase the side effects and reduce the effectiveness of the tricyclic antidepressants (including imipramine).

4. Cimetidine can decrease the breakdown of imipramine in the body, thus increasing the possibility of side effects.

5. Tricyclic antidepressants may increase the side effects of thyroid medication and of over-the-counter (nonprescription) cough, cold, allergy, asthma, sinus, and diet medications.

6. The concurrent use of tricyclic antidepressants and monoamine oxidase (MAO) inhibitors should be avoided because the combination may result in fever, convulsions, or high blood pressure. At least 14 days should separate the use of this drug and the use of an MAO inhibitor.

BE SURE TO TELL YOUR DOCTOR about any medications you are currently taking, especially any of those mentioned above.

WARNINGS

• Tell your doctor if you have had unusual or allergic reactions to any medications, especially to imipramine or any of the other tricyclic antidepressants (such as amitriptyline, doxepin, trimipramine, amoxapine, protriptyline, desipramine, maprotiline, and nortriptyline).

• Tell your doctor if you have a history of alcoholism or if you have ever had asthma, high blood pressure, liver or kidney disease, heart disease, a heart attack, circulatory disease, stomach problems, intestinal problems, difficulty in urinating, enlarged prostate gland, epilepsy, glaucoma, thyroid disease, mental illness, or electroshock therapy.

• If imipramine makes you dizzy or drowsy, do not take part in any activity that requires alertness, such as driving a car or operating potentially dangerous machinery.

• Before having surgery or any other medical or dental treatment, tell your doctor or dentist you are taking this drug.

• Do not stop taking this drug suddenly. Stopping it abruptly can cause nausea, headache, stomach upset, fatigue, or a worsening of your condition. Your doctor may want to reduce the dosage gradually.

• The effects of this medication may last as long as seven days after you stop taking it, so continue to observe all precautions during that period.

• Some of these products contain the color additive FD&C Yellow No. 5 (tartrazine), which can cause allergic-type reactions (skin rash, fainting, difficulty in breathing) in certain susceptible individuals.
• The elderly may be at increased risk for experiencing side effects. Report any such effects, especially dizziness, drowsiness, dry mouth, difficulty urinating, or mental confusion, to your doctor.
• Be sure to tell your doctor if you are pregnant. Adverse effects have been observed in the fetuses of animals that were given large doses of this drug during pregnancy. Also be sure that you tell your doctor if you are breast-feeding an infant. Small amounts of the drug can pass into breast milk and may cause unwanted effects in nursing infants.

---

indinavir

BRAND NAME (Manufacturer)
Crixivan (Merck & Co)
TYPE OF DRUG
Antiviral
INGREDIENT
indinavir
DOSAGE FORM
Capsules (200 mg and 400 mg)
STORAGE
Store at room temperature in a tightly closed, light-resistant container. Do not expose to excess heat or humidity. Moisture may cause indinavir to break down. Do not store medication in the bathroom.

USES

Indinavir is used in the treatment of human immunodeficiency virus (HIV) infection. HIV is the virus that causes AIDS. Indinavir works by inhibiting the reproduction, or growth, of the virus, which slows down the progression of AIDS. Indinavir does not cure HIV infection or AIDS, but it may delay the onset of other infections and diseases caused by AIDS. Indinavir is usually not used alone, but rather in combination with other anti-AIDS medications. These combinations have been shown to make the AIDS virus undetectable in the body.

TREATMENT

This medication works best when the level of medicine in your bloodstream is kept constant. It is best to take the drug at evenly spaced intervals throughout the day. IT IS IMPORTANT NOT TO MISS ANY DOSES OF INDINAVIR. The chances of the AIDS virus becoming resistant to indinavir increase if the level of medication in the bloodstream is low.

If you do miss a dose of this medication, take it as soon as possible. However, if it is almost time for your next dose, skip the missed dose and go back to your regular dosing schedule. Do not double the dose.

Since a meal high in calories, fat, and protein reduces the absorption of this medication, indinavir should be taken with water one hour before or two hours after a heavy meal. Alternatively, it can be taken with a full glass of skim milk, juice, coffee, or tea or with only a light meal. Be sure to discuss with your doctor the appropriate way for you to time and take this medication.

SIDE EFFECTS

Minor. Changes in taste, diarrhea, dizziness, general weak feeling, headache, insomnia or difficulty sleeping, nausea, sleepiness, stomach pain, or vomiting. As your body adjusts to the medication, some of these side effects should diminish or disappear.

To avoid dizziness or light-headedness when you stand, contract and relax the muscles of your legs for a few moments before rising.
Major. Tell your doctor about any side effects that are persistent or particularly bothersome. IT IS ESPECIALLY IMPORTANT TO TELL YOUR DOCTOR about blood in the urine, confusion, dry or itching skin, fat formation on the upper back, fatigue, fruity or unusual mouth odor, increased hunger or thirst, increased urination, sharp back pain just below the ribs, unusual weight loss or fat loss from the face or arms and legs, or vomiting.

INTERACTIONS

Indinavir may interact with a number of other drugs:
1. Indinavir may increase the serious side effects of alprazolam, midazolam, or triazolam if taken concurrently with it.
2. Didanosine may interfere with the absorption of indinavir. These medications should be taken at least one hour apart.
3. Rifampin and grapefruit juice may reduce the effectiveness of indinavir.
4. Clarithromycin, fluconazole, ketoconazole, itraconazole, and rifabutin may increase the amount of indinavir in the body.
5. Indinavir may increase the effects of rifabutin.

WARNINGS

• A small number of patients taking indinavir have developed kidney stones. It is important to drink plenty of water or liquid (about 48 ounces) throughout the day while taking this medication. IF YOU DEVELOP LOW BACK PAIN OR HAVE BLOOD IN THE URINE WHILE TAKING INDINAVIR, CONTACT YOUR DOCTOR.
• Tell your doctor if you have ever had an allergic reaction to any medication, especially to indinavir, ritonavir, nelfinavir, saquinavir, or other drugs used to treat AIDS.
• This medication may cause high blood sugar (or diabetes). Your doctor may want you to check your blood sugar regularly while taking indinavir. Ask your doctor about the signs of high blood sugar and diabetes.
• Your doctor may do regular blood tests to check your cholesterol. Increases in cholesterol may occur with indinavir.
• This medication may cause the fat in your body to be redistributed. There may be a loss of fat from the face, buttocks, arms, and legs and an increase in fatty tissue on the upper back.
• Before taking this medication, be sure to tell your doctor about any medical problems you may have, especially liver problems, diabetes or problems with high blood sugar, high cholesterol, kidney stones, or bleeding problems, especially hemophilia.
• Before having surgery or any medical or dental treatment, be sure to tell your doctor or dentist that you are taking this medication.
• Your doctor may do regular blood tests to see how well this medication is working against the AIDS virus.
• This medication may cause dizziness. You may have a decreased ability to perform tasks that require alertness, such as driving a car or operating heavy machinery. Appropriate caution should be taken.
• Be sure to tell your doctor about any other medications you are taking, both prescription and nonprescription. Indinavir may interact with other medications to produce serious side effects.
• If you are infected with HIV, it is best to avoid any sexual activity involving an exchange of body fluids with other people. If you do have vaginal, anal, or oral sex, always use a latex condom.
• Be sure to tell your doctor if you are pregnant. It is not known if indinavir is safe to use during pregnancy. It is not known if indinavir passes into human breast milk. However, because of the risk of passing HIV to infants, it is recommended that mothers who have HIV infection NOT breast-feed their infants.

insulin

BRAND NAMES (Manufacturers)
Humulin L (Lilly)
Humulin N (Lilly)
Humulin R (Lilly)
Humulin U (Lilly)
Iletin II (Lilly)
Novolin (Novo Nordisk)
Novolin L (Novo Nordisk)
Novolin N (Novo Nordisk)
Novolin R (Novo Nordisk)
Velosulin (Novo Nordisk)
TYPE OF DRUG
Antidiabetic
INGREDIENT
insulin
DOSAGE FORMS
Injectable (all types) (100 units/mL)
Injectable (regular) (500 units/mL)
STORAGE
After opening, keep most forms (except 500 units/mL strength) at room temperature if used within one month. Refrigerate unopened vials of insulin, but never freeze this medication. This medicine should not be exposed to extreme temperatures or direct sunlight.

USES

Insulin is a hormone that is normally produced by the pancreas; it functions in the regulation of blood sugar levels. This medication is used to treat diabetes mellitus (sugar diabetes), a disorder that results from an inability of the pancreas to produce enough insulin. Injectable insulin is used only to treat those patients whose blood sugar levels cannot be controlled by diet and/or by oral antidiabetic medications.

TREATMENT

Your doctor, nurse, dietitian, or pharmacist will show you how to inject insulin, using a specially marked hypodermic syringe. This medication is packaged with printed instructions that should be carefully followed.

Make sure that the insulin you are using is exactly the kind your doctor ordered and that its expiration date has not passed.

Do not shake the bottle; tip it gently, end to end, to mix. ALWAYS CHECK THE DOSE in the syringe at least twice before injecting it.

Clean the site of the injection thoroughly with an antiseptic, such as rubbing alcohol, before giving yourself the shot.

Change the site of the injection daily, and avoid injecting cold insulin.

NEVER use a vial of insulin if there are lumps in it.

Make your injection a regular part of your schedule, so you do not miss any doses. Ask your doctor what to do if you have to take a dose later than the scheduled time.

SIDE EFFECTS

Minor. Insulin can cause redness and rash at the site of injection. Therefore, you should try to rotate injection sites in order to avoid this reaction.
Major. Be sure to tell your doctor about any side effects that are persistent or particularly bothersome. IT IS ESPECIALLY IMPORTANT TO TELL YOUR DOCTOR about fainting, palpitations, shortness of breath, skin rash, or sweating.

Too much insulin can cause hypoglycemia (low blood sugar), which can lead to anxiety, chills, cold sweats, drowsiness, fast heart rate, headache, loss of consciousness, nausea, nervousness, tremors, unusual hunger, or unusual weakness. If you experience these symptoms, you should eat a quick source of sugar (such as table sugar, orange juice, honey, or a nondiet cola). You should also make it a point to tell your doctor that you have had this reaction.

Too little insulin can cause symptoms of hyperglycemia (high blood sugar), such as confusion, drowsiness, dry skin, fatigue, flushing, frequent urination, fruitlike breath odor, loss of appetite, or rapid breathing. If you experience any of these symptoms, contact your doctor; he or she may want to modify your dosing schedule or change your insulin dosage.

INTERACTIONS

Insulin can be expected to interact with several other types of medications:

1. Oral contraceptives (birth control pills), adrenocorticosteroids (cortisonelike medicines), danazol, dextrothyroxine, furosemide, thyroid hormone, thiazide diuretics (water pills), phenothiazine, phenytoin, or nicotine (from smoking) can increase insulin requirements.

2. Monoamine oxidase (MAO) inhibitors, nonsteroidal anti-inflammatory drugs (NSAIDs), lithium, angiotensin converting enzyme (ACE) inhibitors, clofibrate, ketoconazole, guanethidine, disopyramide, sulfinpyrazone, tetracycline, alcohol, anabolic steroids, or large doses of aspirin can increase the effects of insulin, leading to hypoglycemia.

3. Beta blockers (acebutolol, atenolol, betaxolol, carteolol, esmolol, labetalol, metoprolol, nadolol, penbutolol, pindolol, propranolol, timolol) may prolong the effects of insulin and mask the signs of hypoglycemia.

BE SURE TO TELL YOUR DOCTOR about any medications you are currently taking, especially any of the medications listed above.

WARNINGS

- Tell your doctor about unusual or allergic reactions you have had to any medications, especially to insulin.
- Before starting to take this medication, be sure to tell your doctor if you now have or if you have ever had high fevers, infections, kidney disease, liver disease, thyroid disease, or severe nausea and vomiting.
- If your doctor prescribes two types of insulin to achieve better glucose control and recommends mixing the insulin into one syringe, always draw the regular insulin (clear) into the syringe first.
- Some insulin mixtures won't interact with each other for some time. Others react quickly and require immediate injection. Consult your doctor or pharmacist.
- Make sure that your friends and family are aware of the symptoms of an insulin reaction and know what to do should they observe any of the symptoms in you.
- Carry a card or wear a bracelet that identifies you as someone who has diabetes.
- Always have insulin and syringes available.
- When traveling, always carry an ample supply of your diabetic needs and, if possible, a prescription for insulin and syringes. Carry insulin and syringes on your person; baggage can be lost, delayed, or stolen.
- Do not store insulin in your car's glove compartment.
- To avoid the possibility of hypoglycemia (low blood sugar levels), eat on a regular schedule and avoid skipping meals.
- Before having surgery or other medical or dental treatment, tell your doctor or dentist you are taking insulin.
- Check with your doctor or pharmacist before taking any over-the-counter (nonprescription) cough, cold, diet, allergy, asthma, or sinus medications. Some of these products affect blood sugar levels.

• If you become ill, it is possible your insulin requirements may change. Consult your doctor under such circumstances.
• Be sure to tell your doctor if you are pregnant. Insulin dosing requirements often change during pregnancy.

---

insulin aspart

BRAND NAME (Manufacturer)
Novolog (Novo Nordisk)
TYPE OF DRUG
Antidiabetic
INGREDIENT
insulin aspart
DOSAGE FORM
Injectable (100 units/mL vials and cartridges for disposable pens)
STORAGE
Store in the refrigerator, and protect from light. Do not use insulin aspart that has been frozen or exposed to warm temperatures (above 86 degrees Fahrenheit). Any unused insulin should be discarded after the expiration date that is printed on the vial or cartridge.

If refrigeration is not possible, insulin aspart may be stored at room temperature (less than 86 degrees Fahrenheit) for up to 28 days. After 28 days, discard any unused portion. If you are using the cartridge form, the cartridge you are currently using should be stored outside of the refrigerator in a cool place. Discard any unused portion of the cartridge after 28 days.

USES

Insulin is a hormone that is normally produced by the pancreas; it functions in the regulation of blood sugar levels. Insulin aspart is a short-acting human insulin that has undergone small changes in its chemical structure. It is sometimes called an insulin analog. These changes affect the way the insulin is absorbed after it is injected under the skin, making it enter the bloodstream faster than regular human insulin. Insulin aspart is used to treat diabetes mellitus (sugar diabetes), a disorder resulting from an inability of the pancreas to produce enough insulin. Injectable insulin is used only to treat those patients whose blood sugar levels cannot be controlled by diet and/or by oral antidiabetic medications.

TREATMENT

Insulin aspart is given by injection under the skin (subcutaneously). It acts faster than regular insulin and needs to be given just before meals (five to ten minutes). Your doctor, nurse, dietitian, or pharmacist will show you how to inject insulin aspart, using a specially marked hypodermic syringe. This medication is packaged with printed instructions that should be carefully followed.

Make sure that the insulin you are using is exactly the kind that your doctor prescribed for you and that its expiration date has not passed.

ALWAYS CHECK THE DOSE in the syringe at least twice before injecting it.

Clean the site of the injection thoroughly with an antiseptic, such as rubbing alcohol, before giving yourself the shot.

Change the site of the injection daily, and avoid injecting cold insulin aspart.

NEVER use a vial of insulin aspart if there are any particles floating in the vial or if the solution is not clear.

Make your injection a regular part of your daily schedule so that you do not miss any doses. Be sure to ask your doctor what to do if you ever have to take a dose later than the scheduled time.

SIDE EFFECTS

Minor. Insulin aspart can cause redness and rash at the site of injection. Try to rotate injection sites to avoid this reaction.

Major. Tell your doctor about any side effects that are persistent or particularly bothersome. IT IS ESPECIALLY IMPORTANT TO TELL YOUR DOCTOR about palpitations, fainting, shortness of breath, skin rash, or sweating.

Too much insulin aspart can cause hypoglycemia (low blood sugar), which can lead to anxiety, chills, cold sweats, drowsiness, fast heart rate, headache, loss of consciousness, nausea, nervousness, tremors, unusual hunger, or unusual weakness. If you experience these symptoms, eat a quick source of sugar (such as table sugar, orange juice, honey, or a nondiet cola). You should also make it a point to tell your doctor that you have had this reaction.

INTERACTIONS

Insulin aspart can be expected to interact with several other types of medications:

1. Use of albuterol, oral contraceptives (birth control pills), adrenocorticosteroids (cortisonelike medicines), danazol, dextrothyroxine, furosemide, thyroid hormone, thiazide diuretics (water pills), phenothiazine, phenytoin, protease inhibitors (such as indinavir or ritonavir), or nicotine (from smoking) can increase insulin aspart requirements.

2. Monoamine oxidase (MAO) inhibitors, nonsteroidal anti-inflammatory agents, angiotensin converting enzyme (ACE) inhibitors, clofibrate, clonidine, fluoxetine, ketoconazole, guanethidine, disopyramide, sulfinpyrazone, tetracycline, alcohol, anabolic steroids, or large doses of aspirin can increase the effects of insulin aspart, leading to hypoglycemia.

3. Beta blockers (acebutolol, atenolol, betaxolol, carteolol, esmolol, labetalol, metoprolol, nadolol, penbutolol, pindolol, propranolol, timolol) may mask the signs of hypoglycemia.

4. Lithium may either increase or decrease the effects of insulin aspart.

BE SURE TO TELL YOUR DOCTOR about any medications you are currently taking, especially any of the medications listed above.

WARNINGS

• Tell your doctor about unusual or allergic reactions you have had to any medications, especially to insulin aspart or any other types of insulin.

• Too little insulin can cause symptoms of hyperglycemia (high blood sugar), such as confusion, drowsiness, dry skin, fatigue, flushing, frequent urination, fruitlike breath odor, loss of appetite, or rapid breathing. If you experience any of these symptoms, contact your doctor; he or she may want to modify your dosing schedule or change your insulin dosage.

• Before starting to take this medication, be sure to tell your doctor if you now have or ever had high fevers, infections, kidney disease, liver disease, thyroid disease, or severe nausea and vomiting.

• If your doctor prescribes another, longer acting insulin with insulin aspart to achieve better glucose control and recommends mixing the insulins into one syringe, always draw the insulin aspart into the syringe first. The mixed insulins should be used immediately.

• Make sure that your friends and family are aware of the symptoms of an insulin reaction and know what to do should they observe any of the symptoms in you.

• Carry a card or wear a bracelet or pendant that identifies you as someone who has diabetes.

• Always have insulin and syringes available.

• When traveling, always carry an ample supply of your diabetic needs and, if possible, a prescription for insulin and syringes. Carry insulin and syringes on your person; baggage can be lost, delayed, or stolen.

• Do not store insulin aspart in your automobile's glove compartment.
• To avoid the possibility of hypoglycemia (low blood sugar levels), eat on a regular schedule and avoid skipping meals.
• Before having surgery or other medical or dental treatment, tell your doctor or dentist you are taking insulin aspart or any other types of insulin.
• Check with your doctor or pharmacist before taking any over-the-counter (nonprescription) cough, cold, diet, allergy, asthma, or sinus medications. Some of these products affect blood sugar levels.
• If you become ill, your insulin aspart requirements may change. Consult your doctor under such circumstances.
• Be sure to tell your doctor if you are pregnant. Insulin aspart dosing requirements often change during pregnancy.

---

insulin glargine

BRAND NAME (Manufacturer)
Lantus (Aventis)
TYPE OF DRUG
Antidiabetic
INGREDIENT
insulin glargine
DOSAGE FORM
Injectable (100 units/mL vials and cartridges for disposable pens)
STORAGE
Store in the refrigerator and protect from light. Do not use insulin glargine that has been frozen or exposed to warm temperatures (over 86 degrees Fahrenheit). Any unused insulin glargine should be discarded after the expiration date printed on the vial or the cartridge.

If refrigeration is not possible, the 10 mL vial or cartridge of insulin glargine may be stored at room temperature (less than 86 degrees) for up to 28 days. After 28 days, discard any unused portion, whether it has been kept at room temperature or in the refrigerator. The 5 mL vial of insulin glargine may be stored at room temperature (less than 86 degrees) for up to 14 days. After 14 days, discard any unused portion. If kept in the refrigerator, discard the 5 mL vial 28 days after opening.

If you are using the cartridge form of insulin glargine, once a cartridge has been placed in the delivery device, it should be kept at room temperature (less than 86 degrees). Discard any unused portion after 28 days.

USES

Insulin is a hormone that is normally produced by the pancreas; it functions in the regulation of blood sugar levels. Insulin glargine is a long-acting human insulin that has undergone small changes in its chemical structure. It is sometimes called an insulin analog. These changes affect the way the insulin is absorbed after it is injected under the skin, making it get into the bloodstream at a more even rate than other long-acting human insulins. Most long-acting human insulins have a "peak," or high concentration, in the bloodstream shortly after injection. The amount of insulin in the body then slowly falls. Insulin glargine is more slowly absorbed into the bloodstream, resulting in a more constant level of insulin in the blood. In some patients, insulin glargine may stay in the bloodstream longer than other long-acting insulins, giving better control of blood sugar.

Insulin glargine is used to treat diabetes mellitus (sugar diabetes), a disorder that results from an inability of the pancreas to produce enough insulin. Injectable insulin is used only to treat those patients whose blood sugar levels cannot be controlled by diet and/or by oral antidiabetic medications.

TREATMENT

Insulin glargine is given by injection under the skin (subcutaneously). Insulin glargine is usually given once a day to keep blood sugar levels from getting too high. Your doctor, nurse, dietitian, or pharmacist will show you how to inject insulin glargine, using a specially marked hypodermic syringe. This medication is packaged with printed instructions that should be carefully followed.

Make sure that the insulin you are using is exactly the kind your doctor ordered and that its expiration date has not passed. ALWAYS CHECK THE DOSE in the syringe at least twice before injecting it.

Clean the site of the injection thoroughly with an antiseptic, such as rubbing alcohol, before giving yourself the shot.

Change the site of the injection daily, and avoid injecting cold insulin glargine.

NEVER use a vial of insulin glargine if there are any particles floating in the vial or if the solution is not clear.

Make your injection a regular part of your schedule, so that you do not miss any doses. Ask your doctor what to do if you ever have to take a dose later than the scheduled time.

Insulin glargine should NEVER be mixed with other insulins or diluted. Mixing or diluting insulin glargine may result in a loss of control of your blood sugar.

SIDE EFFECTS

Minor. Insulin glargine can cause redness and rash at the site of injection. You should try to rotate injection sites to avoid this reaction.

Major. Be sure to tell your doctor about any side effects that are persistent or particularly bothersome, IT IS ESPECIALLY IMPORTANT TO TELL YOUR DOCTOR about fainting, palpitations, shortness of breath, skin rash, or sweating.

Too much insulin glargine can cause hypoglycemia (low blood sugar), which can lead to anxiety, chills, cold sweats, drowsiness, fast heart rate, headache, loss of consciousness, nausea, nervousness, tremors, unusual hunger, or unusual weakness. If you experience these symptoms, you should eat a quick source of sugar (such as table sugar, orange juice, honey, or a nondiet cola). You should also make it a point to tell your doctor that you have had this reaction.

INTERACTIONS

Insulin glargine can be expected to interact with several other types of medications:

1. Albuterol, oral contraceptive medications (birth control pills), adrenocorticosteroids (cortisonelike medicines), danazol, dextrothyroxine, furosemide, thyroid hormone, thiazide diuretics (water pills), phenothiazine, phenytoin, protease inhibitors (such as ritonavir or indinavir), or nicotine (from smoking) can increase insulin glargine requirements.

2. Monoamine oxidase (MAO) inhibitors, nonsteroidal anti-inflammatory drugs (NSAIDs), angiotensin converting enzyme (ACE) inhibitors, clofibrate, clonidine, fluoxetine, ketoconazole, guanethidine, disopyramide, sulfinpyrazone, tetracycline, alcohol, anabolic steroids, or large doses of aspirin can increase the effects of insulin glargine, leading to hypoglycemia.

3. Beta blockers (acebutolol, atenolol, betaxolol, carteolol, esmolol, labetalol, metoprolol, nadolol, penbutolol, pindolol, propranolol, timolol) may mask the signs of hypoglycemia.

4. Lithium may either increase or decrease the effects of insulin glargine.

BE SURE TO TELL YOUR DOCTOR about any medications you are currently taking, especially any of those listed above.

WARNINGS

• Tell your doctor about unusual or allergic reactions you have had to any medications, especially to insulin glargine or any other types of insulin.

• Too little insulin can cause symptoms of hyperglycemia (high blood sugar), such as confusion, drowsiness, dry skin, fatigue, flushing, frequent urination, fruitlike breath odor, loss of appetite, or rapid breathing. If you experience any of these symptoms, contact your doctor; he or she may want to modify your dosing schedule or change your insulin dosage.
• Before starting to take this medication, be sure to tell your doctor if you now have or ever had high fevers, infections, kidney disease, liver disease, thyroid disease, or severe nausea and vomiting.
• Make sure that your friends and family are aware of the symptoms of an insulin reaction and know what to do should they observe any of the symptoms in you.
• Carry a card or wear a bracelet that identifies you as someone who has diabetes.
• Always have insulin and syringes available.
• When traveling, always carry an ample supply of your diabetic needs and, if possible, a prescription for insulin and syringes. Carry insulin and syringes on your person; baggage can be lost, delayed, or stolen.
• Do not store insulin glargine in your automobile's glove compartment.
• To avoid the possibility of hypoglycemia (low blood sugar levels), eat on a regular schedule and avoid skipping meals.
• Before having surgery or any other medical or dental treatment, tell your doctor or dentist you are taking insulin glargine or any other types of insulin.
• Check with your doctor or pharmacist before taking any over-the-counter (nonprescription) cough, cold, diet, allergy, asthma, or sinus medications. Some of these products affect blood sugar levels.
• If you become ill, your insulin glargine requirements may change. Consult your doctor under such circumstances.
• Be sure to tell your doctor if you are pregnant. Insulin glargine dosing requirements often change during pregnancy.

---

insulin lispro

BRAND NAME (Manufacturer)
Humalog (Lilly)
TYPE OF DRUG
Antidiabetic
INGREDIENT
insulin lispro
DOSAGE FORM
Injectable (100 units/mL vials and cartridges for disposable pens)
STORAGE
Store in the refrigerator and protect from light. Do not use insulin lispro that has been frozen or exposed to temperatures above 86 degrees Fahrenheit. Discard any unused insulin after the expiration date on the vial or cartridge.

If refrigeration is not possible, insulin lispro may be stored at room temperature (less than 86 degrees) for up to 28 days. After 28 days, discard any unused portion. If you are using the cartridge form, store the cartridge you are currently using outside of the refrigerator in a cool place. Discard any unused portion of the cartridge after 28 days.

USES

Insulin is a hormone that is normally produced by the pancreas; it functions in the regulation of blood sugar levels. Insulin lispro is a short-acting human insulin that has undergone small changes in its chemical structure. It is sometimes called an insulin analog. These changes affect the way the insulin is absorbed after it is injected under the skin, making it enter the bloodstream faster than regular human insulin. Insulin lispro is used to treat diabetes mellitus (sugar diabetes), a disorder that results from an inability of the pancreas to produce enough insulin. Injectable insulin is used only to treat those patients whose blood sugar levels cannot be controlled by diet or by oral antidiabetic medications.

TREATMENT

Insulin lispro is given by injection under the skin (subcutaneously). Insulin lispro acts faster than regular insulin and needs to be given just before meals (within 15 minutes). Your doctor, nurse, dietitian, or pharmacist will show you how to inject insulin lispro using a specially marked hypodermic syringe. This medication is packaged with printed instructions that should be carefully followed.

Make sure that the insulin you are using is exactly the kind your doctor ordered and that its expiration date has not passed.

ALWAYS CHECK THE DOSE in the syringe at least twice before injecting it.

Clean the site of the injection thoroughly with an antiseptic, such as rubbing alcohol, before giving yourself the shot.

Change the site of the injection daily, and avoid injecting cold insulin lispro.

NEVER use a vial of insulin lispro if there are any particles floating in the vial or if the solution is not clear.

Make your injection a regular part of your schedule, so that you do not miss any doses. Ask your doctor what to do if you ever have to take a dose later than the scheduled time.

SIDE EFFECTS

Minor. Insulin lispro can cause redness and rash at the site of injection. Try to rotate injection sites in order to avoid this reaction.

Major. Be sure to tell your doctor about any side effects that are persistent or particularly bothersome. IT IS ESPECIALLY IMPORTANT TO TELL YOUR DOCTOR about fainting, palpitations, shortness of breath, skin rash, or sweating.

Too much insulin lispro can cause hypoglycemia (low blood sugar), which can lead to anxiety, chills, cold sweats, drowsiness, fast heart rate, headache, loss of consciousness, nausea, nervousness, tremors, unusual hunger, or unusual weakness. If you experience these symptoms, eat a quick source of sugar (such as table sugar, orange juice, honey, or a nondiet cola). You should also make it a point to tell your doctor that you have had this reaction.

INTERACTIONS

Insulin lispro can be expected to interact with several other types of medications:

1. Albuterol, oral contraceptives (birth control pills), adrenocorticosteroids (cortisonelike medicines), danazol, dextrothyroxine, furosemide, thyroid hormone, thiazide diuretics (water pills), phenothiazine, phenytoin, protease inhibitors (such as ritonavir or indinavir), or nicotine (from smoking) can increase insulin lispro requirements.

2. Monoamine oxidase (MAO) inhibitors, nonsteroidal anti-inflammatory drugs (NSAIDs), angiotensin converting enzyme (ACE) inhibitors, clofibrate, clonidine, fluoxetine, ketoconazole, guanethidine, disopyramide, sulfinpyrazone, tetracycline, alcohol, anabolic steroids, or large doses of aspirin can increase the effects of insulin lispro, leading to hypoglycemia.

3. Beta blockers (acebutolol, atenolol, betaxolol, carteolol, esmolol, labetalol, metoprolol, nadolol, penbutolol, pindolol, propranolol, timolol) may mask the signs of hypoglycemia.

4. Lithium may either increase or decrease the effects of insulin lispro.

BE SURE TO TELL YOUR DOCTOR about any medications you are currently taking, especially any of the medications listed above.

WARNINGS

• Tell your doctor about unusual or allergic reactions you have had to any medications, especially to insulin lispro or any other types of insulin.
• Too little insulin can cause symptoms of hyperglycemia (high blood sugar), such as confusion, drowsiness, dry skin, fatigue, flushing, frequent urination, fruitlike breath odor, loss of appetite, or rapid breathing. If you experience any of these symptoms, contact your doctor; he or she may want to modify your dosing schedule or change your insulin dosage.
• Before starting to take this medication, be sure to tell your doctor if you now have or ever had high fevers, infections, kidney disease, liver disease, thyroid disease, or severe nausea and vomiting.
• If your doctor prescribes another, longer acting insulin with insulin lispro to achieve better glucose control and recommends mixing the insulins into one syringe, always draw the insulin lispro into the syringe first. The mixed insulins should be injected immediately.
• Make sure that your friends and family are aware of the symptoms of an insulin reaction and know what to do should they observe any of the symptoms in you.
• Carry a card or wear a bracelet that identifies you as someone who has diabetes.
• Always have insulin and syringes available.
• When traveling, always carry an ample supply of your diabetic needs and, if possible, a prescription for insulin and syringes. Carry insulin and syringes on your person; baggage can be lost, delayed, or stolen.
• Do not store insulin lispro in your car's glove compartment.
• To avoid the possibility of hypoglycemia (low blood sugar levels), be sure to eat on a regular schedule and avoid skipping meals.
• Before having surgery or other medical or dental treatment, tell your doctor or dentist you are taking insulin lispro or any other types of insulin.
• Check with your doctor or pharmacist before taking any over-the-counter (nonprescription) cough, cold, diet, allergy, asthma, or sinus medications. Some of these products affect blood sugar levels.
• If you become ill, your insulin lispro requirements may change. Consult your doctor under such circumstances.
• Be sure to tell your doctor if you are pregnant. Insulin lispro dosing requirements often change during pregnancy.

---

ipecac

BRAND NAME (Manufacturer)
ipecac* (various manufacturers)
*Available over the counter (without a prescription)
TYPE OF DRUG
Emetic
INGREDIENT
ipecac
DOSAGE FORM
Oral syrup (with 1% or 2% alcohol)
STORAGE
Store at room temperature in a tightly closed container. Do not refrigerate or freeze.

USES

Ipecac is for emergency use to treat drug overdose or poisoning. Ipecac works on the stomach and on the vomiting center in the brain to produce vomiting.

TREATMENT

Before administering ipecac, call a poison control center, emergency room, or physician for advice. You must administer ipecac with adequate amounts of water (½ glass for infants less than 1 year old; 1 to 2 glasses for children and adults) so there is adequate fluid in the stomach. If vomiting does not occur within 20 minutes after a second dose has been given, call again IMMEDIATELY for instructions.

SIDE EFFECTS

Minor. Ipecac can cause diarrhea, drowsiness, nausea, or vomiting that continues for more than 30 minutes. These side effects should disappear within several hours.
Major. Tell your doctor about any side effects that are persistent or particularly bothersome. IT IS ESPECIALLY IMPORTANT TO TELL YOUR DOCTOR about aching or stiffness of the muscles, difficulty in breathing, palpitations, stomach cramps or pain, or weakness as soon as possible.

INTERACTIONS

Ipecac oral syrup should not be administered with milk or with carbonated beverages; these fluids may affect how quickly ipecac works. In addition, activated charcoal will absorb ipecac. If both activated charcoal and ipecac oral syrup are to be administered, give the activated charcoal only after successful vomiting has been produced by the ipecac.

WARNINGS

• Vomiting is not the proper treatment in all cases of possible poisoning: Ipecac should not be used if gasoline, oils, kerosene, acids, alkalies (lye), corrosives, or strychnine has been swallowed, since vomiting of these substances may cause seizures, additional throat burns, or pneumonia.
• Unless otherwise directed by a health professional, ipecac should probably not be used if the poisoned patient has heart disease; is in shock, losing consciousness, or having seizures; or lacks a gag reflex.
• Muscle and heart disorders and at least one death have been reported as a result of the chronic use of ipecac by young women who were using it to induce vomiting for weight loss.
• Ipecac is available over the counter (without a prescription) and can be purchased from most pharmacies. Parents should have on hand a one-ounce bottle of ipecac for each child in the house. Always call a poison control center, emergency room, or physician for instructions BEFORE administering ipecac.
• Be sure to tell your doctor if the overdose or poisoning victim is pregnant. Although ipecac appears to be safe, studies in pregnant women have not been done.

---

irbesartan

BRAND NAME (Manufacturer)
Avapro (Bristol-Myers Squibb)
TYPE OF DRUG
Antihypertensive
INGREDIENT
irbesartan
DOSAGE FORM
Tablets (75 mg, 150 mg, and 300 mg)
STORAGE
Store in a tightly closed container at room temperature, away from heat and direct sunlight. Do not refrigerate or freeze.

USES

Irbesartan is used to treat high blood pressure and potentially may be used for the treatment of congestive heart failure. It is a vasodilator (it widens blood vessels) that blocks the production of chemicals that may be responsible for constricting, or narrowing, blood vessels.

TREATMENT

Take this medication exactly as prescribed by your doctor. It can be taken on an empty stomach or with meals if stomach upset occurs.

While using this medication, try to develop a set schedule for taking it. If you miss a dose and remember within a few hours, take the missed dose and resume your regular schedule. If many hours have passed, skip the dose you missed and then take your next dose as scheduled. Do not double the dose. Irbesartan does not cure high blood pressure, but it will help to control the condition as long as you continue to take the medication.

SIDE EFFECTS

Minor. Abdominal pain, cough, diarrhea, dizziness, drowsiness, fatigue, headache, insomnia, nausea, nervousness, sweating, or vomiting. These side effects should disappear as your body adjusts to the medication.

To avoid dizziness when you stand, contract and relax the muscles of your legs for a few moments before rising. Do this by alternately pushing one foot against the floor while lifting the other foot slightly.

Major. Tell your doctor about any side effects that are persistent or particularly bothersome. IT IS ESPECIALLY IMPORTANT TO TELL YOUR DOCTOR about chest pain; difficulty breathing; fainting; fever; itching; light-headedness (especially during the first few days); muscle cramps; palpitations; rash; sore throat; swelling of the face, eyes, lips, or tongue; tingling in the fingers and toes; or yellowing of the eyes or skin.

INTERACTIONS

Irbesartan interacts with several other types of medications:

1. Diuretics and other antihypertensive medications can cause an excessive drop in blood pressure when they are combined with this medication (especially the first dose).

2. The combination of this medication with amiloride, potassium supplements, salt substitutes, spironolactone, or triamterene can lead to hyperkalemia (dangerously high levels of potassium in the bloodstream).

3. Nonsteroidal anti-inflammatory agents (including ibuprofen, indomethacin, and naproxen) may reduce the effectiveness of this medication.

Before starting to take irbesartan, BE SURE TO TELL YOUR DOCTOR about any medications you are taking, especially those listed above.

WARNINGS

- Tell your doctor about unusual or allergic reactions you have had to any medications, especially to angiotensin-converting enzyme (ACE) inhibitors (including captopril, enalapril, moexipril, ramipril, quinipril, trandolapril, lisinopril, and benazepril), to this medication, or to any other antihypertensive medication.
- Be sure to tell your doctor if you have ever had heart disease, blood disorders, renal or liver disease, or systemic lupus erythematosus.
- Excessive perspiration, dehydration, or prolonged vomiting or diarrhea can lead to an excessive drop in blood pressure while you are taking this medication. Contact your doctor if you have any of these symptoms.
- Before having surgery or other medical or dental treatment, tell your doctor or dentist you are taking this medication.

• If this drug makes you dizzy or drowsy, do not take part in any activity that requires alertness, such as driving a car or operating potentially dangerous equipment.
• If you have high blood pressure, do not take any over-the-counter (nonprescription) medications for weight control or for asthma, sinus, cough, cold, or allergy problems unless you first check with your doctor.
• Be sure to tell your doctor if you are pregnant. This medication is very similar to the class of drugs called ACE inhibitors, which have been shown to cause birth defects, including kidney damage, low blood pressure, and improper skull development, and fetal death when taken in the second and third trimesters. Also tell your doctor if you are breast-feeding an infant. This medication may pass into breast milk and should not be taken by a nursing mother.

---

isoniazid

BRAND NAMES (Manufacturers)
isoniazid (various manufacturers)
Laniazid (Lannett)
TYPE OF DRUG
Antitubercular
INGREDIENT
isoniazid
DOSAGE FORMS
Tablets (50 mg, 100 mg, and 300 mg)
Oral syrup (50 mg per 5-mL spoonful)
STORAGE
Store at room temperature in a tightly closed, light-resistant container. Do not freeze. If the syrup is stored at low temperatures, crystals may form. These should dissolve if the syrup is left at room temperature.

USES

Isoniazid is used to prevent and treat tuberculosis. It acts by severely injuring the cell structure of tuberculosis bacteria, thereby preventing them from growing and multiplying.

TREATMENT

To avoid stomach irritation, you can take isoniazid with food or a full glass of water or milk (unless your doctor directs you to do otherwise).

Antacids prevent the absorption of isoniazid from the gastrointestinal tract, so they should not be taken within an hour of a dose of isoniazid.

Measure each dose of the oral syrup with a specially designed 5-mL measuring spoon. An ordinary kitchen teaspoon is not accurate enough for medical purposes.

It is important to continue to take this medication for the entire time prescribed by your doctor, even if your symptoms disappear before the end of that period. If you stop taking the drug too soon, your infection could recur.

It is common for therapy to last for at least six months and, at times, for as long as two years.

Try not to miss any doses of this medication. If you do miss a dose, take the missed dose as soon as possible. However, if it is almost time for the next dose, do not take the missed dose at all; just return to your regular dosing schedule. Do not double the next dose.

SIDE EFFECTS

Minor. Abdominal pain, dizziness, heartburn, nausea, or vomiting. These side effects should disappear as your body adjusts to the medication.

If you feel dizzy, sit or lie down for a while; get up slowly from a sitting or reclining position; and be careful on stairs.

Major. Tell your doctor about any side effects that are persistent or particularly bothersome. IT IS ESPECIALLY IMPORTANT TO TELL YOUR DOCTOR about blurred vision, breast enlargement (in both sexes), chills, darkening of the urine, eye pain, fever, malaise, memory impairment, numbness or tingling in the fingers or toes, rash, unusual bleeding or bruising, vision changes, weakness, or yellowish discoloration of the eyes or skin.

Your doctor may prescribe supplemental vitamin B_6 (pyridoxine) to help prevent the numbness and tingling that can occur as a side effect of this medication. However, do not take vitamin B_6 without consulting your doctor.

INTERACTIONS

Isoniazid interacts with several other types of medications:

1. Concurrent use of isoniazid and alcohol can decrease the efficacy of isoniazid and increase side effects on the liver.

2. The concurrent use of isoniazid and the drug cycloserine can result in dizziness or drowsiness.

3. The combination of isoniazid and disulfiram can lead to dizziness, loss of coordination, irritable disposition, and insomnia.

4. Isoniazid can decrease the breakdown of phenytoin and carbamazepine in the body, which can lead to an increase in side effects from phenytoin and carbamazepine.

5. Isoniazid can decrease the effectiveness of ketoconazole.

6. In combination, rifampin and isoniazid can increase the risk of liver damage. However, this is a commonly prescribed combination.

7. The effectiveness of isoniazid may be decreased by adrenocorticosteroids (cortisonelike medicines).

8. The side effects of benzodiazepine tranquilizers or meperidine may be increased by isoniazid.

9. Isoniazid may increase the effects of warfarin, a blood thinner, and increase the risk of bleeding.

BE SURE TO TELL YOUR DOCTOR about any medications you are currently taking, especially those listed above.

WARNINGS

• Tell your doctor about unusual or allergic reactions you have had to any medications, especially to isoniazid, ethionamide, pyrazinamide, or niacin (vitamin B_3).

• Before starting to take this medication, be sure to tell your doctor if you have a history of alcoholism or if you now have or ever had kidney disease, liver disease, or seizures.

• If this medication causes you to feel dizzy, avoid tasks that require alertness, such as driving an automobile or operating potentially dangerous equipment.

• Your doctor may want you to have periodic eye examinations while taking this medication, especially if you begin to have vision side effects.

• Isoniazid can interact with several foods (skipjack fish, tuna, yeast extracts, sauerkraut juice, sausages, and certain cheeses), leading to severe reactions. You should, therefore, avoid eating these foods while being treated with isoniazid.

• If you have diabetes and use the Clinitest urine glucose test, you may get erroneously high sugar readings while you are taking this medication. Your doctor may therefore recommend that you temporarily change to the Clinistix or Tes-Tape urine test to avoid this problem.

• Be sure to tell your doctor if you are pregnant. Although isoniazid appears to be safe during pregnancy, it does cross the placenta. Extensive studies in pregnant women have not been conducted. Also be sure to tell your doctor if you are breast-feeding an infant. Small amounts of isoniazid pass into breast milk.

isosorbide dinitrate

BRAND NAMES (Manufacturers)
Dilatrate-SR (Schwarz Pharma)
Iso-Bid (Roberts)
Isordil Tembids (Wyeth)
Isordil Titradose (Wyeth)
isosorbide dinitrate (various manufacturers)
Sorbitrate (Astra Zeneca)
TYPE OF DRUG
Antianginal
INGREDIENT
isosorbide dinitrate
DOSAGE FORMS
Tablets (5 mg, 10 mg, 20 mg, 30 mg, and 40 mg)
Chewable tablets (5 mg and 10 mg)
Sublingual tablets (2.5 mg, 5 mg, and 10 mg)
Sustained-release tablets (40 mg)
Sustained-release capsules (40 mg)
STORAGE
Store in a cool, dry place. This drug loses potency when exposed to heat or moisture.

USES

Isosorbide dinitrate is a vasodilator that relaxes the muscle of the blood vessels, leading to an increase in the oxygen supply to the heart. It is used to relieve (chewable and sublingual tablets) or to prevent (oral tablets and capsules) angina (chest pain). The chewable and sublingual tablets act quickly; they can be used to relieve chest pain after it has begun. The oral tablets and capsules do not act quickly; they are used only to prevent angina attacks.

TREATMENT

Take the chewable or sublingual forms of this medication at the first sign of an angina attack. DO NOT WAIT for the attack to become severe. Then sit down. These tablets are absorbed more completely through the lining of the mouth than from the stomach. Your mouth should be empty when you take these tablets. Do not eat, drink, or smoke with a tablet in your mouth. If the pain of an attack continues, you can take another tablet after five minutes, and a third tablet after another five minutes. If three tablets provide no relief within 15 minutes, CONTACT YOUR DOCTOR IMMEDIATELY or go to the nearest hospital.

The chewable tablet form of this medication should be chewed for at least two minutes before swallowing.

Place the sublingual tablet under the tongue or against the cheek and allow it to dissolve—DO NOT CHEW OR SWALLOW IT. Do not swallow until the drug is dissolved, and do not rinse your mouth for several minutes (this gives a greater opportunity for the drug to be absorbed through the lining of the mouth).

Take the regular tablets and the sustained-release forms of this medication with a full glass of water on an empty stomach. The sustained-release forms should be swallowed whole. Breaking, crushing, or chewing these tablets or capsules destroys their sustained-release activity and possibly increases the side effects.

If you are taking this medication on a regular schedule, try not to miss any doses. If you do miss a dose of this medication, take the missed dose as soon as possible. However, if it is within two hours of the next dose (or six hours for the sustained-release forms), do not take the missed dose at all; return to your regular dosing schedule. Do not double the next dose of medication.

Some doctors may recommend using isosorbide dinitrate prior to expected episodes of physical or emotional stress in order to prevent attacks of angina. Discuss this with your doctor.

SIDE EFFECTS

Minor. Dizziness, flushing, headache, light-headedness, nausea, or vomiting may be experienced. These side effects should diminish or disappear as your body gets accustomed to the medication.

If you feel dizzy or light-headed, sit or lie down for a while; get up slowly from a sitting or reclining position; and be careful on stairs.

To avoid dizziness or light-headedness when you stand, contract and relax the muscles of your legs for a few moments before rising. Do this by pushing one foot against the floor while raising the other foot slightly, alternating feet so that you are "pumping" your legs in a pedaling motion.

Acetaminophen may help relieve headaches caused by this medication.

Major. Tell your doctor about any side effects that are persistent or particularly bothersome. IT IS ESPECIALLY IMPORTANT TO TELL YOUR DOCTOR about fainting spells, heart palpitations, rash, restlessness, sweating, or unusual weakness.

INTERACTIONS

Isosorbide dinitrate can interact with other types of medications:

1. Isosorbide dinitrate, if taken in combination with alcohol, can lead to dizziness and fainting.

2. Over-the-counter (nonprescription) sinus, allergy, cough, cold, asthma, and diet products can block the antianginal effects of isosorbide dinitrate.

3. Do not use this medication with sildenafil (Viagra). Using these medications together has resulted in serious side effects and death.

BE SURE TO TELL YOUR DOCTOR about any medications you are taking at the present time, especially any of those listed above.

WARNINGS

• Tell your doctor about unusual or allergic reactions you have had to any medications, especially to isosorbide dinitrate or to any other nitrate-containing drugs (such as nitroglycerin).

• Before starting to take this medication, tell your doctor if you have ever had severe anemia, glaucoma, a heart attack, or thyroid disease.

• Before using this medication to relieve chest pain, be certain that the pain arises from the heart and is not due to a muscle spasm or to indigestion. If your chest pain is not relieved by use of this drug or if pain arises from a different location or differs in severity, CONSULT YOUR DOCTOR IMMEDIATELY.

• If this drug makes you dizzy or light-headed, do not take part in any activity that requires alertness, such as driving a car or operating potentially dangerous machinery.

• Before having surgery or any other medical or dental treatment, be sure to tell your doctor or dentist that you are taking this medication.

• Tolerance to this medication may develop. If the drug begins to lose its effectiveness, contact your doctor. It may be necessary to change the dosing schedule.

• Isosorbide dinitrate should not be discontinued unless you first consult your doctor. Stopping the drug abruptly may lead to further chest pain. Your doctor may, therefore, want to decrease your dosage gradually.

• If you have frequent diarrhea, you may not be absorbing the sustained-release form of this medication. Discuss this with your doctor.

• Be sure to tell your doctor if you are pregnant. Although this drug appears to be safe to use during pregnancy, extensive studies in pregnant women have not been conducted. Also notify your doctor if you are breast-feeding an infant. It is not known whether or not isosorbide dinitrate passes into breast milk.

isotretinoin

BRAND NAME (Manufacturer)
Accutane (Roche)
TYPE OF DRUG
Acne preparation
INGREDIENT
isotretinoin
DOSAGE FORM
Capsules (10 mg, 20 mg, and 40 mg)
STORAGE
Store at room temperature in a tightly closed, light-resistant container.

USES

This medication is used to treat severe cystic acne. It is not clearly understood how isotretinoin works, but it decreases the production of sebum (an oily skin secretion) and dries up the acne lesions.

TREATMENT

An information leaflet is packaged with this product. Be sure to read it carefully.

Isotretinoin should be taken with meals to obtain maximum benefit.

It may take one to two months before you notice the maximum effects of this medication on your skin.

If you miss a dose of this medication, take the missed dose as soon as possible, and then return to your regular dosing schedule. However, if you do not remember until it is time for your next dose, double the next dose, and then return to your regular dosing schedule.

SIDE EFFECTS

Minor. Changes in skin color, blurred vision or difficulty seeing, drowsiness, dry lips or mouth, fatigue, fluid retention, headache, indigestion, inflammation of the eyelids, inflammation of the lips, irritation of the eyes, or thinning of the hair. These side effects may disappear as your body adjusts to the drug.

You may notice a worsening of your acne for the first few days of treatment.

This medication can cause increased sensitivity to sunlight. Avoid prolonged exposure to sunlight and sunlamps. Wear protective clothing and sunglasses, and also use an effective sunscreen.

To relieve mouth dryness, chew sugarless gum or suck on ice chips or a piece of hard candy. If there is no relief within two weeks, consult your doctor.

Major. Tell your doctor about any side effects that are persistent or particularly bothersome. IT IS ESPECIALLY IMPORTANT TO TELL YOUR DOCTOR about black, tarry stools; bruising; burning or tingling sensation of the skin; changes in the menstrual cycle; depression; dizziness; hives; muscle pain; peeling of the palms and soles; rash; visual disturbances; or weight loss.

INTERACTIONS

This medication interacts with the following substances:

1. The concurrent use of alcohol and isotretinoin can lead to an increase in blood lipid (blood fat) levels, which can be dangerous.

2. Vitamin A and isotretinoin together can result in additive toxic effects.

3. Do not take tetracycline (including minocycline) with isotretinoin. Tetracycline may increase the side effects of this medication.

BE SURE TO TELL YOUR DOCTOR about any medications you are currently taking, especially vitamin A.

WARNINGS

• Tell your doctor about unusual or allergic reactions you have had to any medications, especially to isotretinoin, vitamin A, or the preservative parabens.
• Before starting to take this medication, tell your doctor if you now have or ever had diabetes mellitus (sugar diabetes), hyperlipidemia (high blood lipid levels), or depression.
• If this drug makes you drowsy, do not take part in any activity that requires alertness, such as driving a car or operating potentially dangerous machinery.
• This medication may cause changes in vision that may make driving a car difficult.
• Isotretinoin may cause depression, especially in teenagers and young adults. Suicides have been reported in association with this medication.
• Be sure to tell your doctor if you are or suspect that you might be pregnant. Isotretinoin has been shown to cause birth defects in humans. Also tell your doctor if you are breast-feeding an infant. It is not known whether this medication passes into breast milk. Women of childbearing age should use an effective form of birth control for at least one month before they start taking this drug and continue using it while they are taking this medication and for at least one month after they stop taking it. Within the two weeks before starting this drug, women should have a blood pregnancy test. If the test is negative, the drug will be started on the second or third day of the next normal menstrual period. Women should have a pregnancy test each month while they take this medication. All women must also sign an informed-consent sheet before starting this medication.

---

isradipine

BRAND NAMES (Manufacturers)
DynaCirc Capsules (Novartis)
DynaCirc CR (Novartis)
TYPE OF DRUG
Antianginal (calcium channel blocker) and antihypertensive
INGREDIENT
isradipine
DOSAGE FORMS
Capsules (2.5 mg and 5 mg)
Tablets, extended release (5 mg and 10 mg)
STORAGE
Store at room temperature in a tightly closed container, out of the reach of children and away from moisture and direct light.

USES

Isradipine is used to treat high blood pressure. It belongs to a group of drugs known as calcium channel blockers, which are useful for several cardiovascular conditions. Calcium channel blockers are less likely than beta blockers or thiazide diuretics to have adverse effects on plasma lipids or blood glucose control in hypertensive patients with diabetes, asthma, or hardening of the arteries. It is not fully understood how isradipine works, but by blocking calcium, it relaxes and prevents spasms of the blood vessels of the heart and reduces the oxygen needs of the heart muscle. Isradipine is also a potent vasodilator that relaxes the muscle tissue of the blood vessels, thereby lowering blood pressure.

TREATMENT

If you miss a dose of this medication, take the missed dose as soon as possible. However, if it is almost time for the next dose, do not take the missed dose at all; just return to your regular dosing schedule. Do not double the next dose. If you have a heart condition and have been taking isradipine regularly, it should not be stopped suddenly, as this may worsen your symptoms of heart disease.

This medication does not cure high blood pressure, but it will help to control the condition as long as you continue to take it. It may take several weeks to develop its full effect.

Swallow the extended release tablets whole; do not chew or crush them.

SIDE EFFECTS

Minor. Constipation, dizziness, flushing of the face, headaches, increased heart rate, nervousness, painful extremities, rash, stomach upset, and swollen ankles. These side effects should disappear as your body adjusts to the medication.

To relieve constipation, increase the amount of fiber in your diet (fresh fruits and vegetables, salads, bran, and whole-grain breads), exercise, and drink more water (unless your doctor directs you to do otherwise).

Major. Tell your doctor about any side effects that are persistent or particularly bothersome. IT IS ESPECIALLY IMPORTANT TO TELL YOUR DOCTOR about changes in your menstrual period, confusion, depression, fainting, fatigue, hair loss, itching, loss of balance, palpitations, rapid weight gain (three to five pounds within a week), recurrent infections, shortness of breath, swelling of the hands or feet, tremors, or unusual weakness.

INTERACTIONS

Isradipine interacts with several other drugs:

1. Isradipine may increase the blood-pressure-lowering effect of beta blockers, especially if there is a pre-existing heart condition. Isradipine may also increase the blood levels of the beta blocker propranolol.

2. Other medications that may interact with isradipine include adenosine, cimetidine, digoxin, fentanyl used in conjunction with anesthesia, nonsteroidal anti-inflammatory drugs (NSAIDs), and prazosin.

3. Procainamide and quinidine may increase the effects on the heart if used with isradipine.

4. Large doses of calcium may interfere with the action of isradipine.

WARNINGS

• Tell your doctor about unusual or allergic reactions you have had to any medications, especially to isradipine.

• Before starting to take this medication, be sure to tell your doctor if you now have or ever had any type of heart disease, kidney disease, liver disease, low blood pressure, or a slowed heartbeat.

• Your doctor may want you to check your pulse on a regular basis while you are taking this medication. If your heart rate drops below 50 beats per minute, contact your doctor.

• If you experience angina symptoms, stopping this medication abruptly may lead to a worsening of your chest pain. Your doctor may, therefore, want to reduce your dosage gradually or have you switch to another medication when isradipine is discontinued.

• To prevent dizziness or light-headedness while taking this medication, try not to stand for long periods of time, avoid drinking alcoholic beverages, and try not to become overheated. Avoid exercising strenuously in hot weather, and do not take hot baths, showers, and saunas.

• Be sure to tell your doctor if you are pregnant. There are some indications that israpidine may cause birth defects in animals, but conclusive studies in humans have not been conducted. Also be sure to tell your doctor if you are breast-feeding an infant. It is not known whether isradipine passes into breast milk.

ketoprofen

BRAND NAMES (Manufacturers)
Actron* (Bayer)
ketoprofen (various manufacturers)
Orudis* (Wyeth-Ayerst)
Oruvail (Wyeth-Ayerst)
*Available over the counter (without a prescription) as 12.5-mg tablets.
TYPE OF DRUG
Nonsteroidal anti-inflammatory analgesic
INGREDIENT
ketoprofen
DOSAGE FORMS
Capsules (25 mg, 50 mg, and 75 mg)
Sustained-action capsules (100 mg, 150 mg, and 200 mg)
Tablets (12.5 mg)
STORAGE
Store at room temperature in a tightly closed container.

USES

Ketoprofen is used to treat rheumatoid arthritis and osteoarthritis. Ketoprofen has been shown to block the production of certain body chemicals, called prostaglandins, that trigger pain and inflammation. However, it is not yet fully understood exactly how ketoprofen works.

TREATMENT

Take immediately after meals or with food to reduce stomach irritation. Check with your doctor about taking ketoprofen with an antacid. However, if this medication is being taken for acute pain, take the first one or two doses on an empty stomach (30 to 60 minutes before or 2 hours after a meal) so that it enters your bloodstream quickly.

Swallow the sustained-release capsules whole; do not chew or crush them.

Take ketoprofen on schedule and try not to miss any doses. If you do miss a dose, take the missed dose as soon as possible. However, if it is almost time for the next dose, do not take the missed dose at all; just return to your regular dosing schedule. Do not double the next dose.

Ketoprofen does not cure arthritis, but it will help to control symptoms as long as you take it.

SIDE EFFECTS

Minor. Abdominal pain, changes in taste, constipation, decreased or increased appetite, diarrhea, dizziness, drowsiness, dry mouth, excessive salivation, fatigue, flushing, gas, headache, heartburn, increased heart rate, increased thirst, nausea, nosebleeds, sweating, vomiting, or weight change. These side effects should disappear as your body adjusts to this medication.

Ketoprofen may cause increased sensitivity to sunlight. Therefore, it is important to avoid prolonged exposure to sunlight and sunlamps. Wear protective clothing and sunglasses, and use an effective sunscreen.

To relieve constipation, increase the amount of fiber in your diet (fresh fruits and vegetables, salads, bran, and whole-grain breads). You can also increase your exercise and drink more water (unless your doctor directs you to do otherwise).

If you become dizzy, sit or lie down; get up slowly from a sitting or reclining position; and be careful on stairs.

Major. Tell your doctor about any side effects that are persistent or particularly bothersome. IT IS ESPECIALLY IMPORTANT TO TELL YOUR DOCTOR about black or tarry stools, chills, confusion, decreased or painful urination, hair loss, itching, memory loss, mouth sores, muscle pains, palpitations, rash, shortness of breath, swelling of the feet, tingling in the fingers or toes, unusual bleeding or bruising, unusual weight gain, visual disturbances, or yellowing of the eyes or skin.

INTERACTIONS

Ketoprofen interacts with several other types of medications:

1. Ketoprofen can increase the risk of bleeding complications caused by anticoagulant medications (blood thinners, such as warfarin).

2. Ketoprofen has been known to interfere with the diuretic effects of furosemide and thiazide-type diuretics (water pills).

3. Aspirin, taken concurrently with this medication, can alter the blood levels and elimination of ketoprofen from the body.

4. Probenecid can increase the blood levels of ketoprofen, which in turn can lead to an increased chance of experiencing side effects.

5. The action of beta blockers may be affected by this drug.

6. Ketoprofen taken concurrently with lithium and cyclosporine may increase the amount of these drugs in the body, increasing their toxic effects.

7. Concurrent use of methotrexate and ketoprofen may increase the amount of methotrexate in the body, increasing the risk of toxicity. Do not use these medications together.

BE SURE TO TELL YOUR DOCTOR about any medications you are currently taking, especially those listed above.

WARNINGS

• Tell your doctor about any unusual or allergic reactions you have had to any medications, especially to ketoprofen or to any other chemically related drugs, including aspirin, other salicylates, diclofenac, diflunisal, etodolac, fenoprofen, flurbiprofen, ibuprofen, indomethacin, ketorolac, meclofenamate, mefenamic acid, nabumetone, naproxen, oxaprozin, oxyphenbutazone, phenylbutazone, piroxicam, sulindac, tenoxicam, tiaprofenic acid, or tolmetin.

• Before taking ketoprofen, tell your doctor if you now have or ever had anemia, bleeding problems, gastrointestinal disease, heart failure, hypertension, kidney disease, liver disease, or ulcers.

• If this medication makes you dizzy or drowsy, do not take part in any activity that requires alertness, such as driving an automobile or operating potentially dangerous machinery.

• If vision problems develop while taking this medication, your doctor may refer you to an ophthalmologist.

• Stomach problems are more likely if you take aspirin regularly or drink alcohol while on this drug.

• Before having surgery or any other medical or dental treatment, be sure to tell your doctor or dentist that you are taking this medication. Your doctor or dentist may recommend stopping ketoprofen for several days prior to surgery, to decrease the risk of bleeding complications.

• The elderly may be at increased risk of experiencing some of the side effects of this medication.

• Be sure to tell your doctor if you are pregnant. Although ketoprofen appears to be safe in animals, studies in pregnant women have not been conducted. Ketoprofen should be avoided late in pregnancy because it can alter fetal heart circulation. Also tell your doctor if you are breast-feeding an infant. It is not yet known whether ketoprofen passes into human breast milk.

lamivudine

BRAND NAMES (Manufacturers)
Epivir (GlaxoSmithKline)
Epivir-HBV (GlaxoSmithKline)
TYPE OF DRUG
Antiviral
INGREDIENT
lamivudine
DOSAGE FORMS
Tablets (100 mg and 150 mg)
Oral solution (5 mg per mL and 10 mg per mL)
STORAGE
Store at room temperature in tightly closed, light-resistant containers. Do not freeze.

USES

Lamivudine is used in the treatment of human immunodeficiency virus (HIV) infection. HIV is the virus that causes AIDS. Lamivudine works by inhibiting the reproduction, or growth, of the virus, which slows down the progression of AIDS. Lamivudine does not cure AIDS, but this drug may delay the onset of other infections and diseases caused by AIDS. Lamivudine is used in combination with other anti-AIDS drugs, such as zidovudine. This medication (Epivir-HBV) is also used in the treatment of chronic hepatitis B.

TREATMENT

This medication works best when the level of medicine in your bloodstream is kept constant. It is best to take the drug at evenly spaced intervals throughout the day.

Measure each dose of the solution carefully with a specially designed 5-mL measuring spoon. An ordinary kitchen teaspoon is not accurate enough.

If you miss a dose of this medication, take it as soon as possible. However, if it is almost time for your next dose, skip the missed dose and go back to your regular dosing schedule. Do not double the next dose of the medication.

SIDE EFFECTS

Minor. Cough, dizziness, fatigue, headache, insomnia, nausea, or skin rash. These side effects should diminish or disappear as your body adjusts to the medication.
Major. Tell your doctor about any side effects that are persistent or particularly bothersome. IT IS ESPECIALLY IMPORTANT TO TELL YOUR DOCTOR about nausea; severe abdominal pain; tingling, burning, numbness, or pain in the hands, arms, feet, or legs; or vomiting.

INTERACTIONS

Lamivudine may interact with several other drugs:
1. Sulfamethoxazole and trimethoprim may interfere with your body's ability to eliminate lamivudine and increase the toxicity of lamivudine.
2. Concurrent use of zalcitabine and lamivudine is not recommended. These medications inactivate each other.

BE SURE TO TELL YOUR DOCTOR about any medications you are currently taking, especially any of the medications listed above.

WARNINGS

• Tell your doctor about any unusual or allergic reactions you have had to any medications, especially lamivudine or other medications used to treat HIV infection. Also tell your doctor about any allergic reaction you have had to any foods, preservatives, or dyes.

• During treatment with this medication, you may require periodic blood tests at your physician's office to monitor the effects of lamivudine.

• Be sure to tell your doctor if you have anemia, liver disease, vitamin deficiencies, or kidney disease. If you have kidney disease, your doctor may need to reduce the size or number of your doses of lamivudine.

• If you are taking this medication for hepatitis, it is important to tell your doctor if you believe that you may be at risk for HIV infection.

• Before having surgery or any other medical or dental treatment, tell your doctor or dentist that you are taking this drug.

• If you are infected with HIV, it is best to avoid any sexual activity involving an exchange of body fluids with other people. If you do have vaginal, anal, or oral sex, always use a latex condom.

• If you inject drugs, do not share needles with anyone.

• Although it is not common, lamivudine may cause a condition known as lactic acidosis. IT IS IMPORTANT TO TELL YOUR DOCTOR IMMEDIATELY if you experience severe muscle pain, cramping, diarrhea, shallow or fast breathing, and unusual tiredness or weakness.

• Be sure to tell your doctor if you are pregnant or plan to become pregnant. It is not known if lamivudine is safe to take during pregnancy. Tell your doctor if you are breast-feeding an infant. It is not known if lamivudine passes into breast milk, but the AIDS virus can be transmitted through breast milk. HIV-infected mothers should not breast-feed their infants.

---

lamotrigine

BRAND NAME (Manufacturer)
Lamictal (GlaxoSmithKline)
TYPE OF DRUG
Anticonvulsant
INGREDIENT
lamotrigine
DOSAGE FORMS
Tablets (25 mg, 100 mg, 150 mg, and 200 mg)
Tablets, chewable (2 mg, 5 mg, and 25 mg)
STORAGE
Store at room temperature in a tightly closed, light-resistant container. Do not freeze.

USES

This medication is used alone or in conjunction with other anticonvulsants for the treatment of seizure disorders in adults. Lamotrigine is also useful in infants and children with Lennox-Gastaut syndrome. The mechanism of action of this drug is not related to any other anticonvulsant medication and is not well understood.

TREATMENT

If stomach upset occurs, lamotrigine may be taken with food—unless your doctor instructs you to do otherwise.

Routine monitoring of the level of lamotrigine in your bloodstream is not usually necessary. However, when beginning lamotrigine therapy, it may be necessary to closely monitor the bloodstream levels of other anticonvulsants. The doses of lamotrigine should be administered at evenly spaced intervals day or night, depending on the specific dosage recommended by your doctor. For example, if you take two doses a day, the doses should be spaced 12 hours apart.

Try not to miss any doses of this medication. If you do miss a dose, take the missed dose as soon as possible. However, if it is almost time for your next dose, do not take the missed dose at all; just return to your regular dosing schedule. Do not double the next dose unless your doctor directs you to do so. If you miss two or more doses in a row, be sure to contact your doctor.

SIDE EFFECTS

Minor. Blurred or double vision, constipation, difficulty with balance or walking, dizziness, drowsiness, headache, nausea, or vomiting. These side effects may disappear over time as your body adjusts to the medication.

Lamotrigine can increase your sensitivity to sunlight. It is important to avoid prolonged exposure to sunlight or sunlamps. Wear protective clothing and sunglasses, and use an effective sunscreen.

In order to prevent constipation, increase the amount of fiber in your diet (fresh fruits and vegetables, salads, bran, whole-grain breads), exercise, and drink more water (unless your doctor tells you not to do so).

If you feel dizzy or light-headed, sit or lie down for a while; get up slowly from a sitting or reclining position; and be careful on stairs.

Major. Tell your doctor about any side effects that are persistent or particularly bothersome. IT IS ESPECIALLY IMPORTANT TO TELL YOUR DOCTOR about any type of abnormal balance, abnormal dreaming or hallucinations, depression, difficulty breathing, difficulty in urinating, difficulty walking, double vision, fever, hives, numbness or tingling in the hands or feet, painful sores in the mouth or around the eyes, palpitations, rash, skin discoloration, swelling of the lips or tongue, swollen lymph glands, or tremor.

INTERACTIONS

Lamotrigine interacts with several other types of medications:

1. Concurrent use of this medication with certain anticonvulsants (carbamazepine, oxcarbazepine, phenobarbital, phenytoin, primidone), oral contraceptives (birth control pills), or acetaminophen will result in a decrease in the level of lamotrigine in the bloodstream. The dose of lamotrigine may need to be increased.

2. Use of lamotrigine with valproic acid or carbamazepine may result in increased toxicity of these agents. The dose of these medications may need to be decreased.

Before you start lamotrigine, BE SURE TO TELL YOUR DOCTOR about any medications you are currently taking, especially any of those listed above.

WARNINGS

• Tell your doctor about any unusual or allergic reactions you have had to any medications, especially to lamotrigine or any other anticonvulsant medication.

• Before having surgery or any other medical or dental procedure, be sure to tell your doctor or dentist that you are taking this medication.

• If this medication makes you dizzy or drowsy, do not take part in any activity that requires alertness, such as driving a car or operating potentially dangerous equipment.

• Do not stop taking this medication suddenly. If you stop abruptly, you may experience an uncontrollable seizure.

• Be sure to contact your doctor immediately if you develop a skin rash while taking lamotrigine. It may indicate a serious medical event.

• Be sure to tell your doctor if you now have or if you ever had blood disorders, urinary tract infections, urinary incontinence, glaucoma, heart disease, kidney disease, or liver disease.

• The dose of this medication will need to be reduced if you have any history of kidney or liver disease. Discuss this with your doctor.

• Be sure to tell your doctor if you are pregnant. Although extensive studies of this drug in humans have not been conducted, lamotrigine has been shown to cause side effects in the fetuses of animals that received large doses of the drug during pregnancy. Also tell your doctor if you are breast-feeding an infant. Lamotrigine passes into breast milk, and it is not recommended for nursing women.

---

lansoprazole

BRAND NAME
Prevacid (TAP Pharm)
TYPE OF DRUG
Proton pump inhibitor
INGREDIENT
lansoprazole
DOSAGE FORMS
Capsules, delayed release (15 mg and 30 mg)
Enteric-coated granules for oral suspension, delayed release (15 mg and 30 mg)
STORAGE
Store this medication in a tightly closed container at room temperature. Do not freeze the medication.

USES

Lansoprazole is used to treat peptic and duodenal ulcer, gastroesophageal reflux disease (GERD), and hypersecretory syndromes. This drug suppresses stomach acid secretion.

TREATMENT

For the best treatment results, take lansoprazole with a full glass of water on an empty stomach. This medication is generally taken before breakfast. Do not chew or crush the capsules of medication.

If you have trouble swallowing the capsule, carefully open it and sprinkle the granules on a tablespoonful of applesauce, pudding, cottage cheese, yogurt, or strained pears. Swallow immediately without chewing. The granules may also be emptied into two ounces of apple, cranberry, grape, orange, pineapple, prune, or tomato juice and swallowed immediately without chewing. After swallowing, put an additional two ounces of juice in the cup and drink it to be sure the complete dose of medication has been taken.

If you are using the oral suspension, empty the packet contents into 30 mL (1 oz) water only. Stir well and drink immediately. Do not crush or chew the granules. If any medication remains after drinking, add more water, stir, and drink immediately.

If you miss a dose, take it as soon as possible. However, if it is time for your next dose, do not take the missed dose at all. Just return to your regular dosing schedule. Do not double the next dose.

SIDE EFFECTS

Minor: Abdominal pain, constipation, dizziness, fatigue, headache, or nausea. These side effects should diminish or disappear as your body adjusts to the medication.

If you feel dizzy or light-headed, sit or lie down for a while, stand up slowly, and be careful on stairs.

To relieve constipation, increase the amount of fiber in your diet (fresh fruits and vegetables, salads, bran, and whole-grain breads) and exercise more (unless your doctor directs you to do otherwise).

Major: Tell your doctor about any side effects that are persistent or particularly bothersome. IT IS ESPECIALLY IMPORTANT TO NOTIFY YOUR DOCTOR about cough, depression, diarrhea, flulike symptoms, muscle pain, skin rash, or unusual bruising or bleeding.

INTERACTIONS

Take lansoprazole at least 30 minutes prior to sucralfate to prevent problems with lansoprazole absorption.

Be sure to tell your doctor about any medication you are taking, especially any of those listed above.

WARNINGS

• Tell your doctor about unusual or allergic reactions you have had to any medications, especially to lansoprazole or omeprazole.
• Before starting to take lansoprazole, tell your doctor if you now have or ever had liver disease or stomach cancer.
• If this drug makes you dizzy or drowsy, do not take part in any activities that require mental alertness, such as driving an automobile or operating potentially dangerous machinery or equipment.
• Be sure to tell your doctor if you are pregnant. Adequate studies have not been conducted in human pregnancy. Tell your doctor if you are breast-feeding an infant. It is not known if lansoprazole passes into breast milk; however, this medication should not be used by nursing women.

---

latanoprost

BRAND NAME
Xalatan (Pharmacia)
TYPE OF DRUG
Prostaglandin agonist, antiglaucoma agent
INGREDIENT
latanoprost
DOSAGE FORM
Solution (50 mcg/mL)
STORAGE
Store unopened containers of the solution in the refrigerator. Opened containers of the solution can be stored at room temperature for up to six weeks.

USES

Latanoprost is used in the treatment of glaucoma and ocular hypertension.

TREATMENT

Wash your hands with soap and water before applying this medication. To avoid contaminating the eyedrops, do not touch the tube portion of the dropper or let the tube portion touch your eye, and DO NOT wipe off or rinse the dropper after each use.

To apply the eyedrops, tilt your head back and pull down your lower eyelid with one hand to make a pouch below the eye. Drop the prescribed amount of medicine into this pouch and slowly close your eyes. Try not to blink. Keep your eyes closed, and place one finger at the corner of the eye next to your nose for a minute or two, applying slight pressure (this prevents loss of the medication through the duct that drains fluid from the surface of the eye into the nose and throat). Then wipe away any excess with a clean tissue. Since the drops are somewhat difficult to apply, you may want someone else to apply them for you.

Apply daily, in the evening. Do not take this medication more than once a day, as it may decrease the effectiveness of the medicine. Latanoprost can be taken together with other eyedrops. If more than one medication is to be applied to the eye, wait five minutes before the second medication is applied.

If you miss a dose of this medication, apply the missed dose as soon as possible after you remember. However, if it is almost time for your next dose, do not apply the missed dose at all. Just return to your regular dosing schedule. Do not double the next dose of the medication.

SIDE EFFECTS

Minor: Blurred vision, burning sensation in the eye, crusting of the eyelid, dry eye, excessive tearing, or stinging or bitter taste in the mouth immediately following application. These side effects should lessen as your body adjusts to the medication.

Major: Tell your doctor about any side effects that are persistent or particularly bothersome. IT IS ESPECIALLY IMPORTANT TO NOTIFY YOUR DOCTOR about allergic reactions, changes in eye color, chest pain, cough, depression, eye pain, eye infections, feeling of congestion in the eye, flulike symptoms, muscle pain, sensitivity to light, severe itching of the eyes, skin rash, or unusual bruising or bleeding.

INTERACTIONS

Eyedrops that contain thimerosal can interact with latanoprost. If you use an eyedrop that contains thimerosal, wait at least five minutes before applying latanoprost.

BE SURE TO TELL YOUR DOCTOR about any medication you are taking, especially any of those listed above.

WARNINGS

- Tell your doctor about unusual or allergic reactions you have had to any medications, especially to latanoprost or benzalkonium chloride.
- Before starting to take latanoprost, tell your doctor if you now have or ever had liver or kidney disease, iritis, macular edema, or aphakia.
- If this medication blurs your vision, try to avoid any activities that require visual acuity, such as driving an automobile or operating potentially dangerous machinery.
- This medication may change the color of your eye. Discuss this side effect with your doctor or pharmacist.
- The preservative in latanoprost (benzalkonium chloride) may be absorbed by contact lenses. Do not use this medication while wearing your contact lenses. Instead, remove your contacts before you put in these eyedrops. If necessary, your contact lenses may be reinserted 15 minutes after you have applied the eyedrops.
- Be sure to tell your doctor if you are pregnant. Animal studies have shown that latanoprost, when used in very high doses, can cause problems in pregnancy. Adequate studies have not been conducted in human pregnancy. Be sure to tell your doctor if you are breast-feeding an infant. It is not known if latanoprost passes into breast milk.

---

leflunomide

BRAND NAME (Manufacturer)
Arava (Hoechst-Marion Roussel)
TYPE OF DRUG
Immune modulator
INGREDIENT
leflunomide
DOSAGE FORM
Tablets (10 mg, 20 mg, and 100 mg)
STORAGE
Store this medication in a tightly closed container at room temperature.

USES

Leflunomide is used for the treatment of rheumatoid arthritis. It works by slowing the growth of rapidly proliferating cells. Leflunomide also has anti-inflammatory effects.

TREATMENT

Take it with a full glass of water, with or without meals.

Try not to miss any doses of this medication. If you do miss a dose, take the missed dose as soon as possible. However, if it is almost time for your next dose, do not take the missed dose at all. Just return to your regular dosing schedule. Do not double the next dose.

SIDE EFFECTS

Minor: Diarrhea, dizziness, hair loss, headache, nausea, vomiting, or weight loss. These side effects should diminish or disappear as your body adjusts to the medication.

If you feel dizzy or light-headed, sit or lie down for a while, get up slowly from a sitting or reclining position, and be careful on stairs.

Major: Tell your doctor about any side effects that are persistent or particularly bothersome. IT IS ESPECIALLY IMPORTANT TO NOTIFY YOUR DOCTOR about difficulty swallowing, facial swelling, increased blood pressure, itching, shortness of breath, or skin rash.

INTERACTIONS

Leflunomide can interact with other medications:

1. Charcoal and cholestyramine can decrease the effectiveness of leflunomide.

2. Rifampin may increase the blood levels of leflunomide, which can increase the risk of leflunomide side effects.

3. When leflunomide is combined with drugs that can cause liver damage, there is a risk of increased leflunomide side effects.

Before starting leflunomide, BE SURE TO TELL YOUR DOCTOR about any medication you are taking, especially any of those listed above.

WARNINGS

- Tell your doctor about any unusual or allergic reactions you have had to any medications, especially to leflunomide.
- Before starting to take leflunomide, tell your doctor if you now have or ever had high blood pressure, kidney or liver disease, or cancer.
- If this drug makes you dizzy or drowsy, do not participate in any activities that require mental alertness, such as driving an automobile or operating potentially dangerous machinery or equipment.
- Be sure to tell your doctor if you are pregnant or trying to get pregnant. Leflunomide can harm the fetus. Women of childbearing age should use an effective form of birth control while taking this drug. Women should take a pregnancy test before starting leflunomide. If the test is negative, the medication can be started. If you suspect you may be pregnant while taking this medication, contact your physician immediately. Be sure to tell your doctor if you are breast-feeding an infant. Leflunomide may potentially cause harm to a breast-feeding infant, and it should not be taken by nursing women.

---

levetiracetam

BRAND NAME (Manufacturer)
Keppra (UCB Pharma)
TYPE OF DRUG
Anticonvulsant
INGREDIENT
levetiracetam
DOSAGE FORM
Tablets (250 mg, 500 mg, and 750 mg)

STORAGE

Store in a tightly closed container at room temperature, away from heat and direct sunlight.

USES

Levetiracetam is an antiseizure medication that is used along with other antiseizure medicines to control certain types of seizures in the treatment of epilepsy. Although this medicine will not cure epilepsy, it will help to control your seizures when taken as directed by your doctor.

TREATMENT

This medication works best when the level of medicine in your bloodstream is kept constant. It is best to take the drug at evenly spaced intervals throughout the day and night. For example, if you are to take two doses a day, the doses should be spaced 12 hours apart. IT IS IMPORTANT NOT TO MISS ANY DOSES OF LEVETIRACETAM.

If you do miss a dose of this medication, take it as soon as possible. However, if it is less than two hours until your next dose, take the missed dose right away, and take the next dose one to two hours later. Then go back to your regular dosing schedule. Do not double the doses. Discuss this with your doctor or pharmacist if you are not sure what to do when you miss a dose of levetiracetam.

Take this drug exactly as prescribed by your doctor.

SIDE EFFECTS

Minor. Cough; dizziness; dryness or soreness of the throat; fever; loss of strength or energy; muscle pain or weakness; runny nose; tender, swollen glands in the neck; trouble swallowing; unusual tiredness or weakness; or voice changes. As your body adjusts to the medication, some of these side effects should disappear.

Dry mouth can be relieved by sucking on ice chips or a piece of hard candy or by chewing sugarless gum.

To relieve constipation, increase the amount of fiber in your diet (fresh fruits and vegetables, salads, bran, and whole-grain breads), exercise, and drink more water (unless your doctor directs you to do otherwise).

To avoid dizziness or light-headedness when you stand, contract and relax the muscles in your legs for a few moments before rising. Do this by pushing one foot against the floor while raising the other foot slightly, alternating feet so that you are "pumping" your legs in a pedaling motion.

If you feel dizzy or light-headed, sit or lie down for a while; get up from a sitting or lying position slowly; and be careful on stairs.

Major. Tell your doctor about any side effects that are persistent or particularly bothersome. IT IS ESPECIALLY IMPORTANT TO TELL YOUR DOCTOR about clumsiness or unsteadiness, cough or hoarseness, crying, depression and feelings of sadness, difficulty in breathing or swallowing, double vision, headache, loss of memory or problems with memory, outbursts of anger, pain or tenderness around the eyes and cheekbones, rapidly changing emotional moods, stuffy or runny nose, tightness of the chest, or wheezing.

INTERACTIONS

If used properly, levetiracetam should not interact with other medications.

1. To avoid drug interactions, it is very important that you do not take any over-the-counter (nonprescription) medications or herbal or natural medicines unless you first check with a doctor or pharmacist.

2. Extreme drowsiness can occur when this medication is taken with other central nervous system depressants (such as alcohol, antihistamines, antidepressants, barbiturates, benzodiazepine tranquilizers, muscle relaxants, narcotics, pain medications, and sleeping medications).

Before taking levetiracetam, BE SURE TO TELL YOUR DOCTOR about any medication you are taking.

WARNINGS

• Tell your doctor if you have a history of alcoholism or if you now have or ever had liver or kidney disease. Your dose of this medication may need to be changed.
• Tell your doctor about any unusual or allergic reactions you have had to any medications, especially to levetiracetam or other medicines used in the treatment of epilepsy.
• Levetiracetam may cause extreme fatigue and dizziness. Your ability to perform tasks that require alertness, such as driving a car or operating potentially dangerous machinery, may be decreased. Appropriate caution should be taken.
• Because of your epilepsy, do not take any over-the-counter (nonprescription) medication for weight control or for cough, cold, asthma, allergy, or sinus problems unless you first check with your doctor or pharmacist.
• It is very important to take this medication as directed by your doctor. Do not reduce the dose or take more of this medication at any time. Do not suddenly stop taking levetiracetam; if you do, you may experience uncontrolled seizures.
• Prior to having surgery or any other medical or dental treatment, be sure to tell your doctor or dentist that you are taking levetiracetam.
• Your doctor may do regular blood tests to see how well your other antiseizure medicines are working to control your seizures.
• Be sure to tell your doctor IMMEDIATELY if you are pregnant. Although the effects of this medication during pregnancy have not been thoroughly studied in humans, it has caused toxicity in animal studies. It is also not known if levetiracetam passes into breast milk in humans, so be sure to tell your doctor if you are breast-feeding an infant.

---

levodopa

BRAND NAMES (Manufacturers)
Dopar (Procter & Gamble)
Larodopa (Roche)
TYPE OF DRUG
Antiparkinsonism agent
INGREDIENT
levodopa
DOSAGE FORMS
Tablets (100 mg, 250 mg, and 500 mg)
Capsules (100 mg, 250 mg, and 500 mg)
STORAGE
Store at room temperature in tightly closed, light-resistant containers.

USES

Levodopa is used to treat the symptoms of Parkinson's disease. It is converted in the body to dopamine, a chemical naturally found in the brain that is at diminished levels in patients with Parkinson's disease.

TREATMENT

To avoid stomach irritation, you can take levodopa with food or with a full glass of milk or water (unless your doctor directs you to do otherwise).

You may not observe significant benefit from this drug for two to three weeks after you begin treatment with it.

If you miss a dose, take the missed dose as soon as possible. However, if it is within two hours of the next scheduled dose, do not take the missed dose at all; just return to your regular dosing schedule. Do not double the next dose.

SIDE EFFECTS

Minor. Abdominal pain, anxiety, bitter taste in the mouth, constipation, diarrhea, dizziness, dry mouth, fatigue, flushing, gas, headache, hiccups, hoarseness, increased hand tremors, increased sexual interest, increased sweating, insomnia, loss of appetite, nausea, offensive body odor, salivation, vision changes, vomiting, weakness, or weight gain. These side effects should diminish or disappear as your body adjusts to the medication.

Levodopa can cause a darkening of your urine or sweat. This is a harmless effect.

To relieve constipation, increase the amount of fiber in your diet (fresh fruits and vegetables, salads, bran, and whole-grain breads), drink more water, and exercise (unless your doctor directs you to do otherwise).

If you feel dizzy, sit or lie down for a while; get up slowly from a sitting or reclining position; and be careful on stairs.

To relieve mouth dryness, chew sugarless gum or suck on ice chips or a piece of hard candy.

Major. Tell your doctor about any side effects that are persistent or particularly bothersome. IT IS ESPECIALLY IMPORTANT TO TELL YOUR DOCTOR about bloody or black, tarry stools; confusion; convulsions; depression; fainting; false sense of well-being; loss of coordination; loss of hair; nightmares; painful erection; palpitations; rapid weight gain (three to five pounds within a week); skin rash; visual disturbances; uncontrolled movements; or unusual weakness.

INTERACTIONS

Levodopa interacts with several other types of medications:

1. The dosage of antihypertensive drugs may require adjustment when treatment with levodopa is started.

2. The effectiveness of levodopa may be decreased by the following: benzodiazepine tranquilizers, phenothiazine tranquilizers, haloperidol, thiothixene, phenytoin, papaverine, and reserpine.

3. Methyldopa can increase or decrease the side effects of therapy with levodopa.

4. Use of levodopa and a monoamine oxidase (MAO) inhibitor within 14 days of each other can lead to severe side effects.

5. Levodopa can increase the side effects of tricyclic antidepressants, ephedrine, and amphetamines.

6. Antacids may alter the absorption of levodopa from the gastrointestinal tract.

7. Pyridoxine (vitamin B_6) can decrease the effectiveness of levodopa.

BE SURE TO TELL YOUR DOCTOR about any medications you are taking, especially those listed above.

WARNINGS

• Tell your doctor about unusual or allergic reactions you have had to any medications, especially to levodopa.

• Before starting to take this medication, tell your doctor if you now have or ever had asthma, diabetes mellitus, difficulty in urinating, epilepsy, glaucoma, heart disease, hormone disorders, kidney disease, liver disease, lung disease, melanoma (a type of skin cancer), mental disorders, or peptic ulcers.

• Some of these products contain the color additive FD&C Yellow No. 5 (tartrazine), which can cause allergic-type symptoms (difficulty in breathing, faintness, or rash) in certain susceptible individuals.

• If levodopa makes you dizzy or blurs your vision, avoid activities that require mental alertness, such as driving a car or operating potentially dangerous machinery.

• Notify your doctor if you start to experience any uncontrolled movements of the limbs or face while taking this medication.
• Before having surgery or any other medical or dental treatment, be sure to tell your doctor or dentist that you are taking this medication.
• Levodopa can cause erroneous readings on urine glucose and ketone tests. Therefore, patients who have diabetes and get unusual urine test results while on levodopa should not adjust their dosage of diabetes medications before checking with their doctor.
• Pyridoxine (vitamin B_6) can decrease the effectiveness of levodopa. Persons taking levodopa should avoid taking this vitamin and should avoid foods rich in pyridoxine (including beans, bacon, avocados, liver, dry skim milk, oatmeal, sweet potatoes, peas, and tuna).
• Be sure to tell your doctor if you are pregnant. Although levodopa appears to be safe in humans, birth defects have been reported in the offspring of animals that were administered large doses during pregnancy. Also tell your doctor if you are breast-feeding an infant. Levodopa passes into breast milk and can cause side effects in nursing infants. It should not be used by nursing women.

---

levofloxacin

BRAND NAME (Manufacturer)
Levaquin (McNeil)
TYPE OF DRUG
Quinolone antibiotic
INGREDIENT
levofloxacin
DOSAGE FORM
Tablets (200 mg, 500 mg, and 750 mg)
STORAGE
Store in a tightly closed container at room temperature, away from heat and direct sunlight.

USES

Levofloxacin is an antibiotic used to treat a wide variety of bacterial infections, including pneumonia, sinusitis, urinary tract infections, skin infections, acute bronchitis, and other types of infection. It acts by severely injuring the cell walls of the infecting bacteria, preventing them from growing and multiplying. This medication kills susceptible bacteria, but it is not effective against viruses, parasites, or fungi.

TREATMENT

Take this medication exactly as prescribed by your doctor, even if your symptoms improve. If you stop taking this drug too soon, resistant bacteria are given a chance to grow and the infection may recur. Levofloxacin can be taken either on an empty stomach or with a meal. You should drink several additional glasses of water every day when you are taking this medication unless your doctor directs you to do otherwise. Drinking water will help to prevent unwanted effects from this medication.

It is very important that you do not miss any doses of this medication. While using this medication, try to develop a set schedule for taking it. If you miss a dose and remember within a few hours, take the missed dose and space the following dose halfway through the regular interval between doses, then return to your regular schedule. Try not to skip any doses.

SIDE EFFECTS

Minor. Abdominal pain, diarrhea, dizziness, insomnia, light-headedness, nausea, or vomiting. These side effects should disappear as your body adjusts to the medication.

To avoid dizziness when you stand, contract and relax the muscles of your legs for a few moments before rising. Do this by alternately pushing one foot against the floor while lifting the other foot slightly.

This medication can cause increased sensitivity to sunlight. Avoid prolonged exposure to sunlight and sunlamps. Wear protective clothing and sunglasses, and also use an effective sunscreen.

Major. Tell your doctor about any side effects that are persistent or particularly bothersome. IT IS ESPECIALLY IMPORTANT TO TELL YOUR DOCTOR about agitation, change in your vision, confusion, difficulty breathing, difficulty urinating, headache, muscle or joint pain, restlessness, severe diarrhea (which may be watery or contain blood or pus), skin rash, or swelling of the face. If your symptoms of infection seem to be getting worse rather than improving, contact your doctor.

INTERACTIONS

Levofloxacin interacts with several other types of medications:

1. Antacids, sucralfate, iron- or zinc-containing vitamins, or didanosine may decrease the effectiveness of levofloxacin. To avoid this drug interaction, take these medications two to four hours before or after taking levofloxacin.

2. Levofloxacin can increase the blood levels and adverse effects of digoxin, warfarin, or cyclosporine.

3. Regular consumption of large quantities of caffeine-containing products (coffee, tea, or caffeine-containing soft drinks) with this medication may lead to exaggerated or prolonged effects of caffeine. Your doctor may ask you to restrict your intake of caffeine during treatment.

4. Levofloxacin may cause a decrease in the efficacy of phenytoin, which may therefore result in an increase in seizure activity.

5. Levofloxacin can increase the side effects of nonsteroidal anti-inflammatory medications (including ibuprofen and naproxen). Restlessness and seizures have been reported from concurrent use.

Before starting to take levofloxacin, BE SURE TO TELL YOUR DOCTOR about any medications you are taking, especially those listed above.

WARNINGS

• Tell your doctor about unusual or allergic reactions you have had to any medications, especially to quinolone antibiotics (including ciprofloxacin, sparfloxacin, enoxacin, ofloxacin, norfloxacin, cinoxacin, or nalidixic acid) or to this medication.

• Before starting to take this medication, be sure to tell your doctor if you have ever had brain or spinal cord disease, epilepsy, kidney disease, or liver disease.

• To decrease the potential for harmful effects on your kidneys, increase your intake of fluids (nonalcoholic) unless your doctor directs you to do otherwise.

• This medication can cause dizziness or light-headedness. Make sure you know how you're reacting to this medicine before you operate an automobile or machinery or engage in activities requiring alertness or coordination.

• This medication can make your skin more sensitive to the sun. When you first begin taking it, avoid too much sun and do not use a sunlamp until you see how your skin responds to short periods of sun exposure. This is especially important if you tend to sunburn easily. Using effective sunscreens or sunblocks when taking this medication will help avoid this problem.

• This medication has been prescribed for your current infection only. A subsequent infection, or one that someone else has, may require a different medicine. Do not give your medication to someone else or use it for other infections unless your doctor specifically directs you to do so.

• Be sure to call your doctor immediately if you experience rash, swelling of the face, or difficulty breathing after you take this medication.

• This medication should never be used in young children.
• Be sure to tell your doctor if you are pregnant. This medication and other quinolone antibiotics have been shown to cause serious adverse effects in the developing fetus. Also tell your doctor if you are breast-feeding an infant. This medication may pass into breast milk and should not be taken by a nursing mother.

levothyroxine

BRAND NAMES (Manufacturers)
Levothroid (Forest)
levothyroxine sodium (various manufacturers)
Levoxyl (Jones Pharma)
Synthroid (Abbott)
Thyro-Tabs (Lloyd)
TYPE OF DRUG
Thyroid hormone
INGREDIENT
levothyroxine
DOSAGE FORM
Tablets (0.025 mg, 0.05 mg, 0.075 mg, 0.088 mg, 0.1 mg, 0.112 mg, 0.125 mg, 0.137 mg, 0.15 mg, 0.175 mg, 0.2 mg, and 0.3 mg)
STORAGE
Store this medication at room temperature in a tightly closed, light-resistant container. Do not refrigerate or freeze.

USES

Levothyroxine is prescribed to replace natural thyroid hormones that are absent because of a disorder of the thyroid gland. It is also used to help decrease the size of enlarged thyroid glands and to treat thyroid cancer. This product is prepared synthetically (artificially), but it is exactly like the natural thyroid hormone that is produced by the human body.

TREATMENT

Take this medication on an empty stomach with a full glass of water. If the medication upsets your stomach, however, ask your doctor if you can take it with food or with a glass of milk.

To get accustomed to taking this drug, try to take it at the same time each day. Try not to miss any doses. If you do miss a dose, take it as soon as possible. However, if it is almost time for the next dose, do not take the missed dose at all; just return to your regular dosing schedule. Do not double the next dose. If you miss more than one or two doses, contact your doctor immediately.

SIDE EFFECTS

Minor. Constipation; dry, puffy skin; fatigue; headache; listlessness; or weight gain. These effects are symptoms of an underactive thyroid. They should disappear after your body adjusts to the medication. It could take several weeks for the medication to take effect. Consult your doctor if these symptoms persist.
Major. Tell your doctor about any side effects that are persistent or particularly bothersome. Most of the major side effects associated with this drug are the result of too large a dose. The dosage of this medication may need to be adjusted if you experience any of the following side effects: chest pain, diarrhea, fever, heat intolerance, insomnia, irritability, leg cramps, menstrual irregularities, muscle aches, nervousness, palpitations, shortness of breath, sweating, trembling, or weight loss. CHECK WITH YOUR DOCTOR.

INTERACTIONS

Levothyroxine interacts with several other types of drugs:

1. Dosing requirements for digoxin, insulin, or oral antidiabetic agents may change when levothyroxine is used.

2. The effects of oral anticoagulants (blood thinners, such as warfarin) may be increased by levothyroxine, which could lead to bleeding complications.

3. Cholestyramine and colestipol prevent the body's absorption of levothyroxine. At least four hours should separate doses of levothyroxine and one of these drugs.

4. Oral contraceptives (birth control pills) and estrogen-containing drugs may change dosage requirements of levothyroxine.

5. Phenobarbital may decrease the effects of levothyroxine; but tricyclic antidepressants and over-the-counter (nonprescription) allergy, asthma, cough, cold, sinus, and diet medications may increase its side effects.

BE SURE TO TELL YOUR DOCTOR about any medications you are currently taking, especially any of those listed above.

WARNINGS

- Tell your doctor about unusual or allergic reactions you have had to any medications, especially to thyroid hormone, levothyroxine, or liothyronine or to any other substances such as foods, preservatives, or dyes.
- Tell your doctor if you now have or ever had angina pectoris, diabetes mellitus, heart disease, high blood pressure, kidney disease, or an underactive adrenal or pituitary gland.
- If you have an underactive thyroid gland, you may need to take this medication for life. You should not stop taking it unless you first check with your doctor.
- Before having surgery or any other medical or dental treatment, be sure to tell your doctor or dentist that you are taking levothyroxine.
- Over-the-counter allergy, asthma, cough, cold, sinus, and diet medications can increase the side effects of levothyroxine. Therefore, check with your doctor or pharmacist before taking any of these products.
- Although many thyroid products are on the market, they are not all bioequivalent; that is, they may not all be absorbed into the bloodstream at the same rate or have the same overall activity. DO NOT CHANGE BRANDS of this medication without first consulting your doctor or pharmacist to make sure you are receiving an equivalent product.
- Some of these products contain the color additive FD&C Yellow No. 5 (tartrazine), which can cause allergic-type reactions (fainting, rash, difficulty in breathing) in certain susceptible individuals.
- The use of this medication as part of a weight-control program is not recommended. This practice is not effective for weight loss and may be dangerous.
- Tell your doctor if you are pregnant. Levothyroxine does not readily cross the placenta, and the drug appears to be safe during pregnancy. However, your dosing of levothyroxine may change during pregnancy. Also tell your doctor if you are breast-feeding an infant.

---

lindane

BRAND NAMES (Manufacturers)

G-well (Goldline)

lindane (various manufacturers)

TYPE OF DRUG

Pediculicide and scabicide

INGREDIENT

lindane (formerly known as gamma benzene hexachloride)

DOSAGE FORMS
Lotion (1%)
Shampoo (1%)
STORAGE
Store at room temperature in tightly closed containers. Do not freeze.

USES

This medication is used to eliminate crab lice, head lice, and scabies. Lindane is a central nervous system (brain and spinal cord) stimulant, which causes convulsions and death of the parasites (at the dosage generally used, it is not harmful to humans). Lindane lotion is used to treat only scabies infestations. The shampoo formulation is used to treat only infestations by lice.

TREATMENT

Complete directions for the use of these products are supplied by the manufacturers. Be sure to ask your doctor or pharmacist for these directions, and follow the instructions carefully.

If you are applying this medication to another person, wear plastic or rubber gloves on your hands in order to avoid absorption of this drug through your skin.

Be sure to shake the lotion well before measuring each dose in order to distribute the medication evenly and equalize the doses. The contents of the lotion tend to settle on the bottom of the bottle.

Be sure to rinse off this product according to the directions. If it is not rinsed off COMPLETELY, too much of the medication will be absorbed.

SIDE EFFECTS

Minor. A rash or skin irritation is likely to occur upon application.
Major. Tell your doctor about any side effects that are persistent or particularly bothersome. The serious side effects associated with this medication (clumsiness, convulsions, irritability, muscle cramps, palpitations, restlessness, unsteadiness, unusual nervousness, or vomiting) are due to absorption of this drug through the skin. This should not happen if the product is used according to directions. CONTACT YOUR DOCTOR if you experience any of these symptoms.

INTERACTIONS

Do not use other skin preparations (lotions, ointments, creams, or oils) while you are using lindane. They increase the absorption of this medication through the skin, which can lead to serious side effects.

WARNINGS

• Tell your doctor about unusual or allergic reactions you have had to any medications, especially to lindane.
• This product should NOT be used on the face. If you do get lindane in your eyes, flush it out immediately. To decrease the amount of drug absorbed through the skin, avoid using this product on any open wounds, cuts, or sores.
• Lice are easily transmitted from one person to another. All family members (and sexual partners) should be carefully examined. Personal items (such as clothing and towels) should be machine-washed using the "hot" temperature cycle and then dried. No unusual cleaning measures are required. Combs, brushes, and other washable items may be soaked in boiling water for one hour.
• After using the shampoo for head lice, you must remove the dead nits (eggs). Use a fine-tooth comb to remove them from your hair, or mix a solution of equal parts of water and vinegar and apply it to the affected area. Rub the solution in well. After several minutes, shampoo with your regular shampoo and then brush your hair. This process should remove all of the nits.

• Infants and young children may be at increased risk for side effects (such as seizures) from lindane. Lindane should not be used on premature infants.
• Be sure to tell your doctor if you are pregnant. Lindane is absorbed through the skin and may cause central nervous system side effects in the mother and in the developing fetus. Also tell your doctor if you are breast-feeding an infant. Lindane probably passes into breast milk and may cause central nervous system side effects in nursing infants.

---

linezolid

BRAND NAME (Manufacturer)
Zyvox (Pharmacia)
TYPE OF DRUG
Antibiotic
INGREDIENT
linezolid
DOSAGE FORMS
Tablets (400 mg and 600 mg)
Oral suspension (100 mg per 5-mL teaspoonful)
STORAGE
Store both the tablets and the oral suspension at room temperature in tightly closed, light-resistant containers. Do not freeze. The suspension will lose its potency after 21 days, so discard it at that time.

USES

Linezolid is an antibiotic that is used to treat a variety of serious or difficult-to-treat bacterial infections. It chemically attaches to the bacteria and prevents their growth and multiplication. Linezolid kills susceptible bacteria, but it is not effective against viruses, parasites, or fungi. Therefore, this medicine will not work for colds or the flu.

TREATMENT

Take either on an empty stomach or with food. You should take this medication with plenty of water, unless your doctor directs you to do otherwise. Linezolid is usually taken twice a day.

When taken with certain foods or drinks, this medication can cause an increase in your blood pressure. To prevent this, it is very important to avoid foods that are high in tyramine (including foods that are aged, fermented, pickled, or smoked to increase their flavor, such as cheeses; air-dried, fermented, or smoked fish, meat, or poultry; sauerkraut; soy sauce; red wine; or tap beer). In general, quantities of tyramine consumed should be less than 100 mg per meal. In addition, it is important to note that the tyramine content of any protein-rich food will be increased if it is stored for a long period of time or if it is improperly refrigerated. Your doctor or pharmacist can provide you with a list of foods and drinks to avoid while taking this medication (ask for a list if it is not given to you).

Shake the suspension form of this medication well just before measuring each dose to distribute the ingredients evenly and equalize the doses. The contents tend to settle on the bottom of the bottle. Measure each dose carefully with a specially designed 5-mL measuring spoon, as directed by your doctor or pharmacist. An ordinary kitchen teaspoon is not accurate enough.

It is very important that you do not miss any doses of this medication. Linezolid works best when the level of medicine in your bloodstream is kept constant. It is best to take the drug at the same time(s) every day, at evenly spaced intervals day and night. For example, if you are to take 2 doses a day, space the doses 12 hours apart.

If you miss a dose of this medication, take it as soon as possible. However, if it is almost time for your next dose, skip the missed dose and go back to your regular dosing schedule. Do not double the next dose.

It is important to continue to take linezolid for the entire time prescribed by your doctor (usually five to ten days), even if the symptoms disappear before the end of that period. If you stop taking this drug too soon, resistant bacteria are given a chance to continue growing, and the infection could recur.

SIDE EFFECTS

Minor. Abdominal pain, change in the color of the tongue, constipation, diarrhea, dizziness, drowsiness, dry mouth or bad taste in the mouth, gas, loss of taste, or vomiting. These side effects should disappear as your body adjusts to the medication.

Dry mouth can be relieved by sucking on ice chips or a piece of hard candy or by chewing sugarless gum.

To avoid dizziness or light-headedness when you stand, contract and relax the muscles of your legs for a few moments before rising. Do this by pushing one foot against the floor while raising the other foot slightly, alternating feet so that you are "pumping" your legs in a pedaling motion.

If you feel dizzy, sit or lie down for a while; get up from a sitting or lying position slowly; and be careful on stairs.

Major. Tell your doctor about any side effects that are persistent or particularly bothersome. IT IS ESPECIALLY IMPORTANT TO TELL YOUR DOCTOR about darkened tongue, difficulty in breathing, difficulty in urinating, fever, itching, joint pain, rash, rectal or vaginal itching, severe diarrhea (which can be watery or contain pus or blood), sore mouth, stomach cramps, tingling in the hands or feet, unusual bleeding or bruising, unusual tiredness or weakness, or white patches in the mouth, tongue, or throat. If your symptoms of infection seem to be getting worse rather than improving, you should contact your doctor immediately.

INTERACTIONS

Linezolid interacts with several other types of medications:

1. To avoid drug interactions, it is very important that you do not take any over-the-counter (nonprescription) medications for weight control or for asthma, sinus problems, cough, common cold, or allergy problems unless you first check with a doctor or pharmacist.

2. The side effects of linezolid may be increased by certain drugs including selective serotonin reuptake inhibitors (including fluoxetine, paroxetine, and sertraline), venlafaxine, nefazodone, sibutramine, and monoamine oxidase (MAO) inhibitors (such as selegeline, isocarboxazid, pargyline, phenelzine, and tranylcypromine). Avoid these combinations. Discuss this with your doctor or pharmacist.

Before starting to take this medication, BE SURE TO TELL YOUR DOCTOR about any medications you are currently taking, especially any of those listed above.

WARNINGS

• Tell your doctor about unusual or allergic reactions you have ever had to any medications, especially to linezolid or other antibiotics.

• Tell your doctor if you have ever had hypertension, heart problems, fast or irregular heartbeats, kidney or urinary tract problems, depression, or phenylketonuria.

• Patients with phenylketonuria should be aware that the suspension form of this medication contains 20 mg of phenylalanine per 5-mL teaspoonful. This ingredient can dangerously affect people with phenylketonuria. However, the tablet form of this medication does not contain phenylalanine; discuss this with your doctor or pharmacist.

• This medication has been prescribed for your current infection only. Another infection later on, or one that someone else has, may require a different medicine. You

should not give your medication to other people or use it for other infections, unless your doctor specifically directs you to do so.
• Call your doctor immediately if you experience rash, difficulty breathing, or facial swelling after taking a dose of this medication.
• Before having surgery or any other medical or dental treatment, be sure to tell your doctor or dentist that you are being treated with this medication.
• Be sure to tell your doctor if you are pregnant. This medication has not been thoroughly studied in human pregnancy. Also tell your doctor if you are breast-feeding an infant. This medication passes into breast milk.

---

lisinopril

BRAND NAMES (Manufacturers)
Prinivil (Merck)
Zestril (Zeneca)
TYPE OF DRUG
Antihypertensive
INGREDIENT
lisinopril
DOSAGE FORM
Tablets (2.5 mg, 5 mg, 10 mg, 20 mg, and 40 mg)
STORAGE
Store this medication in a tightly closed container, away from heat, direct light, and moisture.

USES

Lisinopril is used in the treatment of hypertension (high blood pressure) and heart failure and is used after a heart attack. It can also be used for other conditions as determined by your doctor. Lisinopril is a vasodilator (it widens the blood vessels) that acts by blocking the production of chemicals that may be responsible for constricting blood vessels.

TREATMENT

The duration of action of lisinopril permits once-a-day dosing. Lisinopril can be taken either on an empty stomach or with food if it causes stomach irritation.

If you miss a dose of this medication, take the missed dose as soon as possible. However, if it is almost time for the next dose, do not take the missed dose at all; just wait until the next scheduled dose. Do not double the next dose.

In some patients it may require two to four weeks of therapy to achieve maximum therapeutic benefit.

Lisinopril does not cure high blood pressure, but it will help to control the condition as long as you take it according to directions.

SIDE EFFECTS

Minor. Diarrhea; dizziness; dry, hacking cough; fatigue; headache; or nasal congestion. These side effects should diminish or disappear as your body adjusts to the medication.

To avoid dizziness or light-headedness when you stand, contract and relax the muscles of your legs for a few moments before rising. Do this by pushing one foot against the floor while raising the other foot slightly, alternating feet so that you are "pumping" your legs in a pedaling motion.

Major. Tell your physician about any side effects that are persistent or particularly bothersome. IT IS ESPECIALLY IMPORTANT TO TELL YOUR DOCTOR about chest pain; chills; difficult or painful urination; fever; itching; mouth sores; palpitations;

prolonged vomiting or diarrhea; rash; shortness of breath; sore throat; swelling of the face, hands, or feet; tingling in the fingers or toes; unusual bleeding or bruising; or yellowing of the eyes or the skin.

INTERACTIONS

1. Lisinopril tends to cause retention of potassium in the body. Many salt substitutes contain potassium chloride and should only be used with the advice of your physician. Caution should also be observed with low-salt foods, some of which may contain significant amounts of potassium. Other medications such as the diuretics (water pills) triamterene, spironolactone, or amiloride may cause potassium retention. Use of these medications together with lisinopril may lead to excessive levels of potassium in the blood.
2. Nonsteroidal anti-inflammatory drugs (NSAIDs), such as indomethacin, may reduce the effectiveness of lisinopril.
3. Excessive hypotension (low blood pressure) may occur when starting lisinopril in patients on diuretics.

BE SURE TO TELL YOUR DOCTOR about any medications you are currently taking, especially those listed above.

WARNINGS

• Tell your doctor about unusual or allergic reactions you have had to any medications, especially to lisinopril, captopril, quinapril, fosinopril, benazepril, moexipril, ramipril, trandolapril, or enalapril.
• Tell your doctor if you have any other medical problems, such as diabetes, heart disease, kidney disease, liver disease, or systemic lupus erythematosus.
• Tell your doctor if you experience light-headedness, which may be a symptom of excessive hypotension (low blood pressure). This is especially likely to occur during the first few days of therapy. If fainting occurs, stop taking the medication and consult with your physician.
• Excessive perspiration or dehydration during treatment with this medication may cause an excessive drop in blood pressure.
• Report any evidence of infections (such as sore throat or fever) to your physician.
• If you have high blood pressure, do not take any over-the-counter (nonprescription) medication for weight control or for allergy, asthma, sinus, cough, or cold problems unless you first check with your doctor.
• Because lisinopril is eliminated from the body through the kidneys, be sure to report to your physician any symptoms of kidney disease, such as difficulty in urinating. If you have kidney disease, your doctor will need to reduce your dose of this medication.
• Before having surgery or any other medical or dental treatment, be sure to tell your doctor or dentist that you are taking this medication.
• Be sure to tell your doctor if you are pregnant or plan to become pregnant. This drug is not recommended for use during pregnancy. Also tell your doctor if you are breast-feeding an infant. It is not known whether lisinopril passes into breast milk.

lithium

BRAND NAMES (Manufacturers)
Eskalith (SmithKline Beecham)
Eskalith CR (SmithKline Beecham)
lithium carbonate (various manufacturers)
lithium citrate (various manufacturers)
Lithobid (Solvay)
Lithonate (Solvay)
Lithotabs (Solvay)

TYPE OF DRUG
Antimanic (mood stabilizer)
INGREDIENT
lithium
DOSAGE FORMS
Tablets (300 mg)
Extended-release tablets (300 mg and 450 mg)
Capsules (150 mg, 300 mg, and 600 mg)
Syrup (300 mg per 5-mL spoonful, with 0.3% alcohol)
STORAGE
Store at room temperature, away from heat, moisture, and direct sunlight

USES

Lithium is used to treat manic-depressive (bipolar) illness by controlling the manic (excited) phase and by reducing the frequency and severity of depression. Manic-depressive patients often experience unstable emotions ranging from excitement to hostility to depression. The mechanism of the mood-stabilizing effect of lithium is unknown, but it appears to work on the central nervous system to control emotions.

TREATMENT

Lithium should be taken exactly as directed by your doctor. The effectiveness of this medication depends upon the amount of lithium in your bloodstream. Therefore, the medication should be taken every day at regularly spaced intervals in order to keep a constant amount of lithium in your bloodstream. Lithium should be taken immediately after a meal or with food or milk.

The syrup form of this medication must be measured carefully with a specially designed 5-mL measuring spoon. An ordinary kitchen teaspoon is not accurate enough for therapeutic purposes.

If you miss a dose of this medication, take it as soon as possible. However, if it is within two hours (six hours for extended-release tablets) of your next scheduled dose, skip the missed dose and return to your regular schedule. Do not take more than one dose at a time.

If you are taking the long-acting, or slow-release, form of lithium, swallow the tablet or capsule whole. Do not break, crush, or chew before swallowing.

An improvement in your condition may not be seen for several weeks after you begin taking this medication.

SIDE EFFECTS

Minor. Acne, bloating, diarrhea, drowsiness, increased frequency of urination, increased thirst, nausea, trembling of the hands, weakness or tiredness, or weight gain. These side effects should disappear as your body makes an adjustment to this medication.

Major. Blurred vision, clumsiness, confusion, convulsions, difficulty in breathing, dizziness, fainting, palpitations, severe trembling, and slurred speech are possible effects of too much drug in the bloodstream. Dry, rough skin; hair loss; hoarseness; swelling of the feet or lower legs; swelling of the neck; unusual sensitivity to the cold; unusual tiredness; or unusual weight gain may be the result of low thyroid function caused by the medication. CHECK WITH YOUR DOCTOR IMMEDIATELY if you experience any of these side effects.

INTERACTIONS

Lithium interacts with a number of other types of medications:

1. Aminophylline, caffeine, verapamil, acetazolamide, sodium bicarbonate, and theophylline can increase the elimination of lithium from the body, thus decreasing its effectiveness.

2. Diuretics (water pills), especially hydrochlorothiazide, chlorothiazide, chlorthalidone, triamterene and hydrochlorothiazide combination, and furosemide may cause lithium toxicity by delaying the body's lithium elimination.
3. Captopril; chlorpromazine and other phenothiazine tranquilizers; and ibuprofen, indomethacin, naproxen, piroxicam, and the other nonsteroidal anti-inflammatory drugs (NSAIDs) can all slow the elimination of lithium and thereby increase its toxicity.
4. Lithium can increase the side effects of haloperidol and other medications that are used in the treatment of mental illness.
5. Phenytoin, methyldopa, carbamazepine, fluoxetine, and tetracycline can increase the side effects of lithium.
6. Drinking large amounts of caffeine-containing coffees, teas, or colas may reduce the effectiveness of lithium by increasing its elimination from the body through the urine.

BE SURE TO TELL YOUR DOCTOR about any medications you are currently taking, especially any of the medications listed above.

WARNINGS

• Tell your doctor about unusual or allergic reactions you have had to any medications, especially to lithium.
• Tell your doctor if you now have or ever had diabetes mellitus, epilepsy, heart disease, kidney disease, Parkinson's disease, or thyroid disease.
• Elderly patients may be more sensitive to the side effects of lithium than younger patients.
• To maintain a constant level of lithium in your bloodstream, it is important to drink two to three quarts of water or other fluids each day and not to change the amount of salt in your diet, unless your doctor specifically directs you to do so.
• The loss of large amounts of body fluid (from prolonged vomiting or diarrhea or from heavy sweating due to hot weather, fever, exercise, saunas, or hot baths) can result in increased lithium levels in the blood, which can lead to an increase in side effects.
• The toxic dose of lithium is very close to the therapeutic dose, so it is extremely important to follow your correct dosing schedule. Diarrhea, drowsiness, lack of coordination, muscular weakness, and vomiting may be signs of toxicity (overdose). If these symptoms occur for any length of time or begin shortly after taking a dose of lithium, be sure to inform your doctor.
• Lithium is not recommended for use during pregnancy, especially during the first three months, because of possible effects on the thyroid and heart of the developing fetus. Also tell your doctor if you are breast-feeding. Lithium also passes into breast milk and is not recommended for nursing women.
• If this drug makes you drowsy or dizzy, do not participate in any activities that require alertness, such as driving a car or operating potentially dangerous machinery.

---

loperamide

BRAND NAMES (Manufacturers)
Imodium (Janssen)
Imodium A-D* (McNeil CPC)
Kaopectate II* (Upjohn)
loperamide* (various manufacturers)
Maalox Anti-Diarrheal* (RP Rorer)
Neo-Diaral* (Roberts)
Pepto Diarrhea Control* (Procter & Gamble)
*Available over the counter (without a prescription)
TYPE OF DRUG
Antidiarrheal

INGREDIENT
loperamide
DOSAGE FORMS
Capsules (2 mg)
Oral liquid (1 mg per 1 mL and 1 mg per 5-mL spoonful, each with 5.25% alcohol)
Tablets (2 mg)
STORAGE
Store at room temperature in a tightly closed container. Do not freeze.

USES

Loperamide is used to treat acute and chronic diarrhea and to reduce the volume of discharge in patients who have ileostomies. It acts by slowing the movement of the gastrointestinal tract and decreasing the passage of water and other substances into the bowel.

TREATMENT

To avoid stomach upset, you can take loperamide with food or with a full glass of water or milk.

If you miss a dose of this medication, do not take the missed dose at all; just return to your regular dosing schedule. Do not double the next dose.

SIDE EFFECTS

Minor. Constipation, dizziness, drowsiness, dry mouth, fatigue, loss of appetite, nausea, or vomiting. These side effects should diminish or disappear as your body adjusts to the medication.

To relieve constipation, exercise and drink more water (unless your doctor directs you to do otherwise).

To reduce mouth dryness, chew sugarless gum or suck on ice chips or a piece of hard candy.

If you feel dizzy or light-headed, sit or lie down for a while; get up from a sitting or lying position slowly; and be careful on stairs.

Major. Tell your doctor about any side effects that are persistent or particularly bothersome. IT IS ESPECIALLY IMPORTANT TO TELL YOUR DOCTOR about abdominal bloating or pain, fever, rash, or sore throat.

INTERACTIONS

Loperamide should not interact with any other drugs.

WARNINGS

- Tell your doctor about unusual or allergic reactions you have had to any medications, especially to loperamide.
- Tell your doctor if you now have or ever had colitis, diarrhea caused by infectious organisms, drug-induced diarrhea, liver disease, dehydration, or conditions in which constipation must be avoided (such as hemorrhoids, diverticulitis, heart or blood vessel disorders, or blood clotting disorders).
- If this drug makes you dizzy or drowsy, do not take part in any activity that requires alertness.
- Before having surgery or any other medical or dental treatment, be sure to tell your doctor or dentist that you are taking this medication.
- Check with your doctor if your diarrhea does not subside within three days. Unless your doctor prescribes otherwise, do not take this medication for more than ten days at a time.
- While taking this medication, drink lots of fluids to replace those lost because of diarrhea.

• Check with your doctor before administering this medication to a child younger than two years old.
• Be sure to tell your doctor if you are pregnant. The effects of using this medication during pregnancy have not been thoroughly studied in humans. Also be sure to tell your doctor if you are breast-feeding an infant. It is not known whether loperamide passes into breast milk.

---

lopinavir and ritonavir combination

BRAND NAME (Manufacturer)
Kaletra (Abbott)
TYPE OF DRUG
Antiretroviral agent and protease inhibitor
INGREDIENT
lopinavir and ritonavir
DOSAGE FORMS
Capsules (133.3 mg lopinavir and 33.3 mg ritonavir)
Oral solution (400 mg lopinavir and 100 mg ritonavir per 5-mL teaspoonful, contains 42.4% alcohol)
STORAGE
Store both forms in the refrigerator; they will remain potent until the expiration date printed on the label. When stored at room temperature in a tightly closed container, the solution and capsules must be used within two months. Do not expose to excess heat, and do not freeze.

USES

Both lopinavir and ritonavir are used in the treatment of human immunodeficiency virus (HIV) infection. HIV is the virus that causes AIDS. Lopinavir and ritonavir combination works by inhibiting the reproduction, or growth, of the virus, which slows down the progression of AIDS. This medication does not cure HIV infection or AIDS, but it may delay the onset of other infections and diseases caused by AIDS. Lopinavir and ritonavir combination is not usually used alone but rather in combination with other anti-AIDS medications.

TREATMENT

This medication works best when the level of medicine in your bloodstream is kept constant. It is best to take the drug at evenly spaced intervals throughout the day and night. For example, if you are to take 2 doses a day, the doses should be spaced 12 hours apart. IT IS IMPORTANT NOT TO MISS ANY DOSES OF LOPINAVIR AND RITONAVIR COMBINATION. The chances of the AIDS virus becoming resistant to these medications increases if the level of this drug combination in the bloodstream is low. If you miss a dose of this medication, take it as soon as possible. However, if it is almost time for your next dose, skip the missed dose and go back to your regular dosing schedule. Do not double the doses.

It is very important to take lopinavir and ritonavir combination WITH FOOD to make sure that the medication will work properly.

Measure each dose of the solution carefully using the measuring cup provided or with a specially designed 5-mL measuring spoon, as directed by your doctor or pharmacist. An ordinary kitchen teaspoon is not accurate enough.

SIDE EFFECTS

Minor. Abnormal stools, diarrhea, headache, muscle weakness, pain, redistribution of body fat, skin rash, or trouble sleeping. As your body adjusts to the medication, some of these side effects should disappear.

Major. Tell your doctor about any side effects that are persistent or particularly bothersome. IT IS ESPECIALLY IMPORTANT TO TELL YOUR DOCTOR about bloating, blurred vision, chills, constipation, darkened urine, dry mouth, fainting spells, fast heartbeat, fatigue, feeling of extreme weakness or tiredness, fever, flushed or dry skin, fruitlike breath odor, increased hunger or thirst, stomach upset, trouble breathing, unexplained weight loss, unusual muscle aches, vomiting, or yellowing of the skin or the whites of the eyes.

INTERACTIONS

Lopinavir and ritonavir combination may interact with many other drugs.

1. To avoid drug interactions, it is very important that you do not take any over-the-counter (nonprescription) medications for weight control or for asthma, sinus problems, cough, cold, or allergy problems unless you first check with a doctor or pharmacist. It is particularly important to avoid Saint-John's-wort, as it will reduce the efficacy of lopinavir and ritonavir combination.

2. This medication may make birth control pills (oral contraceptives) less effective. A different or additional means of birth control should be used while taking lopinavir and ritonavir combination.

3. The following drugs must NEVER be taken at the same time as lopinavir and ritonavir combination: flecainide, propafenone, dihydroergotamine, ergonovine, ergotamine, methylergonovine, pimozide, midazolam, triazolam, simvastatin, lovastatin, and cisapride. If administered together, these medications can produce very severe side effects.

4. Lopinavir and ritonavir combination may increase the side effects from the following medications: cyclosporine, felodipine, nicardipine, nifedipine, sirolimus, tacrolimus, clarithromycin, and warfarin.

5. The side effects of sildenafil will be increased when taken with lopinavir and ritonavir combination; discuss this with your doctor or pharmacist.

6. If you are being treated with didanosine, it must be taken one hour before OR two hours after you take lopinavir and ritonavir combination.

WARNINGS

• Tell your doctor if you have ever had an allergic reaction to lopinavir and ritonavir combination or to any other medication (especially medications used to treat viral infections or HIV infection, including nelfinavir or indinavir).

• Before taking this medication, be sure to tell your doctor about any medical problems you may have, including liver problems, diabetes, problems with high blood sugar or high cholesterol, or bleeding problems, especially hemophilia.

• You should NEVER stop taking this medication or change the dose unless directed by your doctor.

• Your doctor may order certain blood tests to monitor your liver function while you are taking this drug, especially if you have any history of liver disease or hepatitis.

• This medication may cause the fat in your body to be redistributed. There may be a loss of fat from the face, buttocks, arms, and legs and an increase in fatty tissue on the upper back.

• Be sure to tell your doctor about any other medications or supplements you are taking, both prescription and nonprescription. Lopinavir and ritonavir combination may interact with other medications to produce serious side effects.

• Your doctor may do regular blood tests to check your cholesterol. Increases in cholesterol may occur with lopinavir and ritonavir combination.

• Because the solution form of this medication has a high alcohol content, it is recommended to AVOID drinking any additional alcoholic beverages when you are taking lopinavir and ritonavir combination solution. The combination could produce extreme drowsiness.

• This medication may cause high blood sugar (or worsening of existing diabetes). Your doctor may want you to check your blood sugar regularly while taking this medication. Ask your doctor about the signs of high blood sugar and diabetes.
• Your doctor may do regular blood tests to see how well this medication is working against the AIDS virus.
• Before having surgery or any other medical or dental treatment, be sure to tell your doctor or dentist that you are taking this medication.
• If you are infected with HIV, it is best to avoid any sexual activity involving an exchange of body fluids with other people. If you do have vaginal, anal, or oral sex, always use a latex condom.
• Be sure to tell your doctor if you are pregnant. It is not known if this medication is safe to use during pregnancy, and it is not known if lopinavir and ritonavir combination passes into human breast milk. However, because of the risk of passing HIV to infants, it is recommended that mothers who have HIV infection NOT breast-feed their infants.

---

loracarbef

BRAND NAME (Manufacturer)
Lorabid (Lilly)
TYPE OF DRUG
Cephalosporin antibiotic
INGREDIENT
loracarbef
DOSAGE FORMS
Capsule (200 mg and 400 mg)
Oral suspension (100 mg and 200 mg per 5-mL spoonful)
STORAGE
Store at room temperature in a tightly closed container. Discard any unused portion of the suspension after 14 days because the suspension loses potency after that time. Do not freeze or expose to extreme heat.

USES

Loracarbef is used to treat a wide variety of bacterial infections, including infections of the middle ear, the upper and lower respiratory tract, the skin, and the urinary tract. It is related to the cephalosporin group of antibiotics. This medication acts by binding to essential proteins of the bacterial cell wall, thereby inhibiting the growth and multiplication of the infecting bacteria.

TREATMENT

Loracarbef should be taken on an empty stomach (one hour before or two hours after eating) to avoid a decrease in absorption of the drug.

Shake the suspension well just before measuring each dose to distribute the ingredients evenly and equalize the doses.The contents of the suspension tend to settle on the bottom of the bottle. Measure each dose with a specially designed 5-mL measuring spoon or with the dropper provided. An ordinary kitchen teaspoon is not accurate enough for medical purposes.

Cephalosporin antibiotics work best when the level of medicine in your bloodstream is kept constant. It is best to take the doses at evenly spaced intervals throughout the day and night. For example, if you are to take two doses a day, the doses should be spaced 12 hours apart. If you miss a dose of this medication, take the missed dose immediately. If you do not remember to take the missed dose until it is almost time for your next dose, take it; space the following dose halfway through the regular interval between doses, then return to your regular schedule. Try not to skip any doses of this medication.

It is important to try to take this medication for the entire time prescribed by your doctor (usually 7 to 14 days), even if the symptoms disappear before the end of that period. If you stop taking the drug too soon, resistant bacteria could continue to grow, and infection could recur.

SIDE EFFECTS

Minor. Abdominal pain, diarrhea, dizziness, fatigue, headache, heartburn, loss of appetite, nausea, or vomiting. These side effects should disappear as your body adjusts to the medication.

If you feel dizzy while you are taking this medication, sit or lie down for a while; get up slowly from a sitting or reclining position; and be careful on stairs. Do not operate an automobile or any potentially dangerous equipment or work with any hazardous materials.

Major. Tell your doctor about any side effects that are persistent or particularly bothersome. IT IS ESPECIALLY IMPORTANT TO TELL YOUR DOCTOR about chest pain, darkened tongue, difficulty in breathing, fever, itching, joint pain, rash, rectal or vaginal itching, severe diarrhea (which can be watery or contain pus or blood), sore mouth, stomach cramps, tingling in the hands or feet, or unusual bleeding or bruising. If your symptoms of infection seem to be getting worse rather than improving, contact your doctor.

INTERACTIONS

Loracarbef interacts with several other drugs:

1. Concurrent use of probenecid can increase the blood concentrations and side effects of this medication.

2. The side effects, especially on the kidneys, of diuretics (such as furosemide, bumetanide, or ethacrynic acid), colistin, vancomycin, polymyxin B, and aminoglycoside antibiotics can be increased by loracarbef.

3. Chloramphenicol should be avoided during treatment with loracarbef because of the possibility of an antagonistic (opposing) effect.

BE SURE TO TELL YOUR DOCTOR about any medications you are currently taking, especially any listed above.

WARNINGS

• Tell your doctor about any unusual or allergic reactions you have had to any medications, especially to loracarbef or other cephalosporin antibiotics (such as cefaclor, cefdinir, cefixime, cefmetazole, cefoperazone, cefotaxime, cefpodoxime, cefprozil, ceftazidime, ceftibuten, ceftizoxime, ceftriaxone, cefuroxime, cephradine, and moxalactam) or to penicillin antibiotics.

• Tell your doctor if you have ever had kidney disease or gastrointestinal disease, particularly colitis. If you have kidney disease, your doctor will prescribe a reduced dose of this medication.

• This medication has been prescribed for your current infection only. Another infection later on, or one that someone else has, may require a different medicine. You should not give your medication to other people or use it for other infections, unless your doctor specifically directs you to do so.

• People with diabetes who are taking loracarbef should know that this medication may cause a false-positive sugar reaction with a Clinitest urine glucose test. To avoid this problem while taking loracarbef, switch to Clinistix or Tes-Tape to test urine-sugar content.

• Be sure to tell your doctor if you are pregnant. Although the cephalosporin-related antibiotics appear to be safe during pregnancy, extensive studies in humans have not been conducted. Also tell your doctor if you are breast-feeding an infant. Small amounts of this medication pass into breast milk and may temporarily alter the bacterial balance in the intestinal tract of the nursing infant, resulting in diarrhea.

loratadine

BRAND NAME (Manufacturer)
Claritin (Schering)
TYPE OF DRUG
Antihistamine
INGREDIENT
loratadine
DOSAGE FORMS
Syrup (1 mg per 1 mL)
Tablets (10 mg)
Tablets, rapidly disintegrating (10 mg)
STORAGE
Store at room temperature in a tightly closed, light-resistant container.

USES

Loratadine is a long-acting antihistamine. Antihistamines block the action of histamine, a chemical that is released from the body during an allergic reaction. Loratadine is used to provide symptomatic relief of seasonal allergic rhinitis, such as hay fever.

TREATMENT

Take on an empty stomach to achieve effective blood levels of the drug. The rapidly disintegrating tablet should be placed on the tongue to dissolve and swallowed immediately, either with or without water.

If you miss a dose of this medication, take the missed dose as soon as possible. However, if it is almost time for your next dose, do not take the missed dose at all; just return to your regular dosing schedule. Do not double the next dose.

Loratadine will not cure seasonal allergic rhinitis, but the medication will relieve the symptoms that are associated with the condition.

SIDE EFFECTS

Minor. Blurred vision; breast pain; confusion; constipation; diarrhea; difficult or painful urination; dizziness; dry mouth, throat, or nose; dry skin or hair; headache; increased or decreased appetite; irritability; itching; nausea; restlessness; ringing or buzzing in the ears; stomach upset; or sweating. These side effects should disappear as your body adjusts to the medication.

This medication can cause increased sensitivity to sunlight. It is very important to avoid prolonged exposure to sunlight and sunlamps. Wear protective clothing and use an effective sunscreen.

If you are constipated, increase the amount of fiber in your diet (fresh fruits and vegetables, salads, bran, and whole-grain breads). You can also increase your exercise level and drink more water (unless your doctor directs you not to do so).

Chew sugarless gum or suck on ice chips or a piece of hard candy to reduce mouth dryness.

If you feel dizzy or light-headed, sit or lie down for a while; get up from a sitting or lying position slowly; and be careful on stairs.

Major. Tell your doctor about any side effects that are persistent or particularly bothersome. IT IS ESPECIALLY IMPORTANT TO TELL YOUR DOCTOR about anxiety, change in menstruation, clumsiness, depression, feeling faint, flushing of the face, hallucinations, migraines, palpitations, rash, seizures, shortness of breath, sleeping disorders, sore throat or fever, tightness in the chest or back, trouble breathing, unusual bleeding or bruising, unusual tiredness or weakness, urine discoloration, or yellowing of the eyes or skin.

INTERACTIONS

This drug interacts with several other types of drugs:

1. Concurrent use of this medication with other central nervous system depressants (such as alcohol, barbiturates, benzodiazepine tranquilizers, muscle relaxants, narcotics, pain medications, and phenothiazine tranquilizers) or with tricyclic antidepressants can cause extreme drowsiness.

2. Monoamine oxidase (MAO) inhibitors (such as isocarboxazid, pargyline, phenelzine, selegiline, and tranylcypromine) can be expected to increase the side effects of this medication.

BE SURE TO TELL YOUR DOCTOR about any medications you are currently taking, especially any of those listed above.

WARNINGS

- Be sure to tell your doctor about unusual or allergic reactions you have had to any medications, especially to loratadine, cyproheptadine, azatadine, or any other antihistamines (such as astemizole, brompheniramine, cetirizine, chlorpheniramine, clemastine, dimenhydrinate, diphenhydramine, diphenylpyraline, doxylamine, fexofenadine, hydroxyzine, and terfenadine).
- Tell your doctor if you now have or ever had asthma, blood-vessel disease, glaucoma, high blood pressure, kidney disease, liver disease, peptic ulcers, enlarged prostate gland, or thyroid disease.
- Because loratadine is primarily metabolized by the liver, patients with liver disease may require a lower dosage.
- Although loratadine causes less drowsiness than many of the other medications in its class, your ability to perform tasks that require alertness, such as driving a car or operating potentially dangerous machinery, may be impaired.
- Be sure to tell your doctor if you are pregnant. The effects of this medication during pregnancy have not been thoroughly studied in humans. Also tell your doctor if you are breast-feeding an infant. Loratadine should not be used by nursing mothers.

---

lorazepam

BRAND NAMES (Manufacturers)
Ativan (Wyeth)
lorazepam (various manufacturers)
TYPE OF DRUG
Benzodiazepine sedative/hypnotic
INGREDIENT
lorazepam
DOSAGE FORMS
Tablets (0.5 mg, 1 mg, and 2 mg)
Oral solution (2 mg/mL)
STORAGE
Store the tablet form of this medication at room temperature in a tightly closed, light-resistant container. Keep the solution form of the drug in the refrigerator. Do not take the solution if you notice that it has become discolored or contains a precipitate.

USES

Lorazepam is prescribed to treat symptoms of anxiety and anxiety associated with depression. It is not clear exactly how this medicine works, but it may relieve anxiety by acting as a depressant of the central nervous system (brain and spinal cord). This medication is currently used by many people to relieve nervousness. It is effective for this purpose for short periods, but it is important to try to remove the cause of the anxiety as well.

TREATMENT

Take exactly as your doctor directs. It can be taken with food or a full glass of water if stomach upset occurs. Do not take this medication with a dose of antacids, since they may slow its absorption from the gastrointestinal tract.

If you are taking this medication regularly and miss a dose, take the missed dose immediately if you remember within an hour. If more than an hour has passed, skip the missed dose and wait for the next scheduled dose. Do not double the next dose of the medication.

SIDE EFFECTS

Minor. Bitter taste in the mouth, constipation, diarrhea, dizziness, drowsiness (after a night's sleep), dry mouth, fatigue, flushing, headache, heartburn, excessive salivation, loss of appetite, nausea, nervousness, sweating, or vomiting. As your body adjusts to the medication, these side effects should diminish or disappear.

To relieve constipation, increase the amount of fiber in your diet (fresh fruits and vegetables, salads, bran, and whole-grain breads), exercise, and drink more water (unless your doctor directs you to do otherwise).

Dry mouth can be relieved by chewing sugarless gum or by sucking on ice chips.

If you feel dizzy, sit or lie down for a while. Get up slowly from a sitting or reclining position, and be careful on stairs.

Major. Tell your doctor about any side effects that are persistent or particularly bothersome. IT IS ESPECIALLY IMPORTANT TO TELL YOUR DOCTOR about blurred or double vision, chest pain, depression, difficulty in urinating, fainting, falling, fever, joint pain, hallucinations, memory problems, mouth sores, nightmares, palpitations, rash, shortness of breath, slurred speech, sore throat, uncoordinated movements, unusual excitement, unusual tiredness, or yellowing of the eyes or skin.

INTERACTIONS

Lorazepam interacts with several other types of medications:

1. To prevent oversedation, this drug should not be taken with alcohol, other sedative drugs, antidepressants, or central nervous system depressants (such as antihistamines, barbiturates, muscle relaxants, pain medicines, narcotics, medicines for seizures, and phenothiazine tranquilizers).

2. This medication may decrease the effectiveness of carbamazepine, levodopa, and oral anticoagulants (blood thinners) and may increase the effects of phenytoin.

3. Disulfiram, cimetidine, and isoniazid can increase the blood levels of lorazepam, which can lead to toxic effects.

4. Concurrent use of rifampin may decrease the effectiveness of lorazepam.

BE SURE TO TELL YOUR DOCTOR about any medications you are currently taking, especially any of the medications listed above.

WARNINGS

• Tell your doctor about unusual or allergic reactions you have had to any medications, especially to lorazepam or other benzodiazepine tranquilizers (such as alprazolam, chlordiazepoxide, clorazepate, diazepam, flurazepam, halazepam, midazolam, oxazepam, prazepam, temazepam, and triazolam).

• Tell your doctor if you now have or ever had liver disease, kidney disease, epilepsy, lung disease, myasthenia gravis, porphyria, mental depression, or mental illness.

• This medicine can cause drowsiness. Avoid tasks that require alertness, such as driving a car or using potentially dangerous machinery.

• This medication has the potential for abuse and must be used with caution. Tolerance may develop quickly; do not increase the dosage without first consulting your doctor. It is also important not to stop this medication suddenly if you have been taking it in large amounts or if you have used it for several weeks. Your doctor may want to reduce your dosage gradually.
• This is a safe drug when used properly. When it is combined with other sedative drugs or alcohol, however, serious side effects can develop.
• Be sure to tell your doctor if you are pregnant. This medicine may increase the chance of birth defects if it is taken during the first three months of pregnancy. In addition, too much use of this medicine during the last six months of pregnancy may cause the fetus to become dependent on it, resulting in withdrawal side effects in the newborn. Tell your doctor if you are breast-feeding. This drug can pass into the breast milk and cause drowsiness, slowed heartbeat, and breathing difficulties in the nursing infant.

losartan

BRAND NAME (Manufacturer)
Cozaar (Merck)
TYPE OF DRUG
Antihypertensive
INGREDIENT
losartan
DOSAGE FORM
Tablets (25 mg, 50 mg, and 100 mg)
STORAGE
Store this medication at room temperature in a tightly closed container.

USES

Losartan is used to treat high blood pressure and congestive heart failure. It is a vasodilator (it widens the blood vessels) that acts by blocking the production of chemicals that may be responsible for constricting, or narrowing, the blood vessels.

TREATMENT

Take this drug on an empty stomach or, if it causes stomach upset, with food. To become used to taking this drug, try to take it at the same time(s) every day.

It may be several weeks before you notice the full effects of this medication.

If you miss a dose of this medication, take the missed dose as soon as possible. However, if it is almost time for the next dose, do not take the missed dose at all; just wait until the next scheduled dose. Do not double the next dose of the medication.

Losartan does not cure high blood pressure, but it will help to control the condition as long as you continue to take the medication.

SIDE EFFECTS

Minor. Abdominal pain, cough, diarrhea, dizziness, drowsiness, fatigue, headache, insomnia, nausea, nervousness, sweating, or vomiting. These side effects should diminish or disappear as your body adjusts to the medication.

To avoid dizziness when you stand, contract and relax the muscles of your legs for a few moments before rising. Do this by pushing one foot against the floor while lifting the other foot slightly, alternating feet so that you are "pumping" your legs in a pedaling motion.

Major. Tell your doctor about any side effects that are persistent or particularly bothersome. IT IS ESPECIALLY IMPORTANT TO TELL YOUR DOCTOR about chest pain; difficulty breathing; fainting; fever; itching; light-headedness (especially during the first few days); muscle cramps; palpitations; rash; sore throat; swelling of the face, eyes, lips, or tongue; tingling in the fingers and toes; or yellowing of the eyes or skin.

INTERACTIONS

Losartan interacts with several other types of medications:

1. Diuretics and other antihypertensive medications can cause an excessive drop in blood pressure when they are used concurrently with losartan (especially when the first dose of losartan is taken).

2. The combination of losartan with amiloride, potassium supplements, salt substitutes, spironolactone, or triamterene can lead to hyperkalemia (dangerously high levels of potassium in the bloodstream).

3. Nonsteroidal anti-inflammatory agents (including ibuprofen, indomethacin, and naproxen) may reduce the effectiveness of this medication.

4. Concurrent use of losartan and fluconazole, an antifungal medication, can increase the effects of losartan and may lead to toxicity.

Before starting to take losartan, BE SURE TO TELL YOUR DOCTOR about any medications you are currently taking, especially any of those listed above.

WARNINGS

- Tell your doctor about any unusual or allergic reactions you have had to any medications, especially to losartan.
- Tell your doctor if you now have or ever had blood disorders, heart failure, renal disease, or systemic lupus erythematosus.
- Excessive perspiration, dehydration, or prolonged vomiting or diarrhea can lead to an excessive drop in blood pressure while you are taking this medication. Contact your doctor if you have any of these symptoms.
- Before having surgery or any other medical or dental treatment, tell your doctor or dentist that you are being treated with this medication.
- If this medication makes you feel dizzy or drowsy, do not take part in any activity that requires alertness, such as driving an automobile, operating any potentially dangerous equipment, or using hazardous chemicals.
- If you have high blood pressure, do not take any over-the-counter (nonprescription) medications for weight control or for asthma, sinus, cough, cold, or allergy problems unless you first check with your doctor.
- Be sure to tell your doctor immediately if you are pregnant. Losartan is very similar to the class of drugs called angiotensin-converting enzyme (ACE) inhibitors (including captopril, enalapril, and lisinopril), which have been shown to cause birth defects when taken in the second and third trimesters. Also be sure to tell your doctor if you are breast-feeding an infant. It is not known whether losartan passes into breast milk.

---

lovastatin

BRAND NAMES (Manufacturers)
Altocor (Andrx)
lovastatin (various manufacturers)
Mevacor (Merck)
TYPE OF DRUG
Antihyperlipidemic (lipid-lowering drug)
INGREDIENT
lovastatin
DOSAGE FORM
Tablets (10 mg, 20 mg, and 40 mg)
Tablets, extended release (10 mg, 20 mg, 40 mg, and 60 mg)

STORAGE

Store at room temperature in a tightly closed, light-resistant container. Exposure to heat or moisture may cause this drug to break down.

USES

Lovastatin is used to treat hyperlipidemia (high blood fat levels) and to slow the progression of heart disease. It is prescribed in conjunction with nondrug therapies, such as diet modification and regular exercise, in an attempt to regulate lipid and cholesterol levels. Lovastatin chemically interferes with an enzyme in the body that is responsible for synthesizing cholesterol. This decreases the LDL (low-density lipoprotein) type of cholesterol, which has been associated with coronary heart disease and atherosclerosis.

TREATMENT

Take with food, exactly as prescribed by your doctor. If you are to take the drug once a day, it is best to take the drug in the evening with your dinner.

While using this medication, try to develop a set schedule for taking it. If you miss a dose and remember within a few hours, take the missed dose and resume your regular schedule. If many hours have passed, skip the dose you missed and then take your next dose as scheduled. Do not double the dose.

SIDE EFFECTS

Minor. Abdominal pain or cramps, constipation, diarrhea, gas, nausea, or stomach pain. These side effects should diminish or disappear as your body adjusts to this medication.

To relieve constipation, increase the amount of fiber in your diet (fresh fruits and vegetables, salads, bran, and whole-grain breads), exercise, and drink more water, unless your doctor directs you otherwise.

Major. Tell your doctor about any side effects that are persistent or particularly bothersome. IT IS ESPECIALLY IMPORTANT TO TELL YOUR DOCTOR about blurred vision (or any other visual changes or difficulties) or muscle pain or tenderness, especially if any of these are accompanied by malaise or fever.

INTERACTIONS

Lovastatin can interact with a number of other types of medications:

1. Cholestyramine and colestipol may decrease the absorption of lovastatin. Lovastatin should be taken four hours after these other medications.

2. Cyclosporine, erythromycin, gemfibrozil, niacin, and antifungal agents may increase the risk of serious side effects from lovastatin.

3. Lovastatin may increase the risk of bleeding caused by oral anticoagulants (blood thinners, such as warfarin).

BE SURE TO TELL YOUR DOCTOR about any medications you are currently taking, especially any of those listed above.

WARNINGS

- Tell your doctor about unusual or allergic reactions you have had to any medications. IT IS VERY IMPORTANT TO REPORT ANY SYMPTOMS, including muscle pain, tenderness, or weakness, especially if you also have a fever.
- Tell your doctor if you have ever had liver disease, heart disease, stroke, or disorders of the digestive tract.
- In preliminary studies with lovastatin, some patients were found to have developed eye-related problems during treatment. Although these findings are inconclusive, and it has not yet been determined whether lovastatin is involved in such occurrences, it is advisable to have regular checkups with your ophthalmologist and inform him or her of your use of this medication.

• This medication can increase your sensitivity to sunlight. Avoid prolonged exposure to sunlight and sunlamps, wear protective clothing, and use an effective sunscreen.
• Your doctor may want to test your blood while you are taking this medication to detect any liver problems it may cause.
• Do not take this drug if you are pregnant or breast-feeding an infant.

---

medroxyprogesterone

BRAND NAMES (Manufacturers)
Amen (Carnrick)
Curretab (Solvay)
Cycrin (ESI Lederle)
medroxyprogesterone acetate (various manufacturers)
Provera (Upjohn)
TYPE OF DRUG
Progesterone
INGREDIENT
medroxyprogesterone
DOSAGE FORM
Tablets (2.5 mg, 5 mg, and 10 mg)
STORAGE
Store at room temperature in a tightly closed container. Do not refrigerate.

USES

Medroxyprogesterone is a synthetic progesterone (a female hormone naturally produced by the body) that is used to treat abnormal menstrual bleeding, difficult menstruation, or lack of menstruation. It can be used for other conditions as determined by your doctor.

TREATMENT

This medication may cause stomach irritation. To avoid or minimize this side effect, take medroxyprogesterone with food or immediately after a meal.

If you miss a dose, take the missed dose as soon as possible. However, if it is almost time for the next dose, do not take the missed dose at all; just return to your regular dosing schedule. Do not double the next dose unless directed to do so by your doctor.

SIDE EFFECTS

Minor. Acne, dizziness, hair growth, headache, nausea, or vomiting. These side effects should disappear as your body adjusts to the medication.

This medication can increase your sensitivity to sunlight. Avoid prolonged exposure to sunlight and sunlamps. Wear protective clothing, and use an effective sunscreen.

This medication may cause tenderness, swelling, or bleeding of the gums. Brushing and flossing your teeth regularly may prevent this. You should also see your dentist regularly while you are taking this medicine.

If you feel dizzy or light-headed, sit or lie down for a while; get up slowly from a sitting or reclining position; and be careful on stairs.

Major. Tell your doctor about any side effects that are persistent or particularly bothersome. IT IS ESPECIALLY IMPORTANT TO TELL YOUR DOCTOR about breast tenderness; change in menstrual patterns; chest pain; depression; fainting; hair loss; itching; pain in the calves; rapid weight gain (three to five pounds within a week); rash;

slurred speech; sudden, severe headache; swelling of the feet or the ankles; unusual vaginal bleeding; or yellowing of the eyes or the skin.

INTERACTIONS

Medroxyprogesterone should not interact with other medications if it is used according to directions.

WARNINGS

- Tell your doctor about unusual or allergic reactions you have had to any medications, especially to medroxyprogesterone, progestin, or progesterone.
- Before starting this drug, tell your doctor if you have ever had cancer of the breast or genitals, clotting disorders, diabetes mellitus, depression, epilepsy, gallbladder disease, asthma, heart disease, kidney disease, liver disease, migraines, porphyria, stroke, or vaginal bleeding.
- A package insert should come with this drug. Read it carefully, and if you have any questions, ask your doctor.
- If this drug makes you dizzy or drowsy, do not take part in any activities that require alertness, such as driving a car or operating potentially dangerous machinery.
- It is important to tell your doctor if you are pregnant. Medroxyprogesterone should not be used during the first four months of pregnancy because it has been shown to cause birth defects. Since hormones have long-term effects on the body, this medication should be stopped at least three months before you attempt to become pregnant. Also tell your doctor if you are breast-feeding an infant. Small amounts of medroxyprogesterone pass into breast milk.

---

metformin

BRAND NAMES (Manufacturers)
Glucophage (Bristol-Myers Squibb)
Glucophage XR (Bristol-Myers Squibb)
TYPE OF DRUG
Oral antidiabetic
INGREDIENT
metformin
DOSAGE FORMS
Tablets (500 mg, 850 mg, and 1,000 mg)
Tablets, extended release (500 mg)
STORAGE
Store this medication at room temperature in a tightly closed container. Do not refrigerate or freeze it. Discard any outdated medication.

USES

Metformin is used for the treatment of the form of diabetes mellitus that most commonly appears in adulthood—known as type 2 or non–insulin-dependent diabetes—and that cannot be managed by exercise and dietary therapy alone. Metformin helps to control sugar in the blood by making the body more sensitive to insulin and by reducing the amount of sugar produced by the body. Metformin can be used alone or with other antidiabetic medications (such as sulfonylureas or insulin).

TREATMENT

For this medication to work correctly, it must be taken as directed by your doctor. It is best to take this medication at the same time each day to maintain good blood sugar control. It is important to avoid missing any doses of metformin. If you do miss a dose, take it as soon as possible. However, if it is almost time for your next regular dose of the medication, do not take the missed dose at all; just return to your regular dosing schedule. Do not double the dose. Tell your doctor if you feel any side effects from missing a dose of this drug. Metformin should be taken with a meal to lessen nausea and diarrhea.

Swallow the extended-release tablets whole; do not crush or chew them.

SIDE EFFECTS

Minor. Headache, loss of appetite, metallic taste in mouth, nausea, stomach discomfort, or gas. These side effects should lessen as your body adjusts to the drug.
Major. Tell your doctor about any side effects that are persistent or particularly bothersome. IT IS ESPECIALLY IMPORTANT TO TELL YOUR DOCTOR about anxiousness; cold sweats; diarrhea; excessive hunger; fast, shallow breathing; headache; muscle cramps or pain; rapid pulse; shakiness; unusual sleepiness; or unusual tiredness or weakness.

INTERACTIONS

Metformin interacts with several other types of drugs:
1. Cimetidine, furosemide, nifedipine, amiloride, digoxin, procainamide, quinidine, ranitidine, triamterene, or trimethoprim taken concurrently with metformin may increase the blood concentration of metformin.
2. Alcohol and iodinated contrast material may increase the risk for some of the serious side effects of this medication.
3. Metformin may decrease the amount of glyburide or furosemide in the body.
4. The effectiveness of metformin may be reduced by oral contraceptives, cortisonelike drugs, thiazide diuretics, estrogens, isoniazid, phenothiazines, phenytoin, and thyroid hormones.
5. The actions of metformin may be increased by clofibrate, monoamine oxidase (MAO) inhibitors, probenecid, propranolol, rifabutin, rifampin, salicylates, and sulfonamides.

BE SURE TO TELL YOUR DOCTOR about any medications you are currently taking, especially those listed above.

WARNINGS

- It is important to tell your doctor if you have ever had an unusual or allergic reaction to any medication, especially to metformin.
- It is also important to tell your doctor if you now have or ever had kidney disease, liver disease, or heart disease.
- When taking the extended-release tablets, it is normal for the inactive part of the tablet to be eliminated in the feces as a soft mass.
- Avoid drinking alcohol while taking this medication. Alcohol may increase the risk of serious side effects from metformin.
- Before having surgery or any other medical or dental treatment, be sure to tell your doctor or dentist that you are taking this medication. IT IS ESPECIALLY IMPORTANT TO TELL YOUR DOCTOR that you are taking this medication if you are going to have any type of X-ray or similar medical test. Your doctor may want you to stop taking this medication a few days before such testing is scheduled.
- Follow any special dietary instructions provided by your doctor. This is an important part of controlling your blood sugar levels and is necessary in order for this medication to work properly.
- Test for sugar in your urine as directed by your doctor. It is a convenient way to determine whether your diabetes is being controlled by this medication.
- Eat or drink something containing sugar right away if you experience any symptoms of hypoglycemia (low blood sugar), such as anxiety, chills, cold sweats, cool or pale skin, drowsiness, excessive hunger, headache, nausea, nervousness, rapid heartbeat, shakiness, or unusual tiredness or weakness. It is important for your family and

friends to know the symptoms of low blood sugar. They should understand what to do if they observe any of these symptoms in you.

• Although it is very uncommon, metformin may cause a condition known as lactic acidosis. The symptoms of lactic acidosis are diarrhea, severe muscle pain or cramping, shallow and fast breathing, and unusual sleepiness, tiredness, or weakness. IT IS IMPORTANT TO TELL YOUR DOCTOR IMMEDIATELY if you experience any of these symptoms.

• Be sure to tell your doctor if you are pregnant or plan to become pregnant. This drug has not been studied for use during pregnancy. Your doctor may switch you to insulin while you are pregnant or trying to become pregnant. And be sure to tell your doctor if you are breast-feeding an infant. Small amounts of metformin may pass into breast milk.

---

methadone

BRAND NAMES (Manufacturers)
Dolophine (Roxane)
methadone hydrochloride (various manufacturers)
TYPE OF DRUG
Analgesic
INGREDIENT
methadone
DOSAGE FORMS
Tablets (5 mg, 10 mg, and 40 mg)
Oral concentrate (10 mg per 1-mL dropperful)
Oral solution (5 mg and 10 mg per 5-mL spoonful, with 8% alcohol)
STORAGE
Store at room temperature in tightly closed, light-resistant containers, well out of the reach of children and pets.

USES

Methadone is a narcotic analgesic (pain reliever) that acts directly on the central nervous system (brain and spinal cord). It is used to relieve moderate to severe pain. It is also used to detoxify narcotic addicts and to provide temporary maintenance treatment for them.

TREATMENT

To avoid stomach upset, take methadone with food or milk.

This medication is most effective if you take it at the onset of pain, rather than when the pain becomes intense.

Measure each dose of the solution form of this medication carefully with a specially designed 5-mL measuring spoon. An ordinary kitchen teaspoon is not accurate enough for this purpose.

If you are taking this medication on a regular schedule and you miss a dose, take the missed dose as soon as possible. However, if it is almost time for your next dose, do not take the missed dose at all; just return to your regular dosing schedule. Do not double the next dose.

SIDE EFFECTS

Minor. Constipation, dizziness, drowsiness, dry mouth, false sense of well-being, light-headedness, loss of appetite, nausea, or sweating. These side effects should disappear as your body adjusts to the medication.

If you are constipated, increase the amount of fiber in your diet (eat more fresh fruits and vegetables, salads, bran, and whole-grain breads). You can also increase the amount you exercise and drink more water (unless your doctor directs you to do otherwise).

Chew sugarless gum or suck on ice chips or a piece of hard candy to reduce mouth dryness.

If you feel dizzy or light-headed, sit or lie down for a while; get up from a sitting or lying position slowly; and be careful on stairs. Take special care when driving a car or operating potentially dangerous equipment.

Major. Tell your doctor about any side effects that are persistent or particularly bothersome. IT IS ESPECIALLY IMPORTANT TO TELL YOUR DOCTOR about anxiety, breathing difficulties, excitability, fainting, fatigue, flushing, heart palpitations, painful or difficult urination, pinpoint pupils (of the eyes), rash, restlessness, sore throat and fever, tremors, or weakness.

INTERACTIONS

Methadone interacts with several other types of medications:

1. Concurrent use of methadone with other central nervous system depressants (such as alcohol, antihistamines, barbiturates, benzodiazepine tranquilizers, muscle relaxants, and phenothiazine tranquilizers) or with tricyclic antidepressants can cause extreme drowsiness.

2. A monoamine oxidase (MAO) inhibitor taken within 14 days of this medication can lead to unpredictable and severe side effects.

3. Rifampin and phenytoin can decrease the blood levels and effectiveness of methadone.

4. The combination of cimetidine and this medication can cause confusion, disorientation, and shortness of breath.

BE SURE TO TELL YOUR DOCTOR about any medications you are currently taking, especially any listed above.

WARNINGS

• Tell your doctor about unusual or allergic reactions you have had to any medications, especially to methadone or to any other narcotic analgesic.

• Tell your doctor if you now have or ever had acute abdominal conditions, asthma, brain disease, colitis, epilepsy, gallstones or gallbladder disease, head injuries, heart disease, kidney disease, liver disease, lung disease, mental illness, emotional disorders, enlarged prostate gland, thyroid disease, or urethral stricture.

• If this drug makes you dizzy or drowsy, do not take part in any activity that requires alertness, such as driving a car or operating potentially dangerous machinery.

• Before having surgery or any other medical or dental treatment, be sure to tell your doctor or dentist that you are taking this medication.

• Methadone has the potential for abuse and must be used with caution. Usually, it should not be taken on a regular schedule for longer than ten days (unless your doctor directs you to do so). Tolerance develops quickly; do not increase the dosage or stop taking the drug abruptly unless you first consult your doctor. If you have been taking large amounts of this medication or if you have been taking it for long periods of time, you may experience withdrawal symptoms (muscle aches, diarrhea, gooseflesh, runny nose, nausea, vomiting, shivering, trembling, stomach cramps, sleep disorders, irritability, weakness, excessive yawning, or sweating) when you stop taking it. Your doctor may, therefore, want to reduce the dosage gradually.

• Be sure to tell your doctor if you are pregnant. The effects of this medication during the early stages of pregnancy have not been thoroughly studied in humans. Also tell your doctor if you are breast-feeding an infant. Small amounts of this medication may pass into breast milk and cause excessive drowsiness in the nursing infant.

methotrexate

BRAND NAMES (Manufacturers)
Methotrexate (Lederle)
Rheumatrex Dose Pack (Lederle)
TYPE OF DRUG
Antineoplastic (anticancer drug), antipsoriatic, antirheumatic
INGREDIENT
methotrexate
DOSAGE FORM
Tablets (2.5 mg)
STORAGE
Store at room temperature in a tightly closed container. Do not keep this or any other medication beyond the expiration date marked on the container.

USES

Methotrexate is used to treat certain types of cancer, severe psoriasis, and severe rheumatoid arthritis. It works by slowing the growth rate of rapidly proliferating cells.

TREATMENT

To avoid stomach irritation, take methotrexate with food or with a full glass of water or milk (unless your doctor directs you to do otherwise).

Try not to miss any doses of this medication. If you do miss a dose, take the missed dose as soon as possible. However, if it is almost time for the next dose, do not take the missed dose at all; just return to your regular dosing schedule. Do not double the next dose. If you miss more than two doses in a row, CONTACT YOUR DOCTOR.

SIDE EFFECTS

Minor. Abdominal distress, fatigue, loss of appetite, nasal congestion, nausea, or vomiting. These side effects should diminish or disappear as your body adjusts to the medication. Methotrexate also causes hair loss, which is reversible when the medication is stopped.

This medication can increase your sensitivity to sunlight. You should try to avoid prolonged exposure to sunlight and sunlamps. Wear protective clothing and sunglasses, and use an effective sunscreen.

Major. Tell your doctor about any side effects that are persistent or particularly bothersome. IT IS ESPECIALLY IMPORTANT TO TELL YOUR DOCTOR about back pain, blurred vision, convulsions, diarrhea, difficult or painful urination, drowsiness, fever, headache, itching, menstrual changes, mouth sores, rash, severe abdominal pain, skin color changes, unusual bleeding or bruising, or yellowing of the eyes or skin.

INTERACTIONS

Methotrexate interacts with several other types of medications:

1. Concurrent use of alcohol and methotrexate can lead to an increased risk of liver damage.

2. Methotrexate can block the effectiveness of antigout medications.

3. Nonsteroidal anti-inflammatory drugs, procarbazine, probenecid, phenytoin, tetracycline, aspirin, chloramphenicol, salicylates, and sulfonamide antibiotics can increase the blood levels of methotrexate, which can lead to an increase in serious side effects.

4. Methotrexate has the capability of increasing the effects of the blood thinner warfarin, which can lead to bleeding complications.

5. Folic acid, a B vitamin, may decrease the effect of this medication.

Before starting to take methotrexate, BE SURE TO TELL YOUR DOCTOR about any medications you are currently taking, especially any of those listed above.

WARNINGS

• Tell your doctor about any unusual or allergic reactions you have ever had to any medications, especially any reaction to methotrexate.
• Before starting to take this medication, be sure to tell your doctor if you now have or ever had blood disorders, gout, infection, kidney disease, liver disease, or inflammation of the gastrointestinal tract.
• If this drug makes you dizzy or drowsy, be careful going up and down stairs, and do not take part in any activity that requires alertness, such as driving an automobile or other vehicle or operating potentially dangerous machinery.
• Drink plenty of fluids so that you urinate often (unless your doctor directs you to do otherwise). This helps prevent kidney and bladder problems during therapy.
• Do not get immunized or vaccinated while you are being treated with methotrexate. The vaccination or immunization will not be effective and may lead to an infection if a live-virus vaccine is used.
• Methotrexate is a potent medication that can cause serious side effects. Your doctor will therefore want to monitor your therapy carefully with blood tests.
• It is important to tell your doctor if you are pregnant. Methotrexate has been shown to cause birth defects or death of the fetus. Effective contraception should be used during treatment and for at least eight weeks after treatment is stopped. Also tell your doctor if you are breast-feeding an infant. This medication should never be used by women who are nursing.

---

methylphenidate

BRAND NAMES (Manufacturers)
Concerta (McNeil)
Metadate CD (Celltech)
Methylin (Mallinckrodt)
Methylin ER (Mallinckrodt)
methylphenidate hydrochloride (various manufacturers)
Ritalin (Novartis)
Ritalin-LA (Novartis)
Ritalin-SR (Novartis)
TYPE OF DRUG
Adrenergic
INGREDIENT
methylphenidate
DOSAGE FORMS
Capsules, extended release (20 mg, 30 mg, and 40 mg)
Tablets (5 mg, 10 mg, and 20 mg)
Tablets, sustained-release (10 mg, 18 mg, 20 mg, 27 mg, 36 mg, 54 mg)
STORAGE
Store at room temperature in tightly closed, light-resistant containers.

USES

Methylphenidate is a central nervous system (brain and spinal cord) stimulant that increases mental alertness and decreases fatigue. It is used in the treatment of narcolepsy (a disorder involving the uncontrollable desire to sleep or actual sleep attacks that occur in a rapid, unpredictable, and irresistible manner), mild depression, and abnormal behavioral syndrome in children (attention deficit hyperactivity disorder or attention deficit disorder). The way this medication works to treat abnormal behavioral syndrome in children is not clearly understood.

TREATMENT

This medication should be taken 30 to 45 minutes before meals (unless your doctor directs you otherwise).

If methylphenidate is being used to treat narcolepsy or abnormal behavioral syndrome in children, the first dose should be taken soon after awakening.

To avoid difficulty in falling asleep, take the last dose of the regular tablets four to six hours before bedtime each day. Take the last dose of the sustained-release tablets at least eight hours before bedtime.

Swallow the sustained-release tablets and extended-release capsules whole. Chewing, crushing, or breaking these tablets destroys their sustained-release activity and may increase the side effects. If you are taking the capsule form, you may open the capsule and sprinkle the contents onto a spoonful of applesauce. Swallow completely and immediately without chewing or crushing.

If you miss a dose, take the missed dose as soon as possible. However, if it is almost time for your next dose, do not take the missed dose; just return to your regular dosing schedule. Do not double the next dose.

SIDE EFFECTS

Minor. Abdominal pain, dizziness, drowsiness, dry mouth, headache, insomnia, loss of appetite, nausea, nervousness, vomiting, or weakness. These side effects should disappear as your body adjusts to the medication.

Dry mouth can be relieved by sucking on ice chips or a piece of hard candy or by chewing sugarless gum.

If you feel dizzy, sit or lie down for a while; get up from a sitting or lying position slowly; and be careful on stairs.

Major. Tell your doctor about any side effects you experience that are persistent or particularly bothersome. IT IS ESPECIALLY IMPORTANT TO TELL YOUR DOCTOR about chest pain, fever, hair loss, hallucinations, hives, joint pain, mood changes, palpitations, rash, seizures, sore throat, uncoordinated movements, or unusual bleeding or bruising.

INTERACTIONS

Methylphenidate interacts with several other types of medications:

1. Use of methylphenidate within 14 days of using a monoamine oxidase (MAO) inhibitor (such as isocarboxazid, pargyline, phenelzine, selegiline, and tranylcypromine) can result in severe high blood pressure.

2. Methylphenidate can decrease the blood-pressure-lowering influence of antihypertensive medications (especially guanethidine).

3. Acetazolamide and sodium bicarbonate can decrease the elimination of methylphenidate from the body, thereby prolonging its action and increasing the risk of side effects.

4. Methylphenidate can decrease the elimination and increase the side effects of oral anticoagulants (blood thinners, such as warfarin), tricyclic antidepressants (such as amitriptyline, desipramine, imipramine, and nortriptyline), selective serotonin reuptake inhibitors (such as fluoxetine and paroxetine), anticonvulsants (such as phenytoin, phenobarbital, and primidone), and phenylbutazone.

Before starting to take this medication, BE SURE TO TELL YOUR DOCTOR about any medications you are currently taking, especially any of those listed above.

WARNINGS

• Be sure to tell your doctor about unusual or allergic reactions you have ever had to any medications, especially to methylphenidate.

• Tell your doctor if you now have or if you have ever had epilepsy, glaucoma, high blood pressure, motor tics, Tourette's syndrome, anxiety, or depression or if you have experienced abnormal agitation or tension.
• Methylphenidate can mask the symptoms of extreme fatigue and can cause dizziness. Your ability to perform tasks that require alertness, such as driving a car or operating potentially dangerous machinery, may be decreased. Appropriate caution should, therefore, be taken. A child taking methylphenidate should be careful while engaging in physical activity.
• Before having surgery or any other medical or dental treatment, be sure to tell your doctor or dentist that you are taking this medication.
• Methylphenidate is related to amphetamine and may be habit-forming when taken for long periods of time (both physical and psychological dependence can occur). You should not increase the dosage of this medication or take it for longer than the prescribed time unless you first consult your doctor. It is also important that you not stop taking this medication abruptly; fatigue, sleep disorders, mental depression, nausea, vomiting, or stomach cramps or pain could occur. Your doctor may want to decrease the dosage gradually in order to prevent these side effects.
• Methylphenidate can slow growth in children. Therefore, if this medication is being taken by a child, your doctor may recommend drug-free periods during school holidays and summer vacations. Growth spurts often occur during these drug-free periods.
• Children may be more sensitive to certain side effects from this drug, such as loss of appetite, stomach pain, trouble sleeping, and weight loss.
• If cocaine is being used now or was used in the past, taking methylphenidate may cause severe nervousness, irritability, difficulty sleeping, or possibly irregular heartbeat or seizures.
• Be sure to tell your doctor if you are pregnant. Effects of this drug during pregnancy have not been thoroughly studied in either humans or animals. Also tell your doctor if you are breast-feeding an infant. Small amounts of methylphenidate may pass into breast milk.

---

methylprednisolone (systemic)

BRAND NAMES (Manufacturers)
Medrol (Upjohn)
methylprednisolone (various manufacturers)
TYPE OF DRUG
Adrenocorticosteroid hormone
INGREDIENT
methylprednisolone
DOSAGE FORM
Tablets (2 mg, 4 mg, 8 mg, 16 mg, 24 mg, and 32 mg)
STORAGE
Store at room temperature in a tightly closed container.

USES

Your adrenal glands naturally produce certain cortisonelike chemicals. These chemicals are involved in various regulatory processes in the body (such as those that control the body's fluid balance, temperature, and reactions to inflammation). Methylprednisolone belongs to a group of drugs known as adrenocorticosteroids (or cortisonelike medications). It is used to treat a variety of disorders, including endocrine and rheumatic disorders; asthma; blood diseases; certain cancers; eye disorders; gastrointestinal disturbances, such as ulcerative colitis; respiratory diseases; and inflammations, such as arthritis, dermatitis, and poison ivy. How this drug acts to relieve these disorders is not completely understood.

TREATMENT

To prevent stomach irritation, take methylprednisolone with food or milk.

If you are taking only one dose of this drug each day, try to take it before 9:00 in the morning. This will mimic the body's normal production of this type of chemical.

It is important to try not to miss any doses of methylprednisolone. However, if you do miss a dose of the drug, follow these guidelines:

1. If you are taking this medication more than once a day, take the missed dose as soon as possible and return to your regular schedule. If it is already time for the next dose, double the dose.

2. If you are taking this medication once a day, take the dose you missed as soon as possible, unless you don't remember until the next day. In that case, do not take the missed dose at all; just follow your regular schedule. Do not double the next dose.

3. If you are taking this drug every other day, take it as soon as you remember. If you missed the scheduled time by a whole day, take it when you remember, and then skip a day before you take the next dose. Do not double the dose.

If you miss more than one dose, CONTACT YOUR DOCTOR IMMEDIATELY.

SIDE EFFECTS

Minor. Dizziness, false sense of well-being, increased appetite, increased susceptibility to infections, increased sweating, indigestion, menstrual irregularities, nausea, reddening of the skin on the face, restlessness, sleep disorders, or weight gain. These side effects should disappear as your body adjusts to the medication.

Major. Tell your doctor about any side effects that are persistent or particularly bothersome. IT IS ESPECIALLY IMPORTANT TO TELL YOUR DOCTOR about abdominal enlargement; abdominal pain; acne or other skin problems; back or rib pain; bloody or black, tarry stools; blurred vision; convulsions; eye pain; fever and sore throat; growth impairment (in children); headaches; impaired healing of wounds; increased thirst and urination; mental depression; mood changes; muscle wasting; muscle weakness; nightmares; rapid weight gain (three to five pounds within a week); rash; shortness of breath; thinning of the skin; unusual bleeding or bruising; and unusual weakness.

INTERACTIONS

Methylprednisolone interacts with several other types of medications:

1. Alcohol, aspirin, and anti-inflammatory medications (diclofenac, diflunisal, etodolac, fenoprofen, flurbiprofen, ibuprofen, indomethacin, ketoprofen, ketorolac, mefenamic acid, meclofenamate, naproxen, oxaprozin, piroxicam, sulindac, tenoxicam, tiaprofenic acid, or tolmetin) aggravate the stomach problems that commonly occur with use of methylprednisolone.

2. The dosage of oral anticoagulants (blood thinners, such as warfarin), oral antidiabetic medications, or insulin may need to be altered when therapy with systemic methylprednisolone is started or stopped.

3. The loss of potassium caused by methylprednisolone can lead to serious side effects in individuals taking digoxin. Thiazide diuretics (water pills) can increase the potassium loss caused by methylprednisolone.

4. Phenobarbital, phenytoin, rifampin, and ephedrine can increase the elimination of methylprednisolone from the body, thereby decreasing its effectiveness.

5. Oral contraceptives (birth control pills) and estrogen-containing medications may decrease the elimination of this medication from the body, which can lead to an increase in its side effects.

6. Methylprednisolone can increase the elimination of aspirin and isoniazid, thereby decreasing the effectiveness of these two medications.

7. Cholestyramine and colestipol can chemically bind this medication in the stomach and gastrointestinal tract and prevent its absorption.

BE SURE TO TELL YOUR DOCTOR about any medications you are currently taking, especially any of those listed above.

WARNINGS

• Tell your doctor about unusual or allergic reactions you have had to any medications, especially to methylprednisolone or other adrenocorticosteroids (such as betamethasone, cortisone, dexamethasone, hydrocortisone, prednisolone, prednisone, and triamcinolone).

• Tell your doctor if you now have or if you have ever had bone disease, diabetes mellitus, emotional instability, glaucoma, fungal infections, heart disease, high blood pressure, high cholesterol levels, myasthenia gravis, peptic ulcers, osteoporosis, thyroid disease, tuberculosis, ulcerative colitis, kidney disease, or liver disease.

• To help avoid potassium loss while you are using this medication, take your dose with a glass of fresh or frozen orange juice or eat a banana each day. The use of a salt substitute also helps to prevent potassium loss, but be sure to check with your doctor before using a salt substitute.

• If you are using this medication for longer than a week, you may need to have your dosage adjusted if you are subjected to stress, such as serious infections, injury, or surgery. Discuss this with your doctor.

• If you have been taking this drug for more than a week, do not stop taking it suddenly. If it is stopped suddenly, you may experience abdominal or back pain, dizziness, fainting, fever, muscle or joint pain, nausea, vomiting, shortness of breath, or extreme weakness. Your doctor may therefore want to reduce the dosage gradually. Never increase the dosage or take the drug for longer than the prescribed time, unless you first consult your doctor.

• While you are being treated with methylprednisolone, you should not be vaccinated or immunized. This medication decreases the effectiveness of vaccines and can lead to overwhelming infection if a live-virus vaccine is administered.

• Before having surgery or any other medical or dental treatment, be sure to tell your doctor or dentist that you are taking this medication.

• Because this drug can cause glaucoma and cataracts with long-term use, your doctor may want you to have your eyes examined by an ophthalmologist periodically while undergoing treatment.

• If you are taking this medication for prolonged periods, you should wear or carry a notice or identification stating that you are taking an adrenocorticosteroid.

• This drug can raise blood sugar levels in people with diabetes. Blood sugar levels should therefore be monitored carefully with blood or urine tests when this medication is being taken.

• Some formulations of systemic methylprednisolone contain the color additive FD&C Yellow No. 5 (tartrazine), which can cause an allergic-type reaction in certain susceptible individuals.

• Be sure to tell your doctor if you are pregnant. Systemic methylprednisolone crosses the placenta. Although studies in humans have not been conducted, birth defects have been observed in the fetuses of animals that were given large doses of this type of medication during pregnancy. Also be sure to tell your doctor if you are breastfeeding an infant. Small amounts of methylprednisolone are known to pass into human breast milk and may cause growth suppression or a decrease in natural adrenocorticosteroid production in the nursing infant.

---

metoclopramide

BRAND NAMES (Manufacturers)

Maxolon (SmithKline Beecham)
metoclopramide (various manufacturers)
Reglan (Robins)

TYPE OF DRUG

Dopamine antagonist and antiemetic

INGREDIENT
metoclopramide
DOSAGE FORMS
Tablets (5 mg and 10 mg)
Oral concentrate (10 mg per mL)
Oral syrup (5 mg per 5-mL spoonful)
STORAGE
Store all forms of this medication at room temperature in tightly closed containers. Do not freeze the syrup.

USES

This medication is used to relieve the symptoms associated with diabetic gastric stasis or gastric reflux and to prevent nausea and vomiting. Metoclopramide acts directly on the vomiting center in the brain to prevent nausea and vomiting. Metoclopramide also increases the movement of the stomach and intestines.

TREATMENT

To obtain the best results from treatment, take metoclopramide tablets or syrup 30 minutes before a meal and at bedtime.

Measure each dose of the syrup carefully with a specially designed 5-mL measuring spoon. An ordinary kitchen teaspoon is not accurate enough.

Measure each dose of the concentrate with the specially designed dropper that comes with the medication.

If you miss a dose of this medication, take the missed dose as soon as possible. However, if it is almost time for the next dose, do not take the missed dose at all; just return to your regular dosing schedule. Do not double the next dose.

SIDE EFFECTS

Minor. Diarrhea, dizziness, drowsiness, dry mouth, fatigue, headache, insomnia, nausea, restlessness, or weakness. These side effects should disappear as your body adjusts to the medication.

If you feel dizzy or light-headed, sit or lie down for a while; stand up slowly; and be careful on stairs.

To relieve mouth dryness, chew sugarless gum or suck on ice chips or a piece of hard candy.

Major. Tell your doctor about any side effects that are persistent or particularly bothersome. IT IS ESPECIALLY IMPORTANT TO NOTIFY YOUR DOCTOR about anxiety; confusion; depression; disorientation; involuntary movements of the eyes, face, or limbs; muscle spasms; rash; or trembling of the hands.

INTERACTIONS

Metoclopramide interacts with several types of drugs:

1. Concurrent use of metoclopramide with other central nervous system depressants (such as alcohol, antihistamines, barbiturates, muscle relaxants, narcotics, pain medications, phenothiazine tranquilizers, benzodiazepine tranquilizers, and sleeping medications) or with tricyclic antidepressants can cause extreme drowsiness.

2. Narcotic analgesics may block the effectiveness of metoclopramide.

3. Metoclopramide can block the effectiveness of bromocriptine and pergolide. It can also decrease the absorption of cimetidine and digoxin from the gastrointestinal tract, decreasing their effectiveness.

4. Metoclopramide can increase the body's absorption of acetaminophen, cyclosporine, tetracycline, levodopa, and alcohol.

5. Diabetic patients should know that dosage requirements of insulin may change when metoclopramide is being taken.

6. Use of monoamine oxidase (MAO) inhibitors and metoclopramide may increase blood pressure.

Before starting to take metoclopramide, BE SURE TO NOTIFY YOUR DOCTOR about any medications that you are currently taking, especially any of the medications that are listed above.

WARNINGS

• Tell your doctor about unusual or allergic reactions you have had to any medications, especially to metoclopramide, procaine, or procainamide.

• Before starting to take metoclopramide, be sure to tell your doctor if you now have or ever had epilepsy, kidney disease, liver disease, intestinal bleeding or blockage, Parkinson's disease, or pheochromocytoma.

• If this drug makes you dizzy or drowsy, do not take part in any activities that require mental alertness, such as driving an automobile or operating potentially dangerous machinery or equipment.

• Be sure to tell your doctor about any uncontrolled movements of your eyes, face, legs, arms, or hands.

• Be sure to tell your doctor if you are pregnant. Extensive studies in women during pregnancy have not been conducted. Also tell your doctor if you are breast-feeding an infant. Metoclopramide passes into breast milk.

---

metoprolol

BRAND NAMES (Manufacturers)

Lopressor (Novartis)
metoprolol tartrate (various manufacturers)
Toprol XL (AstraZeneca)

TYPE OF DRUG

Beta-adrenergic blocking agent

INGREDIENT

metoprolol

DOSAGE FORMS

Tablets (50 mg and 100 mg)
Tablets, extended release (25 mg, 50 mg, 100 mg, and 200 mg)

STORAGE

Metoprolol should be stored at room temperature in a tightly closed, light-resistant container.

USES

Metoprolol is used to treat high blood pressure, heart failure, and angina (chest pain) and to prevent additional heart attacks in heart attack patients. Metoprolol belongs to a group of medicines known as beta-adrenergic blocking agents or, as they are more commonly known, beta blockers. This group of medications works by controlling the nerve impulses that travel along certain nerve pathways.

TREATMENT

Metoprolol can be taken with a glass of water, with meals, immediately following meals, or on an empty stomach, depending on your doctor's instructions. Try to take the medication at the same time(s) each day.

Try not to miss any doses of this medicine. If you do miss a dose of the medication, take the missed dose as soon as possible. However, if the next scheduled dose is within eight hours (if you are taking this medicine only once a day) or within four hours (if you are taking this medicine more than once a day), do not take the missed dose at all; just return to your regular dosing schedule. Do not double the next dose of medication.

It is important to remember that metoprolol does not cure high blood pressure, but it will help to control the condition as long as you continue to take it.

SIDE EFFECTS

Minor. Anxiety; cold hands or feet (due to decreased blood circulation to the skin, fingers, and toes); constipation; decreased sexual ability; diarrhea; difficulty in sleeping; drowsiness; dryness of the eyes, mouth, and skin; headache; nausea; nervousness; stomach discomfort; tiredness; or weakness. These side effects should disappear during treatment, as your body adjusts to the medicine.

If you are extra-sensitive to the cold, be sure to dress warmly during cold weather.

To relieve constipation, increase the amount of fiber in your diet (fresh fruits and vegetables, salads, bran, and whole-grain breads) and exercise more (unless your doctor directs you to do otherwise).

Plain, nonmedicated eyedrops (sometimes referred to as artificial tears) may help to relieve eye dryness.

Chew sugarless gum or suck on ice chips or a piece of hard candy to relieve mouth or throat dryness.

Major. Tell your doctor about any side effects that are persistent or particularly bothersome. IT IS ESPECIALLY IMPORTANT TO TELL YOUR DOCTOR about breathing difficulty or wheezing, confusion, dizziness, fever and sore throat, hair loss, hallucinations, light-headedness, mental depression, nightmares, numbness or tingling of the fingers or toes, rapid weight gain (three to five pounds within a week), reduced alertness, skin rash, swelling, or any unusual bleeding or bruising.

INTERACTIONS

Metoprolol interacts with many other types of medications:

1. Nonsteroidal anti-inflammatory drugs, aspirin, or other salicylates may decrease the blood-pressure-lowering effects of beta blockers.

2. Concurrent use of beta blockers and calcium channel blockers, clonidine, guanabenz, or disopyramide can lead to heart failure or very low blood pressure.

3. Cimetidine, certain antibiotics, certain selective serotonin reuptake inhibitor antidepressants, and oral contraceptives (birth control pills) can increase the blood concentrations of metoprolol, which can result in greater side effects.

4. Alcohol, barbiturates, and rifampin can decrease the effectiveness of metoprolol.

5. Side effects may be increased if beta blockers such as metoprolol are taken with clonidine, digoxin, epinephrine, phenylephrine, phenylpropanolamine, phenothiazine tranquilizers, prazosin, or monoamine oxidase (MAO) inhibitors. At least 14 days should separate the use of a beta blocker and the use of an MAO inhibitor.

6. Beta blockers may antagonize (work against) the effects of theophylline, aminophylline, albuterol, isoproterenol, metaproterenol, and terbutaline.

7. Beta blockers can also interact with insulin or oral antidiabetic agents, raising or lowering blood sugar levels and masking the symptoms of low blood sugar.

8. The action of beta blockers may be increased if they are used with chlorpromazine, furosemide, or hydralazine, which may have a negative effect.

BE SURE TO TELL YOUR DOCTOR about any medications you are currently taking, especially any listed above.

WARNINGS

• Tell your doctor if you have ever had unusual or allergic reactions to any medications, especially to metoprolol or any other beta blocker (acebutolol, atenolol, carteolol, esmolol, labetalol, nadolol, penbutolol, pindolol, propranolol, or timolol).

• Tell your doctor if you now have or ever had allergies, asthma, hay fever, eczema, slow heartbeat, bronchitis, diabetes mellitus, emphysema, heart or blood-vessel disease, kidney disease, liver disease, thyroid disease, or poor circulation in the fingers or toes.
• You may want to check your pulse while taking this medication. If your pulse is much slower than your usual rate (or if it is less than 50 beats per minute), you should contact your doctor. A pulse rate that is too slow may cause circulation problems.
• This medicine may affect your body's response to exercise. Make sure you discuss with your doctor a safe amount of exercise for your medical condition.
• It is important that you do not stop taking this medicine without first checking with your doctor. Some conditions may become worse when the medicine is stopped suddenly, and the danger of a heart attack is increased in some patients. Your doctor may want you to reduce gradually the amount of medicine you take before stopping it completely to minimize the potential risks. Make sure that you have enough medicine on hand to last through vacations, holidays, and weekends.
• Before having surgery or any other medical or dental treatment, tell your doctor or dentist that you are being treated with this medication.
• Metoprolol can cause dizziness, drowsiness, light-headedness, or decreased alertness. Be sure to use caution while driving an automobile or operating any potentially dangerous machinery.
• While taking this medicine, do not use any over-the-counter (nonprescription) allergy, asthma, cough, cold, sinus, or diet preparation without first checking with your pharmacist or doctor. Some of these medicines can result in high blood pressure when taken at the same time as a beta blocker.
• Be sure to tell your doctor if you are pregnant. Animal studies have shown that some beta blockers, when used in very high doses, can cause problems in pregnancy. Adequate studies have not been conducted in humans, but there has been some association between beta blockers used during pregnancy and low birth weight, as well as breathing problems and slow heart rate in newborn infants. However, other reports have shown no effects on newborn infants. Also tell your doctor if you are breastfeeding an infant. Although this drug has not been shown to cause problems in breastfed infants, some of the medicine may pass into breast milk, so caution is warranted.

metronidazole

BRAND NAMES (Manufacturers)
Flagyl (Pharmacia)
Flagyl ER (Pharmacia)
Flagyl 375 (Pharmacia)
MetroGel (Galderma)
MetroLotion (Galderma)
metronidazole (various manufacturers)
Noritate (Dermik Laboratories)
Protostat (Ortho)
TYPE OF DRUG
Antibiotic and antiparasitic
INGREDIENT
metronidazole
DOSAGE FORMS
Capsules (375 mg)
Tablets (250 mg and 500 mg)
Tablets, extended release (750 mg)
Topical cream (1%)
Topical gel (0.75%)
Topical lotion (0.75%)

STORAGE
Store at room temperature in a tightly closed, light-resistant container. Do not freeze the topical gel and cream forms of this medication.

USES
Metronidazole is used to treat a wide variety of infections, including infections of the vagina, urinary tract, lower respiratory tract, bones, joints, intestinal tract, and skin. It is also used topically to treat acne rosacea. It acts by killing bacteria and parasites.

TREATMENT
To avoid stomach irritation, take metronidazole with food or with a full glass of water or milk (unless your doctor directs you to do otherwise). However, the extended-release form of this medicine must be taken either one hour or more before a meal or two hours after a meal.

Metronidazole works best when the level of medicine in your bloodstream is kept constant. It is best to take the doses at evenly spaced intervals day and night. For example, if you are to take three doses of the medication each day, the doses should be spaced eight hours apart.

Try not to miss any doses of this medication. If you do miss a dose, take the missed dose as soon as possible. However, if it is almost time for the next dose, do not take the missed dose at all; just return to your regular dosing schedule. Do not double the next dose.

It is important to continue to take this medication for the entire time prescribed by your doctor (usually 7 to 14 days), even if the symptoms disappear before the end of that period. If you stop taking the drug too soon, resistant bacteria and parasites are given a chance to continue growing, and the infection could recur.

SIDE EFFECTS
Minor. Abdominal cramps, constipation, decreased sexual interest, diarrhea, dizziness, dry mouth, headache, insomnia, irritability, joint pain, loss of appetite, metallic taste in the mouth, nasal congestion, nausea, restlessness, or vomiting. These side effects should disappear as your body adjusts to the medication.

To relieve constipation, increase the amount of fiber in your diet (fresh fruits and vegetables, salads, bran, and whole-grain breads), exercise, and drink more water (unless your doctor directs you to do otherwise).

If this medication makes you feel dizzy, sit or lie down for a while; get up slowly from a sitting or lying position; and be careful on stairs.

To relieve mouth dryness, chew sugarless gum or suck on ice chips or a piece of hard candy.

Major. Tell your doctor about any side effects that are persistent or particularly bothersome. IT IS ESPECIALLY IMPORTANT TO TELL YOUR DOCTOR about confusion, convulsions, flushing, hives, itching, joint pain, loss of bladder control, mouth sores, numbness or tingling in the fingers or toes, rash, sense of pressure inside your abdomen, unexplained sore throat and fever, or unusual weakness. If your symptoms of infection seem to be getting worse rather than improving, you should contact your doctor.

INTERACTIONS
Metronidazole interacts with several other types of medications:

1. Concurrent use of alcohol and metronidazole can lead to a severe reaction (abdominal cramps, nausea, vomiting, headache, and flushing), the severity of which is dependent upon the amount of alcohol ingested.

2. Concurrent use of disulfiram and metronidazole can lead to confusion.

3. The effects of oral anticoagulants (blood thinners, such as warfarin) may be increased by metronidazole, which can lead to bleeding complications.

4. Barbiturates can increase the breakdown of metronidazole, which can decrease its effectiveness.
5. Cimetidine can decrease the breakdown of metronidazole, which can increase the chance of side effects.
6. Metronidazole may decrease the breakdown of phenytoin and lithium, which can increase the chance of side effects from these medications.

BE SURE TO TELL YOUR DOCTOR about any medications you are currently taking, especially any of the medications listed above.

WARNINGS

• Tell your doctor about unusual or allergic reactions you have had to any medications, especially to metronidazole.
• Before starting to take this medication, be sure to tell your doctor if you now have or ever had blood disorders, a disease of the central nervous system (brain or spinal cord), or liver disease.
• When metronidazole is used to treat any type of vaginal infection, the woman's sexual partner(s) should receive concurrent therapy in order to prevent reinfection. In addition, sexual intercourse should be avoided or condoms should be used until treatment is completed.
• This medication has been prescribed for your current infection only. Another infection later on, or one that someone else has, may require different drug therapy. Therefore, you should not give your medicine to other people or use it for other infections unless your doctor specifically directs you to do so.
• If this drug makes you dizzy, avoid tasks that require alertness, such as driving a car or operating potentially dangerous machinery.
• Tell your doctor if you experience an unpleasant metallic taste in your mouth while being treated with this medication.
• Before having surgery or any other medical or dental treatment, be sure to tell your doctor or dentist that you are taking this medication.
• Be sure to tell your doctor if you are pregnant. Although metronidazole appears to be safe, it does cross the placenta, and extensive studies in pregnant women have not been conducted. Also tell your doctor if you are breast-feeding an infant. Metronidazole passes into breast milk.

---

miconazole (vaginal)

BRAND NAMES (Manufacturers)
Femizole-M* (Lake Consumer Products)
miconazole nitrate* (various manufacturers)
Monistat Dual Pack (Personal Products)
Monistat 3* (Advanced Care)
Monistat 3 Combination Pack* (Advanced Care)
Monistat 7* (Advanced Care)
Monistat 7 Combination Pack* (Advanced Care)
M-Zole 3 Combination Pack* (Alpharma)
M-Zole 7 Dual Pack* (Alpharma)
*Available without a prescription.
TYPE OF DRUG
Vaginal antifungal agent
INGREDIENT
miconazole
DOSAGE FORMS
Vaginal or topical cream (2%)
Vaginal suppositories (100 mg, 200 mg, and 1,200 mg)

STORAGE

Store this medication at room temperature in a tightly closed container, out of reach of children and pets.

USES

Miconazole is used to treat fungal infections of the vagina. This medication is an antifungal agent that prevents the growth and multiplication of the yeastlike fungus known as candida.

TREATMENT

Miconazole vaginal cream and suppositories are packaged with detailed directions for use. Follow these instructions carefully. An applicator will probably be provided.

Wash the vaginal area thoroughly prior to inserting the cream or suppository.

If you begin to menstruate while being treated with miconazole, continue with your regular dosing schedule.

If you miss a dose of this medication, insert the missed dose as soon as possible. However, if you do not remember until the following day, do not insert the missed dose at all; just return to your regular dosing schedule. Do not double the next dose of the medication.

It is important to finish the entire course of treatment (all of the daily doses included in the package), even if the symptoms disappear before the end of that time. If you stop using the drug too soon, your infection could recur.

Usually, one three-day or one seven-day course is sufficient. However, it may be repeated if your doctor determines that candida is still causing an infection.

SIDE EFFECTS

Minor. You may experience vaginal burning, itching, or irritation when this drug is inserted. This sensation should disappear as your body adjusts to the medication.

Do not treat any side effects that occur in the area of the infection unless you first consult your doctor.

Major. Tell your doctor about any side effects that are persistent or particularly bothersome. IT IS ESPECIALLY IMPORTANT TO TELL YOUR DOCTOR about headache, hives, pelvic cramps, or skin rash.

INTERACTIONS

Miconazole (vaginal) does not interact with other medications if it is used according to directions.

WARNINGS

• Tell your doctor about unusual or allergic reactions you have had to any medications, especially to miconazole.

• Tell your doctor if you have had other vaginal infections, especially if they have been resistant to treatment.

• To prevent reinfection, avoid sexual intercourse during treatment. The use of miconazole cream and suppositories may weaken certain latex products such as condoms, diaphragms, or vaginal spermicides. Do not use these latex products for pregnancy protection during treatment or within three days after your treatment.

• There may be some vaginal drainage while you are using this medication; therefore, you may want to use a sanitary napkin or panty liner to prevent the staining of clothing.

• Wear cotton underpants rather than those made of nylon or other nonporous materials while being treated for a fungal infection of the vagina. To prevent reinfection, always wear freshly laundered underclothes.

• If there is no improvement in your condition, or if irritation in the area continues after several days of treatment, CONTACT YOUR DOCTOR. This medication may

possibly be causing an allergic reaction, or it may not be effective against the organism that is causing your infection.
• Miconazole has been prescribed for your current infection only. Another infection later on, or one that someone else has, may require a different medication. You should not give your medication to other women or use it for other infections you might have unless your doctor specifically directs you to do so.
• Be sure to tell your doctor if you are pregnant. Small amounts of miconazole have been shown to be absorbed from the vagina, so caution is necessary when using this medication during pregnancy. In addition, your doctor may want to change the instructions on how you are to insert this medication if you are pregnant. Also tell your doctor if you are breast-feeding an infant. It is not known whether or not miconazole passes into breast milk.

---

miglitol

BRAND NAME (Manufacturer)
Glyset (Bayer)
TYPE OF DRUG
Antidiabetic agent
INGREDIENT
miglitol
DOSAGE FORM
Tablets (25 mg, 50 mg, and 100 mg)
STORAGE
Store in a tightly closed container at room temperature.

USES

Miglitol is used to treat type 2, or non–insulin-dependent, diabetes. It can be used alone or in combination with oral sulfonylureas in patients whose blood sugar cannot be controlled with diet and exercise alone.

TREATMENT

Take this medication with the start (first bite) of each main meal. Miglitol is usually given three times a day with each main meal. If you miss a dose of the medication, do not take the missed dose if you remember after you have already finished your meal. Take the next scheduled dose with the first bite of your next meal, and check your blood sugar. Do not double the next dose of the medication.

SIDE EFFECTS

Minor: Abdominal pain, diarrhea, gas, nausea, or skin rash. These side effects should diminish or disappear as your body adjusts to the medication.
Major: Tell your doctor about any side effects that are persistent or particularly bothersome. IT IS ESPECIALLY IMPORTANT TO NOTIFY YOUR DOCTOR about low blood sugar or severe abdominal pain.

INTERACTIONS

Miglitol may interact with certain other medications:
1. Miglitol may reduce the effectiveness of digoxin, ranitidine, propranolol, glyburide, and metformin.
2. The effectiveness of miglitol may be reduced by digestive enzyme supplements or charcoal.

Before beginning treatment with miglitol, BE SURE TO TELL YOUR DOCTOR about any medications that you are currently taking, especially any of the medications that are listed above.

WARNINGS

• Tell your doctor about unusual or allergic reactions you have had to any medications, especially to miglitol.

• Before starting to take miglitol, tell your doctor if you now have or ever had inflammatory bowel disease, colonic ulceration, other digestive disorders, or kidney disease.

• Be sure to tell your doctor if you are pregnant. Adequate studies have not been conducted on the use of miglitol during pregnancy in humans. In addition, be sure to tell your doctor if you are breast-feeding an infant. It is not known if miglitol passes into breast milk.

---

minocycline

BRAND NAMES (Manufacturers)
Dynacin (Medicis)
Minocin (Lederle)
minocycline (various manufacturers)
Vectrin (Warner Chilcott)
TYPE OF DRUG
Antibiotic
INGREDIENT
minocycline
DOSAGE FORMS
Capsules (50 mg, 75 mg, and 100 mg)
Capsules, pellet-filled (50 mg and 100 mg)
Oral suspension (50 mg per 5-mL spoonful, with 5% alcohol)
STORAGE
Store this medication at room temperature in a tightly closed, light-resistant container. Do not refrigerate.

USES

Minocycline is used to treat a wide range of bacterial infections and to prevent meningococcal meningitis. It acts by preventing the growth of bacteria. This drug kills susceptible bacteria, but it is not effective against viruses or fungi.

TREATMENT

To avoid stomach upset, you can take this medication with food or before meals (unless your doctor directs you to do otherwise). Take with a full glass of water.

Shake the suspension well just before measuring each dose to distribute the ingredients evenly and equalize the doses. The contents tend to settle on the bottom of the bottle. Measure each dose carefully with a specially designed 5-mL measuring spoon. An ordinary kitchen teaspoon is not accurate enough.

Minocycline works best when the level of medicine in your bloodstream is kept constant. It is best to take the doses at evenly spaced intervals day and night. For example, if you are to take two doses a day, space the doses 12 hours apart.

If you miss a dose of this medication, take the missed dose immediately. However, if you do not remember to take the missed dose until it is almost time for your next dose, take it; space the following dose about halfway through the regular interval between doses; then return to your regular dosing schedule. Try not to skip any doses.

It is important to continue to take this medication for the entire time prescribed by your doctor, even if the symptoms disappear before the end of that period. If you stop taking the drug too soon, resistant bacteria are given a chance to continue growing, and the infection could recur.

SIDE EFFECTS

Minor. Diarrhea, dizziness, headache, light-headedness, loss of appetite, nail discoloration, nausea, stomach cramps and upset, or vomiting. These side effects should disappear as your body adjusts to the medication.

Minocycline can increase your sensitivity to sunlight. You should therefore try to avoid prolonged exposure to sunlight and sunlamps. Wear protective clothing and sunglasses, and use an effective sunscreen.

If this medication makes you feel dizzy or light-headed, sit or lie down for a while; get up from a sitting or lying position slowly; and be careful on stairs.

Major. Tell your doctor about any side effects that are persistent or particularly bothersome. IT IS ESPECIALLY IMPORTANT TO TELL YOUR DOCTOR about darkened tongue, difficulty in breathing, joint pain, mouth irritation, rash, rectal or vaginal itching, sore throat and fever, unusual bleeding or bruising, or yellowing of the eyes or skin. And if your symptoms of infection seem to be getting worse rather than improving, you should contact your doctor.

INTERACTIONS

Minocycline interacts with several other types of medications:

1. Minocycline can increase the absorption of digoxin, which may lead to digoxin toxicity.

2. The gastrointestinal side effects (nausea, vomiting, and stomach upset) of theophylline may be increased when it is used concurrently with minocycline.

3. The dosage of oral anticoagulants (blood thinners, such as warfarin) may need to be adjusted when you begin treatment with minocycline.

4. Minocycline may decrease the effectiveness of oral contraceptives (birth control pills), and pregnancy could result. You should therefore use a different or additional form of birth control while taking minocycline. Discuss this matter with your doctor.

5. Antacids, calcium supplements, iron, choline and magnesium salicylates, magnesium-containing laxatives, cholestyramine, and colestipol may decrease the effects of this drug if they are taken at the same time. Two to three hours should separate doses of any of these medications and minocycline.

BE SURE TO TELL YOUR DOCTOR about any medications you are currently taking, especially any of those listed above.

WARNINGS

- Tell your doctor about unusual or allergic reactions you have had to any medications, especially to minocycline or to oxytetracycline, doxycycline, or tetracycline.
- Tell your doctor if you now have or ever had kidney or liver disease.
- Minocycline can cause dizziness or light-headedness. Your ability to perform tasks that require alertness, such as driving a car or operating potentially dangerous machinery, may be decreased. Take appropriate caution.
- Minocycline can affect tests for syphilis; tell your doctor you are taking this medication if you are also being treated for this disease.
- Make sure that your prescription for this medication is marked with the expiration date. The medication should be discarded after the expiration date. If the drug is used after this date, serious side effects (especially relating to the kidneys) could result.
- This medication has been prescribed for your current infection only. Another infection later on, or one that someone else has, may require a different medicine. You should not give your medicine to other people or use it for other infections, unless your doctor specifically directs you to do so.
- Be sure to tell your doctor if you are pregnant or if you are breast-feeding an infant. Minocycline crosses the placenta, and it passes into breast milk. In addition, minocycline should not be used for infants or for children less than eight years of age. This drug can cause permanent discoloration of the teeth and can inhibit tooth and bone growth if used during their development.

minoxidil (topical)

BRAND NAMES (Manufacturers)
Minoxidil for Men* (Lemmon)
Rogaine* (Pharmacia)
*Available over the counter (without a prescription)
TYPE OF DRUG
Hair growth stimulant
INGREDIENT
minoxidil
DOSAGE FORMS
2% solution (20 mg per mL); 60-mL bottle
STORAGE
Store at room temperature in a tightly closed container. Keep away from heat or flames because the solution is flammable (it contains alcohol).

USES

Minoxidil topical solution is used to stimulate hair growth in people who are balding. The drug seems to exert its maximum effect at the crown of the head. The exact way that it works is not known, but it may stimulate hair growth by improving the blood supply to the hair follicles.

TREATMENT

Before applying topical minoxidil, the hair and scalp should be dry. To avoid skin irritation from the alcohol contained in this product, wait at least 30 minutes after washing or shaving before applying this medication to the scalp. The evening dose of medication should be applied at least 30 minutes before bedtime for more complete absorption of the medication into the scalp. This will prevent the medication from rubbing onto the pillowcase.

Complete directions for the use of this product are supplied with the medication. Be sure to ask your doctor or pharmacist for these directions, and follow the instructions carefully. Apply 1 mL to the balding areas of the scalp twice daily (in the morning and evening), unless directed to do otherwise by your doctor. The rub-on applicator delivers a 1-mL dose when the bottle is squeezed to fill the top chamber to the black line. The full amount in the chamber should then be applied to the scalp. The total daily dosage should not exceed 2 mL. If fingertips are used to apply the solution, wash your hands afterward to avoid spreading the medication.

Two daily applications for up to four months may be required before evidence of hair regrowth is observed. The onset and degree of hair regrowth may be variable among different patients treated with this medicine. If hair regrowth occurs, two daily applications are necessary for additional and continued hair growth (unless your doctor directs otherwise).

First hair growth may be soft, downy, colorless hair that is barely visible. After further treatment, however, the new hair should be the same color and thickness as the other hair on the scalp.

If one or two applications are missed, restart twice daily applications and return to the usual schedule. Do not attempt to make up for missed doses or use more than 1 mL at a time. Do not use on sunburned skin.

It is important to continue to use this medication for the entire time prescribed by your doctor, even if hair growth does not appear within several months.

If there is no hair growth after at least four months or more, consult with your doctor, as this medication may not be effective for you.

SIDE EFFECTS

Minor. Diarrhea, dry skin/scalp, flaking, itching, local redness, nausea, or vomiting. These side effects should disappear as your body adjusts to the medication.

Major. Tell your doctor about any side effects that are persistent or particularly bothersome. IT IS ESPECIALLY IMPORTANT TO TELL YOUR DOCTOR about back pain, chest pain, common cold, cough, dizziness, fluid retention, headache, feeling faint, light-headedness, rapid heartbeat, weight gain, or worsening of hair loss.

INTERACTIONS

Use of abrasive or medicated cleansers or cosmetics or any topical, alcohol-containing preparations (such as aftershave lotions, hairstyling products, or cologne) along with topical minoxidil solution can result in excessive skin dryness and irritation.

WARNINGS

- Tell your doctor about unusual or allergic reactions you have had to any medications, especially to minoxidil.
- Before starting treatment with this medication, be sure to tell your doctor if you now have or have ever had heart disease, high blood pressure, or skin problems such as dermatitis or abrasions of or near the area to be treated.
- Because this medication contains alcohol, it can cause skin irritation to sensitive areas. You should therefore avoid getting this medication in your eyes, nose, or mouth or in areas surrounding scratches or burns.
- Do not apply minoxidil to other areas of the body, because absorption of the drug may be increased and the risk of side effects may become greater. Do not use this medication along with other topical medications on your scalp, unless directed to do so by your doctor.
- If treatment is stopped, new hair growth will probably be shed within a few months.
- More frequent applications or use of larger doses (more than 1 mL twice daily) of this medication will not speed up the process of hair growth and may increase the possibility of side effects.

---

mirtazapine

BRAND NAME (Manufacturer)
Remeron (Organon)
TYPE OF DRUG
Tetracyclic antidepressant
INGREDIENT
mirtazapine
DOSAGE FORMS
Tablets (15 mg, 30 mg, and 45 mg)
Tablets, orally disintegrating (15 mg, 30 mg, and 45 mg)
STORAGE
Store at room temperature in a tightly closed container. Do not expose to excess heat.

USES

Mirtazapine is used to relieve symptoms of mental depression. It is a tetracyclic antidepressant, related to a group of drugs referred to as the tricyclic antidepressants. These medicines are thought to relieve depression by affecting nerve transmission in the brain.

TREATMENT

Take exactly as prescribed by your doctor. To lessen stomach irritation, take with food or a full glass of water (unless your doctor tells you to do otherwise).

If you miss a dose of this medication, take it as soon as you remember, unless it is almost time for your next dose. However, if the dose you missed was a once-a-day bedtime dose, do not take the dose in the morning. Check with your doctor instead. If the dose is taken in the morning, it may cause some unwanted side effects. Do not double the next dose of the medication.

The effects of therapy with this medication may not become apparent for several weeks after treatment is begun.

SIDE EFFECTS

Minor. Constipation, dizziness or light-headedness, dry mouth, increased appetite, nausea, trembling or shaking, vomiting, or weight gain. As your body adjusts to the medication, these side effects should disappear.

This medication may cause increased sensitivity to sunlight. Avoid prolonged exposure to sunlight and sunlamps. Wear protective clothing, and use an effective sunscreen.

Dry mouth can be relieved by chewing sugarless gum or sucking on hard candy.

To avoid dizziness or light-headedness when you stand, contract and relax the muscles of your legs for a few moments before rising.

To relieve constipation, increase the amount of fiber in your diet (fresh fruits and vegetables, salads, bran, and whole-grain breads), exercise, and drink more water (unless your doctor directs you to do otherwise).

Major. Tell your doctor about any side effects that are persistent or particularly bothersome. IT IS ESPECIALLY IMPORTANT TO TELL YOUR DOCTOR about changes in menstruation, chills, confusion, difficulty breathing, fever, hallucinations, mood changes, mouth sores, muscle aches, nervousness or anxiety, seizures, swelling, skin rash, sore throat, unusual movements of the body, or unusual thoughts.

INTERACTIONS

Mirtazapine interacts with several other types of medications:

1. Extreme drowsiness may occur when this medicine is taken with central nervous system depressants (alcohol, antihistamines, barbiturates, benzodiazepine tranquilizers, muscle relaxants, narcotics, pain medications, phenothiazine tranquilizers, and medications to induce sleep) or with other antidepressants.

2. Serious side effects may occur if a monoamine oxidase (MAO) inhibitor (such as selegiline, isocarboxazid, pargyline, phenelzine, procarbazine, or tranylcypromine) is taken with mirtazapine. At least 14 days should separate the use of mirtazapine and the use of an MAO inhibitor.

3. Phenobarbital, carbamazepine, phenytoin, primidone, rifampin, rifabutin, saquinavir, ketoconazole, itraconazole, cimetidine, clarithromycin, erythromycin, fluoxetine, fluvoxamine, nefazodone, or ciprofloxacin may interfere with the effects of mirtazapine when taken concurrently with it.

4. Mirtazapine may decrease the effectiveness of antiseizure medications and may block the blood-pressure-lowering effects of clonidine and guanethidine.

5. Tetracyclic antidepressants may increase the side effects of thyroid medications and over-the-counter (nonprescription) allergy, cough, cold, asthma, sinus, and diet medications. Discuss this with your doctor or pharmacist.

WARNINGS

• Tell your doctor if you have currently have or have a history of drug abuse or alcoholism, seizures, heart disease, asthma, high blood pressure, heart attack, circulatory disease, stomach problems, intestinal problems, liver or kidney problems, difficulty urinating, enlarged prostate gland, seizures, glaucoma, thyroid disease, mental illness, or electroshock therapy.

• Before having surgery or any medical or dental treatment, be sure to tell your doctor or dentist that you are taking mirtazapine.

• Mirtazapine may cause dizziness or light-headedness. Your ability to perform tasks that require alertness, such as driving a car or operating heavy machinery, may be decreased. Appropriate caution should be taken.
• The effects of this medication may last for as long as seven to ten days after you have stopped taking it, so continue to observe all precautions during that time period. Be sure to tell your doctor if the effects continue past that time.
• Elderly patients may be at an increased risk of side effects from this medication.
• Be sure to tell your doctor IMMEDIATELY if you are pregnant or if you are currently breast-feeding an infant. It is not known if mirtazapine is safe to use during pregnancy or if it passes into breast milk. You should discuss the risks and benefits of this medication with your doctor.

---

misoprostol

BRAND NAME (Manufacturer)
Cytotec (Searle)
TYPE OF DRUG
Prostaglandin E1 analog (gastrointestinal protective agent)
INGREDIENT
misoprostol
DOSAGE FORM
Tablets (100 mcg and 200 mcg)
STORAGE
Store this medication at room temperature in a tightly closed container.

USES

Misoprostol is used to prevent stomach ulcers in people who are taking nonsteroidal anti-inflammatory drugs (NSAIDs). NSAIDs (such as aspirin, carprofen, diclofenac, diflunisal, etodolac, fenoprofen, flurbiprofen, ibuprofen, indomethacin, ketoprofen, ketorolac, meclofenamate, mefenamic acid, naproxen, oxaprozin, phenylbutazone, piroxicam, salsalate, sulindac, tenoxicam, tiaprofenic acid, and tolmetin) are frequently prescribed to treat pain or arthritis. NSAIDs have been shown to cause ulcers in some patients. Misoprostol belongs to a group of chemicals called prostaglandins, which protect the stomach by decreasing the secretion of acid and increasing the secretion of mucus. This drug has also been used for other medical conditions; discuss other uses with your doctor.

TREATMENT

Take this medication with meals and at bedtime, unless your doctor directs you to do otherwise.

If you miss a dose, take the missed dose as soon as possible. However, if it is almost time for your next dose, do not take the missed dose at all; just return to your regular dosing schedule. Never take a double dose.

Misoprostol treatment should continue for as long as you take an NSAID. This medication should be taken exactly as prescribed by your doctor.

SIDE EFFECTS

Minor. Abdominal pain, change in appetite, diarrhea, flatulence, gas and bloating, heartburn, menstrual cramps and abnormal bleeding, nausea, or vomiting. Many of these side effects will diminish or disappear as you continue to take the medication.
Major. Tell your doctor about any side effects that are persistent or particularly bothersome. IT IS ESPECIALLY IMPORTANT TO TELL YOUR DOCTOR about chest pain, difficulty in breathing, postmenopausal vaginal bleeding, rash, or severe diarrhea, cramping, or nausea lasting longer than eight days.

INTERACTIONS

Antacids decrease the absorption of misoprostol into the bloodstream. However, antacids do not appear to decrease the beneficial effects of misoprostol in preventing ulcers. Consult your doctor before using antacids with this product.

Before starting to take misoprostol, BE SURE TO TELL YOUR DOCTOR about any other medications you are currently taking.

WARNINGS

- Do not take this medication if you have a history of allergy to prostaglandins.
- Tell your doctor immediately if you develop a rash while taking this medication.
- Women should notify their doctors immediately if they experience any abnormal vaginal bleeding while taking this medication.
- Women of childbearing age must use extreme caution to avoid becoming pregnant while taking misoprostol. This medication may cause miscarriage. Miscarriages caused by misoprostol may be incomplete, which could lead to potentially dangerous bleeding. ANY WOMAN WHO IS PREGNANT OR PLANS TO BECOME PREGNANT SHOULD NOT TAKE MISOPROSTOL. If you are taking misoprostol and discover that you are pregnant, stop taking the drug immediately and call your doctor.
- You should not take misoprostol if you are breast-feeding an infant. The body converts this medication to misoprostol acid, which can pass into breast milk and cause diarrhea in the nursing infant.

---

moexipril

BRAND NAME (Manufacturer)
Univasc (Schwarz Pharma)
TYPE OF DRUG
Antihypertensive
INGREDIENT
moexipril
DOSAGE FORM
Tablets (7.5 mg and 15 mg)
STORAGE
Store this medication in a tightly closed container at room temperature, away from heat and direct sunlight. Do not refrigerate or freeze.

USES

Moexipril is used to treat high blood pressure. It is a vasodilator (it widens blood vessels) that acts by blocking the production of chemicals that may be responsible for constricting or narrowing blood vessels. It is a medication in a class of drugs called the angiotensin-converting enzyme (ACE) inhibitors.

TREATMENT

Take this medication exactly as prescribed by your doctor. Moexipril should be taken on an empty stomach, one hour before a meal (unless your doctor directs you to do otherwise).

While using this medication, try to develop a set schedule for taking it. If you miss a dose and remember within a few hours, take the missed dose and resume your regular dosing schedule. However, if many hours have passed, skip the dose you missed and then take your next dose as scheduled. Do not double the next dose.

Moexipril does not cure high blood pressure, but it will help to control the condition as long as you continue to take it. It may be several weeks before you notice the full effect of this medication.

SIDE EFFECTS

Minor. Abdominal pain, cough, diarrhea, dizziness, drowsiness, fatigue, headache, insomnia, nausea, nervousness, sweating, or vomiting. These side effects should disappear as your body adjusts to the medication.

To avoid dizziness when you stand, contract and relax the muscles of your legs for a few moments before rising. Do this by alternately pushing one foot against the floor while lifting the other foot slightly.

This medication can cause increased sensitivity to sunlight. Avoid prolonged exposure to sunlight and sunlamps, wear protective clothing and sunglasses, and use an effective sunscreen.

Major. Tell your doctor about any side effects that are persistent or particularly bothersome. IT IS ESPECIALLY IMPORTANT TO TELL YOUR DOCTOR about chest pain; difficulty breathing; excessive perspiration; fainting; fever; irregular heartbeat; impaired ability to perceive taste; itching; light-headedness (especially during the first few days); muscle cramps; rash; sore throat; swelling of the face, eyes, lips, or tongue; tingling in the fingers and toes; or yellowing of the eyes or skin.

INTERACTIONS

Moexipril interacts with several other types of medications:

1. Diuretics and other antihypertensive medications can cause an excessive drop in blood pressure when they are combined with this medication (especially with the first dose).

2. The combination of this medication with amiloride, potassium supplements, salt substitutes, spironolactone, or triamterene can lead to hyperkalemia (dangerously high levels of potassium in the bloodstream).

3. Nonsteroidal anti-inflammatory agents (including ibuprofen, indomethacin, and naproxen) may reduce the effectiveness of this medication.

4. Antacids may decrease the effectiveness of moexipril. To avoid this drug interaction, take moexipril either one hour before or two hours after taking antacids.

5. Phenothiazine tranquilizers or probenecid, taken concurrently with moexipril, may increase the blood level and adverse effects of moexipril.

6. Concurrent use of this medication and allopurinol can increase the risk of developing an allergic reaction to these medications.

7. Moexipril can delay the body's elimination of lithium and lead to increased adverse effects from it.

8. This medication can lead to increased blood levels of digoxin and increased adverse effects from it.

Before starting to take moexipril, BE SURE TO TELL YOUR DOCTOR about any medications you are taking, especially those listed above.

WARNINGS

• Tell your doctor about unusual or allergic reactions you have had to any medications, especially to angiotensin-converting enzyme (ACE) inhibitors (including captopril, enalapril, lisinopril, and benazepril) or to this medication.

• Be sure to tell your doctor if you have ever had aortic stenosis, heart attack, stroke, blood disorders, kidney or liver disease, kidney transplant, or systemic lupus erythematosus.

• A persistent dry cough may occur and usually does not subside unless this medication is stopped. If this effect is bothersome, consult your doctor.

• Excessive perspiration, dehydration, or prolonged vomiting or diarrhea can lead to an excessive drop in blood pressure while you are taking this medication. Contact your doctor if you have any of these symptoms.

• Before having surgery or other medical or dental treatment, tell your doctor or dentist you are taking this medication.

• If this drug makes you dizzy or drowsy (sometimes this effect is seen after the first few doses), try to avoid any sudden changes in posture.
• Do not take any over-the-counter (nonprescription) medications for weight control or for asthma, sinus problems, cough, common cold, or allergy problems unless you first check with your doctor.
• Do not stop taking this medication unless you first consult your doctor. Stopping this drug abruptly may lead to a rise in blood pressure.
• Be sure to tell your doctor if you are pregnant. This medication and other drugs in the class called ACE inhibitors (including captopril, enalapril, lisinopril, and benazepril) have been shown to cause birth defects when taken in the second and third trimesters of pregnancy. Also be sure to tell your doctor if you are breast-feeding an infant. This medication may pass into breast milk and should therefore not be taken by a nursing mother.

---

mometasone furoate

BRAND NAME (Manufacturer)
Nasonex (Schering)
TYPE OF DRUG
Nasal adrenocorticosteroid hormone
INGREDIENT
mometasone furoate
DOSAGE FORM
Nasal spray solution (50 mcg per spray)
STORAGE
Store at room temperature in a tightly closed, light-resistant container. Avoid long exposure to sunlight, and do not expose to extreme heat.

USES

Mometasone nasal solution is used to relieve symptoms of rhinitis (inflammation of the nasal passages). How this drug acts to relieve these symptoms is not completely understood. Mometasone belongs to a group of drugs known as adrenocorticosteroids (or cortisonelike medications). Your adrenal glands naturally produce certain cortisonelike chemicals, which are involved in various regulatory processes in the body (such as fluid balance, temperature, and reaction to inflammation).

TREATMENTS

Use this medication only once daily unless your doctor tells you to do otherwise. Clear your nasal passages of secretions just before applying mometasone nasal solution. Then carefully follow the patient instructions, which you should receive when your prescription is dispensed (ask your pharmacist for these instructions if they were not included with your prescription). The instructions will explain how to properly apply this medication. If your doctor recommends that you use a nasal decongestant to clear your nasal passages, use the decongestant just before you use the mometasone nasal solution.

Shake the bottle well before each use to distribute the medicine and equalize the doses.

It may take one to two weeks for symptoms of nasal inflammation to be relieved after starting mometasone. If you have rhinitis at a certain time of the year, you may want to start using mometasone about two to four weeks before you expect to have nasal symptoms. Discuss when you should start taking this medication with your doctor. Mometasone does not cure rhinitis, but it may help relieve the symptoms as long as you continue to use it.

It is best to use mometasone at the same time every day. If you miss a dose of this medication, take it as soon as you remember, unless it is almost time for the next dose. In that case, do not take the missed dose at all; simply return to your regular dosing schedule. Do not double the next dose of the medication.

SIDE EFFECTS

Minor. Cough, diarrhea, headache, joint or muscle aches, nausea, runny or stuffy nose, sneezing, or sore throat. These side effects should diminish or disappear as your body adjusts to the medication.

Major. Tell your doctor about any side effects that are persistent or particularly bothersome. IT IS ESPECIALLY IMPORTANT TO TELL YOUR DOCTOR about chest pain, chest tightness, cold or flulike symptoms, cough, difficulty breathing, earache, increased menstrual cramps or bleeding, nosebleeds, redness or irritation of the eyes, shortness of breath, or white patches or sores in the nose.

INTERACTIONS

This medication should not interact with any other medications as long as it is used according to the directions.

WARNINGS

• Tell your doctor if you have had any unusual or allergic reactions to any other medications, especially to mometasone or to other adrenocorticosteroid medications (such as amcinonide, beclomethasone, betamethasone, clocortolone, cortisone, desonide, desoximetasone, dexamethasone, diflorasone, flumethasone, fluocinonide, fluorometholone, flurandrenolide, halcinonide, hydrocortisone, methylprednisolone, paramethasone, prednisolone, prednisone, or triamcinolone).

• Tell your doctor about any medical conditions that you may have, especially eye problems (such as cataracts or glaucoma), liver or renal problems, any type of infection, recent surgery or injury to the nose, eye infections, tuberculosis, chicken pox, shingles, diabetes, or blood-vessel disease.

• This product contains preservatives. Tell your doctor if you have ever had any type of allergic or adverse reaction to preservatives, such as sulfites, benzalkonium chloride, or phenylethyl alcohol.

• Tell your doctor if you are pregnant. It is not known if mometasone is safe to use during pregnancy. Also tell your doctor if you are breast-feeding an infant. It is not known if mometasone passes into breast milk, but other adrenocorticosteroids do. Discuss the risks and benefits of this medication with your doctor.

---

montelukast

BRAND NAME (Manufacturer)
Singulair (Merck & Co)
TYPE OF DRUG
Antiasthmatic
INGREDIENT
montelukast
DOSAGE FORMS
Granules (4 mg packet)
Tablets (10 mg)
Tablets, chewable (4 mg and 5 mg)
STORAGE
Store this medication at room temperature in tightly closed, light-resistant containers. Do not expose it to excess heat or moisture (do not store it in the bathroom), and do not freeze it.

USES

Montelukast is used to prevent the symptoms of asthma, such as wheezing and shortness of breath. It works by blocking the actions of certain chemicals in the body that cause the airways of the lungs to become inflamed and narrowed. This medication will not stop an asthma attack once it has started, but it does work to prevent acute attacks of asthma.

This medication can also be used for seasonal allergic rhinitis (hay fever) or other medical conditions when prescribed by your doctor.

TREATMENT

Take this medication at the same time each day, usually once a day in the evening. Take it as directed by your doctor, and use it every day, even if you don't have any symptoms of asthma.

If you miss a dose of this medication, take it as soon as you remember. However, if it is almost time for your next dose, do not take the missed dose at all; just return to your regular dosing schedule. Do not double the next dose of the medication.

Do not open the packet of granules until you are ready to take the dose. After opening the packet, the granules must be taken within 15 minutes. The granules can be taken directly in the mouth or sprinkled ONLY on a small quantity of applesauce, cooked carrots or rice, or ice cream. Do not mix the granules with any liquids.

SIDE EFFCTS

Minor. Cough, fever, headache, heartburn, skin rash, stomach pain, stuffy nose, tooth pain, or unusual tiredness. These side effects should diminish or disappear as your body adjusts to the medication.

Major. Tell your doctor about any side effects that are persistent or particularly bothersome. IT IS ESPECIALLY IMPORTANT TO TELL YOUR DOCTOR about flulike symptoms, itching, unusual tiredness, upper abdominal pain, or yellowing of the skin or the whites of the eyes.

INTERACTIONS

Montelukast may interact with other drugs. Rifampin and phenobarbital, when either is taken concurrently with montelukast, may decrease the amount of montelukast in the body and therefore decrease its effectiveness.

WARNINGS

• Be sure to tell your doctor about any unusual or allergic reactions you have had to any medications, including montelukast, zafirlukast, zileuton, aspirin, or nonsteroidal anti-inflammatory drugs (NSAIDs).

• Tell your doctor about any medical problems you currently have, especially any liver or kidney problems.

• The chewable tablets contain the artificial sweetener aspartame, which contains phenylalanine. Each chewable tablet has 0.842 mg of phenylalanine, which can be harmful for those who have phenylketonuria.

• IT IS IMPORTANT TO REMEMBER THAT montelukast will not stop an asthma attack once it has begun. You should not stop taking your other asthma medications unless your doctor tells you to do so.

• Be sure to tell your doctor if you are pregnant. It is not known if montelukast is safe during pregnancy. Also, tell your doctor if you are breast-feeding an infant. Montelukast can pass into human breast milk. You should discuss with your doctor the risks and benefits of this medication if you are breast-feeding an infant.

morphine

BRAND NAMES (Manufacturers)
Kadian (Zeneca)
morphine sulfate (various manufacturers)
MS Contin (Purdue-Pharma)
MSIR (Purdue-Pharma)
Oramorph SR (Roxane)
RMS (Upsher-Smith)
Roxanol (Roxane)
Roxanol SR (Roxane)
TYPE OF DRUG
Analgesic
INGREDIENT
morphine
DOSAGE FORMS
Capsules (15 mg and 30 mg)
Tablets (15 mg and 30 mg)
Tablets, soluble (10 mg, 15 mg, and 30 mg)
Sustained-release capsules (20 mg, 30 mg, 50 mg, 60 mg, and 100 mg)
Sustained-release tablets (15 mg, 30 mg, 60 mg, 100 mg, and 200 mg)
Oral solution (10 mg per 2.5 mL spoonful; 10 mg and 20 mg per 5-mL spoonful; 20 mg per mL; 100 mg per 5-mL spoonful)
Rectal suppositories (5 mg, 10 mg, 20 mg, and 30 mg)
STORAGE
Store the tablets and oral solution at room temperature in tightly closed, light-resistant containers. Keep the rectal suppositories in the refrigerator.

USES

Morphine is a narcotic analgesic that acts directly on the central nervous system (brain and spinal cord). It is used to relieve moderate to severe pain.

TREATMENT

To avoid stomach upset, you can take morphine with food or milk. This medication works most effectively if you take it at the onset of pain, rather than waiting until the pain becomes intense.

The solution form of this medication can be mixed with fruit juices to improve the taste. Be sure to measure each dose carefully with a specially designed 5-mL measuring spoon or with the dropper provided. An ordinary kitchen teaspoon is not accurate enough for this purpose.

Swallow the sustained-release tablets whole. Chewing, crushing, or crumbling the tablets destroys their sustained-release activity and could potentially increase the drug's side effects.

To use the suppository form of this medication, remove the foil wrapper and moisten the suppository with water (if the suppository is too soft to insert, refrigerate it for half an hour or run cold water over it before removing the wrapper). Lie on your left side with your right knee bent. Push the suppository into the rectum, pointed end first. Lie still for a few minutes. Try to avoid having a bowel movement for at least an hour (to give the medication time to be absorbed).

If you are taking this medication on a regular schedule and you miss a dose, take the missed dose as soon as possible after you remember. However, if it is almost time for your next dose of the medication, do not take the missed dose at all; just return to your regular dosing schedule. Do not double the next dose.

SIDE EFFECTS

Minor. Constipation, dizziness, drowsiness, dry mouth, false sense of well-being, flushing, light-headedness, loss of appetite, nausea, rash, or sweating. These side effects should disappear as your body adjusts to the medication.

If you are constipated, increase the amount of fiber in your diet (fresh fruits and vegetables, salads, bran, and whole-grain breads), exercise, and drink more water (unless your doctor directs you to do otherwise).

Chew sugarless gum or suck on ice chips or a piece of hard candy to help reduce mouth dryness.

If you feel dizzy or light-headed, sit or lie down for a while; get up from a sitting or lying position slowly; and be careful on stairs.

Major. Tell your doctor about any side effects that are persistent or particularly bothersome. IT IS ESPECIALLY IMPORTANT TO TELL YOUR DOCTOR about anxiety, difficulty in breathing, excitation, fainting, fatigue, painful or difficult urination, palpitations, restlessness, sore throat and fever, tremors, or weakness.

INTERACTIONS

Morphine interacts with several other types of medications:

1. Concurrent use of this medication with other central nervous system depressants (such as alcohol, antihistamines, barbiturates, benzodiazepine tranquilizers, muscle relaxants, and phenothiazine tranquilizers) or with tricyclic antidepressants can cause extreme drowsiness.

2. A monoamine oxidase (MAO) inhibitor taken within 14 days of this medication can lead to unpredictable and severe side effects.

3. Antihypertensive agents and diuretics may increase the side effects of morphine.

4. The combination of cimetidine and morphine can cause confusion, disorientation, and shortness of breath.

5. Morphine may decrease the effectiveness of metoclopramide.

BE SURE TO TELL YOUR DOCTOR about any medications you are currently taking, especially any of those listed above.

WARNINGS

• Tell your doctor about unusual or allergic reactions you have had to any medications, especially to morphine or to other narcotic analgesics (such as codeine, hydrocodone, hydromorphone, meperidine, methadone, oxycodone, and propoxyphene). In addition, tell your doctor if you have sulfite sensitivity or allergy.

• Tell your doctor if you now have or ever had acute abdominal conditions, asthma, brain disease, colitis, epilepsy, gallstones or gallbladder disease, head injuries, heart disease, kidney disease, liver disease, lung disease, mental illness, emotional disorders, enlarged prostate gland, thyroid disease, or urethral stricture.

• If this drug makes you dizzy or drowsy, do not take part in any activity that requires alertness, such as driving a car or operating potentially dangerous machinery.

• Before having surgery or any other medical or dental treatment, be sure to tell your doctor or dentist that you are taking this medication.

• Morphine has the potential for abuse and must be used with caution. Usually, it should not be taken for longer than ten days (unless your doctor directs you otherwise). Tolerance develops quickly; do not increase the dosage or stop taking the drug abruptly, unless you first consult your doctor. If you have been taking large amounts of this drug, or if you have been taking it for long periods of time, you may experience a withdrawal reaction (muscle aches, diarrhea, gooseflesh, runny nose, nausea, vomiting, shivering, trembling, stomach cramps, sleep disorders, irritability, weakness, excessive yawning, or sweating) when you stop taking it. Your doctor may therefore want to reduce the dosage gradually.

• Be sure to tell your doctor if you are pregnant. The effects of using this medication during the early stages of pregnancy have not been thoroughly studied in humans.

Also be sure to tell your doctor if you are breast-feeding an infant. Small amounts of this medication may pass into breast milk and may result in excessive drowsiness in the nursing infant.

moxifloxacin

BRAND NAME (Manufacturer)
Avelox (Bayer)
TYPE OF DRUG
Antibiotic
INGREDIENT
moxifloxacin
DOSAGE FORM
Tablets (400 mg)
STORAGE
Store this medication at room temperature in a tightly closed, light-resistant container.

USES

Moxifloxacin is an antibiotic that is used to treat a variety of bacterial infections. It chemically attaches to the bacteria and prevents their growth and multiplication. Moxifloxacin kills susceptible bacteria, but it is not effective against viruses, parasites, or fungi. Therefore, this medicine will not work for colds or the flu.

TREATMENT

Moxifloxacin can be taken on an empty stomach or with food. You should take this medication with plenty of water, unless your doctor directs you to do otherwise. It is usually taken once daily.

It is very important that you do not miss any doses of this medication. Moxifloxacin works best when the level of medicine in your bloodstream is kept constant. It is best to take the drug at the same time every day. If you miss a dose of this medication, take it as soon as possible. However, if it is almost time for your next dose of the medication, skip the missed dose and go back to your regular dosing schedule. Do not double the next dose.

It is important to continue to take moxifloxacin for the entire time prescribed by your doctor (usually five to ten days), even if the symptoms disappear before the end of that period. If you stop taking this drug too soon, resistant bacteria are given a chance to continue growing, and the infection could recur.

SIDE EFFECTS

Minor. Abdominal pain, constipation, diarrhea, difficulty sleeping, dizziness, drowsiness, dry mouth, gas, headache, or vomiting. These side effects should disappear as your body adjusts to the medication.

Dry mouth can be relieved by sucking on ice chips or a piece of hard candy or by chewing sugarless gum.

To relieve constipation, increase the amount of fiber in your diet (fresh fruits and vegetables, salads, bran, and whole-grain breads), exercise, and drink more water (unless your doctor directs you to do otherwise).

To avoid dizziness or light-headedness when you stand, contract and relax the muscles of your legs for a few moments before rising.

If you feel dizzy, sit or lie down for a while; get up from a sitting or lying position slowly; and be careful on stairs.

Major. Tell your doctor about any side effects you experience that are persistent or particularly bothersome. IT IS ESPECIALLY IMPORTANT TO TELL YOUR DOCTOR about chest pain, depression, difficulty breathing, difficulty urinating, fainting spells, hallucinations, hives, irregular or fast heartbeat, mood changes, muscle or tendon pain, problems with your vision, rash, seizures, sensitivity to sunlight, swelling of the eyelids, or uncoordinated movements.

INTERACTIONS

Moxifloxacin interacts with several other types of medications:

1. Moxifloxacin interacts with antacids, didanosine, sucralfate, and iron (including multivitamin preparations with iron). These medications reduce the efficacy of moxifloxacin and prevent it from working properly. Therefore, it is important that you take any of these other medications either four hours before OR eight hours after your dose of moxifloxacin.

2. To avoid unwanted drug interactions while you are being treated with moxifloxacin, it is very important that you do not take any over-the-counter (nonprescription) medications for weight control or for asthma, sinus problems, cough, cold, or allergy problems unless you first check with a doctor or pharmacist.

3. The side effects of moxifloxacin on your heart may be increased when it is combined with certain drugs, including quinidine, procainamide, amiodarone, sotolol, cisapride, erythromycin, antipsychotic agents, and tricyclic antidepressants (including amitriptyline, imipramine, and doxepin). These combinations should be avoided. Discuss this with your doctor or pharmacist.

4. Extreme drowsiness can occur when this medication is taken with other central nervous system depressants (such as alcohol, antihistamines, antidepressants, barbiturates, benzodiazepine tranquilizers, muscle relaxants, narcotics, pain medications, and sleeping medications).

Before starting to take this medication, BE SURE TO TELL YOUR DOCTOR about any medications you are currently taking, especially any of those listed above.

WARNINGS

• Tell your doctor about unusual or allergic reactions you have had to any medications, especially to moxifloxacin or other antibiotics.

• Tell your doctor if you have or if you ever had epilepsy, brain or spinal cord disease, diabetes, liver disease, glaucoma, anxiety, agitation, heart problems, fast or irregular heartbeat, high or low blood pressure, kidney or urinary tract problems, depression, or tendinitis.

• Moxifloxacin may cause extreme fatigue and dizziness. Your ability to perform tasks that require alertness, such as driving a car or operating potentially dangerous machinery, may be decreased. Appropriate caution should be taken.

• This medication can make your skin more sensitive to the sun (even for brief periods of time). It is important to limit your exposure to sunlight and sunlamps and wear protective clothing and sunscreen outdoors during the day.

• This medication has been prescribed for your current infection only. Another infection later on, or one that someone else has, may require a different medicine. You should not give your medication to other people or use it for other infections, unless your doctor specifically directs you to do so.

• Call your doctor immediately if you experience rash, breathing difficulties, or swelling of the face after taking this medication.

• Before having surgery or any other medical or dental treatment, be sure to tell your doctor or dentist that you are taking this medication.

• Be sure to tell your doctor if you are pregnant. Although this medication has not been thoroughly studied in humans, it is usually NOT recommended for pregnant women. This type of antibiotic has been reported to cause bone development problems in young animals. Also tell your doctor if you are breast-feeding an infant. Small amounts of moxifloxacin may pass into breast milk; this drug is not recommended for nursing women.

nabumetone

BRAND NAME (Manufacturer)
Relafen (SmithKline Beecham)
TYPE OF DRUG
Nonsteroidal anti-inflammatory analgesic
INGREDIENT
nabumetone
DOSAGE FORM
Tablets (500 mg and 750 mg)
STORAGE
Store in a tightly closed, light-resistant container at room temperature.

USES

Nabumetone is used to treat the inflammation (pain, swelling, stiffness) of rheumatoid arthritis and osteoarthritis. Nabumetone has been shown to block production of certain body chemicals, called prostaglandins, that may trigger pain. This medication may be used for other medical problems when prescribed by your doctor.

TREATMENT

Nabumetone may be taken on an empty stomach or with food or milk. Your doctor may instruct you to take the medication with food or with antacids, however, to decrease stomach upset.

To relieve arthritis symptoms, you must take nabumetone regularly as directed by your doctor. It may take up to two weeks before you feel the full effects of this medication. Nabumetone does not cure arthritis, but it will help to control the condition as long as you continue to take it.

It is important to continue to take nabumetone on schedule and not to miss any doses. If you do miss a dose, take it as soon as possible. However, if it is almost time for your next dose, don't take the missed dose at all; just return to your regular dosing schedule. Do not double the next dose.

SIDE EFFECTS

Minor. Bloating, constipation, diarrhea, difficulty in sleeping, dizziness, drowsiness, headache, heartburn, indigestion, light-headedness, loss of appetite, nausea, nervousness, soreness of the mouth, unusual sweating, or vomiting. As your body adjusts to the drug, these side effects should disappear.

To relieve constipation, increase the amount of fiber in your diet (fresh fruits and vegetables, salads, bran, and whole-grain breads), exercise, and drink more water (unless your doctor directs you to do otherwise).

If you become dizzy or light-headed, sit or lie down for a while; get up slowly from a sitting or reclining position; and be careful on stairs.

Major. If any side effects are persistent or particularly bothersome, report them to your doctor. IT IS ESPECIALLY IMPORTANT TO TELL YOUR DOCTOR about bloody or black, tarry stools; blurred vision; confusion; depression; difficult or painful urination; palpitations; problems with hearing; ringing or buzzing in your ears; skin rash, hives, or itching; stomach pain; swelling of the feet; tightness in the chest; unexplained sore throat and fever; unusual bleeding or bruising; unusual fatigue or weakness; unusual weight gain; wheezing or breathing difficulty; or yellowing of the eyes or skin.

INTERACTIONS

Nabumetone interacts with several other types of medications:

1. Anticoagulants (blood thinners, such as warfarin) can lead to an increase in bleeding complications.

2. Use of aspirin, other salicylates, and other anti-inflammatory medications with nabumetone can increase stomach irritation. Aspirin may also decrease the effectiveness of nabumetone.
3. Nabumetone can interact with diuretics (water pills).
4. Probenecid can increase blood levels of nabumetone, which may increase the risk of side effects.
5. The action of beta blockers may be decreased by this drug.
6. Nabumetone may increase the toxic effects of methotrexate.

BE SURE TO TELL YOUR DOCTOR about any medications you are currently taking, especially any of those listed above.

WARNINGS

- Before you start to take this medication, it is important to tell your doctor if you have ever had any unusual or allergic reactions to nabumetone or any of the other chemically related drugs (aspirin, other salicylates, ibuprofen, diclofenac, diflunisal, etodolac, fenoprofen, indomethacin, ketoprofen, ketorolac, meclofenamate, mefenamic acid, naproxen, oxaprozin, phenylbutazone, piroxicam, sulindac, tenoxicam, or tolmetin).
- Tell your doctor if you now have or ever had bleeding problems, colitis, stomach ulcers or other stomach problems, epilepsy, heart disease, high blood pressure, asthma, kidney disease, liver disease, mental illness, or Parkinson's disease.
- If this medication makes you feel dizzy or drowsy, do not take part in any activity that requires you to be alert, such as driving an automobile or operating any potentially dangerous equipment.
- Because nabumetone can prolong bleeding time, tell your doctor or dentist that you are taking this drug before having surgery or other medical or dental treatment.
- Stomach problems are more likely to occur if you take aspirin regularly or drink alcohol while being treated with this medication. This should be avoided (unless your doctor directs you to do otherwise).
- The elderly may be at increased risk for experiencing side effects from this drug.
- Be sure to tell your doctor IMMEDIATELY if you are pregnant. Studies have shown that this type of medicine, if taken late in pregnancy, may increase the length of pregnancy, prolong labor, or cause other problems during delivery. Also tell your doctor if you are breast-feeding an infant. Small amounts of nabumetone have been known to pass into breast milk, and use of this medicine may not be recommended.

---

naproxen

BRAND NAMES (Manufacturers)
Aleve* (Bayer)
Anaprox (Roche)
Anaprox DS (Roche)
EC-Naprosyn (Roche)
Naprelan (Carnrick Labs)
Naprosyn (Roche)
naproxen (various manufacturers)
* Available over the counter (without a prescription)

TYPE OF DRUG
Nonsteroidal anti-inflammatory analgesic

INGREDIENT
naproxen

DOSAGE FORMS
Tablets (200 mg, 250 mg, 375 mg, and 500 mg)
Oral suspension (125 mg per 5-mL spoonful)

STORAGE

Store all forms of this medication in tightly closed containers at room temperature, away from heat and direct sunlight. Do not freeze.

USES

Naproxen is used to treat the inflammation (pain, swelling, and stiffness) of certain types of arthritis, gout, bursitis, and tendinitis. Naproxen is also used to treat painful menstruation. Naproxen has been shown to block the production of certain body chemicals, called prostaglandins, that may trigger pain. However, it is not yet fully understood how naproxen works to relieve pain.

TREATMENT

Take this medication with or without food. However, to decrease stomach irritation, your doctor may want you to take the medicine with food or antacids.

It is important to take naproxen on schedule and not to miss any doses. If you do miss a dose, take it as soon as possible. However, if it is almost time for your next dose, do not take the missed dose at all; just return to your regular dosing schedule. Do not double the next dose.

If you are taking naproxen to relieve arthritis, you must take it regularly, as directed by your doctor. It may take up to four weeks before you feel the full benefits of this medication. Naproxen does not cure arthritis, but it will help to relieve the discomfort as long as you continue to take it.

SIDE EFFECTS

Minor. Bloating, constipation, diarrhea, difficulty in sleeping, dizziness, drowsiness, headache, heartburn, indigestion, light-headedness, loss of appetite, nausea, nervousness, soreness of the mouth, unusual sweating, or vomiting. As your body adjusts to the medication, these side effects should diminish or disappear.

To relieve constipation, increase the amount of fiber in your diet (fresh fruits and vegetables, salads, bran, and whole-grain breads), exercise, and drink more water (unless your doctor directs you to do otherwise).

If you become dizzy, sit or lie down for a while; get up slowly from a sitting or reclining position; and be careful on stairs.

Major. Tell your doctor about any side effects that are persistent or particularly bothersome. IT IS ESPECIALLY IMPORTANT TO TELL YOUR DOCTOR about bloody or black, tarry stools; blurred vision; confusion; depression; palpitations; ringing or buzzing in the ears or a problem with hearing; shortness of breath or wheezing; skin rash, hives, or itching; stomach pain; sudden decrease in amount of urine; swelling of the feet; tightness in the chest; unexplained sore throat and fever; unusual bleeding or bruising; unusual fatigue or weakness; unusual weight gain; or yellowing of the eyes or skin.

INTERACTIONS

Naproxen interacts with several other types of medications:

1. Concurrent use of naproxen and an anticoagulant (a blood thinner, such as warfarin) can lead to an increase in bleeding complications.

2. Aspirin, salicylates, or other anti-inflammatory medications can cause increased stomach irritation when used concurrently with naproxen.

3. Naproxen can decrease the elimination of lithium and methotrexate from the body, resulting in possible toxicity from these medications.

4. This medication may interfere with the blood-pressure-lowering effects of beta-blocking medications (such as acebutolol, atenolol, betaxolol, carteolol, esmolol, labetalol, metoprolol, nadolol, penbutolol, pindolol, propranolol, and timolol).

5. This medication can also interfere with the diuretic effects of furosemide and of thiazide-type diuretics.

6. Probenecid can increase the amount of naproxen in the bloodstream when both drugs are being taken.

Before starting to take this medication, BE SURE TO TELL YOUR DOCTOR about any medications you are currently taking, especially any of those listed above.

WARNINGS

• Before you take this medication, it is important to tell your doctor if you have ever had unusual or allergic reactions to any medications, especially to naproxen or any of the other chemically related drugs (including aspirin, other salicylates, carprofen, diclofenac, diflunisal, etodolac, fenoprofen, flurbiprofen, indomethacin, ketoprofen, ketorolac, meclofenamate, mefenamic acid, nabumetone, oxaprozin, phenylbutazone, piroxicam, sulindac, tenoxicam, or tolmetin).

• Before taking this medication, it is important to tell your doctor if you now have or ever had bleeding problems, colitis, stomach ulcers or other stomach problems, asthma, epilepsy, heart disease, high blood pressure, kidney disease, liver disease, mental illness, or Parkinson's disease.

• If this medication makes you feel dizzy or drowsy, do not take part in any activity that requires alertness, such as driving an automobile or operating potentially dangerous machinery.

• Because naproxen can prolong your bleeding time, it is important to tell your doctor or dentist that you are taking this drug before having surgery or any other medical or dental treatment.

• Stomach problems are more likely to occur if you take aspirin regularly or drink alcohol while being treated with this medication. You should avoid taking frequent doses of aspirin or drinking alcohol while undergoing treatment with this medication (unless your doctor tells you otherwise).

• Be sure to tell your doctor if you are pregnant. Naproxen may cause unwanted effects to the fetus. Studies have shown that taking naproxen late in pregnancy may increase the length of pregnancy, prolong labor, or cause other problems during delivery. Also be sure to tell your doctor if you are currently breast-feeding an infant. Small amounts of this medication have been shown to pass into breast milk.

---

naratriptan

BRAND NAME (Manufacturer)
Amerge (Glaxo Wellcome)
TYPE OF DRUG
Antimigraine agent
INGREDIENT
naratriptan
DOSAGE FORM
Tablets (1 mg and 2.5 mg)
STORAGE
Store this medication in a tightly closed container at room temperature. Do not freeze this medication.

USES

Although it is not completely understood how naratriptan works, this medication helps to relieve migraine headaches by altering the level of serotonin, a chemical naturally present in the brain. Naratriptan is used to treat migraine headaches in patients who do not get relief from other headache medications such as acetaminophen, aspirin, and nonsteroidal anti-inflammatory drugs (NSAIDs). This drug is not effective for preventing migraine headaches or for the treatment of cluster headaches.

TREATMENT

To obtain the best results from treatment, take each dose of naratriptan with a full glass of water. Naratriptan can be taken either with meals or on an empty stomach. The medication may work better if you lie down in a quiet, darkened room for a while after you take it.

If your migraine headache is less severe after your first naratriptan tablet, your doctor may instruct you to take a second tablet four hours after the first dose if the headache pain starts to come back. It is very important that you obtain specific instructions on the use of this medication from your doctor. Never take a double dose of this medication.

SIDE EFFECTS

Minor. Blurred vision, diarrhea, dizziness, drowsiness, increased tiredness, increased urination, itching, muscle or joint stiffness, nausea, restlessness, or vomiting. These side effects should diminish or disappear as your body adjusts to the medication.

If you feel dizzy or light-headed, sit or lie down for a while, get up slowly from a sitting or reclining position, and be careful on stairs.

Major. Tell your doctor about any side effects that are persistent or particularly bothersome. IT IS ESPECIALLY IMPORTANT TO NOTIFY YOUR DOCTOR about chest pain, difficulty breathing, hives, irregular heartbeat, skin rash, swelling of the eyelids, or tightness in the chest or throat.

INTERACTIONS

Naratriptan interacts with several other medications:

1. Certain antidepressants (such as fluoxetine, paroxetine, sertraline, and fluvoxamine) may produce weakness or incoordination when used with naratriptan.

2. Oral contraceptive medications (birth control pills) may increase the effects of naratriptan.

3. Naratriptan may increase the side effects caused by ergot-containing or ergot-type medications (such as methysergide and dihydroergotamine). Therefore, it is very important that the use of these ergot medications and naratriptan be separated by at least 24 hours.

Before starting naratriptan, BE SURE TO TELL YOUR DOCTOR about any medication you are taking, especially any of those listed above.

WARNINGS

• Tell your doctor about unusual or allergic reactions you have had to any medications, especially to naratriptan, sumatriptan, rizatriptan, or zolmitriptan.

• Naratriptan should not be taken together with other drugs that are in the same class (such as rizatriptan, sumatriptan, or zolmitriptan).

• The safety of using this medicine to treat more than four migraine headaches in a one-month period has not been well established.

• Before starting naratriptan, tell your doctor if you now have or have ever had heart disease, a heart attack, angina, high blood pressure, kidney or liver disease, peripheral vascular disease, or a stroke.

• If this drug makes you dizzy or drowsy, do not take part in any activities that require mental alertness, such as driving an automobile or operating potentially dangerous machinery or equipment.

• This medication can increase your sensitivity to sunlight. Avoid long exposure to sunlight and sunlamps; wear sunglasses and protective clothing, and use an effective sunscreen when outdoors during daylight hours.

• Tell your doctor IMMEDIATELY if you are pregnant. Studies in animals have shown that naratriptan, when used in very high doses, can cause problems in pregnancy. Adequate studies have not been conducted in human pregnancy. Tell your doctor if you are breast-feeding an infant. It is not known if naratriptan passes into breast milk.

nateglinide

BRAND NAME (Manufacturer)
Starlix (Novartis)
TYPE OF DRUG
Antidiabetic agent
INGREDIENT
nateglinide
DOSAGE FORM
Tablets (60 mg and 120 mg)
STORAGE
Store this medication in a tightly closed container at room temperature, away from heat and direct sunlight.

USES

Nateglinide is used for the treatment of the form of diabetes mellitus that appears most frequently in adulthood—known as type 2 or non–insulin-dependent diabetes—that cannot be managed by exercise and control of diet alone. Nateglinide may be added to diet and exercise to manage the disease, or it may be combined with metformin when diet, exercise, and either drug alone cannot provide adequate control of blood sugar.

TREATMENT

Take this medication exactly as prescribed by your doctor. It should be taken with a full glass of water between 1 and 30 minutes BEFORE each meal. If you skip a meal, you must also skip the dose of nateglinide for that meal. If you eat an additional meal, take an additional dose of nateglinide between 1 and 30 minutes before eating. If you miss a dose of this medicine, skip it, and just take the next dose before your next main meal. You should never take a double dose to make up for the one you missed (unless directed to do so by your doctor).

SIDE EFFECTS

Minor. Chills, constipation, cough, diarrhea, hypoglycemia (low blood sugar), itching, muscle aches and pain, nausea, pain in the joints or muscles, runny nose, skin rash, sneezing, sore throat, stomach pain, swelling of the joints, upper respiratory infection, or vomiting. As your body adjusts to the medication, some of these side effects should disappear.

To relieve constipation, increase the amount of fiber in your diet (fresh fruits and vegetables, salads, bran, and whole-grain breads), exercise, and drink more water (unless your doctor directs you to do otherwise).

To avoid dizziness or light-headedness when you stand, contract and relax the muscles of your legs for a few moments before rising. Do this by pushing one foot against the floor while raising the other foot slightly, alternating feet so that you are "pumping" your legs in a pedaling motion.

If you feel dizzy or light-headed, sit or lie down for a while; get up from a sitting or lying position slowly; and be careful on stairs.

Major. Tell your doctor about any side effects that are persistent or particularly bothersome. IT IS ESPECIALLY IMPORTANT TO TELL YOUR DOCTOR about behavioral changes similar to those associated with intoxication; changes in blood pressure; chest pain; cold sweats; cool, pale skin; difficulty breathing or swallowing; difficulty thinking; excessive hunger; fatigue; irregular heartbeat; nervousness; nightmares; rapid pulse; shakiness; skin rash or hives; slurred speech; tooth disorders; or unusual bleeding or bruising.

INTERACTIONS

Nateglinide interacts with several other types of drugs:

1. Beta-blocking agents (including propranolol, metoprolol, and betaxolol) can mask (or hide) some of the symptoms of low blood sugar. If you are taking a beta blocker and nateglinide, it is very important that you discuss this drug interaction with your doctor.

2. Concurrent use of nateglinide with nonsteroidal anti-inflammatory drugs (NSAIDs), including ibuprofen, naproxen, and diclofenac; aspirin or other salicylates; or monoamine oxidase (MAO) inhibitors, such as selegiline, isocarboxazid, pargyline, phenelzine, and tranylcypromine, may increase the potency and action of nateglinide, resulting in blood sugar that is too low. Before taking any of these medications, you should talk to your doctor or pharmacist about the risk of this interaction.

Before taking nateglinide, BE SURE TO TELL YOUR DOCTOR about any medication you are taking, especially any of those listed above.

WARNINGS

• Tell your doctor about any unusual or allergic reactions you have had to any medications, especially to nateglinide, repaglinide, or other antidiabetic agents.

• Tell your doctor if you have a history of alcoholism.

• Tell your doctor if you now have or ever had liver or kidney disease or autonomic neuropathy (a nervous system disorder); if you have type 1 (insulin-dependent) diabetes; or if you've ever experienced a diabetic coma.

• If this medication makes you feel drowsy or dizzy, do not participate in any activity that requires alertness, such as driving an automobile or operating any potentially dangerous equipment.

• Because of your diabetes, do not take any over-the-counter (nonprescription) medication for weight control or for cough, cold, asthma, allergy, or sinus problems unless you first check with your doctor.

• Follow the dietary plan or guidelines provided for you by your doctor, diabetes educator, or dietitian. This is an important part of controlling your blood sugar and is necessary for the medication to work properly.

• Test your blood sugar as directed by your doctor. It is a good way to determine whether your diabetes is being controlled with this medication.

• Eat or drink something containing sugar right away if you experience any symptoms of hypoglycemia (low blood sugar), such as anxiety, chills, cold sweats, cool or pale skin, drowsiness, excessive hunger, headache, nausea, nervousness, rapid heartbeat, shakiness, or unusual tiredness or weakness. It is important for your family and friends to know the symptoms of low blood sugar. Be sure they understand what to do if they observe any of these symptoms in you. Good sources of sugar are orange juice, corn syrup, honey, sugar cubes, and table sugar. Consider purchasing a bracelet that identifies you as a person with diabetes, in case you have a hypoglycemic event away from home.

• Before having surgery or any other medical or dental treatment, be sure to tell your doctor or dentist that you have diabetes and are taking this medication.

• Be sure to tell your doctor if you are pregnant. The effects of this medication during pregnancy have not been thoroughly studied in humans. It is also not known if nateglinide passes into breast milk in humans, so be sure to tell your doctor if you are breast-feeding an infant.

---

nefazodone

BRAND NAME (Manufacturer)
Serzone (Bristol-Myers Squibb)
TYPE OF DRUG
Antidepressant

INGREDIENT
nefazodone
DOSAGE FORM
Tablets (50 mg, 100 mg, 150 mg, 200 mg, and 250 mg)
STORAGE
Store this medication at room temperature in a tightly closed container. Do not expose to excessive heat.

USES

Nefazodone is used to relieve symptoms of mental depression. It is thought to relieve depression by increasing the concentration of certain chemicals (called neurotransmitters) that are involved with nerve transmission in the brain.

TREATMENT

Take this medication exactly as your doctor prescribes. This medicine is best taken on an empty stomach (without food), unless your doctor tells you to do otherwise. The effects of therapy with this medication may not be apparent for several weeks.

If you miss a dose of this medication, take it as soon as you remember. However, if it is almost time for the next dose, do not take the missed dose at all; just return to your regular dosing schedule. Do not double the next dose.

SIDE EFFECTS

Minor. Burning or tingling sensations of the skin, confusion, constipation, cough, diarrhea, dizziness, drowsiness, dry mouth, feeling of warmth, fever or chills, heartburn, increased appetite, sore throat, swelling, trouble sleeping, unusual dreams, or vomiting. These side effects should diminish or disappear as your body adjusts to the medication.

Dry mouth can be relieved by chewing sugarless gum or sucking on hard candy.

To relieve constipation, increase the amount of fiber in your diet (fresh fruits and vegetables, salads, bran, and whole-grain breads), exercise, and drink more water (unless your doctor directs you to do otherwise).

To avoid dizziness or light-headedness when you stand, contract and relax the muscles of your legs for a few moments before rising. Do this by pressing one foot into the floor while raising the other foot slightly, alternating feet so that you are "pumping" your legs in a pedaling motion.

Major. Tell your doctor about any side effects that are persistent or particularly bothersome. IT IS ESPECIALLY IMPORTANT TO TELL YOUR DOCTOR about changes in your eyesight, chest pain, clumsiness or unsteadiness, difficulty breathing, fainting, light-headedness, loss of appetite, muscle weakness, nausea, ringing in the ears, skin rash or itching, swelling of the face, unusual bruising or bleeding, vomiting, or yellowing of the eyes and skin.

INTERACTIONS

Nefazodone may interact with a number of other medications:

1. Extreme drowsiness may occur when this medicine is taken with central nervous system depressants (alcohol, antihistamines, barbiturates, benzodiazepine tranquilizers, muscle relaxants, narcotics, pain medications, phenothiazine tranquilizers, and medications to induce sleep) or with other antidepressants.

2. Serious side effects may occur if a monoamine oxidase (MAO) inhibitor (such as selegiline, isocarboxazid, pargyline, phenelzine, procarbazine, or tranylcypromine) is taken concurrently with nefazodone. At least 14 days should separate the use of nefazodone and the use of an MAO inhibitor.

3. Nefazodone should not be taken with pimozide or cisapride. These combinations may cause the heart to beat irregularly.

4. Nefazodone may increase the serious side effects of some benzodiazepine drugs, such as alprazolam, midazolam, or triazolam. Therefore, nefazodone should not be taken concurrently with any of these drugs.
5. Nefazodone taken concurrently with digoxin may increase the amount of digoxin in the body and increase its side effects.

WARNINGS

• Be sure to tell your doctor about any unusual or allergic reactions you have had to any medications, especially nefazodone and trazodone.
• Tell your doctor if you have a history of drug abuse or alcoholism, seizures, heart disease, low blood pressure, psychiatric illnesses, or liver disease.
• Before having surgery or any other medical or dental treatment, be sure to tell your doctor or dentist that you are taking nefazodone.
• Nefazodone may cause dizziness or light-headedness. You may have decreased ability to perform tasks that require alertness, such as driving a car or operating potentially dangerous machinery. Appropriate caution should be taken.
• Avoid using alcohol while taking this medication. Alcohol may increase the side effects of this medication.
• This medication can increase your sensitivity to sunlight. Avoid long exposure to sunlight and sunlamps, wear sunglasses and protective clothing, and use an effective sunscreen when outdoors during daylight hours.
• Be sure to tell your doctor if you are pregnant or if you are breast-feeding an infant. It is not known if nefazodone is safe to use during pregnancy, nor is it known if nefazodone passes into breast milk. If you are pregnant or breast-feeding an infant, therefore, you should discuss with your doctor or pharmacist the risks and benefits of this medication before starting treatment.

---

nelfinavir

BRAND NAME
Viracept (Agouron)
TYPE OF DRUG
Antiretroviral agent, protease inhibitor
INGREDIENT
nelfinavir
DOSAGE FORMS
Tablets (250 mg)
Powder for oral solution (50 mg per gram)
STORAGE
Store this medication at room temperature in a tightly closed container. Do not expose to excess heat. Once a solution has been prepared from the powder, it should be taken within six hours.

USES

Nelfinavir is used in the treatment of human immunodeficiency virus (HIV) infection. HIV is the virus that causes AIDS. Nelfinavir works by inhibiting the reproduction, or growth, of the virus, which slows down the progression of AIDS. Nelfinavir does not cure HIV infection or AIDS but may delay the onset of other infections and diseases caused by AIDS. Nelfinavir is usually not used alone but rather in combination with other anti-AIDS medications.

TREATMENT

This medication works best when the level of medicine in your bloodstream is kept constant. It is best to take the drug at evenly spaced intervals throughout the day.

IT IS IMPORTANT NOT TO MISS ANY DOSES. The chances of the AIDS virus becoming resistant to nelfinavir increase if the level of medication in the bloodstream is low. If you miss a dose of this medication, take it as soon as possible. However, if it is almost time for your next dose, skip the missed dose and go back to your regular dosing schedule. Do not double the next dose.

Take nelfinavir with food so that it is well absorbed (unless your doctor tells you to do otherwise). The powder for oral solution may be mixed with a small amount of water, milk, formula, soy formula, soy milk, or meal-replacement beverage. It should not be mixed with acidic foods or juices because it may have a bitter taste. Nelfinavir powder should not be mixed with liquid in its original container. Drink all of the solution after it is mixed to be sure you get the entire dose.

SIDE EFFECTS

Minor. Diarrhea, nausea, skin rash, or stomach gas. As your body adjusts to the medication, some of these side effects should disappear.

Major. Tell your doctor about any side effects that are persistent or particularly bothersome. IT IS ESPECIALLY IMPORTANT TO TELL YOUR DOCTOR about confusion, dry or itching skin, fatigue, fruity or unusual mouth odor, increased hunger or thirst, increased urination, unusual weight loss, or vomiting.

INTERACTIONS

Nelfinavir may interact with a number of other drugs:

1. The serious side effects of alprazolam, midazolam, triazolam, ergot drugs, amiodarone, quinidine, or rifabutin may be increased by nelfinavir.

2. Carbamazepine, phenobarbital, phenytoin, grapefruit juice, rifampin, or rifabutin may reduce the amount of nelfinavir in the body, making it less effective.

3. Nelfinavir may make birth control pills (oral contraceptives) less effective. Therefore, a different or additional means of birth control should be used while you are being treated with nelfinavir.

WARNINGS

• Tell your doctor if you ever had an allergic reaction to any medication, especially to nelfinavir, indinavir, ritonavir, saquinavir, or any other medication used to treat AIDS.

• This medication may cause high blood sugar (or diabetes). Your doctor may want you to check your blood sugar regularly while taking nelfinavir. Ask your doctor about the signs of high blood sugar and diabetes.

• Your doctor may do regular blood tests to check your cholesterol. Increases in cholesterol may occur with nelfinavir.

• This medication may cause the fat in your body to be redistributed. This may cause a loss of fat in the face, buttocks, arms, and legs and an increase in fatty tissue on the upper back.

• Before taking this medication, be sure to tell your doctor about any medical problems you may have, especially liver problems, diabetes or problems with high blood sugar, high cholesterol, or bleeding problems, especially hemophilia.

• Before having surgery or any medical or dental treatment, be sure to tell your doctor or dentist that you are taking nelfinavir.

• Your doctor may do regular blood tests to see how well this medication is working against the AIDS virus.

• Nelfinavir powder for solution contains phenylalanine, about 11.2 milligrams per gram of powder. This ingredient can dangerously affect people with phenylketonuria. If you have phenylketonuria, discuss this with your doctor.

• Be sure to tell your doctor about any other medications you are taking, both prescription and nonprescription. Nelfinavir may interact with other medications to produce serious side effects.

• If you are infected with HIV, it is best to avoid any sexual activity involving an exchange of body fluids with other people. If you do have vaginal, anal, or oral sex, always use a latex condom.
• Be sure to tell your doctor if you are pregnant. It is not known if nelfinavir is safe to use during pregnancy. It is not known if nelfinavir passes into human breast milk. However, because of the risk of passing HIV to infants, it is recommended that mothers who have HIV infection NOT breast-feed their infants.

---

neomycin, polymyxin B, and bacitracin or gramicidin combination (ophthalmic)

BRAND NAMES (Manufacturers)
AK-Spore (Akorn)
neomycin, polymyxin B, and bacitracin or gramicidin combination (various manufacturers)
Neosporin (Burroughs Wellcome)
TYPE OF DRUG
Ophthalmic antibiotic
INGREDIENTS
neomycin, polymyxin B, and bacitracin (ointment only) or gramicidin (drops only)
DOSAGE FORMS
Ophthalmic drops (1.75 mg neomycin, 10,000 units polymyxin B, and 0.025 mg gramicidin per mL)
Ophthalmic ointment (3.5 mg neomycin, 10,000 units polymyxin B, and 400 units bacitracin per gram)
STORAGE
Store at room temperature in tightly closed containers. Do not freeze.

USES

This medication is used to treat bacterial infections of the eye. It is an antibiotic combination that is effective against a wide range of bacteria. It acts by preventing the production of nutrients that are required for growth of the infecting bacteria. This medication is not effective against infections caused by viruses or fungi.

TREATMENT

Wash your hands with soap and water before using this medication.

To prevent contamination of the medication, be careful not to touch the tube portion of the dropper, and do not let the dropper touch your eye.

Note that the bottle of eyedrops is not completely full. This is purposely done to allow control of the number of drops dispensed. To apply the eyedrops, tilt your head back and pull down the lower eyelid with one hand to make a pouch below the eye. Drop the prescribed amount of medication into this pouch and slowly close your eyes. Try not to blink. Keep your eyes closed, and place one finger at the corner of the eye next to your nose for a minute or two, applying slight pressure (this is done to prevent loss of medication through the duct that drains fluid from the surface of the eye into the nose and throat). Then wipe away any excess medication with a clean tissue. If you don't think the medicine got into the eye, repeat the process once. If you are using more than one kind of eyedrop, wait at least five minutes before applying a different eye medication.

Follow the same general procedure for the ointment. Tilt your head back, pull down your lower eyelid, and squeeze the ointment in a line along the pouch below the eye. Close the eye and place your finger at the corner of the eye near the nose for a minute or two. Do not rub your eyes. Wipe off excess ointment from around the eye and from the tip of the tube with clean tissues.

Since this medication is somewhat difficult to apply, you may prefer to have someone else apply it for you.

If you miss a dose of this medication, insert the drops or apply the ointment as soon as possible. However, if it is almost time for the next application, do not use the missed dose; just return to your regular dosing schedule.

Continue using this medicine for the entire time prescribed by your doctor, even if the symptoms disappear. If you stop too soon, the infection could recur.

SIDE EFFECTS

Minor. Blurred vision, burning, or stinging. These side effects should disappear as your body adjusts to the drug.

Major. Tell your doctor about any side effects that are persistent or particularly bothersome. IT IS ESPECIALLY IMPORTANT TO TELL YOUR DOCTOR about disturbed or reduced vision and about itching, rash, redness, or swelling in or around your eyes (other than the original symptoms of your infection). If the infection seems to be getting worse rather than improving, contact your doctor.

INTERACTIONS

This medication should not interact with other medications as long as it is used according to directions.

WARNINGS

- Tell your doctor about unusual or allergic reactions you have had to any medications, especially to neomycin, bacitracin, polymyxin B, gramicidin, or any related antibiotics (such as amikacin, colistimethate, colistin, gentamicin, kanamycin, netilmicin, paromomycin, streptomycin, tobramycin, and viomycin).
- Tell your doctor if you now have or if you have ever had kidney disease, an injured cornea, inner ear disease, or myasthenia gravis.
- Do not use this medication for longer than ten consecutive days unless your doctor directs you to do so. Prolonged use of this drug may result in eye damage. If you need to use this medication for six weeks or longer, your doctor may want you to have an eye examination.
- This medication has been prescribed for your current infection only. Another infection later on may require a different medicine. You should not give your medicine to other people or use it for other infections, unless your doctor specifically directs you to do so.
- To allow your eye infection to clear, do not apply makeup to the affected eye.
- Tell your doctor if you are pregnant. The effects of this drug during pregnancy have not been studied.

---

nevirapine

BRAND NAME (Manufacturer)
Viramune (Roxane)
TYPE OF DRUG
Antiviral
INGREDIENT
nevirapine
DOSAGE FORM
Tablets (200 mg)

STORAGE

Store this medication at room temperature in a tightly closed container. Do not expose to excess heat.

USES

Nevirapine is used in the treatment of human immunodeficiency virus (HIV) infection. HIV is the virus that causes AIDS. Nevirapine works by inhibiting the reproduction, or growth, of the virus, which slows down the progression of AIDS. Nevirapine does not cure HIV infection or AIDS, but it may delay the onset of other infections and diseases caused by AIDS.

TREATMENT

This medication works best when the level of medicine in your bloodstream is kept constant. It is best to take the drug at evenly spaced intervals throughout the day. To avoid stomach irritation, you can take nevirapine with food or with a full glass of water (unless your doctor directs you otherwise).

If you miss a dose of this medication, take the missed dose as soon as possible after you remember. However, if it is almost time for your next dose of the medication, do not take the missed dose at all; just return to your regular dosing schedule. Do not double the next dose.

SIDE EFFECTS

Minor. Diarrhea, headache, nausea, or stomach pain. These side effects should diminish or disappear as your body adjusts to the medication.

Major. Tell your doctor about any side effects that are persistent or particularly bothersome. IT IS ESPECIALLY IMPORTANT TO TELL YOUR DOCTOR about fever, skin rash, sores or ulcers in the mouth, or yellowing of the skin or eyes.

INTERACTIONS

Nevirapine may interact with a number of drugs:

1. Rifampin or rifabutin taken concurrently with nevirapine may reduce the effects of nevirapine.

2. Concurrent use of erythromycin, clarithromycin, or cimetidine may increase the effects of nevirapine.

3. Nevirapine may interact with birth control pills, indinavir, ritonavir, nelfinavir, and saquinavir, making these medications less effective.

Before starting this medication, BE SURE TO TELL YOUR DOCTOR about any medications you are currently taking, especially those listed above.

WARNINGS

- Tell your doctor if you have ever had an allergic reaction to nevirapine or to any other medication.
- Before taking this medication, be sure to tell your doctor about any medical problems you may have, especially liver or kidney problems.
- Tell your doctor immediately if you notice any type of skin rash. Nevirapine may cause a serious, life-threatening skin rash, which usually occurs in the first 12 to 16 weeks of treatment. Women are at a higher risk of getting a serious rash.
- Be sure to tell your doctor if you are pregnant. Although birth defects have not been documented in humans, nevirapine does cross the placenta. It is not known whether nevirapine is safe during human pregnancy. Nevirapine passes into human breast milk. Because of the risk of passing HIV to infants, it is recommended that mothers who have HIV infection NOT breast-feed their infants.

nicotine gum

BRAND NAMES (Manufacturers)
Nicorette* (Merrell Dow)
nicotine gum* (various manufacturers)
*Available over the counter (without a prescription)
TYPE OF DRUG
Stop-smoking aid
INGREDIENT
nicotine
DOSAGE FORM
Chewing gum (2 mg and 4 mg)
STORAGE
Keep in the original, child-resistant packaging until it is ready to be chewed.

USES

Nicotine gum is used as a temporary aid for smoking-cessation programs. It helps control the symptoms of nicotine withdrawal (such as irritability, headache, fatigue, and insomnia) and thus helps you concentrate on overcoming the psychological and behavioral aspects of your smoking habit.

TREATMENT

Use nicotine gum when you feel the urge to smoke. Keep the gum with you at all times. Place it where you usually keep your cigarettes. Whenever you feel that you want to smoke, put one piece of gum into your mouth. Chew the gum very slowly, until you taste it or feel a slight tingling in your mouth. As soon as you get the taste of the gum, stop chewing and place it between your cheek and gums. After the taste or tingling is almost gone, chew slowly again until you taste the gum. Then stop chewing again. The gum should be chewed slowly for 30 minutes to release most of the nicotine. You should not expect the gum to give you the same quick satisfaction that smoking does. Do not eat or drink 15 minutes before chewing a piece of nicotine gum or while you are chewing it.

Most people find that 10 to 12 pieces of gum per day are enough to control their urge to smoke. Depending on your needs, you can adjust the rate of chewing and the time between pieces. Do not chew more than 24 pieces per day (unless your doctor directs you to do so).

The risk of smoking again is highest in the first few months after you stop smoking, so it is important that you follow your smoking-cessation program and use nicotine gum as directed during this period.

SIDE EFFECTS

Minor. Because of its nicotine content, the gum does not taste like ordinary chewing gum. During the first several days of chewing the nicotine gum, you may experience mouth sores, jaw muscle aches, headaches, and increased salivation. These side effects should disappear as you continue to use the gum.

If you chew the gum too fast, you may feel effects similar to those experienced when people inhale a cigarette for the first time or when they smoke too fast. These effects include constipation, coughing, dizziness, dry mouth, gas pains, hiccups, hoarseness, insomnia, light-headedness, nausea, redness of the face, sneezing, stomach pain, stomach upset, throat and mouth irritation, and vomiting. Most of these side effects can be controlled by chewing the gum more slowly.

Major. If any of the side effects are persistent or particularly bothersome, report them to your doctor. IT IS ESPECIALLY IMPORTANT TO TELL YOUR DOCTOR about signs of too much nicotine (cold sweats, confusion, difficulty in breathing, disturbed hearing or vision, faintness, marked weakness, palpitations, or seizures).

If you accidently swallow a piece of gum, you should not experience adverse effects. The nicotine is released by chewing and is absorbed primarily in the mouth.

INTERACTIONS

Smoking cessation, with or without nicotine gum, may affect blood levels of certain medications (including aminophylline, caffeine, glutethimide, imipramine, insulin, labetalol, oxazepam, pentazocine, prazosin, propoxyphene, propranolol, and theophylline).

Nicotine can reduce the diuretic effects of furosemide and lessen the blood-pressure-lowering effects of beta blockers.

BE SURE TO TELL YOUR DOCTOR about any medications you are currently taking, especially any listed above.

WARNINGS

- Tell your doctor if you have recently had a heart attack or if you now have or ever had heart palpitations or arrhythmias, angina, active temporomandibular joint (TMJ) disease, cardiovascular disease, endocrine (hormone) disease, thyroid problems, pheochromocytoma, diabetes mellitus, high blood pressure, peptic ulcers, mouth or throat inflammation, or dental problems.
- Be sure to tell your doctor if you are pregnant. Nicotine (from the gum or from cigarette smoke) can harm the fetus. Also tell your doctor if you are breast-feeding an infant. Small amounts of nicotine can pass into breast milk.

---

nicotine transdermal patch

BRAND NAMES (Manufacturers)

NicoDerm CQ* (Glaxo SmithKline Consumer)
nicotine transdermal system* (various manufacturers)
Nicotrol* (Pharmacia)
*Available over the counter (without a prescription)

TYPE OF DRUG

Stop-smoking aid

INGREDIENT

nicotine

DOSAGE FORM

Transdermal patches (5 mg, 7 mg, 10 mg, 14 mg, 15 mg, 21 mg)

STORAGE

Keep this medication in its original, child-resistant packaging until the patch is ready to be applied to the skin. After use, carefully dispose of the patch, as even a used nicotine patch contains a large quantity of residual nicotine that may be harmful to children or pets.

USES

The nicotine patch is used as a temporary aid for smoking-cessation programs. It helps to control the symptoms of nicotine withdrawal (irritability, headache, fatigue, insomnia) and thus helps you to concentrate on overcoming the psychological and behavioral aspects of your smoking habit.

TREATMENT

IT IS IMPORTANT TO STOP SMOKING when therapy with nicotine patches is started. If you continue to smoke and use the nicotine patches, you increase the amount of nicotine in your blood and may be more likely to experience side effects or an overdose. The nicotine patch should be applied daily to a hairless, clean, dry skin site on the upper trunk (chest, back, stomach) or upper outer arm. After 16 or 24 hours, depending on the type of patch, the used patch should be removed and a new patch applied to a different site on your body. (Some nicotine patches, such as the 16-hour variety, should only be worn during the day and removed before bedtime. Other brands should be worn for a full 24 hours. Discuss these options with your doctor or pharmacist.) Try to change the patch at the same time every day, as this may prevent you from forgetting to apply a new patch. Depending on the type of nicotine patch your doctor recommends and the severity of your withdrawal symptoms, you may use the patches daily for 6 to 12 weeks to help you stop smoking. Discuss this with your doctor or pharmacist.

The risk of smoking again is considered highest in the first few months after finishing treatment with nicotine patches. Follow your smoking-cessation program to prevent smoking "relapse."

SIDE EFFECTS

Minor. Abnormal dreams, burning or itching at the patch-application site, diarrhea, difficulty sleeping, dry mouth, hives or swelling at the patch-application site, mood changes, skin rash, or sweating. These side effects should disappear as your body adjusts to the medication.

Major. If any of the side effects are persistent or particularly bothersome, report them to your doctor or pharmacist. IT IS ESPECIALLY IMPORTANT TO TELL YOUR DOCTOR about signs of too much nicotine (cold sweats, confusion, diarrhea, difficulty in breathing, disturbed hearing or vision, nervousness, nightmares, marked weakness, muscle palpitations, severe itching, rash, or seizures).

INTERACTIONS

Smoking cessation, with or without nicotine patches, may affect blood levels of certain medications (including aminophylline, caffeine, furosemide, imipramine, insulin, labetalol, pentazocine, prazosin, propoxyphene, and theophylline). Eliminating nicotine may also increase the blood-pressure-lowering effects of any beta blocker, such as propranolol, you are taking. BE SURE TO TELL YOUR DOCTOR about any medications you are currently taking, especially those listed above.

WARNINGS

- Tell your doctor if you have recently had a heart attack. It is also important to tell your doctor if you now have or if you have ever had heart palpitations or irregular heartbeat, angina, heart disease, a hormone imbalance, kidney problems, thyroid problems, pheochromocytoma, diabetes mellitus, high blood pressure, or stomach ulcers.
- Tell your doctor or pharmacist if you have ever had a rash or irritation from adhesive tape or bandages.
- If you develop a skin rash from the nicotine patch that becomes very swollen and red, contact your doctor for medical advice.
- Be sure to tell your doctor if you are pregnant. Nicotine (from the patches or from smoking cigarettes or chewing tobacco) can cause fetal harm. Also tell your doctor if you are breast-feeding an infant. Small amounts of nicotine have been known to pass into breast milk.

---

nifedipine

BRAND NAMES (Manufacturers)
Adalat (Bayer)
Adalat CC (Bayer)
Nifedical XL (Teva)

nifedipine (various manufacturers)
Procardia (Pfizer)
Procardia XL (Pfizer)

TYPE OF DRUG
Antianginal

INGREDIENT
nifedipine

DOSAGE FORMS
Capsules (10 mg and 20 mg)
Sustained-release tablets (30 mg, 60 mg, and 90 mg)

STORAGE
Store at room temperature in a tightly closed, light-resistant container. Do not freeze.

USES

This medication is used to treat various types of angina (chest pain) and hypertension (high blood pressure). Nifedipine belongs to a group of drugs known as calcium channel blockers. By blocking calcium, nifedipine relaxes and prevents spasms of the blood vessels of the heart and reduces the oxygen needs of the heart muscle.

TREATMENT

Take nifedipine on an empty stomach with a full glass of water one hour before or two hours after a meal (unless your doctor directs you to do otherwise). Swallow the capsules whole to obtain maximum benefit. The sustained-release tablets should also be swallowed whole; do not chew, crush, or bite them.

If you miss a dose of this medication, take the missed dose as soon as possible. However, if it is within two hours of your next scheduled dose, do not take the missed dose at all; just return to your regular dosing schedule. Do not double the next dose.

SIDE EFFECTS

Minor. Bloating, cough, dizziness, flushing, gas, giddiness, headache, heartburn, heat sensation, nasal congestion, nausea, nervousness, sleep disturbances, sweating, or weakness. These side effects should diminish or disappear as your body adjusts to the medication.

If you feel dizzy or light-headed, sit or lie down for a while; get up slowly from a sitting or reclining position; and be careful on stairs. To avoid dizziness or light-headedness when you stand, contract and relax the muscles of your legs for a few moments before rising. Do this by pushing one foot against the floor while raising the other foot slightly, alternating your feet so that you are "pumping" your legs in a pedaling motion.

Major. Tell your doctor about any side effects that are persistent or particularly bothersome. IT IS ESPECIALLY IMPORTANT TO TELL YOUR DOCTOR about blurred vision, chills, confusion, difficulty in breathing, fainting, fever, fluid retention, impotence, mood changes, muscle cramps, palpitations, rash, sore throat, or tremors.

INTERACTIONS

Nifedipine interacts with many other types of medications:

1. Nifedipine can increase the active blood levels of digoxin, warfarin, phenytoin, and quinine, which can lead to an increase in side effects.

2. The combination of nifedipine and beta blockers (acebutolol, atenolol, betaxolol, carteolol, esmolol, labetalol, metoprolol, nadolol, penbutolol, pindolol, propranolol, or timolol) can lead to a severe drop in blood pressure.

3. Nifedipine can lower quinidine blood levels, which can decrease its effectiveness.

4. Cimetidine, cyclosporine, carbamazepine, and antifungal agents can decrease the breakdown of nifedipine in the body, which can increase the risk of side effects from nifedipine.

5. Do not take nifedipine with grapefruit juice; it may result in an increased risk of side effects from nifedipine.

Before starting to take nifedipine, BE SURE TO TELL YOUR DOCTOR about any medications you are currently taking, especially any of those listed above.

WARNINGS

• Tell your doctor about unusual or allergic reactions you have had to any medications, especially to nifedipine.
• Tell your doctor if you have ever had heart disease, kidney disease, low blood pressure, or liver disease.
• If this drug makes you dizzy or drowsy, do not take part in any activity that requires alertness, such as driving a car or operating potentially dangerous machinery.
• Before having surgery or any other medical or dental treatment, tell your doctor or dentist you are taking this drug.
• Do not stop taking this medication unless you first consult your doctor. Stopping this medication abruptly may lead to severe chest pain. Your doctor may, therefore, want to decrease your dosage gradually.
• Be sure to tell your doctor if you are pregnant. Nifedipine has been shown to cause birth defects in the offspring of animals that received large doses of it during pregnancy. This medication has not been studied in pregnant women. Also tell your doctor if you are breast-feeding an infant. Nifedipine passes into breast milk, and your doctor will determine if this medication is appropriate for you.

---

nitrofurantoin

BRAND NAMES (Manufacturers)
Macrobid (Procter & Gamble Pharm.)
Macrodantin (Procter & Gamble Pharm.)
nitrofurantoin (various manufacturers)
TYPE OF DRUG
Antibiotic
INGREDIENT
nitrofurantoin
DOSAGE FORMS
Capsules (25 mg, 50 mg, and 100 mg)
Capsules, dual-release (equivalent to 100 mg)
Oral suspension (25 mg per 5-mL spoonful)
STORAGE
Store at room temperature in tightly closed, light-resistant containers. Do not freeze.

USES

Nitrofurantoin is used to treat bacterial infections of the urinary tract (bladder and kidneys). It kills susceptible bacteria by breaking down their cell membranes and interfering with their production of vital nutrients.

TREATMENT

To avoid stomach irritation and to increase the effectiveness of this drug, you can take it with a meal or with a glass of water or milk.

The tablets and capsules should be swallowed whole to obtain maximum benefit.

Nitrofurantoin works best when the level of medicine in your urine is kept constant. It is best, therefore, to take the doses at evenly spaced intervals day and night. For example, if you are to take three doses a day, the doses should be spaced eight hours apart.

If you miss a dose of this medication, take the missed dose as soon as possible and return to your regular dosing schedule. However, if you do not remember to take the missed dose until it is almost time for your next dose, take it, then space the following dose about halfway through the regular interval between doses; then return to your regular dosing schedule. Try not to skip any doses.

It is important to continue to take this medication for the entire time prescribed by your doctor (usually 7 to 14 days), even if the symptoms disappear before the end of that period. If you stop taking the drug too soon, resistant bacteria are given a chance to continue growing, and the infection could recur.

SIDE EFFECTS

Minor. Abdominal cramps, diarrhea, dizziness, drowsiness, loss of appetite, nausea, or vomiting. These side effects should diminish or disappear as your body adjusts to the medication.

Nitrofurantoin can cause your urine to change color (to rust-yellow or brown). This is a harmless effect, but it may stain your underclothing. The color change will disappear after you stop taking the drug.

If this drug makes you dizzy, sit or lie down; get up slowly; and be careful on stairs.

Major. Tell your doctor about any side effects that are persistent or particularly bothersome. IT IS ESPECIALLY IMPORTANT TO TELL YOUR DOCTOR about chest pain, chills, cough, difficulty in breathing, fainting, fever, hair loss, irritation of the mouth, muscle aches, numbness or tingling, rash, rectal or vaginal itching, unusual bleeding or bruising, weakness, or yellowing of the eyes or skin. If your symptoms of infection seem to be getting worse rather than improving, you should contact your doctor.

INTERACTIONS

Nitrofurantoin interacts with certain other types of medications:

1. Concurrent use of robenecid or sulfinpyrazone can decrease the effectiveness and increase the side effects of nitrofurantoin.

2. Certain antacids (magnesium trisilicate) can decrease the absorption of nitrofurantoin from the gastrointestinal tract.

Before starting to take nitrofurantoin, BE SURE TO TELL YOUR DOCTOR about any medications you are currently taking, especially any of those listed above.

WARNINGS

- Tell your doctor about unusual or allergic reactions you have had to any medications, especially to nitrofurantoin, nitrofurazone, or furazolidone.
- Be sure to tell your doctor if you now have or if you have ever had anemia, diabetes mellitus, electrolyte abnormalities, glucose-6-phosphate dehydrogenase (G6PD) deficiency, kidney disease, lung disease, nerve damage, or vitamin B deficiencies.
- If this drug makes you dizzy or drowsy, do not take part in any activity that requires alertness, such as driving a car.
- Before surgery or other medical or dental treatment, tell your doctor or dentist you are taking this drug.
- People with diabetes should know that nitrofurantoin can cause false-positive results with some urine sugar tests (for example, Clinitest). Be sure to check with your doctor before adjusting your insulin dose.
- This medication has been prescribed for your current infection only. Another infection later on, or one that someone else has, may require a different medicine. You should not give your medicine to other people or use it for other infections unless your doctor specifically directs you to do so.
- Be sure to tell your doctor if you are pregnant. Nitrofurantoin should not be used close to term. It may cause anemia in the newborn infant. Nitrofurantoin should not be used in an infant less than one month of age. Also tell your doctor if you are breast-feeding an infant. Nitrofurantoin passes into the breast milk.

nitroglycerin (systemic)

BRAND NAMES (Manufacturers)
Nitrogard (Forest)
nitroglycerin (various manufacturers)
Nitroglyn (Kenwood)
Nitrolingual (Horizon)
Nitrong (Wharton)
NitroQuick (Ethex)
Nitrostat (Parke-Davis)
TYPE OF DRUG
Antianginal
INGREDIENT
nitroglycerin
DOSAGE FORMS
Sustained-release tablets (2.6 mg, 6.5 mg, and 9 mg)
Sustained-release capsules (2.5 mg, 6.5 mg, 9 mg, and 13 mg)
Sublingual tablets (0.3 mg, 0.4 mg, and 0.6 mg)
Buccal tablets, controlled release (1 mg, 2 mg, 2.5 mg, 3 mg, and 5 mg)
Oral spray (0.4 mg per dose)
STORAGE
Store the sustained-release tablets and capsules, the controlled-release buccal tablets, and the oral spray in tightly capped bottles in a cool, dry place.

Keep the sublingual tablets in their original glass container. A small, temporary supply of tablets can also be stored in a stainless-steel container that is now available. The pendant-type container, which can be worn around your neck, is a convenient storage place for an emergency supply. Never store them in the refrigerator or the bathroom medicine cabinet, because the drug may lose its potency.

USES

This medication is used to prevent and treat angina (chest pain). Nitroglycerin is a vasodilator, which relaxes the muscles of the blood vessels, causing an increase in the oxygen supply to the heart.

The sublingual tablets and oral spray act quickly and can be used to relieve chest pain after it has started. The sustained-release tablets and capsules do not act quickly; they are used to prevent chest pain.

TREATMENT

Be sure to ask your doctor or pharmacist for complete instructions on how and when to use the specific type of nitroglycerin prescribed for you.

The sublingual form of this medication should never be chewed or swallowed. Place the sublingual tablet under the tongue and allow it to dissolve; the medicine is absorbed through the lining of the mouth.

The oral spray form of this medication is absorbed directly through the lining of the mouth. To use the spray, remove the plastic cover on the container. Then, without shaking the container, spray the medication onto or under the tongue. Try not to inhale the spray. Close your mouth after each spray, and try to avoid swallowing right away. Nitroglycerin spray loses its effectiveness if it is swallowed.

Take one sublingual tablet or one or two sprays at the first sign of chest pain. Sit down while you are waiting for the medicine to take effect. Do not eat, drink, or smoke while nitroglycerin is in your mouth. Try not to swallow while nitroglycerin is dissolving, and do not rinse your mouth afterward. Sublingual nitroglycerin or nitroglycerin spray should start working in one to three minutes. If there is no relief, take another tablet or spray dose in five minutes. IF YOU TAKE THREE TABLETS OR THREE

SEPARATE SPRAY DOSES WITHOUT ANY SIGN OF IMPROVEMENT, CALL A DOCTOR IMMEDIATELY OR GO TO A HOSPITAL EMERGENCY ROOM. As a preventive measure, take a nitroglycerin sublingual tablet or a spray dose five or ten minutes before heavy exercise, exposure to high altitudes or extreme cold, or any other potentially stressful situation. Be sure to carry some nitroglycerin sublingual tablets or oral spray with you at ALL times.

The controlled-release buccal tablet form of this medication is absorbed directly through the lining of the mouth. NEVER chew or swallow the sublingual or buccal tablets. Place the buccal tablet between the upper lip and the gum on either side of the front teeth or between the cheek and the gum. The buccal tablet is held in place by a sticky gel seal that develops once the tablet is in contact with saliva. If you wear dentures, the buccal tablet can be placed anywhere between the cheek and the gum. Avoid drinking hot liquids or touching the buccal tablet with your tongue; this can cause the tablet to dissolve faster and could increase the risk of side effects. If the buccal tablet is swallowed by mistake, replace it with another tablet. Nitroglycerin buccal tablets lose their effectiveness when swallowed. Try not to take the buccal tablet at bedtime in order to avoid inadvertently swallowing and choking on the tablet while you are sleeping.

Take the sustained-release tablets or capsules with a full glass of water on an empty stomach one hour before or two hours after a meal. Swallow the sustained-release tablets and capsules whole. Chewing, crushing, or breaking them destroys their sustained-release activity and possibly increases the side effects. If you miss a dose of the sustained-release tablets or capsules, take the missed dose as soon as possible. However, if it is more than halfway through the interval between doses, do not take the missed dose at all; just return to your regular dosing schedule. Do not double the next dose of the sustained-release medication.

SIDE EFFECTS

Minor. Dizziness, flushing of the face, headache, light-headedness, nausea, vomiting, or weakness. These side effects should diminish or disappear as your body adjusts to the medication.

If you feel dizzy or light-headed, sit or lie down for a while; get up slowly from a sitting or reclining position; and be careful on stairs. To avoid dizziness or light-headedness when you stand, contract and relax the muscles of your legs for a few moments before rising. Do this by pushing one foot against the floor while raising the other foot slightly, alternating feet so that you are "pumping" your legs in a pedaling motion.

Acetaminophen may help to relieve headaches caused by this medication.

Major. Tell your doctor about any side effects that are persistent or particularly bothersome. IT IS ESPECIALLY IMPORTANT TO TELL YOUR DOCTOR about diarrhea, fainting, palpitations, rash, or sweating.

INTERACTIONS

Nitroglycerin can interact with other types of medications:

1. The combination of alcohol and nitroglycerin can lead to dizziness and fainting.

2. Nitroglycerin can increase the side effects of the tricyclic antidepressants.

3. Do not use sildenafil (Viagra) with nitroglycerin. The use of this combination may cause serious side effects, even death.

Before starting to take nitroglycerin, BE SURE TO TELL YOUR DOCTOR about any medications you are currently taking, especially tricyclic antidepressants (such as imipramine, desipramine, amitriptyline, and doxepin).

WARNINGS

• Tell your doctor about unusual or allergic reactions you have had to any medications, especially to nitroglycerin or isosorbide dinitrate.

• Before starting to take this medication, be sure to tell your doctor if you now have or ever had anemia, glaucoma, a head injury, low blood pressure, or thyroid disease or if you have recently had a heart attack.
• If this drug makes you dizzy or light-headed, do not take part in any activity that requires alertness, such as driving a car or operating potentially dangerous machinery.
• Before surgery or other medical or dental treatment, tell your doctor or dentist you are taking this drug.
• Tolerance may develop to this medication within one to three months. If it seems to lose its effectiveness, contact your doctor.
• You should not discontinue use of nitroglycerin (if you have been taking it on a regular basis) unless you first consult your doctor. Stopping it abruptly may lead to further chest pain. Your doctor may therefore want to decrease your dosage gradually.
• If you have frequent diarrhea, you may not be absorbing the sustained-release form of this medication. Discuss this with your doctor.
• While taking this medication, do not take any over-the-counter (nonprescription) asthma, allergy, sinus, cough, cold, or diet preparations unless you first check with your doctor or pharmacist. Some of these decrease the effectiveness of nitroglycerin.
• The cotton plug should be removed when the bottle is first opened; it should not be replaced. The cotton plug absorbs some of the medication, decreasing its potency.
• Nitroglycerin is highly flammable. Do not use it in places where it might be ignited.
• Be sure to tell your doctor if you are pregnant. Although the systemic form of nitroglycerin appears to be safe, extensive studies in pregnant women have not been conducted. Also tell your doctor if you are breast-feeding an infant. It is not known whether nitroglycerin passes into breast milk.

---

norfloxacin

BRAND NAME (Manufacturer)
Noroxin (Roberts)
TYPE OF DRUG
Quinolone antibiotic
INGREDIENT
norfloxacin
DOSAGE FORM
Tablets (400 mg)
STORAGE
Store at room temperature in a tightly closed container.

USES

Norfloxacin is an antibiotic that is used to treat bacterial infections of the urinary tract. It works by interfering with the reproduction of the bacteria. Norfloxacin kills susceptible bacteria but is not effective against viruses, parasites, or fungi.

TREATMENT

To obtain the maximum benefit from norfloxacin, it is best to take this drug on an empty stomach (one hour before or two hours after a meal) with a full glass of water. Antacids can decrease the absorption of this medication. Therefore, antacids should not be taken within two hours (before or after) of a dose of norfloxacin, unless otherwise directed by your doctor.

Norfloxacin works best when the level of medicine in your urine is kept constant. It is best to take the doses at evenly spaced intervals day and night. For example, if you are supposed to take two doses a day, the doses should be spaced 12 hours apart.

Try not to miss any doses of this medication. If you do miss a dose, take it as soon as you remember. However, if you do not remember to take the missed dose until it is almost time for your next dose, take it; space the following dose about halfway through the regular interval between doses; then continue with your regular dosing schedule.

Take this medication for the entire time prescribed by your doctor (usually 5 to 14 days), even if the symptoms disappear before the end of that period. If you stop taking the drug too soon, your infection could recur.

SIDE EFFECTS

Minor. Abdominal pain, constipation, diarrhea, dizziness, dry mouth, fatigue, gas, headache, heartburn, nausea, sleeping problems, or vomiting. These side effects should disappear as your body adjusts to this medication.

If you are constipated, increase the amount of fiber in your diet (from fresh fruits and vegetables, salads, bran, and whole-grain breads), exercise, and drink more water (unless your doctor directs you to do otherwise).

To reduce mouth dryness, chew sugarless gum or suck on ice chips or hard candy.

If you feel dizzy or light-headed, sit or lie down for a while; get up slowly from a sitting or reclining position; and be careful on stairs.

Major. Tell your doctor about any side effects that are persistent or particularly bothersome. IT IS ESPECIALLY IMPORTANT TO TELL YOUR DOCTOR about depression, difficult or painful urination, rash, visual disturbances, or a yellowish discoloration of the skin or eyes. If the symptoms of your infection seem to be getting worse rather than improving, contact your doctor.

INTERACTIONS

Norfloxacin can interact with several other types of drugs:

1. Probenecid can block the excretion of norfloxacin into the urinary tract, decreasing its effectiveness in treating infections located there.

2. Antacids, didanosine, sucralfate, iron, calcium, magnesium, and zinc can decrease the absorption of norfloxacin from the gastrointestinal tract.

3. Nitrofurantoin may antagonize (act against) the effectiveness of norfloxacin.

4. This drug may increase the actions and side effects of the blood thinner warfarin.

5. Norfloxacin may increase the side effects of cyclosporine.

BE SURE TO TELL YOUR DOCTOR about any medications you are currently taking, especially any of the medications mentioned above.

WARNINGS

• Tell your doctor about unusual or allergic reactions you have had to any medications, especially to norfloxacin, to other fluoroquinolones, or to the related antibiotics cinoxacin and nalidixic acid.

• Before starting norfloxacin, tell your doctor if you now have or ever had liver disease or seizures.

• If this drug makes you dizzy, do not take part in any activity that requires alertness, such as driving a car or operating potentially dangerous machinery. Be especially careful when going up and down stairs.

• To prevent the formation of crystals in the kidneys, try to drink plenty of fluids (at least eight glasses of water or fruit juice each day) while you are taking this medication (unless your doctor directs you to do otherwise).

• This medication has been prescribed for your current infection only. A subsequent infection, or one that someone else has, may require a different kind of antibiotic. Do not give your medicine to other people or use it to treat other infections unless your doctor directs you to do so.

• Be sure to tell your doctor if you are pregnant. Studies in pregnant women have not been conducted. However, problems with bone formation have occurred in the immature offspring of animals that received large doses of norfloxacin during pregnancy. Also tell your doctor if you are breast-feeding an infant. It is not yet known if norfloxacin passes into breast milk.

nortriptyline

BRAND NAMES (Manufacturers)
Aventyl (Lilly)
nortriptyline (various manufacturers)
Pamelor (Novartis)
TYPE OF DRUG
Tricyclic antidepressant
INGREDIENT
nortriptyline
DOSAGE FORMS
Capsules (10 mg, 25 mg, 50 mg, and 75 mg)
Oral solution (10 mg per 5-mL spoonful with 4% alcohol)
STORAGE
Store at room temperature in a tightly closed, light-resistant container. Do not freeze the oral solution.

USES

Nortriptyline is used to relieve the symptoms of mental depression. It is thought to relieve depression by increasing the concentration of certain chemicals necessary for nerve transmission in the brain.

TREATMENT

Take this medication exactly as your doctor prescribes. It can be taken with water or with food to lessen the chance of stomach irritation, unless your doctor tells you to do otherwise.

If you miss a dose of this medication, take the missed dose as soon as possible, then return to your regular dosing schedule. However, if the dose you missed was a once-a-day bedtime dose, do not take that dose in the morning; check with your doctor instead. If the dose is taken in the morning, it may cause unwanted side effects. Never double the dose.

The effects of therapy with this medication may not become apparent for two or three weeks.

SIDE EFFECTS

Minor. Anxiety, blurred vision, confusion, constipation, cramps, diarrhea, dizziness, drowsiness, dry mouth, fatigue, heartburn, insomnia, loss of appetite, nausea, peculiar tastes in the mouth, restlessness, sweating, vomiting, weakness, or weight gain or loss. As your body adjusts to the medication, these side effects should disappear.

This medication may increase your sensitivity to sunlight. Avoid prolonged exposure to sunlight or sunlamps, wear protective clothing, and use sunscreen.

Dry mouth caused by this medication can be relieved by chewing sugarless gum or by sucking on ice chips or a piece of hard candy.

To relieve constipation, increase the amount of fiber in your diet (fresh fruits and vegetables, salads, bran, and whole-grain breads), exercise, and drink more water (unless your doctor directs you to do otherwise).

To avoid dizziness or light-headedness when you stand, contract and relax the muscles of your legs for a few moments before rising. Do this by pushing one foot against the floor while raising the other foot slightly, alternating feet so that you are "pumping" your legs in a pedaling motion.

Major. Tell your doctor about any side effects that are persistent or particularly bothersome. IT IS ESPECIALLY IMPORTANT TO TELL YOUR DOCTOR about agitation, chest pain, convulsions, difficulty in urinating, enlarged or painful breasts (in both sexes), fainting, fever, fluid retention, hair loss, hallucinations, headaches, impotence, mood changes, mouth sores, nervousness, nightmares, numbness in the fingers or toes, palpitations, ringing in the ears, seizures, skin rash, sleep disorders, sore throat, swelling, tremors, uncoordinated movements or balance problems, unusual bleeding or bruising, or yellowing of the eyes or skin.

INTERACTIONS

Nortriptyline interacts with a number of other types of medications:

1. Extreme drowsiness can occur when this drug is taken with central nervous system depressants (such as alcohol, antihistamines, barbiturates, benzodiazepine tranquilizers, muscle relaxants, narcotics, pain medications, phenothiazine tranquilizers, and sleeping medications) or other tricyclic antidepressants.

2. Nortriptyline may decrease the effectiveness of antiseizure medications and may block the blood-pressure-lowering effects of clonidine and guanethidine.

3. Birth control pills and estrogen-containing drugs can increase the side effects and reduce the effectiveness of the tricyclic antidepressants (including nortriptyline).

4. Tricyclic antidepressants may increase the side effects of thyroid medication and over-the-counter (nonprescription) cough, cold, asthma, allergy, sinus, and diet medications.

5. The concurrent use of tricyclic antidepressants and monoamine oxidase (MAO) inhibitors should be avoided because the combination may result in fever, convulsions, or high blood pressure. At least 14 days should separate the use of this drug and the use of an MAO inhibitor.

6. Cimetidine can decrease the elimination of nortriptyline from the body, increasing the possibility of side effects.

7. Fluoxetine taken concurrently with nortriptyline may increase the side effects of nortriptyline.

8. The use of probucol or pimozide and nortriptyline may increase the risk of side effects on the heart.

Before starting to take nortriptyline, BE SURE TO TELL YOUR DOCTOR about any medications you are currently taking, especially any of those listed above.

WARNINGS

• Tell your doctor if you have had unusual or allergic reactions to any medications, especially to nortriptyline or to any of the other tricyclic antidepressants (including amitriptyline, imipramine, doxepin, trimipramine, amoxapine, protriptyline, desipramine, or maprotiline).

• Tell your doctor if you have a history of alcoholism or if you have ever had asthma, high blood pressure, liver or kidney disease, heart disease, a heart attack, circulatory disease, stomach problems, intestinal problems, difficulty in urinating, enlarged prostate gland, epilepsy, glaucoma, thyroid disease, mental illness, or electroshock therapy.

• If this drug makes you dizzy or drowsy, do not take part in any activity that requires alertness, such as driving a car or operating potentially dangerous machinery.

• Before having surgery or other medical or dental treatment, be sure to tell your doctor or dentist that you are being treated with this medication.

• Do not stop taking this drug suddenly. Abruptly stopping it can cause nausea, headache, stomach upset, fatigue, or a worsening of your condition. Your doctor may want to reduce the dosage gradually.

• The effects of nortriptyline may last as long as seven days after you have stopped taking it, so continue to observe all precautions during that period.

• Be sure to tell your doctor if you are pregnant. Problems in humans have not been reported; however, studies in animals have shown that this type of medication can cause side effects in the fetus when given to the mother in large doses during pregnancy. Also tell your doctor if you are breast-feeding an infant. Small amounts of this drug can pass into breast milk and may cause unwanted effects, such as irritability or sleeping problems, in nursing infants.

nystatin

BRAND NAMES (Manufacturers)
Mycostatin (Squibb)
Nilstat (Lederle)
nystatin (various manufacturers)
Nystex (Savage)
TYPE OF DRUG
Antifungal
INGREDIENT
nystatin
DOSAGE FORMS
Oral tablets (500,000 units)
Oral suspension (100,000 units per mL with not more than 1% alcohol)
Oral lozenges (200,000 units)
Vaginal tablets (100,000 units)
Topical cream, ointment, and powder (100,000 units per gram)
STORAGE
Store the oral tablets, suspension, topical cream, ointment, and powder forms of this medication at room temperature in tightly closed, light-resistant containers. Keep the oral lozenges and vaginal tablets in the refrigerator. Do not freeze any form of this medication.

USES

Nystatin is used to treat fungal infections of the mouth, throat, gastrointestinal tract, skin, and vagina. By chemically binding to the cell membranes of fungal organisms, this medication causes the cell contents to leak out, which kills the infecting fungi.

TREATMENT

You can take the oral tablet form of this medication either on an empty stomach or with food or milk (as directed by your doctor).

Shake the oral suspension well just before using each dose to distribute the ingredients evenly and equalize the doses. The contents tend to settle at the bottom of the bottle. Measure each dose of the oral suspension carefully with a specially designed 5-mL measuring spoon or dropper. An ordinary kitchen teaspoon is not accurate enough. Place half of the dose in each side of your mouth. Try to hold the suspension in the mouth or swish it through the mouth for as long as possible before swallowing it.

Allow the oral lozenge to dissolve slowly in the mouth.

The vaginal tablets are packaged with instructions and an applicator for inserting the tablets into the vagina. Read the instructions carefully before using this product.

Occasionally, the vaginal tablets are prescribed to be taken orally (to treat mouth or throat infections). The tablets are sucked on to increase contact time with the mouth and throat.

Carefully wash the region where you are to apply the topical cream, ointment, or powder and pat dry. Then apply a sufficient amount of medication to the affected area. Do NOT apply an occlusive dressing (like kitchen plastic wrap) over the medication (unless your doctor directs you to do so).

If you are using the powder form to treat a foot infection, sprinkle it liberally into your shoes and socks as well as on your feet.

Try not to miss any doses of this medication. If you do miss a dose, take (or apply) the missed dose as soon as possible after you remember. However, if it is almost time for the next dose, do not take (or apply) the missed dose at all; just return to your regular dosing schedule. Do not double the next dose of this medication.

Take this drug for the entire time prescribed by your doctor (usually a period of 7 to 14 days), even if the symptoms disappear before the end of that time. If you stop taking the drug too soon, resistant fungi may be given a chance to continue growing, and your infection could recur.

SIDE EFFECTS

Minor. Oral forms: diarrhea, nausea, or vomiting. Topical and vaginal forms: itching. These side effects should disappear as your body adjusts to the drug.

Major. Tell your doctor about any side effects that are persistent or particularly bothersome. IT IS ESPECIALLY IMPORTANT TO TELL YOUR DOCTOR about a rash. If symptoms of your infection seem to be getting worse rather than improving, tell your doctor.

INTERACTIONS

Nystatin should not interact with other medications if it is used according to directions.

WARNINGS

• Tell your doctor about unusual or allergic reactions you have had to any medications, especially to nystatin.

• If you are using this drug to treat a vaginal infection, avoid sexual intercourse or ask your partner to wear a condom until treatment has been completed. These measures help prevent reinfection. Use the vaginal tablets continuously, even during a menstrual period. Unless instructed otherwise by your doctor, do not douche during treatment or until three weeks after you stop using the vaginal tablets. Wear cotton underpants, rather than nylon or other nonporous materials, when you are being treated for a fungal infection of the vagina. There may be some vaginal drainage while using the vaginal tablets, so you may wish to use a sanitary napkin or panty liner.

• This medication has been prescribed for your current infection only. Another infection later on, or one that someone else has, may require a different medicine. You should not give your medicine to other people or use it for other infections unless your doctor specifically directs you to do so.

• If the symptoms of infection do not begin to improve within two or three days after starting nystatin, BE SURE TO CONTACT YOUR DOCTOR. This medication may not be effective against the organism that is causing your infection.

• Be sure to tell your doctor if you are pregnant. Although nystatin appears to be safe during pregnancy, extensive and conclusive studies in humans have not been conducted. Also tell your doctor if you are breast-feeding an infant. It is not known whether this medication passes into breast milk.

---

ofloxacin

BRAND NAME (Manufacturer)
Floxin (McNeil)
TYPE OF DRUG
Quinolone antibiotic
INGREDIENT
ofloxacin
DOSAGE FORM
Tablets (200 mg, 300 mg, and 400 mg)
STORAGE
Store in a tightly closed container at room temperature, away from heat and direct sunlight.

USES

Ofloxacin is an antibiotic that is used to treat skin and bone infections, sexually transmitted diseases, urinary tract and prostate infections, and respiratory and gastrointestinal infections. Ofloxacin acts by severely injuring the cell walls of the infecting bacteria, thereby preventing them from growing and multiplying. This medication kills susceptible bacteria, but it is not effective against viruses, parasites, or fungi.

TREATMENT

Take exactly as prescribed by your doctor, even if your symptoms improve. If you stop taking this drug too soon, resistant bacteria are given the chance to grow and the infection may recur. Ofloxacin is usually taken twice a day for 7 to 14 days, although it may be given for longer periods of time. This medication can be taken with meals or a full glass of water if stomach upset occurs.

If you miss a dose of ofloxacin, take the missed dose as soon as possible. If it is almost time for your next dose, take the missed dose and space the following dose halfway through the regular interval between doses, then return to your regular dosing schedule. Try not to skip any doses.

SIDE EFFECTS

Minor. Abdominal pain, diarrhea, dizziness, insomnia, light-headedness, nausea, or vomiting. These side effects should disappear as your body adjusts to the drug.

Major. Tell your doctor about any side effects that are persistent or particularly bothersome. IT IS ESPECIALLY IMPORTANT TO TELL YOUR DOCTOR about agitation; confusion; headache; irregular heartbeat; joint pain; restlessness; severe diarrhea (which may be watery or contain blood or pus); skin rash, itching, or redness; or swelling of the lower leg. If your symptoms of infection seem to be getting worse rather than improving, contact your doctor.

INTERACTIONS

Ofloxacin interacts with several other types of medications:

1. Probenecid can increase the concentrations of this drug in the blood.

2. Ofloxacin may increase the effects of theophylline or oral anticoagulants. Closer monitoring of the effects of these medications is recommended.

3. Avoid using quinidine, procainamide, amiodarone, and sotalol because of the increased risk of side effects when used with ofloxacin.

4. Antacids, iron, magnesium, sucralfate, zinc, and didanosine may decrease the absorption of ofloxacin. Thus, ofloxacin should be taken at least two hours before or two hours after a dose of any of those medications.

BE SURE TO TELL YOUR DOCTOR about any medications you are currently taking, especially any of the medications listed above.

WARNINGS

- Tell your doctor about any unusual or allergic reactions you have had to any medications, especially to ofloxacin, other quinolones, or quinolone-related antibiotics.
- Tell your doctor if you now have or if you have ever had liver disease, kidney disease, or epilepsy.
- This medication may increase your sensitivity to sunlight. Avoid prolonged exposure to sunlight or sunlamps, wear protective clothing, and use sunscreen.
- To avoid dizziness or light-headedness when you stand, contract and relax the muscles of your legs for a few moments before rising. Do this by pushing one foot against the floor while raising the other foot slightly, alternating feet so that you are "pumping" your legs in a pedaling motion.
- If you feel dizzy or light-headed, sit or lie down for a while; get up slowly from a sitting or reclining position; and be careful on stairs.

• If this drug makes you dizzy or drowsy, do not take part in any activities that require alertness, such as driving a car or operating potentially dangerous machinery.
• Be sure to tell your doctor if you are pregnant. Studies in pregnant women have not been conducted. However, lameness has occurred in the mature offspring of animals that received large doses of ofloxacin during pregnancy. Also tell your doctor if you are breast-feeding an infant. Ofloxacin passes into breast milk.

olanzapine

BRAND NAME (Manufacturer)
Zyprexa (Lilly)
TYPE OF DRUG
Antipsychotic
INGREDIENT
olanzapine
DOSAGE FORM
Tablets (2.5 mg, 5 mg, 7.5 mg, 10 mg, 15 mg, and 20 mg)
Tablets, orally disintegrating (5 mg, 10 mg, 15 mg, and 20 mg)
STORAGE
Store in a tightly closed container at room temperature, away from heat and direct sunlight. Keep the orally disintegrating tablets in their original packaging.

USES

Olanzapine is prescribed to treat symptoms of mental illness, such as the emotional symptoms of psychosis and schizophrenia. It is also given for the short-term treatment of acute mania in patients who have manic-depressive (bipolar) disorder. This medication is thought to relieve the symptoms of mental illness by blocking certain chemicals involved with nerve transmission in the brain.

TREATMENT

Take this medication exactly as prescribed by your doctor. It is usually taken once a day, and it can be taken either with or without food. To decrease stomach irritation, take this medication with food unless your doctor tells you otherwise.

The full effects of this medication for the control of emotional or mental symptoms may not become apparent for two weeks after you begin treatment.

It is not necessary to take the orally disintegrating tablet with water. When placed on your tongue, the tablet will dissolve completely and can be swallowed with or without water. Before you open the blister packet, make sure your hands are dry; do not open the packet until it is time for you to take the tablet.

If you miss a dose of this medicine, take the missed dose as soon as possible, then return to your regular dosing schedule. However, if it is almost time for your next dose, skip the one you missed and then return to your regular dosing schedule. Never take a double dose unless directed to do so by your doctor.

SIDE EFFECTS

Minor. Blurred vision, constipation, diarrhea, dizziness or light-headedness, drooling, drowsiness, dry mouth, headache, jerking or stiffness, lack of strength, nausea, problems sleeping, rash, restlessness, uncontrolled body movements, vomiting, weakness, or weight gain. These side effects may diminish or disappear as your body adjusts to the medication.

Dry mouth can be relieved by chewing sugarless gum or sucking on hard candy.

To relieve constipation, increase the amount of fiber in your diet (fresh fruits and vegetables, salads, bran, and whole-grain breads), exercise, and drink more water (unless your doctor directs you to do otherwise).

To avoid dizziness or light-headedness when you stand, contract and relax the muscles in your legs for a few moments before rising. Do this by pushing one foot against the floor while raising the other foot slightly, alternating feet so that you are "pumping" your legs in a pedaling motion.

If you feel dizzy or light-headed, sit or lie down for a while; get up slowly from a sitting or reclining position; and be careful on stairs.

Major. Tell your doctor about any side effects that are persistent or particularly bothersome. IT IS ESPECIALLY IMPORTANT TO TELL YOUR DOCTOR about chest pain; difficulty in breathing or swallowing; extreme dizziness; fainting or feeling faint; fast or pounding heartbeat; frequent urination; heart palpitations; painful erection; seizures; skin rash or hives; or uncontrolled or involuntary movements of the face, mouth, tongue, or jaw.

INTERACTIONS

Olanzapine interacts with several other types of drugs:

1. Extreme drowsiness can occur when this medication is taken with other central nervous system depressants (such as alcohol, antihistamines, antidepressants, barbiturates, benzodiazepine tranquilizers, muscle relaxants, narcotics, pain medications, and sleeping medications).

2. Fluvoxamine may increase the adverse effects caused by olanzapine.

3. Olanzapine can increase the blood-pressure-lowering effects of antihypertensive medications and possibly increase their side effects.

4. Carbamazepine, omeprazole, levodopa, and rifampin can reduce the efficacy of this medication. Discuss this with your doctor or pharmacist.

Before taking olanzapine, BE SURE TO TELL YOUR DOCTOR about any medication you are taking, especially any of those listed above.

WARNINGS

• Tell your doctor about any unusual or allergic reactions you have had to any medications, especially to olanzapine, clozapine, or other antipsychotics.

• Tell your doctor if you now have or ever had a history of heart attack, heart disease, irregular heartbeats, heart failure, low potassium or magnesium in your blood, Alzheimer's disease, epilepsy, alcoholism, circulatory disease, or liver or kidney disease.

• To prevent oversedation, avoid drinking alcoholic beverages while taking this medication.

• If this medication makes you drowsy or dizzy, do not take part in any activity that requires alertness, such as driving a car or operating dangerous equipment.

• This medication may decrease sweating and heat release from the body. Therefore, avoid getting overheated by strenuous exercise in hot weather and avoid taking hot baths, showers, or saunas.

• While taking this medication, do not take any over-the-counter (nonprescription) medication for weight control or for cough, cold, asthma, allergy, or sinus problems unless you first check with your doctor.

• Before having surgery or any other medical or dental treatment, be sure to tell your doctor or dentist that you are taking olanzapine.

• Olanzapine may increase your sensitivity to sunlight, so limit your exposure to sunlight and wear protective clothing and an effective sunscreen when you are outdoors during daylight hours. Also, avoid exposure to sunlamps.

• Be sure to tell your doctor if you are pregnant. Although olanzapine has not been adequately studied in humans, it has caused birth defects in animals. Discuss the risks and benefits of using this medication during pregnancy with your doctor. Olanzapine can also pass into human breast milk. Be sure to tell your doctor if you are nursing an infant and discuss the risks and benefits of this medication.

omeprazole

BRAND NAME (Manufacturer)
Prilosec (AstraZeneca)
TYPE OF DRUG
Gastric-acid-secretion inhibitor
INGREDIENT
omeprazole
DOSAGE FORM
Delayed-release capsules (20 mg)
STORAGE
Store at room temperature in a tightly closed container.

USES

Omeprazole is prescribed to treat peptic ulcer, gastroesophageal reflux disease (GERD), and hypersecretory syndromes. This medication suppresses stomach-acid secretion.

TREATMENT

Do not open, chew, or crush the capsules. Take them with a glass of water on an empty stomach. It is best to take the dose one hour before meals or two hours after meals.

Try to take the medication at the same time(s) each day. If you miss a dose of the medication, take the missed dose as soon as possible. However, if it is almost time for the next dose, skip the missed dose and return to your regular schedule. Do not double the next dose of the medication (unless your doctor directs you to do so).

It is important that you take this medication for the exact amount of time prescribed by your doctor.

SIDE EFFECTS

Minor. Abdominal pain, burning sensation in mouth, constipation, diarrhea, dizziness, dry mouth, fatigue, headache, or palpitations. These side effects should diminish or disappear as your body adjusts to the medication.

To relieve constipation while you are being treated with this medication, increase the amount of fiber in your diet (eat more fresh fruits and vegetables, salads, bran, and whole-grain breads), exercise, and drink more water (unless your doctor directs you to do otherwise).

To avoid dizziness when you stand, contract and relax the muscles of your legs for a few moments before rising. Do this by pushing one foot against the floor while raising the other foot slightly, alternating feet so that you are "pumping" your legs in a pedaling motion.

To help relieve dry mouth, chew sugarless gum or suck on ice chips or a piece of hard candy.

Major. Tell your doctor about any side effects that are persistent or particularly bothersome. IT IS ESPECIALLY IMPORTANT TO TELL YOUR DOCTOR about itching, rash, tingling of fingers or toes, unusual tiredness, or yellowing of the eyes or skin.

INTERACTIONS

Omeprazole may interact with several medications.

1. Omeprazole may increase the effects and the side effects of diazepam, warfarin, and phenytoin.

2. Omeprazole may decrease the absorption of ketoconazole, itraconazole, iron, and certain forms of ampicillin.

Be sure to tell your doctor about any medications you are currently taking, especially any of those listed above.

WARNINGS

- Tell your doctor about unusual or allergic reactions you have had to any drugs, especially to omeprazole.
- Tell your doctor if you now have or if you have ever had thyroid disease, liver disease, Addison's disease, or Cushing's disease.
- This medication may cause dizziness or light-headedness, so use caution while driving a car or operating potentially dangerous equipment.
- If you feel dizzy or light-headed, sit down for a while; get up slowly from a sitting or reclining position; and be careful on stairs.
- Long-term and high-dose treatment with omeprazole has been associated with higher incidences of gastric tumors. Consult your doctor if you need to take high doses of omeprazole for a long time.
- Be sure to tell your doctor if you are pregnant. Adequate studies on the use of omeprazole during human pregnancy have not been conducted. Also be sure to tell your doctor if you are breast-feeding an infant.

---

ondansetron

BRAND NAMES (Manufacturers)
Zofran (GlaxoSmithKline)
Zofran ODT (GlaxoSmithKline)
TYPE OF DRUG
Antiemetic
INGREDIENT
ondansetron
DOSAGE FORMS
Solution (4 mg per 5 mL)
Tablets (4 mg and 8 mg)
Tablets, orally disintegrating (4 mg and 8 mg)
STORAGE
Store in a tightly closed container at room temperature, away from heat and direct sunlight. Keep the orally disintegrating tablets in their original packaging.

USES

Ondansetron is used to prevent the nausea, vomiting, and retching associated with cancer chemotherapy or radiation therapy. It is also used to prevent the nausea and vomiting that may occur following surgery. Though it is unclear precisely how ondansetron acts, it appears to work by blocking the release of certain chemicals in the brain that stimulate the impulse to vomit.

TREATMENT

Take this medication exactly as prescribed by your doctor. Ondansetron can be taken with meals or with a full glass of water if you are bothered by stomach upset (unless your doctor directs you otherwise).

Measure the solution with a specially designed 5-mL measuring spoon. An ordinary kitchen teaspoon is not accurate enough for this purpose.

With dry hands, carefully remove an orally disintegrating tablet from its packaging. Place the tablet on the tip of the tongue; it will dissolve in seconds and can be swallowed with saliva.

The effectiveness of this treatment is thought to be related to keeping a steady level of ondansetron in the bloodstream. It is very important not to skip any doses of this medication.

SIDE EFFECTS

Minor. Constipation, diarrhea, dizziness, drowsiness, dry mouth, fever or chills, headache, light-headedness, or skin rash. These side effects should diminish or disappear as your body adjusts to the medication.

To relieve constipation, increase the amount of fiber in your diet (fresh fruits and vegetables, salads, bran, and whole-grain breads), exercise, and drink more water (unless your doctor directs you to do otherwise).

Major. Tell your doctor about any side effects that are persistent or particularly bothersome. IT IS ESPECIALLY IMPORTANT FOR YOU TO TELL YOUR DOCTOR about shortness of breath, tightness of the chest, troubled breathing, or wheezing.

INTERACTIONS

Agents that increase serotonin, a chemical in the body, may increase the risk of serious side effects when taken with ondansetron. These agents include antimigraine agents and antidepressants such as fluoxetine, fluvoxamine, nefazodone, venlafaxine, sertraline, paroxetine, citalopram, and escitalopram. Be sure to tell your doctor about these or any other medications you may be taking.

WARNINGS

- Tell your doctor about unusual, unexpected, or allergic reactions you have had to any medications, especially ondansetron, granisetron, dolasetron, or other medications used for nausea or vomiting.
- Tell your doctor if you have or if you have ever had liver or kidney disease or phenylketonuria.
- If this drug makes you drowsy or dizzy, avoid taking part in any activity that requires alertness, such as driving an automobile or operating potentially dangerous equipment, tools, or machinery.
- If you feel dizzy or light-headed, sit or lie down for a while; get up slowly from a sitting or reclining position; and be careful on stairs.
- Be sure to tell your doctor if you are pregnant. Extensive studies in pregnant women have not been conducted. Be sure to tell your doctor if you are breast-feeding an infant. It is not known if ondansetron passes into breast milk.

---

oral contraceptives

BRAND NAMES (Manufacturers)

Alesse (Wyeth-Ayerst)
Brevicon (Watson)
Demulen (Pharmacia)
Desogen (Organon)
Genora (Rugby)
Jenest (Organon)
Levlen (Berlex)
Levora (Watson)
Loestrin (Parke-Davis)
Lo/Ovral (Wyeth-Ayerst)
Mircette (Organon)
Modicon (Ortho)
Nordette (Monarch)
Norinyl (Watson)

Norlestrin (Parke-Davis)
Ortho-Cept (Ortho)
Ortho-Cyclen (Ortho)
Ortho-Novum (Ortho)
Ortho-Tricyclen (Ortho)
Ovcon (Bristol-Myers)
Ovral (Wyeth-Ayerst)
Tri-Levlen (Berlex)
Tri-Norinyl (Watson)
Triphasil (Wyeth-Ayerst)

TYPE OF DRUG
Oral contraceptive

INGREDIENTS
estrogens and progestins

DOSAGE FORM
Tablets (in packages of 21 or 28 tablets; when 28 tablets are present, seven of the tablets are either placebos or iron pills)

STORAGE
Store at room temperature in their original container, which is designed to help you keep track of your dosing schedule.

USES

Oral contraceptives change the hormone balance of the body to prevent pregnancy.

TREATMENT

To avoid stomach irritation, you can take oral contraceptives with food or with a full glass of water or milk.

To become accustomed to taking this medication, try to take it at the same time every day.

Use a supplemental method of birth control for the first week after you start taking oral contraceptives. The medication takes time to become fully effective. Discuss this with your doctor.

Even if you do not start to menstruate on schedule at the end of the pill cycle, begin the next cycle of pills at the prescribed time. Many women taking oral contraceptives have irregular menstruation.

If you miss a dose of this medication and you are on a 21-day schedule, take the missed dose as soon as you remember. If you don't remember until the next day, take the dose of that day plus the one you missed; then return to your regular dosing schedule. If you miss two days' doses, you should take two tablets a day for the next two days; then return to your regular dosing schedule. You should also use another form of birth control for at least seven days following the missed pills. If you miss your dose three days in a row, you should stop taking this drug and use a different method of birth control until you check with your doctor. Your doctor may want you to start a new package seven days after the last tablet was missed and use an additional method of birth control until the start of your next period.

If you are on the 28-day schedule and you miss taking any one of the first 21 tablets, you should follow the instructions for the 21-day schedule. If you missed taking any of the last seven tablets, there is no danger of pregnancy, but you should take the first pill of the next month's cycle on the regularly scheduled day.

SIDE EFFECTS

Minor. Abdominal cramps, acne, backache, bloating, change in appetite, changes in sexual desire, diarrhea, dizziness, fatigue, headache, nasal congestion, nausea, nervousness, vaginal irritation, or vomiting. These side effects should disappear as your body adjusts to the medication.

This medication can increase your sensitivity to sunlight. Avoid prolonged exposure to sunlight and sunlamps, wear protective clothing, and use a sunscreen.

If you feel dizzy or light-headed, sit or lie down for a while; get up slowly from a sitting or reclining position; and be careful on stairs.

To avoid dizziness or light-headedness when you stand, contract and relax the muscles in your legs for a few moments before rising. Do this by pressing one foot into the floor while raising the other foot slightly, alternating feet so that you are "pumping" your legs in a pedaling motion.

Major. Tell your doctor about any side effects that are persistent or particularly bothersome. IT IS ESPECIALLY IMPORTANT TO TELL YOUR DOCTOR about abdominal pain; breakthrough vaginal bleeding (spotting); changes in menstrual flow; chest pain; depression; difficult or painful urination; enlarged or tender breasts; hearing changes; increase or decrease in hair growth; migraine headaches; numbness or tingling; pain in your calves; rash; skin color changes; swelling of the feet, ankles, or lower legs; unusual bleeding or bruising; vaginal itching; weight changes; or yellowing of the eyes or the skin.

INTERACTIONS

These drugs interact with several other medications:

1. Pain relievers, antimigraine preparations, rifampin, barbiturates, phenytoin, primidone, carbamazepine, isoniazid, neomycin, griseofulvin, penicillins, tetracycline, chloramphenicol, sulfonamide antibiotics, nitrofurantoin, theophylline, ritonavir, and ampicillin can reduce the effectiveness of oral contraceptives and increase the risk of pregnancy. Your doctor may advise you to use an extra form of contraception, such as a condom, if you take one of these drugs.

2. Oral contraceptives can reduce the effectiveness of oral anticoagulant medications (blood thinners, such as warfarin), anticonvulsants, tricyclic antidepressants, antihypertensive medications, oral antidiabetic medications, lorazepam, oxazepam, and vitamins.

3. Oral contraceptives can increase the blood levels of caffeine, diazepam, chlordiazepoxide, metoprolol, propranolol, adrenocorticosteroid drugs, imipramine, clomipramine, cyclosporine, and phenytoin, which can lead to an increase in side effects.

BE SURE TO TELL YOUR DOCTOR about any medications you are currently taking, especially any of the medications listed above.

WARNINGS

• Tell your doctor about unusual or allergic reactions you have had to any medications, especially to estrogens, progestins, or progesterones.

• Before you start to take this medication, be sure to tell your doctor if you now have or if you have ever had asthma, bleeding problems, breast cancer, clotting disorders, diabetes mellitus, endometriosis, epilepsy, gallbladder disease, heart disease, high blood pressure, kidney disease, liver disease, mental depression, migraine headaches, porphyria, a stroke, thyroid disease, uterine tumors, unexplained vaginal bleeding, or vitamin deficiencies.

• Some women who have used an oral contraceptive have had difficulty becoming pregnant after discontinuing use. Most of these women had had scanty or irregular periods before starting oral contraceptives. Possible subsequent difficulty in becoming pregnant is a matter you should discuss with your doctor before deciding to use an oral contraceptive.

• Every prescription comes with a booklet that explains birth control pills. Read this booklet carefully. It contains exact directions on how to use this medicine correctly and describes the risks involved.

• Do not smoke while taking oral contraceptives. Smoking may reduce the effectiveness of the contraceptives and increase the risk of side effects.

• Women who are over age 30 and women who smoke while taking this medication have an increased risk of developing serious heart or blood-vessel side effects.
• If this drug makes you dizzy, avoid taking part in any activity that requires alertness, such as driving an automobile or operating potentially dangerous tools, equipment, or machinery. Be careful on stairs.
• Before surgery or other medical or dental treatment, tell your doctor or dentist you are taking this drug.
• Be sure to tell your doctor if you are pregnant. Oral contraceptives have been associated with birth defects in animals and in humans. Because hormones have long-term effects on the body, women should stop taking oral contraceptives at least three months prior to becoming pregnant. Another method of birth control should be used for those three months. Also tell your doctor if you are breast-feeding an infant. This medication passes into breast milk.

---

orlistat

BRAND NAME (Manufacturer)
Xenical (Roche)
TYPE OF DRUG
Antiobesity agent
INGREDIENT
orlistat
DOSAGE FORM
Capsules (120 mg)
STORAGE
Store in a tightly closed container at room temperature.

USES

Orlistat is used as part of an overall treatment plan for weight loss. Successful weight-loss programs require diet modification and exercise. Orlistat works by blocking the absorption of fat from the gastrointestinal tract.

TREATMENT

This medication can be taken with a full glass of water. The dose should be taken either with each meal that contains fat or within one hour of such a meal. If you skip a meal or eat a meal with no fat, you may omit your orlistat dose.

If you miss a dose, do not take the missed dose. Take the next scheduled dose with your next meal. Do not double the next dose.

SIDE EFFECTS

Minor: Abdominal pain, diarrhea, fatty stools, fecal incontinence, gas with discharge, oily spotting, rectal pain, or urgency to defecate. These side effects may diminish or disappear as your body adjusts to the medication.
Major: Tell your doctor about any side effects that are persistent or particularly bothersome. IT IS ESPECIALLY IMPORTANT TO NOTIFY YOUR DOCTOR about severe abdominal pain or severe diarrhea.

INTERACTIONS

Orlistat may interact with several medications:
1. Orlistat may reduce the effectiveness of fat-soluble vitamins. Take vitamin supplements at least two hours before or after a dose of orlistat.
2. Orlistat may reduce the effectiveness of cyclosporine. Take your dose of cyclosporine at least two hours before or after your dose of orlistat.

3. Orlistat may alter the effect of warfarin (a blood thinner). The effect of warfarin should be monitored carefully while you are taking orlistat.
4. Orlistat may increase the absorption of pravastatin, increasing its effects.

Before starting orlistat, BE SURE TO TELL YOUR DOCTOR about any medication you are taking, especially any of those listed above.

WARNINGS

• Tell your doctor about unusual or allergic reactions you have had to any medications, especially to orlistat.
• Before starting to take orlistat, tell your doctor if you now have or ever had gallbladder problems, chronic malabsorption, kidney stones, or an eating disorder.
• Be sure to tell your doctor if you are pregnant. Orlistat should not be used during pregnancy. Be sure to tell your doctor if you are breast-feeding an infant. It is not known if orlistat passes into breast milk.

---

oxaprozin

BRAND NAME (Manufacturer)
Daypro (Pharmacia)
TYPE OF DRUG
Nonsteroidal anti-inflammatory drug (NSAID)
INGREDIENT
oxaprozin
DOSAGE FORM
Caplets (600 mg)
STORAGE
Store in a tightly closed, light-resistant container at room temperature.

USES

Oxaprozin is used to treat the inflammation (pain, swelling, and stiffness) of certain types of arthritis. Oxaprozin has been shown to block the production of certain body chemicals called prostaglandins that may trigger pain.

TREATMENT

If you are taking oxaprozin to relieve arthritis, you must take it regularly as directed by your physician. It may take up to several weeks before you feel the full benefits of this medication. Oxaprozin does not cure arthritis, but it will help to relieve the condition as long as you continue to take it.

It is important to take oxaprozin on schedule and not to miss any doses. If you miss a dose, take it as soon as possible. However, if it is almost time for your next dose, do not take the missed dose at all; just return to your regular dosing schedule. Do not double the next dose.

This medication should be taken with food or milk to avoid stomach irritation, unless your doctor tells you otherwise. If you are using the medication for acute pain, the first one or two doses can be taken on an empty stomach so that the medicine gets into your bloodstream faster.

SIDE EFFECTS

Minor: Abdominal pain, bloating, constipation, diarrhea, headache, heartburn, indigestion, light-headedness, nausea, nervousness, soreness of the mouth, or vomiting. These side effects should diminish or disappear as your body adjusts to the drug.

To relieve constipation, increase the amount of fiber in your diet (fresh fruits and vegetables, salads, bran, and whole-grain breads) and drink more water (unless your doctor directs you to do otherwise).

To avoid dizziness or light-headedness when you stand, contract and relax the muscles of your legs for a few moments before rising. Do this by pushing one foot against the floor while raising the other foot slightly, alternating feet so that you are "pumping" your legs in a pedaling motion.

If you feel dizzy or light-headed, sit or lie down for a while, get up slowly from a sitting or reclining position, and be careful on stairs.

Major: Tell your doctor about any side effects that are persistent or particularly bothersome. IT IS ESPECIALLY IMPORTANT TO TELL YOUR DOCTOR about bloody or black stools, blurred vision, confusion, hives or itching, ringing or buzzing in the ears, shortness of breath, skin rash, sore throat and fever, stomach pain, swelling of the feet, tightness of the chest, unusual bleeding or bruising, unusual fatigue or weakness, wheezing, or yellowing of the eyes or skin.

INTERACTIONS

Oxaprozin interacts with several other types of medications:

1. Anticoagulants (blood thinners, such as warfarin) and valproic acid can lead to an increase in bleeding complications when used with oxaprozin.

2. Aspirin, other salicylates, and other nonsteroidal anti-inflammatory drugs (NSAIDs) can cause increased stomach irritation if taken concurrently with this drug.

3. Oxaprozin can decrease the elimination of methotrexate from the body, resulting in possible toxicity from this medication. Avoid using methotrexate with oxaprozin.

4. Oxaprozin may interfere with the blood-pressure-lowering effects of beta blockers (such as acebutolol, atenolol, betaxolol, carteolol, esmolol, labetalol, metoprolol, nadolol, penbutolol, pindolol, propranolol, and timolol).

5. This medication may decrease the diuretic effects of furosemide and thiazide.

6. Probenecid may increase the blood level of oxaprozin, which may increase the risk of side effects from oxaprozin.

7. Oxaprozin may increase the side effects of cyclosporine and lithium.

Before starting this medication, BE SURE TO TELL YOUR DOCTOR about any medications you are taking, especially those listed above.

WARNINGS

• Before taking this medication, it is important to tell your doctor if you have ever had an unusual or allergic reaction to any medication, especially to oxaprozin or any of the other chemically related drugs (including aspirin, salicylates, diclofenac, etodolac, fenoprofen, flurbiprofen, ibuprofen, indomethacin, ketoprofen, meclofenamate, mefenamic acid, nabumetone, naproxen, piroxicam, sulindac, or tolmetin).

• Before taking this medication, it is important to tell your doctor if you now have or if you ever had bleeding problems, asthma, epilepsy, heart disease, high blood pressure, kidney disease, liver disease, mental illness, stomach ulcer, or Parkinson's disease.

• Since oxaprozin can prolong bleeding time, it is important to tell your doctor or dentist that you are taking this medication before having surgery or any other medical or dental treatment.

• If oxaprozin makes you feel dizzy or drowsy, do not take part in any activity that requires alertness, such as driving a car or operating potentially dangerous machinery.

• Oxaprozin may increase your sensitivity to sunlight. Avoid prolonged exposure to the sun or sunlamps, and wear protective clothing and an effective sunscreen when you are outdoors during daylight hours.

• Stomach problems are more likely to occur if you take aspirin regularly or drink alcohol while being treated with this medication. Avoid taking frequent doses of aspirin or drinking alcohol while undergoing treatment with this medication (unless your doctors directs you otherwise).

• Be sure to tell your physician if you are pregnant. Oxaprozin may cause unwanted effects on the heart or blood flow of the fetus. Also, be sure to tell your physician if you are breast-feeding an infant. Small amounts of this medication have been shown to pass into breast milk.

---

oxcarbazepine

BRAND NAME (Manufacturer)
Trileptal (Novartis)
TYPE OF DRUG
Antiseizure agent
INGREDIENT
oxcarbazepine
DOSAGE FORMS
Tablets (150 mg, 300 mg, and 600 mg)
Oral suspension (300 mg per 5-mL spoonful)
STORAGE
Store at room temperature in a tightly closed container. Do not expose to excess heat. Discard any unused portion of the oral suspension after seven weeks.

USES

Oxcarbazepine is used to prevent seizures in patients with epilepsy. It is thought that oxcarbazepine works to stop or stabilize some of the electrical activity of the brain, keeping the nerve cells of the brain from becoming overexcited. Seizures occur when there is too much electrical activity in the brain.

TREATMENT

Take this medication exactly as prescribed by your doctor. Oxcarbazepine may be taken either on an empty stomach or with food or milk, unless your doctor directs you to do otherwise.

Shake the suspension well just before measuring each dose to distribute the ingredients evenly and equalize the doses. The medication may settle to the bottom of the container. Measure each dose with a specially designed 5-mL measuring spoon. An ordinary kitchen teaspoon is not accurate enough to measure the medication.

It is important not to stop taking this medication abruptly. Stopping oxcarbazepine suddenly may result in a return of seizures. If this medication needs to be stopped, it should be done gradually. Discuss this with your doctor before stopping oxcarbazepine.

The full effects of this medication may not be apparent for several weeks. Usually the dose of oxcarbazepine is slowly increased over two to four weeks.

If you miss a dose of this medication, take the missed dose as soon as possible. However, if it is almost time for your next dose, do not take the missed dose at all; just return to your regular dosing schedule. Do not double the doses or take more than prescribed by your doctor. If you miss more than two doses, contact your doctor.

SIDE EFFECTS

Minor. Change in sense of taste, constipation, diarrhea, dizziness, drowsiness, dry mouth, insomnia, nausea, nervousness, runny or stuffy nose, stomach pain, or vomiting. Most of these effects should disappear as your body adjusts to the medication.

Dry mouth can be relieved by chewing sugarless gum or sucking on hard candy.

To avoid dizziness or light-headedness when you stand, contract and relax the muscles of your legs for a few moments before rising. Do this by pushing one foot against the floor while raising the other foot slightly, alternating feet so that you are "pumping" your legs in a pedaling motion.

If you feel dizzy or light-headed, sit or lie down for a while; get up from a sitting or lying position slowly; and be careful on stairs.

To relieve constipation, increase the amount of fiber in your diet (fresh fruits and vegetables, salads, bran, and whole-grain breads), exercise, and drink more water (unless your doctor directs you to do otherwise).

Major. Tell your doctor about any side effects that are persistent or particularly bothersome. IT IS ESPECIALLY IMPORTANT TO TELL YOUR DOCTOR about being unusually emotional or depressed, bruising, changes in vision, chills, difficulty walking or feelings of clumsiness, excessive thirst, falling, fever, muscle pain, seizures, skin rash, sore throat, or swollen glands.

INTERACTIONS

Oxcarbazepine may interact with a number of other medications:

1. Concurrent use of this medication with other central nervous system depressants (such as alcohol, barbiturates, benzodiazepine tranquilizers, muscle relaxants, narcotics, pain medications, and phenothiazine tranquilizers) or with tricyclic antidepressants can cause extreme drowsiness.

2. Use of over-the-counter (nonprescription) cough, cold, or allergy medications may increase the side effects of this medication and should be avoided.

3. Other antiseizure medications (such as valproic acid, carbamazepine, and phenytoin) may affect the actions of oxcarbazepine, possibly decreasing its effectiveness.

4. Oxcarbazepine may also reduce the effects of certain antiseizure medications, such as phenobarbital.

5. This medication may reduce the effectiveness of oral contraceptive medications (birth control pills). Therefore, an additional or alternative method of birth control (such as a barrier method) may be needed during treatment with oxcarbazepine. Discuss this with your doctor.

6. Oxcarbazepine may reduce the effectiveness of medications called calcium channel blockers, such as felodipine, verapamil, nifedipine, and others.

BE SURE TO TELL YOUR DOCTOR about these or any other medications you are currently taking.

WARNINGS

• Tell your doctor if you have ever had an allergic reaction to oxcarbazepine, carbamazepine, other antiseizure medications, or any other medications.

• Tell your doctor if you now have or ever had kidney or liver disease, too low a sodium level, or thyroid disease.

• While taking this medication, your ability to perform tasks that require alertness, such as driving a car or operating potentially dangerous machinery, may be impaired.

• It is important to see your doctor regularly while you are taking this medication to make sure that your seizures are being controlled.

• Be sure to tell your doctor if you are pregnant. Oxcarbazepine may cause birth defects; it is similar to carbamazepine, another medication for seizures, which is known to cause birth defects. You should discuss with your doctor the risks and benefits of using this medication during pregnancy. Oxcarbazepine can also pass into human breast milk. Be sure to tell your doctor if you are breast-feeding an infant, and discuss the risks and benefits of this medication.

---

oxybutynin

BRAND NAMES (Manufacturers)

Ditropan (Alza)
Ditropan XL (Alza)
oxybutynin (various manufacturers)

TYPE OF DRUG

Antispasmodic

INGREDIENT
oxybutynin
DOSAGE FORMS
Tablets (5 mg)
Extended-release tablets (5 mg, 10 mg, and 15 mg)
Oral syrup (5 mg per 5-mL spoonful)
STORAGE
Store all forms of this medication at room temperature in a tightly closed container. Do not freeze the syrup form of this medication.

USES

Oxybutynin is used to relieve the symptoms associated with urinary incontinence (inability to control the bladder) or urinary frequency.

TREATMENT

Oxybutynin can be taken either on an empty stomach with water only or, to reduce stomach irritation, with food or milk (as directed by your doctor).

Swallow the extended-release tablets whole; do not crush or chew them.

Measure each dose of the oral syrup carefully with a specially designed 5-mL measuring spoon. An ordinary kitchen teaspoon is not accurate enough.

If you miss a dose of this medication, take the missed dose as soon as possible. However, if it is almost time for the next dose, do not take the missed dose at all; just return to your regular dosing schedule. Do not double the next dose of this medication.

SIDE EFFECTS

Minor. Bloating, blurred vision, constipation, decreased sweating, dizziness, drowsiness, dry mouth, insomnia, nausea, vomiting, or weakness. These side effects should disappear as your body adjusts to the medication.

This medication can cause increased sensitivity of your eyes to sunlight. Sunglasses may help relieve the discomfort caused by bright lights.

To relieve constipation, increase the amount of fiber in your diet (fresh fruits and vegetables, salads, bran, and whole-grain breads) and exercise (unless your doctor directs you to do otherwise).

If you feel dizzy, sit or lie down for a while; get up slowly from a sitting or reclining position; and be careful on stairs.

To avoid dizziness or light-headedness when you stand, contract and relax the muscles of your legs for a few moments before rising. Do this by pressing one foot into the floor while raising the other foot slightly, alternating feet so that you are "pumping" your legs in a pedaling motion.

To help relieve mouth dryness, chew sugarless gum or suck on ice chips or a piece of hard candy.

Major. Tell your doctor about any side effects that are persistent or particularly bothersome. IT IS ESPECIALLY IMPORTANT TO TELL YOUR DOCTOR about decreased sexual ability, difficult or painful urination, eye pain, itching, palpitations, rapid rise in body temperature, or skin rash.

INTERACTIONS

Oxybutynin may interact with several medications:

1. Oxybutynin can cause extreme drowsiness when combined with alcohol or other central nervous system depressants (such as antihistamines, barbiturates, benzodiazepine tranquilizers, narcotics, and pain medications).

2. The side effects of oxybutynin may be increased if taken with tricyclic antidepressants, glycopyrrolate, dicyclomine, or ipratropium.

BE SURE TO TELL YOUR DOCTOR about these or any other medications you are currently taking.

WARNINGS

• Tell your doctor about unusual or allergic reactions you have had to any medications, especially to oxybutynin.
• Before you begin treatment with this medication, be sure to tell your doctor if you now have or have ever had bleeding disorders, glaucoma, heart disease, hiatal hernia, high blood pressure, intestinal blockage, kidney disease, liver disease, myasthenia gravis, enlarged prostate gland, rapid heart rate, thyroid disease, toxemia of pregnancy, ulcerative colitis, or urinary retention.
• If this drug makes you dizzy or blurs your vision, avoid taking part in any activity that requires alertness, such as driving an automobile or operating any potentially dangerous machinery.
• This medication can decrease sweating and heat release from the body. Try not to become overheated. Avoid strenuous exercise in hot weather, and do not take hot baths, showers, and saunas.
• To prevent oversedation, avoid drinking alcoholic beverages while you are taking this medication.
• Be sure to tell your doctor if you are pregnant. Although oxybutynin appears to be safe during pregnancy, extensive studies in humans have not been conducted. Also tell your doctor if you are breast-feeding an infant. This drug may decrease milk production. It is not known whether oxybutynin passes into breast milk.

---

pancreatin

BRAND NAME (Manufacturer)
Creon (Solvay)
TYPE OF DRUG
Digestive enzymes
INGREDIENTS
pancreatin, lipase, protease, and amylase
DOSAGE FORM
Capsules (in various strengths)
STORAGE
Store at room temperature in a tightly closed container.

USES

This medication is a combination of specific digestive (pancreatic) enzymes obtained from pigs or cows. These enzymes aid in the digestion and absorption of fats and starches. Pancreatin is given for the treatment of various pancreatic-enzyme deficiencies resulting from conditions such as pancreatitis, cystic fibrosis, or gastrointestinal bypass surgery.

TREATMENT

To obtain the maximum benefit from this medication, take pancreatin just before or with meals or snacks. If you miss a dose of this medication, do not take the missed dose at all; just return to your regular dosing schedule. Do not double the next dose.

SIDE EFFECTS

Minor. Diarrhea, nausea, or stomach cramps. These side effects should disappear as your body adjusts to pancreatin.
Major. Tell your doctor about any side effects that are persistent or particularly bothersome. IT IS ESPECIALLY IMPORTANT TO TELL YOUR DOCTOR about bloody urine, hives, joint pain, skin rash, or swelling of the feet or legs.

INTERACTIONS

Pancreatin may interact with several medications:

1. Pancreatin can decrease the absorption of iron from the gastrointestinal tract, which may lead to a nutritional deficiency.

2. Calcium- or magnesium-containing antacids decrease the effectiveness of pancreatin and should therefore be avoided during treatment with this medication.

BE SURE TO TELL YOUR DOCTOR about these or any other medications you are currently taking.

WARNINGS

• Tell your doctor about any unusual or allergic reactions you have had to any medications, especially to pancreatin, pancrelipase, or any other digestive enzymes.

• Since pancreatin may reduce the absorption of iron, an iron supplement may be needed. Talk to your doctor about whether an iron supplement would be appropriate for you during treatment with pancreatin.

• Patients who have allergies to pork or beef products may also be allergic to pancreatin.

• Your doctor may prescribe medication that lowers stomach acid, such as cimetidine or ranitidine, to increase the absorption of pancreatin.

• Be sure to tell your doctor if you are pregnant. Although pancreatin appears to be safe during pregnancy, extensive studies have not been conducted. Also tell your doctor if you are breast-feeding an infant. It is not known whether pancreatin passes into breast milk.

---

pancrelipase

BRAND NAMES (Manufacturers)

Cotazym (Organon)
Ku-Zyme (Schwarz Pharma)
Ku-Zyme-HP (Schwarz Pharma)
Pancrease (Ortho-McNeil)
Pancrease MT (Ortho-McNeil)
Ultrase (Axcan Scandipharm)
Ultrase MT (Axcan Scandipharm)
Viokase (Axcan Scandipharm)
Zymase (Organon)

TYPE OF DRUG

Digestive enzymes

INGREDIENTS

lipase, protease, and amylase

DOSAGE FORMS

Tablets (in various strengths)
Capsules (in various strengths)
Powder packets (in various strengths)

STORAGE

Pancrelipase tablets, capsules, and powder should be stored at room temperature in tightly closed containers, away from moisture. Do not refrigerate any form of pancrelipase.

USES

This medication is a combination of specific digestive (pancreatic) enzymes obtained from pigs. These enzymes aid in the digestion and absorption of starches and fats. Pancrelipase is used in the treatment of various pancreatic-enzyme deficiencies resulting from conditions such as pancreatitis, cystic fibrosis, or gastrointestinal bypass surgery.

TREATMENT

To obtain the maximum benefit, take pancrelipase just before or with meals or snacks. The powder can be added to food; the tablets can be crushed and mixed with food.

If you are taking the capsules containing the enteric-coated microspheres, swallow the capsules whole. Chewing, crushing, or breaking the capsules decreases their effectiveness and increases the side effects. However, if you have difficulty swallowing the capsules, you can open them and sprinkle the contents on a small amount of liquid or soft food, which you should then swallow without chewing. Do not mix this medication with alkaline foods (such as dairy products); they can reduce its effectiveness.

If you miss a dose of this medication, do not take the missed dose at all; just return to your regular dosing schedule. Do not double the next dose.

SIDE EFFECTS

Minor. Diarrhea, nausea, or stomach cramps. These side effects should disappear over time as your body adjusts to the medication.

Major. Tell your doctor about any side effects you experience that are persistent or particularly bothersome. IT IS ESPECIALLY IMPORTANT TO TELL YOUR DOCTOR about bloody urine, hives, joint pain, shortness of breath, skin rash, or swelling of the feet.

INTERACTIONS

Pancrelipase may interact with several medications:

1. Pancrelipase can decrease the absorption of iron from the gastrointestinal tract, which may lead to nutritional deficiency.

2. Antacids that contain calcium or magnesium decrease pancrelipase's effectiveness and should be avoided.

BE SURE TO TELL YOUR DOCTOR about these or any other medications you are currently taking.

WARNINGS

• Tell your doctor about unusual or allergic reactions you have had to any medications, especially to pancrelipase, pancreatin, or any other digestive enzymes.

• Patients who have allergies to pork products may also be allergic to pancrelipase, since it is obtained from pigs.

• Since pancrelipase may reduce the absorption of iron, an iron supplement may be needed. Talk to your doctor about whether an iron supplement would be appropriate for you during treatment with pancreatin.

• The powder form as well as the powder from opened capsules of this medication can be very irritating to the nose and throat. Avoid inhaling the particles.

• Be sure to tell your doctor if you are pregnant. Although pancrelipase appears to be safe during pregnancy, extensive studies have not been conducted. Also tell your doctor if you are breast-feeding an infant. It is not known whether pancrelipase passes into breast milk.

---

pantoprazole

BRAND NAME (Manufacturer)
Protonix (Wyeth)
TYPE OF DRUG
Gastric-acid-secretion inhibitor

INGREDIENT
pantoprazole
DOSAGE FORM
Tablets (40 mg)
STORAGE
Store at room temperature in a tightly closed container. Do not expose this medication to extreme temperatures.

USES

Pantoprazole is prescribed to treat peptic ulcer disease, gastroesophageal reflux disease (GERD), and hypersecretory syndromes; it suppresses stomach-acid secretion.

TREATMENT

This medication may be taken before, during, or following a morning meal, unless your doctor directs you to do otherwise. Swallow the tablets whole; do not chew or crush them.

If you miss a dose of this medication, take it as soon as you remember. However, if it is almost time for your next dose, do not take the missed dose at all; just return to your regular dosing schedule. Do not double the next dose of the medication.

It is important to take this medication for as long as prescribed by your doctor.

SIDE EFFECTS

Minor. Abdominal pain, burning sensation in the mouth, constipation, diarrhea, dizziness, fatigue, headache, insomnia, joint pain, or skin rash. Most of these effects should disappear as your body adjusts to the medication.

Dry mouth can be relieved by chewing sugarless gum or sucking on hard candy.

To avoid dizziness or light-headedness when you stand, contract and relax the muscles of your legs for a few moments before rising. Do this by pressing one foot against the floor while raising the other foot slightly, alternating feet so that you are "pumping" your legs in a pedaling motion.

If you feel dizzy or light-headed, sit or lie down for a while; get up slowly from a sitting or reclining position; and be careful on stairs.

To relieve constipation, increase the amount of fiber in your diet (fresh fruits and vegetables, salads, bran, and whole-grain breads), exercise, and drink more water (unless your doctor directs you to do otherwise).

Major. Tell your doctor about any side effects that are persistent or particularly bothersome. IT IS ESPECIALLY IMPORTANT TO TELL YOUR DOCTOR about abdominal pain with nausea and vomiting, changes in vision, chest pain, difficulty breathing, itching, joint pain with skin rash or blistering of the skin, rash, shortness of breath, swelling of the face or mouth, unusual tiredness, or yellowish discoloration of the eyes and skin.

INTERACTIONS

Pantoprazole may interact with a number of other medications.

1. Use of pantoprazole with ketoconazole, itraconazole, some forms of penicillin, digoxin, or iron may alter the absorption of these medications and reduce or increase their effectiveness.

2. Pantoprazole may increase the effects of warfarin (a blood thinner), increasing the side effects of this medication.

BE SURE TO TELL YOUR DOCTOR about these or any other medications you are currently taking.

WARNINGS

- Tell your doctor about any unusual reactions you have had to any medication, especially pantoprazole or any medication used for ulcers or acid reflux (GERD).

• Tell your doctor if you now have or if you have ever had liver disease or kidney disease.
• While taking this medication, your ability to perform tasks that require alertness, such as driving a car or operating potentially dangerous machinery, may be impaired.
• Long-term and high-dose treatment with medications similar to pantoprazole have been associated with a higher incidence of gastric tumors. Discuss this with your doctor if you need to take high doses of pantoprazole for a long time.
• Be sure to tell your doctor if you are pregnant. Adequate studies of the use of pantoprazole during human pregnancy have not been conducted, and animal studies have shown pantoprazole to cause birth defects. Also be sure to tell your doctor if you are breast-feeding an infant. Pantoprazole passes into breast milk and may cause side effects in a nursing infant.

paroxetine

BRAND NAMES (Manufacturers)
Paxil (GlaxoSmithKline)
Paxil CR (GlaxoSmithKline)
TYPE OF DRUG
Antidepressant
INGREDIENT
paroxetine
DOSAGE FORMS
Tablets (20 mg and 30 mg)
Tablets, extended release (12.5 mg, 25 mg, and 37.5 mg)
Oral suspension (10 mg per 5 mL)
STORAGE
Store in a tightly closed container at room temperature, away from heat and direct sunlight. Do not store in the bathroom. Heat or moisture can cause this medicine to break down.

USES

Paroxetine is used to treat the symptoms of mental depression and some forms of anxiety. It is also used to treat obsessive-compulsive disorder. Paroxetine increases the concentration of certain chemicals that are necessary for nerve transmission in the brain. Having too low an amount of a certain chemical, called serotonin, may cause some of the symptoms of depression and anxiety.

TREATMENT

Take this medication exactly as prescribed by your doctor. To avoid stomach irritation, take paroxetine with food or with a full glass of water (unless your doctor directs you to do otherwise).

Shake the oral suspension well before measuring each dose to distribute the contents evenly and equalize the doses. The contents tend to settle at the bottom of the bottle. Measure each dose carefully with a specially designed 5-mL measuring spoon. An ordinary kitchen teaspoon is not accurate enough for this purpose.

Swallow the extended-release tablets whole; do not chew or crush them.

The effects of treatment with this medication may not become apparent for one to three weeks after you begin taking it.

If you miss a dose of this medicine, take it as soon as you remember. However, if it is almost time for your next dose, do not take the missed dose at all; just return to your regular dosing schedule. You should never take a double dose to make up for one you missed.

SIDE EFFECTS

Minor. Agitation, changes in taste perception, constipation, decreased concentration, decreased sex drive, diarrhea, dizziness, drowsiness, dry mouth, fast heartbeat, flushing, frequent urination, headache, increased sweating, loss of appetite, nausea, stuffy nose, vision changes, or weight gain or loss. These side effects should diminish or disappear as your body adjusts to the medication.

Dry mouth can be relieved by chewing sugarless gum or sucking on ice chips or a piece of hard candy.

To relieve constipation, increase the amount of fiber in your diet (fresh fruits and vegetables, salads, bran, and whole-grain breads), exercise, and drink more water (unless your doctor directs you to do otherwise).

To avoid dizziness when you stand, contract and relax the muscles in your legs for a few moments before rising. Do this by pressing one foot against the floor while raising the other foot slightly, alternating feet so that you are "pumping" your legs in a pedaling motion.

If you feel dizzy or light-headed, sit or lie down for a while; get up slowly from a sitting or reclining position; and be careful on stairs.

Major. Tell your doctor about any side effects you experience that are persistent or particularly bothersome. IT IS ESPECIALLY IMPORTANT TO TELL YOUR DOCTOR about anxiety, chills or fever, confusion, convulsions (seizures), enlarged lymph glands (swelling under the jaw, in the armpits, or in the groin area), difficulty in breathing, joint or muscle pain, rapid heartbeat, skin rash or hives, swelling of the feet or lower legs, or unusual weakness or tiredness.

INTERACTIONS

Paroxetine will interact with several other types of medications:

1. Extreme drowsiness can occur when this medication is taken with other central nervous system depressants (such as alcohol, antihistamines, barbiturates, benzodiazepine tranquilizers, muscle relaxants, narcotics, pain medications, phenothiazine tranquilizers, and sleeping medications) or with other antidepressants.

2. Paroxetine may increase the effects of oral anticoagulants (blood thinners, such as warfarin) and certain heart medications (such as digoxin).

3. Serious side effects may occur if a monoamine oxidase (MAO) inhibitor (such as furazolidone, isocarboxazid, pargyline, phenelzine, procarbazine, selegiline, or tranylcypromine) is taken concurrently with paroxetine. At least 14 days should separate the use of paroxetine and the use of an MAO inhibitor.

4. Paroxetine should not be given together with drugs that have serotonergic action (other antidepressants, tryptophan, some migraine drugs, and certain medications used for nausea and vomiting). Such a combination can result in agitation, restlessness, confusion, seizures, and possibly death.

5. Paroxetine may interfere with the action of tricyclic antidepressants and phenothiazines, possibly increasing the side effects from these medications.

Before taking paroxetine, BE SURE TO TELL YOUR DOCTOR about any medication you are taking, especially any of those listed above.

WARNINGS

- Tell your doctor immediately if you develop a skin rash or hives while taking this medication or if you have ever had a reaction to paroxetine before.
- Tell your doctor if you have a history of alcoholism or if you now have or ever had a heart attack, asthma, circulatory disease, difficulty in urinating, electroshock therapy, enlarged prostate gland, epilepsy, glaucoma, high blood pressure, intestinal problems, liver or kidney disease, mental illness, or thyroid disease.
- If this medication makes you drowsy or dizzy, do not take part in any activity that requires mental alertness, such as driving a car or operating dangerous equipment.

• Do not stop taking this medication suddenly. Abruptly stopping it can cause nausea, headache, stomach upset, or a worsening of your condition. Your doctor may want to reduce your dose gradually.
• Elderly individuals may be at greater risk for side effects. They should use this drug cautiously and report any mental-status changes to their doctor immediately.
• The effects of this medication may be present for as long as five weeks after you stop taking it, so continue to observe all precautions during this period.
• Be sure to tell your doctor if you are pregnant. Although birth defects have not been documented in animal studies, it is not known if paroxetine is safe during human pregnancy. It is not known if paroxetine passes into breast milk, so be sure to tell your doctor if you are breast-feeding an infant.

---

penicillin VK

BRAND NAMES (Manufacturers)
Beepen-VK (GlaxoSmithKline)
Betapen-VK (Bristol-Myers Squibb)
penicillin VK (various manufacturers)
Pen-Vee K (Wyeth-Ayerst)
V-Cillin K (Lilly)
Veetids (Bristol-Myers Squibb)
TYPE OF DRUG
Penicillin antibiotic
INGREDIENT
penicillin v potassium
DOSAGE FORMS
Tablets (250 mg and 500 mg)
Oral solution (125 mg and 250 mg per 5-mL spoonful)
STORAGE
Store the tablets at room temperature in a tightly closed container. Keep the oral solution in the refrigerator in a tightly closed container. Discard any unused portion of the solution after 14 days because the solution loses potency after that time. Do not freeze this medication.

USES

Penicillin VK is used to treat a wide variety of bacterial infections, including infections of the middle ear, the skin, the respiratory tract, and the urinary tract. It acts by severely injuring the cell membranes of infecting bacteria, thereby preventing them from growing and multiplying. Penicillin VK kills susceptible bacteria, but it is not effective against viruses, parasites, or fungi.

TREATMENT

Take this medication on an empty stomach or with a glass of water one hour before or two hours after a meal. Never take it with fruit juices or carbonated beverages because the acidity of these drinks destroys the drug in the stomach.

Shake the oral solution well just before measuring each dose. Measure each dose carefully with a specially designed 5-mL measuring spoon. An ordinary kitchen teaspoon is not accurate enough.

Penicillin VK works best when the level of medicine in your bloodstream is kept constant. It is best, therefore, to take the doses at evenly spaced intervals throughout the day and night. For example, if you are to take four doses a day, the doses should be spaced six hours apart.

If you miss a dose of this medication, take the missed dose immediately. However, if you do not remember to take the missed dose until it is almost time for the next dose, take it; space the following dose about halfway through the regular interval between doses; then return to your regular dosing schedule. Try not to skip any doses of this medication.

It is important that you continue to take this medication for the entire time prescribed by your doctor (usually a period of 7 to 14 days), even if the symptoms of infection disappear before the end of that time. If you stop taking this medication too soon, resistant bacteria will be given a chance to continue growing, and the infection could recur.

SIDE EFFECTS

Minor. Diarrhea, heartburn, nausea, or vomiting. These side effects should disappear as your body adjusts to the drug.

Major. Tell your doctor about any side effects that are persistent or particularly bothersome. IT IS ESPECIALLY IMPORTANT TO TELL YOUR DOCTOR about bloating, chills, cough, darkened tongue, difficulty in breathing, fever, irritation of the mouth, muscle aches, rash, rectal or vaginal itching, severe diarrhea, or sore throat. If the infection seems to be getting worse rather than getting better, you should contact your physician.

INTERACTIONS

Penicillin VK will interact with several other types of medications:

1. Probenecid can increase the blood concentrations of this medication.

2. Colestipol and cholestyramine may decrease the absorption of penicillin from the gastrointestinal tract. Several hours should separate doses of these medications.

3. Penicillin VK may decrease the effectiveness of oral contraceptives (birth control pills), and pregnancy could result. You should therefore use an alternative or additional form of birth control while you are taking this medication. Discuss this with your doctor.

4. Concurrent use of methotrexate and penicillin VK may increase the toxicity of methotrexate. Discuss this with your doctor if you need to take methotrexate while you are taking penicillin VK.

BE SURE TO TELL YOUR DOCTOR about any medications you are currently taking, especially any of those listed above.

WARNINGS

- Tell your doctor about unusual or allergic reactions you have had to any medications, especially to penicillin or other related antibiotics (such as ampicillin and amoxicillin), cephalosporin antibiotics, penicillamine, or griseofulvin.
- CALL YOUR DOCTOR IMMEDIATELY if you experience any swelling of the face, tongue, or mouth; shortness of breath; or a rash after taking the medication.
- Tell your doctor if you now have or if you have ever had kidney disease, asthma, or allergies.
- This medication has been prescribed for your current infection only. Another infection later on, or one that someone else has, may require a different medicine. You should not give your medicine to other people or use it for other infections, unless your doctor specifically directs you to do so.
- People with diabetes who are taking penicillin VK should know that this drug can cause a false-positive sugar reaction with a Clinitest urine glucose test. To avoid this problem while taking penicillin, they should switch to Clinistix or Tes-Tape to test their urine for sugar.
- Be sure to tell your doctor if you are pregnant. Although penicillin appears to be safe during pregnancy, extensive studies in humans have not been conducted. Also tell your doctor if you are breast-feeding an infant. Small amounts of this medication pass into breast milk and may temporarily alter the bacterial balance in the intestinal tract of a nursing infant, resulting in diarrhea.

pentoxifylline

BRAND NAMES (Manufacturers)
Trental (Hoechst)
pentoxifylline (various manufacturers)
TYPE OF DRUG
Hemorrheologic
INGREDIENT
pentoxifylline
DOSAGE FORM
Sustained-release tablets (400 mg)
STORAGE
Store at room temperature in a tightly closed container.

USES

Pentoxifylline is used to treat intermittent claudication (leg pain caused by poor blood circulation) or peripheral vascular disease.

TREATMENT

Take pentoxifylline with meals. Swallow the tablets whole; chewing, crushing, or breaking them will destroy the controlled-release activity and increase the risk of side effects.

If you miss a dose, take it as soon as possible. However, if it is almost time for the next dose, do not take the missed dose at all; just wait until the next scheduled dose. Do not double the dose.

The benefits from pentoxifylline may be seen within two to four weeks after starting the medication.

SIDE EFFECTS

Minor. Abdominal pain, altered taste, belching, bloating, constipation, diarrhea, dizziness, drowsiness, dry mouth, excessive salivation, flushing, gas, headache, heartburn, insomnia, nasal congestion, nausea, nosebleeds, trembling of the hands, vomiting, or weight change. As your body adjusts to pentoxifylline, these side effects should disappear.

If you are constipated, increase the amount of fiber in your diet (fresh fruits and vegetables, salads, bran, and whole-grain breads), exercise, and drink more water (unless your doctor directs you to do otherwise).

To reduce mouth dryness, chew sugarless gum or suck on ice chips or a piece of hard candy.

If you feel dizzy or light-headed, lie or sit down for a while; get up slowly from a sitting or reclining position; and be careful on stairs.

To avoid dizziness when you stand, contract and relax the muscles in your legs for a few moments before rising. Do this by pressing one foot against the floor while raising the other foot slightly, alternating feet so that you are "pumping" your legs in a pedaling motion.

Major. Tell your doctor about any side effects that are persistent or particularly bothersome. IT IS ESPECIALLY IMPORTANT TO TELL YOUR DOCTOR about chest pain, confusion, earache, flulike symptoms, itching, palpitations, rash, shortness of breath, sore throat, unusual bleeding or bruising, unusual weight gain, visual disturbances, or yellowing of the eyes or skin.

INTERACTIONS

Pentoxifylline interacts with other types of medications:

1. Anticoagulants (blood thinners, such as warfarin) in combination with pentoxifylline can increase the risk of bleeding complications.
2. This drug can add to the blood-pressure-lowering effects of antihypertensives.
3. The combination of pentoxifylline and xanthines, such as theophylline, or other drugs that stimulate the central nervous system may result in increased side effects.
4. Concurrent use of cimetidine may increase the side effects of this medication.

BE SURE TO TELL YOUR DOCTOR about any medications you are currently taking, especially any of the drugs that are listed above.

WARNINGS

• Before you take this medication, it is important to tell your doctor if you have ever had unusual or allergic reactions to any medications, especially to pentoxifylline or chemically related compounds, such as caffeine, dyphylline, oxtriphylline, theophylline, and aminophylline.
• Tell your doctor if you now have or ever had liver disease, kidney disease, or peptic ulcer disease.
• Before having surgery or any other medical or dental treatment, be sure to tell your doctor or dentist that you are taking this medication. Pentoxifylline can increase bleeding complications.
• If pentoxifylline makes you dizzy or drowsy, do not take part in any activity that requires alertness, such as driving a car or operating dangerous machinery.
• Smoking cigarettes may worsen your condition; do not smoke.
• Be sure to tell your doctor if you are pregnant. Although pentoxifylline appears to be safe in animals, studies in pregnant women have not been conducted. Also tell your doctor if you are breast-feeding an infant. Small amounts of pentoxifylline pass into human breast milk.

---

perindopril

BRAND NAME (Manufacturer)
Aceon (Solvay)
TYPE OF DRUG
Antihypertensive
INGREDIENT
perindopril
DOSAGE FORM
Tablets (2 mg, 4 mg, and 8 mg)
STORAGE
Store at room temperature in a tightly closed container. Do not expose to excess heat.

USES

Perindopril is used to treat high blood pressure. It is a vasodilator (it widens the blood vessels) that acts by blocking the production of chemicals that may be responsible for constricting, or narrowing, the blood vessels.

TREATMENT

Perindopril may be taken either on an empty stomach or with food or milk (unless your doctor directs you to do otherwise). To become accustomed to this medication, it should be taken at the same time every day.

It may take several weeks before you notice the full effects of this medication.

If you miss a dose of this medication, take the missed dose as soon as possible. However, if it is almost time for your next dose, do not take the missed dose at all; just return to your regular dosing schedule. Do not double the next dose or take more than prescribed by your doctor.

It is important that you take this medication on a regular basis as prescribed by your doctor. Perindopril does not cure high blood pressure, but it will help you to control the condition for as long as you continue to take it.

SIDE EFFECTS

Minor. Abdominal pain, constipation, cough, diarrhea, dizziness, dry mouth, fatigue, flushing, headache, insomnia, loss of appetite, loss of taste perception, nausea, or vomiting. Most of these effects should diminish or disappear as your body adjusts to the medication.

Dry mouth can be relieved by chewing sugarless gum or sucking on hard candy.

To avoid dizziness or light-headedness when you stand, contract and relax the muscles of your legs for a few moments before rising. Do this by pushing one foot against the floor while raising the other foot slightly, alternating feet so that you are "pumping" your legs.

If you feel dizzy or light-headed, sit or lie down for a while; get up from a sitting or lying position slowly; and be careful on stairs.

To relieve constipation, increase the amount of fiber in your diet (fresh fruits and vegetables, salads, bran, and whole-grain breads), exercise, and drink more water (unless your doctor directs you to do otherwise).

Major. Tell your doctor about any side effects that are persistent or particularly bothersome. IT IS ESPECIALLY IMPORTANT TO TELL YOUR DOCTOR about chest pains; chills; difficult or painful urination; fever; heart palpitations; itching; mouth sores; prolonged vomiting or diarrhea; rash; sore throat; swelling of the face, hands, or feet; tingling of the fingers or toes; unusual bleeding or bruising; or yellowing of the skin or the whites of the eyes.

INTERACTIONS

Perindopril may interact with a number of other medications:

1. Diuretics (water pills) and other antihypertensive medications can cause an excessive drop in blood pressure when combined with perindopril (especially with the first dose).

2. The combination of perindopril with spironolactone, triamterene, amiloride, potassium supplements, or salt substitutes can lead to hyperkalemia (dangerously high levels of potassium in the bloodstream).

3. Antineoplastic agents (anticancer drugs) or chloramphenicol can increase the bone-marrow side effects of perindopril.

4. Concurrent use of perindopril and the antigout medication allopurinol can increase the risk of developing an allergic reaction.

5. Indomethacin and other nonsteroidal anti-inflammatory drugs (such as ibuprofen or naproxen) may decrease the blood-pressure-lowering effects of perindopril.

6. Perindopril can delay the body's elimination of lithium. Concurrent use of perindopril and lithium may cause lithium toxicity.

7. Alcohol should be avoided while taking perindopril. This combination may cause too low a blood pressure.

8. Use of over-the-counter (nonprescription) cough, cold, or allergy medications may reduce the effectiveness of this medication and should be avoided.

BE SURE TO TELL YOUR DOCTOR about these or any other medications you are currently taking.

WARNINGS

• Tell your doctor if you have ever had an allergic reaction to perindopril, any medication used to treat high blood pressure, or any other medications.

• Tell your doctor if you now have or if you have ever had kidney disease, liver disease, heart disease, swelling of the face or the mouth, aortic stenosis, lupus or scleroderma, diabetes mellitus, too high levels of potassium in your blood (hyperkalemia), or any type of blood disorder.

• Call your doctor immediately if you experience any swelling of the face or mouth or difficulty breathing or swallowing after taking this medication.

• While taking this medication, your ability to perform tasks that require alertness, such as driving a car or operating potentially dangerous machinery, may be impaired.

• If you are having surgery or undergoing any type of dental procedure, be sure to tell your doctor or dentist that you are taking perindopril.

• Excessive perspiration, dehydration, or prolonged vomiting or diarrhea can lead to an excessive drop in blood pressure while you are taking this medication. Contact your doctor if you have any of these symptoms.

• Do not stop taking this medication unless you first consult your doctor. Stopping this drug abruptly may lead to a rise in blood pressure.

• The first few doses of this medication may cause dizziness. Try to avoid any sudden changes in posture.

• Be sure to tell your doctor if you are pregnant. Perindopril may cause birth defects if taken during the second or third trimester of pregnancy. Also perindopril can pass into human breast milk. Be sure to tell your doctor if you are breast-feeding an infant and discuss the risks and benefits of taking this medication.

---

phenelzine

BRAND NAME (Manufacturer)
Nardil (Parke-Davis)
TYPE OF DRUG
Monoamine oxidase (MAO) inhibitor
INGREDIENT
phenelzine
DOSAGE FORM
Tablets (15 mg)
STORAGE
Store at room temperature in a tightly closed, light-resistant container.

USES

This medication is used to treat clinical depression. Phenelzine belongs to a group of drugs known as monoamine oxidase (MAO) inhibitors. It is not clearly understood how it works, but it is thought to increase the amounts of certain chemicals in the brain that act to relieve depression.

TREATMENT

Phenelzine can be taken either on an empty stomach or, to avoid stomach irritation, with food or milk (as directed by your doctor).

If you are taking a single daily dose, it is best to take the dose in the morning.

If you miss a dose of this medication, take it as soon as you remember. However, if it's almost time for your next dose, do not take the missed dose at all; just return to your regular dosing schedule. Do not double the next dose.

The full therapeutic benefits of this medication may not be observed for up to four weeks after you start to take it.

SIDE EFFECTS

Minor. Constipation, diarrhea, dizziness, drowsiness, dry mouth, fatigue, headache, insomnia, nausea, restlessness, stomach upset, sweating, or weakness. These side effects should diminish or disappear as your body gets accustomed to the medication.

Phenelzine can increase your sensitivity to sunlight. Avoid prolonged exposure to sunlight and sunlamps, wear protective clothing and sunglasses, and use an effective sunscreen.

If you feel dizzy, sit or lie down for a while; get up slowly from a sitting or reclining position; and be careful on stairs.

To relieve constipation, increase the amount of fiber in your diet (fresh fruits and vegetables, salads, bran, and whole-grain breads) and drink more water (unless your doctor directs you to do otherwise).

To relieve mouth dryness, chew sugarless gum or suck on ice chips or a piece of hard candy.

Major. Tell your doctor about any side effects that are persistent or particularly bothersome. IT IS ESPECIALLY IMPORTANT TO TELL YOUR DOCTOR about anxiety, blurred vision, changes in sexual ability, chills, confusion, convulsions, darkened tongue, difficult or painful urination, fainting, false sense of well-being, hallucinations, jitteriness, mental disorders, rapid weight gain (three to five pounds within a week), uncoordinated movements, or yellowing of the eyes or the skin.

If you experience a severe headache, stiff neck, chest pains, palpitations, or vomiting while taking this medication, CONTACT YOUR DOCTOR OR AN EMERGENCY ROOM IMMEDIATELY. These symptoms may be the result of a food or drug interaction.

INTERACTIONS

Phenelzine interacts with a number of medications and foods:

1. Concurrent use of phenelzine with central nervous system depressants (such as alcohol, barbiturates, benzodiazepine tranquilizers, muscle relaxants, narcotics, pain medications, phenothiazine tranquilizers, and sleeping medications) or with tricyclic antidepressants can lead to extreme drowsiness.

2. The dosage of anticonvulsant medications may need to be adjusted when phenelzine is started.

3. Serious, and sometimes fatal, side effects can result if phenelzine is used within 14 days of another monoamine oxidase inhibitor, a beta blocker, carbamazepine, cyclobenzaprine, methyldopa, guanethidine, reserpine, levodopa, meperidine or another narcotic, amphetamines, ephedrine, methylphenidate, phenylpropanolamine, pseudoephedrine, sumatriptan or a similar medication for migraine, bupropion, buspirone, dextromethorphan, nefazodone, trazodone, clomipramine, fluoxetine, fluvoxamine, paroxetine, sertraline, citalopram, escitalopram, or a tricyclic antidepressant.

4. Tyramine-containing foods and beverages (aged cheeses, sour cream, yogurt, pickled herring, chicken livers, canned figs, raisins, bananas, avocados, soy sauce, broad bean pods, yeast extracts, beer, and certain wines), excessive amounts of caffeine-containing beverages (coffee, tea, cocoa, and cola), or chocolate can also cause serious reactions in patients on phenelzine therapy.

5. Phenelzine can increase the blood-sugar-lowering effects of insulin and oral antidiabetic medications.

6. Phenelzine may increase the action of warfarin (a blood thinner), increasing the risk of bleeding.

Before starting treatment with this medication, BE SURE TO TELL YOUR DOCTOR about any medications that you are currently taking, especially any of the medications that are listed above.

Be sure you are aware of the foods that interact with phenelzine.

WARNINGS

• Tell your doctor about unusual or allergic reactions you have had to any medications, especially to phenelzine or other MAO inhibitors.

• Before starting to take this medication, be sure to tell your doctor if you now have or if you have ever had asthma, bronchitis, diabetes mellitus, epilepsy, glaucoma, severe headaches, heart disease, blood-vessel disease, kidney disease, liver disease, mental disorders, Parkinson's disease, pheochromocytoma, or thyroid disease.

• If this drug makes you dizzy or drowsy, do not take part in any activity that requires alertness, such as driving a car or operating potentially dangerous machinery.

• Before having surgery or any other medical or dental treatment, be sure to tell your doctor or dentist that you are taking this medication.

• Check with your doctor or pharmacist before taking any nonprescription asthma, allergy, cough, cold, diet, or sinus preparations. Using these products in combination with phenelzine may cause serious side effects.

• If you also have angina, do not increase your amount of physical activity unless you first check with your doctor. Phenelzine can decrease the symptoms of angina without decreasing the risks of strenuous exercise.

• Be sure to tell your doctor if you are pregnant. Studies in animals have shown that phenelzine can cause birth defects if it is taken in high doses during pregnancy. Studies in humans have not been conducted. Also tell your doctor if you are breast-feeding an infant. Small amounts of phenelzine may pass into breast milk.

---

phenytoin

BRAND NAMES (Manufacturers)
Dilantin (Parke-Davis)
Dilantin Infatab (Parke-Davis)
Dilantin Kapseals (Parke-Davis)
phenytoin (various manufacturers)
TYPE OF DRUG
Anticonvulsant
INGREDIENT
phenytoin
DOSAGE FORMS
Capsules (30 mg and 100 mg)
Chewable tablets (50 mg)
Oral suspension (125 mg per 5-mL spoonful, with less than 0.6% alcohol)
STORAGE
Store all forms of this drug at room temperature in tightly closed, light-resistant containers. This medication should not be refrigerated and should never be frozen.

USES

Phenytoin is used to control certain types of convulsions, or seizures. It is not clear exactly how phenytoin works to control convulsions, but it appears to prevent the spread of seizure activity in the brain. Phenytoin may also be used to treat other conditions as determined by your physician.

TREATMENT

To avoid stomach irritation, take phenytoin with food or with a full glass of water or milk (unless your doctor directs you to do otherwise). This medication should be taken at the same time in relation to meals to make sure that the drug is absorbed consistently.

Chew the tablet form of this medication before swallowing.

Shake the suspension well just before measuring each dose to distribute the ingredients evenly and equalize the doses. The contents tend to settle on the bottom of the bottle. Measure each dose carefully with a specially designed 5-mL measuring spoon. An ordinary kitchen teaspoon is not accurate enough.

Phenytoin works best when the level of medicine in your bloodstream is kept constant. It is best to take the doses at evenly spaced intervals day and night. For example, if you are taking three doses a day, the doses should be spaced eight hours apart.

If you miss a dose of this medication, take the missed dose as soon as possible. However, if it is almost time for the next dose, do not take the missed dose at all; just return to your regular dosing schedule. Do not double the next dose. If you miss two or more doses in a row, contact your doctor.

SIDE EFFECTS

Minor. Constipation, drowsiness (mild), headache, insomnia, nausea, or vomiting. These side effects should begin to disappear as your body gets accustomed to the medication.

To relieve constipation, increase the amount of fiber in your diet (fresh fruits and vegetables, salads, bran, and whole-grain breads), exercise, and drink more water (unless your doctor directs you to do otherwise).

Major. Tell your doctor about any side effects that are persistent or particularly bothersome. IT IS ESPECIALLY IMPORTANT TO TELL YOUR DOCTOR about blurred vision, change in facial features, change in the color of your urine, chest pain, confusion, dizziness, gum enlargement, increased hair growth, joint pain, muscle twitching, nervousness, numbness, rash, slurred speech, sore throat, swollen glands, uncoordinated movements, unusual bleeding or bruising, or yellowing of the eyes or skin.

INTERACTIONS

Phenytoin can be expected to interact with a number of other types of medications:

1. The effectiveness of phenytoin can be decreased by concurrent use of alcohol, barbiturates, tricyclic antidepressants, phenothiazines, bupropion, antipsychotics (such as clozipine), and haloperidol. Concurrent use of these medications with phenytoin may increase the risk of seizures.

2. Phenytoin can decrease the effectiveness of amiodarone, calcifediol, warfarin, quinidine, disopyramide, dexamethasone, doxycycline, lamotrigine, levodopa, and theophylline.

3. The active blood levels and also the side effects of phenytoin can be increased by other anticonvulsants, chloramphenicol, cimetidine, disulfiram, isoniazid, aspirin, fluoxetine, metronidazole, amiodarone, trimethoprim, sulfonamide antibiotics, tolbutamide, benzodiazepines, tricyclic antidepressants, phenothiazines, estrogens, warfarin, omeprazole, ticlopidine, methylphenidate, fluconazole, itraconazole, or ketoconazole.

4. Valproic acid can either increase or decrease the effects of phenytoin.

5. The dosage of oral antidiabetic medications or insulin may need to be adjusted when phenytoin is started.

6. Phenytoin may decrease the absorption of furosemide from the gastrointestinal tract, decreasing furosemide's effectiveness.

7. Antacids, calcium supplements, sucralfate, didanosine, and medicines for diarrhea may decrease the gastrointestinal absorption and effectiveness of phenytoin. Do not take phenytoin within two to three hours of taking an antacid or antidiarrheal.

8. Phenytoin may decrease the effectiveness of oral contraceptives (birth control pills). An alternative method of birth control may be needed. Check with your doctor.

9. Concurrent use of folic acid, leucovorin, rifampin, paroxetine, or enteral feeding (such as drinking Ensure) may decrease the effectiveness of phenytoin by lowering the amount of medication in the bloodstream.

Before starting to take phenytoin, BE SURE TO TELL YOUR DOCTOR about any medications you are currently taking, especially any of those listed above.

WARNINGS

- Tell your doctor about unusual or allergic reactions you have had to any medications, especially to phenytoin, ethotoin, or mephenytoin.
- Before starting to take this medication, be sure to tell your doctor if you now have or ever had blood disorders, diabetes mellitus, or liver disease.

• If this drug makes you dizzy or drowsy, do not take part in any activity that requires alertness, such as driving a car or operating potentially dangerous machinery. Children should be careful while playing.
• Before surgery or other medical or dental treatment, tell your doctor or dentist you are taking phenytoin.
• Do not stop taking this medication unless you first consult your doctor. If this drug is stopped abruptly, you may experience uncontrollable seizures. Your doctor may want to reduce your dosage gradually. Be sure you have enough on hand for holidays and vacations.
• Although several generic versions of this medication are available, you should not switch from one brand to another without your doctor's prior assessment and approval. If you have your medication refilled and it looks different, be sure to consult with your pharmacist.
• Therapy with phenytoin may cause your gums to enlarge enough to cover your teeth. This can be minimized, at least partially, by frequent brushing and massaging of the gums with the rubber tip of a good toothbrush.
• Be sure to tell your doctor if you are pregnant. Birth defects have been reported more often in infants whose mothers have seizure disorders. It is unclear if the increased risk of birth defects is associated with the seizure disorders or with anticonvulsant medications such as phenytoin that are used to treat them. Discuss this with your doctor. Also tell your doctor if you are breast-feeding an infant. Phenytoin passes into breast milk.

---

pioglitazone

BRAND NAME (Manufacturer)
Actos (Eli Lilly)
TYPE OF DRUG
Oral antidiabetic
INGREDIENT
pioglitazone
DOSAGE FORM
Tablets (15 mg, 30 mg, and 45 mg)
STORAGE
Store at room temperature in a tightly closed container. Do not store in the bathroom or expose to moisture or extreme temperatures.

USES

Pioglitazone is used for the treatment of diabetes mellitus (sugar diabetes), which appears in adulthood and cannot be managed by control of diet alone. This type of diabetes is known as type 2 diabetes (sometimes called maturity-onset or non-insulin-dependent diabetes). Pioglitazone lowers blood sugar levels by increasing the actions of insulin already present in the bloodstream. Unlike other oral medications for diabetes, pioglitazone does not increase the release of insulin from the pancreas; it helps your body make better use of the insulin you have.

TREATMENT

This medication is usually taken once a day, with or without meals (unless your doctor directs you to do otherwise). It is best to take this medication at the same time each day.

It is important to try not to miss any doses of this medication. If you do miss a dose, take it as soon as you remember within the same day. Otherwise, do not take the missed dose at all; just return to your regular dosing schedule. Do not double the next dose. Tell your doctor if you feel any side effects from missing a dose of this drug.

SIDE EFFECTS

Minor. Drowsiness, headache, muscle soreness, runny or stuffy nose, sore throat, or upper respiratory infections. These side effects usually go away during treatment, as your body adjusts to the medicine.

Major. If any side effects are persistent or particularly bothersome, it is important to notify your doctor. IT IS ESPECIALLY IMPORTANT TO TELL YOUR DOCTOR about abdominal pain; anemia; dark urine; feelings of tiredness or fatigue; loss of appetite; nausea; shortness of breath; swelling of the legs, feet, hands, or arms; tooth problems; vomiting; weight gain; or yellowing of the skin or eyes.

INTERACTIONS

Pioglitazone interacts with a number of other medications:

1. Ketoconazole and itraconazole may reduce the body's ability to break down pioglitazone, resulting in a higher level of the medication in the bloodstream. This may increase the side effects of pioglitazone.

2. Although studies have not been done, medications such as erythromycin, clarithromycin, amiodarone, cimetidine, fluvoxamine, nefazodone, fluoxetine, delavirdine, protease inhibitors (amprenavir, indinavir, nelfinavir, ritonavir, and saquinavir), and fluconazole may increase the effects and toxicities of pioglitazone.

3. Grapefruit juice and grapefruit may interfere with the breakdown and removal of pioglitazone from the body. This may increase the side effects of pioglitazone. Do not consume grapefruit juice and grapefruit while taking pioglitazone.

4. The effects of oral contraceptives (birth control pills) may be reduced with pioglitazone. An additional or alternative form of contraception may be needed. Discuss this with your doctor.

5. Beta-blocking medications (atenolol, metoprolol, nadolol, pindolol, propranolol, and timolol) can mask the symptoms of low blood sugar, which can be dangerous.

BE SURE TO TELL YOUR DOCTOR about these or any other medications you may be taking.

WARNINGS

• It is important to tell your doctor if you have ever had any unusual or allergic reaction to pioglitazone, any other oral antidiabetics, or any other medication.

• It is also important to tell your doctor if you now have or ever had kidney disease, liver disease, swelling of the hands or feet, heart disease, heart failure, or type 1 (insulin-dependent) diabetes.

• Avoid drinking alcoholic beverages while taking this medication (unless directed otherwise by your doctor). Large amounts of alcohol can lower blood sugar to dangerously low levels and also damage your liver.

• Medications similar to pioglitazone have caused damage to the liver. Your doctor may want to perform regular blood tests before and during therapy with pioglitazone to make sure your liver is working properly. If liver problems develop while taking pioglitazone, the medication should be stopped.

• Follow the special diet that your doctor gave you. This is an important part of controlling your blood sugar and is necessary for this medicine to work properly.

• Be sure to tell your doctor or dentist that you are taking this medicine before having any kind of surgery or other medical or dental treatment.

• Test for sugar in your blood or urine as directed by your doctor. It is a convenient way to determine if your diabetes is being controlled by this medicine.

• When pioglitazone is taken alone, the chance of hypoglycemia is low. However, it may occur when this medication is taken with other oral antidiabetic medications or with insulin. Eat or drink something containing sugar right away if you experience any symptoms of low blood sugar (such as anxiety, chills, cold sweats, cool or pale skin, drowsiness, excessive hunger, headache, nausea, nervousness, rapid heartbeat, shakiness, or unusual tiredness or weakness). It is important that your family and friends know the symptoms of low blood sugar and what to do if they recognize any of these symptoms in you. Check with your doctor as soon as possible, even if these symptoms are corrected by the sugar. The blood-sugar-lowering effects of some medications can last for hours, and the symptoms may return during this period. Good sources of sugar are orange juice, corn syrup, honey, sugar cubes, and table sugar. You are at greatest risk of developing low blood sugar if you skip or delay meals, exercise more than usual, cannot eat because of nausea or vomiting, or drink large amounts of alcohol.

• Be sure to tell your doctor if you are pregnant. Studies have not yet been completed in humans and it is unknown if pioglitazone can cause birth defects. Also tell your doctor if you are breast-feeding an infant. The use of pioglitazone while breast-feeding is not recommended.

---

potassium chloride

BRAND NAMES (Manufacturers)
Kaochlor (Pharmacia)
Kaon (Pharmacia)
Kay Ciel (Berlex)
K-Dur (Key)
K-Lor (Abbott)
Klor-Con (Upsher-Smith)
Klorvess (Novartis)
Klotrix (Bristol-Myers Squibb)
K-Lyte/Cl (Bristol-Myers Squibb)
K-Tab (Abbott)
Micro-K (Ther-Rx)
Micro-K Extencaps (Ther-Rx)
potassium chloride (various manufacturers)
Slow-K (Novartis)
Ten-K (Novartis)

TYPE OF DRUG
Potassium replacement

INGREDIENT
potassium chloride

DOSAGE FORMS
Effervescent tablets (20 mEq, 25 mEq, and 50 mEq)
Sustained-release tablets (6.7 mEq, 8 mEq, 10 mEq, and 20 mEq)
Sustained-release capsules (8 mEq and 10 mEq)
Oral liquid (10 mEq, 20 mEq, 30 mEq, and 40 mEq per 15-mL spoonful; alcohol content varying from 0% to 5%)
Oral powder (20 mEq per packet)

STORAGE
Store at room temperature in a tightly closed container. Do not refrigerate.

USES

This medication is used to prevent or treat potassium deficiency, especially potassium deficiency that is caused by the use of diuretics (water pills).

TREATMENT

To avoid stomach irritation, take potassium chloride with food or immediately after a meal. Take this medication at the same time(s) each day.

Measure each dose of the liquid carefully with a specially designed 5-mL measuring spoon. An ordinary kitchen teaspoon is not accurate enough.

If you are taking the liquid, powder, or effervescent tablet, dilute each dose in at least four ounces (half cup) of cold water or juice. Be sure the medication has dissolved completely and has stopped fizzing before you drink it. Then sip it slowly. DO NOT use tomato juice to dissolve this medication (unless your doctor specifically directs you to do so). Tomato juice contains a great deal of sodium.

Swallow the sustained-release tablets and capsules whole. Chewing, crushing, or breaking these tablets or capsules destroys their sustained-release activity and possibly increases the side effects.

If you miss a dose of this medication, take the missed dose as soon as possible. However, if it is almost time for the next scheduled dose, do not take the missed dose at all; just return to your regular dosing schedule. Do not double the next dose of the medication.

SIDE EFFECTS

Minor. Diarrhea, nausea, stomach pains, or vomiting. These should disappear over time as your body makes an adjustment to the medicine.

Major. Tell your doctor about any side effects that are persistent or particularly bothersome. IT IS ESPECIALLY IMPORTANT TO TELL YOUR DOCTOR about anxiety; bloody or black, tarry stools; confusion; difficulty in breathing; numbness or tingling in the arms, legs, or feet; palpitations; severe abdominal pain; or unusual weakness.

INTERACTIONS

Potassium chloride can be expected to interact with several other types of medications:

1. The combination of potassium chloride with amiloride, spironolactone, salt substitutes, ACE inhibitors, or triamterene can lead to hyperkalemia (high levels of potassium in the bloodstream).

2. The combination of digoxin and high doses of potassium chloride can lead to heart problems.

3. Use of potassium chloride and nonsteroidal anti-inflammatory drugs, such as ibuprofen, may increase the risk of stomach ulcers.

Before starting to take potassium chloride, BE SURE TO TELL YOUR DOCTOR about any medications you are currently taking, especially any of those listed above.

WARNINGS

• Tell your doctor about unusual or allergic reactions you have had to any medications, especially to potassium.

• Before starting to take this medication, be sure to tell your doctor if you now have or ever had Addison's disease, dehydration, heart disease, heat cramps, hyperkalemia, intestinal blockage, kidney disease, or peptic ulcers.

• Ask your doctor about using a salt substitute instead of potassium chloride; salt substitutes are similar but less expensive and more convenient. However, salt substitutes should only be used with your doctor's approval. Too much potassium can be dangerous.

• If you are taking the sustained-release tablets and you find something that looks like a tablet in your stool, there is no reason for concern. The drug is contained in a wax core that is designed to release the medication slowly. This wax core is eliminated in the stool.

• Some of these products contain the color additive FD&C Yellow No. 5 (tartrazine), which can cause an allergic-type reaction (rash, shortness of breath, or fainting) in certain susceptible individuals.

• Be sure to tell your doctor if you are pregnant. Although this drug appears to be safe, extensive studies in pregnant women have not been conducted. Also tell your doctor if you are breast-feeding an infant.

pramipexole

BRAND NAME (Manufacturer)
Mirapex (Pharmacia)
TYPE OF DRUG
Antiparkinson's agent (dopamine-receptor agonist)
INGREDIENT
pramipexole
DOSAGE FORM
Tablets (0.125 mg, 0.25 mg, .50 mg, 1 mg, and 1.5 mg)
STORAGE
Store in a tightly closed container at room temperature, away from heat and direct sunlight. Do not refrigerate or freeze.

USES

This medication is used alone or in combination with levodopa/carbidopa therapy to treat Parkinson's disease. Although the exact mechanism of action is not known, this drug may work by stimulating dopamine receptors in the striatum portion of the brain.

TREATMENT

Take this medication exactly as prescribed by your doctor. This medication can be taken either on an empty stomach or with a meal. Taking this medication with food may help to reduce nausea. It is very important to follow your doctor's instructions for taking this medication, especially if you are taking levodopa/carbidopa with pramipexole. It is possible that as the pramipexole dose is gradually increased, the levodopa/carbidopa dose may be gradually decreased to avoid additional adverse effects. While using pramipexole, try to develop a set schedule for taking it.

If you miss a dose and remember within a few hours, take the missed dose and resume your regular dosing schedule. However, if it is almost time for your next scheduled dose, do not take the missed dose at all; just return to your regular dosing schedule. Do not double the next dose.

This medication does not cure Parkinson's disease, but it will help to control the condition as long as you continue to take it. It may be several weeks before you notice the full effect of this medication.

SIDE EFFECTS

Minor. Constipation, diarrhea, dry mouth, flushing, gas, headache, heartburn, tremor, and yawning. These side effects should diminish or disappear as your body adjusts to the medication.

To relieve constipation, increase the amount of fiber in your diet (fresh fruits and vegetables, salads, bran, and whole-grain breads) and exercise more (unless your doctor directs you to do otherwise.)

Plain, nonmedicated eyedrops (artificial tears) may help to relieve eye dryness that may be caused by this medication.

Chew sugarless gum or suck on ice chips or a piece of hard candy to relieve mouth or throat dryness.

Major. Tell your doctor about any side effects that are persistent or particularly bothersome. IT IS ESPECIALLY IMPORTANT TO TELL YOUR DOCTOR about abdominal pain, chest pain, clumsiness or unsteadiness, confusion, dizziness, drowsiness, fainting, falling, hallucinations, insomnia, loss of appetite, low blood pressure, muscle pain, nasal congestion, nausea, runny nose, sneezing, sore throat, swelling in the legs, trouble breathing, twisting or other unusual body movements, twitching, unusual tiredness or weakness, or worsening of Parkinson's.

To avoid dizziness when you stand, contract and relax the muscles of your legs for a few moments before rising. Do this by pushing one foot against the floor while lifting the other foot slightly, alternating feet so that you are "pumping" your legs in a pedaling motion that helps to get your blood circulating. If this medication makes you feel dizzy, sit or lie down for a while, get up slowly from a sitting or reclining position, and use caution on stairs.

INTERACTIONS

Pramipexole may interact with other types of medications:

1. Cimetidine, ranitidine, diltiazem, triamterene, verapamil, quinine, or quinidine may increase the blood level and adverse effects of pramipexole.

2. Phenothiazine tranquilizers, haloperidol, metoclopramide, or antipsychotics may antagonize (work against) the effects of this medication and reduce its effectiveness for treating Parkinson's disease.

3. Concurrent use of this medication with other central nervous system depressants (such as antihistamines, barbiturates, tranquilizers, tricyclic antidepressants, sleeping medications, muscle relaxants, and other pain medications) or with alcohol can cause extreme drowsiness.

Before starting to take this medication, BE SURE TO TELL YOUR DOCTOR about any medications you are taking, especially those listed above.

WARNINGS

• Tell your doctor about unusual or allergic reactions you have had to any medications, especially to ropinirole, pramipexole, or any other medications used for Parkinson's disease.

• Be sure to tell your doctor if you have ever had hallucinations, kidney disease, liver disease, low blood pressure, or eye disorders.

• Before having surgery or other medical or dental treatment, tell your doctor or dentist you are taking this medication.

• While taking this medication, your doctor will want to check your progress at regular visits, especially during the first few months of treatment. Your doctor will need to adjust your dosage gradually to find the best level of medicine for your Parkinson's disease.

• Do not stop taking this medication without first checking with your doctor. Your doctor may want to gradually reduce the amount of medicine you are taking over seven days before completely stopping the drug. Make sure that you have enough medicine on hand to last through vacations, holidays, and weekends.

• Do not drink any alcohol-containing beverages or take any over-the-counter (nonprescription) medications for weight control or for asthma, sinus, cough, cold, or allergy problems unless you first check with your pharmacist or doctor.

• This medication can cause dizziness, drowsiness, light-headedness, and decreased alertness. Use caution while driving a car or operating potentially dangerous machinery. Be especially careful when going up or down stairs or getting up from a sitting or lying position.

• Hallucinations may occur in some patients. This is more common in very elderly patients (older than 75 years).

• After you stop taking this medicine, your body may need time to adjust. The length of time this takes depends on the amount of medicine you were taking and how long you used it. During this time, it is important to tell your doctor if you experience confusion, fever, or extreme muscle stiffness.

• Be sure to tell your doctor if you are pregnant. This medication has been shown to cause birth defects in the offspring of animals that received large doses of it during pregnancy. Adequate studies have not been done in human pregnancy. Also tell your doctor if you are breast-feeding an infant. It is not known if this medication passes into breast milk.

pravastatin

BRAND NAME (Manufacturer)
Pravachol (Bristol-Myers Squibb)
TYPE OF DRUG
Antihyperlipidemic (lipid-lowering drug)
INGREDIENT
pravastatin
DOSAGE FORM
Tablets (10 mg, 20 mg, and 40 mg)
STORAGE
Store in a tightly closed container at room temperature, away from heat and direct sunlight.

USES

Pravastatin is used to treat hyperlipidemia (high blood fat levels). It may be prescribed with nondrug therapies such as diet control and exercise in an attempt to regulate lipid and cholesterol levels. Pravastatin chemically interferes with an enzyme in the body that is responsible for synthesizing cholesterol. This enzyme blockade decreases the LDL (low-density lipoprotein) type of cholesterol, which has been associated with coronary artery disease and atherosclerosis.

TREATMENT

Take this medication exactly as prescribed by your doctor. If you are to take pravastatin once a day, it is best to take the drug in the evening. If stomach upset occurs, pravastatin can be taken with meals or with a full glass of water.

While using this medication, try to develop a set schedule for taking it. If you miss a dose and remember within a few hours, take the missed dose and then simply resume your regular dosing schedule. If many hours have passed, however, skip the dose you missed, and take your next dose of the medication as scheduled. Do not double the next dose.

SIDE EFFECTS

Minor. Abdominal pain or cramps, constipation, diarrhea, gas, nausea, or stomach pain. These effects may be relieved by taking pravastatin with a meal. To relieve constipation, increase the amount of water and fiber in your diet (eat more fresh fruit, vegetables, bran, and whole-grain bread) and exercise more, unless your doctor directs you to do otherwise.
Major. Tell your doctor about any side effects that are persistent or particularly bothersome. IT IS ESPECIALLY IMPORTANT TO TELL YOUR DOCTOR about blurred vision (or any other visual changes or difficulties) or about muscle pain or tenderness, especially with malaise or fever.

INTERACTIONS

Pravastatin interacts with certain other medications:
1. Pravastatin may increase the effectiveness of oral anticoagulants (blood thinners, such as warfarin) and digoxin.
2. Because of the risk of severe myopathy (muscle weakness), the combined use of pravastatin with gemfibrozil or clofibrate should generally be avoided.
3. Cyclosporine, erythromycin, nicotinic acid, ketoconazole, itraconazole, fluconazole, clarithromycin, or niacin may increase the side effects of pravastatin and should be used with extreme caution.

BE SURE TO TELL YOUR DOCTOR about any medications you are currently taking, especially those listed above.

WARNINGS

• Tell your doctor about unusual or allergic reactions you have had to any medications, especially pravastatin or other agents to reduce cholesterol.
• Tell your doctor if you have ever had liver disease, heart disease, stroke, or disorders of the digestive tract.
• Patients taking another drug in this same class developed eye-related problems during treatment. It is advisable to have regular check-ups with your ophthalmologist, who should be informed that you are taking this drug.
• This drug should not be taken if you are pregnant. Serious side effects have been reported in the offspring of animals that received this drug during pregnancy. Also be sure to tell your doctor if you are breast-feeding an infant. This drug should not be used while breast-feeding.

---

prazosin

BRAND NAMES (Manufacturers)
Minipress (Pfizer)
prazosin (various manufacturers)
TYPE OF DRUG
Antihypertensive
INGREDIENT
prazosin
DOSAGE FORM
Capsules (1 mg, 2 mg, and 5 mg)
STORAGE
Store this medication at room temperature in a tightly closed, light-resistant container. Do not refrigerate.

USES

Prazosin is used to treat high blood pressure. It is a vasodilator that relaxes the muscle tissue of blood vessels, which in turn lowers blood pressure. This drug is also sometimes used to treat a condition in men called benign prostatic hyperplasia, or BPH.

TREATMENT

To avoid stomach irritation, you can take prazosin with food or with a full glass of water or milk. To become accustomed to taking this medication, try to take it at the same time(s) each day.

The first dose of this medication can cause fainting, so it is often recommended that the very first dose of the medication be taken at bedtime.

If you miss a dose of this medication, take the missed dose as soon as possible. However, if it is almost time for the next dose, do not take the missed dose at all; just return to your regular dosing schedule. Do not double the next dose of this medication.

Prazosin does not cure high blood pressure, but it will help to control the condition as long as you continue to take the medication.

The effects of this medication may not become apparent for two weeks.

SIDE EFFECTS

Minor. Abdominal pain, constipation, diarrhea, dizziness, drowsiness, dry mouth, frequent urination, headache, impotence, nasal congestion, nausea, nervousness, sweating, tiredness, vomiting, or weakness. These side effects should disappear as your body adjusts to the medication.

To relieve constipation, increase the amount of fiber in your diet (fresh fruits and vegetables, salads, bran, and whole-grain breads), exercise, and drink more water (unless your doctor directs you to do otherwise).

To relieve mouth dryness, chew sugarless gum or suck on ice chips or a piece of hard candy.

If you feel dizzy or light-headed, sit or lie down for a while; get up slowly from a sitting or reclining position; and be careful on stairs.

To avoid dizziness or light-headedness when you stand, contract and relax the muscles of your legs for a few moments before rising. Do this by pushing one foot against the floor while raising the other foot slightly, alternating feet so that you are "pumping" your legs in a pedaling motion.

Major. Tell your doctor about any side effects that are persistent or particularly bothersome. IT IS ESPECIALLY IMPORTANT TO TELL YOUR DOCTOR about blurred vision; chest pain; constant erection; depression; difficulty in breathing; difficulty in urinating; fainting; hallucinations; itching; loss of hair; nosebleeds; palpitations; rapid weight gain (three to five pounds within a week); rash; ringing in the ears; swelling of the feet, legs, or ankles; or tingling of the fingers or toes.

INTERACTIONS

Prazosin may interact with other types of medications:

1. The combination of prazosin and alcohol or prazosin and another antihypertensive agent can lead to a severe drop in blood pressure and fainting.

2. The severity and duration of the blood-pressure-lowering effects of the first dose of prazosin may be enhanced by a beta blocker.

BE SURE TO TELL YOUR DOCTOR about any medications you are currently taking, especially any of the medications that are listed above.

WARNINGS

- Tell your doctor about unusual or allergic reactions you have had to any medications, especially to doxazosin, prazosin, or terazosin.
- Before starting to take this medication, be sure to tell your doctor if you now have or ever had angina (chest pain) or kidney disease.
- Because initial therapy with this drug may cause dizziness or fainting, your doctor will probably start you on a low dosage and increase the dosage gradually.
- If this drug makes you dizzy or drowsy or blurs your vision, do not take part in any activity that requires alertness, such as driving an automobile or operating potentially dangerous machinery.
- To avoid dizziness or fainting while taking this drug, try not to stand for long periods of time, avoid drinking excessive amounts of alcohol, and try not to get overheated (avoid exercising strenuously in hot weather and taking hot baths, showers, or saunas).
- Before taking any over-the-counter (nonprescription) sinus, allergy, asthma, cough, cold, or diet preparations, check with your doctor or pharmacist. Some of these products can cause an increase in blood pressure.
- Do not stop taking this medication unless you first check with your doctor. If you stop taking this drug you may experience a rise in blood pressure. Your doctor may, therefore, want to decrease your dosage gradually.
- Be sure to tell your doctor if you are pregnant. Although this drug appears to be safe, there have been only limited studies in pregnant women. Also tell your doctor if you are breast-feeding an infant.

---

prednisolone (systemic)

BRAND NAMES (Manufacturers)

Delta-Cortef (Pharmacia)
Orasone (Solvay)
prednisolone (various manufacturers)
Prelone (Muro)

TYPE OF DRUG
Adrenocorticosteroid hormone
INGREDIENT
prednisolone
DOSAGE FORMS
Tablets (5 mg)
Oral syrup (5 mg per 5-mL and 15 mg per 5-mL spoonful, with 0.4 % to 5% alcohol)
STORAGE
Store at room temperature in a tightly closed container. Do not freeze.

USES

Your adrenal glands naturally produce certain cortisonelike chemicals. These chemicals are involved in various regulatory processes in the body (such as those involving fluid balance, temperature, and reaction to inflammation). Prednisolone belongs to a group of drugs known as adrenocorticosteroids (or cortisonelike medications). It is used to treat a variety of disorders, including endocrine and rheumatic disorders; asthma; blood diseases; certain cancers; eye disorders; gastrointestinal disturbances, such as ulcerative colitis; respiratory diseases; and inflammations, such as arthritis, dermatitis, and poison ivy. How this drug acts to relieve these disorders is not completely understood.

TREATMENT

To prevent stomach irritation, you can take prednisolone with food or milk.

Measure each dose of the oral syrup carefully with a specially designed 5-mL measuring spoon. An ordinary kitchen teaspoon is not accurate enough.

If you are taking only one dose of this medication each day, try to take it before 9:00 in the morning. Taking the medication in this way will mimic the body's normal production of this type of chemical.

It is important to try not to miss any doses of prednisolone. However, if you do miss a dose, follow these guidelines:

If you are taking this medication more than once a day, take the missed dose as soon as possible and return to your regular dosing schedule. If it is already time for the next dose, double it.

If you are taking this medication once a day, take the dose you missed as soon as possible, unless you don't remember until the next day. In that case, do not take the missed dose at all; just follow your regular dosing schedule. Do not double the next dose of the medication.

If you are taking this drug every other day, take the missed dose as soon as you remember it. If you missed the scheduled time by a whole day, take the dose when you remember, then skip a day before you take the next dose. Do not double the next dose of the medication.

If you miss more than one dose of prednisolone, CONTACT YOUR DOCTOR.

SIDE EFFECTS

Minor. Dizziness, false sense of well-being, increased appetite, indigestion, menstrual irregularities, nausea, reddening of the skin on the face, restlessness, sleep disorders, sweating, or weight gain. These effects should begin to disappear as your body adjusts to the medication.

Major. Tell your doctor about any side effects that are persistent or particularly bothersome. IT IS ESPECIALLY IMPORTANT TO TELL YOUR DOCTOR about abdominal enlargement; abdominal pain; acne or other skin problems; back or rib pain; bloody or black, tarry stools; blurred vision; convulsions; eye pain; fever and sore throat; growth impairment (in children); headaches; impaired healing of wounds; increased thirst and urination; mental depression; mood changes; muscle wasting or weakness; rapid weight gain (three to five pounds within a week); rash; shortness of breath; thinning of the skin; unusual bruising or bleeding; or unusual weakness.

INTERACTIONS

Prednisolone interacts with several other types of medications:

1. Alcohol, aspirin, and anti-inflammatory medications (such as diclofenac, diflunisal, etodolac, fenoprofen, flurbiprofen, ibuprofen, indomethacin, ketoprofen, meclofenamate, mefenamic acid, nabumetone, naproxen, oxaprozin, piroxicam, sulindac, and tolmetin) aggravate the stomach problems that commonly accompany use of this medication.

2. The dosage of oral anticoagulants (blood thinners, such as wafarin), oral antidiabetic drugs, or insulin may require adjustment when this medication is being taken.

3. The loss of potassium caused by prednisolone can lead to serious side effects in individuals taking digoxin.

4. Thiazide diuretics (water pills) can increase the potassium loss caused by this medication.

5. Phenobarbital, phenytoin, rifampin, or ephedrine can increase the elimination of prednisolone from the body, thereby decreasing its effectiveness.

6. Oral contraceptives (birth control pills) and estrogen-containing drugs may decrease the elimination of this drug from the body, which can lead to an increase in side effects.

7. Prednisolone can increase the elimination of aspirin and isoniazid, thereby decreasing the effectiveness of these two medications.

8. Cholestyramine, colestipol, and antacids can chemically bind this medication in the stomach and gastrointestinal tract, preventing its absorption.

BE SURE TO TELL YOUR DOCTOR about any medications you are currently taking, especially any listed above.

WARNINGS

• Tell your doctor about unusual or allergic reactions you have had to any medications, especially to prednisolone or other adrenocorticosteroids (such as betamethasone, cortisone, dexamethasone, hydrocortisone, methylprednisolone, prednisone, and triamcinolone).

• Tell your doctor if you now have or ever had bone disease, diabetes mellitus, emotional instability, glaucoma, fungal infections, heart disease, high blood pressure, high cholesterol levels, myasthenia gravis, peptic ulcers, osteoporosis, thyroid disease, tuberculosis, ulcerative colitis, kidney disease, or liver disease.

• To help avoid potassium loss while you are using this medication, you can take your dose of the drug with a glass of fresh or frozen orange juice, or eat a banana each day. The use of a salt substitute also helps prevent potassium loss. Check with your doctor, however, before making any dietary changes or using a salt substitute.

• If you are using this medication for longer than a week and you are subjected to stress (as a result of serious infections, injury, or surgery), you may need to have your dosage adjusted. Discuss this with your doctor.

• If you have been taking this drug for more than a week, do not stop taking it suddenly. If it is stopped abruptly, you may experience abdominal or back pain, dizziness, fainting, fever, muscle or joint pain, nausea, vomiting, shortness of breath, or extreme weakness. Your doctor may, therefore, want to reduce the dosage gradually. Never increase the dosage or take the drug for longer than the prescribed time unless you first consult your doctor.

• While you are taking this drug, you should not be vaccinated or immunized. Prednisolone decreases the effectiveness of vaccines and increases the risk of infection if a live-virus vaccine is administered.

• Before having surgery or any other medical or dental treatment, be sure to tell your doctor or dentist that you are taking this medication.

- Because this medication can cause glaucoma and cataracts with long-term use, your doctor may want you to have your eyes examined by an ophthalmologist periodically during treatment.
- If you are taking prednisolone for prolonged periods, you should wear or carry an identification card or notice stating that you are taking an adrenocorticosteroid.
- This medication can raise blood sugar levels in people who have diabetes. Blood sugar levels should be monitored carefully with blood or urine tests when this medication is being taken.
- Some of these products contain the color additive FD&C Yellow No. 5 (tartrazine), which can cause allergic-type reactions (shortness of breath, wheezing, rash, fainting) in certain susceptible individuals.
- Be sure to tell your doctor if you are pregnant. This drug crosses the placenta, and its safety in human pregnancy has not been established. Birth defects have been observed in the fetuses of animals who were given large doses of this type of drug during pregnancy. Also tell your doctor if you are breast-feeding an infant. Small amounts of this medication do pass into breast milk and may cause growth suppression or a decrease in natural adrenocorticosteroid-hormone production in the nursing infant.

---

prednisone (systemic)

BRAND NAMES (Manufacturers)
Deltasone (Upjohn)
Liquid Pred (Muro)
Meticorten (Schering)
Orasone (Solvay)
Panasol-S (Seatrace)
Prednicen-M (Central)
prednisone (various manufacturers)
TYPE OF DRUG
Adrenocorticosteroid hormone
INGREDIENT
prednisone
DOSAGE FORMS
Tablets (1 mg, 2.5 mg, 5 mg, 10 mg, 20 mg, and 50 mg)
Oral solution (5 mg per 5-mL spoonful, with 5% alcohol)
Oral intensol solution (5 mg per mL, with 30% alcohol)
STORAGE
Store at room temperature in a tightly closed container. Do not freeze.

USES

Your adrenal glands naturally produce certain cortisonelike chemicals. These chemicals are involved in various regulatory processes in the body (such as those involving fluid balance, temperature, and reaction to inflammation). Prednisone belongs to a group of drugs known as adrenocorticosteroids (or cortisonelike medications). It is used to treat a variety of disorders, including endocrine and rheumatic disorders; asthma; blood diseases; certain cancers; eye disorders; gastrointestinal disturbances, such as ulcerative colitis; respiratory diseases; and inflammations, such as arthritis, dermatitis, and poison ivy. How this drug acts to relieve these disorders is not completely understood.

TREATMENT

To prevent stomach irritation, you can take prednisone with food or milk.

If you are taking only one dose of this medication each day, try to take it before 9:00 in the morning.

Measure the oral solution carefully with the specially designed dropper (for the intensol solution) or a 5-mL measuring spoon. An ordinary kitchen teaspoon is not accurate enough for therapeutic purposes.

It is important to try not to miss any doses of prednisone. However, if you do miss a dose, follow these guidelines:

If you are taking this medication more than once a day, take the missed dose as soon as possible and return to your regular dosing schedule. If it is already time for the next dose, double it.

If you are taking this medication once a day, take the dose you missed as soon as possible. However, if you don't remember until the next day, do not take the missed dose at all; just follow your regular dosing schedule. Do not double the next dose of this medication.

If you are taking this drug every other day, take it when you remember. If you missed the scheduled dose by a whole day, take it; then skip a day before you take the next dose. Do not double the dose.

If you miss more than one dose of prednisone, CONTACT YOUR DOCTOR.

SIDE EFFECTS

Minor. Dizziness, false sense of well-being, increased appetite, increased sweating, indigestion, menstrual irregularities, nausea, reddening of the skin on the face, restlessness, sleep disorders, or weight gain. These side effects should disappear as your body adjusts to the medication.

Major. Tell your doctor about any side effects that are persistent or particularly bothersome. IT IS ESPECIALLY IMPORTANT TO TELL YOUR DOCTOR about abdominal enlargement; abdominal pain; acne or other skin problems; back or rib pain; bloody or black, tarry stools; blurred vision; convulsions; eye pain; fever and sore throat; growth impairment (in children); headaches; impaired healing of wounds; increased thirst and urination; mental depression; mood changes; muscle wasting or weakness; rapid weight gain (three to five pounds within a week); rash; shortness of breath; thinning of the skin; unusual bruising or bleeding; or unusual weakness.

INTERACTIONS

Prednisone interacts with several other types of medications:

1. Alcohol, aspirin, and anti-inflammatory medications (such as diclofenac, diflunisal, etodolac, fenoprofen, flurbiprofen, ibuprofen, indomethacin, ketoprofen, meclofenamate, mefenamic acid, nabumetone, naproxen, oxaprozin, piroxicam, sulindac, or tolmetin) aggravate the stomach problems that are common with this drug.

2. The dosage of oral anticoagulant medications (blood thinners, such as warfarin), oral antidiabetic drugs, or insulin may need to be adjusted when this medication is being taken.

3. The loss of potassium caused by prednisone can lead to serious side effects in individuals taking digoxin.

4. Thiazide diuretics (water pills) can increase the potassium loss caused by this medication.

5. Phenobarbital, phenytoin, rifampin, and ephedrine can increase the elimination of prednisone from the body, thereby decreasing its effectiveness.

6. Oral contraceptives (birth control pills) and estrogen-containing drugs may decrease the elimination of this drug from the body, which can lead to an increase in side effects.

7. Prednisone can increase the elimination of aspirin and isoniazid, decreasing the effectiveness of these two drugs.

8. Cholestyramine, colestipol, and antacids can chemically bind this medication in the stomach and gastrointestinal tract, preventing its absorption.

BE SURE TO TELL YOUR DOCTOR about any medications you are currently taking, especially any of those listed above.

WARNINGS

• Tell your doctor about unusual or allergic reactions you have had to any medications, especially to prednisone or other adrenocorticosteroids (such as betamethasone, cortisone, dexamethasone, hydrocortisone, methylprednisolone, prednisolone, and triamcinolone).
• Tell your doctor if you now have or ever had bone disease, diabetes mellitus, emotional instability, glaucoma, fungal infections, heart disease, high blood pressure, high cholesterol levels, kidney disease, liver disease, myasthenia gravis, peptic ulcers, osteoporosis, thyroid disease, tuberculosis, or ulcerative colitis.
• To help avoid potassium loss while using this drug, take your dose with a glass of fresh or frozen orange juice or eat a banana each day. The use of a salt substitute also helps prevent potassium loss. Check with your doctor before making any dietary changes.
• If you are using this medication for longer than a week, you may need to have your dosage adjusted if you are subjected to stress, such as serious infection, injury, or surgery.
• If you have been taking this drug for more than a week, do not stop taking it suddenly. If it is stopped abruptly, you may experience abdominal or back pain, dizziness, fainting, fever, muscle or joint pain, nausea, vomiting, shortness of breath, or extreme weakness. Your doctor may therefore want to reduce the dosage gradually. Never increase the dosage or take the drug for longer than the prescribed time unless you first consult your doctor.
• While you are taking this drug, you should not be vaccinated or immunized. This medication decreases the effectiveness of vaccines and can increase the risk of infection if a live-virus vaccine is administered.
• Before surgery or other medical or dental treatment, tell your doctor or dentist you are taking this drug.
• Because this drug can cause glaucoma and cataracts with long-term use, your doctor may want you to have your eyes examined by an ophthalmologist.
• If you are taking this medication for prolonged periods, you should wear or carry an identification card or notice stating that you are taking an adrenocorticosteroid.
• This drug can raise blood sugar levels in people with diabetes. Blood sugar should be monitored carefully with blood or urine tests when this drug is started.
• Be sure to tell your doctor if you are pregnant. Birth defects have been observed in the fetuses of animals that were given large doses of this drug during pregnancy. Also tell your doctor if you are breast-feeding an infant. It has been shown that small amounts of this drug pass into breast milk and may cause growth suppression or a decrease in natural adrenocorticosteroid production in the nursing infant.

---

prochlorperazine

BRAND NAMES (Manufacturers)
Compazine (GlaxoSmithKline)
Compazine Spansules (GlaxoSmithKline)
prochlorperazine maleate (various manufacturers)
TYPE OF DRUG
Phenothiazine tranquilizer and antiemetic
INGREDIENT
prochlorperazine
DOSAGE FORMS
Tablets (5 mg, 10 mg, and 25 mg)
Sustained-release capsules (10 mg and 15 mg)
Suppositories (2.5 mg, 5 mg, and 25 mg)
Oral solution (5 mg per 5-mL spoonful)

STORAGE

Store the tablet, capsule, and oral solution forms of this medication at room temperature in tightly closed, light-resistant containers. The suppositories may be stored in the refrigerator in tightly closed, light-resistant containers. Prochlorperazine should never be frozen.

If the oral solution turns slightly yellow, the medicine is still effective and can be used. However, if the solution changes color markedly or has particles floating in it, it should not be used; rather, it should be discarded down the sink.

USES

Prochlorperazine is prescribed to treat the symptoms of certain types of mental illness, such as the emotional symptoms of psychosis, the manic phase of manic-depressive illness, and severe behavioral problems in children. This medication is thought to relieve the symptoms of mental illness by blocking certain chemicals involved with nerve transmission in the brain. Prochlorperazine is also frequently used to treat nausea and vomiting (this medication works at the vomiting center in the brain to relieve nausea and vomiting).

TREATMENT

To avoid stomach irritation, you can take the tablet or capsule form of this medication with a meal or with a glass of water or milk (unless your doctor directs you to do otherwise).

Antacids and antidiarrheal medicines may decrease the absorption of this medication from the gastrointestinal tract. Therefore, at least one hour should separate doses of any of these medicines and prochlorperazine.

Swallow the sustained-release capsules whole; do not crush, break, or open them. Breaking these capsules releases the medication into your system all at once, destroying their sustained-release activity.

Measure the oral syrup carefully with a specially designed 5-mL measuring spoon. An ordinary kitchen teaspoon is not accurate enough.

To use the suppository form, remove the foil wrapper (if the suppository is too soft to insert, refrigerate it for half an hour or run cold water over it before removing the wrapper), and moisten the suppository with water. Lie on your left side with your right knee bent. Push the suppository into the rectum, pointed end first. Lie still for a few minutes. Try to avoid having a bowel movement for at least an hour (to give the medication time to be absorbed).

If you miss a dose of this medication, take the missed dose as soon as possible. However, if it is almost time for your next dose, do not take the missed dose at all; just return to your regular dosing schedule. Do not double the next dose (unless your doctor directs you to do so).

The full effects of this medication for the control of emotional or mental symptoms may not become apparent for two weeks after you start to take it.

SIDE EFFECTS

Minor. Blurred vision, constipation, decreased sweating, diarrhea, dizziness, drooling, drowsiness, dry mouth, fatigue, jitteriness, menstrual irregularities, nasal congestion, restlessness, vomiting, or weight gain. As your body adjusts to the medication, these side effects should disappear.

Prochlorperazine can also cause discoloration of the urine, turning it a red, pink, or red-brown color. This color change is a harmless side effect.

This medication can cause increased sensitivity to sunlight. It is important to avoid prolonged exposure to sunlight and sunlamps. Wear protective clothing and sunglasses, and use an effective sunscreen.

Chew sugarless gum or suck on ice chips or a piece of hard candy to reduce mouth dryness.

If you are constipated, increase the amount of fiber in your diet (fresh fruits and vegetables, salads, bran, and whole-grain breads), exercise, and drink more water (unless your doctor directs you to do otherwise).

To avoid dizziness or light-headedness when you stand, contract and relax the muscles of your legs for a few moments before rising. Do this by pushing one foot against the floor while raising the other foot slightly, alternating feet so that you are "pumping" your legs in a pedaling motion.

If you feel dizzy or light-headed, sit or lie down for a while; get up slowly from a sitting or reclining position; and be careful on stairs.

Major. Tell your doctor about any side effects that are persistent or particularly bothersome. IT IS ESPECIALLY IMPORTANT TO TELL YOUR DOCTOR about breast enlargement (in both sexes); chest pain; convulsions; darkened skin; difficulty in swallowing or breathing; fainting; fever; impotence; involuntary movements of the face, mouth, jaw, or tongue; palpitations; rash; sleep disorders; sore throat; tremors; uncoordinated movements; unusual bleeding; visual disturbances; or yellowing of the eyes or skin.

INTERACTIONS

Prochlorperazine interacts with several other types of medications:

1. This medication can cause drowsiness when combined with alcohol or central nervous system depressants (drugs that slow the activity of the brain and spinal cord), such as barbiturates, benzodiazepine tranquilizers, muscle relaxants, narcotics, and pain medications, or with tricyclic antidepressants.

2. Prochlorperazine can decrease the effectiveness of amphetamines, guanethidine, anticonvulsants, and levodopa.

3. The side effects of epinephrine, monoamine oxidase (MAO) inhibitors, propranolol, phenytoin, fluoxetine, fluvoxamine, paroxetine, sertraline, citalopram, escitalopram, and tricyclic antidepressants may be increased by this medication. At least 14 days should separate the use of this drug and the use of an MAO inhibitor.

4. Lithium may increase the side effects and decrease the effectiveness of this medication.

5. Thiazide diuretics can enhance the blood-pressure-lowering side effects of prochlorperazine.

6. The effects of prochlorperazine on the heart may be increased by disopyramide, erythromycin, probucol, procainamide, and quinidine.

Before starting to take prochlorperazine, BE SURE TO TELL YOUR DOCTOR about any medications you are currently taking, especially any of the medications listed above.

WARNINGS

• Tell your doctor about unusual reactions you have had to any drugs, especially to prochlorperazine or other phenothiazine tranquilizers (such as chlorpromazine, fluphenazine, mesoridazine, perphenazine, promazine, thioridazine, trifluoperazine, and triflupromazine) or to loxapine.

• Tell your doctor if you have a history of alcoholism or if you now have or ever had any blood disease, bone marrow disease, brain disease, breast cancer, blockage in the urinary or digestive tracts, drug-induced depression, epilepsy, high or low blood pressure, diabetes mellitus, glaucoma, heart or circulatory disease, liver disease, lung disease, Parkinson's disease, peptic ulcers, or an enlarged prostate gland.

• Tell your doctor about any recent exposure to a pesticide or an insecticide. Prochlorperazine may increase the side effects from the exposure.

• To prevent oversedation, avoid drinking alcoholic beverages while taking this medication.

• If this medication makes you dizzy or drowsy, do not take part in any activity that requires alertness, such as driving a car or operating potentially dangerous machinery.

• Before having surgery or any other medical or dental treatment, be sure to tell your doctor or dentist that you are taking this medication.
• Some of the side effects caused by this drug can be prevented by taking an antiparkinsonism drug. Discuss this with your doctor.
• This medication can decrease sweating and heat release from the body. You should try not to get overheated (avoid exercising strenuously in hot weather, and avoid taking hot baths, showers, or saunas).
• Do not stop taking prochlorperazine suddenly if you have been taking it for a prolonged period. If the medication is stopped abruptly, you may experience nausea, vomiting, stomach upset, headache, increased heart rate, insomnia, tremors, or a worsening of your condition. Your doctor may therefore want to reduce your dosage gradually to avoid these effects of abrupt withdrawal.
• If you are planning to have a myelogram, or any other procedure in which dye will be injected into your spinal cord, be sure to tell your doctor ahead of time that you are taking this medication.
• Avoid spilling the oral solution on your skin; it may cause redness and irritation.
• While taking this medication, do not take any over-the-counter (nonprescription) medications for weight control or for cough, cold, allergy, asthma, or sinus problems unless you first check with your doctor. The combination of these medications with prochlorperazine may cause an increase in blood pressure.
• Be sure to tell your doctor if you are pregnant. Although there have been reports of safe use of this medication during pregnancy, there have also been reports of liver disease and tremors in newborn infants whose mothers received this type of medication close to the end of their pregnancy. In addition, be sure to inform your doctor if you are breast-feeding an infant.

---

promethazine

BRAND NAMES (Manufacturers)
Phenergan (Wyeth-Ayerst)
promethazine (various manufacturers)
TYPE OF DRUG
Antihistamine and antiemetic
INGREDIENT
promethazine
DOSAGE FORMS
Tablets (12.5 mg, 25 mg, and 50 mg)
Oral syrup (6.25 mg per 5-mL spoonful, with 7% alcohol; 25 mg per 5-mL spoonful, with 1.5% alcohol)
Rectal suppositories (12.5 mg, 25 mg, and 50 mg)
STORAGE
Store the tablet and oral syrup forms of this medication at room temperature in tightly closed, light-resistant containers. Do not freeze. Keep the suppositories in the refrigerator in a tightly closed container.

USES

Promethazine, a phenothiazine derivative, is prescribed for a wide range of conditions. It belongs to a group of drugs known as antihistamines, which block the action of histamine, a chemical that is released by the body during an allergic reaction. It is therefore used to treat or prevent symptoms of allergy or hay fever. Promethazine also (1) works at the vomiting center in the brain and can be used for the prevention or treatment of nausea and vomiting; (2) is a central nervous system (brain and spinal cord) depressant, which produces light sleep or mild sedation; and (3) prevents motion sickness.

TREATMENT

To avoid stomach irritation, you can take the tablet or oral syrup with a meal or a glass of water or milk (unless your doctor directs otherwise).

Measure the oral syrup carefully with a specially designed 5-mL measuring spoon. An ordinary kitchen teaspoon is not accurate enough.

To use the suppository, remove the foil wrapper (if the suppository is too soft to insert, refrigerate it for half an hour or run cold water over it before removing the wrapper), and moisten the suppository with water. Lie on your left side with your right knee bent. Push the suppository into the rectum, pointed end first. Lie still for a few minutes. Try to avoid having a bowel movement for at least an hour (to give the medication time to be absorbed).

If you are taking this medication regularly and miss a dose, take the missed dose as soon as possible. However, if it is almost time for the next dose, do not take the missed dose at all; just return to your regular schedule. Do not double the next dose.

SIDE EFFECTS

Minor. Blurred vision, diarrhea, dizziness, drowsiness, dry mouth, light-headedness, nausea, or vomiting. These side effects should diminish or disappear as your body adjusts to this drug.

This medication can cause increased sensitivity to sunlight. It is important to avoid prolonged exposure to sunlight and sunlamps. Wear protective clothing and sunglasses, and use an effective sunscreen.

To reduce mouth dryness, chew sugarless gum or suck on ice chips or hard candy.

To avoid dizziness or light-headedness when you stand, contract and relax the muscles of your legs for a few moments before rising. Do this by alternately pushing one foot against the floor while raising the other foot slightly, so that you are "pumping" your legs in a pedaling motion.

If you feel dizzy or light-headed, sit or lie down for a while; get up slowly from a sitting or reclining position; and be careful on stairs.

Major. Tell your doctor about any side effects that are persistent or particularly bothersome. IT IS ESPECIALLY IMPORTANT TO TELL YOUR DOCTOR about confusion; disorientation; involuntary movements of the face, mouth, jaw, or tongue; rash; uncoordinated movements; unusual bleeding or bruising; or yellowing of the eyes or skin.

INTERACTIONS

This medication will interact with several other types of medications:

1. Promethazine can cause extreme drowsiness when combined with alcohol or other central nervous system depressants (drugs that slow the activity of the brain and spinal cord), such as barbiturates, benzodiazepine tranquilizers, muscle relaxants, narcotics, and pain medications, or with tricyclic antidepressants.

2. Promethazine can decrease the effectiveness of amphetamines, guanethidine, anticonvulsants, and levodopa.

3. The side effects of epinephrine, monoamine oxidase (MAO) inhibitors, propranolol, fluoxetine, fluvoxamine, paroxetine, citalopram, escitalopram, and tricyclic antidepressants may be increased by this medication. At least 14 days should separate the use of this medication and the use of an MAO inhibitor.

4. The effects of promethazine on the heart may be increased by disopyramide, erythromycin, pimozide, probucol, procainamide, or quinidine.

BE SURE TO TELL YOUR DOCTOR about any medications you are currently taking, especially any of the medications that are listed above.

WARNINGS

• Tell your doctor about any unusual or allergic reactions you have had to any medications, especially to promethazine or any chemically related phenothiazine drug

(chlorpromazine, fluphenazine, mesoridazine, perphenazine, prochlorperazine, promazine, thioridazine, trifluoperazine, triflupromazine).
• Before starting treatment with promethazine, tell your doctor if you now have or ever had asthma, blockage of the urinary or digestive tract, diabetes mellitus, enlarged prostate gland, epilepsy, glaucoma, heart disease, liver disease, peptic ulcers, or sleep apnea.
• To prevent oversedation, avoid drinking alcoholic beverages while taking this medication.
• If this medication makes you dizzy or drowsy, do not take part in any activity that requires alertness, such as driving a car or operating potentially dangerous machinery.
• Prior to having surgery or any other medical or dental treatment, be sure to tell your doctor or dentist that you are taking this medication.
• Be sure to tell your doctor if you are pregnant. Small amounts of this medication cross the placenta. Although there are reports of safe use of this drug during pregnancy, there are also reports of liver disease and tremors in newborns whose mothers received this medication close to term. Also tell your doctor if you are breast-feeding. Small amounts of this medication pass into breast milk and may cause unwanted effects in nursing infants, such as sudden infant death syndrome (SIDS) or sleep apnea.

---

propoxyphene

BRAND NAMES (Manufacturers)
Darvon (Lilly)
Darvon-N (Lilly)
Dolene (Wyeth)
propoxyphene hydrochloride (various manufacturers)
TYPE OF DRUG
Analgesic
INGREDIENT
propoxyphene
DOSAGE FORMS
Capsules (65 mg)
Tablets (100 mg)
Oral suspension (10 mg per mL)
STORAGE
Store at room temperature in tightly closed containers. Do not refrigerate or freeze.

USES

Propoxyphene is a narcotic analgesic that acts on the central nervous system (brain and spinal cord) to relieve mild to moderate pain.

TREATMENT

To avoid stomach upset, you can take propoxyphene with food or milk.

Shake the suspension well just before measuring each dose to distribute the ingredients evenly and equalize the doses. The contents tend to settle on the bottom of the bottle. Measure each dose carefully with a specially designed 5-mL measuring spoon. An ordinary kitchen teaspoon is not accurate enough.

This medication works best if taken at the first sign of pain. Do not wait for the pain to become severe.

If your doctor has prescribed this medication to be taken on a regular schedule and you miss a dose, take the missed dose as soon as possible. However, if it is almost time for your next dose, do not take the missed dose at all; just return to your regular dosing schedule. Do not double the next dose.

SIDE EFFECTS

Minor. Blurred vision, constipation, dizziness, drowsiness, indigestion, light-headedness, nausea, nervousness, restlessness, vomiting, or weakness. As your body adjusts to the medication, these side effects should disappear.

If you are constipated, increase the amount of fiber in your diet (fresh fruits and vegetables, salads, bran, and whole-grain breads), exercise, and drink more water (unless your doctor directs you to do otherwise).

If you feel dizzy or light-headed, sit or lie down for a while; get up slowly; and be careful on stairs.

Major. Tell your doctor about any troublesome side effects. IT IS ESPECIALLY IMPORTANT TO TELL YOUR DOCTOR about confusion, convulsions, darkening of the urine, depression, difficulty in breathing, hallucinations, palpitations, ringing in the ears, skin rash, yellowing of the eyes or skin, or yellow stools.

INTERACTIONS

Propoxyphene can interact with several types of drugs:

1. Concurrent use of propoxyphene with other central nervous system depressants (such as antihistamines, barbiturates, tranquilizers, sleeping medications, muscle relaxants, and other pain medications) or with tricyclic antidepressants can cause extreme drowsiness.

2. Propoxyphene can increase carbamazepine blood levels, which in turn can result in greater side effects.

3. A monoamine oxidase (MAO) inhibitor taken within 14 days of this medication can lead to unpredictable and severe side effects.

4. Propoxyphene also interacts with alcohol, increasing its intoxicating effects. You should therefore avoid drinking alcoholic beverages while taking this medicine.

5. Naltrexone will block the action of propoxyphene and may cause serious side effects in patients addicted to propoxyphene.

TELL YOUR DOCTOR about any medications you are currently taking, especially any of those listed above.

WARNINGS

• Tell your doctor about unusual or allergic reactions you have had to any medications, especially to propoxyphene or to other narcotic analgesics (such as codeine, hydrocodone, hydromorphone, meperidine, methadone, morphine, or oxycodone).

• Tell your doctor if you now have or ever had acute abdominal conditions, asthma, brain disease, colitis, epilepsy, gallstones or gallbladder disease, head injuries, heart disease, kidney disease, liver disease, lung disease, mental illness, emotional disorders, enlarged prostate gland, thyroid disease, or urethral stricture.

• If this drug makes you dizzy or drowsy, do not take part in any activity that requires alertness, such as driving a car or operating potentially dangerous machinery.

• Before having surgery or any other medical or dental treatment, be sure to tell your doctor or dentist that you are taking this medication.

• Propoxyphene has the potential for abuse and must be used with caution. Usually you should not take it on a regular schedule for longer than ten days (unless your doctor directs you to do so). Tolerance develops quickly; do not increase the dosage or stop taking the drug abruptly, unless you first consult your doctor. If you have been taking large amounts of this medication or have been taking it for long periods of time, you may experience a withdrawal reaction (muscle aches, diarrhea, gooseflesh, runny nose, nausea, vomiting, shivering, trembling, stomach cramps, sleep disorders, irritability, weakness, excessive yawning, or sweating) when you stop taking it. Your doctor may therefore want to reduce the dosage gradually.

• Be sure to tell your doctor if you are pregnant. The effects of taking this medication during the early stages of pregnancy have not been thoroughly studied in humans.

However, regular use of propoxyphene in large doses during the later stages of pregnancy can result in addiction of the fetus, leading to withdrawal symptoms (irritability, excessive crying, tremors, fever, vomiting, diarrhea, sneezing, or excessive yawning) in the newborn. Also tell your doctor if you are breast-feeding an infant. Small amounts of this medication may pass into breast milk and cause excessive drowsiness in the nursing infant.

---

propranolol

BRAND NAMES (Manufacturers)
Inderal (Wyeth-Ayerst)
Inderal LA (Wyeth-Ayerst)
propranolol (various manufacturers)
TYPE OF DRUG
Beta-adrenergic blocking agent
INGREDIENT
propranolol
DOSAGE FORMS
Tablets (10 mg, 20 mg, 40 mg, 60 mg, 80 mg, and 90 mg)
Extended-release capsules (60 mg, 80 mg, 120 mg, and 160 mg)
Oral solution (20 mg and 40 mg per 5-mL spoonful)
Oral concentrated solution (80 mg per mL)
STORAGE
Store at room temperature in a tightly closed, light-resistant container. The solutions should never be frozen.

USES

Propranolol is used to treat high blood pressure, angina pectoris (chest pain), and irregular heartbeats. It is also useful in preventing migraine headaches and controlling tremors. Propranolol belongs to a group of medicines known as beta-adrenergic blocking agents or, more commonly, beta blockers. These drugs work by controlling nerve impulses along certain nerve pathways.

TREATMENT

Propranolol can be taken with a glass of water, with meals, immediately following meals, or on an empty stomach (depending on your doctor's instructions). Try to take the medication at the same time(s) each day.

Swallow the extended-release capsules whole. Do not chew or crush them. Breaking the capsule releases the medication all at once, defeating the purpose of extended-release capsules.

Measure the oral solution with a specially designed 5-mL measuring spoon or dropper. An ordinary kitchen teaspoon is not accurate enough.

Mix the oral concentrated solution in four ounces (half cup) of water, juice, or soda before drinking. Then refill the cup with more of the liquid and drink it to ensure that you have taken the entire dose. This form of the medication may also be mixed with applesauce or pudding.

It is important to remember that propranolol does not cure high blood pressure, but it will help control the condition as long as you continue to take it.

Try not to miss any doses of this medicine. If you do miss a dose, take the missed dose as soon as possible after you remember. However, if it is within eight hours (if you are taking this medicine only once a day) or within four hours (if you are taking this medicine more than once a day) of your next scheduled dose, do not take the missed dose at all; just return to your regular dosing schedule. Do not double the next dose of the medication.

SIDE EFFECTS

Minor. Anxiety; constipation; decreased sexual ability; diarrhea; difficulty in sleeping; drowsiness; dryness of the eyes, mouth, and skin; headache; nausea; nervousness; stomach discomfort; tiredness; or weakness. These side effects should disappear with time.

To relieve constipation, increase the amount of fiber in your diet (fresh fruits and vegetables, salads, bran, and whole-grain breads) and drink more water (unless your doctor directs you to do otherwise).

If you are extra-sensitive to the cold, be sure to dress warmly during cold weather.

Plain, nonmedicated eyedrops (sometimes called artificial tears) may help to relieve eye dryness.

Chewing sugarless gum or sucking on ice chips or a piece of hard candy can help to relieve mouth and throat dryness.

Major. Tell your doctor about any side effects you experience that are persistent or particularly bothersome. IT IS ESPECIALLY IMPORTANT TO TELL YOUR DOCTOR about breathing difficulty or wheezing, cold hands or feet (due to decreased blood circulation to skin, fingers, and toes), confusion, depression, dizziness, hair loss, hallucinations, light-headedness, nightmares, numbness or tingling of the fingers or toes, rapid weight gain (three to five pounds within a week), reduced alertness, skin rash, sore throat and fever, swelling, or unusual bleeding or bruising.

INTERACTIONS

Propranolol interacts with a number of other types of medications:

1. Indomethacin, aspirin, or other salicylates lessen the blood-pressure-lowering effects of beta blockers.

2. Concurrent use of beta blockers and calcium channel blockers (diltiazem, nifedipine, or verapamil) or disopyramide can lead to heart failure or very low blood pressure.

3. Cimetidine and oral contraceptives (birth control pills) can increase the blood concentrations of propranolol, which can result in greater side effects.

4. Side effects may also be increased when beta blockers are taken with clonidine, digoxin, epinephrine, phenylephrine, phenylpropanolamine, phenothiazine tranquilizers, prazosin, reserpine, or monoamine oxidase (MAO) inhibitors. At least 14 days should separate the use of a beta blocker and an MAO inhibitor.

5. Barbiturates, alcohol, and rifampin can increase the breakdown of propranolol in the body, which can lead to a decrease in its effectiveness.

6. When used concurrently, beta blockers may antagonize (work against) the effects of theophylline, aminophylline, albuterol, isoproterenol, metaproterenol, salmeterol, formoterol, or terbutaline.

7. Beta blockers can also interact with insulin or oral antidiabetic agents, raising or lowering blood sugar levels or masking the symptoms of low blood sugar.

8. The action of beta blockers may be excessively increased if they are used with chlorpromazine, furosemide, or hydralazine.

BE SURE TO TELL YOUR DOCTOR about any medications you are currently taking, especially any of those listed above.

WARNINGS

• Before starting to take this medication, it is important to tell your doctor if you have ever had unusual or allergic reactions to any beta blocker (acebutolol, atenolol, betaxolol, carteolol, esmolol, labetalol, metoprolol, nadolol, penbutolol, pindolol, propranolol, or timolol).

• Tell your doctor if you now have or if you have ever had allergies, asthma, hay fever, eczema, slow heartbeat, bronchitis, diabetes mellitus, emphysema, heart or blood-vessel disease, kidney disease, liver disease, thyroid disease, or poor circulation in the fingers or toes.

• You may want to check your pulse while taking this medication. If your pulse is much slower than your usual rate (or if it is less than 50 beats per minute), check with your doctor. A pulse rate that is too slow may cause circulation problems.
• This medicine may affect your body's response to exercise. Make sure you ask your doctor what an appropriate amount of exercise would be for you, taking into account your medical condition.
• It is important that you do not stop taking this medicine without first checking with your doctor. Some conditions may become worse when the medicine is stopped suddenly, and the danger of a heart attack is increased in some patients. Your doctor may want you to gradually reduce the amount of medicine you take before stopping completely. Make sure that you have enough medicine on hand to last through vacations, holidays, and weekends.
• Before having surgery or any other medical or dental treatment, tell your physician or dentist that you are taking this medicine. Often, this medication will be discontinued 48 hours prior to any major surgery.
• Propranolol can cause drowsiness, light-headedness, and decreased alertness. Use caution while driving a car or operating dangerous machinery. Be especially careful on stairs.
• While taking this medicine, do not use any over-the-counter (nonprescription) allergy, asthma, cough, cold, sinus, or diet preparations without first checking with your pharmacist or doctor. The combination of these medicines with a beta blocker can result in high blood pressure.
• Be sure to tell your doctor if you are pregnant. Animal studies have shown that some beta blockers can cause problems in pregnancy when used at very high doses. Adequate studies have not been done in humans, but there has been some association between use of beta blockers during pregnancy and low birth weight, as well as breathing problems and slow heart rate in newborn infants. However, other reports have shown no effects in newborn infants. Also tell your doctor if you are breast-feeding an infant. Although this medicine has not been shown to cause problems in breast-fed infants, some of the medicine may pass into breast milk, so caution is warranted.

---

quetiapine

BRAND NAME (Manufacturer)
Seroquel (Zeneca)
TYPE OF DRUG
Antipsychotic
INGREDIENT
quetiapine
DOSAGE FORM
Tablets (25 mg, 100 mg, and 200 mg)
STORAGE
Store this medication at room temperature in a tightly closed container. Do not expose to excess heat.

USES

Quetiapine is used in the treatment of schizophrenia in patients who have not been helped by or who could not tolerate other medications. It is not known exactly how this medication works to relieve the symptoms of schizophrenia, but it is thought to affect certain chemicals in the brain.

TREATMENT

Take this medication exactly as prescribed by your doctor. Never increase the dose unless your doctor tells you to do so. To lessen stomach irritation, this medication may be taken with food (unless your doctor tells you to do otherwise). The effects of this medication may not become apparent for several days.

If you miss a dose of this medication, take it as soon as you remember. However, if it is almost time for your next dose, do not take the missed dose at all; just return to your regular dosing schedule. Do not double the next dose.

SIDE EFFECTS

Minor. Constipation; dizziness; drowsiness; dry mouth; fast heartbeat; increased sweating; indigestion; light-headedness, especially when getting up from sitting or lying down; sore throat; stuffy or runny nose; or weight gain. As your body adjusts to the medication, these side effects should diminish or disappear.

Dry mouth can be relieved by chewing sugarless gum or sucking on hard candy.

If you feel dizzy or light-headed, sit or lie down for a while; get up slowly from a sitting or reclining position; and be careful on stairs.

To avoid dizziness or light-headedness when you stand, contract and relax the muscles of your legs for a few moments before rising. Do this by pressing one foot against the floor while raising the other foot slightly, alternating feet so that you are "pumping" your legs in a pedaling motion.

To relieve constipation, increase the amount of fiber in your diet (fresh fruits and vegetables, salads, bran, and whole-grain breads), exercise, and drink more water (unless your doctor directs you to do otherwise).

Major. Tell your doctor about any side effects that are persistent or particularly bothersome. IT IS ESPECIALLY IMPORTANT TO TELL YOUR DOCTOR about breast changes (in women), changes in menstruation, chills, difficulty speaking or breathing, dryness of the skin, fast breathing, fever, increased sweating, irregular heartbeat, loss of appetitie, loss of balance, muscle aches, muscle stiffness, shuffling walk, seizures, skin rash, slowness of movements, sore throat, stiffness of the arms or legs, swelling of the feet or ankles, trembling or shaking, or weight gain.

INTERACTIONS

Quetiapine may interact with a number of medications.

1. Extreme drowsiness may occur when this medicine is taken with central nervous system depressants (alcohol, antihistamines, barbiturates, benzodiazepine tranquilizers, muscle relaxants, narcotics, pain medications, phenothiazine tranquilizers, and medications to induce sleep) or with antidepressants.

2. Quetiapine may block the effects of levodopa and other drugs used to treat Parkinson's disease.

3. Erythromycin, fluconazole, itraconazole, diltiazem, nefazodone, ketoconazole, verapamil, and clarithromycin may increase some of the side effects of quetiapine.

4. Quetiapine may increase the blood-pressure-lowering effects of drugs used to treat high blood pressure, such as beta blockers, ACE inhibitors, calcium channel blockers, or diuretics (water pills).

WARNINGS

• Be sure to tell your doctor about any unusual or allergic reactions you have had to medications, especially to quetiapine or other drugs used to treat schizophrenia.

• Tell your doctor if you now have or have ever had a blood disease, breast cancer, heart disease, irregular heartbeats, stroke, low blood pressure, glaucoma, stomach or intestinal problems, enlarged prostate, depression, circulatory disease, liver or kidney disease, seizures, or Alzheimer's disease. Also tell your doctor if you have ever abused drugs or alcohol.

• This medication may cause changes in the lenses of your eyes or cataracts. Your doctor may want you to have regular eye examinations by an ophthalmologist. You should discuss this with your doctor.

• Before having surgery or any medical or dental treatment, be sure to tell your doctor or dentist that you are taking this medication.
• Quetiapine may cause dizziness or light-headedness. Your ability to perform tasks that require alertness, such as driving a car or operating heavy machinery, may be decreased. Take appropriate caution.
• This medication may affect your body's ability to regulate temperature. Be careful when doing activities that may raise your body's temperature, such as strenuous exercise. If you do exercise, make sure you drink plenty of water to avoid becoming overheated or dehydrated. You should also avoid exposure to extreme heat.
• Be sure to tell your doctor if you are pregnant. It is not known if quetiapine is safe to use during pregnancy. Also tell your doctor if you are breast-feeding an infant. Quetiapine passes into breast milk. You should discuss with your doctor the risks and benefits of using this medication when you are pregnant or are breast-feeding an infant.

---

quinapril

BRAND NAME (Manufacturer)
Accupril (Parke-Davis)
TYPE OF DRUG
Antihypertensive
INGREDIENT
quinapril
DOSAGE FORM
Tablets (5 mg, 10 mg, 20 mg, and 40 mg)
STORAGE
Store this medication at room temperature in a tightly closed container. Do not refrigerate.

USES

Quinapril is used to treat high blood pressure. It is a vasodilator (it widens the blood vessels) that acts by blocking the production of chemicals that may be responsible for constricting or narrowing the blood vessels. Quinapril is in a class of drugs called the angiotensin-converting enzyme (ACE) inhibitors.

TREATMENT

Quinapril can be taken either on an empty stomach or, if the drug causes stomach irritation, with food. To avoid a decrease in the absorption of quinapril, food that has a high fat content should be avoided. In order to become accustomed to taking this medication, you should take quinapril at the same time(s) every day.

It may be several weeks before you notice the full effects of this medication.

If you miss a dose of quinapril, take the missed dose as soon as possible. However, if it is almost time for the next dose, do not take the missed dose at all; just wait until the next scheduled dose. Do not double the next dose.

Quinapril does not cure high blood pressure, but it will help to control the condition for as long as you continue to take the medication.

SIDE EFFECTS

Minor. Abdominal pain, constipation, cough, diarrhea, dizziness, dry mouth, fatigue, flushing, headache, insomnia, loss of appetite, loss of taste perception, nausea, or vomiting. These side effects should disappear as your body adjusts to the drug.

Quinapril can increase your sensitivity to sunlight. It is important to avoid prolonged exposure to sunlight and sunlamps. Wear protective clothing and sunglasses, and use an effective sunscreen.

To relieve constipation, increase the amount of fiber in your diet (fresh fruits and vegetables, salads, bran, and whole-grain breads), exercise, and drink more water (unless your doctor directs you to do otherwise).

To relieve mouth dryness, suck on ice chips or a piece of hard candy, or chew sugarless gum.

To avoid dizziness or light-headedness when you stand, contract and relax the muscles of your legs for a few moments before rising. Do this by pushing one foot against the floor while raising the other foot slightly, alternating feet so that you are "pumping" your legs. If you feel dizzy or light-headed, sit or lie down for a while; get up slowly from a sitting or reclining position; and be careful on stairs.

Major. Tell your doctor about any side effects that are persistent or especially bothersome. IT IS ESPECIALLY IMPORTANT TO TELL YOUR DOCTOR about chest pains; chills; difficult or painful urination; fever; heart palpitations; itching; mouth sores; prolonged vomiting or diarrhea; skin rash; sore throat; swelling of the face, hands, or feet; tingling in the fingers or toes; unusual bleeding or bruising; or yellowing of the eyes or skin.

INTERACTIONS

Quinapril interacts with several other types of medications:

1. Diuretics (water pills) and other antihypertensive medications can cause an excessive drop in blood pressure when combined with quinapril (especially with your first dose of it).

2. The combination of quinapril with spironolactone, triamterene, amiloride, potassium supplements, or salt substitutes can lead to hyperkalemia (dangerously high levels of potassium in the bloodstream).

3. Antineoplastic agents (anticancer medications) or chloramphenicol can increase the bone-marrow side effects of quinapril.

4. Concurrent use of quinapril and the antigout medication allopurinol can increase the risk of developing an allergic reaction.

5. Indomethacin and other nonsteroidal anti-inflammatory drugs (NSAIDs) can decrease the blood-pressure-lowering effects of quinapril.

6. Quinapril can delay the body's elimination of lithium. Concurrent use of quinapril and lithium may therefore cause lithium toxicity.

7. Quinapril may reduce the amount of tetracycline absorbed by the body, possibly because of quinapril's high magnesium content; a similar effect may occur with other medications that interact with magnesium.

8. Antacids may decrease the absorption of quinapril. Take quinapril either one hour before or two hours after taking antacids.

Before starting quinapril, BE SURE TO TELL YOUR DOCTOR about any drugs you are taking, especially any of those listed above.

WARNINGS

• Tell your doctor about any unusual or allergic reactions you have had to medications, especially to benazepril, captopril, enalapril, fosinopril, lisinopril, moexipril, quinapril, or ramipril.

• Tell your doctor if you now have or if you have ever had aortic stenosis, blood disorders, kidney disease, a kidney transplant, liver disease, systemic lupus erythematosus, a heart attack, or a stroke.

• Excessive perspiration, dehydration, or prolonged vomiting or diarrhea can lead to an excessive drop in blood pressure while you are taking this medication. Contact your doctor if you have any of these symptoms.

• Before having surgery or other medical or dental treatment, tell your doctor or dentist that you are taking this drug.

• The first few doses of this medication may cause dizziness. Try to avoid any sudden changes in posture. In addition, you should avoid driving an automobile or operating any potentially dangerous equipment during this initial stage of treatment with quinapril.

• If you have high blood pressure, do not take any over-the-counter (nonprescription) medications for weight control or for allergy, asthma, sinus, cough, or cold problems unless you first check with your doctor.

• Do not stop taking this medication unless you first consult your doctor. Stopping this drug abruptly may lead to a rise in blood pressure.

• A persistent dry cough may occur and usually does not subside unless the medication is stopped. If this effect is bothersome, consult your doctor.

• Be sure to tell your doctor if you are pregnant. Quinapril may cause birth defects in the fetus if taken during the second or third trimester of pregnancy. Also tell your doctor if you are breast-feeding an infant. Quinapril may pass into breast milk. The effects of this drug on the nursing infant have not been determined.

rabeprazole

BRAND NAME (Manufacturer)
Aciphex (Eisai)
TYPE OF DRUG
Gastric-acid-secretion inhibitor
INGREDIENT
rabeprazole
DOSAGE FORM
Tablets (20 mg)
STORAGE
Store this medication at room temperature in a tightly closed container. Do not expose this medication to extreme temperatures.

USES

Rabeprazole is prescribed for the treatment of peptic ulcer disease, gastroesophageal reflux disease (GERD), and hypersecretory syndromes. This medication suppresses stomach-acid secretion.

TREATMENT

This medication should be taken once each day with your morning meal, unless your doctor directs you to do otherwise. Swallow the tablets whole; do not chew or crush them before swallowing.

If you miss a dose of this medication, take it as soon as you remember. However, if it is almost time for your next dose, do not take the missed dose at all; just return to your regular dosing schedule. Do not double the next dose of the medication.

It is important to take this medication for as long as prescribed by your doctor.

SIDE EFFECTS

Minor. Abdominal pain, constipation, diarrhea, dizziness, feeling of weakness, headache, heartburn, insomnia, itching, numbness or tingling of the hands or feet, or sleepiness. Most of these effects should disappear as your body adjusts to the medication.

Dry mouth can be relieved by chewing sugarless gum or sucking on hard candy.

To avoid dizziness or light-headedness when you stand, contract and relax the muscles of your legs for a few moments before rising. Do this by pressing one foot against the floor while raising the other foot slightly, alternating feet so that you are "pumping" your legs in a pedaling motion.

If you feel dizzy or light-headed, sit or lie down for a while; get up from a sitting or lying position slowly; and be careful on stairs.

To relieve constipation, increase the amount of fiber in your diet (fresh fruits and vegetables, salads, bran, and whole-grain breads), exercise, and drink more water (unless your doctor directs you to do otherwise).
Major. Tell your doctor about any side effects that are persistent or particularly bothersome. IT IS ESPECIALLY IMPORTANT TO TELL YOUR DOCTOR about bloody urine, difficulty breathing, itching, mouth sores, seizures, swelling of the face or mouth, unusual bleeding or bruising, unusual tiredness or weakness, or yellowing of the skin or eyes.

INTERACTIONS

Rabeprazole may interact with certain other medications:
1. Use of rabeprazole with ketoconazole, itraconazole, some forms of penicillin, digoxin, or iron may alter the absorption of these medications and may thereby either reduce or increase their effectiveness.
2. Rabeprazole may increase the effects of cyclosporine and warfarin (a blood thinner), increasing the side effects of these medications.
BE SURE TO TELL YOUR DOCTOR about these or any other medications you are currently taking.

WARNINGS

• Tell your doctor about any unusual reactions you have had to any medication, especially rabeprazole or any medication used for ulcers or acid reflux (GERD).
• Tell your doctor if you now have or ever had liver disease or kidney disease.
• While taking this medication, your ability to perform tasks that require alertness, such as driving a car or operating potentially dangerous machinery, may be impaired.
• Long-term use and high-dose treatment with medications similar to rabeprazole have been associated with a higher than normal incidence of gastric tumors. Discuss this with your doctor if you need to take high doses of rabeprazole for a long time.
• Be sure to tell your doctor if you are pregnant. Adequate human studies have not been conducted with rabeprazole, and animal studies have shown rabeprazole to cause birth defects. Also be sure to tell your doctor if you are breast-feeding an infant. Rabeprazole passes into breast milk and may cause side effects in a nursing infant.

---

raloxifene

BRAND NAME (Manufacturer)
Evista (Lilly)
TYPE OF DRUG
Selective estrogen-receptor modulator (SERM)
INGREDIENT
raloxifene
DOSAGE FORM
Tablets (60 mg)
STORAGE
Store this medication in a tightly closed container at room temperature.

USES

Raloxifene is used to prevent osteoporosis in postmenopausal women. After menopause, estrogen levels decrease. This decrease in estrogen leads to increased bone loss. Raloxifene works by decreasing bone loss.

TREATMENT

This medication can be taken with or without meals. It is important to take raloxifene on schedule and not to miss any doses. If you miss a dose, take it as soon as possible. However, if it is almost time for your next dose, do not take the missed dose at all; just return to your regular dosing schedule. Do not double the next dose.

SIDE EFFECTS

Minor: Bloating, gas, depression, hot flashes, insomnia, nausea, pain in the joints, stomach upset, swollen joints, vomiting, or weight gain. These side effects should decrease as your body adjusts to the medicine.

Major: Tell your doctor about any side effects that are persistent or particularly bothersome. IT IS ESPECIALLY IMPORTANT TO TELL YOUR DOCTOR about chest pain, cloudy or bloody urine, fever, flulike symptoms, hives, itching, leg cramps, loss of coordination, migraine headache, numbness of the chest or arm, shortness of breath, skin rash, swelling of the legs or hands, or vaginal itching.

INTERACTIONS

Raloxifene interacts with other types of medications:

1. Raloxifene may decrease the effectiveness of the anticoagulant (blood thinner) warfarin if they are taken concurrently.

2. Cholestyramine may significantly decrease absorption of raloxifene. The two should not be used together.

3. Raloxifene use should be monitored when used in combination with highly protein-bound medications such as naproxen, ibuprofen, indomethacin, clofibrate, and diazepam. Raloxifene is also highly plasma-protein bound.

4. Raloxifene should not be used with estrogen.

Before starting this medication, BE SURE TO TELL YOUR DOCTOR about any medications you are taking, especially those listed above.

WARNINGS

• Before taking this medication, it is important to tell your doctor if you have ever had an unusual or allergic reaction to any medication, especially to raloxifene.

• Before taking this medication, it is important to tell your doctor if you now have or ever had blood clots in your legs or lungs, heart disease, liver disease, or cancer.

• Before any surgical procedure, tell your doctor that you are taking this medication. Raloxifene should be discontinued at least 72 hours before surgery and should not be restarted until you are able to walk and move around. It is important to avoid raloxifene use if you are on prolonged bedrest or if you are taking a long trip during which you will be immobile. If you are planning a long trip or surgery that will require prolonged bedrest, discuss this with your physician.

• This medication should only be used by postmenopausal women.

• If raloxifene makes you dizzy or drowsy, do not take part in any activity that requires alertness, such as driving an automobile or operating any potentially dangerous machinery.

• Be sure to tell your physician if you are pregnant or trying to become pregnant. Raloxifene should not be used by women who are pregnant or who may become pregnant. In animal studies, raloxifene caused abnormal fetal development. If you think you may be pregnant, stop this medication and contact your physician. Also, tell your physician if you are breast-feeding an infant. Raloxifene should be avoided by breast-feeding women. It is not known if raloxifene passes into breast milk.

---

ramipril

BRAND NAME (Manufacturer)
Altace (Hoechst-Roussel/Upjohn)
TYPE OF DRUG
Antihypertensive

INGREDIENT
ramipril
DOSAGE FORM
Capsules (1.25 mg, 2.5 mg, 5 mg, and 10 mg)
STORAGE
Store in a tightly closed container at room temperature, away from heat and direct sunlight. Do not refrigerate.

USES

Ramipril is used to treat high blood pressure and congestive heart failure in patients after a heart attack. It is a vasodilator (it widens blood vessels) that blocks the production of chemicals that may be responsible for constricting, or narrowing, blood vessels. Ramipril is in a class of drugs called the angiotensin-converting enzyme (ACE) inhibitors.

TREATMENT

This medication should be taken exactly as prescribed by your doctor. Ramipril can be taken either on an empty stomach or with a meal.

While using this medication, try to develop a set schedule for taking it. If you miss a dose and remember within a few hours, take the missed dose and resume your regular dosing schedule. If many hours have passed, skip the dose you missed and then take your next dose as scheduled. Do not double the next dose.

Ramipril does not cure high blood pressure, but it will help control the condition as long as you continue to take it. It may be several weeks before you notice the full effect of this medication.

SIDE EFFECTS

Minor. Abdominal pain, cough, diarrhea, dizziness, drowsiness, fatigue, headache, insomnia, nausea, nervousness, sweating, or vomiting. These side effects should disappear as your body adjusts to the medication.

To avoid dizziness when you stand, contract and relax the muscles of your legs for a few moments before rising. Do this by pushing one foot against the floor while raising the other foot slightly, alternating feet so that you are "pumping" your feet in a pedaling motion.

If you feel dizzy, sit or lie down; get up slowly from a sitting or reclining position; and be careful on stairs.

This medication can cause increased sensitivity to sunlight. Avoid prolonged exposure to sunlight and sunlamps, wear protective clothing and sunglasses, and use an effective sunscreen.

Major. Tell your doctor about any side effects that are persistent or particularly bothersome. IT IS ESPECIALLY IMPORTANT TO TELL YOUR DOCTOR about chest pain; difficulty breathing; excessive perspiration; fainting; fever; impaired taste perception; irregular heartbeat; itching; light-headedness (especially during the first few days); muscle cramps; rash; sore throat; swelling of the face, eyes, lips, or tongue; tingling in the fingers and toes; or yellowing of the eyes or skin.

INTERACTIONS

Ramipril interacts with several other types of medications:

1. Diuretics and other antihypertensive medications can cause an excessive drop in blood pressure when they are combined with this medication (especially with the first dose).

2. The combination of this medication with amiloride, potassium supplements, salt substitutes, spironolactone, or triamterene can lead to hyperkalemia (dangerously high levels of potassium in the bloodstream).

3. Nonsteroidal anti-inflammatory agents (including ibuprofen, indomethacin, and naproxen) may reduce the effectiveness of this medication.
4. Antacids may decrease the effectiveness of ramipril. To avoid this drug interaction, take ramipril either one hour before or two hours after taking antacids.
5. Phenothiazine tranquilizers or probenecid may increase the blood level and adverse effects of ramipril.
6. Concurrent use of this medication and allopurinol can increase the risk of developing an allergic reaction to these medications.
7. Ramipril can delay the body's elimination of lithium and lead to increased adverse effects from lithium.
8. Concurrent administration of this medication with digoxin can lead to increased blood levels of and adverse effects from digoxin.

Before starting to take ramipril, BE SURE TO TELL YOUR DOCTOR about any medications you are taking, especially those listed above.

WARNINGS

• Tell your doctor about unusual or allergic reactions you have had to any medications, especially to angiotensin-converting enzyme (ACE) inhibitors (including captopril, enalapril, lisinopril, quinapril, fosinopril, moexipril, and benazepril) or to this medication.
• Be sure to tell your doctor if you have ever had aortic stenosis, heart attack, stroke, blood disorders, kidney or liver disease, kidney transplant, or systemic lupus erythematosus.
• A persistent dry cough may occur and usually does not subside unless this medication is stopped. If this effect is bothersome, consult your doctor,
• Excessive perspiration, dehydration, or prolonged vomiting or diarrhea can lead to an excessive drop in blood pressure while you are taking this medication. Contact your doctor if you have any of these symptoms.
• Before having surgery or other medical or dental treatment, tell your doctor or dentist you are taking this medication.
• If this drug makes you dizzy or drowsy (sometimes this effect occurs after the first few doses), try to avoid any sudden changes in posture.
• Do not take any over-the-counter (nonprescription) medications for weight control or for asthma, sinus, cough, cold, or allergy problems unless you first check with your doctor.
• Do not stop taking this medication unless you first consult your doctor. Stopping this drug abruptly may lead to a rise in blood pressure.
• Be sure to tell your doctor if you are pregnant. This medication and other drugs in the class called ACE inhibitors have been shown to cause birth defects, including kidney damage, low blood pressure, improper skull development, and fetal death, when taken in the second and third trimesters. Also tell your doctor if you are breast-feeding an infant. This medication may pass into breast milk and should not be taken by a nursing mother.

---

ranitidine

BRAND NAMES (Manufacturers)
Zantac (GlaxoSmithKline)
Zantac EFFERdose (GlaxoSmithKline)
Zantac GELdose (GlaxoSmithKline)
Zantac 75* (GlaxoSmithKline)
*Available over the counter.
TYPE OF DRUG
Gastric-acid-secretion inhibitor (decreases stomach acid)

INGREDIENT
ranitidine
DOSAGE FORMS
Capsules (150 mg and 300 mg)
Granules, effervescent (150 mg)
Tablets (75 mg, 150 mg, and 300 mg)
Tablets, effervescent (150 mg)
Oral syrup (15 mg per mL)
STORAGE
Store this medication, regardless of dosage form, at room temperature in a tightly closed, light-resistant container. Do not freeze.

USES

Ranitidine is used in the treatment of duodenal and gastric ulcers. It is also used in the long-term treatment of excessive stomach-acid secretion, in the prevention of recurrent ulcers, and in the treatment of reflex esophagitis (inflammation of the esophagus). Ranitidine works by blocking the effects of histamine on the stomach, thereby reducing stomach-acid secretion.

TREATMENT

You can take ranitidine either on an empty stomach or with food or milk.

If you miss a dose of this medication, take the missed dose as soon as possible. However, if it is almost time for the next dose, do not take the missed dose at all; just return to your regular dosing schedule. Do not double the next dose of the medication.

The prescribed dose of the granule or the effervescent tablet form of this medication must be dissolved in six to eight ounces of water before being swallowed. Be sure the granules or tablets are completely dissolved first.

Measure each dose of the oral syrup carefully with a specially designed 5-mL measuring spoon. An ordinary kitchen teaspoon is not accurate enough.

SIDE EFFECTS

Minor. Constipation, diarrhea, dizziness, headache, nausea, or stomach upset. These side effects should disappear as your body adjusts to the medication.

To relieve constipation, exercise, drink more water, and add more fiber (from vegetables, fresh fruit, whole-grain breads, and bran) to your diet, unless your doctor directs you to do otherwise.

To avoid dizziness or light-headedness when you stand, contract and relax the muscles of your legs for a few moments before rising. Do this by pressing one foot against the floor while raising the other foot slightly, alternating feet so that you are "pumping" your legs in a pedaling motion.

If you feel dizzy while taking this medication, sit or lie down for a while; get up slowly from a sitting or reclining position; and be careful on stairs.

Major. Tell your doctor about any side effects that are persistent or particularly bothersome. IT IS ESPECIALLY IMPORTANT TO TELL YOUR DOCTOR about confusion, decreased sexual ability, unusual bleeding or bruising, or weakness.

INTERACTIONS

Ranitidine can interact with other types of medications:

1. Ranitidine may increase the blood-sugar-lowering effects of glipizide or glyburide.
2. Ranitidine can decrease the elimination of warfarin (a blood thinner) from the body, which can increase the risk of bleeding complications.
3. Ranitidine can increase blood levels of procainamide, metoprolol, phenytoin, or midazolam.
4. Ranitidine may cause a false-positive result with the Multistix urine protein test.

5. Ranitidine may decrease the absorption of ketoconazole and etaconazole, reducing their effectiveness.
6. Antacids can block the absorption of ranitidine. If you are taking antacids as well as ranitidine, at least one hour should separate doses of the two medications.
7. Sucralfate may reduce the absorption of ranitidine, reducing its effect.
BE SURE TO TELL YOUR DOCTOR about any medications you are currently taking, especially any of the medications that are listed above.

WARNINGS

- Tell your doctor about unusual or allergic reactions you have had to any medications, especially to ranitidine.
- Tell your doctor if you now have or ever had kidney or liver disease.
- Ranitidine should be taken continuously for as long as your doctor prescribes. To do otherwise may result in ineffective therapy.
- The granule and the effervescent tablet forms of this medication contain aspartame, which is broken down to phenylalanine; these should be used with caution in patients with phenylketonuria.
- Cigarette smoking may block the beneficial effects of ranitidine.
- If this drug makes you dizzy, do not take part in any activity that requires alertness, such as driving an automobile or operating potentially dangerous equipment.
- Be sure to tell your doctor if you are pregnant. Ranitidine appears safe during pregnancy; however, extensive testing has not been conducted. Also tell your doctor if you are breast-feeding an infant. Small amounts of ranitidine pass into breast milk.

---

repaglinide

BRAND NAME (Manufacturer)
Prandin (Novo Nordisk)
TYPE OF DRUG
Antidiabetic agent
INGREDIENT
repaglinide
DOSAGE FORM
Tablets (0.5 mg, 1 mg, and 2 mg)
STORAGE
Store in a tightly closed container at room temperature.

USES

Repaglinide is used for the treatment of the form of diabetes mellitus that appears most commonly in adulthood—known as type 2, or non–insulin-dependent, diabetes—when it cannot be managed by exercise and control of diet alone. Repaglinide can be used in combination with metformin in patients whose blood sugar cannot be controlled with diet, exercise, and either agent alone.

TREATMENT

For the medication to work correctly, take it exactly as directed by your physician. Repaglinide can be taken with a full glass of water 15 to 30 minutes before eating. If you skip a meal, omit the dose of repaglinide for that meal. If you eat an extra meal, you should take an extra dose of repaglinide 15 to 30 minutes before eating.

SIDE EFFECTS

Minor. Constipation, diarrhea, hypoglycemia (low blood sugar), itching, muscle aches and pains, nausea, skin rash, upper respiratory infection, or vomiting. These side effects should diminish or disappear as your body adjusts to the drug.

To relieve constipation, increase the amount of fiber in your diet (fresh fruits and vegetables, salads, bran, and whole-grain breads) and drink more water (unless your doctor directs you to do otherwise).

Major. Tell your doctor about any side effects that are persistent or particularly bothersome. IT IS ESPECIALLY IMPORTANT TO NOTIFY YOUR DOCTOR about changes in blood pressure, chest pain, cold sweats, fatigue, irregular heartbeat, rapid pulse, shakiness, tooth disorders, or unusual bruising or bleeding.

INTERACTIONS

Repaglinide can interact with other medications:

1. Macrolide antibiotics (including erythromycin, clarithromycin, and azithromycin) and azole antifungals (such as ketoconazole, fluconazole, and itraconazole) may increase the blood level of repaglinide, which may increase its side effects.

2. Carbamazepine, barbiturates, and rifampin may decrease the effectiveness of repaglinide.

3. Beta blockers, chloramphenicol, guanethidine, monoamine oxidase (MAO) inhibitors, nonsteroidal anti-inflammatory drugs (NSAIDs), probenecid, and aspirin or other salicylates can sometimes lower blood sugar when used with oral antidiabetic agents. Use caution when these medications are begun or discontinued during treatment with repaglinide.

4. Thiazide and other diuretics, corticosteroids, thyroid agents, phenothiazines, estrogens, oral contraceptives, phenytoin, calcium channel blockers, and isoniazid may increase blood sugar when used together with oral antidiabetic agents. Use caution when these drugs are begun or discontinued during treatment with repaglinide.

Before starting repaglinide, BE SURE TO TELL YOUR DOCTOR about any medication you are taking, especially any of those listed above.

WARNINGS

• Tell your doctor about unusual or allergic reactions you have had to any medications, especially to repaglinide.

• Avoid drinking alcohol while taking this medication. Alcohol may increase the side effects of repaglinide.

• Follow the special diet provided by your doctor. This is an important part of controlling your blood sugar and is necessary for the medication to work properly.

• Test your blood sugar as directed by your physician. It is a good way to determine whether your diabetes is being controlled with this medication.

• Eat or drink something containing sugar right away if you experience any symptoms of hypoglycemia (low blood sugar), such as anxiety, chills, cold sweats, cool or pale skin, drowsiness, excessive hunger, headache, nausea, nervousness, rapid heartbeat, shakiness, or unusual tiredness or weakness. It is important for your family and friends to know the symptoms of low blood sugar. They should understand what to do if they observe any of these symptoms in you. Good sources of sugar are orange juice, corn syrup, honey, sugar cubes, and table sugar.

• Before starting to take repaglinide, tell your doctor if you now have or ever had type 1 diabetes, diabetic coma, or kidney or liver disease.

• Be sure to tell your doctor if you are pregnant. Adequate studies of repaglinide use during pregnancy have not been conducted in humans. And tell your doctor if you are breast-feeding an infant. It is not known if repaglinide passes into breast milk.

---

rifampin

BRAND NAMES (Manufacturers)

Rifadin (Aventis)
Rimactane (Novartis)

TYPE OF DRUG
Antibiotic
INGREDIENT
rifampin
DOSAGE FORM
Capsules (150 mg and 300 mg)
STORAGE
Store at room temperature in a tightly closed, light-resistant container.

USES

Rifampin is an antibiotic that is used to treat tuberculosis and to prevent meningococcal meningitis. This medication works by preventing the growth and multiplication of susceptible bacteria. Rifampin is not effective against viruses, parasites, or fungi.

TREATMENT

Take rifampin with a full glass of water on an empty stomach one hour before or two hours after a meal. If this medication causes stomach irritation, check with your doctor to see if you can take it with food.

Try not to miss any doses of this medication. If you do miss a dose, take the missed dose as soon as possible. However, if it is almost time for your next dose, do not take the missed dose at all; just return to your regular dosing schedule. Do not double your next dose.

Continue to take this medication for the entire time prescribed by your doctor (which may be months to years), even if the symptoms disappear before the end of that period. If you stop taking the drug too soon, resistant bacteria will continue to grow, and your infection could recur.

SIDE EFFECTS

Minor. Diarrhea, dizziness, drowsiness, gas, headache, heartburn, loss of appetite, nausea, stomach irritation, or vomiting. These side effects should disappear as your body adjusts to the medication.

If you feel dizzy, sit or lie down for a while; get up slowly from a sitting or reclining position; and be careful on stairs.

To avoid dizziness when you stand, contract and relax the muscles of your legs for a few moments before rising. Do this by pressing one foot against the floor while raising the other foot slightly, alternating feet so that you are "pumping" your legs in a pedaling motion.

Major. Tell your doctor about any side effects that are persistent or particularly bothersome. IT IS ESPECIALLY IMPORTANT TO TELL YOUR DOCTOR about confusion, difficult or painful urination, fatigue, fever, flushing, itching, muscle weakness, numbness, skin rash, uncoordinated movements, visual disturbances, or yellowing of the eyes or skin. And if your symptoms of infection seem to be worsening rather than improving, tell your doctor.

INTERACTIONS

Rifampin interacts with several other types of medications:

1. Rifampin can decrease the blood levels and therefore the effectiveness of metoprolol, propranolol, verapamil, aminophylline, theophylline, oxtriphylline, quinidine, adrenocorticosteroids (cortisonelike medicines), progestins, clofibrate, methadone, oral anticoagulants (blood thinners, such as warfarin), oral antidiabetic medicines, barbiturates, benzodiazepine tranquilizers, dapsone, trimethoprim, phenytoin, delavirdine, efavirenz, nevirapine, digoxin, estrogen, disopyramide, mexiletine, propafenone, quinidine, tocainide, amprenavir, indinavir, nelfinavir, netonavir, saquinavir, itraconazole, ketoconazole, fluconazole, and chloramphenicol.

2. Concurrent use of rifampin with alcohol or isoniazid can lead to an increased risk of liver damage.
3. Rifampin may decrease the effectiveness of oral contraceptives (birth control pills), and pregnancy could result. You should therefore use a different or additional form of birth control while you are being treated with rifampin. Discuss available options with your doctor.

BE SURE TO TELL YOUR DOCTOR about any medications you are currently taking, especially any of those listed above.

WARNINGS

- Tell your doctor about unusual or allergic reactions you have had to any medications, especially to rifampin.
- Before beginning a course of treatment with this medication, be sure to tell your doctor if you have a history of alcoholism or liver disease.
- Rifampin has been prescribed for your current infection only. Another infection later on, or one that someone else has, may require a different medicine. You should not give your medicine to other people or use it for other infections unless your doctor specifically directs you to do so.
- If this drug makes you dizzy or drowsy, do not take part in any activity that requires alertness, such as driving an automobile or operating potentially dangerous tools, machinery, or other equipment.
- Rifampin can cause reddish-orange to reddish-brown discoloration of your urine, feces, saliva, sputum, sweat, and tears. This is a harmless effect. The drug may also permanently discolor soft contact lenses. You might want to stop wearing them while you are taking this medication. Discuss this with your ophthalmologist.
- Do not stop taking this medication unless you first check with your doctor. Stopping this medication and then restarting it at a later time can lead to an increase in side effects.
- Be sure to tell your doctor if you are pregnant. Although rifampin appears to be safe in humans, birth defects have been reported in the offspring of animals that received large doses of the drug during pregnancy. Also tell your doctor if you are breast-feeding an infant. Small amounts of rifampin pass into breast milk.

---

risperidone

BRAND NAME (Manufacturer)
Risperdal (Janssen)
TYPE OF DRUG
Antipsychotic
INGREDIENT
risperidone
DOSAGE FORMS
Tablets (0.25 mg, 0.5 mg, 1 mg, 2 mg, 3 mg, and 4 mg)
Oral solution (1 mg per mL)
STORAGE
Store in a tightly closed container at room temperature, away from heat and direct sunlight. Do not freeze.

USES

Risperidone is prescribed to treat symptoms of mental illness, such as the emotional symptoms of psychosis. This medication is thought to relieve the symptoms of mental illness by blocking certain chemicals that are involved with nerve transmission in the brain, although the exact way in which it works is not yet completely understood.

TREATMENT

Take this medication exactly as prescribed by your doctor. To prevent stomach irritation, take all forms of this drug with or soon after meals (unless your doctor directs you to do otherwise).

Measure each dose of the oral solution carefully using the special dropper provided. Mix each dose with three to four ounces of water, coffee, low-fat milk, or orange juice. It should not be mixed with cola or tea.

The full effects of this medication for the control of emotional or mental symptoms may not become apparent for two weeks after you begin treatment.

If you miss a dose of this medicine, take the missed dose as soon as possible. However, if it is almost time for your next dose, skip the one you missed; just return to your regular schedule. You should never take a double dose to make up for the one you missed unless directed to do so by your doctor.

SIDE EFFECTS

Minor. Blurred vision, changes in blood pressure, constipation, decreased sweating, diarrhea, dizziness, drooling, drowsiness, dry mouth, fatigue, jitters, menstrual irregularities, restlessness, stuffy nose, vomiting, or weight gain. These side effects should diminish or disappear as your body adjusts to the medication.

This medication can cause increased sensitivity to sunlight. It is important to avoid prolonged exposure to sunlight or sunlamps. Wear protective clothing and use an effective sunscreen.

Dry mouth can be relieved by chewing sugarless gum or sucking on hard candy.

To relieve constipation, increase the amount of fiber in your diet (fresh fruits and vegetables, salads, bran, and whole-grain breads), exercise, and drink more water (unless your doctor directs you to do otherwise).

If this medication makes you feel dizzy, sit or lie down for a while, get up slowly from a sitting or reclining position, and use caution on stairs.

To avoid dizziness or light-headedness when you stand, contract and relax the muscles in your legs for a few moments before rising. Do this by pushing one foot against the floor while raising the other foot slightly, alternating feet so that you are "pumping" your legs in a pedaling motion.

Major. Tell your doctor about any side effects that are persistent or particularly bothersome. IT IS ESPECIALLY IMPORTANT TO TELL YOUR DOCTOR about breast enlargement (in both sexes); chest pain; convulsions (seizures); darkened skin; difficulty in breathing or swallowing; fainting; fever; impotence; involuntary movements of the face, mouth, tongue, or jaw; palpitations; skin rash or hives; sleep disorders; sore throat; tremors; uncoordinated movements; unusual bleeding or bruising; visual disturbances; or yellowing of either the eyes or the skin.

INTERACTIONS

Risperidone interacts with several other types of drugs:

1. Extreme drowsiness can occur when this medication is taken with other central nervous system depressants (such as alcohol, antihistamines, antidepressants, barbiturates, benzodiazepine tranquilizers, muscle relaxants, narcotics, pain medications, and sleeping medications).

2. Carbamazepine may reduce the effectiveness of resperidone.

3. Risperidone may increase the effects of some blood-pressure-lowering medicines.

4. The side effects of monoamine oxidase (MAO) inhibitors and tricyclic antidepressants may be increased when combined with this medication.

5. Clozapine may increase the risk of side effects from resperidone.

6. Resperidone may reduce the effect of levodopa, pergolide, and medications used for Parkinson's disease.

Before taking risperidone, BE SURE TO TELL YOUR DOCTOR about any medication you are taking, especially any of those listed above.

WARNINGS

- Tell your doctor about any unusual or allergic reactions you have had to any medications, especially to risperidone.
- Tell your doctor if you have a history of alcoholism or if you now have or ever had heart or circulatory disease, difficulty in urinating, enlarged prostate gland, epilepsy, glaucoma, liver disease, or Parkinson's disease.
- To prevent oversedation, avoid drinking alcoholic beverages while taking this medication.
- If this medication makes you drowsy or dizzy, do not take part in any activity that requires alertness, such as driving a car or operating dangerous equipment.
- Do not stop taking this medication suddenly. Stopping it abruptly can cause nausea, vomiting, headache, stomach upset, increased heart rate, insomnia, trembling, or a worsening of your condition. Your doctor may want to reduce the dose gradually.
- Some of the side effects of this drug can be prevented by taking an antiparkinson drug. Discuss this matter with your doctor.
- This medication may decrease sweating and heat release from the body. Therefore avoid getting overheated by strenuous exercise in hot weather and avoid taking hot baths, showers, or saunas.
- While taking this medication, do not take any over-the-counter (nonprescription) medication for weight control or for cough, cold, asthma, allergy, or sinus problems unless you first check with your doctor.
- Before having surgery or any other medical or dental treatment, be sure to tell your doctor or dentist that you are taking risperidone.
- Be sure to tell your doctor if you are pregnant. The effects of this medication during pregnancy have not been thoroughly studied in humans. It is also not known if risperidone passes into breast milk in humans, so be sure to tell your doctor if you are breastfeeding an infant.

---

ritonavir

BRAND NAME (Manufacturer)
Norvir (Abbott)
TYPE OF DRUG
Antiviral
INGREDIENT
ritonavir
DOSAGE FORMS
Capsules (100 mg)
Solution (80 mg per mL)
STORAGE
Keep the capsule form of this medication in the refrigerator in a tightly closed, light-resistant container. Do not freeze the capsules. Store the solution form at room temperature in the original container. Do not expose the solution to excess heat, and never freeze it.

USES

Ritonavir is used in the treatment of human immunodeficiency virus (HIV) infection. HIV is the virus that causes AIDS. Ritonavir works by inhibiting the reproduction, or growth, of the virus, which slows down the progression of AIDS. Ritonavir does not cure HIV infection or AIDS, but it may delay the onset of other infections and diseases caused by AIDS. Ritonavir is usually not used alone but rather in combination with other anti-AIDS medications. These combinations have been shown to make the AIDS virus undetectable in the body.

TREATMENT

This medication works best when the level of medicine in your bloodstream is kept constant. It is best, therefore, to take the medication at evenly spaced intervals throughout the day. IT IS IMPORTANT NOT TO MISS ANY DOSES OF RITONAVIR. The chances of the AIDS virus becoming resistant to ritonavir increase if the level of medication in the bloodstream is low.

Take ritonavir with food unless otherwise directed by your doctor.

If you miss a dose of this medication, take it as soon as possible. However, if it is almost time for your next dose, skip the missed dose and go back to your regular dosing schedule. Do not double the next dose.

SIDE EFFECTS

Minor. Changes in taste perception, diarrhea, dizziness, general feeling of weakness, headache, nausea, sleepiness, stomach pain, or vomiting. As your body adjusts to the medication, some of these side effects should disappear.

To avoid dizziness or light-headedness when you stand, contract and relax the muscles of your legs for a few moments before rising. Do this by pressing one foot against the floor while raising the other foot slightly, alternating feet so that you are "pumping" your legs in a pedaling motion.

If you feel dizzy or light-headed, sit or lie down for a while; get up slowly from a sitting or reclining position; and be careful on stairs.

Major. Tell your doctor about any side effects that are persistent or particularly bothersome. IT IS ESPECIALLY IMPORTANT TO TELL YOUR DOCTOR about confusion, dry or itching skin, fatigue, fruity or unusual mouth odor, increased hunger or thirst, increased urination, numbness or tingling around the mouth or in the hands or feet, unexplained weight loss, or vomiting.

INTERACTIONS

Ritonavir may interact with a number of other drugs:

1. Ritonavir may increase the serious side effects of alprazolam, midazolam, triazolam, clorazepate, diazepam, estazolam, flurazepam, quinidine, zolpidem, amiodarone, bepridil, bupropion, clozapine, ergot drugs, meperidine, pimozide, piroxicam, propafenone, propoxyphene, rifabutin, or clarithromycin. Therefore, ritonavir should not be used concurrently with any of these medications.

2. Ritonavir may make birth control pills (oral contraceptives) less effective. A different or additional method of birth control should be used during treatment with ritonavir.

WARNINGS

• Tell your doctor if you have ever had an allergic reaction to any medication, especially ritonavir, indinavir, saquinavir, nelfinavir, or any other medication used to treat AIDS.

• This medication may cause high blood sugar (or diabetes). Your doctor may want you to check your blood sugar regularly while you're taking ritonavir. Ask your doctor about the signs of high blood sugar and diabetes.

• Your doctor may do regular blood tests to check your cholesterol. Increases in cholesterol may occur with ritonavir.

• This medication may cause the fat in your body to be redistributed. There may be a loss of fat from the face, buttocks, arms, and legs and an increase in fatty tissue on the upper back.

• Before taking this medication, be sure to tell your doctor about any medical problems you may have, especially liver problems, diabetes or problems with high blood sugar, high cholesterol, or bleeding problems, especially hemophilia.

• Your doctor may do regular blood tests to see how well this medication is working against the AIDS virus.

• Before having surgery or any medical or dental treatment, be sure to tell your doctor or dentist that you are taking this medication.
• Be sure to tell your doctor about any other medications you are taking, both prescription and nonprescription. Ritonavir may interact with other medications to produce serious side effects.
• If you are infected with HIV, it is best to avoid any sexual activity involving an exchange of body fluids with other people. If you do have vaginal, anal, or oral sex, always use a latex condom.
• Be sure to tell your doctor if you are pregnant. It is not known if ritonavir is safe to use during pregnancy. It is not known if ritonavir passes into human breast milk. However, because of the risk of passing HIV to infants, it is recommended that mothers who have HIV infection NOT breast-feed their infants.

---

rivastigmine

BRAND NAME (Manufacturer)
Exelon (Novartis)
TYPE OF DRUG
Acetylcholinesterase inhibitor
INGREDIENT
rivastigmine
DOSAGE FORM
Capsules (1.5 mg, 3 mg, 4.5 mg, and 6 mg)
STORAGE
Store the capsules at room temperature in a tightly closed container. Do not expose this medication to extreme temperatures.

USES

Rivastigmine is used to treat Alzheimer's disease. This medication works by preventing the breakdown of a certain chemical in the brain called acetylcholine. Acetylcholine is important in maintaining thinking and other cognitive abilities. In patients who have Alzheimer's disease, there is less acetylcholine present in the brain than there normally would be. Rivastigmine helps to increase the amount of this chemical in the brain. Rivastigmine will not cure Alzheimer's disease, but it may slow its progression, especially when used in the early stages of the disease.

TREATMENT

Take this medication exactly as prescribed by your doctor. It is best to take rivastigmine at regular intervals, with meals if possible. Usually, rivastigmine is started at a low dose and gradually increased over several weeks. If for any reason this medication is stopped for more than several days, it may be necessary to start at a low dose again and gradually increase it; check with your doctor.

If you miss a dose of this medication, take it as soon as possible after you remember. However, if it is almost time for your next dose, do not take the missed dose at all; just return to your regular dosing schedule. Do not double the next dose of the medication.

SIDE EFFECTS

Minor. Abdominal bloating, confusion, constipation, depression, dizziness, fatigue, hallucinations, headache, increased sweating, insomnia, nausea, or stomach cramps. These side effects should diminish or disappear as your body adjusts to the medication.

To avoid dizziness or light-headedness when you stand, contract and relax the muscles of your legs for a few moments before rising. Do this by pushing one foot against the floor while raising the other foot slightly, alternating feet so that you are "pumping" your legs in a pedaling motion.

If you feel dizzy or light-headed, sit or lie down for a while; get up from a sitting or reclining position slowly; and be careful on stairs.

To relieve constipation, increase the amount of fiber in your diet (fresh fruits and vegetables, salads, bran, and whole-grain breads), exercise, and drink more water (unless your doctor directs you to do otherwise).

Major. Tell your doctor about any side effects that are persistent or particularly bothersome. IT IS ESPECIALLY IMPORTANT TO TELL YOUR DOCTOR about abdominal pain, aggressive behavior, difficulty breathing, difficulty urinating, fainting, loss of appetite, loss of strength, seizures, severe vomiting or diarrhea, slow or irregular heartbeats, tremors, very low blood pressure, or weight loss.

INTERACTIONS

Rivastigmine may interact with a number of other medications:

1. Use of rivastigmine with bethanechol may increase the side effects of both medications.

2. Taking rivastigmine with nonsteroidal anti-inflammatory drugs (NSAIDs), such as ibuprofen, may increase stomach irritation and the risk of stomach ulcers.

BE SURE TO TELL YOUR DOCTOR about any medications you are currently taking, especially any of those listed above.

WARNINGS

• Tell your doctor about any unusual reactions you have had to any medication, especially to rivastigmine or to other medications that are used in the treatment of Alzheimer's disease.

• Tell your doctor if you now have or if you have ever had asthma, heart disease or problems with too slow a heart rate, low blood pressure, seizures or epilepsy, urinary problems, or stomach ulcers.

• If you are having surgery or undergoing any type of dental procedure, be sure to tell your doctor or dentist that you are taking rivastigmine.

• While taking this medication, your ability to perform tasks that require alertness, such as driving a car or operating potentially dangerous machinery, may be impaired.

• Be sure to tell your doctor if you are pregnant. Adequate studies of rivastigmine use in human pregnancy have not been conducted. This medication should not be used by women who are breast-feeding an infant.

---

rizatriptan

BRAND NAMES (Manufacturers)

Maxalt (Merck)

Maxalt-LT (Merck)

TYPE OF DRUG

Antimigraine agent

INGREDIENT

rizatriptan

DOSAGE FORMS

Tablets (5 mg and 10 mg)

Tablets, orally disintegrating (5 mg and 10 mg)

STORAGE

Store this medication in a tightly closed container at room temperature. Keep the orally disintegrating tablets in the blister pack in the original outer aluminum pouch until ready for use.

USES

Although it is not completely understood how rizatriptan works, this medication helps to relieve migraine headaches by altering the level of a chemical in the brain called serotonin. Rizatriptan is used for the treatment of migraine headaches for those patients who do not get relief from other headache medicine such as acetaminophen, aspirin, and nonsteroidal anti-inflammatory drugs (NSAIDs). This drug is not effective for preventing migraine headaches or for the treatment of cluster headaches.

TREATMENT

When taking the orally disintegrating tablets, be sure your hands are dry. Peel open the blister pack and place the tablet on your tongue. It is not necessary to drink any liquid, as the tablet will melt from the saliva in the mouth. This medication may work better if you lie down in a quiet, darkened room after taking it.

If your migraine is less severe after your first rizatriptan tablet, your doctor may instruct you to take a second tablet two hours after the first dose if the headache pain starts to come back. It is very important that you obtain specific instructions from your doctor on how to use this drug properly. Never double the dose of this medication, and do not take more than 15 milligrams (mg) of rizatriptan in any 24-hour period.

SIDE EFFECTS

Minor. Blurred vision, diarrhea, dizziness, drowsiness, increased tiredness, increased urination, itching, muscle or joint stiffness, nausea, restlessness, or vomiting. These side effects should diminish or disappear as your body adjusts to the medication.

If you feel dizzy or light-headed, sit or lie down for a while, stand up slowly, and be careful on stairs.

To avoid dizziness or light-headedness when you stand, contract and relax the muscles of your legs for a few moments before rising. Do this by pressing one foot against the floor while raising the other foot slightly, alternating feet so that you are "pumping" your legs in a pedaling motion.

Major. Tell your doctor about any side effects that are persistent or particularly bothersome. IT IS ESPECIALLY IMPORTANT TO NOTIFY YOUR DOCTOR about any chest pain, irregular heartbeats, or tightness of the chest or throat.

INTERACTIONS

Rizatriptan may interact with several medications:

1. Rizatriptan can produce dangerous side effects when taken with a class of drugs called monoamine oxidase (MAO) inhibitors. It is very important that rizatriptan and MAO inhibitors not be taken together. At least two weeks should separate a dose of an MAO inhibitor and a dose of rizatriptan in order to avoid this potentially dangerous drug interaction.

2. Certain antidepressants (fluoxetine, paroxetine, sertraline, fluvoxamine, citalopram, and escitalopram) used concurrently with rizatriptan may produce weakness or an unusual lack of coordination.

3. Rizatriptan may increase the side effects caused by ergot-containing or ergot-type drugs (such as methysergide and dihydroergotamine). It is very important that at least 24 hours separate the use of any of these ergot drugs and rizatriptan.

4. Propranolol may increase the blood levels of rizatriptan when it is taken concurrently. If you are taking propranolol, your doctor may recommend that you use a lower dose (5 mg) of rizatriptan.

Before starting rizatriptan, BE SURE TO TELL YOUR DOCTOR about any medication you are taking, especially any of those listed above.

WARNINGS

• Tell your doctor about unusual or allergic reactions you have had to any medications, especially to rizatriptan or any other medication for migraine.

• Rizatriptan should not be taken together with other drugs that are in the same class (such as naratriptan, sumatriptan, zolmitriptan) or any other medications for migraine.
• Before starting to take rizatriptan, tell your doctor if you now have or ever had heart disease, a heart attack, angina, high blood pressure, kidney or liver disease, peripheral vascular disease, or a stroke.
• The safety of using this medication to treat more than four headaches in any one-month period has not been well established. Talk to your doctor about this if you experience more than three headaches in a month.
• If this drug makes you dizzy or drowsy, do not take part in any activities that require mental alertness, such as driving an automobile or operating potentially dangerous machinery or equipment.
• Be sure to tell your doctor if you are pregnant. Adequate studies have not been conducted in human pregnancy. Be sure to tell your doctor if you are breast-feeding an infant. It is not known if rizatriptan passes into breast milk.

---

rofecoxib

BRAND NAME (Manufacturer)
Vioxx (Merck)
TYPE OF DRUG
Nonsteroidal anti-inflammatory drug (NSAID)
INGREDIENT
rofecoxib
DOSAGE FORMS
Tablets (12.5 mg and 25 mg)
Oral suspension (12.5 mg per 5-mL spoonful and 25 mg per 5-mL spoonful)
STORAGE
Store either form of this medication at room temperature in a tightly closed container. Do not expose this medication to extreme temperatures.

USES

Rofecoxib is used to treat the signs and symptoms of osteoarthritis and rheumatoid arthritis. This medication is also used for the short-term treatment of acute pain, such as following dental surgery. Rofecoxib is also used for pain and discomfort associated with menstrual periods. Rofecoxib works by blocking the formation of prostaglandins, which are chemicals in the body that cause swelling and inflammation in tissues and joints.

TREATMENT

This medication is usually taken once a day, with or without meals. However, to avoid stomach irritation, your doctor may direct you to take this medication with food or milk. It is best to take this medication at the same time each day.

Shake the suspension well just before measuring each dose, since some of the medicine may settle at the bottom of the container. Measure each dose with a specially designed 5-mL measuring spoon. An ordinary kitchen teaspoon is not accurate enough.

It is important to try not to miss any doses of this medication. If you do miss a dose, take it as soon as you remember. However, if it is almost time for your next dose of the medication, do not take the missed dose at all; just return to your regular dosing schedule. Do not double the next dose of this medication.

SIDE EFFECTS

Minor. Back pain, blurred vision, constipation, diarrhea, dizziness, feeling of weakness, heartburn, or nausea. These side effects usually go away during treatment, as your body adjusts to the medicine.

To avoid dizziness or light-headedness when you stand, contract and relax the muscles of your legs for a few moments before rising. Do this by pressing one foot against the floor while raising the other foot slightly, alternating feet so that you are "pumping" your feet in a pedaling motion.

If you feel dizzy or light-headed, sit or lie down for a while; get up from a sitting or reclining position slowly; and be careful on stairs.

To relieve constipation, increase the amount of fiber in your diet (fresh fruits and vegetables, salads, bran, and whole-grain breads), exercise, and drink more water (unless your doctor directs you to do otherwise).

Major. If any side effects are persistent or particularly bothersome, it is important to notify your doctor. IT IS ESPECIALLY IMPORTANT THAT YOU TELL YOUR DOCTOR about black, tarry stools; chest congestion or tightness; chills, fever, or muscle aches; severe or bloody diarrhea; shortness of breath; skin rash; swelling of the legs, feet, hands, or arms; vomiting of blood or material that looks like coffee grounds; or weight gain.

INTERACTIONS

Rofecoxib interacts with a number of other medications:

1. Concurrent use of rofecoxib with aspirin or other nonsteroidal anti-inflammatory drugs (NSAIDs), such as ibuprofen, indomethacin, or naproxen, may increase the risk of stomach ulcers or bleeding. These medications should not be taken together.

2. Concurrent use of this medication and warfarin (a blood thinner) may increase the effects of warfarin and increase the risk of bleeding.

3. Rofecoxib may increase the risk of side effects from lithium and theophylline when used concurrently with either of these medications.

4. Rifampin may lower the amount of rofecoxib in the body and reduce its effectiveness when the two drugs are used at the same time.

5. Sucralfate and antacids that contain calcium, aluminum, or magnesium may reduce the amount of rofecoxib that is absorbed, possibly making this medication less effective.

6. The effects of diuretics (water pills) such as thiazide diuretics and furosemide may be reduced by concurrent use of rofecoxib.

7. The antihypertensive effects of ACE inhibitors may be reduced if they are taken concurrently with rofecoxib.

BE SURE TO TELL YOUR DOCTOR about any medications you are currently taking, especially any of those listed above.

WARNINGS

• It is important that you tell your doctor if you have ever had any unusual or allergic reactions to rofecoxib, aspirin, other medications that are used for arthritis or pain, or any other medication.

• It is also important to tell your doctor if you now have or ever had kidney disease, liver disease, swelling of the hands or feet, heart disease, heart failure, high blood pressure, anemia, asthma, nasal polyps, or stomach ulcers.

• Avoid drinking alcoholic beverages while taking this medication (unless directed otherwise by your doctor). Large amounts of alcohol can affect your liver and also increase the risk of stomach irritation or ulcers.

• Be sure to tell your doctor or dentist that you are taking this medicine before having any kind of surgery or other medical or dental treatment.

• Be sure to tell your doctor if you are pregnant. Rofecoxib should not be used during late pregnancy because it may cause harm to the fetus. Also be sure to tell your doctor if you are breast-feeding an infant. The use of rofecoxib while breast-feeding is not recommended.

ropinirole

BRAND NAME (Manufacturer)
Requip (GlaxoSmithKline)
TYPE OF DRUG
Antiparkinson agent (dopamine receptor agonist)
INGREDIENT
ropinirole
DOSAGE FORM
Tablets (0.25 mg, 0.5 mg, 1 mg, 2 mg, and 5 mg)
STORAGE
Store this medication in a tightly closed container at room temperature, away from heat and direct sunlight. Do not refrigerate or freeze.

USES

This medication is used alone or in combination with levodopa/carbidopa therapy to treat Parkinson's disease. Although the exact mechanism of action is not known, this drug may work by stimulating dopamine receptors in the striatum portion of the brain.

TREATMENT

Take this medication exactly as prescribed by your doctor. It can be taken either on an empty stomach or with a meal. Taking this medication with food may help to reduce nausea. It is very important to follow your doctor's instructions for taking this medication. If you are taking levodopa/carbidopa with ropinirole, it is possible that as the ropinirole dose is gradually increased, the levodopa/carbidopa dose may be gradually decreased to avoid additional adverse effects.

While using this medication, try to develop a set schedule for taking it. If you miss a dose and remember within a few hours, take the missed dose and resume your regular dosing schedule. However, if it is almost time for your next scheduled dose, do not take the missed dose at all; just return to your regular dosing schedule. Do not double the next dose of this medication.

This medication does not cure Parkinson's disease, but it will help to control the condition as long as you continue to take it. It may be several weeks before you notice the full effect of this medication.

SIDE EFFECTS

Minor. Constipation, diarrhea, dry mouth, flushing, gas, headache, heartburn, hot flashes, increased sweating, tremor, or yawning. These side effects should disappear as your body adjusts to the medication.

To relieve constipation, increase the amount of fiber in your diet (fresh fruits and vegetables, salads, bran, and whole-grain breads), drink more water, and exercise more (unless your doctor directs you to do otherwise.)

Plain, nonmedicated eyedrops (artificial tears) may help to relieve any eye dryness caused by this medication.

Chew sugarless gum or suck on ice chips or a piece of hard candy to relieve mouth or throat dryness.

Major. Tell your doctor about any side effects that are persistent or particularly bothersome. IT IS ESPECIALLY IMPORTANT TO TELL YOUR DOCTOR about abdominal pain; chest pain; clumsiness or unsteadiness; confusion; difficulty breathing; dizziness; drowsiness; fainting; falling; hallucinations; loss of appetitie; low blood pressure; muscle pain; nasal congestion; nausea; runny nose; sneezing; sore throat; swelling in the legs; twitching, twisting, or other unusual body movements; unusual tiredness or weakness; or worsening of Parkinson's.

To avoid dizziness when you stand, contract and relax the muscles of your legs for a few moments before rising. Do this by pressing one foot against the floor while raising the other foot slightly, alternating feet so that you are "pumping" your legs in a pedaling motion.

If you feel dizzy, sit or lie down for a while, get up slowly from a sitting or reclining position, and be careful on stairs.

INTERACTIONS

Ropinirole may interact with other types of medications:

1. Cimetidine, diltiazem, enoxacin, erythromycin, fluvoxamine, mexiletine, norfloxacin, ciprofloxacin, tacrine, or estrogen may increase the blood level and adverse effects of ropinirole. It is very important to tell your doctor if you are taking any of these medications in addition to ropinirole.

2. Phenothiazine tranquilizers, haloperidol, antipsychotics, and metoclopramide may antagonize (work against) the effects of this medication and reduce its effectiveness for treating Parkinson's disease.

3. Concurrent use of other central nervous system depressants (such as antihistamines, barbiturates, tranquilizers, tricyclic antidepressants, sleep medications, muscle relaxants, and other pain medications) or alcohol can cause extreme drowsiness.

Before starting to take this medication, BE SURE TO TELL YOUR DOCTOR about any medications you are taking, especially any of those listed above.

WARNINGS

- Tell your doctor about unusual or allergic reactions you have had to any medications, especially to ropinirole or pramipexole.
- Be sure to tell your doctor if you have ever had hallucinations, kidney disease, liver disease, or low blood pressure.
- Before having surgery or other medical or dental treatment, tell your doctor or dentist you are taking this medication.
- While taking this medication, your doctor will want to check your progress at regular visits, especially during the first few months of treatment. Your doctor will need to adjust your dosage gradually to find the best level of medicine for your Parkinson's disease.
- Do not stop taking this medication without first checking with your doctor. Your doctor may want to gradually reduce the amount of medicine you are taking over several days before completely stopping the treatment. Make sure that you have enough medicine on hand to last through vacations, holidays, and weekends.
- Do not drink any alcohol-containing beverages or take any over-the-counter (nonprescription) medications for weight control or for asthma, sinus, cough, cold, or allergy problems unless you first check with your pharmacist or doctor.
- This medication can cause dizziness, drowsiness, light-headedness, and decreased alertness. Therefore, use caution while driving a car or operating dangerous machinery. Be especially careful when going up or down stairs or getting up from a sitting or lying position.
- Hallucinations may occur in some patients. This is more common in very elderly patients (older than 75 years).
- Smoking may reduce the efficacy of ropinirole; tell your doctor if you smoke cigarettes or use other forms of tobacco.
- After you stop taking this medicine, your body may need time to adjust. The length of time this takes depends on the amount of medicine you were taking and how long you used it. During this time, it is important to tell your doctor if you experience confusion, fever, or extreme muscle stiffness.
- Be sure to tell your doctor if you are pregnant. This medication has been shown to cause birth defects in the offspring of animals that received large doses of it during

pregnancy. Adequate studies have not been done on the use of this medication in human pregnancy. Also tell your doctor if you are breast-feeding an infant. It is not known if this medication passes into breast milk.

---

rosiglitazone

BRAND NAME (Manufacturer)
Avandia (GlaxoSmithKline)
TYPE OF DRUG
Oral antidiabetic
INGREDIENT
rosiglitazone
DOSAGE FORM
Tablets (2 mg, 4 mg, and 8 mg)
STORAGE
Store this medication at room temperature in a tightly closed, light-resistant container. Do not expose it to extreme temperatures.

USES

Rosiglitazone is used for the treatment of the type of diabetes that most often appears in adulthood—known as type 2 adult-onset, or non–insulin-dependent, diabetes—and that cannot be managed by exercise and control of diet alone. Rosiglitazone lowers blood sugar levels by increasing the actions of insulin that is already present in your bloodstream. Unlike other oral medications for diabetes, rosiglitazone does not increase the release of insulin from the pancreas; it helps your body make better use of the insulin you have.

TREATMENT

This medication can be taken once daily or divided into two doses each day and taken with or without meals (depending on your doctor's directions for use). It is best to take this medication at the same time each day.

It is important to try not to miss any doses of this medication. If you do miss a dose and are taking this medication once daily, take it as soon as you remember within the same day. Otherwise, do not take the missed dose at all; just return to your regular dosing schedule. Never double the dose of rosiglitazone.

If you are taking this medication twice a day and you miss a dose, take the missed dose as soon as you remember, then return to your regular dosing schedule. However, if it is almost time for your next dose, skip the missed dose and return to your regular dosing schedule. Never double the dose of rosiglitazone or take more than two doses a day to make up for a missed dose. Be sure to tell your doctor if you notice any side effects from missing a dose of this drug.

SIDE EFFECTS

Minor. Drowsiness, headache, muscle soreness, runny or stuffy nose, sore throat, or upper respiratory infections. These side effects usually go away during treatment, as your body adjusts to the medicine.

Major. If any side effects are persistent or particularly bothersome, it is important to notify your doctor. IT IS ESPECIALLY IMPORTANT TO TELL YOUR DOCTOR about abdominal pain; anemia; dark urine; feeling of tiredness or fatigue; loss of appetite; nausea; shortness of breath; swelling of the legs, feet, hands, or arms; tooth problems; vomiting; weight gain; or yellowing of the skin or eyes.

INTERACTIONS

Rosiglitazone interacts with a number of other medications:

1. Medications similar to rosiglitazone have reduced the effectiveness of oral contraceptives (birth control pills). Therefore, a second form of contraception may be required during treatment with rosiglitazone. Be sure to discuss this with your doctor.
2. Beta-blocking medications (atenolol, metoprolol, nadolol, pindolol, propranolol, and timolol) can mask the symptoms of low blood sugar, which can be dangerous.

BE SURE TO TELL YOUR DOCTOR about any medications you are taking, especially any of those listed above.

WARNINGS

• It is important to tell your doctor if you have ever had any unusual or allergic reaction to rosiglitazone, any other oral antidiabetics, or any other medication.
• It is also important to tell your doctor if you now have or ever had kidney disease, liver disease, swelling of the hands or feet, heart disease, heart failure, or type 1 (insulin-dependent) diabetes.
• Avoid drinking alcoholic beverages while taking this medication (unless directed otherwise by your doctor). Large amounts of alcohol can lower blood sugar to dangerously low levels and also adversely affect your liver.
• Medications similar to rosiglitazone have caused damage to the liver. Your doctor may want to perform regular blood tests before and during therapy with rosiglitazone to make sure your liver is working properly. If liver problems develop during treatment with rosiglitazone, the medication should be stopped.
• Follow the special diet that your doctor gave you. This is an important part of controlling your blood sugar and is necessary in order for this drug to work properly.
• Be sure to tell your doctor or dentist that you are taking this medicine before having any kind of surgery or other medical or dental treatment.
• Test for sugar in your blood or urine as directed by your doctor. It is a convenient way to determine if your diabetes is being controlled by this medicine.
• When rosiglitazone is taken alone, the risk of hypoglycemia is low. However, hypoglycemia may occur when this medication is taken with other oral antidiabetic medications or with insulin. Eat or drink something containing sugar right away if you experience any symptoms of low blood sugar (such as anxiety, chills, cold sweats, cool or pale skin, drowsiness, excessive hunger, headache, nausea, nervousness, rapid heartbeat, shakiness, or unusual tiredness or weakness). It is important that your family and friends know the symptoms of low blood sugar and what to do if they recognize any of these symptoms in you. Also check with your doctor as soon as possible, even if these symptoms are corrected by the sugar. The blood-sugar-lowering effects of some medications can last for hours, and the symptoms may return during this period. Good sources of sugar are orange juice, corn syrup, honey, sugar cubes, and table sugar. You are at greatest risk of developing low blood sugar if you skip or delay meals, exercise more than usual, cannot eat because of nausea or vomiting, or drink large amounts of alcohol.
• Be sure to tell your doctor if you are pregnant. Studies have not yet been completed on the safety of using this medication during human pregnancy, and it is unknown if rosiglitazone can cause birth defects. Also tell your doctor if you are breast-feeding an infant. The use of rosiglitazone while breast-feeding is not recommended.

---

salmeterol

BRAND NAME (Manufacturer)
Serevent (GlaxoSmithKline)
TYPE OF DRUG
Bronchodilator
INGREDIENT
salmeterol

DOSAGE FORM
Inhalation aerosol (each spray delivers 21 mcg)
STORAGE
Store this medication at room temperature, away from excessive heat. The contents are pressurized and can explode if heated.

USES

Salmeterol is used to relieve the wheezing and shortness of breath caused by lung diseases such as asthma and emphysema. This drug acts directly on the muscles of the bronchi (breathing tubes) to relieve bronchospasm (muscle contractions of the breathing tubes in the lungs). This action reduces airway resistance and allows air to move more freely to and from the lungs.

TREATMENT

Take this medication exactly as prescribed by your doctor. Salmeterol is usually packaged with an instruction sheet. Read the directions carefully before using. Shake the container well just before each use to distribute the ingredients evenly and equalize the doses. The contents tend to settle on the bottom. If more than one inhalation is prescribed, wait one full minute between inhalations to receive the full benefit from the first dose.

If you miss a dose of this medicine, take the missed dose as soon as possible, then follow your regular dosing schedule for the next dose. Do not double the next dose.

Do not use salmeterol for acute asthma symptoms. This medication has a slow onset of action and is not effective for immediate symptom relief. Use a short-acting bronchodilator (such as albuterol) for acute symptoms. Be sure you discuss this with your doctor ahead of time, so you know when to use different asthma medications.

Salmeterol can be used to prevent exercise-induced bronchospasm. It should be administered 30 to 60 minutes before exercise.

SIDE EFFECTS

Minor. Anxiety, dizziness, drowsiness, dryness or irritation of the mouth or throat, fast heartbeat, flushing, loss of appetite, muscle cramps, nausea, sweating, tremors, vomiting, or weakness. These side effects should diminish or disappear as your body adjusts to the medication.

To help prevent dryness or irritation of the mouth or throat, rinse your mouth with water after each dose.

If you feel dizzy, sit or lie down for a while; get up slowly from a sitting or reclining position; and be careful on stairs.

Major. Tell your doctor about any side effects that are persistent or particularly bothersome. IT IS ESPECIALLY IMPORTANT TO TELL YOUR DOCTOR about chest pain, increased blood pressure, itching or rash, or palpitations.

INTERACTIONS

Salmeterol interacts with several other types of medications:

1. A beta blocker (such as acebutolol, atenolol, labetalol, metoprolol, nadolol, pindolol, propranolol, timolol), when used concurrently with salmeterol, antagonizes (acts against) it, thus decreasing the effectiveness of salmeterol.

2. Monoamine oxidase (MAO) inhibitors, tricyclic antidepressants, antihistamines, levothyroxine, and over-the-counter (nonprescription) cough, cold, asthma, allergy, diet, and sinus medications may increase the side effects of this medication. At least four weeks should separate the use of MAO inhibitors and salmeterol.

3. If you use insulin or other antidiabetic medications, your dosage may need to be adjusted when you begin taking salmeterol.

4. The use of salmeterol with other bronchodilator drugs (oral or inhalation) may have additive side effects. Discuss this potential with your doctor.

Before taking salmeterol, BE SURE TO TELL YOUR DOCTOR about any medication you are taking, especially any of those listed above.

WARNINGS

• Tell your doctor about any unusual or allergic reactions you have had to medications, especially to salmeterol or any related drugs (albuterol, amphetamines, ephedrine, epinephrine, isoproterenol, metaproterenol, norepinephrine, phenylephrine, phenylpropanolamine, pseudoephedrine, or terbutaline).
• Tell your doctor if you have ever had heart disease, enlarged prostate gland, epilepsy, glaucoma, high blood pressure, or thyroid disease.
• If this medication makes you drowsy or dizzy, do not take part in any activity that requires mental alertness, such as driving a car or operating dangerous equipment.
• DO NOT EXCEED THE RECOMMENDED DOSE OF THIS MEDICATION; excessive use of salmeterol may lead to serious side effects.
• Do not puncture, break, or burn the aerosol container. The contents are under pressure and may explode.
• Be sure to tell your doctor if you are pregnant. The effects of treatment with this medication during pregnancy have not been well studied in humans, but salmeterol has caused side effects in the offspring of animals that received large doses during pregnancy. Also be sure to tell your doctor if you are breast-feeding an infant. It is not known if salmeterol passes into breast milk.

---

saquinavir

BRAND NAMES (Manufacturers)
Fortovase (Roche)
Invirase (Roche)
TYPE OF DRUG
Antiviral
INGREDIENT
saquinavir
DOSAGE FORMS
Capsules (200 mg)
Capsules, softgel (200 mg)
STORAGE
Store the capsules at room temperature in a tightly closed, light-resistant container and do not expose them to excess heat. Keep the softgel capsules in the refrigerator in a tightly closed container. If the softgel capsules are stored at room temperature, they should be used within three months.

USES

Saquinavir is used in the treatment of human immunodeficiency virus (HIV) infection. HIV is the virus that causes AIDS. Saquinavir works by inhibiting the reproduction, or growth, of the virus, which slows down the progression of AIDS. Saquinavir does not cure HIV infection or AIDS, but it may delay the onset of other infections and diseases caused by AIDS. Saquinavir is usually not used alone but rather in combination with other anti-AIDS medications. These combinations have been shown to make the AIDS virus undetectable in the body.

TREATMENT

This medication works best when the level of medicine in your bloodstream is kept constant. Therefore, it is best to take the drug at evenly spaced intervals throughout the day. IT IS IMPORTANT NOT TO MISS ANY DOSES OF SAQUINAVIR. The chances of the AIDS virus becoming resistant to saquinavir increase if the level of medication in the bloodstream is low. Saquinavir should be taken within two hours of a full meal to ensure that it is well absorbed (unless your doctor directs you otherwise).

If you miss a dose of this medication, take it as soon as possible. However, if it is almost time for your next dose, skip the missed dose and go back to your regular dosing schedule. Do not double the next dose.

SIDE EFFECTS

Minor. Diarrhea, general weak feeling, headache, mouth ulcers, nausea, or stomach pain. As your body adjusts to the medication, some of these side effects should diminish or disappear.

Major. Tell your doctor about any side effects that are persistent or particularly bothersome. IT IS ESPECIALLY IMPORTANT TO TELL YOUR DOCTOR about burning or prickling sensations in the skin or skin rash.

INTERACTIONS

Saquinavir may interact with a number of other drugs:

1. The serious side effects of alprazolam, midazolam, triazolam, quinidine, ergot derivatives, or calcium channel blockers may be increased if used concurrently with saquinavir.

2. Carbamazepine, dexamethasone, phenobarbital, phenytoin, rifabutin, rifampin, or grapefruit juice may reduce the effectiveness of saquinavir.

3. Concurrent use of clarithromycin, fluconazole, ketoconazole, itraconazole, and rifabutin may increase the amount of saquinavir in the body.

4. Saquinavir may increase the side effects of atorvastatin, lovastatin, simvastatin, and sildenafil, increasing the risk of side effects from these drugs.

WARNINGS

- Tell your doctor if you have ever had an allergic reaction to any medication, especially saquinavir, indinavir, ritonavir, nelfinavir, or any other medication used to in the treatment of AIDS.
- This medication may cause high blood sugar (or diabetes). Your doctor may want you to check your blood sugar regularly while taking saquinavir. Ask your doctor about the signs of high blood sugar and diabetes.
- Your doctor may do regular blood tests to check your cholesterol. Increases in cholesterol may occur with saquinavir.
- This medication may cause the fat in your body to be redistributed. The result may be a loss of fat from the face, buttocks, arms, and legs and an increase in fatty tissue on the upper back.
- Before taking this medication, be sure to tell your doctor about any medical problems you may have, especially liver problems, diabetes or problems with high blood sugar, high cholesterol, or bleeding problems, especially hemophilia.
- Your doctor may do regular blood tests to see how well this medication is working against the AIDS virus.
- Before having surgery or any medical or dental treatment, be sure to tell your doctor or dentist that you are taking saquinavir.
- Be sure to tell your doctor about any other medications you are taking, both prescription and nonprescription. Saquinavir may interact with other medications to produce serious side effects.
- If you are infected with HIV, it is best to avoid any sexual activity involving an exchange of body fluids with other people. If you do have vaginal, anal, or oral sex, always use a latex condom.
- Be sure to tell your doctor if you are pregnant. It is not known if saquinavir is safe to use during pregnancy. It is not known if saquinavir passes into human breast milk. However, because of the risk of passing HIV to infants, it is recommended that mothers who have HIV infection NOT breast-feed their infants.

scopolamine (transdermal)

BRAND NAME (Manufacturer)
Transderm-Scop (Novartis Consumer Health)
TYPE OF DRUG
Antiemetic and antivertigo
INGREDIENT
scopolamine
DOSAGE FORM
Transdermal system (the patch delivers 1 mg of scopolamine over three days)
STORAGE
Store at room temperature in the original container, away from direct heat and light.

USES

Scopolamine is used to prevent nausea and vomiting associated with motion sickness. Transdermal scopolamine is a small patch that is applied to the skin. Transdermal application (i.e., application of medicine through the skin) delivers reduced doses of scopolamine, which decreases the risk of adverse side effects.

TREATMENT

The transdermal system (patches) allows controlled continuous release of scopolamine. Patches are easy to use and convenient. For best results, wash and dry your hands thoroughly before handling the patch. Apply the patch to the hairless area of the skin behind the ear at least four hours before the antiemetic effect is required. Do not place it over any cuts or irritations. Wash your hands thoroughly after handling the patch to prevent direct contact of the medication with the eyes. The medication should last up to three days. If treatment is needed for more than three days, discard the used patch, and replace with a new patch behind the other ear. It is okay to bathe or shower with a patch in place. If the patch becomes displaced at any time during treatment, it should be discarded and a fresh patch placed on the hairless area behind the other ear. If redness or irritation develops at the application site, consult your physician. Do not trim or cut the patches.

SIDE EFFECTS

Minor. Blurred vision and enlargement of pupils; drowsiness; or dryness of mouth, nose, and throat. These side effects should diminish or disappear as your body adjusts to the medication.

To relieve mouth dryness, chew sugarless gum or suck on ice chips or hard candy.

If you feel dizzy or light-headed, sit or lie down for a while; get up slowly from a sitting or reclining position; and be careful on stairs

Major. Tell your doctor about any side effects that are persistent or particularly bothersome. IT IS ESPECIALLY IMPORTANT TO TELL YOUR DOCTOR about blurred vision (severe); confusion (severe); convulsions; difficulty in breathing; dizziness; drowsiness (severe); dry mouth, nose, or throat (severe); eye pain (severe); fast heartbeat; fever; rash; slurred speech; unusual excitement or restlessness; unusual warmth, dryness, or flushing of the skin.

INTERACTIONS

Scopolamine can interact with several other types of medications:

1. This medication can cause additive drowsiness when combined with alcohol or other central nervous system depressants (such as antihistamines, barbiturates, benzodiazepine tranquilizers, muscle relaxants, narcotics, and pain medications) or with tricyclic antidepressants.

2. Scopolamine can cause additive anticholinergic effects (such as dryness of the mouth, nose, and throat or difficulty in urinating) when combined with drugs such as belladonna alkaloids, antidepressants, and antihistamines.

Before starting treatment with scopolamine, BE SURE TO TELL YOUR DOCTOR about any medications that you are currently taking, especially any of the medications that are listed above.

WARNINGS

- Tell your doctor about any unusual or allergic reactions you have had to any medications, especially any reactions to scopolamine.
- Tell your doctor if you now have or ever had blockage of the urinary tract, stomach, or intestinal tract.
- Tell your doctor if you now have or ever had metabolic, liver, or kidney disease.
- Tell your doctor if you have glaucoma (increased pressure in the eyeball).
- This medication may cause drowsiness or blurred vision. Make sure you know how you react to this medication before attempting activities such as driving a car or operating potentially dangerous equipment.
- Patients who use the patch for more than three days are more likely to experience dizziness, headache, nausea, or vomiting for a short period of time following discontinuation of the drug.
- Do not use the transdermal system on children.
- Elderly patients may be especially susceptible to the central nervous system effects (confusion, sedation, memory impairment, unusual excitement) of scopolamine.
- Be sure to tell your doctor if you are pregnant. Extensive studies in pregnant women have not been conducted. Also tell your doctor if you are breast-feeding. It is not known whether scopolamine passes into breast milk.

---

selegiline

BRAND NAME (Manufacturer)
Eldepryl (Somerset)
TYPE OF DRUG
Antiparkinson agent
INGREDIENT
selegiline
DOSAGE FORM
Tablets (5 mg)
STORAGE
Store this medication at room temperature in a tightly closed container.

USES

This medication is used either alone or in combination with levodopa or levodopa/carbidopa to treat the symptoms of Parkinson's disease. This drug helps to increase and extend the beneficial effects of levodopa. Recent studies suggest that selegiline may help to slow the progression of Parkinson's disease when taken early in the course of the disease. This drug has also been used to treat depression.

TREATMENT

Take this medication exactly as your doctor prescribes. You can take it with food to decrease the chance of stomach irritation unless your doctor tells you otherwise.

If you miss a dose of this medication, take the missed dose as soon as possible, then return to your regular dosing schedule. However, if you do not remember the missed dose until late afternoon or evening, skip the missed dose. If the drug is taken late in the afternoon, it may cause some unwanted side effects. Never double the next dose of medication.

The full effects of this medication may not be apparent for two to three days. At that time, your doctor may change your dose of levodopa or levodopa/carbidopa.

SIDE EFFECTS

Minor. Dizziness, drowsiness, dryness of mouth, headache, heartburn, light-headedness, nausea, nervousness, restlessness, stomach pain, trouble sleeping, or vomiting. These side effects should lessen or disappear as your body adjusts to the medication.

Dry mouth can be relieved by chewing sugarless gum or by sucking on ice chips or a piece of hard candy.

To avoid dizziness or light-headedness when you stand, contract and relax the muscles of your legs for a few moments before rising. Do this by pushing one foot against the floor while raising the other foot slightly, alternating feet so that you are "pumping" your legs in a pedaling motion.

If you feel dizzy or light-headed, sit or lie down for a while, get up slowly from a sitting or reclining position, and be careful on stairs.

Major. Tell your doctor about any side effects that are persistent or particularly bothersome. IT IS ESPECIALLY IMPORTANT TO TELL YOUR DOCTOR about blood in your urine; chest pain; convulsions; dark or tarry stools; difficulty in breathing; difficulty in speaking; difficulty in urination; fast heartbeat; feelings of euphoria; hallucinations; mood changes; persistent restlessness; severe stomach pain; stiff neck; or uncontrolled movements of your arms, legs, or face.

INTERACTIONS

Selegiline may interact with several medications:

1. Tell your doctor if you have taken the drug meperidine in the two to three weeks before starting selegiline. The combination may cause severe side effects, including sweating, severe high blood pressure, and seizure.

2. Concurrent use of this medication and fluoxetine, fluvoxamine, nefazodone, paroxetine, sertraline, venlafaxine, citalopram, escitalopram, or tricyclic antidepressants may cause serious side effects, including severe agitation, delirium, restlessness, tremor, fever, diarrhea, and incoordination. You should wait at least 14 days after stopping selegiline before starting one of these other medications.

Be sure to tell your doctor about any medications, including over-the-counter products, that you are currently taking, especially any of those listed above.

WARNINGS

- Tell your doctor if you have had unusual or allergic reactions to any medications, especially to selegiline or to any monoamine oxidase (MAO) inhibitors (such as furazolidone, isocarboxazid, pargyline, phenelzine, procarbazine, or tranylcypromine).
- Tell your doctor if you have a history of stomach problems, intestinal problems, asthma, high blood pressure, or seizure disorders.
- If this drug makes you dizzy or drowsy, do not take part in any activity that requires alertness, such as driving a car or operating potentially dangerous equipment.
- Before having surgery or any other medical or dental treatment, be sure to tell your doctor or dentist you are taking this medication.
- Your doctor may give you a list of foods that you should either avoid or limit in your diet. These foods or beverages may include those containing caffeine (coffee, tea, cola, or chocolate) or those containing a substance called tyramine (found in certain cheeses and meats).
- Be sure to tell your doctor if you are pregnant. This drug has not caused adverse effects to the fetuses in animal studies, and problems in humans have not been reported. Also tell your doctor if you are breast-feeding an infant.

sertraline

BRAND NAME (Manufacturer)
Zoloft (Roerig)
TYPE OF DRUG
Antidepressant
INGREDIENT
sertraline
DOSAGE FORMS
Tablets (25 mg, 50 mg, and 100 mg)
Oral concentrate (20 mg/mL with 12% alcohol)
STORAGE
Store in a tightly closed container at room temperature, away from heat and direct sunlight. Do not store in the bathroom. Heat or moisture can cause this medicine to break down.

USES

Sertraline is used to treat the symptoms of mental depression, obsessive-compulsive disorder (OCD), panic attacks, and other mental health problems. It increases the concentration of certain chemicals that are necessary for nerve transmission in the brain.

TREATMENT

Take this medication exactly as prescribed by your doctor. To avoid stomach irritation, you can take sertraline with food or a full glass of water (unless your doctor directs you to do otherwise).

The effects of treatment with this medication may not become apparent for one to three weeks. It is important to continue to take this medication, even if you feel better.

The oral concentrate can be diluted or mixed with 4 ounces (half cup) of water, ginger ale, lemon-lime soda, lemonade, or orange juice ONLY. After you prepare the dose, it must be taken immediately. Do not store or mix in advance, as the medication will not be stable.

If you miss a dose of this medicine, it is not necessary to make up the missed dose. Skip that dose and continue at the next scheduled time. You should never take a double dose to make up for one you missed.

SIDE EFFECTS

Minor. Agitation, changes in taste, constipation, decreased concentration, decreased sex drive, diarrhea, dizziness, drowsiness, dry mouth, fast heartbeat, flushing, frequent urination, headache, increased sweating, loss of appetite, nausea, stuffy nose, vision changes, or weight gain or loss. These side effects should diminish or disappear as your body adjusts to the medication.

Dry mouth can be relieved by chewing sugarless gum or sucking on ice chips or a piece of hard candy.

To relieve constipation, increase the amount of fiber in your diet (fresh fruits and vegetables, salads, bran, and whole-grain breads), exercise, and drink more water (unless your doctor directs you to do otherwise).

To avoid dizziness when you stand, contract and relax the muscles in your legs for a few moments before rising.

Major. Tell your doctor about any side effects that are persistent or particularly bothersome. IT IS ESPECIALLY IMPORTANT TO TELL YOUR DOCTOR about anxiety, chills or fever, convulsions (seizures), enlarged lymph glands (swelling under the jaw, in the armpits, or in the groin area), difficulty in breathing, joint or muscle pain, skin rash or hives, or swelling of the feet or lower legs.

INTERACTIONS

Sertraline interacts with several other types of drugs:

1. Extreme drowsiness can occur when this medication is taken with other central nervous system depressants (such as alcohol, antihistamines, barbiturates, benzodiazepine tranquilizers, muscle relaxants, narcotics, pain medications, phenothiazine tranquilizers, or sleeping medications) or with other antidepressants.

2. Sertraline may increase the effects of oral anticoagulants (blood thinners, such as warfarin) and certain heart medications (such as digoxin, beta blockers including propranolol and metoprolol, and diltiazem).

3. Serious side effects may occur if a monoamine oxidase (MAO) inhibitor (such as furazolidone, isocarboxazid, pargyline, phenelzine, procarbazine, selegiline, or tranylcypromine) is taken with sertraline. At least 14 days should separate the use of sertraline and the use of an MAO inhibitor.

Before taking sertraline, BE SURE TO TELL YOUR DOCTOR about any medication you are taking, especially any of those listed above.

WARNINGS

• Tell your doctor immediately if you develop a skin rash or have hives while taking this medication or if you have ever had a reaction to sertraline or to any of the other selective serotonin-reuptake inhibitors, including fluoxetine, paroxetine, and citalopram.

• Be sure that you tell your doctor if you have a history of alcoholism or if you have or ever had a heart attack, asthma, circulatory disease, difficulty in urinating, electroshock therapy, enlarged prostate gland, epilepsy, glaucoma, high blood pressure, intestinal problems, liver or kidney disease, mental illness, or thyroid disease.

• If this medication makes you drowsy or dizzy, do not take part in any activity that requires mental alertness, such as driving a car or operating dangerous equipment.

• Do not stop taking this medication suddenly. Stopping it abruptly can cause nausea, headache, stomach upset, or a worsening of your condition. Your doctor may want to reduce the dose gradually.

• Elderly individuals may be at greater risk of experiencing unwanted or otherwise bothersome side effects. Use this drug cautiously and report any mental status changes to your doctor immediately.

• The effects of this medication may be present for as long as five weeks after you discontinue treatment with it. It is important, therefore, that you continue to observe all precautions during this period.

• This medication will make your skin more sensitive to the sun. Avoid prolonged exposure to the sun or sunlamps, and wear protective clothing, sunscreen, and sunglasses when outdoors during daylight hours.

• Be sure to tell your doctor if you are pregnant. Although birth defects have not been documented in animal studies, it is not known if sertraline is safe during human pregnancy. It is not known if sertraline passes into breast milk, so be sure to tell your doctor if you are breast-feeding an infant.

---

sibutramine

BRAND NAME (Manufacturer)
Meridia (Knoll)
TYPE OF DRUG
antiobesity
INGREDIENT
sibutramine
DOSAGE FORM
Capsules (5 mg, 10 mg, and 15 mg)

STORAGE
Store at room temperature in a tightly closed, light-resistant container. Do not expose to excess heat or moisture. Do not store in the bathroom.

USES
Sibutramine is used as an appetite suppressant to help you lose weight and maintain weight loss and is used together with a low-calorie diet. This medication is thought to work by altering certain chemicals in the brain (neurotransmitters) that affect the appetite. How long sibutramine is effective in decreasing appetite is not known, but its effects after two years have not been well studied.

TREATMENT
Sibutramine can be taken with or without food, usually in the morning, or as directed by your doctor.

If you miss a dose of this medicine, take it as soon as possible if you remember on that day. Otherwise, skip that day's dose and return to your regular dosing schedule on the next day. Do not double the next dose.

SIDE EFFECTS
Minor. Changes in taste perception, constipation, diarrhea, difficulty sleeping, dizziness, drowsiness, dry mouth, headache, increased sweating or thirst, indigestion, nausea, nervousness or anxiety, skin flushing, stomach pain, stuffy or runny nose, or tingling or burning of the skin. These side effects should diminish or disappear as your body adjusts to the medication.

Dry mouth can be relieved by chewing sugarless gum or sucking on ice chips or, with your doctor's approval, hard candy.

To relieve constipation, increase the amount of fiber in your diet (fresh fruits and vegetables, salads, bran, and whole-grain breads), exercise, and drink more water (unless your doctor directs you to do otherwise).

To avoid dizziness or light-headedness when you stand, contract and relax the muscles of your legs for a few moments before rising. Do this by pressing one foot against the floor while raising the other foot slightly, alternating feet so that you are "pumping" your legs in a pedaling motion.

Major. Tell your doctor about any side effects that you find are persistent or particularly bothersome. IT IS ESPECIALLY IMPORTANT THAT YOU TELL YOUR DOCTOR about achiness, changes in mood, chills, depression, fast or irregular heartbeat, hives, increased blood pressure, painful menstruation, seizures, skin rash, swelling of the feet or ankles, unusual bleeding, unusual bruising or purple spots on the skin, or unusual weight gain.

INTERACTIONS
Sibutramine may interact with a number of other drugs:

1. Use of this medication within 14 days of a monoamine oxidase (MAO) inhibitor (such as phenelzine, isocarboxazid, pargyline, tranylcypromine, procarbazine, selegiline, or furazolidone) may result in severe, life-threatening reactions.

2. Sibutramine should not be taken with medications that may increase blood pressure, such as ephedrine, phenylpropanolamine, pseudoephedrine, or over-the-counter (nonprescription) weight-loss, allergy, asthma, sinus, cough, or cold products.

3. Erythromycin, clarithromycin, itraconazole, or ketoconazole may increase the side effects of sibutramine.

4. The risk of serious side effects will be increased if sibutramine is taken with other appetite suppressants, antidepressants, or antimigraine agents. It is important to avoid these medications while you are taking sibutramine.

5. Extreme drowsiness may occur when this medication is taken with central nervous system depressants, such as alcohol, antihistamines, barbiturates, benzodiazepine tranquilizers, muscle relaxants, narcotics, pain medications, phenothiazine tranquilizers, and medications to induce sleep.

Before taking sibutramine, BE SURE TO TELL YOUR DOCTOR about any medication you are taking, especially any of those listed above.

WARNINGS

- Tell your doctor if you have ever had any unusual or allergic reaction to sibutramine or any other medication.
- It is important to tell your doctor about any medical conditions you currently have or have ever had, especially heart disease, irregular heartbeats, liver or kidney problems, glaucoma, high blood pressure, stroke, seizures, eating disorders, or gallstones. Also inform your doctor if you have a history of, or current problems with, drug abuse.
- Before having surgery or any medical or dental treatment, be sure to tell your doctor or dentist that you are taking sibutramine.
- Sibutramine should not be used in children under 16 years of age.
- Sibutramine may cause dizziness or light-headedness. Your ability to perform tasks that require alertness, such as driving a car or operating heavy machinery, may be decreased. Appropriate caution should be taken.
- It is important to see your doctor regularly while taking sibutramine. This medication may affect your blood pressure and your heart.
- This medicine should be taken exactly as prescribed by your doctor. Do not increase the dose of this medicine unless your doctor tells you to do so.
- Be sure to tell your doctor if you are pregnant. Studies in animals indicate that sibutramine may cause problems if taken during pregnancy. The effects of sibutramine during human pregnancy are unknown. In addition, tell your doctor if you are breast-feeding an infant. The effects of sibutramine during breast-feeding are unknown. You should discuss the risks and benefits of sibutramine with your doctor.

---

sildenafil

BRAND NAME (Manufacturer)
Viagra (Pfizer)
TYPE OF DRUG
Impotence therapy agent
INGREDIENT
sildenafil
DOSAGE FORM
Tablets (25 mg, 50 mg, and 100 mg)
STORAGE
Store this medication at room temperature in a tightly closed container. Do not expose it to extreme temperatures.

USES

This medication is used for the treatment of erectile dysfunction (ED), or impotence, in men. Sildenafil works by increasing the chemicals in the body that are needed for a man to have an erection. Sildenafil is used to treat impotence that occurs as a result of a disease such as diabetes, surgery on the prostate, or injury to the spinal cord or that stems from psychological difficulties.

TREATMENT

Take this medication exactly as directed by your doctor. Do not increase the dose unless your doctor tells you to. Sildenafil is usually taken about one hour before sexual intercourse, unless your doctor directs you to do otherwise.

SIDE EFFECTS

Minor. Clumsiness, diarrhea, dizziness, dry mouth, flushing of the skin, frequent urination, headache, indigestion or stomach upset, nasal congestion, sleepiness, or swelling or bleeding of the gums. These side effects should diminish or disappear as your body adjusts to the medication.

Dry mouth can be relieved by chewing sugarless gum or sucking on hard candy.

If this medication makes you feel dizzy, sit or lie down for a while, get up slowly from a sitting or reclining position, and be careful on stairs.

To avoid dizziness or light-headedness when you stand, contract and relax the muscles of your legs for a few moments before rising. Do this by pressing one foot against the floor while raising the other foot slightly, alternating feet so that you are "pumping" your legs in a pedaling motion.

Major. Tell your doctor about any side effects that are persistent or particularly bothersome to you. IT IS ESPECIALLY IMPORTANT THAT YOU TELL YOUR DOCTOR about bladder pain; changes in your eyesight, such as blurred vision, changes in your color perception, or sensitivity to light; chest pain; cloudy or bloody urine; confusion; convulsions; dizziness; enlargement of the breasts; feeling faint or anxious; hives; increased need to urinate or pain with urination; itching; migraine headaches; rapid or irregular heartbeats; or skin rash.

INTERACTIONS

Sildenafil may interact with a number of other medications:

1. Sildenafil may increase the effects of medications that lower blood pressure, especially nitroglycerin or other nitrates and alpha-blockers including doxazosin, terazosin, and prazosin.

2. Cimetidine, erythromycin, clarithromycin, saquinavir, ritonavir, indinavir, nelfinavir, itraconazole, or ketoconazole may increase the side effects of sildenafil.

Before taking sildenafil, BE SURE TO TELL YOUR DOCTOR about any medication you are taking, especially any of those listed above.

WARNINGS

• Be sure to tell your doctor about any unusual or allergic reactions that you have had to any medications, especially to sildenafil.

• IT IS ESSENTIAL THAT YOU INFORM YOUR DOCTOR about any medications you are taking, especially medications for the heart or for blood pressure.

• DEATHS AND SERIOUS ADVERSE EFFECTS (HEART ATTACK, STROKE, IRREGULAR HEARTBEATS, HIGH BLOOD PRESSURE) HAVE OCCURRED shortly after taking this medication in men with heart disease and in those taking medications for heart disease and high blood pressure. You should discuss the risks of this medication with your doctor.

• Tell your doctor about any medical problems you now have or have ever had, especially heart, kidney, or liver problems; heart attack or stroke; bleeding problems; cancers; blood diseases; eye or vision problems; or high or low blood pressure.

• This medication will not protect you against sexually transmitted disease, such as HIV infection.

• This medication may, infrequently, cause prolonged erections (priapism), which can be painful and result in permament damage to the penis. You should discuss these risks with your doctor. Call your doctor immediately if your erection lasts more than four hours.

• This medication may cause dizziness. Your ability to perform tasks that require alertness, such as driving a car or operating dangerous machinery, may be decreased. Appropriate caution should be taken.

• If you begin to experience chest pain, dizziness, or nausea upon the start of sexual activity, do not continue with this activity. Call your doctor immediately.

simvastatin

BRAND NAME (Manufacturer)
Zocor (Merck Sharp & Dohme)
TYPE OF DRUG
Antihyperlipidemic (lipid-lowering drug)
INGREDIENT
simvastatin
DOSAGE FORM
Tablets (5 mg, 10 mg, 20 mg, 40 mg, and 80 mg)
STORAGE
Store in a tightly closed container at room temperature, away from heat and direct sunlight. Do not refrigerate.

USES

Simvastatin is used to treat hyperlipidemia (high blood-fat levels). It may be prescribed with nondrug therapies such as diet modification and exercise in an attempt to regulate lipid and cholesterol levels. Simvastatin chemically interferes with an enzyme in the body that is responsible for synthesizing cholesterol. This enzyme blockade decreases the LDL (low-density lipoprotein) type of cholesterol, which has been associated with coronary artery disease and atherosclerosis. It may be used for other medical reasons when prescribed by your doctor.

TREATMENT

Take this medication exactly as prescribed by your doctor. If you are to take simvastatin once a day, it is best to take the drug in the evening. Simvastatin can be taken with meals or with a full glass of water if stomach upset occurs (unless your doctor directs you otherwise).

While using this medication, try to develop a set schedule for taking it. If you miss a dose and remember within a few hours, take the missed dose and resume your regular schedule. If many hours have passed, skip the dose you missed and then take your next dose as scheduled. Do not double the next dose.

SIDE EFFECTS

Minor. Abdominal pain or cramps, constipation, diarrhea, gas, nausea, or stomach pain. These effects may be relieved by taking simvastatin with a meal, adding fiber to your diet, or using mild stool softeners.

To relieve constipation, increase the amount of fiber in your diet (fresh fruits and vegetables, bran, and whole-grain breads), exercise, and drink more water (unless your doctor directs you to do otherwise).

Major. Tell your doctor about any side effects that are persistent or particularly bothersome. IT IS ESPECIALLY IMPORTANT TO TELL YOUR DOCTOR about blurred vision (or any other visual changes or difficulties) or muscle pain or tenderness, especially with malaise or fever.

INTERACTIONS

Simvastatin may interact with other medications:

1. Simvastatin may increase the effectiveness of oral anticoagulants (blood thinners, such as warfarin) and digoxin.

2. Because of the risk of severe myopathy (muscle weakness), the combined use of simvastatin and gemfibrozil, fenofibrate, or certain doses of niacin should generally be avoided.

3. Cyclosporine, erythromycin, amiodarone, and verapamil may increase the side effects of simvastatin and therefore should be used with extreme caution during treatment with simvastatin.

BE SURE TO TELL YOUR DOCTOR about any medications that you are taking, especially any of the medications listed above.

WARNINGS

• Tell your doctor about unusual or allergic reactions you have had to any medications, particularly simvastatin or other medications to lower your blood cholesterol levels.
• Be sure to tell your doctor if you have ever had liver disease, kidney disease, heart disease, a stroke, or digestive-tract problems. Having a history of any of these medical problems may influence the dose of simvastatin that is prescribed for you.
• Be sure to call your doctor immediately if you experience muscle pain, muscle weakness, extreme fatigue, and fever.
• Limit your intake of alcoholic beverages while taking this medication to avoid increased side effects from it.
• Patients taking another drug in this same class developed eye-related problems during treatment. It is advisable, therefore, to have regular checkups with your ophthalmologist, who should be informed that you are being treated with this medication.
• This medication can make your skin more sensitive to the sun, even during brief periods of exposure. It is important, therefore, to limit your exposure to sunlight and to avoid sunlamps. Also, wear protective clothing and sunscreen when you are outdoors during daylight hours.
• This drug should NOT be taken if you are pregnant. Serious side effects have been reported in the offspring of animals given this drug during pregnancy. Also be sure to tell your doctor if you are breast-feeding an infant. This drug should NOT be used while breast-feeding.

---

sodium sulfacetamide (ophthalmic)

BRAND NAMES (Manufacturers)
AK-Sulf Forte (Akorn)
Bleph-10 (Allergan)
Cetamide (Alcon)
Isopto Cetamide (Alcon)
Sodium Sulamyd (Schering)
sodium sulfacetamide (various manufacturers)
Sulf-10 (Novartis)
TYPE OF DRUG
Ophthalmic antibiotic
INGREDIENT
sodium sulfacetamide
DOSAGE FORMS
Ophthalmic drops (1%, 10%, 15%, and 30%)
Ophthalmic ointment (10%)
STORAGE
Store this medication at room temperature in tightly closed containers. This medication should never be frozen. If the eyedrops turn brown or otherwise become discolored, they should be discarded.

USES

Sodium sulfacetamide is used to treat bacterial eye infections and corneal ulcers. Sodium sulfacetamide is an antibiotic that is effective against a wide range of bacteria.

It acts by preventing production of the nutrients that are required for growth of the infecting bacteria. This medication, however, is not effective against infections that are caused by viruses, parasites, or fungi.

TREATMENT

Wash your hands with soap and water before applying this medication. To avoid contamination of the eyedrops or ointment, be careful not to touch the tube of the dropper or the tip of the ointment tube or let them touch your eyes; do not wipe off or rinse the dropper after use.

To apply the drops, tilt your head back and pull down the lower eyelid with one hand to make a pouch below the eye. Drop the prescribed amount of medicine into this pouch and slowly close your eyes. Try not to blink. Keep your eyes closed, and place one finger at the corner of the eye next to your nose for a minute or two, applying a slight pressure (this is done to prevent loss of medication through the duct that drains fluid from the surface of the eye into the nose and throat). Then wipe away any excess with a clean tissue.

To apply the ointment form of this medication, tilt the head back, pull down the lower lid to form a pouch below the eye, and squeeze a small amount of ointment (½ inch) in a line along the pouch. Close the eyes, and place your finger at the corner of the eye next to your nose for a minute or two, but do not rub your eyes. Then wipe off any excess ointment with a clean tissue.

Since this medication is somewhat difficult to apply, you may want to have someone else apply it for you.

It is important to continue to take this medication for the entire time prescribed by your doctor, even if the symptoms disappear before the end of that period. If you stop applying the drug too soon, resistant bacteria are given a chance to continue growing, and the infection could recur.

If you miss a dose of this medication, apply the missed dose as soon as possible. However, if it is almost time for your next dose, do not apply the missed dose at all; just return to your regular dosing schedule. Do not use twice as much medication at the next dose.

SIDE EFFECTS

Minor. Sodium sulfacetamide may cause blurred vision or burning or stinging in the eyes immediately after it is applied (especially the 30% solution). This effect should last only a few minutes.

Major. Tell your doctor about any side effects that are persistent or particularly bothersome. IT IS ESPECIALLY IMPORTANT TO TELL YOUR DOCTOR about signs of irritation in the eyes (such as redness, swelling, or itching) that last more than several minutes, chills, fever, itching, or difficulty in breathing. If your symptoms of infection are getting worse rather than improving, contact your doctor.

INTERACTIONS

This drug should not be used concurrently with preparations containing silver, such as silver nitrate ophthalmic.

Be sure to tell your doctor about any medications that you are currently taking, especially any of the type mentioned above.

WARNINGS

- Tell your doctor about unusual or allergic reactions that you have had to any medications, especially to sodium sulfacetamide or to any other sulfa medication (diuretics, oral antidiabetic medications, sulfonamide antibiotics).
- This medication may cause allergic-type symptoms, such as hives, itching, wheezing, or anaphylaxis, in patients sensitive to sulfite.

• Sodium sulfacetamide may cause your eyes to become unusually sensitive to bright light; this sensitivity is temporary and will resolve itself once treatment with this medication is complete. Wearing sunglasses may help to lessen your discomfort during treatment.
• This medication has been prescribed for your current infection only. Another infection later on or one that someone else has may require a different medicine. You should not give your medicine to other people or use it for other infections, unless your doctor specifically directs you to do so.
• In order to allow your eye infection to clear, do not apply makeup to the affected eye.
• If there is no change in your condition two or three days after starting to take this medication, contact your doctor.
• Do not stop using sodium sulfacetamide eyedrops without consulting with your doctor first.
• Be sure to tell your doctor if you are pregnant. The safe use of this medication in human pregnancy has not been established. Although it is an ophthalmic, if large amounts of this medication are applied for prolonged periods, some of it may be absorbed into the bloodstream. Also tell your doctor if you are breast-feeding an infant. If this medication is absorbed, small amounts may pass into the breast milk and may temporarily alter the bacterial balance in the intestinal tract of the nursing infant, resulting in diarrhea.

---

sparfloxacin

BRAND NAME (Manufacturer)
Zagam (Rhone-Poulenc Rorer)
TYPE OF DRUG
Quinolone antibiotic
INGREDIENT
sparfloxacin
DOSAGE FORM
Tablets (200 mg)
STORAGE
Store in a tightly closed container at room temperature, away from heat and direct sunlight.

USES

This medication is an antibiotic that is used to treat a wide variety of bacterial infections, including pneumonia and acute attacks of chronic bronchitis. This medication acts by severely injuring the cell walls of the infecting bacteria, preventing them from growing and multiplying. This medication kills susceptible bacteria, but it is not effective against viruses, parasites, or fungi.

TREATMENT

Take this medication exactly as prescribed by your doctor, even if your symptoms improve. If you stop taking this medication too soon, resistant bacteria are given a chance to grow, and the infection may recur. Sparfloxacin can be taken either on an empty stomach or with a meal. You should drink several additional glasses of water every day when you are taking this medication, unless your doctor directs you to do otherwise. Drinking water will help to prevent unwanted side effects.

It is very important that you do not miss any doses of this medication. While using this medication, try to develop a set schedule for taking it. If you miss a dose and remember within a few hours, take the missed dose and space the following dose halfway through the regular interval between doses; then return to your regular schedule. Try not to skip any doses.

SIDE EFFECTS

Minor. Abdominal pain, diarrhea, dizziness or light-headedness, insomnia, nausea, or vomiting. These side effects should diminish or disappear as your body adjusts to the medication.

If this medication makes you feel dizzy or light-headed, sit or lie down for a while, get up slowly from a sitting or reclining position, and be careful on stairs.

To avoid dizziness when you stand, contract and relax the muscles of your legs for a few moments before rising. Do this by pressing one foot against the floor while lifting the other foot slightly, alternating feet so that you are "pumping" your legs in a pedaling motion.

This medication can cause increased sensitivity to sunlight. Avoid prolonged exposure to sunlight and sunlamps; wear protective clothing and sunglasses, and use an effective sunscreen when you are outdoors during daylight hours.

Major. Tell your doctor about any side effects that are persistent or particularly bothersome. IT IS ESPECIALLY IMPORTANT TO TELL YOUR DOCTOR about agitation, change in your vision, confusion, difficulty breathing, difficulty urinating, headache, muscle or joint pain, restlessness, severe diarrhea (which may be watery or contain blood or pus), skin rash, or swelling of the face. Also, if your symptoms of infection seem to be getting worse rather than improving, contact your doctor.

INTERACTIONS

Sparfloxacin interacts with several other types of medications:

1. Sparfloxacin should NEVER be taken with the following medications: amiodarone, disopyramide, procainamide, quinidine, sotalol, bepridil, erythromycin, tricyclic antidepressants (including amitriptyline, desipramine, or imipramine), or phenothiazine tranquilizers (including thioridazine and chlorpromazine). Discuss this with your doctor or pharmacist if you take any of these medications and sparfloxacin has been prescribed for you.

2. Concurrent use of antacids, iron- or zinc-containing vitamins, or didanosine with this medication may result in decreased effectiveness of sparfloxacin. To avoid this drug interaction, take these medications two to four hours either before or after taking sparfloxacin.

3. Sucralfate decreases the efficacy of sparfloxacin if it is taken at the same time. To avoid this drug interaction, take your dose of sucralfate at least six hours after taking your dose of sparfloxacin.

4. Sparfloxacin can lead to increased blood levels of and adverse effects from digoxin, warfarin, or cyclosporine.

5. Sparfloxacin can lead to increased blood levels and adverse effects of theophylline.

6. Sparfloxacin may decrease the efficacy of phenytoin, which may result in an increase in seizure activity.

Before starting to take sparfloxacin, BE SURE TO TELL YOUR DOCTOR about any medications you are taking, especially those listed above.

WARNINGS

• Tell your doctor about unusual or allergic reactions you have had to any medications, especially to quinolone antibiotics (including ciprofloxacin, enoxacin, ofloxacin, norfloxacin, cinoxacin, or nalidixic acid) or to this medication.

• Before starting to take this medication, be sure to tell your doctor if you have or have ever had brain or spinal cord disease, epilepsy, kidney disease, liver disease, or irregular heartbeats.

• To decrease the potential for harmful effects on your kidneys, increase your intake of fluids (nonalcoholic) unless your doctor directs you to do otherwise.

• Sparfloxacin can cause dizziness or light-headedness. Be sure you know how you're reacting to this medicine before you drive an automobile, operate machinery, or perform any other activities requiring alertness or coordination.

• This medication can make your skin more sensitive to the sun. When you first begin to take this medicine, avoid too much sun and do not use a sunlamp until you see how your skin responds to short periods of sun exposure. This is especially important if you tend to sunburn easily. Using an effective sunscreen or sunblock on your skin will help avoid this problem. Continue to avoid direct and indirect sunlight for several weeks AFTER you stop taking this medication. Increased skin problems still may occur, and you should take precautions to prevent sunburn.
• This medication has been prescribed for your current infection only. A subsequent infection, or one that someone else has, may require a different medicine. Do not give your medication to someone else or use it for other infections unless your doctor specifically directs you to do so.
• Be sure to call your doctor immediately if you experience rash, swelling of the face, or difficulty breathing after you take this medication.
• This drug should never be used in young children.
• Be sure to tell your doctor if you are pregnant. This medication and other quinolone antibiotics have been shown to cause serious adverse effects in the developing fetus when taken by pregnant women. Also tell your doctor if you are breast-feeding an infant. This medication may pass into breast milk and should not be taken by a nursing mother.

---

spironolactone

BRAND NAMES (Manufacturers)
Aldactone (Searle)
spironolactone (various manufacturers)
TYPE OF DRUG
Diuretic and antihypertensive
INGREDIENT
spironolactone
DOSAGE FORM
Tablets (25 mg, 50 mg, and 100 mg)
STORAGE
Store at room temperature in a tightly closed, light-resistant container.

USES

This drug is used to treat high blood pressure. It is also used to reduce fluid accumulation in the body caused by conditions such as heart failure, cirrhosis of the liver, kidney disease, and the long-term use of some drugs.

Spironolactone reduces fluid accumulation by increasing the elimination of salt and water through the kidneys. It may be used in combination with other diuretics to prevent potassium loss. Since spironolactone blocks the effects of a chemical (aldosterone) released from the adrenal gland, it can also be used to diagnose and treat an overactive adrenal gland.

TREATMENT

To decrease stomach irritation from this medication, you can take spironolactone with a glass of milk or with a meal (unless your doctor directs you to do otherwise). Try to take it at the same time every day. Avoid taking a dose after 6:00 in the evening; otherwise, you may have to get up during the night to urinate.

This medication does not cure high blood pressure, but it will help to control the condition as long as you continue to take it.

If you miss a dose of this medication, take the missed dose as soon as possible. However, if it is almost time for the next dose, do not take the missed dose at all; just wait until the next scheduled dose. Do not double the next dose.

SIDE EFFECTS

Minor. Cramping, diarrhea, dizziness, drowsiness, dry mouth, headache, increased urination, nausea, rash, restlessness, vomiting, or weakness. As your body adjusts to the medication, these side effects should disappear.

Dry mouth can be relieved by chewing sugarless gum or sucking on hard candy.

If this medication makes you feel dizzy or light-headed, sit or lie down for a while, get up slowly from a sitting or reclining position, and be careful on stairs.

To avoid dizziness or light-headedness when you stand, contract and relax the muscles of your legs for a few moments before rising. Do this by pushing one foot against the floor while raising the other foot slightly, alternating feet so that you are "pumping" your legs in a pedaling motion.

Major. Tell your doctor about any side effects that are persistent or particularly bothersome. IT IS ESPECIALLY IMPORTANT TO TELL YOUR DOCTOR about anxiety; clumsiness; confusion; deepening of the voice (in women); enlarged breasts (in both sexes); fever; impotence; increased hair growth; menstrual disturbances; muscle cramps; numbness or tingling in the hands, feet, or lips; palpitations; postmenopausal bleeding; rapid weight gain (three to five pounds within a week); stomach cramps; uncoordinated movements; or unusual tiredness or weakness.

INTERACTIONS

Spironolactone may interact with several other medications as well as with certain food products:

1. Concurrent use of spironolactone with amiloride, antihypertensive agents (such as benazepril, captopril, enalapril, fosinopril, lisinopril, quinapril, and ramipril) triamterene, potassium salts, low-salt milk, salt substitutes, or laxatives can cause serious side effects such as hyperkalemia (high blood levels of potassium).

2. Spironolactone may increase the side effects of lithium, digoxin, digitoxin, and ammonium chloride.

3. The effectiveness of oral anticoagulants (blood thinners) may be decreased by this medication.

4. Concurrent use of aspirin may decrease the diuretic effects of spironolactone.

5. Extreme drowsiness can occur when this medication is taken with other central nervous system depressants, such as alcohol, antihistamines, antidepressants, barbiturates, benzodiazepine tranquilizers, muscle relaxants, narcotics, pain medications, and sleeping medications.

Before starting to take spironolactone, BE SURE TO TELL YOUR DOCTOR about any medications you are currently taking, especially any of those listed above.

WARNINGS

• Tell your doctor about unusual or allergic reactions you have had to any medications, especially to spironolactone or to any other diuretic.

• Tell your doctor if you have ever had kidney or urination problems, heart disease, hyperkalemia (high blood levels of potassium), liver disease, menstrual abnormalities, breast enlargement, or diabetes mellitus.

• Spironolactone can cause hyperkalemia. Signs of hyperkalemia include palpitations; confusion; numbness or tingling in the hands, feet, or lips; anxiety; or unusual tiredness or weakness. However, do not alter your diet in an effort to avoid this problem unless your doctor tells you to do so. Elderly patients may be more susceptible to hyperkalemia.

• There are several generic brands of this drug. Consult your pharmacist about these items; some of them are not equivalent to the brand-name medications.

• Limit your intake of alcoholic beverages to prevent dizziness and light-headedness while taking this drug.

• Do not take any over-the-counter (nonprescription) medications for weight control or for allergy problems, asthma, cough, cold, or sinus problems unless you first get your doctor's approval.
• This medication may cause extreme fatigue and dizziness. Your ability to perform tasks that require alertness, such as driving a car or operating potentially dangerous machinery, may be decreased. Take appropriate caution.
• To prevent severe water loss (dehydration) while taking this medication, check with your doctor if you have or develop any illness that causes severe or continuous nausea, vomiting, or diarrhea.
• Be sure to tell your doctor if you are pregnant. This drug crosses the placenta, and its safety in human pregnancy has not been established. Adverse effects have been observed in the fetuses of animals that were given large doses of this drug during pregnancy. Also tell your doctor if you are breast-feeding an infant.

---

stavudine

BRAND NAMES (Manufacturers)
Zerit (BMS Virology)
Zerit XR (BMS Virology)
TYPE OF DRUG
Antiviral
INGREDIENT
stavudine
DOSAGE FORMS
Capsules (15 mg, 20 mg, 30 mg, and 40 mg)
Capsules, extended release (37.5 mg, 50 mg, 75 mg, and 100 mg)
Powder for oral solution (1 mg/mL)
STORAGE
Store at room temperature in a tightly closed container. Do not expose to excess heat. Once a solution has been prepared from the powder, keep it in the refrigerator. Discard any unused portion after 30 days.

USES

Stavudine is used in the treatment of human immunodeficiency virus (HIV) infection. HIV is the virus that causes AIDS. Stavudine works by inhibiting the reproduction, or growth, of the virus, which slows down the progression of AIDS. Stavudine does not cure HIV infection or AIDS, but it may delay the onset of other infections and diseases caused by AIDS. Stavudine is usually not used alone but rather in combination with other anti-AIDS medications.

TREATMENT

This medication works best when the level of medicine in your bloodstream is kept constant. It is best to take the drug at evenly spaced intervals throughout the day. IT IS IMPORTANT NOT TO MISS ANY DOSES OF STAVUDINE. The chances of the AIDS virus becoming resistant to stavudine increase if the level of medication in the bloodstream is low. To lessen stomach irritation, stavudine may be taken with food, unless your doctor tells you to do otherwise.

If you have been prescribed the extended-release capsule and have a difficult time swallowing it, you can open the capsule and mix the contents with 30 mL of yogurt or applesauce. Be careful not to chew or crush the beads while swallowing.

If you miss a dose of this medication, take it as soon as possible. However, if it is almost time for your next dose, skip the missed dose and go back to your regular dosing schedule. Do not double the next dose.

SIDE EFFECTS

Minor. Diarrhea, difficulty sleeping, general weak feeling, headache, loss of appetite, nausea, or vomiting. As your body adjusts to the medication, some of these side effects should diminish or disappear.

Major. Tell your doctor about any side effects that are persistent or particularly bothersome. IT IS ESPECIALLY IMPORTANT TO TELL YOUR DOCTOR about fat accumulation on your back; fever; joint or muscle pain; severe abdominal pain with nausea and vomiting; skin rash; tingling, burning, numbness, or pain in the hands or feet; or unusual tiredness or weakness.

INTERACTIONS

Stavudine may interact with a number of other drugs:

Stavudine may cause lactic acidosis and a condition known as peripheral neuropathy, which is numbness, pain, burning, or tingling, usually in the hands or feet. Because of this, stavudine should not be taken with other drugs that may cause these conditions, including chloramphenicol, cisplatin, dapsone, didanosine, ethambutol, ethionamide, hydralazine, isoniazid, lithium, metronidazole, nitrofurantoin, phenytoin, vincristine, zalcitabine, or hydroxyurea.

Before starting to take stavudine, BE SURE TO TELL YOUR DOCTOR about any medications, both prescription and over-the-counter (nonprescription), you are currently taking, especially any of those listed above.

WARNINGS

- Tell your doctor if you have ever had an allergic reaction to any medication, especially to stavudine or any other medication used to treat AIDS.
- This medication may cause a condition known as peripheral neuropathy, which is tingling, burning, pain, or numbness in the hands or feet. It usually stops when the drug is stopped. If you have these symptoms while taking stavudine, be sure to tell your doctor immediately.
- Although uncommon, stavudine may also cause inflammation of the pancreas (known as pancreatitis). You should contact your doctor immediately if you develop abdominal pain, nausea, and vomiting. Also, your doctor may do regular blood tests to determine if stavudine is adversely affecting your pancreas.
- Before taking this medication, be sure to tell your doctor about any medical problems you may have, especially liver or renal problems, problems with the pancreas, or tingling, numbness, burning, or pain in the hands or feet.
- Before having surgery or any other medical or dental treatment, be sure to tell your doctor or dentist that you are taking this medication.
- Your doctor may do regular blood tests to see how well this medication is working against the AIDS virus.
- If you are infected with HIV, it is best to avoid any sexual activity involving an exchange of body fluids with other people. If you do have vaginal, anal, or oral sex, always use a latex condom.
- Be sure to tell your doctor if you are pregnant. It is not known if stavudine is safe to use during pregnancy. It is not known if stavudine passes into human breast milk. However, because of the risk of passing HIV to infants, it is recommended that mothers who have HIV infection NOT breast-feed their infants.

---

sucralfate

BRAND NAMES (Manufacturers)

Carafate (Aventis)
sucralfate (various manufacturers)

TYPE OF DRUG
Antiulcer
INGREDIENT
sucralfate
DOSAGE FORMS
Tablets (1 g)
Suspension (1 g per 10 mL)
STORAGE
Store at room temperature in a tightly closed container. Do not refrigerate.

USES

Sucralfate is used for the short-term treatment of ulcers. This medication binds to the surface of the ulcer, thereby protecting it from stomach acid and promoting healing. This medication may be used for other medical conditions when prescribed by your doctor.

TREATMENT

To obtain maximum benefit from this drug, swallow the tablets whole with a full glass of water. Shake the suspension well just before measuring each dose to distribute the ingredients evenly and equalize the doses. The contents tend to settle on the bottom of the bottle. Then measure each dose carefully with a specially designed 5-mL measuring spoon, as directed by your doctor or pharmacist. An ordinary kitchen teaspoon is not accurate enough.

Take your dose on an empty stomach one hour before or two hours after a meal and at bedtime. Do not take antacids for 30 minutes before or after taking sucralfate.

Continue to take sucralfate for the full length of time prescribed by your doctor, even if your symptoms disappear before you have finished the prescribed amount of the drug. Your ulcer may not yet be healed. However, do not take sucralfate for longer than eight weeks without your doctor's authorization.

If you miss a dose of this medication, take the missed dose as soon as possible. However, if it is almost time for the next dose, do not take the missed dose at all; just return to your regular dosing schedule. Do not double the next dose.

SIDE EFFECTS

Minor. Back pain, constipation, diarrhea, dizziness, drowsiness, dry mouth, indigestion, nausea, or stomach pain. These side effects should disappear as your body adjusts to the medication.

To relieve constipation, exercise and drink more water (unless your doctor directs you to do otherwise).

If this medication makes you feel dizzy, sit or lie down for a while; get up slowly from a sitting or reclining position; and be careful on stairs.

To avoid dizziness when you stand, contract and relax the muscles of your legs for a few moments before rising. Do this by pressing one foot against the floor while raising the other foot slightly, alternating feet so that you are "pumping" your legs in a pedaling motion.

To relieve mouth dryness, chew sugarless gum or suck on ice chips or a piece of hard candy.

Major. Tell your doctor about any side effects that are persistent or particularly bothersome. IT IS ESPECIALLY IMPORTANT TO TELL YOUR DOCTOR about itching or rash. If your condition does not improve or seems to be getting worse, you should contact your doctor.

INTERACTIONS

Sucralfate interacts with several other medications:

1. Sucralfate may prevent the absorption of tetracycline, warfarin, digoxin, phenytoin, ranitidine, ketoconazole, quinidine, and fat-soluble vitamins (vitamins A, D, E, and K) from the gastrointestinal tract. At least two hours should separate doses of any of these medications and sucralfate.
2. Sucralfate may decrease stomach absorption of quinolone antibiotics, including ciprofloxacin, norfloxacin, and ofloxacin. At least two hours should separate doses of these medications and sucralfate.

BE SURE TO TELL YOUR DOCTOR about any medications that you are taking, especially any of the medications that are listed above.

WARNINGS

• Tell your doctor about unusual or allergic reactions you have had to any medications, especially to sucralfate.
• Tell your doctor if you now have or if you have ever had kidney disease.
• If sucralfate makes you dizzy or drowsy, do not take part in any activity that requires mental alertness, such as driving an automobile or operating potentially dangerous machinery or equipment.
• Be sure to tell your doctor if you are pregnant. Although sucralfate appears to be safe to use during pregnancy, extensive studies in pregnant women have not been conducted. In addition, be sure to tell your doctor if you are breast-feeding an infant. It is not known whether sucralfate passes into breast milk.

---

sulfamethoxazole and trimethoprim combination

BRAND NAMES (Manufacturers)
Bactrim (Roche)
Bactrim DS (Roche)
Bactrim Pediatric (Roche)
Bethaprim DS (Major)
Cotrim (Lemmon)
Cotrim DS (Lemmon)
Cotrim Pediatric (Lemmon)
Septra (Glaxo-Wellcome)
Septra DS (Glaxo-Wellcome)
sulfamethoxazole and trimethoprim (various manufacturers)
Sulfatrim (various manufacturers)
TYPE OF DRUG
Antibiotic
INGREDIENTS
sulfamethoxazole and trimethoprim
DOSAGE FORMS
Tablets (400 mg sulfamethoxazole and 80 mg trimethoprim)
Double-strength (DS) tablets (800 mg sulfamethoxazole and 160 mg trimethoprim)
Oral suspension (200 mg sulfamethoxazole and 40 mg trimethoprim per 5-mL spoonful)
STORAGE
Store at room temperature in tightly closed, light-resistant containers. The oral suspension does not need to be refrigerated. This medication should never be frozen.

USES

Sulfamethoxazole and trimethoprim combination is used to treat a broad range of infections, including urinary tract infections, certain respiratory and gastrointestinal infections, and otitis media (middle-ear infection). Sulfamethoxazole and trimethoprim acts by preventing production of the nutrients that are required for growth of the infecting bacteria.

TREATMENT

It is best to take the tablets with a full glass of water on an empty stomach, either one hour before or two hours after a meal. However, if this drug causes stomach upset, check with your doctor to see if you can take it with food or milk.

Shake the oral suspension well just before measuring each dose to distribute the ingredients evenly and equalize the doses. The contents tend to settle on the bottom of the bottle. Measure each dose carefully with a specially designed 5-mL measuring spoon. An ordinary kitchen teaspoon is not accurate enough.

This medication works best when the level of medicine in your system is kept constant. Therefore, it is best to take the doses at evenly spaced intervals day and night. For example, if you are to take two doses a day, the doses should be spaced 12 hours apart. Try not to skip any doses.

If you miss a dose of this medication, take the missed dose immediately. However, if you do not remember to take the missed dose until it is almost time for your next dose, take the missed dose immediately; space the following dose about halfway through the regular interval between doses (wait about six hours if you are taking two doses a day); and then return to your regular dosing schedule.

It is important to continue to take this medication for the entire time prescribed by your doctor (usually 7 to 14 days), even if the symptoms disappear before the end of that period. If you stop taking the drug too soon, resistant bacteria are given a chance to continue growing, and the infection could recur.

SIDE EFFECTS

Minor. Abdominal pain, diarrhea, dizziness, headache, loss of appetite, nausea, sore mouth, or vomiting. These side effects should diminish or disappear as your body adjusts to the drug.

Sulfamethoxazole and trimethoprim combination can cause increased sensitivity to sunlight. It is, therefore, important to avoid prolonged exposure to sunlight and sunlamps while you are being treated with this medication. Wear protective clothing and sunglasses and use sunscreen when outdoors during daylight hours. However, do not use a sunscreen that contains para-aminobenzoic acid (PABA), which interferes with the antibacterial activity of this medication.

If this medication makes you feel dizzy, sit or lie down for a while; get up slowly from a sitting or reclining position; and be careful on stairs.

To avoid dizziness when you stand, contract and relax the muscles in your legs for a few moments before rising. Do this by pressing one foot against the floor while raising the other foot slightly, alternating feet so that you are "pumping" your legs in a pedaling motion.

Major. Tell your doctor about any side effects that are persistent or particularly bothersome. IT IS ESPECIALLY IMPORTANT TO TELL YOUR DOCTOR about bloody urine, convulsions, difficult or painful urination, difficulty in breathing, difficulty in swallowing, fever, hallucinations, itching, joint pain, lower back pain, pale skin, rash, ringing in the ears, sore throat, swelling of the front part of the neck, swollen or inflamed tongue, tingling in the hands or feet, unusual bleeding or bruising, unusual fatigue, or yellowing of the eyes or skin. If your infection seems to be getting worse rather than improving, contact your doctor.

INTERACTIONS

This medicine will interact with several other types of medications:

1. Sulfamethoxazole can increase the blood levels of oral anticoagulants (blood thinners, such as warfarin), oral antidiabetic agents, methotrexate, aspirin, cyclosporine, zidovudine, and phenytoin, which can lead to serious side effects from these medications.

2. Probenecid and sulfinpyrazone can increase the blood levels of sulfamethoxazole, which can lead to an increase in side effects.

3. Concurrent use of trimethoprim with antineoplastic agents (anticancer drugs) can increase the risk of developing blood disorders.

BE SURE TO TELL YOUR DOCTOR about any medications you are currently taking, especially any of the medications that are listed above.

WARNINGS

• Tell your doctor about unusual or allergic reactions you have had to any medications, especially to trimethoprim, sulfamethoxazole, or other sulfa drugs (other sulfonamide antibiotics, diuretics, dapsone, sulfoxone, oral antidiabetic medications, oral antiglaucoma medication, or acetazolamide).

• Tell your doctor if you now have or ever had glucose–6-phosphate dehydrogenase (G6PD) deficiency, kidney disease, liver disease, porphyria, or megaloblastic anemia (folate-deficiency anemia).

• This medication has been prescribed for your current infection only. Another infection you develop later on, or one that someone else develops, may require a different medicine. You should not give your medicine to other people or use it for other infections, unless your doctor specifically directs you to do so.

• This drug should be taken with plenty of water to avoid kidney stone formation.

• If this medication tends to make you dizzy or drowsy, do not take part in any activity that requires mental alertness, such as driving an automobile or operating potentially hazardous machinery or equipment.

• If there is no improvement in your condition several days after starting treatment with this medication, check with your doctor. This medication may not be effective against the bacteria causing your infection.

• Before having surgery or any other medical or dental treatment, be sure to tell your doctor or dentist that you are taking this medication.

• Be sure to tell your doctor if you are pregnant. Small amounts of sulfamethoxazole and trimethoprim cross the placenta. Although these drugs appear to be safe during pregnancy, extensive studies in humans have not been conducted. Trimethoprim has been shown to cause birth defects in the offspring of animals that received very large doses during pregnancy. Tell your doctor if you are breast-feeding. Small amounts of sulfamethoxazole pass into breast milk and may temporarily alter the bacterial balance in the intestinal tract of the nursing infant, resulting in diarrhea. Small amounts of trimethoprim also pass into breast milk, and there is a chance that it may cause anemia in the nursing infant. This combination medication should not be used in an infant less than two months of age (to avoid side effects involving the liver).

---

sulfasalazine

BRAND NAMES (Manufacturers)
Azulfidine (Kabi Pharmacia)
Azulfidine EN-tabs (Kabi Pharmacia)
sulfasalazine (various manufacturers)
TYPE OF DRUG
Sulfonamide and anti-inflammatory
INGREDIENT
sulfasalazine
DOSAGE FORMS
Tablets (500 mg)
Enteric-coated tablets (500 mg)

STORAGE
Store at room temperature in a tightly closed, light-resistant container. Do not refrigerate.

USES
This medication is used to treat inflammatory bowel disease (regional enteritis or ulcerative colitis) and rheumatoid arthritis in adults and children. In the intestine, sulfasalazine is converted to 5-aminosalicylic acid, an aspirinlike drug, which acts to relieve inflammation.

TREATMENT
To avoid stomach irritation while you are being treated with this medication, take your doses with a full glass of water, with food, or after meals (unless your doctor directs you to do otherwise).

Swallow the enteric-coated tablets whole. The enteric coating is added to lessen stomach irritation. Chewing, breaking, or crushing these tablets destroys the coating.

If you miss a dose of this medication, take the missed dose as soon as possible. However, if it is almost time for the next dose, do not take the missed dose at all; just return to your regular dosing schedule. Do not double the next dose.

SIDE EFFECTS
Minor. Diarrhea, dizziness, drowsiness, insomnia, loss of appetite, mild headache, nausea, stomach upset, or vomiting. These side effects should diminish or disappear as your body adjusts to the medication.

This medication can increase your sensitivity to sunlight. Avoid prolonged exposure to sunlight and sunlamps during treatment. Wear protective clothing and use a sunscreen when you are outdoors during daylight hours. However, do not use a sunscreen that contains para-aminobenzoic acid (PABA), because it interferes with this medication's action.

Sulfasalazine can discolor contact lenses. You may want to stop wearing them while taking this medication. Discuss this with your ophthalmologist.

Sulfasalazine can cause your urine to change to an orange-yellow color. This is a harmless effect.

If you feel dizzy while being treated with sulfasalazine, sit or lie down for a while; get up slowly from a sitting or reclining position; and be careful on stairs.

To avoid dizziness when you stand, contract and relax the muscles of your legs for a few moments before rising. Do this by pressing one foot against the floor while raising the other foot slightly, alternating feet so that you are "pumping" your legs in a pedaling motion.

Major. Tell your doctor about any side effects that are persistent or particularly bothersome. IT IS ESPECIALLY IMPORTANT TO TELL YOUR DOCTOR about blood in the urine, convulsions, depression, difficulty in swallowing, difficult or painful urination, fatigue, fever, hallucinations, hearing loss, itching, joint pain, lower back pain, mouth sores, pale skin, rash or peeling skin, ringing in the ears, severe headache, sore throat, swelling of the front part of the neck, tingling sensations, unusual bleeding or bruising, or a yellowish discoloration of the eyes or skin.

INTERACTIONS
Sulfasalazine interacts with a number of other types of medications:

1. Sulfasalazine can increase the side effects of oral anticoagulants (blood thinners, such as warfarin), oral antidiabetic agents, methotrexate, aspirin, and phenytoin.

2. The blood levels and effectiveness of digoxin and folic acid are decreased by concurrent use of sulfasalazine.

BE SURE TO TELL YOUR DOCTOR about any medications you are currently taking, especially any listed above.

WARNINGS

• Tell your doctor about any unusual or allergic reactions you have had to any medications, especially any reactions to sulfasalazine, aspirin or other salicylates, or any sulfa drug (diuretics, oral antidiabetic medications, sulfonamide antibiotics, oral antiglaucoma medication, acetazolamide, sulfoxone, dapsone).
• Before starting to take this drug, be sure to tell your doctor if you now have or ever had blood disorders, blockage of the urinary tract or intestine, glucose–6-phosphate dehydrogenase (G6PD) deficiency, kidney disease, liver disease, or porphyria.
• To help prevent formation of kidney stones, drink at least 8 to 12 glasses of water or fruit juice each day while taking this drug (unless your doctor directs you otherwise).
• Before having surgery or other medical or dental treatment, tell your doctor or dentist you are taking this drug.
• If your condition does not improve within a month or two after starting to take sulfasalazine, check with your doctor. It may be necessary to change your medication.
• Be sure to tell your doctor if you are pregnant. Although sulfasalazine appears to be safe during most of pregnancy, extensive studies in humans have not been conducted. There is also concern that if this drug is taken during the ninth month of pregnancy, it may cause liver or brain disorders in the infant. In addition, notify your physician if you are breast-feeding an infant. Small amounts of sulfasalazine pass into breast milk, so caution is warranted.

---

sumatriptan

BRAND NAME (Manufacturer)
Imitrex (Cerenex)
TYPE OF DRUG
Antimigraine agent
INGREDIENT
sumatriptan
DOSAGE FORMS
Injection (6 mg per 0.5 mL)
Nasal solution (5 mg and 20 mg per spray)
Tablets (25 mg, 50 mg, and 100 mg)
STORAGE
Store this medication at room temperature in a tightly closed container. Protect this medication from heat and light, and do not freeze it. Also, check the expiration date on the label; do not use if the expiration date has passed.

USES

Although it is not completely known how sumatriptan works, this medicine helps to stop migraine headaches by altering the level of a chemical in the brain called serotonin. Sumatriptan is used for the treatment of migraine headaches for those patients who do not get relief from other antiheadache medicines, such as acetaminophen, aspirin, and nonsteroidal anti-inflammatory drugs (NSAIDs). This medication is not effective for preventing migraine headaches or for the treatment of cluster headaches.

TREATMENT

Sumatriptan may be taken with or without food. This medication may work more effectively if you lie down in a quiet, darkened room after taking it.

The tablet form of this medication must be swallowed whole (without crushing or chewing). If your migraine headache is less severe after your first sumatriptan tablet, your doctor may instruct you to take a second tablet two hours after the first tablet if the headache pain starts to come back. It is very important that you obtain specific instructions on the use of this medicine from your doctor. Never double the dose.

The injection should be given under the skin (subcutaneously). If you are using the injection form, your doctor, pharmacist, or other health care professional will teach you exactly how and when to use this medication.

The nasal solution should be administered in 5 to 10 mg doses (1 to 2 sprays) in each nostril or as a single 20 mg dose (1 spray) into one nostril. Additional sprays should not be given for at least two hours. Be sure that you get a thorough explanation and/or demonstration of how to properly administer the nasal spray from your doctor, pharmacist, or other health care professional.

SIDE EFFECTS

Minor. Bad taste in your mouth; dizziness; ear, nose, or throat discomfort; flushing; muscle pain; nausea; skin rash; stiff neck; tingling; or weakness. These side effects should diminish or disappear as your body adjusts to the medication.

Major. Tell your doctor about any side effects that are persistent or particularly bothersome. IT IS ESPECIALLY IMPORTANT TO TELL YOUR DOCTOR about chest pain, irregular heartbeats, and tightness or heaviness in the chest.

INTERACTIONS

Sumatriptan interacts with several other medications:

1. Sumatriptan can interact with a class of drugs called monoamine oxidase (MAO) inhibitors to produce dangerous side effects. It is very important, therefore, that sumatriptan and MAO inhibitors (including isocarboxazid, pargyline, phenelzine, selegilene, or tranylcypromine) not be taken together. At least 14 days must separate a dose of an MAO inhibitor and sumatriptan. If you take an MAO inhibitor and sumatriptan has been prescribed for you, be sure to discuss this with your doctor.

2. The concurrent use of sumatriptan and certain antidepressants (including fluoxetine, paroxetine, sertraline, citalopram, and fluvoxamine) or sibutramine may produce weakness, incoordination, and other adverse effects. Discuss this risk with your doctor or pharmacist if you take any of these medications and sumatriptan has been prescribed for you.

3. Sumatriptan may increase the side effects caused by ergot-containing or ergot-type medications (such as methysergide and dihydroergotamine). Therefore, it is very important that the use of these ergot medications and sumatriptan be separated by at least 24 hours.

Before starting to take sumatriptan, BE SURE TO TELL YOUR DOCTOR about any medications you are currently taking, especially any of those listed above.

WARNINGS

• Tell your doctor about any unusual or allergic reactions you have had to any medications, especially to sumatriptan, zolmitriptan, naratriptan, or rizatriptan.

• Tell your doctor if you have or have ever had a stroke, hardening of the arteries, high blood pressure, high blood cholesterol, or diabetes.

• Notify your doctor if you are or have been a smoker or if you have a family history of heart disease.

• Be sure to tell your doctor IMMEDIATELY if you are pregnant. The effects of this medication in human pregnancy have not been thoroughly studied. In addition, be sure to tell your doctor if you are breast-feeding an infant. Small amounts of sumatriptan pass into breast milk.

---

tamoxifen

BRAND NAMES (Manufacturers)

Nolvadex (AstraZeneca)

tamoxifen (various manufacturers)

TYPE OF DRUG
Antiestrogen and antineoplastic (anticancer drug)
INGREDIENT
tamoxifen
DOSAGE FORM
Tablets (10 mg and 20 mg)
STORAGE
Store at room temperature in a tightly closed, light-resistant container.

USES

This medication is used in the prevention and treatment of breast cancer. Tamoxifen is a nonsteroidal antiestrogen drug. It is not yet fully understood how tamoxifen works, but it is possible that the drug acts to block estrogen from binding to the breast tissue. This action would work to inhibit further tumor growth.

TREATMENT

Tamoxifen can be taken either on an empty stomach or with food or a glass of milk, unless your doctor directs you to do otherwise.

If you miss a dose of this medication, take the missed dose as soon as possible. However, if it is almost time for the next dose, do not take the missed dose at all; just return to your regular dosing schedule. Do not double the next dose of this medication.

SIDE EFFECTS

Minor. Distaste for food, dizziness, headache, hot flashes, light-headedness, nausea, vaginal itching, or vomiting. These side effects should disappear as your body adjusts to the medication.

It is extremely important to take this medication in spite of any nausea or vomiting that you may experience. If you do vomit immediately after taking a dose of tamoxifen, call your physician; it may be necessary for you to repeat the dose.

It is possible that you may experience an increase in bone and tumor pain when you first start treatment with tamoxifen. The pain generally subsides rapidly but may require the temporary use of analgesics (pain relievers). Be sure to consult your doctor if you experience any unusual pain after starting therapy with tamoxifen.

If you feel dizzy or light-headed, sit or lie down for a while; get up slowly from a sitting or reclining position; and be careful on stairs.

To help avoid dizziness when you stand, contract and relax the muscles in your legs for a few moments before rising. Do this by pressing one foot against the floor while raising the other foot slightly, alternating feet so that you are "pumping" your legs in a pedaling motion.

Major. Tell your doctor about any side effects that are persistent or particularly bothersome. IT IS ESPECIALLY IMPORTANT TO TELL YOUR DOCTOR about blurred vision; chills; depression; fever; new breast lumps; pain, swelling, or tenderness in your legs; rapid weight gain (three to five pounds within a week); rash; sore throat; unusual weakness; or vaginal bleeding or discharge.

INTERACTIONS

The activity and anticoagulant (blood-thinning) effects of drugs such as warfarin can be increased when they are taken at the same time as tamoxifen. Be sure to tell your doctor if you are taking an anticoagulant.

BE SURE TO TELL YOUR DOCTOR about any medications, whether prescription or over-the-counter (nonprescription), that you are taking.

WARNINGS

- Be sure to tell your doctor about any unusual or allergic reactions you have had to any medications, especially to tamoxifen.

• Before starting to take this medication, be sure to tell your doctor if you now have or ever had blood disorders or visual disturbances.
• Before starting to take this medication, it is very important for you to tell your doctor if you are pregnant. Although there have been no studies done on the effects of this medication in pregnant women, isolated reports of problems have been documented when pregnant women have been using tamoxifen. Also be sure to notify your physician if you are breast-feeding. This medication should not be taken by nursing women.

---

tamsulosin

BRAND NAME (Manufacturer)
Flomax (Boehringer Ingelheim)
TYPE OF DRUG
Benign-prostatic-hyperplasia agent
INGREDIENT
tamsulosin
DOSAGE FORM
Capsules (0.4 mg)
STORAGE
Store at room temperature in a tightly closed container. Do not expose to excess heat.

USES

Tamsulosin is used to reduce urinary obstruction and relieve the symptoms associated with symptomatic benign prostatic hyperplasia (BPH). The drug can effectively relieve the hesitancy, dribbling of urine, and sensation of incomplete bladder emptying often associated with BPH.

TREATMENT

Take this medication about 30 minutes after the same meal each day unless your doctor tells you to do otherwise. Swallow the capsules whole; do not chew, crush, or open them. The effects of this medication may not be apparent for two to four weeks.

If you miss a dose of this medication, take it as soon as you remember. However, if it is almost time for the next dose, do not take the missed dose at all; just return to your regular dosing schedule. Do not double the next dose.

SIDE EFFECTS

Minor. Back pain, diarrhea, dizziness, drowsiness, faintness when getting up after sitting or lying down, headache, nausea, sexual problems, stuffy or runny nose, or unusual weakness. As your body adjusts to the medication, some of these side effects should disappear.

If this medication makes you feel dizzy, sit or lie down for a while, get up slowly from a sitting or recling position, and be careful on stairs.

To avoid dizziness or light-headedness when you stand, contract and relax the muscles of your legs for a few moments before rising. Do this by pressing one foot against the floor while raising the other foot slightly, alternating feet so that you are "pumping" your legs in a pedaling motion.

Major. Tell your doctor about any side effects that are persistent or particularly bothersome. IT IS ESPECIALLY IMPORTANT TO TELL YOUR DOCTOR about difficulty urinating, light-headedness, or sexual difficulties.

INTERACTIONS

Tamsulosin may interact with a number of other drugs:
1. Tamsulosin may interfere with the actions of warfarin, a blood thinner.

2. The drug cimetidine may increase the amount of tamsulosin in the body.
3. Tamsulosin may increase the blood-pressure-lowering effects of other antihypertensive medications.
4. To avoid drug interactions, it is very important that you do not take any over-the-counter (nonprescription) medications for weight control or for asthma, sinus problems, cough, cold, or allergy problems unless you first check with a doctor or pharmacist.
5. It is important to avoid drinking alcohol when you are taking tamsulosin. If you drink alcohol at the same time that you are being treated with this medication, your blood pressure may become dangerously low.

WARNINGS

- Be sure to tell your doctor about any unusual or allergic reactions you may have had to any medications, including tamsulosin, terazosin, doxazosin, or prazosin.
- You should tell your doctor about any medical problems you may have, especially heart or kidney problems and high or low blood pressure.
- This medication may cause dizziness. Your ability to perform tasks that require alertness, such as driving a car or operating heavy machinery, may be decreased. Appropriate caution should be taken.

---

tegaserod

BRAND NAME (Manufacturer)
Zelnorm (Novartis)
TYPE OF DRUG
Irritable bowel agent
INGREDIENT
tegaserod
DOSAGE FORM
Tablets (2 mg and 6 mg)
STORAGE
Store at room temperature in a tightly closed container. Do not expose to extreme temperatures.

USES

Tegaserod is used for the treatment of irritable bowel syndrome (IBS) in women who have constipation as their main symptom. It should never be taken by women who have diarrhea as their main symptom of IBS. The drug works to increase the activity of the bowels by altering certain chemicals and hormones in your bowels. When taken as directed, this medication will help to lessen the constipation, abdominal bloating, and pain associated with IBS. Tegaserod does not cure IBS, but it will help to manage the symptoms as long as you take the medication.

TREATMENT

This medication is usually taken twice a day. It is best to take tegaserod on an empty stomach, shortly before a meal. In addition, it is best to take this medication at approximately the same time each day.

It is important to try not to miss any doses of this medication. If you do miss a dose, skip the missed dose and return to your regular dosing schedule. Do not double the next dose of this medication.

SIDE EFFECTS

Minor. Back pain, bloated feeling, gas, headache, mild dizziness, or nausea. These side effects usually go away during treatment, as your body adjusts to the medicine.

To avoid dizziness or light-headedness when you stand, contract and relax the muscles of your legs for a few moments before rising. Do this by pressing one foot against the floor while raising the other foot slightly, alternating feet so that you are "pumping" your legs in a pedaling motion.

If you feel dizzy or light-headed, sit or lie down for a while; get up from a sitting or lying position slowly; and be careful on stairs.

Major. Tell your doctor if any side effects are persistent or particularly bothersome. IT IS ESPECIALLY IMPORTANT TO TELL YOUR DOCTOR about cold sweats; confusion; diarrhea; feeling of warmth; itching skin; shortness of breath; stomach pain or cramps; swelling or redness of the legs, feet, hands, or arms; or vomiting.

INTERACTIONS

Tegaserod has not been reported to cause any drug interactions. However, to avoid drug interactions, it is very important that you do not take any over-the-counter (nonprescription) medications for weight control or for asthma, sinus, cough, cold, or allergy problems unless you first check with your doctor or pharmacist.

BE SURE TO TELL YOUR DOCTOR about any medications you may be taking.

WARNINGS

- It is important to tell your doctor if you have ever had any unusual or allergic reaction to tegaserod or to any other medication.
- When you first start to take this medication, your doctor may have you return frequently to see how the medication is working. It is important to tell your doctor if you have any abdominal pain after you begin to take tegaserod.
- This drug should only be used in adult women; it has not been tested in males.
- It is also important to tell your doctor if you now have or if you have ever had kidney disease, liver disease, gallbladder disease, bowel obstructions or intestinal blockage, sphincter of Oddi dysfunction (severe stomach pain with nausea and vomiting), or swelling of the hands or feet.
- While taking this medication, your ability to perform tasks that require alertness, such as driving a car or operating potentially dangerous machinery, may be impaired.
- Be sure to tell your doctor or dentist that you are taking this medicine before having any kind of surgery or other medical or dental treatment.
- Tell your doctor if you are pregnant. Studies in human pregnancy have not yet been completed, and it is unknown if tegaserod can cause birth defects. Also tell your doctor if you are breast-feeding an infant, and discuss the risks and benefits of this drug.

---

telmisartan

BRAND NAME (Manufacturer)
Micardis (Boehringer)
TYPE OF DRUG
Antihypertensive agent
INGREDIENT
telmisartan
DOSAGE FORM
Tablets (20 mg, 40 mg, and 80 mg)
STORAGE
Store at room temperature in a tightly closed container. Do not expose to excess heat. Do not remove tablets from the blister packet until you are ready to take the tablet.

USES

Telmisartan is used to treat high blood pressure. It is a vasodilator (it widens the blood vessels) that acts by blocking the production of chemicals that may be responsible for constricting or narrowing the blood vessels. It may be used for other medical conditions, including heart failure, when prescribed by your doctor.

TREATMENT

Telmisartan may be taken either on an empty stomach or with food or milk (unless your doctor directs you to do otherwise). To become accustomed to this medication, take telmisartan at the same time every day.

It may take several weeks before you notice the full effects of this medication.

If you miss a dose of this medication, take the missed dose as soon as possible. However, if it is almost time for your next dose, do not take the missed dose at all; just return to your regular dosing schedule. Do not double the next dose or take more than prescribed by your doctor.

It is important that you take this medication on a regular basis as prescribed by your doctor. Telmisartan does not cure high blood pressure, but it will help you to control the condition for as long as you continue to take it.

SIDE EFFECTS

Minor. Abdominal pain, constipation, cough, diarrhea, dizziness, dry mouth, fatigue, flushing, headache, insomnia, loss of appetite, loss of sense of taste, nausea, or vomiting. Most of these side effects should diminish or disappear as your body adjusts to the medication.

Dry mouth can be relieved by chewing sugarless gum or sucking on hard candy.

To avoid dizziness or light-headedness when you stand, contract and relax the muscles of your legs for a few moments before rising. Do this by pushing one foot against the floor while raising the other foot slightly, alternating feet so that you are "pumping" your legs in a pedaling motion.

If you feel dizzy or light-headed, sit or lie down for a while; get up from a sitting or lying position slowly; and be careful on stairs.

To relieve constipation, increase the amount of fiber in your diet (fresh fruits and vegetables, salads, bran, and whole-grain breads), exercise, and drink more water (unless your doctor directs you to do otherwise).

Major. Tell your doctor about any side effects that are persistent or particularly bothersome. IT IS ESPECIALLY IMPORTANT TO TELL YOUR DOCTOR about chest pains; chills; difficult or painful urination; fever; itching; mouth sores; palpitations; prolonged vomiting or diarrhea; skin rash; sore throat; swelling of the face, hands, or feet; tingling of the fingers or toes; unusual bleeding or bruising; or yellowing of the skin or the whites of the eyes.

INTERACTIONS

Telmisartan may interact with a number of other medications:

1. Diuretics (water pills) and other antihypertensive drugs can cause an excessive drop in blood pressure when combined with telmisartan (especially the first dose).

2. The combination of telmisartan with spironolactone, triamterene, amiloride, potassium supplements, or salt substitutes can lead to hyperkalemia (dangerously high levels of potassium in the bloodstream).

3. Indomethacin and other nonsteroidal anti-inflammatory drugs (such as ibuprofen or naproxen) may decrease the blood-pressure-lowering effects of telmisartan.

4. Concurrent use of telmisartan and digoxin can delay the body's elimination of digoxin and may cause digoxin toxicity. Discuss this with your doctor or pharmacist.

5. Alcohol should be avoided during treatment with telmisartan. This combination may cause your blood pressure to become too low.

6. Use of over-the-counter (nonprescription) cough, cold, or allergy medications may reduce the effectiveness of this medication and should be avoided.

BE SURE TO TELL YOUR DOCTOR about these or any other medications you are currently taking.

WARNINGS

• Be sure to tell your doctor if you have ever experienced an allergic reaction to telmisartan, to any medication that is used to treat high blood pressure, or to any other medications, especially to angiotensin-converting enzyme (ACE) inhibitors (including captopril, enalapril, lisinopril, and benazepril), candesartan, eprosartan, irbesartan, losartan, olmesartan, or valsartan.
• Tell your doctor if you now have or ever had kidney or liver disease, heart disease, swelling of the face or mouth, aortic stenosis, lupus or scleroderma, diabetes mellitus, too high potassium levels in your blood, or any type of blood disorder.
• Call your doctor immediately if you experience any swelling of the face or mouth or difficulty breathing or swallowing after taking this medication.
• While taking this medication, your ability to perform tasks that require alertness, such as driving an automobile or operating potentially dangerous machinery, may be impaired. Caution is required.
• If you are having surgery or undergoing any type of dental procedure, be sure to tell your doctor or dentist that you are taking telmisartan.
• Excessive perspiration, dehydration, or prolonged vomiting or diarrhea can lead to an excessive drop in blood pressure while you are taking this medication. Contact your doctor if you have any of these symptoms.
• Do not stop taking this medication unless you first consult your doctor. Stopping this drug abruptly may lead to a rise in blood pressure.
• The first few doses of this medication may cause dizziness. Try to avoid any sudden changes in posture.
• Be sure to tell your doctor if you are pregnant. Telmisartan may cause birth defects if taken during the second or third trimester of pregnancy. Telmisartan can also pass into human breast milk. Be sure to tell your doctor if you are breast-feeding an infant, and be sure to discuss the risks and benefits of this medication.

---

terazosin

BRAND NAMES (Manufacturers)
Hytrin (Abbott)
terazosin (various manufacturers)
TYPE OF DRUG
Antihypertensive
INGREDIENT
terazosin
DOSAGE FORMS
Capsules (1 mg, 2 mg, 5 mg, and 10 mg)
Tablets (1 mg, 2 mg, 5 mg, and 10 mg)
STORAGE
Store at room temperature in a tightly closed, light-resistant container.

USES

Terazosin is used to treat high blood pressure. It relaxes the muscle tissue of the blood vessels, which in turn lowers blood pressure.

Terazosin is also used to reduce urinary obstruction and relieve the symptoms associated with symptomatic benign prostatic hyperplasia (BPH). The drug can effectively relieve the hesitancy, dribbling of urine, and sensation of incomplete bladder emptying often associated with BPH.

TREATMENT

The first dose of this medication may cause fainting, especially in the elderly. Your doctor will gradually increase your dose to avoid this adverse effect.

If you miss a dose of this medication, take it as soon as possible. However, if it is almost time for your next dose, do not take the missed dose at all; just wait until the next scheduled dose. Do not double the next dose.

This medication does not cure high blood pressure or BPH, but it will help to control the condition as long as you continue to take it. In order to become accustomed to taking this medication, try to take it at the same time(s) each day.

A minimum of four to six weeks may be needed to see a response from the medication for the treatment of BPH.

SIDE EFFECTS

Minor. Cold symptoms, constipation, diarrhea, dizziness, drowsiness, dry mouth, fluid retention, frequent urination, headache, itching, lack of energy, malaise, nasal congestion, nausea, nervousness, rash, sweating, or weight gain. These side effects should disappear as your body adjusts to the medication.

To prevent constipation, increase the amount of fiber in your diet (eat more fresh fruits and vegetables, salads, bran, and whole-grain breads), unless your doctor tells you otherwise.

If this medication makes you feel dizzy, sit or lie down for a while, get up slowly from a sitting or reclining position, and be careful on stairs.

To avoid dizziness or light-headedness when you stand, contract and relax the muscles of your legs for a few moments before rising. Do this by pushing one foot against the floor while raising the other foot slightly, alternating feet so that you are "pumping" your legs.

Major. Tell your doctor about any side effects that are persistent or particularly bothersome. IT IS ESPECIALLY IMPORTANT TO TELL YOUR DOCTOR about blurred vision, chest pain, difficulty breathing, difficulty urinating, fever, flulike symptoms, heart-rate disturbance, impotence, nose bleeds, palpitations, persistent malaise or fatigue, postural effects (dizziness, light-headedness, vertigo leading to reductions in blood pressure or fainting), ringing in the ears, or swelling.

INTERACTIONS

Terazosin has been known to interact with certain other types of medications:

1. The combination of terazosin and alcohol or verapamil can lead to a severe drop in blood pressure and fainting.

2. The severity and duration of the blood-pressure-lowering effects of the initial dose of terazosin may be enhanced by a beta blocker.

3. To avoid drug interactions, do not take any over-the-counter (nonprescription) medications for weight control or for asthma, sinus problems, cough, cold, or allergy problems unless you first check with your doctor or pharmacist.

BE SURE TO TELL YOUR DOCTOR about any medications you are currently taking, especially any of the medications listed above.

WARNINGS

- Tell your doctor about unusual or allergic reactions you have had to any medications, especially to terazosin, prazosin, or doxazosin.
- Before starting to take this medication, be sure to tell your doctor if you now have or ever had angina (chest pain), kidney disease, or liver disease.
- Because initial therapy with this drug may cause dizziness or fainting, your doctor will probably start you on a low dosage and increase the dosage gradually.
- If this drug makes you dizzy or drowsy or blurs your vision, do not take part in any activity that requires alertness, such as driving a car or operating potentially dangerous tools or machinery.
- To avoid dizziness or fainting while taking this drug, try not to stand for long periods of time, avoid drinking excess amounts of alcohol, and try not to get overheated (avoid exercising strenuously in hot weather and taking hot baths, showers, or saunas).

• Before taking any over-the-counter (nonprescription) sinus, allergy, asthma, cough, cold, or diet preparations, check with your doctor or pharmacist. Some of these products can cause an increase in blood pressure.
• Terazosin is only indicated for hypertension and benign prostatic hyperplasia (BPH). This agent is not for symptoms or conditions that appear to be similar to BPH, such as cancer of the prostate.
• Do not stop taking this medication unless you first check with your doctor. If you stop taking this drug, you may experience a rise in blood pressure. Your doctor may want to decrease your dose gradually.
• Be sure to tell your doctor if you are pregnant. Although this medication appears to be safe, there have been only limited studies in pregnant women. Also be sure to tell your doctor if you are breast-feeding an infant; terazosin should be used with caution in nursing women.

---

terbinafine

BRAND NAME (Manufacturer)
Lamisil (Novartis)
TYPE OF DRUG
Antifungal
INGREDIENT
terbinafine
DOSAGE FORM
Tablets (250 mg)
STORAGE
Store this medication at room temperature in a tightly closed container. Do not expose to excess heat.

USES

Terbinafine is used to treat fungal infections of the nail, scalp, skin, groin, and feet. This medication acts by severely damaging the cell walls of the infecting fungus, preventing the fungus from growing and multiplying. Terbinafine is only effective against certain fungi and does not affect bacteria, parasites, or viruses.

TREATMENT

Terbinafine may be taken either on an empty stomach or with food or milk (unless your doctor directs you to do otherwise). Terbinafine should be taken exactly as prescribed by your doctor.

If you are taking terbinafine more than once a day, it is important to take it at evenly spaced intervals throughout the day. If you are taking this medication once a day, it should be taken at the same time each day.

It is important to finish the full course of therapy your doctor prescribes. If you stop taking this medication too soon, resistant fungi can grow and the infection may return. Depending on where the infection is, you may have to take terbinafine for several months.

If you miss a dose of this medication, take it as soon as you remember, unless it is almost time for the next dose. In that case, do not take the missed dose at all; just return to your regular dosing schedule. Do not double the next dose of the medication.

SIDE EFFECTS

Minor. Changes in taste perception, diarrhea, loss of appetite, nausea, stomach upset, or vomiting. As your body adjusts to the medication, these side effects should diminish or disappear.

Major. Tell your doctor about any side effects that are persistent or particularly bothersome. IT IS ESPECIALLY IMPORTANT TO TELL YOUR DOCTOR about aching joints or muscles; blistering, reddening, or peeling of the skin; dark or brown urine; difficulty swallowing; fever, chills, or sore throat; light-colored stools; skin rash or itching; unusual bleeding or bruising; unusual tiredness or weakness; or yellowing of the eyes or skin.

INTERACTIONS

Terbinafine may interact with a number of other medications:
1. Use of alcohol with terbinafine may increase the risk of liver damage.
2. Caffeine, cimetidine, itraconazole, ketoconazole, clarithromycin, erythromycin, fluoxetine, fluvoxamine, indinavir, nefazodone, paroxetine, ritonavir, saquinavir, sertraline, and venlafaxine may increase the risk of side effects from terbinafine.
3. Phenobarbital, carbamazepine, griseofulvin, phenytoin, primidone, and rifampin may lessen the amount of terbinafine in the body and reduce its effectiveness.

WARNINGS

• Be sure to tell your doctor about any unusual or allergic reactions you may have had to any medications, including terbinafine.
• You should tell your doctor about any medical problems you may have, especially alcohol or drug abuse, liver problems, or kidney problems.
• Before starting terbinafine, tell your doctor about any other drugs you are taking.
• Avoid using alcohol while taking this medication because it may increase the risk of liver damage.
• It is important to see your doctor regularly while taking terbinafine to be sure that the medication is working effectively against the infection. Your doctor may want to do blood tests to make sure that the drug is not affecting your liver.
• Be sure to tell your doctor if you are pregnant. It is not known if terbinafine is safe during pregnancy. Terbinafine can pass into human breast milk. This medication is not recommended for nursing mothers.

---

tetracycline

BRAND NAMES (Manufacturers)
Robitet Robicaps (Robins)
Sumycin 250 (Par)
Sumycin 500 (Par)
tetracycline hydrochloride (various manufacturers)
TYPE OF DRUG
Tetracycline antibiotic
INGREDIENT
tetracycline
DOSAGE FORMS
Capsules (250 mg and 500 mg)
Oral suspension (125 mg per 5-mL spoonful)
STORAGE
Store at room temperature in tightly closed, light-resistant containers. Discard any unused portion of the suspension after 14 days because the drug loses its potency after that period. Discard any medication that is outdated or no longer needed. This medication should never be frozen.

USES

Tetracycline is used to treat acne (bacteria may be partly responsible for the development of acne lesions) and a wide variety of bacterial infections. It acts by inhibiting the growth of bacteria. Tetracycline kills susceptible bacteria, but it is not effective against viruses or fungi.

TREATMENT

Ideally, this medication should be taken on an empty stomach one hour before or two hours after a meal. It should be taken with a full glass of water to avoid irritating the throat or esophagus (swallowing tube). If this drug causes stomach upset, however, you can take it with food (unless your doctor directs you to do otherwise).

Avoid consuming dairy products (milk, cheese, etc.) within two hours of any dose of this drug. Avoid taking antacids and laxatives that contain aluminum, calcium, or magnesium within an hour or two of a dose. Avoid taking any medication containing iron within three hours of a dose. These products, including vitamins, chemically bind tetracycline in the stomach and gastrointestinal tract, preventing the drug from being absorbed into the body.

Shake the oral suspension well just before measuring each dose to distribute the ingredients evenly and equalize the doses. The contents tend to settle on the bottom of the bottle. Measure each dose carefully with a specially designed 5-mL measuring spoon. An ordinary kitchen teaspoon is not accurate enough. Do not mix the oral suspension with any other substance unless your doctor tells you to do so.

Tetracycline works best when the level of medicine in your bloodstream is kept constant. It is best to take the doses at evenly spaced intervals day and night. For example, if you are to take four doses a day, the doses should be spaced six hours apart.

If you miss a dose of this medication, take the missed dose immediately. However, if you do not remember to take the missed dose until it is almost time for your next dose, take it; space the following dose about halfway through the regular interval between doses; and then return to your regular dosing schedule.

It is important to continue to take this medication for the entire time prescribed by your doctor, even if the symptoms disappear before the end of that period. If you stop taking the drug too soon, resistant bacteria are given a chance to continue growing, and the infection could recur.

SIDE EFFECTS

Minor. Diarrhea, discoloration of the nails, dizziness, loss of appetite, nausea, stomach cramps and upset, or vomiting. These side effects should diminish or disappear as your body adjusts to the medication.

To avoid dizziness or light-headedness when you stand, contract and relax the muscles of your legs for a few moments before rising. If you feel dizzy, sit or lie down for a while; get up slowly from a sitting or reclining position; and be careful on stairs.

Tetracycline can increase your sensitivity to sunlight. Avoid prolonged exposure to sunlight or sunlamps during treatment with this medication. Wear protective clothing and sunglasses, and use an effective sunscreen.

Major. Tell your doctor about any side effects that are persistent or particularly bothersome. IT IS ESPECIALLY IMPORTANT TO TELL YOUR DOCTOR about darkened tongue, difficulty in breathing, joint pain, mouth irritation, rash, rectal or vaginal itching, sore throat and fever, unusual bleeding or bruising, or yellowing of the eyes or skin. And if your symptoms of infection seem to be getting worse rather than improving, contact your doctor.

INTERACTIONS

Tetracycline interacts with other types of medications:

1. It can increase the absorption of digoxin, which may lead to digoxin toxicity.

2. The gastrointestinal side effects (nausea, vomiting, or stomach upset) of theophylline may be increased by tetracycline.

3. The dosage of oral anticoagulants (blood thinners, such as warfarin) may need to be adjusted when treatment with tetracycline is started.

4. Tetracycline may decrease the effectiveness of oral contraceptives (birth control pills), and pregnancy could result. You should, therefore, use a different or additional form of birth control while taking tetracycline. Discuss this matter with your doctor.

BE SURE TO TELL YOUR DOCTOR about any medications that you are currently taking, especially any of the medications that are listed above.

WARNINGS

• Tell your doctor about unusual or allergic reactions you have had to any medications, especially to tetracycline or to oxytetracycline, doxycycline, or minocycline.
• Tell your doctor if you now have or ever had kidney or liver disease.
• This medication may cause extreme fatigue and dizziness. Your ability to perform tasks that require alertness, such as driving a car or operating potentially dangerous machinery, may be decreased. Take appropriate caution.
• Tetracycline can affect tests for syphilis; tell your doctor you are taking this drug if you are being tested for syphilis.
• Make sure that your prescription for this medication is marked with the expiration date. Discard the medication after the expiration date has passed. If tetracycline is used after it has expired, serious side effects (especially to the kidneys) could result.
• This medication has been prescribed for your current infection only. Another infection later on, or one that someone else has, may require a different medicine. You should not give your medicine to other people or use it for other infections unless your doctor specifically directs you to do so.
• Be sure to tell your doctor if you are pregnant or if you are breast-feeding. Tetracycline crosses the placenta and passes into breast milk. If used during tooth development, this drug can cause permanent tooth discoloration. It can also inhibit tooth and bone growth in the fetus. It should NOT be used in pregnant or nursing women or in children less than eight years of age.

theophylline

BRAND NAMES (Manufacturers)
Aquaphyllin (Ferndale)
Asmalix (Century)
Bronkodyl (Winthrop)
Elixophyllin (Forest)
Lanophyllin (Lannett)
Quibron-T (Roberts)
Slo-bid Gyrocaps (Rorer)
Slo-Phyllin (Rorer)
Sustaire (Pfizer)
Theochron (Inwood)
Theoclear (Central)
Theo-Dur (Key)
Theolair (3M)
theophylline (various manufacturers)
Theospan (Laser)
Theo-24 (Whitby)
Theovent (Schering)
Uniphyl (Purdue Frederick)
TYPE OF DRUG
Bronchodilator
INGREDIENT
theophylline

DOSAGE FORMS

Tablets (100 mg, 125 mg, 200 mg, 250 mg, and 300 mg)
Capsules (100 mg and 200 mg)
Sustained-release tablets and capsules (50 mg, 65 mg, 75 mg, 100 mg, 125 mg, 130 mg, 200 mg, 250 mg, 260 mg, 300 mg, 400 mg, and 500 mg)
Oral liquid (80 mg per 15-mL spoonful or 150 mg per 15 mL spoonful, some with alcohol of varying amounts, including 1%, 7.5%, and 20%)

STORAGE

Store this medication in a tightly closed, light-resistant container at room temperature. Do not freeze. Discard any outdated medication.

USES

Theophylline is prescribed to treat breathing problems (wheezing and shortness of breath) caused by asthma, bronchitis, or emphysema. It relaxes the smooth muscle of the bronchial airways (breathing tubes), which opens the air passages to the lungs and thereby allows air to move in and out more easily.

TREATMENT

Theophylline should be taken on an empty stomach 30 to 60 minutes before a meal or two hours after a meal. If this medication causes stomach irritation, however, you can take it with food or with a full glass of water or milk (unless your doctor directs you to do otherwise).

Antidiarrheal medications and some antacids prevent the absorption of theophylline from the gastrointestinal tract. Therefore, at least one hour should separate doses of one of these medications and theophylline.

Swallow the sustained-release tablet or capsule form of this medication whole. Chewing, crushing, or crumbling them destroys their sustained-release activity and possibly increases the side effects. If the tablet is scored for breaking, you can break it along those lines. If the regular capsules are too large to swallow, they can be opened and the contents mixed with jam, jelly, or applesauce. Swallow the mixture without chewing.

Measure each dose of the oral liquid carefully with a 5-mL measuring spoon or a dose cup designed for that purpose. Ordinary kitchen spoons are not accurate enough.

Theophylline works best when the level of the medicine in your bloodstream is kept constant. It is best, therefore, to take it at evenly spaced intervals day and night. For example, if you are to take four doses a day, the doses should be spaced six hours apart. Try to take your medication at the same time(s) each day.

Try not to miss any doses of this medication. If you do miss a dose, take the missed dose as soon as possible. However, if it is almost time for the next dose, do not take the missed dose at all; just return to your regular dosing schedule. Do not double the next dose.

SIDE EFFECTS

Minor. Diarrhea, dizziness, flushing, headache, heartburn, increased urination, insomnia, irritability, loss of appetite, nausea, nervousness, stomach pain, or vomiting. These side effects should disappear over time as your body adjusts to the medication.

If you feel dizzy or light-headed, sit or lie down for a while; get up slowly from a sitting or reclining position; and be careful on stairs.

To help avoid dizziness when you stand, contract and relax the muscles of your legs for a few moments before rising. Do this by pressing one foot against the floor while raising the other foot slightly, alternating feet so that you are "pumping" your legs in a pedaling motion.

Major. Tell your doctor about any side effects that are persistent or particularly bothersome. IT IS ESPECIALLY IMPORTANT TO TELL YOUR DOCTOR about black, tarry stools; confusion; convulsions; difficulty in breathing; fainting; muscle twitches; palpitations; rash; severe abdominal pain; or unusual weakness.

INTERACTIONS

Theophylline interacts with several other types of drugs:
1. Theophylline can increase the diuretic effect of the medication furosemide.
2. Beta blockers (acebutolol, atenolol, betaxolol, carteolol, esmolol, labetalol, metoprolol, nadolol, penbutolol, pindolol, propranolol, or timolol) can decrease the effectiveness of theophylline.
3. Theophylline can increase the side effects of over-the-counter (nonprescription) sinus, cough, cold, asthma, allergy, and diet products; digoxin; and oral anticoagulants (blood thinners, such as warfarin).
4. Theophylline can decrease the effectiveness of phenytoin and lithium.
5. Phenobarbital, carbamazepine, and rifampin can increase the elimination of theophylline from the body, decreasing its effectiveness.
6. Cimetidine, ciprofloxacin, clarithromycin, erythromycin, norfloxacin, troleandomycin, oral contraceptives (birth control pills), allopurinol, and thiabendazole can decrease the elimination of theophylline from the body and increase its side effects.
7. Concurrent use of verapamil can cause an increase in the effects of theophylline.

Before you start to take this medication, BE SURE TO TELL YOUR DOCTOR about any medications that you are currently taking, especially any of the medications that are listed above.

WARNINGS

• Tell your doctor about unusual or allergic reactions you have had to any medications, especially to theophylline, aminophylline, caffeine, dyphylline, oxtriphylline, or theobromine.
• Tell your doctor if you now have or ever had an enlarged prostate gland, fibrocystic breast disease, heart disease, kidney disease, low or high blood pressure, liver disease, stomach ulcers, or thyroid disease.
• Cigarette or marijuana smoking may affect this drug's action. BE SURE TO TELL YOUR DOCTOR if you smoke. However, if you decide to quit smoking, be sure to inform your doctor first.
• High fever, diarrhea, flu, and influenza vaccination can affect the action of this medication. Therefore, be sure to tell your doctor if you experience any episodes of high fever or prolonged diarrhea while you are being treated with this medication. Before having any vaccinations, especially those to prevent the flu, BE SURE TO TELL YOUR DOCTOR that you are taking this medication.
• Avoid drinking large amounts of caffeine-containing beverages (coffee, cocoa, tea, or cola drinks), and avoid eating large amounts of chocolate. These products may increase the side effects of theophylline.
• Do not change your diet without first consulting your doctor. A high-protein, low-carbohydrate diet or char-broiled foods may affect the action of this drug.
• Before having surgery or any other medical or dental treatment, be sure to tell your doctor or dentist that you are taking this medication.
• Before taking any over-the-counter (nonprescription) asthma, allergy, cough, cold, sinus, or diet products, ask your doctor or pharmacist. These products may add to the side effects of theophylline.
• Do not change brands or dosage forms of this medication without your doctor's permission. If your medication refill looks different, check with your doctor.
• The elderly and young children may be more sensitive to the effects of theophylline.
• Your doctor may require you to have periodic blood tests to be sure your medication is working properly.
• Be sure to tell your doctor if you are pregnant. Although theophylline appears to be safe when used during pregnancy, extensive studies in humans have not been con-

ducted. Also be sure to tell your doctor if you are breast-feeding an infant. Small amounts of theophylline pass into breast milk and may cause irritability or insomnia in nursing infants. Be sure that you discuss the risks and benefits of this medication with your doctor.

---

tiagabine

BRAND NAME (Manufacturer)
Gabitril (Abbott)
TYPE OF DRUG
Anticonvulsant
INGREDIENT
tiagabine
DOSAGE FORM
Tablets (4 mg, 12 mg, 16 mg, and 20 mg)
STORAGE
Store at room temperature in a tightly closed, light-resistant container. Do not expose to excess heat or moisture. Do not store in the bathroom.

USES

This medication is used for the treatment of seizure disorders. The mechanism through which tiagabine works against seizures is unknown, but it is thought to work by altering chemical messengers (called neurotransmitters) in the brain. Tiagabine is usually used in combination with other antiseizure medications.

TREATMENT

Take this medication exactly as your doctor prescribes. Tiagabine works best when the level of medicine in your bloodstream is kept constant. It is best, therefore, to take this medication at evenly spaced intervals day and night. For example, if you are to take three doses a day, the doses should be spaced about eight hours apart. To lessen stomach irritation, you can take tiagabine with food (unless your doctor tells you to do otherwise).

Try not to miss any doses of this medication. If you do miss a dose, take it as soon as you remember. However, if it is almost time for your next dose of this medication, do not take the missed dose at all; just return to your regular dosing schedule. Do not double the next dose of the medication. If you miss more than two doses of this medication, contact your doctor.

SIDE EFFECTS

Minor. Chills, diarrhea, dizziness or light-headedness, drowsiness, fever, headache, muscle aches, nervousness, sore throat, trembling of the hands, unusual tiredness or weakness, or vomiting. As your body adjusts to the medication, some of these side effects should disappear.

If this medication makes you feel dizzy, sit or lie down for a while, get up slowly from a sitting or reclining position, and be careful on stairs.

To avoid dizziness or light-headedness when you stand, contract and relax the muscles of your legs for a few moments before rising.

Major. Tell your doctor about any side effect that is persistent or particularly bothersome. IT IS ESPECIALLY IMPORTANT TO TELL YOUR DOCTOR about agitation; bloody or cloudy urine; blue or purple spots on the skin; burning, numbness, or tingling sensations of the skin; burning or pain when urinating; difficulty concentrating or paying attention; difficulty talking; difficulty urinating; frequent urge to urinate; itching; loss of memory; mental depression; mood changes; rash; unusual or uncontrollable eye movements; or weakness.

INTERACTIONS

Tiagabine may interact with a number of other medications:

1. Central nervous system depressants (such as alcohol, antihistamines, barbiturates, benzodiazepine tranquilizers, muscle relaxants, narcotics, pain medications, phenothiazine tranquilizers, and medications to induce sleep) or antidepressants may cause extreme drowsiness when taken with this medication.

2. Other antiseizure medications (carbamazepine, phenobarbital, phenytoin, primidone, or valproic acid) may alter the amount of tiagabine in the body.

Before you start this medication, BE SURE TO TELL YOUR DOCTOR about any medications you are currently taking, especially any that are listed above.

WARNINGS

- Tell your doctor about any unusual or allergic reactions you have had to other medications, including tiagabine and other antiseizure medications.
- Tell your doctor if you now have or ever had liver problems, blood disorders, status epilepticus, mental disorders, or other types of seizures.
- Before having surgery or any medical or dental treatment, be sure to tell your doctor or dentist that you are taking tiagabine.
- Do not stop taking this medication suddenly. If you stop abruptly, you may experience an increase in seizures. Your doctor may want to gradually reduce your dosage of the medication before stopping it.
- This medication may cause dizziness. Your ability to perform tasks that require alertness, such as driving an automobile or operating potentially dangerous machinery, may be decreased. Take appropriate caution.
- Be sure to tell your doctor if you are pregnant. Tiagabine has been shown to cause birth defects in animals, and it is not known if it is safe to take during human pregnancy. Also tell your doctor if you are breast-feeding an infant. It is not known if tiagabine passes into breast milk. Discuss the risks and benefits with your doctor.

---

ticlopidine

BRAND NAME (Manufacturer)
Ticlid (Roche)
TYPE OF DRUG
Antiplatelet agent
INGREDIENT
ticlopidine
DOSAGE FORM
Tablets (250 mg)
STORAGE
Store at room temperature in a tightly closed container. Do not expose to excess heat.

USES

Ticlopidine is used to lessen the risk of having a heart attack or stroke. It works by preventing red blood cells (platelets) from sticking or adhering to each other. It is usually used for patients who cannot take aspirin.

TREATMENT

Take this medication exactly as prescribed by your doctor. Using more than your doctor prescribed may increase the chance of bleeding or other side effects. To avoid stomach irritation, take it with food (unless your doctor tells you to do otherwise).

If you miss a dose, take the missed dose as soon as possible. However, if it is almost time for the next dose, do not take the missed dose at all. Just return to your regular dosing schedule. Do not double the doses.

SIDE EFFECTS

Minor. Bloating or gas, diarrhea, dizziness, indigestion, nausea, stomach pain, or vomiting. These side effects should disappear as your body adjusts to the medication.

If this medication makes you feel dizzy, sit or lie down for a while, get up slowly from a sitting or reclining position, and be careful on stairs.

To avoid dizziness or light-headedness when you stand, contract and relax the muscles of your legs for a few moments before rising. Do this by pressing one foot against the floor while raising the other foot slightly, alternating feet so that you are "pumping" your legs in a pedaling motion.

Major. Tell you doctor about any side effects that are persistent or particularly bothersome. IT IS ESPECIALLY IMPORTANT TO TELL YOUR DOCTOR about black, tarry stools; blood in the urine or stools; purple or red spots on the skin; severe or bloody diarrhea; severe stomach pain; signs of an infection (fever, chills, sore throat, or white spots in the mouth); skin rash; sudden or severe headaches; unusual bleeding or bruising; vomiting of blood or coffee-groundlike material; or yellowing of the eyes or skin.

INTERACTIONS

Ticlopidine may interact with a number of other drugs.

1. Aspirin or nonsteroidal anti-inflammatory agents (NSAIDs), such as ibuprofen and similar medications, may increase the risk of bleeding.

2. Ticlopidine may increase the side effects of phenytoin.

3. The use of warfarin (a blood thinner) during treatment with ticlopidine may increase the risk of bleeding.

4. Ticlopidine may reduce the effects of theophylline, aminophylline, or digoxin.

5. Antacids may prevent the absorption of this medicine from the stomach. You should wait one to two hours after taking any antacids before taking ticlopidine.

WARNINGS

- Tell your doctor if you have ever had an allergic reaction to ticlopidine or to any other medication.
- Before starting this medication, be sure to tell your doctor if you now have or ever had any major medical problems, especially bleeding problems, stomach or ulcer problems, or liver problems.
- Tell your doctor immediately if you notice any unusual bleeding while taking ticlopidine, including bleeding from the gums, nosebleeds, blood in the urine or stool, or vomiting of blood or coffee-groundlike material.
- Because of the risk of bleeding, be sure to tell your doctor or dentist that you are taking this drug before having any surgical, dental, or other medical procedure. Your doctor may want you to stop taking this medication before undergoing surgery or dental procedures.
- If this drug makes you dizzy or drowsy, do not take part in any activity that requires alertness, such as driving a car or operating potentially dangerous equipment.
- Be sure to tell your doctor if you are pregnant. Although birth defects have not been documented in animals, it is unknown if the drug is safe to take during human pregnancy. It is also not known if ticlopidine passes into human breast milk. Tell your doctor if you are breast-feeding an infant and discuss the risks and benefits of the drug.

---

timolol maleate (systemic)

BRAND NAMES (Manufacturers)

Blocadren (Merck & Co.)

timolol maleate (various manufacturers)

TYPE OF DRUG

Beta-adrenergic blocking agent

INGREDIENT
timolol
DOSAGE FORM
Tablets (5 mg, 10 mg, and 20 mg)
STORAGE
Store at room temperature in a tightly closed, light-resistant container.

USES

Timolol is used to treat high blood pressure and to prevent additional heart attacks in heart attack patients. This drug belongs to a group of medicines known as beta-adrenergic blocking agents or, more commonly, beta blockers. These drugs work by controlling nerve impulses along certain nerve pathways.

TREATMENT

Timolol tablets can be taken with a glass of water, with meals, immediately following meals, or on an empty stomach, depending on your doctor's instructions. Try to take your dose(s) of the medication at the same time(s) each day.

Try not to miss any doses of this medication. If you do miss a dose, take the missed dose as soon as possible. However, if the next scheduled dose is within eight hours (if you are taking this medicine only once a day) or within four hours (if you are taking this medicine more than once a day), do not take the missed dose at all; just return to your regular dosing schedule. Do not double the next dose.

It is important to remember that timolol maleate does not cure high blood pressure, but it will help to control the condition as long as you continue to take it.

SIDE EFFECTS

Minor. Anxiety; constipation; decreased sexual ability; diarrhea; difficulty in sleeping; drowsiness; dryness of the eyes, mouth, and skin; headache; nausea; nervousness; stomach discomfort; tiredness; or weakness. These side effects should disappear during treatment as your body adjusts itself to the medicine.

If you are extra-sensitive to the cold, be sure to dress warmly during cold weather.

To relieve constipation, increase the fiber in your diet (fresh fruits and vegetables, salads, bran, and whole-grain breads) unless your doctor directs otherwise.

Plain, nonmedicated eyedrops (artificial tears) may help to relieve eye dryness.

Chew gum or suck on hard candy to relieve mouth and throat dryness.

Major. Tell your doctor about any side effects that are persistent or particularly bothersome. IT IS ESPECIALLY IMPORTANT TO TELL YOUR DOCTOR about cold hands or feet (due to decreased blood circulation to skin, fingers, and toes), confusion, depression, dizziness, fever and sore throat, hair loss, hallucinations, light-headedness, nightmares, numbness or tingling of the fingers or toes, rapid weight gain (three to five pounds within a week), reduced level of alertness, skin rash, swelling, unusual bleeding or bruising, or wheezing or difficulty in breathing.

INTERACTIONS

Timolol may interact with many other types of drugs:

1. Indomethacin has been shown to decrease the effect of the beta blockers in lowering blood pressure. This may also happen with aspirin or other salicylates.

2. Concurrent use of beta blockers and calcium channel blockers (diltiazem, nifedipine, or verapamil) or disopyramide can lead to heart failure or very low blood pressure.

3. Cimetidine and oral contraceptives (birth control pills) can increase the blood concentrations of timolol, which can result in greater side effects.

4. Side effects may also be increased when beta blockers are taken with clonidine, digoxin, epinephrine, phenylephrine, phenylpropanolamine, phenothiazine tran-

quilizers, prazosin, reserpine, or monoamine oxidase (MAO) inhibitors. At least 14 days should separate the use of a beta blocker and the use of an MAO inhibitor.
5. Alcohol, barbiturates, and rifampin can decrease the blood concentrations of beta blockers, which can result in a decrease in effectiveness.
6. Beta blockers may antagonize (work against) the effects of theophylline, aminophylline, albuterol, isoproterenol, metaproterenol, salmeterol, and terbutaline.
7. Beta blockers can also interact with insulin or oral antidiabetic agents, raising or lowering blood-sugar levels or masking the symptoms of low blood sugar.
8. The action of beta blockers may be increased if they are used with chlorpromazine, furosemide, or hydralazine.

BE SURE TO TELL YOUR DOCTOR about any medications you are currently taking, especially any of those listed above.

WARNINGS

• Before starting to take this medication, it is important to tell your doctor if you have ever had unusual or allergic reactions to timolol or to any beta blocker (acebutolol, atenolol, betaxolol, carteolol, esmolol, labetalol, metoprolol, nadolol, penbutolol, pindolol, or propranolol).

• Tell your doctor if you now have or ever had allergies, asthma, hay fever, eczema, slow heartbeat, bronchitis, diabetes mellitus, emphysema, heart or blood-vessel disease, kidney disease, liver disease, thyroid disease, or poor circulation in the fingers or toes.

• You may want to check your pulse on a regular basis while you are being treated with this medication. If your pulse is much slower than your usual rate (or if it is less than 50 beats per minute), check with your doctor. A pulse rate that is too slow may cause circulation problems.

• This medication may affect your body's response to exercise. Therefore, be sure you discuss with your doctor how much exercise is safe for you, taking into account your medical condition as well as the effects of this drug.

• It is important that you do not stop taking this medicine unless you first check with your doctor. Some conditions may become worse when the medicine is stopped suddenly, and the danger of a heart attack is increased in some patients. Your doctor may want you to gradually reduce the amount of medicine you take before stopping completely. Make sure that you have enough medicine on hand to last through weekends, vacations, and holidays.

• Before having surgery or any other medical or dental treatment, tell your doctor or dentist that you are taking this medication. Often, this medication will be discontinued 48 hours prior to major surgery.

• This medication can cause dizziness, drowsiness, light-headedness, or decreased alertness. Exercise caution while driving an automobile or using any potentially dangerous machinery.

• While taking this medicine, do not use any over-the-counter (nonprescription) allergy, asthma, cough, cold, sinus, or diet preparations unless you first check with your pharmacist or doctor. Some of these medications can bring about high blood pressure when combined with timolol.

• This medication can make your skin more sensitive to the sun, even after only brief exposure. It is important to limit your exposure to sunlight and sunlamps. Wear protective clothing, and apply sunblock as needed.

• Be sure to tell your doctor if you are pregnant. Animal studies have shown that some beta blockers can cause problems during pregnancy when used at very high doses. There has been some association between use of beta blockers during pregnancy and low birth weight, as well as breathing problems and slow heart rate in newborn infants. However, other reports have shown no effects on newborn infants. Also tell your doctor if you are breast-feeding. Small amounts of timolol may pass into breast milk.

timolol (ophthalmic)

BRAND NAMES (Manufacturers)
Betinol (Ciba Vision)
timolol ophthalmic solution (various manufacturers)
Timoptic (Merck & Co.)
Timoptic XE (Merck & Co.)
TYPE OF DRUG
Antiglaucoma ophthalmic solution
INGREDIENT
timolol
DOSAGE FORMS
Ophthalmic drops (0.25% and 0.5%)
Ophthalmic gel-forming solution (0.25% and 0.5%)
STORAGE
Store this medication at room temperature in a tightly closed container. Do not freeze. If timolol (ophthalmic) discolors or turns brown, it should be discarded; a color change indicates a loss of potency.

USES

Timolol (ophthalmic) is used to reduce pressure in the eye caused by glaucoma or other eye conditions. This medication belongs to a group of medications that are known as beta blockers. When applied to the eye, timolol (ophthalmic) reduces pressure within the eye by decreasing eye-fluid (aqueous humor) production and perhaps by increasing the outflow of fluid from the eye.

TREATMENT

Be sure to wash your hands with soap and water before applying this medication. To avoid contamination of the medication, be careful not to touch the tube portion of the dropper or let it touch your eye, and do not wipe off or rinse the dropper after you use it. The gel solution should be shaken once before each use.

If you are using timolol ophthalmic gel-forming solution along with other eyedrops, administer the other eyedrops ten minutes (or more) BEFORE you put the timolol ophthalmic gel-forming solution in your eye. Discuss this with your doctor or pharmacist.

To apply the ophthalmic drops or solution, tilt your head back and pull down your lower eyelid with one hand to make a pouch below the eye. Drop the prescribed amount of medicine into this pouch and slowly close your eyes. Try not to blink. Keep your eyes closed, and place one finger at the corner of the treated eye next to your nose for a minute or two, applying a slight pressure (this is done to prevent loss of medication through the duct that drains fluid from the surface of the eye into the nose and throat). Then wipe away any excess medication with a clean tissue. Since applying the medication is somewhat difficult to do, you may want to have someone else apply the ophthalmic drops for you.

If you miss a dose of this medication, apply the missed dose as soon as possible. However, if it is almost time for your next dose, do not apply the missed dose at all; just return to your regular dosing schedule. If the medication is used only once a day and you do not remember missing a dose until the following day, skip the missed dose. Do not double the next dose.

SIDE EFFECTS

Minor. When you apply this medication for the first time, you may feel a stinging sensation in your eyes. This should stop in a few minutes.

Major. Tell your doctor about any side effects that are persistent or particularly bothersome. IT IS ESPECIALLY IMPORTANT TO TELL YOUR DOCTOR about itching, skin rash, hives, or irritation of the eye that lasts more than a few minutes after application. Major side effects are rare when this product is administered correctly. However, rare occurrences of anxiety, confusion, depression, dizziness, drowsiness, generalized rash, indigestion, loss of appetite, nausea, weakness, and a slight reduction of the resting heart rate have been observed in some users of this drug. If you have any of these symptoms, it is important that you contact your doctor as soon as possible.

INTERACTIONS

Timolol (ophthalmic) may interact with certain other medications: It may increase the side effects of reserpine, oral beta blockers, calcium channel blockers, digoxin, quinidine, and phenothiazine tranquilizers.

Before you begin treatment with timolol (ophthalmic), BE SURE THAT YOU TELL YOUR DOCTOR about any medications that you are currently taking, especially any of the medications that are listed above.

WARNINGS

- Tell your doctor about unusual or allergic reactions you have had to any medications, especially to timolol or to any other beta blockers (acebutolol, atenolol, betaxolol, carteolol, esmolol, labetalol, metoprolol, nadolol, penbutolol, pindolol, or propranolol).
- Tell your doctor if you now have or if you have ever had asthma, diabetes mellitus, heart disease, or myasthenia gravis.
- Your doctor should check your eye pressure regularly to be sure the glaucoma is under control.
- Tell your doctor if you are pregnant. Small amounts of timolol may be absorbed into the bloodstream, and its safety in pregnancy has not been established. Birth defects have been observed in the fetuses of animals that were given large doses of this drug during pregnancy. Also tell your doctor if you are breast-feeding. If this drug reaches the bloodstream and passes into the breast milk, it can cause a slowed heart rate in the nursing infant.

---

tobramycin (ophthalmic)

BRAND NAMES (Manufacturers)
AK-Tob (Akron)
tobramycin ophthalmic solution (various manufacturers)
Tobrex (Alcon)
TYPE OF DRUG
Ophthalmic antibiotic
INGREDIENT
tobramycin
DOSAGE FORMS
Ophthalmic drops (0.3% tobramycin)
Ophthalmic ointment (0.3% tobramycin)
STORAGE
Store at room temperature in tightly closed containers. Discard any medication that is outdated or no longer needed.

USES

Tobramycin ophthalmic is used for the short-term treatment of bacterial infections of the eyes. Tobramycin is an aminoglycoside antibiotic, which acts to prevent the growth and multiplication of infecting bacteria.

TREATMENT

Wash your hands with soap and water before using this medication. To prevent contamination of the medicine, be careful not to touch the tube portion of the dropper and do not let it touch the eye.

Note that the bottle of the eyedrops is not completely full; this is to allow control of the number of drops used.

To apply the drops, tilt your head back and pull down the lower eyelid with one hand to make a pouch below the eye. Drop the prescribed amount of medicine into the pouch and slowly close your eyes. Try not to blink. Keep your eyes closed, and place one finger at the corner of the eye next to your nose for a minute or two, applying a slight pressure (this is done to prevent loss of medication through the duct that drains fluid from the surface of the eye into the nose and throat). Then wipe away any excess with a clean tissue. If you think that the medicine did not get into your eye, repeat the process once. If you are using more than one type of eyedrop, wait at least five minutes between doses of the two types of medication.

Follow the same general procedure for applying the ointment. Tilt your head back, pull down the lower eyelid, and squeeze the prescribed amount of ointment in a line along the pouch below the eye. Close your eyes, and place your finger at the corner of the eye, near the nose, for a minute or two. Do not rub your eyes. Wipe off excess ointment and the tip of the tube with clean tissues.

Since applying the medication is somewhat difficult to do, you may want someone else to administer the drops or ointment for you.

If you miss a dose of this drug, insert the drops or apply the ointment as soon as possible. However, if it is almost time for the next application, do not use the missed dose at all; just return to your regular dosing schedule.

It is important to continue to take this medication for the entire time prescribed by your doctor, even if the symptoms of infection disappear before the end of that period. If you stop applying the medication too soon, resistant bacteria are given a chance to continue growing, and the infection could recur.

SIDE EFFECTS

Minor. Blurred vision, burning, or stinging. These side effects should disappear as your body gets accustomed to the drug.

Major. Tell your doctor about any side effects that are persistent or particularly bothersome. IT IS ESPECIALLY IMPORTANT TO TELL YOUR DOCTOR about disturbed or reduced vision; eye pain, itching, or swelling; severe irritation; or rash.

INTERACTIONS

This medication should not interact with other medications as long as it is used according to directions.

WARNINGS

- Tell your doctor about any reactions you have had to drugs, especially to tobramycin or to any other aminoglycoside antibiotic (amikacin, gentamicin, kanamycin, neomycin, netilmicin, paromomycin, or streptomycin).
- Before starting tobramycin (ophthalmic), tell your doctor if you now have or ever had fungal or viral infections of the eye, kidney disease, or myasthenia gravis.
- If there is no change in your condition two or three days after starting to take this drug, contact your doctor. The drug may not be effective for your infection.
- This medication has been prescribed for your current infection only. A subsequent infection that you may develop, or one that someone else has, may require a different medicine. You should not give your medicine to other people or use it to treat other infections unless your doctor specifically directs you to do so.
- To allow your eye infection to clear, do not apply makeup to the affected eye. Do not use these drops with contact lenses in place; discuss this with your doctor.

• Be sure to tell your doctor if you are pregnant. Extensive studies in pregnant women have not been conducted. Also tell your doctor if you are breast-feeding an infant. Small amounts of tobramycin may pass into the breast milk.

tolcapone

BRAND NAME (Manufacturer)
Tasmar (Roche)
TYPE OF DRUG
Antiparkinson agent
INGREDIENT
tolcapone
DOSAGE FORM
Tablets (100 mg and 200 mg)
STORAGE
Store in a tightly closed container at room temperature, away from heat and direct sunlight. Do not refrigerate or freeze.

USES

Tolcapone is a medicine used in combination with levodopa/carbidopa therapy to treat Parkinson's disease. Although the exact mechanism of action is not known, this drug may work by inhibiting an enzyme in the body called catechol-O-methyltransferase (COMT), which may increase the effectiveness of levodopa/carbidopa therapy.

TREATMENT

Take this medication exactly as prescribed by your doctor. Tolcapone can be taken either on an empty stomach or with a meal in combination with levodopa/carbidopa therapy. It is very important to follow your doctor's instructions for taking this medication and levodopa/carbidopa, because it is likely that as the tolcapone dose is gradually increased, the dose of levodopa/carbidopa may be gradually decreased to avoid additional adverse effects.

Try to develop a set schedule for taking this medication. If you miss a dose and remember within a few hours, take the missed dose and resume your regular schedule. However, if it is almost time for your next scheduled dose, do not take the missed dose at all; just return to your regular dosing schedule. Do not double the next dose.

Tolcapone does not cure Parkinson's disease, but it will help to control the condition as long as you continue to take it. It may be several weeks before you notice the full effect of this medication.

SIDE EFFECTS

Minor. Constipation, discoloration of the urine (to bright yellow), dryness of the mouth, excessive dreaming, gas, heartburn, or increased sweating. These side effects (except discolored urine) should disappear as your body adjusts to the medication.

To relieve constipation, increase the amount of fiber in your diet (fresh fruits and vegetables, salads, bran, and whole-grain breads) and exercise more (unless your doctor directs you to do otherwise.)

Plain, nonmedicated eyedrops (artificial tears) may help to relieve eye dryness.

Chew sugarless gum or suck on ice chips or a piece of hard candy to relieve mouth or throat dryness.

Major. Tell your doctor about any side effects that are persistent or particularly bothersome. IT IS ESPECIALLY IMPORTANT TO TELL YOUR DOCTOR about abdominal pain; blood in your urine; chest pain; clay-colored stools; confusion; cough; diarrhea; dizziness; drowsiness; fainting; fever; hallucinations (seeing, hearing, or feeling things that are not there); headache; light-headedness; loss of appetite; low blood pressure;

muscle pain; nasal congestion; nausea; runny nose; sneezing; sore throat; trouble breathing; trouble sleeping; twitching, twisting, or other unusual body movements; or vomiting.

To avoid dizziness when you stand, contract and relax the muscles of your legs for a few moments before rising. Do this by pressing one foot against the floor while raising the other foot slightly, alternating feet so that you are "pumping" your legs in a pedaling motion.

If this medication makes you feel dizzy or light-headed, sit or lie down for a while, get up slowly from a sitting or reclining position, and be careful on stairs.

INTERACTIONS

Tolcapone may interact with other types of medications:

Tolcapone may result in an altered response to the blood-thinning medication warfarin. Therefore, your doctor may want to monitor your warfarin therapy more frequently during concurrent treatment with tolcapone in order to avoid additional adverse effects.

Before starting to take tolcapone, BE SURE TO TELL YOUR DOCTOR about any medications you are taking, especially the medication listed above.

WARNINGS

- Tell your doctor about unusual or allergic reactions you have had to any medications, especially to tolcapone.
- Be sure to tell your doctor if you have ever had hallucinations, kidney disease, liver disease, or low blood pressure.
- Before having surgery or any other medical or dental treatment, tell your doctor or dentist that you are taking this medication.
- While taking this medication, your doctor will want you to have blood tests to ensure that tolcapone is not harming your liver. Your doctor will tell you how long these blood tests will be necessary.
- Do not stop taking tolcapone without first checking with your doctor. Your doctor may want to gradually reduce the amount of medicine you are taking before completely stopping it. Make sure that you have enough medicine on hand to last through vacations, holidays, and weekends.
- Do not take any over-the-counter (nonprescription) medications for weight control or for asthma, sinus, cough, cold, or allergy problems unless you first check with your pharmacist or doctor.
- This medication can cause dizziness, drowsiness, light-headedness, and decreased alertness. Therefore, you should exercise caution while driving an automobile or operating dangerous machinery. Be especially careful when going up or down stairs or when getting up from a sitting or lying position.
- Hallucinations may occur in some patients being treated with tolcapone. This is more common in very elderly patients (older than 75 years).
- Tolcapone will cause your urine to turn bright yellow. This is a harmless side effect that will disappear after you stop treatment with tolcapone.
- After you stop taking tolcapone, your body may need time to adjust. The length of time this takes depends on the amount of medicine you were taking and how long you used it. During this time, it is important to tell your doctor if you experience confusion, fever, or extreme muscle stiffness.
- Be sure to tell your doctor if you are pregnant. This medication has been shown to cause birth defects in the offspring of animals that received large doses of it during pregnancy. Adequate studies have not been done in human pregnancies. Also be sure to tell your doctor if you are breast-feeding an infant. It is not known if this medication passes into breast milk.

tolterodine

BRAND NAMES (Manufacturers)
Detrol (Pharmacia)
Detrol LA (Pharmacia)
TYPE OF DRUG
Antispasmodic
INGREDIENT
tolterodine
DOSAGE FORMS
Tablets (1 mg and 2 mg)
Capsules, extended-release (2 mg and 4 mg)
STORAGE
Store at room temperature in a tightly closed container. Do not expose to excess heat or light.

USES

Tolterodine is used to relieve symptoms associated with urinary incontinence (inability to control the bladder) or urinary frequency or urgency.

TREATMENT

To reduce stomach irritation, this medication may be taken with food (unless your doctor tells you to do otherwise).

If you miss a dose of this medication, take it as soon as you remember, unless it is almost time for your next dose of the medication. In that case, do not take the missed dose at all; just return to your regular dosing schedule. Do not double the next dose of this medication.

SIDE EFFECTS

Minor. Constipation, diarrhea, dizziness, drowsiness, dry eyes, dry mouth, gas, headache, joint pain, nausea, stomach pain, tiredness, or upset stomach. As your body adjusts to the medication, some of these side effects should disappear.

Dry mouth can be relieved by chewing sugarless gum or sucking on hard candy.

If this medication makes you feel dizzy, sit or lie down for a while, get up slowly from a sitting or reclining position, and be careful on stairs.

To avoid dizziness or light-headedness when you stand, contract and relax the muscles of your legs for a few moments before rising. Do this by pressing one foot against the floor while raising the other foot slightly, alternating feet so that you are "pumping" your legs in a pedaling motion.

To relieve constipation, increase the amount of fiber in your diet (fresh fruits and vegetables, salads, bran, and whole-grain breads), exercise, and drink more water (unless your doctor directs you to do otherwise).

Major. Tell your doctor about any side effects that are persistent or particularly bothersome. IT IS ESPECIALLY IMPORTANT TO TELL YOUR DOCTOR about bloody or cloudy urine; difficult, burning, or painful urination; the urge to urinate frequently; or vision changes, such as blurred vision or difficulty adjusting your focus to see long distances.

INTERACTIONS

Extreme drowsiness may occur when this medicine is taken concurrently with central nervous system depressants (alcohol, antihistamines, barbiturates, benzodiazepine tranquilizers, muscle relaxants, narcotics, pain medications, phenothiazine tranquilizers, and medications to induce sleep) or with antidepressants.

2. Erythromycin, clarithromycin, miconazole, itraconazole, or ketoconazole may increase the amount of tolterodine in the body and its side effects. Your doctor will likely need to lower your dosage of tolterodine during treatment with any of these medications.

WARNINGS

• Tell your doctor about any unusual or allergic reactions you have had to any medications, especially to tolterodine or oxybutynin.
• Before you start treatment with this medication, tell your doctor if you have or have ever had stomach or intestinal problems, glaucoma, liver or kidney disease, intestinal blockage, high blood pressure, an enlarged prostate gland, urinary problems, or asthma.
• This medication can decrease sweating and heat release from the body. Try not to become overheated: Avoid strenuous exercise in hot weather, and do not take hot baths, showers, and saunas.
• This medication may cause blurred vision or dizziness. As a result, your ability to perform tasks that require alertness, such as driving an automobile or operating potentially dangerous machinery, may be decreased. Appropriate caution should be taken.
• Be sure to tell your doctor if you are pregnant. It is not known if tolterodine is safe to use during pregnancy. Also be sure to tell your doctor if you are breast-feeding an infant. It is not known if tolterodine passes into breast milk. You should discuss the risks and benefits of this medication with your doctor.

---

topiramate

BRAND NAME (Manufacturer)
Topamax (Ortho-McNeil)
TYPE OF DRUG
Antiseizure agent
INGREDIENT
topiramate
DOSAGE FORMS
Tablets (25 mg, 100 mg, and 200 mg)
Capsules, sprinkle (15 mg and 25 mg)
STORAGE
Store this medication at room temperature in a tightly closed container. Avoid exposing this medication to moisture or excessive heat. Do not store it in the glove compartment of your car. And do not refrigerate or freeze the medication.

USES

Topiramate is used along with other medications to prevent seizures in patients with epilepsy. It is thought that this medication works to stop or stabilize some of the electrical activity of the brain, keeping the nerve cells of the brain from becoming overexcited. Seizures occur when the electrical activity of the brain is overactive. This medication will not cure your epilepsy but will help to control your seizures when taken as directed by your doctor.

TREATMENT

Take this medication exactly as prescribed by your doctor. Topiramate may be taken either on an empty stomach or with food or milk (unless your doctor directs you to do otherwise). It is important to swallow the tablets whole; do not chew, break, or crush them. The sprinkle capsules may be swallowed whole or their contents can be sprinkled onto a teaspoonful of soft food (such as applesauce, yogurt, pudding, ice cream, oatmeal, or custard) and swallowed immediately. Do not prepare the capsule/food mixture ahead of time or store any of it for a later dose. Be careful not to chew or crush the pellets from the capsule before you swallow.

Drink plenty of water or other fluids (unless your doctor directs you to do otherwise). This will help to prevent kidney stones from forming.

It is important not to stop taking this medication abruptly. Suddenly stopping topiramate may result in a return of seizures. If this medication needs to be stopped, it should be done gradually. Talk with your doctor before you attempt to stop treatment.

The full effects of this medication may not be apparent for several weeks. Usually, the dose of topiramate is slowly increased over several weeks.

If you miss a dose of this medication, take the missed dose as soon as possible. However, if it is almost time for your next dose, do not take the missed dose at all; just return to your regular dosing schedule. Do not double the next dose or take more than prescribed by your doctor.

SIDE EFFECTS

Minor. Back pain, breast pain in women, chest pain, constipation, heartburn, hot flashes, increased sweating, leg pain, nausea, or tremors. Most of these effects should disappear as your body adjusts to the medication.

To relieve constipation, increase the amount of fiber in your diet (fresh fruits and vegetables, salads, bran, and whole-grain breads), exercise, and drink more water (unless your doctor directs you to do otherwise).

Major. Tell your doctor about any side effects that are persistent or particularly bothersome. IT IS ESPECIALLY IMPORTANT TO TELL YOUR DOCTOR about being unusually emotional, depressed, or nervous; difficulty walking or feelings of clumsiness; problems with your eyes or vision, including blurred vision, seeing double, eye pain, eye redness, difficult-to-control eye movements, or increased eye pressure; speech or language problems; unusual tiredness or weakness; or weight loss.

INTERACTIONS

Topiramate may interact with a number of other medications:

1. Concurrent use of this medication with other central nervous system depressants (such as alcohol, barbiturates, benzodiazepine tranquilizers, muscle relaxants, narcotics, pain medications, and phenothiazine tranquilizers) or with tricyclic antidepressants can cause extreme drowsiness.

2. Concurrent use of topiramate and any over-the-counter (nonprescription) medication for weight loss or for cough, cold, sinus problems, asthma, or allergies may increase the side effects of topiramate. Combining topiramate with any of these medications should be avoided.

3. The effects of oral contraceptive medications (birth control pills) may be reduced by concurrent use of topiramate. An additional method of birth control (such as a barrier method) may be needed while you are being treated with topiramate. Discuss this with your doctor or pharmacist.

4. Acetazolamide will increase your chances of having kidney stones when taken with topiramate; avoid concurrent use of these two medications.

BE SURE TO TELL YOUR DOCTOR about any medications that you are currently taking, especially any of the medications that are listed above.

WARNINGS

• Tell your doctor if you have ever had an allergic reaction to topiramate or another antiseizure medication or any other medications.

• Tell your doctor if you now have or if you have ever had kidney or liver disease, too low of a sodium level in your blood, or thyroid disease.

• While taking this medication, your ability to perform tasks that require alertness, such as driving an automobile or operating potentially dangerous machinery, may be impaired. Caution should be taken.

• It is important to see your doctor regularly while you are being treated with this medication to make sure your seizures are being controlled.
• Be sure to tell your doctor if you are pregnant. Although it has not been adequately studied in humans, topiramate has caused birth defects in animals given large doses. You should discuss the risks and benefits of using this medication during pregnancy with your doctor. Topiramate can also pass into human breast milk. Be sure to tell your doctor if you are breast-feeding an infant and discuss the risks and benefits of this medication.

---

tramadol

BRAND NAMES (Manufacturers)
tramadol (various manufacturers)
Ultram (Ortho-McNeil)
TYPE OF DRUG
Analgesic
INGREDIENT
tramadol
DOSAGE FORM
Tablets (50 mg)
STORAGE
Store at room temperature in a tightly closed, light-resistant container. Do not refrigerate or freeze.

USES

Tramadol is used for the treatment of moderate to moderately severe pain. It acts on the central nervous system (brain and spinal cord) to relieve pain. The mechanism of action of tramadol is not related to any other analgesics, and the mechanism of action is poorly understood.

TREATMENT

Tramadol should be taken every four to six hours as needed for pain (unless your doctor specifically instructs you to do otherwise). It can be taken with food or on an empty stomach.

This medication works most effectively if you take it at the onset of pain, rather than waiting until the pain becomes intense.

If you are taking this medication on a schedule and you miss a scheduled dose, take the missed dose as soon as possible. However, if it is almost time for your next dose, do not take the missed dose at all; just return to your regular schedule. Do not double the next dose unless your doctor directs you to do so.

SIDE EFFECTS

Minor. Constipation, diarrhea, dizziness, dry mouth, fatigue, itching, nausea or vomiting, nervousness, restlessness, sleep disorders, sweating, or upset stomach. These side effects should disappear as your body adjusts to the medication.

Dry mouth can be relieved by sucking on ice chips or a piece of hard candy or by chewing sugarless gum.

If you feel dizzy or light-headed, sit or lie down for a while; get up from a sitting or lying position slowly; and be careful on stairs.

To avoid dizziness when you stand, contract and relax the muscles of your legs for a few moments before rising. Do this by pressing one foot against the floor while raising the other foot slightly, alternating feet so that you are "pumping" your legs in a pedaling motion.

To prevent constipation, increase the amount of fiber in your diet (fresh fruits and vegetables, salads, bran, whole-grain breads), exercise, and drink more water (unless your doctor tells you not to do so).

Major. Tell your doctor about any side effects that are persistent or particularly bothersome. IT IS ESPECIALLY IMPORTANT TO TELL YOUR DOCTOR about black, tarry stools; chest tightness; difficulty urinating; hallucinations; headaches; loss of coordination; mental depression; palpitations; rash; seizures; tremors; or trouble breathing.

INTERACTIONS

Tramadol interacts with several other types of medications:

1. Use of tramadol within 14 days of a monoamine oxidase (MAO) inhibitor (isocarboxazid, furazolidone, pargyline, phenelzine, procarbazine, or tranylcypromine) can result in high blood pressure along with other side effects.

2. This medication may increase the sedative effects of alcohol or other drugs that interact with central nervous system action (such as anesthetic medications, opioids, phenothiazines, sedative hypnotics, or tranquilizers).

3. Tramadol may increase the risk of seizures in patients with epilepsy or in those patients that receive medications that may increase the risk of seizure (medications such as MAO inhibitors and neuroleptics).

4. Higher doses of tramadol may be necessary in patients who are also taking carbamazepine.

5. Tramadol may increase your chances of having side effects from certain antidepressants. Discuss this with your doctor or pharmacist.

BE SURE TO TELL YOUR DOCTOR about any medications you are currently taking, especially any listed above.

WARNINGS

- Tell your doctor about any unusual or allergic reactions you have had to any medications, especially to tramadol or to other analgesics.
- Before having surgery or other medical or dental procedures, tell your doctor or dentist that you are taking this drug.
- Tell your doctor if you have a history of drug abuse or if you have or ever had abdominal disease, peptic ulcers, epilepsy, head injuries, heart disease, kidney disease, or liver disease.
- Tramadol can cause drowsiness or dizziness. Your ability to perform tasks that require alertness, such as driving an automobile or operating potentially dangerous machinery, may be decreased. Caution is required.
- Do not drink any alcohol while you are being treated with tramadol.
- Be sure to tell your doctor if you are pregnant. Although extensive studies in human pregnancy have not been conducted, tramadol has been shown to cause side effects in the fetuses of animals that received large doses of the drug during pregnancy. Tramadol is known to cross the placenta. Also tell your doctor if you are nursing an infant. It is not known if tramadol passes into breast milk.

---

trandolapril

BRAND NAME (Manufacturer)
Mavik (Abbot Labs)
TYPE OF DRUG
Antihypertensive (blood-pressure-lowering drug)
INGREDIENT
trandolapril
DOSAGE FORM
Tablets (1 mg, 2 mg, and 4 mg)

STORAGE

Store in a tightly closed container at room temperature, away from heat and direct sunlight. Do not refrigerate.

USES

Trandolapril is used to treat high blood pressure and congestive heart failure after a heart attack. It is a vasodilator (it widens blood vessels) that acts by blocking the production of chemicals that may be responsible for constricting or narrowing blood vessels. It is a medication in a class of drugs called the angiotensin-converting enzyme (ACE) inhibitors.

TREATMENT

Take this medication exactly as prescribed by your doctor. Trandolapril can be taken either on an empty stomach or with a meal.

While using this medication, try to develop a set schedule for taking it. If you miss a dose and remember within a few hours, take the missed dose and resume your regular dosing schedule. If many hours have passed, skip the dose you missed and then take your next dose as scheduled. Do not double the next dose.

Trandolapril does not cure high blood pressure, but it will help to control the condition as long as you continue to take it. It may be several weeks before you notice the full effects of this medication.

SIDE EFFECTS

Minor. Abdominal pain, cough, diarrhea, dizziness, drowsiness, fatigue, headache, insomnia, nausea, nervousness, sweating, or vomiting. These side effects should disappear as your body adjusts to the medication.

If this medication makes you feel dizzy, sit or lie down for a while, get up slowly from a sitting or reclining position, and be careful on stairs.

To avoid dizziness when you stand, contract and relax the muscles of your legs for a few moments before rising. Do this by pressing one foot against the floor while lifting the other foot slightly, alternating feet so that you are "pumping" your legs in a pedaling motion.

This medication can cause increased sensitivity to sunlight. Avoid prolonged exposure to sunlight and sunlamps, wear protective clothing and sunglasses, and use an effective sunscreen.

Major. Tell your doctor about any side effects that are persistent or particularly bothersome. IT IS ESPECIALLY IMPORTANT TO TELL YOUR DOCTOR about chest pain; difficulty breathing; excessive perspiration; fainting; fever; impaired taste perception; irregular heartbeat; itching; light-headedness (especially during the first few days); muscle cramps; rash; sore throat; swelling of the face, eyes, lips, or tongue; tingling in the fingers and toes; or yellowing of the eyes or skin.

INTERACTIONS

Trandolapril interacts with several other types of medications:

1. Diuretics and other antihypertensive medications can cause an excessive drop in blood pressure when they are combined with this drug (especially the first dose).

2. Concurrent use of amiloride, potassium supplements, salt substitutes, spironolactone, or triamterene can lead to hyperkalemia (dangerously high blood-potassium levels).

3. Nonsteroidal anti-inflammatory agents (NSAIDs), including ibuprofen, indomethacin, and naproxen, may reduce the effectiveness of this medication.

4. Antacids may decrease the effectiveness of trandolapril. To avoid this drug interaction, it is recommended that trandolapril be taken either one hour before or two hours after taking antacids.

5. Phenothiazine tranquilizers or probenecid may increase the blood level and adverse effects of trandolapril.

6. Concurrent use of this medication and allopurinol can increase the risk of developing an allergic reaction to these medications.
7. This medication can delay the body's elimination of lithium and lead to increased adverse effects from lithium.
8. The concurrent use of this medication and digoxin can lead to increased blood levels of and adverse effects from digoxin.

Before starting to take trandolapril, BE SURE TO TELL YOUR DOCTOR about any medications you are taking, especially those listed above.

WARNINGS

• Tell your doctor about unusual or allergic reactions you have had to any medications, especially to any angiotensin-converting enzyme (ACE) inhibitors (including captopril, enalapril, lisinopril, and benazepril) or to this medication.
• Be sure to tell your doctor if you have or ever had aortic stenosis, heart attack, stroke, blood disorders, kidney or liver disease, kidney transplant, or systemic lupus erythematosus.
• A persistent dry cough may occur during treatment with this medication and usually does not subside unless this medication is stopped. If the coughing is bothersome to you, consult your doctor about it.
• Excessive perspiration, dehydration, or prolonged vomiting or diarrhea can lead to an excessive drop in blood pressure while you are taking this medication. Contact your doctor if you have any of these symptoms.
• Before having surgery or other medical or dental treatment, tell your doctor or dentist you are taking this medication.
• If this drug makes you dizzy or drowsy (sometimes this effect is seen after the first few doses), try to avoid any sudden changes in posture.
• Do not take any over-the-counter (nonprescription) medications for weight control or for asthma, sinus, cough, cold, or allergy problems unless you first check with your doctor.
• Do not stop taking this medication unless you first consult your doctor. Stopping this drug abruptly may lead to a rise in blood pressure.
• Be sure to tell your doctor if you are pregnant. This medication and other drugs in the class called ACE inhibitors (including captopril, enalapril, lisinopril, and benazepril) have been shown to cause birth defects, including kidney damage, low blood pressure, improper skull development, and death, when taken in the second and third trimesters. Also tell your doctor if you are breast-feeding an infant. This medication may pass into breast milk and should not be taken by a nursing mother.

---

trazodone

BRAND NAMES (Manufacturers)
Desyrel (Apothecon)
Desyrel Dividose (Apothecon)
trazodone (various manufacturers)
TYPE OF DRUG
Antidepressant
INGREDIENT
trazodone
DOSAGE FORM
Tablets (50 mg, 100 mg, 150 mg, and 300 mg)
STORAGE
Store this medication at room temperature in a tightly closed, light-resistant container. Like all medications, trazodone should be stored well out of the reach of children and pets.

USES

Trazodone is used to relieve the symptoms of mental depression. It is thought to relieve depression by increasing the concentration of certain chemicals (called neurotransmitters) involved with nerve transmission in the brain. Trazodone may also be used for other medical problems when prescribed by your doctor.

TREATMENT

Take this drug exactly as your doctor prescribes. It can be taken with water, milk, or food to lessen stomach irritation (unless your doctor tells you to do otherwise).

If you miss a dose of this medication, take the missed dose as soon as possible and return to your regular dosing schedule. However, if the dose you missed was a once-a-day bedtime dose, do not take that dose in the morning; check with your doctor instead. If the dose is taken in the morning, it may cause some unwanted side effects. Never double the next dose of this medication.

The benefits of therapy may not become apparent for two to four weeks.

SIDE EFFECTS

Minor. Blurred vision, constipation, diarrhea, dizziness, drowsiness, dry mouth, gas, headache, heartburn, light-headedness, nausea, sleep disorders, vomiting, or weight gain or loss. These side effects should diminish or disappear as your body adjusts to trazodone.

This medication can cause increased sensitivity to sunlight. It is important to avoid prolonged exposure to sunlight and sunlamps. Wear protective clothing and sunglasses, and use an effective sunscreen.

Dry mouth can be relieved by chewing sugarless gum or by sucking on ice chips or a piece of hard candy.

To relieve constipation, increase the amount of fiber in your diet (fresh fruits and vegetables, salads, bran, and whole-grain breads), exercise, and drink more water (unless your doctor directs you to do otherwise).

If this medication makes you feel dizzy or light-headed, sit or lie down for a while, get up slowly from a sitting or reclining position, and be careful on stairs.

To avoid dizziness and light-headedness when you stand, contract and relax the muscles of your legs for a few moments before rising. Do this by pushing one foot against the floor while raising the other foot slightly, alternating feet so you are "pumping" your legs in a pedaling motion.

Major. Tell your doctor about any side effects that are persistent or particularly bothersome. IT IS ESPECIALLY IMPORTANT TO TELL YOUR DOCTOR about chest tightness, confusion, difficult or painful urination, hallucinations, loss of coordination, mood changes, muscle aches or pains, palpitations, prolonged or inappropriate erection of the penis, rash, ringing in the ears, shortness of breath, tingling in the fingers or toes, tremors, unusual bleeding or bruising, or unusual tiredness or weakness.

INTERACTIONS

Trazodone interacts with several other types of medications:

1. Extreme drowsiness can occur when trazodone is taken with central nervous system depressants (drugs that slow the activity of the brain and spinal cord), including alcohol, antihistamines, barbiturates, benzodiazepine tranquilizers, muscle relaxants, narcotics, pain medications, phenothiazine tranquilizers, medications to promote sleep, or with tricyclic antidepressants.

2. The concurrent use of trazodone and monoamine oxidase (MAO) inhibitors should be avoided because the combination can result in fever, convulsions, or high blood pressure. At least 14 days should separate the use of this drug and the use of an MAO inhibitor.

3. Trazodone may increase the blood levels of digoxin and phenytoin, which may, in turn, lead to an increase in side effects from these medications.

4. The blood-pressure-lowering effects of antihypertensives may be increased by trazodone, which can be dangerous.

BE SURE TO TELL YOUR DOCTOR about any medications you are currently taking, especially those mentioned above.

WARNINGS

• Tell your doctor if you have had unusual or allergic reactions to any medications, especially to trazodone.
• Be sure to tell your doctor if you have a history of alcoholism or if you now have or have ever had electroshock therapy, heart disease, a heart attack, kidney disease, or liver disease.
• If this drug makes you dizzy or drowsy, do not take part in any activity that requires alertness, such as driving a car or operating potentially dangerous tools, equipment, or machinery.
• Before having surgery or any other medical or dental treatment, be sure to tell your doctor or dentist that you are taking this medication.
• Do not stop taking this drug suddenly. Stopping this medication abruptly may cause nausea, headache, stomach upset, fatigue, or worsening of your condition. Your doctor may therefore want to reduce the dosage gradually to help prevent or minimize these effects.
• The effects of this medication may last as long as seven days after you stop taking it, so continue to observe all precautions during that period.
• Be sure to tell your doctor if you are pregnant. The safe use of this medication in pregnancy has not been established. Side effects have been observed in the offspring of animals that were given this medication in large doses during pregnancy. Also tell your doctor if you are breast-feeding an infant. Small amounts of this drug pass into breast milk and may cause unwanted effects, such as irritability or sleeping problems, in nursing infants.

---

tretinoin

BRAND NAMES (Manufacturers)
Altinal (Upsher-Smith)
Avital (Bertek)
Renova (Ortho)
Retin-A (Ortho)
Retin-A Micro (Ortho)
tretinoin (various manufacturers)
TYPE OF DRUG
Acne preparation
INGREDIENT
tretinoin (retinoic acid; vitamin A acid)
DOSAGE FORMS
Cream (0.02%, 0.025%, 0.05%, and 0.1%)
Gel (0.01%, 0.025%, 0.04%, and 0.1% with 90% alcohol)
Liquid (0.05% with 55% alcohol)
STORAGE
Store all forms of this drug at room temperature in a tightly closed, light-resistant container. Keep this and all medications out of the reach of children and pets.

USES

Tretinoin is used topically (on the skin) to treat acne vulgaris. It appears to work by increasing the turnover (death and replacement) of skin cells. It is also used to lessen the appearance of fine wrinkles on the face.

TREATMENT

Instructions for the patient should be included with this product. Be sure that you get them (ask your pharmacist for them if they are not included with your prescription) and read them carefully before you apply this medication.

Wash your skin gently with a mild or hypoallergenic soap and warm water. Pat dry with a clean towel. Then wait about 30 minutes before applying tretinoin cream, gel, or liquid. The medication should be applied once a day just before going to bed.

Apply this medication only to the skin where the acne lesions appear, unless you are directed to do otherwise by your doctor. Be sure to cover the entire affected area lightly. You may use a fingertip, gauze pad, or cotton swab to apply the liquid. To avoid applying too much medication, be careful not to oversaturate the gauze pad or cotton swab. To avoid contamination, use a gauze pad or cotton swab only once and then throw it away.

During the early weeks of treatment with this medication, there may be an apparent increase in skin lesions. This is usually not a reason to discontinue use of the drug. However, your doctor may want to change the concentration of the medication prescribed for you. Some improvement may be noted within two to three weeks of starting treatment, although more than six weeks may be required before definite benefits are observed.

If you miss a dose of this medication, apply the missed dose as soon as possible, then return to your regular dosing schedule. If you do not remember until the following day, do not apply the missed dose at all; just return to your regular dosing schedule.

SIDE EFFECTS

Minor. Immediately after applying tretinoin to your skin, you may experience a sensation of warmth or a mild stinging sensation, or your skin may become reddened. After a few days of treatment, some peeling of the skin is to be expected. You may also find that you have a heightened sensitivity to sunlight, wind, or cold.

If this drug does increase your sensitivity to sunlight, try to avoid prolonged exposure to sunlight and sunlamps, wear protective clothing, and use an effective sunscreen.

Major. Tell your doctor about any side effects that are persistent or particularly bothersome. IT IS ESPECIALLY IMPORTANT TO TELL YOUR DOCTOR about blistering; crusting; marked darkening or lightening of the skin; severe burning; severe redness; or swelling.

INTERACTIONS

Tretinoin interacts with several other products:

1. Abrasive or medicated soaps or cleaners.

2. Other acne preparations (particularly peeling agents containing sulfur, resorcinol, benzoyl peroxide, or salicylic acid).

3. Cosmetics and skin cleansers that have a strong drying effect on the skin.

4. Locally applied products containing high amounts of alcohol, spices, or lime.

These products should be used with caution during treatment, since they can increase the extent of irritation.

WARNINGS

• Tell your doctor about unusual or allergic reactions you have had to any drugs, especially to tretinoin, isotretinoin, etretinate, or vitamin A and its derivatives.

• Before starting to take this medication, be sure to tell your doctor if you have eczema.

• This drug should not be used if you are sunburned; it may increase the irritation.

• Keep tretinoin away from the eyes, the mouth, the creases on either side of the nose, open cuts, and mucous membranes; it can severely irritate these sensitive areas.

• Avoid washing your face too often while using tretinoin. Be sure to use a mild or hypoallergenic soap.

- Normal use of nonmedicated cosmetics is permissible, but the skin should be cleaned thoroughly before the medication is applied.
- This medication has been prescribed for your current condition only. Do not give this medication to other people or use it for any purpose other than the one for which it was prescribed by your doctor.
- Be sure to tell your doctor if you are pregnant. The safety of using this medication in human pregnancy or during breast-feeding has not been established.

triamcinolone (inhalation)

BRAND NAME (Manufacturer)
Azmacort (Aventis)
TYPE OF DRUG
Corticosteroid inhalant (antiasthmatic)
INGREDIENT
triamcinolone
DOSAGE FORM
Inhalation aerosol (each actuation or puff delivers approximately 100 mcg)
STORAGE
Store at room temperature away from excessive heat. The contents are pressurized and can explode if heated. Do not puncture the container. This product should not be refrigerated or frozen.

USES

Inhalation corticosteroids are cortisonelike medicines. They are used to help prevent the symptoms of asthma. When used regularly every day, inhalation corticosteroids decrease the number and severity of asthma attacks. However, they will not relieve an asthma attack that has already started. This medicine works by preventing certain cells in the lungs and breathing passages from releasing substances that cause asthma symptoms.

TREATMENT

This medication should be packaged with an instruction sheet. Read the directions carefully before using this medication. You may wish to consult your doctor or pharmacist about the proper administration of this drug. Shake the container well just before each use to evenly distribute the ingredients and equalize the doses, as the contents tend to settle on the bottom of the bottle. If more than one inhalation is necessary, wait at least one full minute between doses to receive the full benefit of the first dose.

Take this medication exactly as prescribed by your doctor. Do not use more of it and do not use it more often than recommended by your doctor. To do so may increase the chance of side effects.

While using this medication, try to develop a set schedule for taking it. If you miss a dose and remember within a few hours, take the missed dose and use any remaining doses for that day at evenly spaced intervals. Do not double the next dose.

This medication does not cure asthma, but it will help to control the condition as long as you continue to take it. It may be several weeks before you notice the full effect of this medication.

SIDE EFFECTS

Minor. Cough, dry mouth, hoarseness or other voice changes, sore throat, or unpleasant taste in the mouth. These side effects should diminish or disappear as your body adjusts to the medication.

Chew sugarless gum or suck on ice chips or a piece of hard candy to relieve mouth or throat dryness.

To prevent dryness and irritation of the mouth and throat and to prevent possible infection of the mouth, rinse or gargle with water after each dose. DO NOT SWALLOW the water after rinsing.

Major. Tell your doctor about any side effects that are persistent or particularly bothersome. IT IS ESPECIALLY IMPORTANT TO TELL YOUR DOCTOR about behavior changes; creamy white, curd-like patches in the mouth or throat; depression; difficulty breathing; nervousness; pain or burning in the chest; pain when eating or swallowing; restlessness; tightness in the chest; or wheezing.

INTERACTIONS

This medication should not interact with other medications when used according to directions.

Before starting to take this medication, BE SURE TO TELL YOUR DOCTOR about any medications you are taking.

WARNINGS

• Tell your doctor about unusual or allergic reactions you have had to any cortisone-like medications, especially to this medication.

• Be sure to tell your doctor if you have ever had bone disease of any sort (including osteoporosis), diabetes mellitus, emotional instability, glaucoma, fungal infections, heart disease, high blood pressure, high cholesterol levels, myasthenia gravis, ulcerative colitis, peptic ulcers, kidney disease, liver disease, or tuberculosis.

• Before having surgery or other medical or dental treatment, tell your doctor or dentist you are taking this medication. Depending on how long you have been taking this medication, you may need to receive higher doses if you are under stress, such as from a serious infection, injury, or surgery. Discuss this with your doctor or dentist.

• Avoid contact of the aerosol inhalation with your eyes.

• Do not puncture, break, or burn the aerosol container. The contents are under pressure and may explode. In addition, avoid exposure of this medication to cold or freezing temperatures; this medication may be less effective if it is cold when you use it.

• Do not stop taking this medication without first checking with your doctor. Your doctor may want to gradually reduce the amount of medicine you are taking before completely stopping it. Make sure that you have enough medicine on hand to last through vacations, holidays, and weekends.

• Do not take any over-the-counter (nonprescription) medications for weight control or for asthma, sinus, cough, cold, or allergy problems unless you first check with your pharmacist or doctor.

• Your doctor may want you to carry a medical identification card stating that you are using this medicine and that you may need additional medicine during times of emergency, stress, severe asthma attack, or other illness.

• If you are using a bronchodilator (albuterol, metaproterenol, etc.) by inhalation, you must use the bronchodilator several minutes BEFORE this medication (corticosteroid inhaler). Discuss this with your doctor or pharmacist.

• Notify your doctor immediately if you are exposed to any person with chicken pox or the measles.

• This medication is for preventative therapy only. DO NOT use it to treat an acute asthmatic attack. This medication should be used at regularly scheduled intervals throughout the day as prescribed by your doctor, even if you are not having any symptoms of asthma.

• Be sure to tell your doctor if you are pregnant. This medication has been shown to cause birth defects in the offspring of animals that received large doses of it during pregnancy. Adequate studies have not been done in humans. Also tell your doctor if you are breast-feeding an infant. Small amounts of this medication pass into breast milk and may cause growth suppression or a decrease in natural corticosteroid production in the nursing infant.

triamcinolone (topical)

BRAND NAMES (Manufacturers)
Aristocort (Fujisawa)
Aristocort A (Fujisawa)
Flutex (Syosset)
Kenalog (Westwood-Squibb)
Kenalog-H (Westwood-Squibb)
Triacet (Lemmon)
triamcinolone acetonide (various manufacturers)

TYPE OF DRUG
Adrenocorticosteroid hormone

INGREDIENT
triamcinolone

DOSAGE FORMS
Ointment (0.025%, 0.1%, and 0.5%)
Cream (0.025%, 0.1%, and 0.5%)
Lotion (0.025% and 0.1%)
Paste, dental (0.1%)
Aerosol (two seconds of spray delivers approximately 0.2 mg of drug, with 10.3% alcohol)

STORAGE
Store at room temperature in a tightly closed container. Do not freeze.

The spray (foam) form of this medication is packaged under pressure. It should not be stored near heat or an open flame or in direct sunlight, and the container should never be punctured.

USES

Your adrenal glands naturally produce certain cortisonelike chemicals. These chemicals are involved in various processes in the body (such as maintenance of fluid balance, regulation of temperature, and reaction to inflammation). Triamcinolone belongs to a group of drugs known as adrenocorticosteroids (or cortisonelike medications). It is used to relieve the skin inflammation (redness, swelling, itching, and discomfort) associated with conditions such as dermatitis, eczema, and poison ivy. How this drug acts to relieve these disorders is not completely understood.

TREATMENT

Before applying this medication, wash your hands. Then, unless your doctor gives you different instructions, gently wash the area of the skin where the medication is to be applied. With a clean towel, pat the area almost dry; it should be slightly damp when you put the medicine on.

Shake the lotion well before pouring, to distribute the ingredients evenly and equalize the doses. The contents tend to settle on the bottom of the bottle.

Apply a small amount of the medication to the affected area in a thin layer. Do not bandage the area unless your doctor tells you to do so. If you are to apply an occlusive dressing (such as kitchen plastic wrap), be sure you understand the instructions. Wash your hands again after application.

If you are using the aerosol spray form of this medication, shake the can in order to disperse the medication evenly. Hold the can upright six to eight inches from the area to be sprayed, and spray the area for one to three seconds. DO NOT SMOKE while using the aerosol spray.

Apply the dental paste with a cotton applicator, pressing (not rubbing) the paste onto the affected area. It is best applied after meals and at bedtime, unless directed otherwise by your doctor or dentist.

If you miss a dose of this medication, apply the dose as soon as possible. However, if it is almost time for the next application, do not apply the missed dose; just return to your regular dosing schedule. Do not put twice as much of the medication on your skin at the next application.

SIDE EFFECTS

Minor. Acne, burning sensation, irritation of the affected area, or skin dryness. These side effects should diminish or disappear as your body adjusts to the medication.

If the affected area is extremely dry or scaling, the skin may be moistened by soaking in water or by applying water with a clean cloth before applying the medication. The ointment form is probably better for dry skin.

A mild, temporary stinging sensation may occur after this medication is applied. If this persists, contact your doctor.

Major. Tell your doctor about any side effects that are persistent or particularly bothersome. IT IS ESPECIALLY IMPORTANT TO TELL YOUR DOCTOR about blistering of the skin, increased hair growth, itching, loss of skin color, rash, secondary infection in the area being treated, or thinning of the skin with easy bruising.

INTERACTIONS

This medication should not interact with other medications as long as it is used according to the directions given to you by your doctor or pharmacist.

Before starting to take this medication, BE SURE TO TELL YOUR DOCTOR about any medications that you are currently taking.

WARNINGS

• Tell your doctor about unusual or allergic reactions you have had to any medications, especially to triamcinolone or other adrenocorticosteroids (such as amcinonide, betamethasone, clocortolone, cortisone, desonide, desoximetasone, dexamethasone, diflorasone, flumethasone, fluocinolone, fluocinonide, fluorometholone, flurandrenolide, halcinonide, hydrocortisone, methylprednisolone, prednisolone, and prednisone).

• Tell your doctor if you now have or ever had blood-vessel disease, chicken pox, diabetes mellitus, fungal infection, peptic ulcers, shingles, tuberculosis of the lungs or skin, vaccinia, or any other infection, especially at the site currently being treated.

• If any kind of irritation develops while you are using this medication, immediately discontinue applying it and notify your doctor.

• This product is intended for topical use only. It is not for use in the eyes or on the mucous membranes; contact may result in side effects.

• Do not use this product with an occlusive wrap unless your doctor directs you to do so. Systemic absorption of this drug is increased if extensive areas of the body are treated, particularly if occlusive bandages are used. If it is necessary for you to use this drug under a wrap, follow your physician's instructions exactly. Do not leave the wrap in place longer than specified.

• If you are using this medication on a child's diaper area, it is important not to put tight-fitting diapers or plastic pants on the child. This may lead to increased systemic absorption of the medication and an increase in side effects.

• To avoid freezing skin tissue when using the aerosol form, do not spray for more than three seconds, and hold the container at least six inches away from the skin.

• To prevent side effects when using the aerosol form of this medication near the face, cover your eyes, and do not inhale the spray.

• Do not use this medication for longer than the time prescribed by your doctor.

• It is very important that you tell your doctor if you are pregnant. If large amounts of triamcinolone are applied for prolonged periods, some of it will be absorbed and may cross the placenta. Although extensive studies in human pregnancy have not yet been conducted, birth defects have been observed in the offspring of animals that were given large oral doses of this type of drug during pregnancy. Also notify your doctor if you are breast-feeding an infant. If absorbed through the skin, small amounts of this drug pass into breast milk and may cause growth suppression or a decrease in the production of natural adrenocorticosteroid hormones in the nursing infant.

---

triamterene

BRAND NAME (Manufacturer)
Dyrenium (SmithKline Beecham)
TYPE OF DRUG
Diuretic and antihypertensive
INGREDIENT
triamterene
DOSAGE FORM
Capsules (50 mg and 100 mg)
STORAGE
Store at room temperature in a tightly closed, light-resistant container.

USES

Triamterene is prescribed to treat high blood pressure. It is also used to reduce fluid accumulation in the body caused by conditions such as heart failure, cirrhosis of the liver, kidney disease, and the long-term use of certain medications. Triamterene reduces fluid accumulation by increasing the elimination of salt and water through the kidneys. It may also be used in combination with other diuretics to prevent potassium loss.

TREATMENT

To decrease stomach irritation, you can take triamterene with a glass of milk or with a meal (unless your doctor directs you to do otherwise). Try to take it at the same time(s) every day. Avoid taking a dose after 6:00 in the evening; otherwise, you may have to get up during the night to urinate.

This medication does not cure high blood pressure, but it will help to control the condition as long as you take it.

If you miss a dose of this medication, take the missed dose as soon as possible. However, if it is almost time for the next dose, do not take the missed dose at all; just wait until the next scheduled dose. Do not double the next dose.

SIDE EFFECTS

Minor. Diarrhea, dizziness, drowsiness, dry mouth, headache, increased thirst, increased urination, nausea, tiredness, upset stomach, or vomiting. As your body adjusts to triamterene, these side effects should diminish or disappear.

Triamterene can cause increased sensitivity to sunlight. It is therefore important to avoid prolonged exposure to sunlight and sunlamps while you are taking this medication. Wear protective clothing and use sunscreen whenever you are outdoors during daylight hours.

Triamterene may cause your urine to turn bluish; this is a harmless side effect.

Dry mouth can be relieved by sucking on ice chips or a piece of hard candy or by chewing sugarless gum.

If this medication makes you feel dizzy, sit or lie down for a while, get up slowly from a sitting or reclining position, and be careful on stairs.

To avoid dizziness or light-headedness when you stand, contract and relax the muscles of your legs for a few moments before rising. Do this by pushing one foot against the floor while raising the other foot slightly, alternating feet so that you are "pumping" your legs in a pedaling motion.

Major. Tell your doctor about any side effects that are persistent or particularly bothersome. IT IS ESPECIALLY IMPORTANT TO TELL YOUR DOCTOR about anxiety; back or flank (side) pain; confusion; cracking at the corners of the mouth; difficulty in breathing; extreme weakness; fever; mouth sores; numbness or tingling in the hands, feet, or lips; painful urination; palpitations; rash; a red or inflamed tongue; sore throat; unusual bleeding or bruising; or unusual tiredness.

INTERACTIONS

Triamterene will interact with several foods and other types of medications:

1. Concurrent use of triamterene with antihypertensives, such as benazepril, captopril, enalapril, fosinopril, lisinopril, and ramipril, or with spironolactone, amiloride, potassium salts, low-salt milk, salt substitutes, or laxatives can cause serious side effects from hyperkalemia (high levels of potassium in the blood).

2. Triamterene may decrease the effectiveness of antigout medications, insulin, and oral antidiabetic medications.

3. Triamterene has been known to increase the side effects of lithium and amantadine when taken concurrently.

4. Indomethacin should never be taken concurrently with triamterene. Discuss this with your doctor if both have been prescribed for you.

5. Cimetidine may increase the side effects of triamterene.

Before starting to take triamterene, BE SURE TO TELL YOUR DOCTOR about any medications you are currently taking, especially any of those listed above.

WARNINGS

- Before starting to take this medication, be sure to tell your doctor if you have ever had an unusual or allergic reaction to any medication, especially to triamterene or to any other diuretic.
- Be sure to tell your doctor if you now have or ever had kidney disease, kidney stones, urination problems, hyperkalemia, diabetes mellitus, liver disease, acidosis, or gout.
- Triamterene can cause hyperkalemia (high blood levels of potassium). Signs of hyperkalemia include palpitations; confusion; numbness or tingling in the hands, feet, or lips; anxiety; or unusual tiredness or weakness. Discuss this possible effect with your doctor and ask if there are any steps you should take or foods you should avoid in order to help prevent this problem.
- You should limit your intake of alcoholic beverages while taking this drug in order to prevent dizziness and the feeling of light-headedness.
- Do not take any over-the-counter (nonprescription) medications for weight control or for allergy, asthma, cough, cold, or sinus problems unless you first check with your doctor. Some of these products can lead to an increase in blood pressure.
- It is possible that treatment with this medication will cause severe water loss (dehydration). In order to prevent this, be sure to check with your doctor if you have any illness that causes severe or continuous nausea, vomiting, or diarrhea.
- If you are taking quinidine (an antiarrhythmic heart medication), it is important to know that triamterene may interfere with the laboratory determination of your blood quinidine concentration. Before you undergo this type of test, be sure to tell your doctor that you are also taking the drug triamterene.
- Your doctor may schedule regular office visits to monitor your progress and possibly adjust your dosage.
- Be sure to tell your doctor if you are pregnant. This medication crosses the placenta, and its safety in human pregnancy has not been thoroughly investigated. Effects have been reported in the fetuses of animals that received large doses of this medication during pregnancy. Also be sure to tell your doctor if you are breast-feeding an infant. It has been established that small amounts of triamterene do pass into breast milk.

triazolam

BRAND NAMES (Manufacturers)
Halcion (Upjohn)
triazolam (various manufacturers)
TYPE OF DRUG
Benzodiazepine sedative/hypnotic
INGREDIENT
triazolam
DOSAGE FORM
Tablets (0.125 mg and 0.25 mg)
STORAGE
Store at room temperature in a tightly closed, light-resistant container.

USES

Triazolam is prescribed to treat insomnia, including problems with falling asleep, waking during the night, and early morning wakefulness. It is not clear exactly how this medicine works, but it may relieve insomnia by acting as a depressant of the central nervous system (brain and spinal cord).

TREATMENT

Take this medicine 30 to 60 minutes before bedtime. It can be taken with a full glass of water or with food if stomach upset occurs. Do not take this medication with a dose of antacid, which may slow its absorption.

If you are taking this medication regularly and you miss a dose, take the missed dose immediately if you remember within an hour. If more than an hour has passed, skip the dose you missed and wait for the next scheduled dose. Do not double the next dose.

SIDE EFFECTS

Minor. Bitter taste in mouth, constipation, diarrhea, dizziness, drowsiness (after a night's sleep), dry mouth, excessive salivation, fatigue, flushing, headache, heartburn, loss of appetite, nausea, nervousness, sweating, or vomiting. As your body adjusts to the medication, these side effects should diminish or disappear.

To relieve constipation, increase the amount of fiber in your diet (fresh fruits and vegetables, salads, bran, and whole-grain breads), exercise, and drink more water (unless your doctor directs you to do otherwise).

Dry mouth can be relieved by chewing sugarless gum or by sucking on ice chips.

If you feel dizzy, sit or lie down for a while; get up slowly from a sitting or reclining position; and be careful on stairs. To help avoid dizziness when you stand, contract and relax the muscles in your legs for a few moments before rising. Do this by pressing one foot against the floor while raising the other foot slightly, alternating feet so that you are pumping your legs in a pedaling motion.

Major. Tell your doctor about any side effects that are persistent or particularly bothersome. IT IS ESPECIALLY IMPORTANT TO TELL YOUR DOCTOR about blurred or double vision, chest pain, depression, difficulty in urinating, fainting, falling, fever, hallucinations, joint pain, mouth sores, nightmares, palpitations, rash, shortness of breath, slurred speech, sore throat, uncoordinated movements, unusual excitement, unusual tiredness, or yellowing of the eyes or skin.

INTERACTIONS

Triazolam interacts with a number of other types of drugs:

1. To prevent oversedation, triazolam should not be taken with alcohol, other sedative drugs, central nervous system depressants (such as antihistamines, barbiturates, mus-

cle relaxants, pain medicines, narcotics, medicines for seizures, and phenothiazine tranquilizers), or antidepressants.
2. It may decrease the effectiveness of carbamazepine, levodopa, and oral anticoagulants (blood thinners, such as warfarin) and increase the side effects of phenytoin.
3. Disulfiram, oral contraceptives (birth control pills), isoniazid, and cimetidine can increase the blood levels of triazolam, which can lead to toxic effects.
4. Concurrent use of rifampin may decrease the effectiveness of triazolam.
BE SURE TO TELL YOUR DOCTOR about any medications you are taking.

WARNINGS

• Tell your doctor about unusual or allergic reactions you have had to any medications, especially to triazolam or other benzodiazepine tranquilizers (such as alprazolam, chlordiazepoxide, clorazepate, diazepam, flurazepam, halazepam, lorazepam, prazepam, and temazepam).
• Tell your doctor if you now have or ever had liver disease, kidney disease, epilepsy, lung disease, myasthenia gravis, porphyria, mental depression, or mental illness.
• This medicine can cause considerable drowsiness. Avoid tasks that require mental alertness, such as driving an automobile or operating potentially dangerous machinery or equipment.
• Triazolam has the potential for abuse and must be used with caution. Tolerance may develop quickly; do not increase the dosage unless you first consult your doctor. It is also important not to stop taking this drug suddenly if you have been taking it in large amounts or if you have used it for several weeks. Your doctor may want to reduce your dosage of the medication gradually.
• This is a safe drug when used properly. When it is combined with other sedative drugs or with alcohol, however, serious side effects can develop.
• Be sure to tell your doctor if you are pregnant. This type of medicine may increase the chance of birth defects if it is taken during the first three months of pregnancy. In addition, use of too much of this medicine during the last six months of pregnancy may lead to addiction of the fetus, resulting in withdrawal side effects in the newborn. Use of this medicine during the last weeks of pregnancy may cause excessive drowsiness, slowed heartbeat, and breathing difficulties in the infant. Tell your doctor if you are breast-feeding an infant. This medicine can pass into breast milk and cause unwanted side effects in nursing infants.

---

valacyclovir

BRAND NAME (Manufacturer)
Valtrex (GlaxoSmithKline)
TYPE OF DRUG
Antiviral
INGREDIENT
valacyclovir
DOSAGE FORM
Tablets (500 mg and 1g)
STORAGE
Store at room temperature in a tightly closed, light-resistant container. Do not expose to excess heat.

USES

Valacyclovir is used to treat genital herpes, herpes zoster (shingles) infections of the skin, and cold sores caused by the herpes virus. Valacyclovir prevents the growth and multiplication of the herpes virus. This drug does not cure a herpes infection, but it may relieve the pain associated with the viral infection and may shorten its duration.

TREATMENT

To lessen stomach upset, take valacyclovir tablets with food (unless your doctor tells you to do otherwise).

Take valacyclovir as soon as possible after the symptoms of a herpes virus infection appear. This medication works best when it is started within 48 hours of the onset of the rash that appears with shingles or within 24 hours of the onset of the symptoms of genital herpes. It works best for cold sores when it is started at the earliest sign of a cold sore (tingling, itching, and burning).

Complete the full course of therapy, even if your symptoms disappear sooner. The length of your treatment will depend on your specific medical problem.

If you miss a dose of this medication, take it as soon as possible. However, if it is almost time for your next dose, do not take the missed dose at all; just return to your regular dosing schedule. Do not double the next dose.

SIDE EFFECTS

Minor. Constipation, diarrhea, dizziness, headache, joint pain, loss of appetite, nausea, stomach pain, unusual tiredness or weakness, or vomiting. These side effects should diminish or disappear as your body adjusts to the medication.

To relieve constipation, increase the amount of fiber in your diet (fresh fruits and vegetables, salads, bran, and whole-grain breads), exercise, and drink more water (unless your doctor directs you to do otherwise).

If this medication makes you feel dizzy, sit or lie down for a while, get up slowly from a sitting or reclining position, and be careful on stairs.

To avoid dizziness or light-headedness when you stand, contract and relax the muscles of your legs for a few moments before rising. Do this by pressing one foot against the floor while raising the other foot slightly, alternating feet so that you are "pumping" your legs in a pedaling motion.

Major. Tell your doctor about any side effects that are persistent or particularly bothersome. IT IS ESPECIALLY IMPORTANT TO TELL YOUR DOCTOR about abdominal cramps, prolonged diarrhea or nausea, or severe menstrual cramps.

INTERACTIONS

Valacyclovir may interact with other medications: Probenecid and cimetidine may increase the amount of valacyclovir in the body.

BE SURE TO TELL YOUR DOCTOR about any medications you are currently taking, especially either of the medications that are listed above.

WARNINGS

- Be sure to tell your doctor about any unusual or allergic reactions you have had to any medications, especially any reactions to acyclovir.
- Before starting therapy with this medication, be sure to tell your doctor if you have any other medical problems, especially kidney or liver problems or any problems with your immune system.
- Try to avoid sexual activity while you have signs or symptoms of genital herpes; this medication does not prevent transmission of herpes to other people, nor does it prevent recurrence.
- This medication has been prescribed for your current infection only. An infection that someone else has may require a different medication. Do not use your medication to treat other types of infections unless your doctor specifically directs you to do so.
- If this drug makes you dizzy or drowsy, do not participate in any activity that requires alertness, such as driving a car or operating potentially dangerous equipment.
- Be sure to tell your doctor if you are pregnant. Although this medication appears to be safe in animals, there is no information on its use in humans during pregnancy. In addition, be sure to tell your doctor if you are breast-feeding an infant. It is not known if valacyclovir is safe to use when you are breast-feeding.

valdecoxib

BRAND NAME (Manufacturer)
Bextra (Pharmacia)
TYPE OF DRUG
Nonsteroidal anti-inflammatory agent, analgesic
INGREDIENT
valdecoxib
DOSAGE FORM
Tablets (10 mg and 20 mg)
STORAGE
Store at room temperature, away from heat, in a tightly closed container. Do not freeze.

USES

Valdecoxib is used to treat the signs and symptoms of osteoarthritis and rheumatoid arthritis. It may also be used for the short-term treatment of acute pain, such as following dental surgery. Valdecoxib is also used for pain and discomfort associated with menstruation. Valdecoxib works by blocking the formation of prostaglandins, which are chemicals in the body that cause swelling and inflammation in tissues and joints.

TREATMENT

This medication is usually taken once a day, with or without meals. However, to avoid stomach irritation, your doctor may direct you to take this medication with food or milk. It is best to take this medication at the same time each day.

It is important to try not to miss any doses of this medication. If you do miss a dose, take it as soon as you remember. However, if it is almost time for your next dose, do not take the missed dose; just return to your regular dosing schedule. Do not double the next dose of this medication.

SIDE EFFECTS

Minor. Back pain, blurred vision, constipation, diarrhea, dizziness, ear congestion, feeling weak, heartburn, or nausea. These side effects usually go away during treatment, as your body adjusts to the medicine.

To avoid dizziness or light-headedness when you stand, contract and relax the muscles of your legs for a few moments before rising. Do this by pressing one foot against the floor while raising the other foot slightly, alternating feet so that you are "pumping" your legs in a pedaling motion.

If you feel dizzy or light-headed, sit or lie down for a while; get up from a sitting or lying position slowly; and be careful on stairs.

To relieve constipation, increase the amount of fiber in your diet (fresh fruits and vegetables, salads, bran, and whole-grain breads), exercise, and drink more water (unless your doctor directs you to do otherwise).

Major. If any side effects are persistent or particularly bothersome to you, it is important to notify your doctor. IT IS ESPECIALLY IMPORTANT TO TELL YOUR DOCTOR about black tarry stools; chest congestion or tightness; chills; fever; muscle aches; severe or bloody diarrhea; shortness of breath; skin rash; swelling of the legs, feet, hands, or arms; vomiting of blood or material that looks like coffee grounds; or weight gain.

INTERACTIONS

Valdecoxib interacts with a number of other medications:

1. Concurrent use of aspirin or other nonsteroidal anti-inflammatory drugs (NSAIDs), such as ibuprofen, indomethacin, or naproxen, with this medication may increase the risk of stomach ulcers or bleeding. They should not be taken with valdecoxib.

2. Use of valdecoxib and warfarin (a blood thinner) may increase the effects of warfarin and thereby increase the risk of bleeding.
3. Concurrent use of valdecoxib may increase the risk of side effects from lithium and dextromethorphan.
4. Antifungal agents (including ketoconazole and fluconazole) may increase the amount of valdecoxib in the body and increase the side effects from valdecoxib.
5. The effects of diuretics (water pills), such as thiazide diuretics and furosemide, may be reduced by valdecoxib.
6. The antihypertensive effects of ACE inhibitors may be reduced with valdecoxib.

BE SURE TO TELL YOUR DOCTOR about any medications you are taking, especially those mentioned above.

WARNINGS

• It is important to tell your doctor if you have ever had any unusual or allergic reaction to valdecoxib, celecoxib, rofecoxib, aspirin, nonsteroidal anti-inflammatory drugs (such as ibuprofen, indomethacin, or naproxen), any other medication used for arthritis or pain, or any other medication.
• It is also important to tell your doctor if you now have or ever had kidney disease, liver disease, swelling of the hands or feet, heart disease, heart failure, high blood pressure, anemia, asthma, nasal polyps, or stomach ulcers.
• Avoid drinking alcoholic beverages while taking this medication (unless directed otherwise by your doctor). Large amounts of alcohol can affect your liver and also increase the risk of stomach irritation or ulcers.
• Be sure to tell your doctor or dentist that you are taking this medicine before having any kind of surgery or other medical or dental treatment.
• Be sure to tell your doctor if you are pregnant. Valdecoxib should not be used during the later part of pregnancy because it may cause harm to the fetus. Also, be sure to tell your doctor if you are breast-feeding an infant, and discuss the risks and benefits of using this medication when nursing.

---

valproic acid

BRAND NAMES (Manufacturers)
Depakene (Abbott)
Depakote* (Abbott)
valproic acid (various manufacturers)
*Note: Divalproex sodium, sold under the brand name Depakote, is chemically and therapeutically similar to valproic acid. It has been formulated as an enteric-coated tablet to prolong its effects and to decrease stomach irritation.
TYPE OF DRUG
Anticonvulsant
INGREDIENT
valproic acid
DOSAGE FORMS
Capsules (250 mg)
Enteric-coated tablets (125 mg, 250 mg, and 500 mg)
Oral syrup (250 mg per 5-mL spoonful)
Sprinkle capsule (125 mg)
STORAGE
Store at room temperature in a tightly closed container. Do not freeze.

USES

Valproic acid is used to treat various seizure disorders. It prevents seizures or convulsions by increasing concentrations of a certain chemical (gamma aminobutyric acid) in the brain. It is also used to help prevent migraine headaches and in the treatment and prevention of mania in persons with bipolar disorder (manic-depression).

TREATMENT

To avoid stomach irritation, take valproic acid with food or milk (unless your doctor directs you to do otherwise). Your doctor may advise you to take this medication at bedtime to avoid any stomach discomfort.

Swallow the capsules or enteric-coated tablets whole. Chewing or opening the capsules before swallowing them releases their contents, which may cause irritation of the mouth and throat.

Measure each dose of the oral syrup carefully with a specially designed 5-mL measuring spoon. An ordinary kitchen teaspoon is not accurate enough.

Only the specially designed sprinkle capsules should be opened before swallowing. Place the entire contents of the sprinkle capsule on a teaspoonful of applesauce or pudding, and swallow it immediately. Do not chew the food-drug mixture, and do not prepare it ahead of time.

Valproic acid works best when the level of medication in the bloodstream is kept constant. Therefore, it is best to take the doses at evenly spaced intervals day and night. For example, if you are to take 2 doses each day, the doses should be spaced 12 hours apart.

It is important to try not to miss any doses of this medication. If you do miss a dose and remember within six hours, take the missed dose immediately. If more than six hours have passed, do not take the missed dose at all; just return to your regular dosing schedule. Do not double the next dose of this medication. If you miss two or more consecutive doses of this medication, contact your doctor as soon as possible for further instructions.

SIDE EFFECTS

Minor. Constipation, diarrhea, dizziness, drowsiness, hair loss, headache, increased or decreased appetite, insomnia, nausea, stomach upset, vomiting, or weight gain or loss. These side effects should disappear as your body adjusts to the medication.

To relieve constipation, increase the amount of fiber in your diet (fresh fruits and vegetables, salads, bran, and whole-grain breads), exercise, and drink more water (unless your doctor directs you to do otherwise).

If you feel dizzy, sit or lie down for a while; stand up slowly from a sitting or reclining position; and be careful when climbing or descending stairs.

To help prevent dizziness when you stand, contract and relax the muscles of your legs for a few moments before rising. Do this by pressing one foot against the floor while raising the other foot slightly, alternating feet so that you are "pumping" your legs in a pedaling motion.

Major. Tell your doctor about any side effects that are persistent or particularly bothersome. IT IS ESPECIALLY IMPORTANT TO TELL YOUR DOCTOR about blurred vision, cramps, depression, facial edema (swelling), loss of coordination, menstrual disorders, mental disorders, skin rash, tremors, unusual bleeding or bruising, weakness, or a yellowish discoloration of the eyes or skin.

INTERACTIONS

Valproic acid interacts with several other types of drugs:

1. Concurrent use of valproic acid with other central nervous system depressants (medications or other substances that slow the activity of the brain and spinal cord), such as alcohol, antihistamines, barbiturates, muscle relaxants, narcotics, pain medications, phenothiazine tranquilizers, sleeping medications, or with tricyclic antidepressants can lead to drowsiness.

2. It can lead to bleeding complications when combined with oral anticoagulants (blood thinners, such as warfarin), aspirin, dipyridamole, or sulfinpyrazone.

3. Valproic acid can increase the blood levels and side effects of phenobarbital and primidone.
4. The combination of valproic acid and clonazepam or phenytoin can lead to an increase in seizure activity.
5. Aspirin may interfere with the metabolism of valproic acid, which in turn may result in increased toxicity and increased side effects.

Before beginning treatment with valproic acid, BE SURE TO TELL YOUR DOCTOR about any medications that you are currently taking, especially any of those medications listed above.

WARNINGS

- Be sure to tell your doctor about unusual or allergic reactions you have had to any medications, especially to valproic acid, sodium valproate, or divalproex sodium.
- Be sure to tell your doctor if you now have or ever had blood disorders, kidney disease, or liver disease.
- If this drug makes you dizzy or drowsy, do not take part in any activity that requires alertness, such as driving a car or operating potentially dangerous machinery.
- Before having surgery or any other medical or dental treatment, be sure to tell your doctor or dentist that you are taking this medication.
- Do not stop taking this medication unless you first check with your doctor. Stopping the drug abruptly may lead to a worsening of your condition. Your doctor may want to reduce your dosage gradually or start you on another medication when valproic acid is discontinued. Make sure you have enough medication on hand to last through weekends, holidays, and vacations.
- Diabetic patients should know that valproic acid can interfere with urine tests for ketones. You should therefore check with your doctor before adjusting your insulin dose to determine if any increase or decrease is necessary.
- Be sure to tell your doctor if you are pregnant. Valproic acid has been shown to cause birth defects in the offspring of animals that received large doses of the medication during pregnancy. Valproic acid has also been associated with spinal cord birth defects in humans when used during the first three months of pregnancy. The risks and benefits of treatment should be discussed with your doctor. Also be sure to tell your doctor if you are breast-feeding an infant. Small amounts of valproic acid pass into breast milk.

---

valsartan

BRAND NAME (Manufacturer)
Diovan (Novartis)
TYPE OF DRUG
Antihypertensive (blood-pressure-lowering drug)
INGREDIENT
valsartan
DOSAGE FORM
Capsules (40 mg, 80 mg, 160 mg, and 320 mg)
STORAGE
Store in a tightly closed container at room temperature, away from heat and direct sunlight. Do not refrigerate or freeze.

USES

Valsartan is used to treat high blood pressure as well as for the treatment of congestive heart failure. Valsartan is a vasodilator (it widens blood vessels) that acts by blocking the production of chemicals that may be responsible for constricting or narrowing blood vessels.

TREATMENT

Take this medication exactly as prescribed by your doctor. Valsartan can be taken on an empty stomach or with meals if stomach upset occurs.

While using this medication, try to develop a set schedule for taking it. If you miss a dose and remember within a few hours, take the missed dose and resume your regular schedule. If many hours have passed, skip the dose you missed and then take your next dose as scheduled. Do not double the next dose.

Valsartan does not cure high blood pressure or heart failure, but it will help to control the condition as long as you continue to take it.

SIDE EFFECTS

Minor. Abdominal pain, cough, diarrhea, dizziness, drowsiness, fatigue, headache, insomina, nausea, nervousness, sweating, or vomiting. These side effects should disappear as your body adjusts to the medication.

If this medication makes you feel dizzy, sit or lie down for a while, get up slowly from a sitting or reclining position, and be careful on stairs.

To avoid dizziness when you stand, contract and relax the muscles of your legs for a few moments before rising. Do this by alternately pushing one foot against the floor while lifting the other foot slightly.

Major. Tell your doctor about any side effects that are persistent or particularly bothersome. IT IS ESPECIALLY IMPORTANT TO TELL YOUR DOCTOR about chest pain; difficulty breathing; fainting; fever; itching; light-headedness (especially during the first few days); muscle cramps; palpitations; rash; sore throat; swelling of the face, eyes, lips, or tongue; tingling in the fingers and toes; or yellowing of the eyes or skin.

INTERACTIONS

Valsartan interacts with several other types of medications:

1. Diuretics and other antihypertensive medications can cause an excessive drop in blood pressure when they are combined with this medication, especially with the first dose.

2. Amiloride, potassium supplements, salt substitutes, spironolactone, or triamterene can lead to hyperkalemia (dangerously high levels of potassium in the bloodstream) when used with this drug.

3. Nonsteroidal anti-inflammatory drugs (NSAIDs), including ibuprofen, indomethacin, and naproxen, may reduce the effectiveness of this medication.

Before starting to take valsartan, BE SURE TO TELL YOUR DOCTOR about any medications you are taking, especially those listed above.

WARNINGS

• Tell your doctor about unusual or allergic reactions you have had to any medications, especially to valsartan or to angiotensin-converting enzyme (ACE) inhibitors (including captopril, enalapril, lisinopril, and benazepril), candesartan, eprosartan, irbesartan, losartan, olmesartan, or telmisartan.

• Be sure to tell your doctor if you have or ever had heart disease, blood disorders, renal or liver disease, or systemic lupus erythematosus.

• Excessive perspiration, dehydration, or prolonged vomiting or diarrhea can lead to an excessive drop in blood pressure while you are taking this medication. Contact your doctor if you have any of these symptoms.

• Before having surgery or any other medical or dental treatment, be sure to tell your doctor or dentist that you are taking this medication.

• If this drug makes you dizzy or drowsy, do not participate in any activity that requires alertness, such as driving a car or operating potentially dangerous equipment.

• If you have high blood pressure, do not take any over-the-counter (nonprescription) medications for weight control or for asthma, sinus, cough, cold, or allergy problems unless you first check with your doctor.

• Be sure to tell your doctor if you are pregnant. This medication is very similar to the class of drugs called ACE inhibitors (including captopril, enalapril, lisinopril, and benazepril), which have been shown to cause birth defects when taken in the second and third trimesters of pregnancy. Also tell your doctor if you are breast-feeding an infant. This medication may pass into breast milk and should not be taken by a nursing mother.

---

venlafaxine

BRAND NAMES (Manufacturers)
Effexor (Wyeth-Ayerst)
Effexor-XR (Wyeth-Ayerst)
TYPE OF DRUG
Antidepressant
INGREDIENT
venlafaxine
DOSAGE FORMS
Tablets (25 mg, 37.5 mg, 50 mg, 75 mg, and 100 mg)
Capsules (37.5 mg, 75 mg, and 150 mg)
STORAGE
Store in a tightly closed container at room temperature, away from heat and direct sunlight. Do not store in the bathroom. Heat or moisture can cause this medicine to break down.

USES

Venlafaxine is used to treat the symptoms of clinical mental depression and anxiety. It increases the concentration of certain chemicals (called neurotransmitters) that are necessary for nerve transmission in the brain.

TREATMENT

Take this drug exactly as prescribed by your doctor. To avoid stomach irritation, you should take venlafaxine with food (unless your doctor directs you to do otherwise).

The effects of treatment with this medication may not become apparent for several weeks after you begin treatment.

If you miss a dose of this medicine, it is not necessary to make up the missed dose. Skip that dose and continue at the next scheduled time. Never take a double dose to make up for the one you missed.

SIDE EFFECTS

Minor. Agitation, changes in taste perception, constipation, decreased concentration, decreased sex drive, diarrhea, dizziness, drowsiness, dry mouth, fast heartbeat, flushing, frequent urination, headache, increased sweating, loss of appetite, nausea, tremors, unusual dreams, vision changes, or weight gain or loss. These side effects should diminish or disappear as your body adjusts to the medication.

Dry mouth can be relieved by chewing sugarless gum or sucking on ice chips or a piece of hard candy.

To relieve constipation, increase the amount of fiber in your diet (fresh fruits and vegetables, salads, bran, and whole-grain breads). You can also increase your level of exercise and drink more water (unless your doctor directs you to do otherwise).

If you feel dizzy, sit or lie down for a while, get up slowly from a sitting or reclining position, and be careful on stairs. To avoid dizziness when you stand, contract and relax your leg muscles for a few moments before rising. Do this by pressing one foot against the floor while raising the other foot slightly, alternating feet so that you are pumping your legs in a pedaling motion.

Major. Tell your doctor about any side effects that are persistent or particularly bothersome. IT IS ESPECIALLY IMPORTANT TO TELL YOUR DOCTOR about anxiety, chills or fever, convulsions (seizures), difficulty in breathing, enlarged lymph glands (swelling under the jaw, in the armpits, or in the groin area), joint or muscle pain, noticeable swelling of the feet or lower legs, or skin rash or hives.

INTERACTIONS

Venlafaxine can interact with several other types of medications:
1. Extreme drowsiness can occur when this medication is taken with other central nervous system depressants (such as alcohol, antihistamines, barbiturates, benzodiazepine tranquilizers, muscle relaxants, narcotics, pain medications, phenothiazine tranquilizers, and sleeping medications) or with other antidepressants.
2. Serious side effects may occur if a monoamine oxidase (MAO) inhibitor (such as furazolidone, isocarboxazid, pargyline, phenelzine, procarbazine, selegiline, or tranylcypromine) is used concurrently with venlafaxine. At least 14 days should separate the use of venlafaxine and the use of an MAO inhibitor.
3. When this drug is combined with cimetidine and taken by the elderly or those with high blood pressure or liver disease, there may be a higher risk of side effects.
4. When venlafaxine is combined with trazodone, sibutramine, sumatriptan, haloperidol, Saint-John's-wort, or desipramine, serious side effects may develop. Discuss this with your doctor or pharmacist.

Before taking venlafaxine, BE SURE TO TELL YOUR DOCTOR about any medications you are currently taking, especially any of those listed above.

WARNINGS

• Tell your doctor immediately if you develop a skin rash or have hives while taking this drug or if you have ever had a reaction to venlafaxine before.
• Tell your doctor if you have a history of alcoholism or if you have or have ever had a heart attack, asthma, circulatory disease, difficulty in urinating, electroshock therapy, enlarged prostate gland, epilepsy, glaucoma, high blood pressure, intestinal problems, liver or kidney disease, mental illness, or thyroid disease.
• If this drug makes you dizzy or drowsy, do not take part in any activity that requires mental alertness, such as driving a car or operating potentially dangerous equipment.
• Do not stop taking this medication suddenly. Stopping it abruptly can cause nausea, headache, stomach upset, or a worsening of your condition. Your doctor may want to reduce the dose gradually.
• Elderly individuals may be at greater risk for side effects. Use this drug cautiously and report any changes in mental status to your doctor immediately.
• The effects of this medication may be present for as long as five weeks after you stop taking it, so continue to observe all precautions during this period.
• Be sure to tell your doctor if you are pregnant. Although birth defects have not been documented in animal studies, it is not known if venlafaxine is safe during pregnancy. It is not known if venlafaxine passes into breast milk, so be sure to tell your doctor if you are breast-feeding an infant.

---

verapamil

BRAND NAMES (Manufacturers)
Calan (Searle)
Calan SR (Searle)
Isoptin (Knoll)
Isoptin SR (Knoll)
verapamil (various manufacturers)
Verelan (Lederle)

TYPE OF DRUG
Antianginal (calcium channel blocker) and antihypertensive
INGREDIENT
verapamil
DOSAGE FORMS
Tablets (40 mg, 80 mg, and 120 mg)
Sustained-release tablets (120 mg, 180 mg, and 240 mg)
Sustained-release or extended-release capsules (100 mg, 120 mg, 180 mg, 200 mg, 240 mg, and 360 mg)
STORAGE
Store at room temperature in a tightly closed container. Do not refrigerate it.

USES

Verapamil is used to treat angina pectoris (chest pain), high blood pressure, and irregular heartbeats (arrhythmia). It belongs to a group of drugs known as calcium channel blockers. It is not clearly understood how verapamil works, but it is thought to increase the blood supply to the heart. It is also a vasodilator that relaxes the muscle tissue of the blood vessels, thereby lowering blood pressure.

TREATMENT

Verapamil can be taken either on an empty stomach or with meals, as directed by your doctor or pharmacist. Do not crush or chew the sustained-release tablets or capsules; they must be swallowed whole.

The sustained-release and extended-release capsules may be opened and the contents sprinkled onto a spoonful of applesauce that is either at room temperature or cold from the refrigerator (not hot). After swallowing this mixture, be sure to drink a glass of water to ensure that all the pellets have been swallowed. Never crush or chew the pellets. Do not prepare the applesauce-pellet mixture ahead of time. It must be taken immediately after it is prepared.

If you miss a dose of this medication, take the missed dose as soon as possible. However, if it is almost time for the next dose, do not take the missed dose at all; just return to your regular dosing schedule. Do not double the next dose.

This medication does not cure your medical condition, but it will help to control the condition as long as you continue to take it.

SIDE EFFECTS

Minor. Abdominal pain, blurred vision, constipation, dizziness, headache, muscle cramps, nausea, sleeplessness, or sweating. These side effects should disappear as your body adjusts to the medication.

To relieve constipation, increase the amount of fiber in your diet (fresh fruits and vegetables, salads, bran, and whole-grain breads), and drink more water (unless your doctor directs you to do otherwise).

If this medication makes you feel dizzy, sit or lie down for a while, get up slowly from a sitting or reclining position, and be careful on stairs.

To avoid dizziness when you stand, contract and relax the muscles of your legs for a few moments before rising. Do this by pressing one foot against the floor while raising the other foot slightly, alternating feet so that you are "pumping" your legs in a pedaling motion.

In addition, to help prevent dizziness or fainting while taking this medication, try not to stand for long periods of time, avoid drinking alcoholic beverages, and try not to become overheated (avoid exerting yourself or exercising strenuously in hot weather, and do not take hot baths, showers, or saunas).

Major. Tell your doctor about any side effects that are persistent or particularly bothersome. IT IS ESPECIALLY IMPORTANT TO TELL YOUR DOCTOR about changes in menstruation, confusion, depression, fainting, fatigue, hair loss, itching, loss of balance, palpitations, rapid weight gain (three to five pounds within a week), shortness of breath, swelling of the hands or feet, tremors, or unusual weakness.

INTERACTIONS

This drug will interact with a number of other types of medications:

1. The concurrent use of alcohol, quinidine, or prazosin and verapamil can cause a severe drop in blood pressure and result in fainting.

2. Beta blockers (acebutolol, atenolol, betaxolol, carteolol, esmolol, labetalol, metoprolol, nadolol, penbutolol, pindolol, propranolol, or timolol) and digoxin should be used cautiously with verapamil, because side effects to the heart may be increased.

3. Disopyramide should not be taken within 48 hours of verapamil; the combination of these medications could lead to heart failure.

4. Cimetidine and ranitidine can decrease the elimination of verapamil from the body, which can lead to an increased risk of side effects.

5. Sulfinpyrazone and rifampin can increase the elimination of verapamil from the body, which can lead to a decrease in its effectiveness.

6. Verapamil can increase the effects of carbamazepine, theophylline, cyclosporine, sirolimus, tacrolimus, amiodarone, prazosin, and drugs that treat high cholesterol (including lovastatin, atorvastatin, and pravastatin).

BE SURE TO TELL YOUR DOCTOR about any medications you are taking.

WARNINGS

• Tell your doctor about unusual or allergic reactions you have had to any medications, especially to verapamil.

• Before starting therapy with this medication, be sure to tell your doctor if you have ever had any type of heart disease, kidney disease. liver disease, low blood pressure, or a slowed heartbeat.

• Your doctor may want you to check your pulse while you are taking this drug. If your heart rate drops below 50 beats per minute, contact your doctor.

• Verapamil is not effective for an attack of chest pain that has already started; this medication is only effective in preventing attacks from occurring.

• It is extremely important that you do not stop taking this medication without first consulting your doctor. Stopping abruptly may lead to a worsening of your chest pain. Your doctor may, therefore, want to reduce your dosage gradually or have you switch to another similar medication when verapamil is discontinued.

• Do not become concerned if you notice the outer shell of certain verapamil tablets in your stools. This is normal and to be expected.

• Be sure to tell your doctor if you are pregnant. Extensive studies in pregnant women have not been conducted. Also be sure to tell your doctor if you are breast-feeding an infant. Small amounts of verapamil pass into breast milk and may cause unwanted side effects in the nursing infant.

---

vitamins, multiple, with fluoride

BRAND NAMES (Manufacturers)

Florvite (Everett)
Poly-Vi-Flor (Mead Johnson)
polyvitamins with fluoride drops and tablets (various manufacturers)
Polyvite with Fluoride Drops (Major)
Vi-Daylin F (Ross)

TYPE OF DRUG

Multivitamin and fluoride supplement

INGREDIENTS

vitamins A, D, E, C, B_6, B_{12}, folic acid, riboflavin, niacin, fluoride, and thiamine

DOSAGE FORMS

Chewable tablets (2,500 IU [international units] vitamin A; 400 IU vitamin D; 15 IU vitamin E; 60 mg vitamin C; 0.3 mg folic acid; 1.0 mg thiamine; 1.2 mg riboflavin; 13.5 mg niacin; 1.0 mg vitamin B_6; 4.5 mcg vitamin B_{12}; and 0.25 mg, 0.5 mg, or 1.0 mg fluoride)

Oral drops (1,500 IU vitamin A; 400 IU vitamin D; 4.1 or 5 IU vitamin E; 35 mg vitamin C; 0.5 mg thiamine; 0.6 mg riboflavin; 8 mg niacin; 0.4 mg vitamin B_6; 2 mcg vitamin B_{12}; and 0.25 mg or 0.5 mg fluoride per mL)

Oral tablets (2,500 IU vitamin A; 400 IU vitamin D; 15 IU vitamin E; 60 mg vitamin C; 0.3 mg folic acid; 1.05 mg thiamine; 1.2 mg riboflavin; 13.5 mg niacin; 1.05 mg vitamin B_6; 4.5 mcg vitamin B_{12}; 0.5 mg or 1.0 mg fluoride)

STORAGE

Store the regular and chewable tablets at room temperature in a tightly closed, light-resistant container. Store the oral drops at room temperature in the original plastic container (glass containers interact with and destroy the fluoride in the solution). A slight darkening in the color of the drops does not indicate a loss in potency of the vitamins or fluoride; the solution can still be used safely. Do not refrigerate or freeze any form of these vitamins.

USES

Multiple vitamins with fluoride added are used to protect against tooth decay and vitamin deficiencies in children. Fluoride has been found to be helpful in preventing cavities in the teeth.

TREATMENT

Crush or have your child chew the tablets before swallowing. To provide maximum protection, the tablets should be given at bedtime after the teeth have been brushed. Do not allow the child to eat for at least 15 minutes after chewing the tablets in order to allow the fluoride to work on the teeth.

The oral drops can be taken directly, or they can be mixed with juice or foods. Measure the dose carefully with the dropper provided. Do not use kitchen utensils; they are not accurate enough.

Do not give this medication with milk. Milk prevents the absorption of fluoride from the gastrointestinal tract.

If your child misses a dose of this medication, administer the missed dose as soon as possible. However, if it is almost time for the next dose, do not give the missed dose at all; just return to the child's regular dosing schedule. Do not double the next dose of the vitamin.

SIDE EFFECTS

Minor. Occasionally, this product causes constipation, diarrhea, drowsiness, fatigue, loss of appetite, nausea, vomiting, or weakness. These side effects should disappear as the body adjusts to the medication.

To relieve constipation, increase the amount of fiber in your child's diet (with fresh fruits and vegetables, salads, bran, and whole-grain breads) and encourage your child to drink more water (unless your child's doctor directs you to do otherwise).

Major. Tell your doctor about any side effects that are persistent or particularly bothersome. IT IS ESPECIALLY IMPORTANT TO TELL YOUR DOCTOR about bloody or black, tarry stools; difficulty in swallowing; discoloration of the teeth; excessive drooling; excitation; mouth sores; rash; stomach cramps; or tremors.

INTERACTIONS

This product should not interact with other medications if it is used according to directions. But be sure that your child's doctor knows about any medications that your child currently takes.

WARNINGS

• Tell your doctor about any unusual or allergic reactions your child has had to vitamins, fluoride, or any other medications or supplements.
• Be sure to tell your doctor if your child now has or ever had one or more of the following: bone, heart, kidney, or thyroid disease.
• If the fluoride content of your drinking water is 0.7 parts per million or more, do not use the chewable tablets. Do not give the oral drops to children younger than three years of age in areas where the drinking water contains 0.3 parts per million or more of fluoride. If you are not sure of the fluoride content of your drinking water, ask your doctor or call the county health department.
• Vitamins with fluoride are often prescribed for infants who are not being given any source of fluoridated water. Once your infant is given fluorinated water consistently, ask your doctor if you should still continue to give this medication to your child.
• Never call this medication "candy" or "candy-flavored vitamins." Your child may take you literally and attempt to eat them like candy, swallowing too many of them. An overdosage of vitamins can have dangerous consequences and requires immediate medical attention. Call your local poison control center or emergency services

---

vitamins, prenatal

BRAND NAMES (Manufacturers)
Prenatal-1 + iron tablets (various manufacturers)
Stuartnatal Plus (Wyeth-Ayerst)
TYPE OF DRUG
Multivitamin and mineral supplement
INGREDIENTS
calcium, iron, folic acid, zinc, copper, niacin, riboflavin, thiamine, and vitamins A, D, E, B_6, B_{12}, and C
DOSAGE FORM
Tablets (200 mg, 250 mg, or 300 mg calcium; 60 mg, 65 mg, or 90 mg iron; 1.0 mg folic acid; 4,000 IU [international units] or 5,000 IU vitamin A; 400 IU vitamin D; 11 IU vitamin E; 1.5 mg thiamine; 3 mg riboflavin; 20 mg niacin; 10 mg vitamin B_6; 12 mcg vitamin B_{12}; 120 mg vitamin C; zinc, copper, and other ingredients)
STORAGE
Store the prenatal vitamins at room temperature in a tightly closed, light-resistant container. Do not refrigerate or freeze the vitamins.

USES

This product is a multivitamin and mineral supplement for use during pregnancy and nursing.

TREATMENT

To avoid stomach irritation, you can take this product with food or with a full glass of water or milk, unless your doctor directs you otherwise.

If you miss a dose of the prenatal vitamins, take the missed dose as soon as possible after you remember. However, if it is almost time for the next dose, do not take the missed dose at all; just return to your regular dosing schedule. Do not double the next dose.

SIDE EFFECTS

Minor. Constipation, diarrhea, nausea, stomach upset, or vomiting. These side effects should disappear as your body adjusts to the medication.

To relieve constipation, increase the amount of fiber in your diet (fresh fruits and vegetables, salads, bran, and whole-grain breads), exercise, and drink more water (unless your doctor directs you to do otherwise).

Black stools are a normal consequence of iron therapy and do not indicate that a problem has developed from the vitamin therapy.

Major. Tell your doctor about any side effects that are persistent or particularly bothersome. IT IS ESPECIALLY IMPORTANT TO TELL YOUR DOCTOR about bloody or tarry stools or severe abdominal pain.

INTERACTIONS

This product should not interact with other medications if it is used according to directions. However, be sure that your doctor knows about any medications or supplements that you are currently taking.

WARNINGS

- Tell your doctor about unusual or allergic reactions you have had to any medications, especially to any vitamin, mineral, or iron products.
- Be sure to tell your doctor if you have ever had bone disease, liver disease, kidney disease, or stomach ulcers.
- Because this product may mask the symptoms of pernicious anemia, it should be used only under a doctor's supervision.

---

warfarin

BRAND NAMES (Manufacturers)
Coumadin (Bristol-Myers Squibb)
warfarin (various manufacturers)
TYPE OF DRUG
Anticoagulant
INGREDIENT
warfarin
DOSAGE FORM
Tablets (1 mg, 2 mg, 2.5 mg, 3 mg, 4 mg, 5 mg, 6 mg, 7.5 mg, and 10 mg)
STORAGE
Store this medication at room temperature in a tightly closed, light-resistant container. Do not refrigerate.

USES

Warfarin is used to prevent blood-clot formation by decreasing the production of blood-clotting substances by the liver.

TREATMENT

You can take warfarin with a full glass of water. In order to become accustomed to taking this medication, try to take it at the same time each day.

If you miss a dose, take the missed dose as soon as possible. However, if it is almost time for the next dose, do not take the missed dose at all; just return to your regular dosing schedule. Do not double the next dose. If you miss more than two doses of this medication in a row, contact your doctor as soon as possible.

SIDE EFFECTS

Minor. Blurred vision, cramps, decreased appetite, diarrhea, or nausea. These side effects should disappear as your body adjusts to the medication. This medication may produce a red-orange discoloration of the urine; this is a harmless side effect that goes away when the drug is discontinued.

Major. Tell your doctor about any side effects that are persistent or particularly bothersome. IT IS ESPECIALLY IMPORTANT TO TELL YOUR DOCTOR about bloody or black, tarry stools; blood in your sputum; fever; heavy bleeding from cuts; internal bleeding (signs of internal bleeding include abdominal pain or swelling and vomiting of blood or material that resembles coffee grounds); loss of hair; mouth sores; nausea; nosebleeds; rash; red urine; severe bruising; severe headache; swelling of joints; unusually heavy menstrual bleeding; or yellowing of the eyes or skin.

INTERACTIONS

Warfarin interacts with many other types of drugs:
1. Alcohol, allopurinol, amiodarone, anabolic steroids, antibiotics, chloral hydrate, chloramphenicol, chlorpropamide, cimetidine, clofibrate, danazol, disulfiram, erythromycin, glucagon, isoniazid, ketoconazole, methyldopa, methylphenidate, metronidazole, monoamine oxidase (MAO) inhibitors, nalidixic acid, propoxyphene, quinidine, quinine, salicylates, sulfamethoxazole and trimethoprim combination, sulfinpyrazone, sulfonamides, sulindac, tetracycline, thyroid hormones, and tolbutamide can increase the effects of warfarin, which can be dangerous.
2. Azathioprine, barbiturates, carbamazepine, cholestyramine, colestipol, estrogens, ethchlorvynol, griseofulvin, oral contraceptives (birth control pills), phenytoin, propylthiouracil, rifampin, sucralfate, and vitamin K can decrease the effectiveness of warfarin when taken concurrently.
3. Adrenocorticosteroids (cortisonelike medications), anticancer drugs, aspirin, diflunisal, dipyridamole, fenoprofen, ibuprofen, indomethacin, oxyphenbutazone, phenylbutazone, potassium, quinidine, quinine, and salicylates can increase the bleeding complications of warfarin.
4. Warfarin can increase the side effects of oral antidiabetic agents and phenytoin.
5. Diuretics may either increase the effects or decrease the effectiveness of warfarin. Be sure to ask your doctor about the safety of concurrent use of diuretics and warfarin.
6. While taking warfarin, do not start or stop taking any over-the-counter (nonprescription) medications or supplements, including herbal products such as Saint-John's-wort, ginseng, garlic, or coenzyme Q_{10}, unless recommended by your doctor or pharmacist.

Before starting to take warfarin, BE SURE TO TELL YOUR DOCTOR about any medications (both prescription and nonprescription) you are currently taking, especially any of those listed above.

WARNINGS

• Tell your doctor about unusual or allergic reactions you have had to any medications, especially to warfarin.
• Before starting treatment with this medication, BE SURE TO TELL YOUR DOCTOR if you now have or ever had any condition for which bleeding is an added risk, such as an aneurysm, blood disorders, cancer, diabetes mellitus, congestive heart failure, edema, endocarditis, high blood pressure, indwelling catheters, intestinal infections, kidney or liver disease, malnutrition, menstrual difficulties, pericarditis, surgery, thyroid disease, tuberculosis, ulcers, vasculitis, or wounds and injuries.
• Before having surgery or any other medical or dental treatment, BE SURE TO TELL YOUR DOCTOR OR DENTIST that you are taking warfarin.
• Do not take any aspirin-containing products or any over-the-counter products while you are on warfarin, unless you first check with your doctor or pharmacist. Aspirin can increase the risk of bleeding complications from warfarin.
• Avoid any activity, such as a contact sport, that might lead to physical injury. Tell your doctor about any fall or blow that occurs. Warfarin can cause heavy bleeding from cuts.
• Use an electric razor while shaving to reduce the risk of cutting yourself, and be especially gentle and careful while brushing your teeth.

• Since factors as diverse as travel, diet, the environment, and your general health can affect your body's response to warfarin, your dosage level should be carefully monitored by your doctor.
• Do not stop taking warfarin unless you first consult your doctor. If you stop taking this drug abruptly, you may experience unwanted blood clotting. Your doctor may, therefore, want to reduce your dosage gradually.
• Do not change brands of this medication without consulting your doctor.
• Avoid changes in your diet, as this can affect how warfarin works. It is particularly important not to eat more or less foods with a high content of vitamin A (such as green, leafy vegetables). Discuss this with your doctor or pharmacist.
• Some of these products contain the color additive FD&C Yellow No. 5 (tartrazine), which can cause allergic-type reactions in certain susceptible individuals.
• Be sure to tell your doctor if you are pregnant. Warfarin has been associated with birth defects and bleeding complications in fetuses. Also tell your doctor if you are breast-feeding an infant.

---

zafirlukast

BRAND NAME (Manufacturer)
Accolate (AstraZeneca)
TYPE OF DRUG
Antiasthmatic
INGREDIENT
zafirlukast
DOSAGE FORM
Tablets (10 mg and 20 mg)
STORAGE
Store at room temperature in a tightly closed, light-resistant container. Do not expose to excess heat or moisture. Do not store in the bathroom.

USES

Zafirlukast is used to prevent the symptoms of asthma, such as wheezing and shortness of breath. Zafirlukast works by blocking the actions of certain chemicals in the body that cause the airways of the lungs to become inflamed and narrowed. This drug will not stop an asthma attack once it has started but works to prevent acute attacks of asthma.

TREATMENT

Take this medication at the same time each day. Zafirlukast should be taken on an empty stomach (either one hour before or two hours after a meal) to make sure it is completely absorbed, unless your doctor tells you to do otherwise.

Take zafirlukast as directed by your doctor and use it every day even if you don't have any symptoms of asthma. If you miss a dose, take it as soon as you remember. However, if it is almost time for the next dose, do not take the missed dose at all; just return to your regular dosing schedule. Do not double the next dose.

SIDE EFFECTS

Minor. Headache or nausea. These side effects should diminish or disappear as your body adjusts to the medication.

Major. Tell your doctor about any side effects that are persistent or particularly bothersome. IT IS ESPECIALLY IMPORTANT TO TELL YOUR DOCTOR about abdominal pain; decreased appetite; difficulty breathing; extreme fatigue; flulike symptoms (fever, muscle aches, weight loss); heart problems; itching; nausea; rash; tingling in the hands, fingers, or toes; or yellowing of the eyes or skin.

INTERACTIONS

Zafirlukast may interact with other drugs:

1. Zafirlukast may increase the serious side effects of midazolam, triazolam, alprazolam, nifedipine, isradipine, nicardipine, nifedipine, nimodipine, carbamazepine, phenytoin, tolbutamide, and cyclosporine.

2. Zafirlukast may increase the actions of warfarin (a blood thinner) and increase the risk of bleeding.

3. Concurrent use of erythromycin or theophylline may reduce the actions of zafirlukast.

4. To avoid drug interactions, it is very important that you do not take any over-the-counter (nonprescription) medications for weight control or for asthma, sinus, cough, cold, or allergy problems unless you first check with a doctor or pharmacist.

Before taking zafirlukast, BE SURE TO TELL YOUR DOCTOR about any medications you are currently taking, especially any of those listed above.

WARNINGS

• Be sure to tell your doctor about any unusual or allergic reactions you may have had to any medications, including zafirlukast, montelukast, or zileuton.

• You should tell your doctor about any medical problems you now have or have had, especially any liver or kidney problems.

• IT IS IMPORTANT TO REMEMBER THAT zafirlukast will not stop an asthma attack once it has begun. You should not stop taking your other asthma medications unless your doctor tells you to do so.

• A small number of patients have experienced a potentially serious side effect while they were taking zafirlukast and reducing or stopping their use of inhaled corticosteroids. BE SURE TO TALK WITH YOUR DOCTOR before stopping or reducing the use of any other asthma medications.

• Be sure to tell your doctor if you are pregnant. It is not known if zafirlukast is safe during pregnancy. Zafirlukast can pass into human breast milk. Because of the risk of some long-term effects in a nursing infant, zafirlukast should not be used if you are breast-feeding an infant.

---

zalcitabine

BRAND NAME (Manufacturer)
Hivid (Roche)
TYPE OF DRUG
Antiviral
INGREDIENT
zalcitabine
DOSAGE FORM
Tablets (0.375 mg and 0.75 mg)
STORAGE
Store at room temperature in a tightly closed container. Do not expose to excess heat.

USES

Zalcitabine is used in the treatment of human immunodeficiency virus (HIV) infection. HIV is the virus that causes AIDS. Zalcitabine works by inhibiting the reproduction, or growth, of the virus, which slows down the progression of AIDS. Zalcitabine does not cure HIV infection or AIDS, but it may delay the onset of other infections and diseases caused by AIDS. Zalcitabine is usually not used alone but rather in combination with other anti-AIDS medications. These combinations have been shown to make the AIDS virus undetectable in the body.

TREATMENT

This medication works best when the level of medicine in your bloodstream is kept constant. It is best to take the medication at evenly spaced intervals throughout the day. IT IS IMPORTANT NOT TO MISS ANY DOSES OF ZALCITABINE. The chances of the AIDS virus becoming resistant to zalcitabine increase if the level of medication in the bloodstream is low. Zalcitabine should be taken on an empty stomach so that it is well absorbed (unless your doctor tells you to do otherwise).

If you miss a dose of this medication, take it as soon as possible. However, if it is almost time for your next dose, skip the missed dose and go back to your regular dosing schedule. Do not double the next dose.

SIDE EFFECTS

Minor. Diarrhea, headache, nausea, stomach pain, or vomiting. As your body adjusts to the medication, some of these side effects should disappear.

Major. Tell your doctor about any side effects that are persistent or particularly bothersome. IT IS ESPECIALLY IMPORTANT TO TELL YOUR DOCTOR about fever and sore throat; joint or muscle pain; severe abdominal pain with nausea and vomiting; skin rash; sores in the mouth; tingling, burning, numbness, or pain in the hands or feet; or yellowing of the skin or eyes.

INTERACTIONS

Zalcitabine may interact with a number of other drugs:

1. Zalcitabine may cause a condition known as peripheral neuropathy, which is numbness, pain, burning, or tingling usually in the hands or feet, and lactic acidosis. Because of this, zalcitabine should not be taken with other drugs that may cause these conditions, including chloramphenicol, cisplatin, dapsone, didanosine, ethambutol, ethionamide, hydralazine, isoniazid, lithium, metronidazole, nitrofurantoin, phenytoin, vincristine, stavudine, or hydroxyurea.

2. Zalcitabine may also cause a condition known as pancreatitis, an inflammation of the pancreas. Because of this, zalcitabine should not be taken with other drugs that may cause pancreatitis, including alcohol, asparaginase, azathioprine, estrogens, furosemide, nitrofurantoin, methyldopa, pentamidine, sulfonamide, sulindac, tetracycline, thiazide diuretics (water pills), or valproic acid.

3. Gentamicin, tobramycin, amikacin, amphotericin B, cimetidine, probenecid, or foscarnet may increase the amount of zalcitabine in the body, increasing its side effects.

4. Antacids, sucralfate, or drugs that contain magnesium or aluminum may lessen the absorption of zalcitabine and make the drug less effective.

5. To avoid drug interactions, do not take any over-the-counter (nonprescription) medications for weight control or for asthma, sinus problems, cough, cold, or allergy problems unless you first check with a doctor or pharmacist.

Before taking zalcitabine, BE SURE TO TELL YOUR DOCTOR about any drugs that you are currently taking, especially any of the medications that are listed above.

WARNINGS

- Tell your doctor if you have ever had an allergic reaction to any medication, especially to zalcitabine or any other medication used to treat AIDS.
- This drug may cause peripheral neuropathy, which is tingling, burning, pain, or numbness in the hands or feet. It usually stops when the drug is stopped. If you have these symptoms while taking zalcitabine, be sure to tell your doctor immediately.
- Zalcitabine may cause inflammation of the pancreas. Contact your doctor immediately if you develop abdominal pain, nausea, and vomiting. Also, your doctor may do regular blood tests to determine if zalcitabine is affecting your pancreas.
- Before taking this medication, be sure to tell your doctor about any medical problems you may have, especially liver or renal problems; problems with the pancreas; alcoholism; high cholesterol; or tingling, numbness, burning, or pain in the hands or feet.

• Before having surgery or any medical or dental treatment, be sure to tell your doctor or dentist that you are being treated with zalcitabine.
• Your doctor may do regular blood tests to see how well this medication is working against the AIDS virus.
• If you are infected with HIV, it is best to avoid any sexual activity involving an exchange of body fluids with other people. If you do have vaginal, anal, or oral sex, always use a latex condom.
• Be sure to tell your doctor if you are pregnant. It is not known if zalcitabine is safe to use during pregnancy. It is not known if zalcitabine passes into human breast milk. However, because of the risk of passing HIV to infants, it is recommended that mothers who have HIV infection NOT breast-feed their infants.

---

zaleplon

BRAND NAME (Manufacturer)
Sonata (Wyeth)
TYPE OF DRUG
Sedative/hypnotic
INGREDIENT
zaleplon
DOSAGE FORM
Capsules (5 mg and 10 mg)
STORAGE
Store in a tightly closed container at room temperature, away from heat and direct sunlight.

USES

Zaleplon is prescribed to treat insomnia, including problems with falling asleep, waking during the night, and early morning wakefulness. It is not clear how zaleplon works, but it may relieve insomnia by acting as a depressant of the central nervous system (brain and spinal cord). This medication should only be used for a short time (usually no longer than two weeks) to treat insomnia.

TREATMENT

Take this medicine immediately before bedtime. Since it works quickly, you should be ready to go to bed right after you take it. This medicine should be taken on an empty stomach so that it works quickly. Taking it after a heavy or high-fat meal will make the medication work less effectively to help you fall asleep.

If you miss a dose, take the missed dose as soon as possible. However, if it is almost time for your next dose, skip the one you missed and then return to your regular schedule. You should never take a double dose to make up for the one you missed unless directed to do so by your doctor. Discuss this with your doctor or pharmacist if you are not sure about what to do when you miss a dose of zaleplon.

Only use this medication if you plan to get at least four hours of sleep. If you wake before four hours, you may feel drowsy and have problems with your memory.

It is important not to stop taking this medication abruptly. Suddenly stopping this medication may result in an increase in side effects. If this medication needs to be stopped, it should be done gradually. Talk with your doctor before stopping zaleplon.

This medication should be taken exactly as prescribed by your doctor.

SIDE EFFECTS

Minor. Constipation, dizziness, dryness of the mouth, headache, muscle pain, or nausea. As your body adjusts to the medication, some of these side effects should diminish or disappear.

Dry mouth can be relieved by sucking on ice chips or a piece of hard candy or by chewing sugarless gum.

To relieve constipation, increase the amount of fiber in your diet (fresh fruits and vegetables, salads, bran, and whole-grain breads), exercise, and drink more water (unless your doctor directs you to do otherwise).

To avoid dizziness or light-headedness when you stand, contract and relax the muscles in your legs for a few moments before rising. Do this by pushing one foot against the floor while raising the other foot slightly, alternating feet so that you are "pumping" your legs in a pedaling motion.

If you feel dizzy or light-headed, sit or lie down for a while; get up from a sitting or lying position slowly; and be careful on stairs.

Major. Tell your doctor about any persistent or particularly bothersome side effects. IT IS ESPECIALLY IMPORTANT TO TELL YOUR DOCTOR about anxiety, blurred or double vision, clumsiness or unsteadiness, confusion, delusions, difficulty in breathing or swallowing, hallucinations, headache, loss of memory or problems with memory, nosebleed, not feeling like yourself, or tightness of the chest or wheezing.

If you experience abdominal cramping, seizures, unexplained sadness, increased sweating, shaking or trembling, or vomiting after you stop taking this medication, call your doctor immediately.

INTERACTIONS

Zaleplon may interact with a few other medications:

1. Concurrent use of this medication with other central nervous system depressants (such as alcohol, barbiturates, benzodiazepine tranquilizers, muscle relaxants, narcotics, pain medications, and phenothiazine tranquilizers) or with tricyclic antidepressants can cause extreme drowsiness.

2. Concurrent use of over-the-counter (nonprescription) medications for weight control or for cough, cold, asthma, sinus, or allergy problems may increase the adverse side effects of this medication.

3. Antiseizure medications (such as primidone, carbamazepine, and phenytoin) may be affected by the actions of zaleplon, possibly changing their effectiveness.

4. Cimetidine will increase the blood levels and side effects of zaleplon; your doctor may need to reduce your zaleplon dose in order to avoid this drug interaction. Discuss this with your doctor or pharmacist.

5. Rifampin will decrease the blood levels and efficacy of zaleplon. Discuss this drug interaction with your doctor or pharmacist.

Before you begin treatment with zaleplon, BE SURE TO TELL YOUR DOCTOR about any medications that you are currently taking, especially any of the medications that are listed above.

WARNINGS

• Tell your doctor if you now have or ever had a history of drug abuse or dependence, alcoholism, liver disease, kidney disease, mental depression, or any problems with your breathing. Your dose of this medication may need to be changed if you have liver disease.

• Tell your doctor about any unusual or allergic reactions you have had to any medications, especially to zaleplon.

• Zaleplon may cause extreme fatigue and dizziness. Your ability to perform tasks that require alertness, such as driving an automobile or operating potentially dangerous machinery, may be decreased. Take appropriate caution.

• While you are taking zaleplon, do not take any over-the-counter (nonprescription) medication for weight control or for cough, cold, asthma, allergy, or sinus problems unless you first check with your doctor or pharmacist.

• It is very important for you to take this medication exactly as directed by your doctor. Do not reduce the dose or take more of this medication at any time unless your doctor has specifically directed you to change the amount of medication you take. Do not suddenly stop taking zaleplon; if you do, you may experience an increase in adverse effects.

• Prior to having surgery or any other medical or dental treatment, be sure to tell your doctor or dentist that you are taking zaleplon.

• If you have a seizure disorder and are taking medications to control it, your doctor may do regular blood tests to see how well your antiseizure medicines are working to control your seizures while you are being treated with zaleplon.

• Be sure to tell your doctor IMMEDIATELY if you are pregnant. Although the effects of this medication during pregnancy have not been thoroughly studied in humans, zaleplon has caused toxicity in studies done on pregnant animals. Because small amounts of zaleplon pass into the breast milk, it is also important to tell your doctor if you are breast-feeding an infant.

---

zidovudine (AZT)

BRAND NAME (Manufacturer)
Retrovir (GlaxoSmithKline)
TYPE OF DRUG
antiviral
INGREDIENT
zidovudine (AZT, azidothymidine)
DOSAGE FORMS
Capsules (100 mg)
Tablets (300 mg)
Syrup (50 mg per 5 mL)
STORAGE
Store all forms of this drug at room temperature in tightly closed, light-resistant containers. Do not refrigerate or freeze this medication.

USES

Zidovudine (formerly called azidothymidine, or AZT) is used in the treatment of human immunodeficiency virus (HIV) infection. HIV is the virus that causes AIDS. Zidovudine works by inhibiting the reproduction, or growth, of the virus, which slows down the progression of AIDS. Zidovudine does not cure AIDS, but this drug may delay the onset of other infections and diseases caused by AIDS. This medication is also used to reduce the spread of HIV to the fetus in the HIV-positive pregnant women.

TREATMENT

This medication works best when the level of medicine in your bloodstream is kept constant. It is best to take the drug at evenly spaced intervals throughout the day, as directed by your doctor.

Use a special 5-mL dosing spoon to measure doses of the syrup. Kitchen teaspoons are not accurate enough.

If you miss a dose of this medication, take it as soon as possible. However, if it is almost time for your next dose of the medication, just skip the missed dose and go back to your regular dosing schedule. Do not double the next dose.

SIDE EFFECTS

Minor. Blue or brown bands on nails, difficulty sleeping, headache, muscle soreness, or nausea. Some of these side effects may go away during treatment, as your body adjusts to the medicine.

Major. Abdominal discomfort, chills, confusion, convulsions, fever, loss of appetite, mania, muscle tenderness or weakness, pale skin, sore throat, or unusual tiredness.

INTERACTIONS

Zidovudine interacts with many other drugs:

1. Concurrent use of certain other antibiotic, antifungal, or antiviral medications may increase the toxicity of zidovudine.

2. Methadone, ganciclovir, and probenecid can interfere with your body's ability to eliminate zidovudine and may increase the toxicity of zidovudine.

3. Zidovudine taken concurrently with phenytoin can alter the level of phenytoin in your body.

4. To avoid drug interactions, do not take any over-the-counter (nonprescription) medications for weight control or for asthma, sinus problems, cough, cold, or allergy problems unless you first check with a doctor or pharmacist.

Before you begin treatment with zidovudine, BE SURE TO TELL YOUR DOCTOR about these or any medications that you are currently taking.

WARNINGS

• Tell your doctor about unusual or allergic reactions you have had to any medications, especially zidovudine. Also tell your doctor about any allergic reaction you have had to any foods, preservatives, or dyes.

• You may require periodic blood sample checks at your physician's office to monitor the effects of zidovudine.

• Tell your doctor if you have anemia, liver disease, or any vitamin deficiencies.

• Before having surgery or any other medical or dental treatment, tell your doctor or dentist that you are being treated with this medication.

• If you are infected with HIV, it is best to avoid any sexual activity involving an exchange of body fluids with other people. If you do have vaginal, anal, or oral sex, always use a latex condom.

• If you inject drugs, do not share needles with anyone else; dispose of used needles safely.

• Be sure to tell your doctor if you are pregnant. In addition, be sure to tell your doctor if you are breast-feeding an infant. It is not known if zidovudine passes into breast milk, but HIV or the AIDS virus can be transmitted through breast milk. It is therefore recommended that women who are infected with the HIV virus or who have AIDS should NOT breast-feed.

---

zileuton

BRAND NAME (Manufacturer)
Zyflo (Abbott)
TYPE OF DRUG
Antiasthmatic
INGREDIENT
zileuton
DOSAGE FORM
Tablets (600 mg)
STORAGE
Store this medication at room temperature in a tightly closed, light-resistant container. Do not expose the medication to excess heat.

USES

Zileuton is used to prevent the symptoms of asthma, such as wheezing and shortness of breath. Zileuton works by blocking the production of certain chemicals in the body that cause the airways of the lungs to become inflamed and narrowed. This drug will not stop an asthma attack once it has started, but it does work to prevent acute attacks of asthma from occurring in the first place.

TREATMENT

Take this medication at the same time each day. Zileuton should be taken as directed by your doctor and used every day, even if you don't have any symptoms of asthma.

If you miss a dose of this drug, take the missed dose as soon as you remember. However, if it is almost time for the next dose, do not take the missed dose at all; just return to your regular dosing schedule. Do not double the next dose of the medication.

SIDE EFFECTS

Minor. Nausea, stomach pain, upset stomach, or weakness. These side effects should diminish or disappear as your body adjusts to the medication.

Major. Tell your doctor about any side effects that are persistent or particularly bothersome. IT IS ESPECIALLY IMPORTANT TO TELL YOUR DOCTOR about difficulty breathing, flulike symptoms, itching, loss of appetite, nausea, unusual tiredness, upper abdominal pain, or yellowing of the eyes or skin.

INTERACTIONS

Zileuton may interact with certain other medications:

1. Zileuton may increase the serious side effects and actions of midazolam, triazolam, alprazolam, nifedipine, isradipine, nicardipine, nifedipine, nimodipine, propranolol, theophylline, carbamazepine, phenytoin, tolbutamide, and cyclosporine.

2. Zileuton may increase the actions of warfarin (a blood thinner) and increase the risk of bleeding.

3. To avoid drug interactions, do not take any over-the-counter (nonprescription) medications for weight control or for asthma, sinus problems, cough, cold, or allergy problems unless you first check with a doctor or pharmacist.

Before taking zileuton, BE SURE TO TELL YOUR DOCTOR about any medications you are currently taking, especially any of those listed above.

WARNINGS

- Be sure to tell your doctor about any unusual or allergic reactions you may have had to any medications, including zileuton, montelukast, or zafirlukast.
- Tell your doctor about any medical problems you may have, especially liver or kidney problems or problems with alcohol or drug abuse.
- When taking this medication, it is necessary for your doctor to test your blood regularly to see what effect zileuton is having on your liver.
- IT IS IMPORTANT TO REMEMBER THAT zileuton will not stop an asthma attack once it has begun. You should not stop taking your other asthma medications unless your doctor tells you to do so.
- Be sure to tell your doctor if you are pregnant. When given at high doses, zileuton reduced the survival of some newborn animals. Studies in humans have not been done, and it is not known if zileuton is safe during human pregnancy. It is not known if zileuton passes into human breast milk. Because of the chance of long-term effects in infants, zileuton should not be used if you are breast-feeding an infant.

---

ziprasidone

BRAND NAME (Manufacturer)
Geodon (Pfizer)
TYPE OF DRUG
Antipsychotic
INGREDIENT
ziprasidone
DOSAGE FORM
Capsules (20 mg, 40 mg, 60 mg, and 80 mg)

STORAGE

Store in a tightly closed container at room temperature, away from heat and direct sunlight.

USES

Ziprasidone is prescribed to treat the symptoms of mental illness, such as the emotional symptoms of psychosis and schizophrenia. This medication is thought to relieve the symptoms of mental illness by blocking certain chemicals (called neurotransmitters) that are involved with nerve transmission in the brain.

TREATMENT

Take this medication exactly as prescribed by your doctor. Ziprasidone is usually taken twice a day, and it should always be taken with a meal (unless your doctor directs you to do otherwise).

The full effects of this medication for the control of emotional or mental symptoms may not become apparent for two weeks after you begin treatment.

If you miss a dose of this medicine, take the missed dose as soon as possible. However, if it is almost time for your next dose, skip the one you missed and return to your regular schedule. Never take a double dose to make up for the one you missed unless directed to do so by your doctor.

SIDE EFFECTS

Minor. Blurred vision, constipation, diarrhea, dizziness or light-headedness, drooling, dry mouth, headache, jerking or stiffness, lack of strength, nausea, problems sleeping, rash, restlessness, sleepiness, uncontrolled movements of the body, vomiting, weakness, or weight gain. These side effects are likely to diminish or disappear as your body adjusts to the medication.

Dry mouth can be relieved by chewing sugarless gum or sucking on hard candy.

To relieve constipation, increase the amount of fiber in your diet (fresh fruits and vegetables, salads, bran, and whole-grain breads), exercise, and drink more water (unless your doctor directs you to do otherwise).

To avoid dizziness or light-headedness when you stand, contract and relax the muscles in your legs for a few moments before rising. Do this by pushing one foot against the floor while raising the other foot slightly, alternating feet so that you are "pumping" your legs in a pedaling motion.

If you feel dizzy or light-headed, sit or lie down for a while; get up from a sitting or reclining position slowly; and be careful on stairs.

Major. Tell your doctor about any side effects that are persistent or particularly bothersome. IT IS ESPECIALLY IMPORTANT TO TELL YOUR DOCTOR about chest pain; difficulty breathing or swallowing; extreme dizziness; fainting or feeling faint; fast or pounding heartbeat; hives; irregular heartbeat or pulse; movements of the face, mouth, tongue, or jaw that you cannot control; painful erection; seizures; or skin rash.

INTERACTIONS

Ziprasidone interacts with several other types of drugs:

1. Extreme drowsiness can occur when this medication is taken with other central nervous system depressants (such as alcohol, antihistamines, antidepressants, barbiturates, benzodiazepine tranquilizers, muscle relaxants, narcotics, pain medications, and sleeping medications).

2. The adverse side effects of ziprasidone may be increased and lead to very serious irregular heartbeats when it is taken concurrently with any of the following medications: chlorpromazine, antiarrhythmics (any drug given to treat irregular heartbeats), droperidol, dolasetron, gatifloxacin, levomethadyl acetate, mefloquine, mesoridazine, moxifloxacin, pentamidine, pimozide, probucol, quinidine, tacrolimus, or thioridazine. Ziprasidone should NEVER be taken with any of these medications.

3. Ziprasidone will increase the blood-pressure-lowering effects of antihypertensive medications and possibly increase their side effects if it is taken concurrently with them. If you are currently taking any blood-pressure-lowering drugs and ziprasidone has been prescribed for you, discuss this potential interaction with your doctor.

Before taking ziprasidone, BE SURE TO TELL YOUR DOCTOR about any medication you are taking, especially any of those listed above.

WARNINGS

• Tell your doctor about any unusual or allergic reactions you have had to any medications, especially to ziprasidone or other antipsychotics.
• Tell your doctor if you now have or ever had a history of heart attack, heart disease, irregular heartbeats, heart failure, low potassium or magnesium in your blood, Alzheimer's disease, epilepsy, alcoholism, circulatory disease, or liver or kidney disease.
• To prevent oversedation, avoid drinking alcohol while taking this medication.
• If this medication makes you drowsy or dizzy, do not take part in any activity that requires alertness, such as driving a car or operating dangerous equipment.
• This medication may decrease sweating and heat release from the body. Avoid getting overheated by strenuous exercise in hot weather and taking hot baths, showers, or saunas.
• While taking this medication, do not take any over-the-counter (nonprescription) medication for weight control or for cough, cold, asthma, allergy, or sinus problems unless you first check with your doctor.
• Prior to having surgery or any other medical or dental treatment, be sure to tell your doctor or dentist that you are taking this medication.
• Ziprasidone may increase your sensitivity to sunlight. It is important to use caution during exposure to the sun. Avoid exposure to sunlamps. When you are outdoors during daylight hours, wear protective clothing and an effective sunscreen.
• Be sure to tell your doctor if you are pregnant. Although it has not been adequately studied in human pregnancy, ziprasidone has caused birth defects in animals. You should discuss the risks and benefits of using this medication during pregnancy with your doctor. Ziprasidone can also pass into human breast milk. So be sure to tell your doctor if you are breast-feeding an infant, and discuss the risks and benefits of this medication thoroughly.

---

zolmitriptan

BRAND NAMES (Manufacturers)
Zomig (AstraZeneca)
Zomig ZMT (AstraZeneca)
TYPE OF DRUG
Antimigraine agent
INGREDIENT
zolmitriptan
DOSAGE FORMS
Tablets (2.5mg and 5mg)
Tablets, orally disintegrating (2.5mg)
STORAGE
Store this medication in a tightly closed container at room temperature.

USES

Although it is not completely understood how zolmitriptan works, this medication helps to relieve migraine headaches by altering the level of a chemical in the brain called serotonin. Zolmitriptan is used for the treatment of migraine headaches for those patients who do not get relief from other medicines used to treat headache, such as acetaminophen, aspirin, and nonsteroidal anti-inflammatory drugs (NSAIDs). This medication is not effective for preventing migraine headaches or for the treatment of cluster headaches.

TREATMENT

This medication should be taken with a full glass of water. If your doctor prescribed a dose smaller than 2.5 mg, you may break the 2.5 mg tablet in half. This medication may work better if you lie down in a quiet, darkened room after you take it.

It is not necessary to take the orally disintegrating tablet with water. Open the blister pack containing the tablet just before you take it; the tablet will dissolve when placed on your tongue.

If your migraine is less severe after your first zolmitriptan tablet, your doctor may instruct you to take a second tablet two hours after the first dose if the headache pain starts to come back. It is very important that you obtain specific instructions on the use of this medicine from your doctor. Never double the dose.

SIDE EFFECTS

Minor: Blurred vision, diarrhea, dizziness, drowsiness, increased tiredness, increase in urination, itching, muscle or joint stiffness, nausea, restlessness, or vomiting.

If this medication makes you feel dizzy or light-headed, sit or lie down for a while, get up slowly from a sitting or reclining position, and be careful on stairs.

To help prevent dizziness or light-headedness when you stand, contract and relax the muscles of your legs for a few minutes. Do this by pressing one foot against the floor while raising the other foot slightly, alternating feet so that you are "pumping" your legs in a pedaling motion.

Major: Tell your doctor about any side effects that are persistent or particularly bothersome. IT IS ESPECIALLY IMPORTANT TO NOTIFY YOUR DOCTOR about chest pain, irregular heartbeat, or tightness of the chest or throat.

INTERACTIONS

Zolmitriptan can interact with several other types of medications:

1. Zolmitriptan can interact with a class of medications called monoamine oxidase (MAO) inhibitors to produce dangerous side effects. It is very important that zolmitriptan and MAO inhibitors not be taken together. If you were taking an MAO inhibitor, you must not take any doses of zolmitriptan for at least two weeks in order to avoid this potentially dangerous drug interaction.

2. Zolmitriptan should not be taken together with other medications that are in the same class, such as naratriptan, sumatriptan, or rizatriptan.

3. Concurrent use of some antidepressants (fluoxetine, paroxetine, sertraline, fluvoxamine, or sibutramine) and zolmitriptan may produce weakness or incoordination.

4. Zolmitriptan may increase the side effects caused by ergot-containing or ergot-type drugs (such as methysergide and dihydroergotamine). Therefore, it is very important that the use of these ergot drugs and zolmitriptan be separated by a minimum of 24 hours.

5. Propranolol and cimetidine may increase the blood levels of zolmitriptan when either drug is given concurrently with zolmitriptan.

6. To avoid drug interactions, do not take any over-the-counter (nonprescription) medications for weight control or for asthma, sinus problems, cough, cold, or allergy problems unless you first check with a doctor or pharmacist.

Before you begin treatment with zolmitriptan, BE SURE THAT YOU TELL YOUR DOCTOR about any medications that you are taking, especially any of the medications that are listed above.

WARNINGS

• Tell your doctor about unusual or allergic reactions you have had to any medications, especially to zolmitriptan, naratriptan, sumatriptan, or rizatriptan.

• Before starting to take zolmitriptan, tell your doctor if you now have or ever had heart disease, heart attack, angina, high blood pressure, kidney or liver disease, peripheral vascular disease, or stroke.
• The safety of using this medication to treat more than four headaches in a one-month period has not been well established. If you are experiencing more than four headaches in a one-month period, discuss this with your doctor.
• This medication can make your skin more sensitive to the sun, even when exposed for brief periods of time. It is important to limit your exposure to sunlight and to avoid sunlamps. When you are outdoors during daylight hours, wear protective clothing and an effective sunscreen.
• If this medication makes you dizzy or drowsy, do not participate in any activities that require mental alertness, such as driving an automobile or operating potentially dangerous machinery or equipment.
• Be sure to tell your doctor if you are pregnant. Adequate studies have not been conducted on the use of this medication during human pregnancy. In addition, be sure to tell your doctor if you are breast-feeding an infant. It is not known if zolmitriptan passes into breast milk.

---

zolpidem

BRAND NAME (Manufacturer)
Ambien (Searle)
TYPE OF DRUG
Sedative/hypnotic
INGREDIENT
zolpidem
DOSAGE FORM
Tablet (5 mg and 10 mg)
STORAGE
Store at room temperature in a tightly closed container. Do not expose to excess heat.

USES

Zolpidem is prescribed to treat insomnia, including problems with falling asleep, waking during the night, and early morning wakefulness. It is not clear how zolpidem works, but it may relieve insomnia by acting as a depressant of the central nervous system (brain and spinal cord).

TREATMENT

This medicine should be taken immediately before bedtime. Since it works quickly, you should be ready to go to bed right after you take it. This medicine should be taken on an empty stomach so that it works quickly. However, it may be taken with food or a full glass of water to lessen stomach upset (unless your doctor tells you to do otherwise).

If you are taking this medicine regularly and miss a dose, just skip it and return to your regular dosing schedule. Do not double the next dose.

SIDE EFFECTS

Minor. Diarrhea, drowsiness during the day, double or blurred vision, dryness of the mouth, headache, nausea, stomach pain, unusual dreams or nightmares, or vomiting. These side effects should diminish or disappear as your body adjusts to the medication.

Dry mouth can be relieved by chewing sugarless gum or sucking on hard candy.

Major. It is important to tell your doctor about any side effects that are persistent or particularly bothersome. IT IS ESPECIALLY IMPORTANT TO TELL YOUR DOCTOR about confusion, dizzinesses or light-headedness, feeling depressed, hallucinations, irritability, trouble sleeping, or unusual excitedness or nervousness.

If this medication makes you feel dizzy, sit or lie down for a while, get up slowly from a sitting or reclining position, and be careful on stairs.

To help prevent dizziness or light-headedness when you stand, contract and relax the muscles of your legs for a few moments before rising. Do this by pressing one foot against the floor while raising the other foot slightly, alternating feet so that you are pumping your legs in a pedaling motion.

INTERACTIONS

Zolpidem may interact with a number of other medications:

1. Extreme drowsiness may occur when this medicine is taken with central nervous system depressants (alcohol, antihistamines, barbiturates, benzodiazepine tranquilizers, muscle relaxants, narcotics, pain medications, phenothiazine tranquilizers, and medications to induce sleep) or with antidepressants.

2. Zolpidem taken concurrently with chlorpromazine may increase the side effects of chlorpromazine.

3. To avoid drug interactions, it is very important that you do not take any over-the-counter (nonprescription) medications for weight control or for asthma, sinus problems, cough, cold, or allergy problems unless you first check with a doctor or pharmacist.

Before taking zolpidem, BE SURE TO TELL YOUR DOCTOR about any medications you are currently taking, especially any of those listed above.

WARNINGS

• Be sure to tell your doctor about any unusual or allergic reactions you may have had to zolpidem or to any other medications.

• It is important that you take this medication only in the amount prescribed by your doctor. Zolpidem has the potential for abuse and must be used with caution. Do not increase the dose without consulting your doctor. It is important not to stop taking this drug suddenly if you have been taking large amounts or if you have used it for several weeks. Your doctor may want you to reduce the dosage slowly to avoid withdrawal reactions, such as stomach cramps, nervousness or panicky feelings, sweating, uncontrolled crying, vomiting, nausea, or unusual tiredness or weakness.

• This drug is safe when used properly. However, serious side effects may develop if zolpidem is taken with alcohol or other sedative drugs.

• If this drug makes you dizzy or drowsy, do not participate in any activity that requires alertness, such as driving a car or operating potentially dangerous equipment.

• Be sure to tell your doctor if you are pregnant. Although no serious effects from zolpidem have been seen in animal studies, the effects during human pregnancy are not known. Also tell your doctor if you are breast-feeding an infant. Zolpidem does pass into breast milk, and its effects on infants are not known. You should discuss the risks and benefits of the medicine with your doctor.

---

zonisamide

BRAND NAME (Manufacturer)
Zonegra (Elan)
TYPE OF DRUG
Anticonvulsant
INGREDIENT
zonisamide
DOSAGE FORM
Capsules (100 mg)

STORAGE
Store in a tightly closed container at room temperature, away from heat and direct sunlight.

USES
Zonisamide is an antiseizure medication that is usually used along with other antiseizure medicines to control certain types of seizures in the treatment of epilepsy. Although this medicine will not cure epilepsy, it will help to control your seizures when taken as directed by your doctor.

TREATMENT
Zonisamide is usually taken once a day, either with or without food. Swallow the capsule whole; do not break, chew, or crush it.

This medication works best when the level of medicine in your bloodstream is kept constant. It is therefore best to take the medication at evenly spaced intervals throughout the day and night. For example, if you have been prescribed a once-a-day dose of zonisamide, you should try to take that dose at the same time every day. IT IS IMPORTANT NOT TO MISS ANY DOSES OF ZONISAMIDE.

If you miss a dose of this medication, take the missed dose as soon as possible and return to your regular dosing schedule. However, if it is almost time for your next dose, skip the one you missed and return to your regular schedule. Never take a double dose to make up for the one you missed unless directed to do so by your doctor. Discuss this with your doctor or pharmacist if you are not sure about what to do when you miss a dose.

During treatment with zonisamide, be sure to drink plenty of water or other fluids (unless your doctor directs you to do otherwise). This will help to prevent kidney stones from forming.

Do not stop taking this medication abruptly. Suddenly stopping zonisamide may result in a return of seizures. If this medication needs to be stopped, the dosage should be reduced gradually. Talk with your doctor before stopping zonisamide on your own.

The full effects of this medication may not be apparent for several weeks. Usually, the dose of zonisamide is slowly increased over several weeks.

Take zonisamide exactly as prescribed by your doctor.

SIDE EFFECTS
Minor. Anxiety, constipation, dizziness, dry mouth, loss of appetite, restlessness, sleepiness, or unusual tiredness or weakness. As your body adjusts to the medication, some of these side effects should diminish or disappear.

Dry mouth can be relieved by sucking on ice chips or a piece of hard candy or by chewing sugarless gum.

To relieve constipation, increase the amount of fiber in your diet (fresh fruits and vegetables, salads, bran, and whole-grain breads), exercise, and drink more water (unless your doctor directs you to do otherwise).

To avoid dizziness or light-headedness when you stand, contract and relax the muscles in your legs for a few moments before rising. Do this by pushing one foot against the floor while raising the other foot slightly, alternating feet so that you are "pumping" your legs in a pedaling motion.

If this medication makes you feel dizzy or light-headed, sit or lie down for a while; get up from a sitting or lying position slowly; and be careful on stairs.

Major. Tell your doctor about any side effects that are persistent or that you find particularly bothersome. IT IS ESPECIALLY IMPORTANT TO TELL YOUR DOCTOR about agitation, any type of skin rash, clumsiness or unsteadiness, delusions, difficulty breathing, difficulty swallowing, easy bruising, fever, hallucinations, headache, loss of memory or problems with memory, sore throat, tightness in the chest, ulcers in the mouth, or wheezing.

INTERACTIONS

Zonisamide may interact with a number of other medications.

1. Concurrent use of this medication with other central nervous system depressants (such as alcohol, barbiturates, benzodiazepine tranquilizers, muscle relaxants, narcotics, pain medications, and phenothiazine tranquilizers) or with tricyclic antidepressants can cause extreme drowsiness.

2. Use of over-the-counter (nonprescription) medications for weight loss or for cough, cold, sinus problems, asthma, or allergy problems may increase the side effects of this medication. Concurrent use of any of these medications and zonisamide should be avoided.

3. Concurrent use of zonisamide with any of the other antiseizure medications (such as valproic acid, carbamazepine, or phenytoin) may alter the effectiveness of the medication.

4. The effects of oral contraceptive medications (birth control pills) may be reduced by zonisamide. An additional or alternative method of birth control (such as a barrier method) may be needed during treatment with zonisamide. Discuss this with your doctor or pharmacist.

5. Acetazolamide will increase your chances of having kidney stones when taken with zonisamide; this drug combination should be avoided.

Before you begin treatment with zonisamide, BE SURE TO TELL YOUR DOCTOR about any medications that you are currently taking, especially any of the medications that are listed above.

WARNINGS

• Tell your doctor if you have a history of alcoholism and if you now have or have ever had liver or kidney disease. Your dose of this medication may need to be changed if you have kidney disease.

• Tell your doctor about any unusual or allergic reactions you have had to any medications, especially to zonisamide, other medications to control your seizure disorder, or any sulfonamide or sulfa drugs. Since zonisamide is a sulfonamide-type medication, it should not be taken if you have had an allergic reaction to sulfa drugs in the past. Discuss this with your doctor or pharmacist.

• Zonisamide may cause extreme fatigue and dizziness. Your ability to perform tasks that require alertness, such as driving an automobile or operating potentially dangerous machinery, may be decreased. Take appropriate caution.

• Because of your epilepsy, do not take any over-the-counter (nonprescription) medication for weight control or for cough, cold, asthma, allergy problems, or sinus problems unless you first check with your doctor or pharmacist.

• It is very important to take this medication as directed by your doctor. Do not reduce the dose or take more of this medication at any time. Do not suddenly stop taking zonisamide; if you do, you may experience uncontrolled seizures.

• Prior to having surgery or any other medical or dental treatment, be sure to tell your doctor or dentist that you are taking zonisamide.

• Contact your doctor IMMEDIATELY if you experience a rash, fever, sore throat, oral ulcers, or easy bruising after taking this medication.

• Your doctor may do regular blood tests to see how well your other antiseizure medicines are working to control your seizures.

• Be sure to tell your doctor IMMEDIATELY if you are pregnant. Although the effects of this medication during pregnancy have not been thoroughly studied in humans, it has caused toxicity in studies of animal pregnancy. It is also not known if zonisamide passes into breast milk in humans, so be sure to tell your doctor if you are breastfeeding an infant.

Canadian Brand Names

Following is a list of commonly prescribed Canadian brand-name medications and their manufacturers. Also listed is the generic-drug profile in this publication under which you can find information about each brand-name drug. Please note that in Canada acetaminophen is known as paracetamol, albuterol is known as salbutamol, metaproterenol is known as orciprenaline, and meperidine is known as pethidine.

BRAND NAME (Manufacturer)	Profile
Aerius® (Schering)	**desloratadine**
Albert Glyburide® (Albert Pharma)	**glyburide**
Alti-Alprazolam® (AltiMed)	**alprazolam**
Alti-Ticlopidine® (AltiMed)	**ticlopidine**
Ampicin® (Bristol-Myers Squibb)	**ampicillin**
Ansaid® (Upjohn)	**flurbiprofen**
Apo-Allopurinal® (Apotex)	**allopurinal**
Apo-Alpraz® (Apotex)	**alprazolam**
Apo-Ampi® (Apotex)	**ampicillin**
Apo-ASA® (Apotex)	**aspirin**
Apo-Benztropine® (Apotex)	**benztropine**
Apo-Diazepam® (Apotex)	**diazepam**
Apo-Fluphenazine® (Apotex)	**fluphenazine**
Apo-Hydro® (Apotex)	**hydrochlorothiazide**
Apo-Ibuprofen® (Apotex)	**ibuprofen**
Apo-Pen-VK® (Apotex)	**penicillin VK**
Becloforte® (Glaxo Wellcome)	**beclomethasone**
Candistatin® (Westwood-Squibb)	**nystatin**
Canesten® (Bayer)	**clotrimazole (vaginal)**
Carbolith® (ICN)	**lithium**
Chlorpromanyl® (Technilab)	**chlorpromazine**
Chronovera® (Serle)	**verapamil**
Clavulin® (GlaxoSmithKline)	**amoxicillin and clavulanic acid combination**
Clonapam® (ICN)	**clonazepam**
Clotrimaderm® (Taro)	**clotrimazole (topical)**
Coronex® (Wyeth-Ayerst)	**isosorbide dinitrate**

BRAND NAME (Manufacturer)	Profile
Coumadin® (DuPont)	**warfarin**
Coversyl® (Servier)	**perindopril**
Cytotec® (Pharmacia)	**misoprostol**
Dalacin C® (Pharmacia)	**clindamycin (systemic)**
Detensol® (Desbergers)	**propranolol**
Diuchlor H® (Medic)	**hydrochlorothiazide**
Dixarit® (Boehringer Ingelheim)	**clonidine**
Doxycin® (Riva)	**doxycycline**
Doxytec® (Technilab)	**doxycycline**
Eltroxin® (GlaxoSmithKline)	**levothyroxine**
Emex® (GlaxoSmithKline)	**metoclopramide**
Eprex® (Janssen-Ortho)	**erythropoietin**
Erythromid® (Abbott)	**erythromycin**
Euglucon® (Boehringer Mannheim)	**glyburide**
Flexitec® (Technilab)	**cyclobenzaprine**
Fluoderm® (Taro)	**fluocinolone (topical)**
Froben® (Abbott)	**flurbiprofen**
Gen-Alprazolam® (Genpharm)	**alprazolam**
Gen-Amoxicillin® (Genpharm)	**amoxicillin**
Gen-Atenolol® (Genpharm)	**atenolol**
Gen-Buspirone® (Genpharm)	**buspirone**
Hibidil 1:2000® (Zeneca)	**chlorhexidine gluconate**
Hibitane® Gluconate 20% (Zeneca)	**chlorhexidine gluconate**
Hibitane® Skin Cleanser 2% and 4% (Zeneca)	**chlorhexidine gluconate**
Impril® (ICN)	**imipramine**
Isotrex® (Steifel)	**isotretinoin**
Kwellada® (R & C)	**lindane**
Largactil® (Rhone-Poulenc Rorer)	**chlorpromazine**
Lenoltec with codeine No. 4® (Technilab)	**acetaminophen and codeine combination**
Levate® (ICN)	**amitriptyline**

BRAND NAME (Manufacturer)	Profile
Lidemol® (Roche)	**fluocinonide (topical)**
Lin-Buspiron® (Linson)	**buspirone**
Lin-Nefazodone® (Linson)	**nefazodone**
Lin-Pravastatin® (Linson)	**pravastatin**
Lithane® (Pfizer)	**lithium**
Lithizine® (Maney)	**lithium**
Loperacap® (ICN)	**loperamide**
Losec® (AstraZeneca)	**omeprazole**
Lovenox-HP® (Aventis)	**enoxaparin**
Maxeran® (Aventis)	**metoclopramide**
M-Eslon® (Rhone-Poulenc Rorer)	**morphine**
Metadol® (Pharmascience)	**methadone**
Micozole® (Taro)	**miconazole (vaginal)**
Minestrin 1/20® (Pfizer)	**oral contraceptives**
Min-Ovral® (Wyeth-Ayerst)	**oral contraceptives**
Minox® (Riva)	**minoxidil (topical)**
Modecate® (Squibb)	**fluphenazine**
Moditen HCl® (Squibb)	**fluphenazine**
M.O.S.-Sulfate® (ICN)	**morphine**
Myclo® (Boehringer Ingelheim)	**clotrimazole (topical), clotrimazole (vaginal)**
Nadopen-V® (Nadeau)	**penicillin VK**
Nalcrom® (Rhone-Poulenc Rorer)	**cromolyn sodium**
Naxen® (Altimed)	**naproxen**
Neo-Codema® (Neolab)	**hydrochlorothiazide**
Norventyl® (ICN)	**nortriptyline**
Novamoxin® (Novopharm)	**amoxicillin**
Novo-Ampicillin® (Novopharm)	**ampicillin**
Novo-Carbamaz® (Novopharm)	**carbamazepine**
Novo-Cholamine® (Novopharm)	**cholestyramine**
Novo-Cimetine® (Novopharm)	**cimetidine**
Novo-Dipam® (Novopharm)	**diazepam**
Novo-Doxylin® (Novopharm)	**doxycycline**
Novo-Hydrazide® (Novopharm)	**hydrochlorothiazide**

BRAND NAME (Manufacturer)	Profile
Novo-Lexin® (Novopharm)	**cephalexin**
Novo-Naprox® (Novopharm)	**naproxen**
Novo-Nidazole® (Novopharm)	**metronidazole**
Novo-Pen-VK® (Novopharm)	**penicillin VK**
Novo-Poxide® (Novopharm)	**chlordiazepoxide**
Novo-Pramine® (Novopharm)	**imipramine**
Novo-Pranol® (Novopharm)	**propranolol**
Novo-Profen® (Novopharm)	**ibuprofen**
Novo-Semide® (Novopharm)	**furosemide**
Novo-Sertraline® (Novopharm)	**sertraline**
Novo-Sorbide® (Novopharm)	**isosorbide dinitrate**
Novo-Spiroton® (Novopharm)	**spironolactone**
Novo-Tetra® (Novopharm)	**tetracycline**
Novo-Trimel® (Novopharm)	**sulfamethoxazole and trimethoprim combination**
Novo-Triptyn® (Novopharm)	**amitriptyline**
Nu-Cimet® (Nu-Pharm)	**cimetidine**
Nu-Pravastatin® (Nu-Pharm)	**pravastatin**
Nu-Prochlor® (Nu-Pharm)	**prochlorperazine**
Nu-Ranit® (Nu-Pharm)	**ranitidine**
Nyaderm® (Taro)	**nystatin**
Oracort® (Taro)	**triamcinolone (inhalation)**
Oxycocet® (Technilab)	**acetaminophen and oxycodone combination**
Oxycodan® (Technilab)	**aspirin and oxycodone combination**
Pantoloc® (Solvay Pharma/Byk Canada)	**pantoprazole**
Penbritin® (Wyeth-Ayerst)	**ampicillin**
Peptol® (Horner)	**cimetidine**
Peridol® (Technilab)	**haloperidol**
Pertofrane® (Novartis)	**desipramine**
PMS-Fluphenazine® (Pharmascience)	**fluphenazine**
PMS-Prochlorperazine® (Pharmascience)	**prochlorperazine**

BRAND NAME (Manufacturer)	Profile
Prandase® (Bayer)	**acarbose**
Prevex HC® (TCD)	**hydrocortisone**
Purinol® (Horner)	**allopurinol**
PVF® (Frosst)	**penicillin VK**
Rhinalar® (Roche)	**flunisolide (nasal)**
Rhodis® (Rhodiapharm)	**ketoprofen**
Rho-Metformin FC® (RhoxalPharma)	**metformin**
Rhovail® (RHO-Pharma)	**ketoprofen**
Riphenidate® (Technilab)	**methylphenidate**
Rivotril® (Roche)	**clonazepam**
Rofact® (ICN)	**rifampin**
Roubac® (Rougier)	**sulfamethoxazole and trimethoprim combination**
Rounox® with Codeine (Rougier)	**acetaminophen and codeine combination**
Rynacrom® (Aventis)	**cromolyn sodium (nasal)**
Salazopyrin® (Pharmacia)	**sulfasalazine**
Solium® (Horner)	**chlordiazepoxide**
Statex® (Pharmascience)	**morphine**
Stemetil® (Aventis)	**prochlorperazine**
Stieva-A® (Stiefel)	**tretinoin**
Sulcrate® (Aventis)	**sucralfate**
Tamofen® (Rhone-Poulenc Rorer)	**tamoxifen**
Tenolin® (Technilab)	**atenolol**
Topsyn® (Medicis)	**fluocinonide**
Transderm-V® (Novartis)	**scopolamine (transdermal)**
Triadapin® (Aventis)	**doxepin**
Uritol® (Horner)	**furosemide**
Urozide® (ICN)	**hydrochlorothiazide**
Vitinoin® (Pharmascience)	**tretinoin**
Vivol® (Horner)	**diazepam**
Warfilone® (Frosst)	**warfarin**
Winpred® (ICN)	**prednisone (systemic)**

Index

This comprehensive index includes both the brand names (in **boldface** type) and generic names of the drugs profiled in this publication, all in alphabetical order. To find information on a brand-name drug, first look up the brand name. The brand-name listing will give you the drug's generic name. Look up the generic name to find the page number of the appropriate drug profile.

A

B

C

D

J

K

L

M

N

O

P

Q

R

S

T

U

V

W